To Uncle Benja

THE SPORTSPAGES
ALMANAC 1991

So you can be even
more horribly 'right' for
A Question of Sport.

love,
Dominick, Jane, Charlotte
+ George
xxxx.

THE SPORTSPAGES
ALMANAC 1991

THE COMPLETE SPORTING FACTBOOK

**Matthew Engel and
Ian Morrison**

SIMON & SCHUSTER

A SPORTSPAGES BOOK

First published in Great Britain by
Simon and Schuster Ltd in 1990
A Paramount Communications Company

Copyright © Matthew Engel and Ian Morrison 1990

SPORTSPAGES
The Specialist Sports Bookshop
Caxton Way
94-96 Charing Cross Road
London WC2H 0JG

Simon & Schuster Ltd
West Garden Place
Kendal Street
London W2 2AQ

Simon & Schuster of Australia Pty Ltd
Sydney

British Library Cataloguing-in-Publication Data available
ISBN 0-671-71600-X

Typeset by Learning Curve, Watford
Printed and bound in Great Britain
by Billing & Sons, Worcester

CONTENTS

INTRODUCTION

The 1991 edition of *The Sportspages Almanac* is, like the first edition, an attempt to provide a sports reference book like no other. It contains details of all the major events due to happen in 1991, those that did happen in 1990 and everything worthwhile that happened before that.

It is aimed at all sports followers - fanatical or casual - especially those of an irreverent turn of mind. It has a lot of facts, a decent number of laughs and probably the occasional mistake.

The 1991 edition contains the full story of the soccer World Cup, of the run-crazy English cricket season and Nick Faldo's triumphant summer. It also tells the tale of Yannick Noah and the witchdoctor, reveals what Wally Lewis put in his urine sample and what happened when Miss Batt met Mr Ball.. It contains all the news of frog-jumping, ferret racing and nun-running.

The words are again mine, the statistics almost all Ian's. The Sportspages year runs roughly from October to October so this edition contains some late results from 1989 as well. We have tried as hard as humanly possible to eliminate any mistakes. Apologies in advance for any that might have crept in; please let us know gently. We should stress that the 1991 fixtures in particular are only provisional and it is wise to check venues and timings. Any suggestions for inclusions in the 1992 edition will be welcome plus any cuttings, oddities and quotes, especially from any foreign or local papers.

Producing this second edition represents a triumph of hope over experience and of willpower over normal production schedules. Thanks again to everyone who helped us including all the officials from various sports. Particular thanks go to our better halves, Ann and Hilary, for their love, support and above all tolerance; to John Gaustad for his constant enthusiasm; to Jane Prendergast for her editorial assistance; and to everyone at Simon and Schuster especially Richard Wigmore, Fenella Smart, Sarah Baker-Smith, Brian Perman, Jacks Thomas, Jessica Cuthbert-Smith and Jonathan Atkins. I hope they all recover soon.

We would also like to thank Jeremy Alexander, Mike Averis, Simon Barnes, Steve Barnett, Colin Bateman, Stephen Bierley, Mike Calvin, Jane Court, Andy Davies, Steph Fincham, Paul Fitzpatrick, David Frith, Mike Getty, Cat Gibbon, Peter Gillman, Vivien Green, Tony Greer, Declan Hamblin, Alan Hodder, David Irvine, Nick Johnston, Jonathan Keates, Tim Lamb, James Lawton, Richard Lockwood, Andrew Madgett, Sean Magee, Yuri Matischen, Norman de Mesquita, Keith Murphy, Andrew Nickolds, Josie Peer, Vic Robbie, Nicholas Soames, Rob Steen, John Trachim, Tai Wai Cheung, Georgina Wald, Paul Weaver, Mike Weiss, Alan Wilkes, everyone at *Learning Curve*, everyone on *The Guardian* sports desk and the inventor of the fax machine. Bless them all.

Mathew Engel, October 1990
c/o Simon and Schuster, West Garden Place Kendal St, London W2 2AQ.

ABBREVIATIONS

List of abbreviations for countries commonly used in this book.

Alb	Albania
Alg	Algeria
Arg	Argentina
Aus	Australia
Aut	Austria
Bah	Bahamas
Bar	Barbados
Bel	Belgium
Ber	Bermuda
Boh	Bohemia
Bol	Bolivia
Bra	Brazil
Bul	Bulgaria
Bur	Burma
Cam	Cameroon
Can	Canada
Chi	Chile
Chn	China
Col	Colombia
Cub	Cuba
Cyp	Cyprus
Cze	Czechoslovakia
Den	Denmark
Dji	Djibouti
Dom	Dominican Republic
Ecu	Ecuador
Egy	Egypt
Eng	England
Est	Estonia
Eth	Ethiopia
Fij	Fiji
Fin	Finland
Fra	France
FRG	West Germany
GB	Great Britain
GDR	East Germany
Ger	Germany
Gha	Ghana
Gre	Greece
Gue	Guernsey
Guy	Guyana
Hai	Haiti
Haw	Hawaii
HK	Hong Kong
Hol	The Netherlands
Hun	Hungary
Ice	Iceland
Ina	Indonesia
Ind	India
IOM	Isle of Man
Ire	Republic of Ireland
Irn	Iran
Irq	Iraq
Isr	Israel
Ita	Italy
Jam	Jamaica
Jap	Japan
Jer	Jersey
Ken	Kenya
Kuw	Kuwait
Lie	Liechtenstein
Lux	Luxembourg
Mal	Malta
Mex	Mexico
Mon	Mongolia
Mor	Morocco
NI	Northern Ireland
Nic	Nicaragua
Nig	Nigeria
NKo	North Korea
Nor	Norway
NRo	Northern Rhodesia
NZ	New Zealand
Pak	Pakistan
Pan	Panama
Par	Paraguay
Per	Peru
Phi	Philippines
Pol	Poland
Por	Portugal
PR	Puerto Rico
Rho	Rhodesia
Rom	Romania
SA	South Africa
Sco	Scotland
Sen	Senegal
Sin	Singapore
SKo	South Korea
Som	Somalia
Spa	Spain
Sri	Sri Lanka
SRo	Southern Rhodesia
Sud	Sudan
Sur	Surinam
SVi	St Vincent
Swe	Sweden
Swi	Switzerland
Syr	Syria
Tah	Tahiti
Tai	Taiwan
Tan	Tanzania
Tha	Thailand
Tri	Trinidad & Tobago
Tun	Tunisia
Tur	Turkey
UAR	United Arab Emirates
Uga	Uganda
Uru	Uruguay
US	United States
USSR	Soviet Union
Ven	Venezuela
VI	Virgin Islands
Wal	Wales
Yug	Yugoslavia
Zai	Zaire
Zam	Zambia
Zim	Zimbabwe

SPORTS ROUND-UP

AFGHAN RACING

This sport was reported to be staged regularly and seriously in West Germany and, more occasionally and frivolously, in Britain. The dogs have to be securely muzzled to stop them wounding each other. Among the other breeds being raced in Europe are salukis, poodles and Jack Russells. The sport of terrier racing, popular in the Lake District for about 30 years, was given a new status in 1990 when there was a demonstration at Crufts.

ARM-WRESTLING

Televised by the ITV company TSW and expected to be networked nationwide in 1991. "It's about time the sport had more respectability," said Frank Pittal, who makes special arm-wrestling tables. "It takes violence off the street."

ASIAN GAMES

Eleven criminals were executed "to make Beijing peaceful, safe and happy for foreign friends to visit during the Asian Games," according to the *Beijing Daily*. Games officials tried to train 60,000 doves to make ceremonial peace flights. Hundreds were shot dead by hunters.

BARE-KNUCKLE FIGHTING

Illegal, but reported to be flourishing in London and Birmingham with £1000 prizes. Hospitals are habitually told the losers have fallen downstairs. For larger sums, some of the fighters take on rottweilers.

BETTING

Gareth Trueson of Llangollen was one of the few men in the world annoyed by the reopening of the Berlin Wall. He asked the bookmakers William Hill in October 1989 for odds on the Wall reopening. He was offered 12-1 that it would happen before the end of the century but he declined the bet. In 1988 Hills offered 200-1 without getting any takers.

Peter Babka, 63, an Australian professional punter, won a Federal Court ruling that his winnings - £700,000 in ten years - should not be subject to tax. Officials had claimed his gambling was a business.

BULLFIGHTING

Strike action in Spain by the picadors and bandilleros was narrowly averted after they received guarantees that social security would cover them when they were gored. In Britain the Cable TV authority wanted to censor bullfights after complaints from viewers; Spain protested that the fights were a tradition and shown mainly for Spaniards abroad.

CAGE FIGHTING

Reported to be run secretly in various Chinese communities in the Far East and US, apparently under gangster control. There are said to be no rules and the loser sometimes dies.

CHICKEN-FLYING

At the World Championships in Ohio, Judy, the 1989 winner with a record flight of 542ft 9in, shocked her supporters by flying backwards and had to be rescued from the top of a tent.

CLUEDO

Ivan Lee, a Malaysian student, won the first World Cluedo Championship in Torquay by correctly guessing the answer: Professor Plum with the candlestick in the conservatory.

COURSE A L'ANGLAISE

It was reported that a race in which the slowest runner is deemed the winner is known among Parisian schoolchildren as *course à l' anglaise* - racing, English style.

COURSING

Illegal hare-coursing - with the hares given no chance of escape - run by gangs of men, some armed, was reported to be taking place in Wiltshire, Cambridgeshire and Hertfordshire. Bets of up to £5000 were recorded. The maximum fine is £50.

DOG FIGHTING

Barry Raj, a self-employed car dealer living in a Hell's Angel chapter house in Sunderland, was jailed for four months for being involved in dog-fighting. Police had arrested 36 men after raiding a farm in Fife.

FERRET RACING

Only two animals turned up at the World Championships held at Yapton, Sussex instead of the expected 30. Both were owned by Mr Ron Marner from Barnham.

FROG JUMPING

The annual Frog Jump Jubilee in Calaveras County, California was transformed when Andy Koffman brought along three foot-long African giant frogs to outleap the other entrants. Organisers were afraid the interlopers would either (a) win ridiculously easily, (b) leap out of the arena and hit a spectator or (c) eat the other frogs. They compromised by changing the rules to ban the largest frogs (from Cameroon) but allow all those small enough to fit on the launch pad. In the event, the giants fell far short of the Americans in the final, all finishing way behind the winning jump (19ft 3in) by a bullfrog called Help Mr Wizard. Koffman blamed the cold weather.

GREASED PIG-CATCHING

Animal rights activists in Florida called for contests to be stopped because they were traumatic for the pigs.

HANG GLIDING

Legalised in East Germany after being banned for years to prevent people escaping.

INDOOR CLIMBING

Scaling indoor walls up to 50ft high became increasingly popular. This is known in California as "Rock til You Drop".

KING OF THE TINKERS

Dan Rooney from London beat Dennis McGinley from Ballinasloe, County Galway after a 15-minute fist fight for the title ended in a cut eye in Crossmaglen, County Armagh. Hundreds of travellers watched and Rooney's supporters carried him shoulder-high through the streets though McGinley insisted: "I'm still the King."

LAWN-MOWER RACING

Invented at the Cricketers' Arms, Wisborough Green, Sussex and now attracting teams from Wales, Scotland, France - plus lunatics from Zimbabwe who bring their dismantled mowers as hand baggage.

MARTIAL ARTS

Legalised in Romania, which banned all except judo under the Ceausescu regime - though there were known to be secret karate courses at several sports clubs.

MIDGET BOWLING

In New York, Mike Anderson, a 3ft Australian, was regularly strapped to a skateboard and hurled at skittles. "My pals and I like it," he said. "I don't find it demeaning." However, state legislators disagreed and said any bar which staged such contests would have its liquor licence revoked. Local promoter Bryce Jones described this as censorship. He said the sport was "a performance art designed to satirise the values of mainstream America". He added that it was not a revolting sport like naked females wrestling in jelly.

NUN RUNNING

The International Nun Run was held at the Trim Pony Races, County Meath with eight pony-riding sisters. Sister Mary Joy won; Sister Malen del Garcia of Puerto Rico, who weighs 23 stone, came last on Have Mercy on Me. £4,000 was wagered on the race; the first prize went to Sister Mary Joy's nominated charity, the Peru Missions.

SPORTS ROUND-UP

OFF-ROAD MOTOR CYCLING

Three big races through the Mojave Desert in California were banned because they posed a threat to the habitat of the desert tortoise.

PIGEON RACING

Thomas Waddell of Baltimore was arrested after being seen walking down the street oddly. He was found to be carrying 26 racing pigeons in his trousers, stolen from enthusiast John Styron. 21 were live, five dead. Waddell was charged with grand theft, malicious destruction of property and cruelty to animals.
A homing pigeon beat a fax machine in a special one-mile challenge race between Heathrow and the pigeon's loft in West Drayton, Middlesex.

PIT BULL TERRIER FIGHTING

Flourishing near Scunthorpe with contests lasting $1^3/_4$ hours or more. "When you watch them fighting," said one enthusiast, "their little tails are going all the time. They love it."

POKER

In Las Vegas, Phil Hellmuth, the 1989 World Series champion, played the first ever man v computer game for money. Hellmuth cleaned the computer out in two hours.

PRAIRIE DOG SHOOTING

At the World Championship Prairie Dog Shoot in Nucla, Colorado 106 hunters killed 2,956 animals. The 25 protesters survived, just.

ROBOT OLYMPICS

A machine called Trolleyman carried the Olympic flame from the Parthenon Restaurant in Glasgow to Strathclyde University to start the first International Robot Olympics.

ROTTWEILER RACING

Supposed to be filmed for a TV comedy sketch at Crayford dog track but the track's general manager, Roger Lakey, was sacked by owners Ladbrokes for agreeing to the idea. Filming moved to Hackney instead.

SCRABBLE

New smooth tiles were introduced at the North American Scrabble Championship to prevent players cheating by recognising letters by their feel as they rummaged in the bag. Unfortunately, the tiles turned out to be transparent.

SPORTS ROUND-UP

SEX

An anonymous American clay pigeon shooter, 59, claimed to have regular multiple orgasms in a study by scientists in New York. He was so excited when he first had the experience he shouted "Doublee!", the term for shooting two clay pigeons with a double-barrelled gun.

Dr Anne McLaren, director of the Medical Research Council's Mammalian Development Unit, predicted that eventually sports would no longer be divided by sex but into three groups - high, medium and low potential, depending on competitors' heart-lung capacity.

SUBBUTEO

Armed guards were called to the World Cup in Italy to separate warring TV crews.

SUMO

Yasokichi Konishiki, 35 stone, of Hawaii, became the third foreigner in the three-century history of professional sumo to win a tournament when he won the annual competition at Fukuoka. Konishiki's name means "little brocade"; his nickname is "the dump truck". Meanwhile, Chiyonofuji, "the wolf", became the first sumo to achieve 1,000 wins. Ms Mayumi Moriyama, Japan's chief cabinet secretary, wanted to break a centuries-old taboo that women never step inside a sumo ring by presenting the Prime Minister's Cup at a major tournament. Never, said the head of the Sumo Association.

TROTTING

Delvin Miller, a 76-year-old American trotting driver, drove in his eighth decade of competitive racing, having started in 1929 at the Burgettstown Fair in Ohio.

WOMEN'S BOXING

Sue Atkins, 28, retained the women's British lightweight title against Jane Johnson in a pub gym in South London. Atkins was fighting with a damaged left hand; she hurt it gardening.

YOGIC FLYING

The fifth annual European Yogic Flying competition was held at the Maharishi Golden Dome in Skelmersdale, Lancashire, home of the Maharishi Mahesh Yogi's community. Events included a 50-metre race, high and long jumps and a 25-metre hurdle, all conducted from the lotus position. Yogic flying involves lifting oneself off the ground while in a state of transcendental meditation. Britain was said not to be very good at it.

1891 - 1991

CRICKET

In 1891 Dr W G Grace went to Australia for the first time, captaining England in an unsuccessful attempt to retain the Ashes. Surrey won the County Championship. George Hirst scored the first of his 36,323 first-class runs.

HORSE RACING

The pari-mutuel was established in Paris. Gouverneur became the first French-trained winner of The Derby. Come Away won the Grand National; his jockey was Harry Beasley, the only man to breed, train and ride a Grand National winner.

GOLF

Hugh Kirkaldy won the 31st British Open over his home course at St Andrews and won £10.

LAWN TENNIS

Mabel Cahill of Ireland won the US singles title at Philadelphia to become the first overseas winner of an event now regarded as part of the Grand Slam. Wilfred Baddeley and Lottie Dod were the All-England champions.

BOXING

James J Corbett and Peter Jackson fought each other to a standstill after 61 rounds. The $10,000 prize money was split.

ASSOCIATION FOOTBALL

The Football Association invented the penalty after an incident at the Notts County v Stoke City Cup quarter-final at Trent Bridge. In the last minute, Stoke were denied an equaliser when the left-back Hendry punched away a shot that had the goalkeeper beaten. The first-ever penalty was scored by Alex McCall of Renton against Leith Athletic on August 22 and the first in the English League by John Heath of Wolves against Accrington Stanley on September 14. Blackburn Rovers equalled the Wanderers' record of five FA Cup wins, beating Notts County 3-1 at The Oval. Crowd: 23,000. Receipts: £1,454.

The referee replaced the two umpires and a Liverpool engineer John Brodie patented goalnets, which became compulsory in the League the same year.

CRICKET

In 1991 Graham Gooch will be leading England in Australia in an attempt to get The Ashes back, and England will then face the West Indies and Sri Lanka at home. The full cricket fixtures for 1991 start on page 170.

HORSE RACING

In 1991 the Derby will be run at Epsom on June 5 and the Grand National at Aintree on April 6. The full racing fixtures for 1991 start on page 245.

GOLF

In 1991 The 120th Open will be held at Royal Birkdale from July 18-21. The golf fixtures are on page 211.

LAWN TENNIS

In 1991 the All-England Championships at Wimbledon will be held from June 24 to July 7. The tennis fixtures are on page 337.

BOXING

In 1991 the heavyweight champion will fight fewer rounds for more money. The most amazing sporting event of 1990 is described on page 90.

ASSOCIATION FOOTBALL

In 1991 the FA Cup final will be held at Wembley on May 19. The football fixtures start on page 54. The story of the 1990 World Cup and the preceding season starts on page 16.

MOTOR RACING

Not invented in 1891. The fixtures for 1991 are on page 272.

49...AND COUNTING

The San Francisco 49ers won Superbowl XXIV by a record margin when they beat the Denver Broncos 55-10 in the Louisiana Superdome. The game was expected to be lopsided - bookmakers settled on a 12-point spread - but not that lopsided: advertisers who had paid up to $1.4 million a minute were furious as viewers switched off long before the end.

Though George Seifert had taken over from Bill Walsh as the 49ers' coach, the club's pattern and, above all, the quarterback remained unchanged: 33-year-old Joe Montana was brilliant yet again. He had a record five touchdown passes before leaving the field 11 minutes from the end. The Broncos' quarterback John Elway, meanwhile, had a nightmare. Two crucial Broncos' passes, just after half-time, were intercepted, first by linebacker Michael Walter then by Chet Brooks.

Montana offered his fourth Superbowl ring to his wife Jennifer. "I'll take the next one," he said casually. This was the eighth Superbowl to go to the NFC team in nine years, and the lopsidedness was thought to be starting to damage the event's appeal and financial strength. The TV ratings - 39 per cent of US sets were switched on - were the lowest since 1969. Gary Holloway of Jonesboro, Georgia left home to watch the game at his mother-in-law's just after his wife shot herself dead. "I can't explain this wild story," said Clayton County investigator Jim Mabe. "That game was so boring."

The 49ers were the dominant team through the regular season as well. But the others were closely matched. A week before the regular season ended, 17 of the 28 NFL teams were still in contention for play-off places. The most prominent exceptions were Mike Ditka's Chicago Bears, who were showing signs of decay: a local newspaper poll showed a majority in favour of Ditka's departure and club president Mike McCaskey warned him not to be so bad-tempered. The worst by far, however, were the once-mighty Dallas Cowboys who lost their first eight games under the new coach Jerry Jones, beat the Washington Redskins 13-3, and then lost the remaining seven. The franchise was said to be having trouble paying routine bills.

Paul Tagliabue, a lawyer, succeeded Paul Rozelle as Commissioner. The NFL suspended 13 more players who tested positive for anabolic steroids. Dexter Manley, the Washington Redskins defensive end, was banned for life after failing a drugs test - for cocaine - for the third time. Manley also said that he spent four years at Oklahoma State University despite being unable to read. Of the 30 players suspended for drugs in 1988 and 1989 only four were white; a former drugs-tester said three white quarterbacks were being protected by the NFL. Rev Jesse Jackson demanded an immediate congressional enquiry.

Art Shell took over the Los Angeles Raiders and became the NFL's first black manager. The Raiders' owner Al Davis announced that the club would be moving back to Oakland after nine years. However, the Oakland City Council cancelled an offer of $602 million over 15 years and other sweeteners, and the club decided to stay where they were. Chris Silcox, 39, a Birmingham, England, nightclub owner, was named Raiders' Supporter of the Year after he travelled an estimated 250,000 miles to watch the team.

The Philadelphia Eagles followed Phoenix and Dallas by banning beer sales at home games because of fears of rowdyism. The University of South Carolina banned visiting bands from playing "Louie, Louie" at games because people danced and made the stands shake. The University of Michigan banned spectators from bringing in marshmallows to games after a fashion developed for throwing them at cheerleaders and the band.

A federally-protected witness, Donald "Tony the Greek" Frankos, said that the union leader Jimmy Hoffa, who was reputedly murdered, lies buried in an oil drum beneath one of the end zones at Giants' Stadium. Dr Andy Reiss asked everyone in America to concentrate by repeating "Come to us. We welcome you. We await you in Soldiers Field at half-time. We await you in Chicago. Please come." in the hope of persuading a UFO to land on the pitch at the Bears-Eagles game.

1989-90

NATIONAL FOOTBALL LEAGUE (NFL)

FINAL NFL STANDINGS

American Conference (AFC)

EAST	W	L	T	F	A
1 (1) Buffalo Bills	9	7	0	409	317
2 (5) Miami Dolphins	8	8	0	331	379
3 (2) Indianapolis Colts	8	8	0	298	301
4 (3) New England Patriots	5	11	0	297	391
5 (4) New York Jets	4	12	0	253	411
CENTRAL					
1 (1) Cleveland Browns	9	6	1	334	254
2 (3) Houston Oilers (*)	9	7	0	365	412
3 (4) Pittsburgh Steelers(*)	9	7	0	265	326
4 (2) Cincinnati Bengals	8	8	0	405	285
WEST					
1 (2) Denver Broncos	11	5	0	362	226
2 (3) Los Angeles Raiders	8	8	0	315	297
3 (5) Kansas City Chiefs	8	7	1	318	286
4 (1) Seattle Seahawks	7	9	0	241	327
5 (4) San Diego Chargers	6	10	0	266	290

National Conference (NFC)

EAST	W	L	T	F	A
1 (2) New York Giants	12	4	0	368	252
2 (1) Philadelphia Eagles(*)	11	5	0	342	274
3 (3) Washington Redskins	10	6	0	386	308
4 (4) Phoenix Cardinals	5	11	0	258	377
5 (5) Dallas Cowboys	1	15	0	204	393
CENTRAL					
1 (2) Minnesota Vikings	10	6	0	351	276
2 (5) Green Bay Packers	10	6	0	362	356
3 (4) Detroit Lions	7	9	0	312	364
4 (1) Chicago Bears	6	10	0	358	377
5 (3) Tampa Bay Buccaneers	5	11	0	320	419
WEST					
1 (1) San Francisco 49ers	14	2	0	442	253
2 (2) Los Angeles Rams(*)	11	5	0	426	344
3 (3) New Orleans Saints	9	7	0	386	301
4 (4) Atlanta Falcons	3	13	0	279	437

Last season's positions in brackets. (*) indicates wild card berth in play-offs.

Play-offs

AFC

Wild Card Game
PITTSBURGH STEELERS 26 Houston Oilers 23 (OT)
Semi-finals
CLEVELAND BROWNS 34 Buffalo Bills 30
DENVER BRONCOS 24 Pittsburgh Steelers 23
Championship Game
DENVER BRONCOS 37 Cleveland Browns 21

NFC

Wild Card Game
LOS ANGELES RAMS 21 Philadelphia Eagles 17
Semi-finals
LOS ANGELES RAMS 19 New York Giants 13
SAN FRANCISCO 49ers 41 Minnesota Vikings 13
Championship Game
SAN FRANCISCO 49ers 30 Los Angeles Rams 3

How the teams reached the Superbowl

SAN FRANCISCO 49ers

Home		Away	
12-13	LA Rams	30-24	Indianapolis
37-20	New England	20-16	Tampa Bay
31-13	New Orleans	38-28	Philadelphia
45-3	Atlanta	24-20	New Orleans
17-21	Green Bay	31-14	Dallas
34-24	NY Giants	23-10	NY Jets
21-10	Buffalo	23-10	Atlanta
26-0	Chicago	30-27	LA Rams

DENVER BRONCOS

Home		Away	
34-20	Kansas City	28-14	Buffalo
31-21	LA Raiders	13-16	Cleveland
16-10	San Diego	24-21	Seattle
14-3	Indianapolis	16-13	Kansas City
24-28	Philadelphia	14-10	Washington
34-7	Pittsburgh	13-16	LA Raiders
41-14	Seattle	37-0	Phoenix
7-14	NY Giants	16-19	San Diego

SUPERBOWL XX1V

Louisiana Superdome, New Orleans, Jan 28

San Francisco 49ers   13   14   14   14 - 55
Touchdowns: Rice (3), Ratman (2), Jones, Taylor, Craig
Points After : Cofer (7)

Denver Broncos   3   0   7   0 - 10
Touchdowns: Elway
Field Goals: Treadwell
Points After: Treadwell
Attendance: 72,919
Most Valuable Player: Joe Montana (49ers QB)

THE NOT-SO-SUPERBOWL

"If the Broncos had been a real horse, instead of playing like the rear end of one, they would have shot it."
Martin Walker, The Guardian

"We don't get a lot of credit, but that's OK. We don't care about the credit, only the winning."
Ronnie Lott of the 49ers

"They were just all over us. They beat us to death."
John Elway of the Broncos

"God would have had trouble beating them today. In fact they had God."
Pat Bowlen, Broncos owner

"I could play till I'm 40 if the offensive line plays like that."
Joe Montana

"Montana is the best there is, the best there ever has been."
Bubba Paris of the 49ers

20TH AFC–NFC PRO BOWL
Honolulu, Feb 4

NFC   3   3   21   0   -   27
Touchdowns: Meggett, Gray, Millard
Points After: Murray 3
Field Goals: Murray 2

AFC   0   7   0   14   -   21
Touchdowns: Okaye, Edmunds, Johnson
Points After: Treadwell 3
Attendance: 50,445

JOE MONTANA'S FIVE SUPERBOWLS

Most passes attempted: 122
Most passes completed: 83
Highest completion percentage completed: 68%
Most yards passing: 1,142
Most touch down passes: 11
Most attempts without an interception: 122
Most touch down passes – single game: 5
Most consecutive completions – single game: 13
Most MVP Awards: 3

1989–90 BOWL GAMES

California Bowl FRESNO STATE 27 Bull State 6 (31,610)
Independence State Bowl OREGON 27 Tulsa 24 (30,333)
Aloha Bowl MICHIGAN STATE 33 Hawaii 13 (50,000)
All American Bowl TEXAS TECH 49 Duke 21 (47,750)
Liberty Bowl MISSISSIPPI 42 Air Force 29 (60,128)
Holiday Bowl PENN STATE 50 BYU 39 (61,113)
John Hancock Bowl PITTSBURGH 31 Texas A&M 28 (44,887)
Anaheim Freedom Bowl WASHINGTON 34 Florida 7 (33,858)
Peach Bowl SYRACUSE 19 Georgia 18 (44,991)
Gator Bowl CLEMSON 27 West Virginia 7 (82,911)
Copper Bowl ARIZONA 17 North Carolina State 10 (37,237)
Hall of Fame Bowl AUBURN 31 Ohio State 14 (52,535)
Florida Citrus Bowl ILLINOIS 31 Virginia 21 (60,016)
Cotton Bowl TENNESSEE 31 Arkansas 27 (74,358)
Fiesta Bowl FLORIDA STATE 41 Nebraska 17 (73,953)
Rose Bowl UNIV. OF SOUTHERN CALIFORNIA 17 Michigan 10 (103,450)
Orange Bowl NOTRE DAME 21 Colorado 6 (81,190)
Sugar Bowl MIAMI 33 Alabama 25 (77,452)
Michigan won the College Football Championships (decided by a poll of journalists) for the third time in seven years.

———— CHAMPIONS ————

The National Football League (NFL) has been constituted as follows:
1921-32 One League only; 1933-49 Two divisions (Eastern and Western); 1950-52 Two Divisions and National Conferences; 1953-59 Two Divisions (Eastern and Western Conferences); 1960-69 Two Leagues (American Football League (AFL) and National Football League (NFL); 1970-Two (American Football Conference (AFC) and National Football Conference (NFC)
Play-offs introduced in 1933

Champions:

Year	Champion		
1921	Chicago Staleys		
1922	Canton Bulldogs (Ohio)		
1923	Canton Bulldogs (Ohio)		
1924	Cleveland Bulldogs		
1925	Chicago Cardinals		
1926	Frankford Yellowjackets (Philadelphia)		
1927	New York Giants		
1928	Providence Streamroller		
1929	Green Bay Packers		
1930	Green Bay Packers		
1931	Green Bay Packers		
1932	Chicago Bears		

NFL Play-off

Year	Winner	Score	Runner-up
1933	Chicago Bears	23-21	New York Giants
1934	New York Giants	30-13	Chicago Bears
1935	Detroit Lions	26-7	New York Giants
1936	Green Bay Packers	21-6	Boston Redskins
1937	Washington Redskins	28-21	Chicago Bears
1938	New York Giants	23-17	Green Bay Packers
1939	Green Bay Packers	27-0	New York Giants
1940	Chicago Bears	73-0	Washington Reds
1941	Chicago Bears	37-9	New York Giants
1942	Washington Redskins	14-6	Chicago Bears
1943	Chicago Bears	41-21	Washington Reds
1944	Green Bay Packers	14-7	New York Giants
1945	Cleveland Rams	15-14	Washington Reds
1946	Chicago Bears	24-14	New York Giants
1947	Chicago Cardinals	28-21	Philadelphia Eagles
1948	Philadelphia Eagles	7-0	Chicago Cardinals
1949	Philadelphia Eagles	14-0	Los Angeles Rams
1950	Cleveland Browns	30-28	Los Angeles Rams
1951	Los Angeles Rams	24-17	Cleveland Browns
1952	Detroit Lions	17-7	Cleveland Browns
1953	Detroit Lions	17-16	Cleveland Browns
1954	Cleveland Browns	56-10	Detroit Lions
1955	Cleveland Browns	38-14	Los Angeles Rams
1956	New York Giants	47-7	Chicago Bears
1957	Detroit Lions	59-14	Cleveland Browns
1958	Baltimore Colts	23-17	New York Giants
1959	Baltimore Colts	31-16	New York Giants

AFL/AFC Championship

Year	Winner	Score	Runner-up
1960	Houston Oilers	24-16	LA Chargers
1961	Houston Oilers	10-3	S.Diego Chargers
1962	Dallas Texans	20-17	Houston Oilers
1963	San Diego Chargers	51-10	Boston Patriots
1964	Buffalo Bills	20-7	S.Diego Chargers
1965	Buffalo Bills	23-0	S.Diego Chargers
1966	Kansas City Chiefs	31-7	Buffalo Bills
1967	Oakland Raiders	40-7	Houston Oilers
1968	New York Jets	27-23	Oakland Raiders
1969	Kansas City Chiefs	17-7	Oakland Raiders
1970	Baltimore Colts	27-17	Oakland Raiders
1971	Miami Dolphins	21-0	Baltimore Colts
1972	Miami Dolphins	21-17	Pitt. Steelers
1973	Miami Dolphins	27-10	Oakland Raiders
1974	Pittsburgh Steelers	24-13	Oakland Raiders
1975	Pittsburgh Steelers	16-10	Oakland Raiders
1976	Oakland Raiders	24-7	Pitt. Steelers
1977	Denver Broncos	20-17	Oakland Raiders
1978	Pittsburgh Steelers	34-5	Houston Oilers
1979	Pittsburgh Steelers	27-13	Houston Oilers
1980	Oakland Raiders	34-27	S.Diego Chargers
1981	Cincinnati Bengals	27-7	S.Diego Chargers
1982	Miami Dolphins	14-0	New York Jets
1983	Los Angeles Raiders	30-14	Seattle Seahawks
1984	Miami Dolphins	45-28	Pitt. Steelers
1985	New England Pats	31-14	Miami Dolphins
1986	Denver Broncos	23-20	Cleveland Browns
1987	Denver Broncos	38-33	Cleveland Browns
1988	Cincinnati Bengals	21-10	Buffalo Bills
1989	Denver Broncos	37-21	Cleveland Browns

NFL/NFC Championship

1960	Philadelphia Eagles	17-13	Green Bay Packers
1961	Green Bay Packers	37-0	New York Giants
1962	Green Bay Packers	16-7	New York Giants
1963	Chicago Bears	14-10	New York Giants
1964	Cleveland Browns	27-0	Baltimore Colts
1965	Green Bay Packers	23-12	Cleveland Browns
1966	Green Bay Packers	34-27	Dallas Cowboys
1967	Green Bay Packers	21-17	Dallas Cowboys
1968	Baltimore Colts	34-0	Cleveland Browns
1969	Minnesota Vikings	27-7	Cleveland Browns
1970	Dallas Cowboys	17-10	San Fran 49ers
1971	Dallas Cowboys	14-3	San Fran 49ers
1972	Washington Redskins	26-3	Dallas Cowboys
1973	Minnesota Vikings	27-10	Dallas Cowboys
1974	Minnesota Vikings	14-10	Los Angeles Rams
1975	Dallas Cowboys	37-7	Los Angeles Rams
1976	Minnesota Vikings	24-13	Los Angeles Rams
1977	Dallas Cowboys	23-6	Minnesota Vikings
1978	Dallas Cowboys	28-0	Los Angeles Rams
1979	Los Angeles Rams	9-0	Tampa Bay Buccs
1980	Philadelphia Eagles	20-7	Dallas Cowboys
1981	San Francisco 49ers	28-27	Dallas Cowboys
1982	Washington Redskins	31-17	Dallas Cowboys
1983	Washington Redskins	24-21	San Fran 49ers
1984	San Francisco 49ers	23-0	Chicago Bears
1985	Chicago Bears	24-0	Los Angeles Rams
1986	New York Giants	17-0	Washington Reds
1987	Washington Redskins	17-10	Minnesota Vikings
1988	San Francisco 49ers	28-3	Chicago Bears
1989	San Francisco 49ers	30-3	Los Angeles Rams

Superbowl

1967	Green Bay Packers	35-10	Kansas City Chiefs
	Memorial Coliseum, Los Angeles		
1968	Green Bay Packers	33-14	Oakland Raiders
	Orange Bowl, Miami		
1969	New York Jets	16-7	Baltimore Colts
	Orange Bowl, Miami		
1970	Kansas City Chiefs	23-7	Minnesota Vikings
	Tulane Stadium, New Orleans		
1971	Baltimore Colts	16-13	Dallas Cowboys
	Orange Bowl, Miami		
1972	Dallas Cowboys	24-3	Miami Dolphins
	Tulane Stadium, New Orleans		
1973	Miami Dolphins	14-7	Washington Redskins
	Memorial Coliseum, Los Angeles		
1974	Miami Dolphins	24-7	Minnesota Vikings
	Rice Stadium, Houston		
1975	Pittsburgh Steelers	16-6	Minnesota Vikings
	Tulane Stadium, New Orleans		
1976	Pittsburgh Steelers	21-17	Dallas Cowboys
	Orange Bowl, Miami		
1977	Oakland Raiders	32-14	Minnesota Vikings
	Rose Bowl, Pasadena		
1978	Dallas Cowboys	27-10	Denver Broncos
	Louisiana Superdome, New Orleans		
1979	Pittsburgh Steelers	35-31	Dallas Cowboys
	Orange Bowl, Miami		
1980	Pittsburgh Steelers	31-19	Los Angeles Rams
	Rose Bowl, Pasadena		
1981	Oakland Raiders	27-10	Philadelphia Eagles
	Louisiana Superdome, New Orleans		
1982	San Francisco 49ers	26-21	Cincinnati Bengals
	Pontiac Silverdome, Pontiac		
1983	Washington Redskins	27-17	Miami Dolphins
	Rose Bowl, Pasadena		
1984	Los Angeles Raiders	38-9	Washington Redskins
	Tampa Stadium, Tampa		
1985	San Francisco 49ers	38-16	Miami Dolphins
	Stanford Stadium, Stanford		
1986	Chicago Bears	46-10	New England Patriots
	Louisiana Superdome, New Orleans		
1987	New York Giants	39-20	Denver Broncos
	Rose Bowl, Pasadena		
1988	Washington Redskins	42-10	Denver Broncos
	Jack Murphy Stadium, San Diego		
1989	San Francisco 49ers	20-16	Cincinnati Bengals
	John Robbie Stadium, Miami		
1990	San Francisco 49ers	55-10	Denver Broncos
	Louisiana Superdome, New Orleans		

Wins: 4 Pittsburgh Steelers, San Francisco 49ers; 3 Oakland/LA Raiders, 2 Green Bay Packers, Washington Redskins, Dallas Cowboys, Miami Dolphins; 1 Chicago Bears, New York Giants, Baltimore Colts, Kansas City Chiefs.

Appearances: 5 Dallas Cowboys, Miami Dolphins; 4 Minnesota Vikings; Oakland/LA Raiders, Pittsburgh Steelers, San Francisco 49ers Washington Redskins; 3 Denver Broncos, 2 Baltimore Colts, Green Bay Packers, Kansas City Chiefs, Cincinnati Bengals; 1 Chicago Bears, Los Angeles Rams, New Patriots, New York Giants, New York Jets, Philadelphia Eagles.

Note: all Superbowls are played in the calendar year after the season they refer to. Thus the 1988 champions played the 1989 Superbowl.

> **❝ I refuse to sit back and give the credit to the other people. Because we stink.❞**
>
> *Mike Ditka, Chicago Bears coach, after losing to the Washington Redskins*

> **"I think he knows I'm doing one hell of a job. I've told him enough times."**
> *Buddy Ryan, Philadelphia Eagles coach, on relations with owner Norman Braman*

> **"If Buddy told me to jump off a bridge, well, I wouldn't do it, but I'd think about it."**
> *Jerome Brown, Eagles defensive tackle, on Ryan*

> **"Football combines the two worst things about American life. It is violence punctuated by committee meetings."**
> *George F. Will, US columnist*

> **"A sport in which grotesquely overdressed and often grossly overweight men run very short distances before thudding and blundering into each other en masse; whereupon the game stops dead, often for minutes at a time."**
> *Geoffrey Moorhouse, British author*

> **"Having had a lot of late nights by myself, I've become an addict of American Football.❞**
> *Salman Rushdie, British author*

ROSE BOWL

First played in 1902, and regularly since 1916.
All games played at the Rose Bowl, Pasadena, except 1942 at Durham, N. Carolina.

Results since 1981:

1981	Michigan	23-6	Washington
1982	Washington	28-0	Iowa
1983	UCLA	24-14	Michigan
1984	UCLA	45-9	Illinois
1985	USC	20-17	Ohio State
1986	UCLA	45-28	Iowa
1987	Arizona State	22-15	Michigan
1988	Michigan	20-17	So. California
1989	Michigan	22-14	So. California
1990	So. California	17-10	Michigan

AMERICAN BOWL

All Played at Wembley Stadium

1983	Minnesota Vikings	28-10	St Louis Cardinals
1986	Chicago Bears	17-6	Dallas Cowboys
1987	Los Angeles Rams	28-27	Denver Broncos
1988	Miami Dolphins	27-21	San Francisco 49ers
1989	Philadelphia Eagles	17-3	Cleveland Browns
1990	New Orleans Saints	17-10	Los Angeles Raiders

COCA-COLA BOWL (formerly Budweiser Bowl)

1986	London Ravens	20-12	Streatham Olympians
1987	London Ravens	40-23	Manchester All Stars
1988	Birmingham Bulls	30-6	London Olympians
1989	Manchester Spartans	21-14	Birmingham Bulls
1990	Manchester Spartans	27-25	Northampton Storm

EUROPEAN CHAMPIONSHIPS

1983	Italy	18-6	Finland
1985	Finland	13-2	Italy
1987	Italy	24-22	West Germany
1989	Great Britain	26-0	Finland

—— RECORDS ——

TEAM RECORDS

Record scores

Washington Redskins 0 Chicago Bears 73, 1940; Washington Redskins 72 New York Giants 41, 1966; Los Angeles Rams 70 Baltimore Colts 27, 1950; New York Bulldogs 20 Chicago Cardinals 65, 1949; Los Angeles Rams 65 Detroit Lions 24, 1950.

Most seasons as league champions

11 Green Bay; 9 Chicago Bears; 5 New York Giants

Most games won in regular season

15 San Francisco (1984); Chicago (1985) 14 Miami (1972, 1984); Pittsburgh (1970); Washington (1983); Chicago (1986); NY Giants (1986) San Francisco 49ers (1989)

Most consecutive games won (regular season)

14 Miami (1972); 13 Chicago Bears (1934); 12 Minnesota (1969); 12 Chicago (1985)

Passing - most passes completed (career)

3686 (6467) Fran Tarkenton (Minnesota, NY Giants) 1961-71; 3297 (5604) Dan Fouts (San Diego) 1973-87; 2830 (5186) Johnny Unitas (Baltimore, San Diego) 1956-73

(figures in brackets are passes attempted)

Passing - most yards gained (career)

47,003 Fran Tarkenton (Minnesota, NY Giants) 1961-71; 43,040 Dan Fouts (San Diego) 1973-87; 40,239 Johnny Unitas (Baltimore, San Diego) 1956-73.

Most consecutive home games without defeat

30 Green Bay (1928-33); 27 Miami (1971-74); 18 Chicago Bears (1932-35, 1941-44); Oakland (1969-70); Dallas (1979-81).

Most consecutive away games without defeat

13 Chicago Bears (1941-43); 12 Green Bay (1928-30); 11 LA/San Diego Chargers (1960-61); Los Angeles Rams (1966-68).

INDIVIDUAL RECORDS

Most games played in career

340 George Blanda (Chicago Bears, Baltimore, Houston, Oakland) 1949-75; 282 Jim Marshall (Cleveland, Minnesota) 1960-79; 263 Jan Stenerud (Kansas City, Green Bay, Minnesota) 1967-85.

Most seasons as coach

40 George Halas (Chicago Bears) 1920-67; 33 Earl Lambeau (Green Bay, Chicago Cardinals, Washington) 1921-53; 29 Tom Landry (Dallas) 1960-88.

Most points (career)

2002 George Blanda (Chicago Bears, Baltimore, Houston, Oakland) 1949-75; 1699 Jan Stenerud (Kansas City, Green Bay, Minnesota) 1967-85; 1439 Jim Turner (NY Jets, Denver) 1964-79.

Most points (season)

176 Paul Hornung (Green Bay) 1960; 161 Mark Moseley (Washington) 1983; 155 Gino Cappelletti (Boston) 1964.

Most points (game)

40 Ernie Havers Chicago Cardinals v Chicago Bears 1929; 36 Dub Jones Cleveland v Chicago Bears 1951; 36 Gale Sayers Chicago v San Francisco 1965; 33 Paul Hornung Green Bay v Baltimore 1961.

Rushing - most yards gained (career)

16,726 Walter Payton (Chicago) 1975-87; 12.739 Tony Dorsett (Dallas) 1977-89 12,312 Jim Brown (Cleveland) 1957-65; 12,120 Franco Harris (Pittsburgh, Seattle) 1972-84.

—— 1991 ——

Jan 5-6 Jan 12-13 AFC and NFC Divisional play-offs; Jan 20 AFC and NFC Championships; Jan 27 SUPERBOWL XXV (Tampa, Florida); Mar 23 World League of American Football starts; Aug 4 (prov) American Bowl (Wembley).

ANGLING

——— 1990 ———

WORLD FRESHWATER CHAMPIONSHIPS
River Drava, nr. Maribor, Yugoslavia, Sep 3

Individual
1 Bob Nudd (Eng) 2 pts
2 Kevin Ashurst (Eng) 4 pts
3 Romain Koenit (Lux) 5 pts

Team
1 France 60 pts
2 England 89 pts
3 Italy 89 pts

WORLD FLY FISHING CHAMPIONSHIPS
River Dee & Llyn Brenig, Wales, Sep 20-21

Individual
1 Franciszek Szajnik (Pol) 30,160 pts
2 Adam Sikora (Pol) 28,920 pts
3 A Bigare (Bel) 25,690 pts

Team
1 Czechoslovakia
2 Poland
3 Belgium

NATIONAL LEAGUE FIRST DIVISION
River Witham, Sep 8

Individual
1 Stuart Cheetham (Middle Nene) 20kg 390g
2 Dave Lutkin (Oundle AS) 16kg 131g
3 Chris Insley (Marazion AS) 14kg 390g

Team
1 Trevs AS
2 Isaak Walton, Preston
3 Leicester AS

——— CHAMPIONS ———

WORLD FRESHWATER CHAMPIONS
(since 1981)

	Individual	Team
1981	Dave Thomas (Eng)	France
1982	Kevin Ashurst (Eng)	Holland
1983	Wolf-Rudiger Kremkus (FRG)	Belgium
1984	Bobby Smithers (Ire)	Luxembourg
1985	Dave Roper (Eng)	England
1986	Lud Wever (Hol)	Italy
1987	Clive Branson (Wal)	England
1988	Jean-Pierre Fouquet (Fra)	England
1989	Tom Pickering (Eng)	France
1990	Bob Nudd (Eng)	France

Most wins - *Individual:* **3** Robert Tesse (Fra) 1959-60, 1965; Team: **12** France

———1991———

Sep 28 National League First Division (Leeds-Liverpool Canal, Wigan)

ARCHERY

——— 1990 ———

EUROPEAN CHAMPIONSHIPS
Barcelona, Jul 25-26
Men - *Individual*: Stanislav Zabrodsky (USSR) 335 pts
Men - *Team*: Soviet Union 984 pts
Women - *Individual*: Natalya Nasaridze (USSR) 330 pts
Women - *Team*: Soviet Union 987 pts

BRITISH TARGET CHAMPIONSHIPS
Lichfield, Aug 11-12
Men: Steve Hallard (Dunlop Archers) 2,284 pts
Women: Pauline Edwards (Atkins Archers) 2,278 pts

UK MASTERS
Lilleshall, Jun 9-10
Men: Steve Hallard (Dunlop Archers) 1,254 pts
Women: Pauline Edwards (Atkins Archers) 1,247 pts

——— CHAMPIONS ———

WORLD CHAMPIONS
(past 10 years)
Men

	Individual	Team
1981	Kysti Laasonen (Fin)	United States
1983	Richard McKinney (US)	United States
1985	Richard McKinney (US)	South Korea
1987	Vladimir Yesheyev (USSR)	South Korea
1989	Stanislav Zabrodsky (USSR)	USSR

Women

	Individual	Team
1981	Natalya Butuzova	USSR
1983	Kim Jin-Ho (SKo)	South Korea
1985	Irina Soldatova (USSR)	USSR
1987	Ma Xiagjun (Chn)	USSR
1989	Soo Nyung-Kim (SKo)	South Korea

OLYMPIC CHAMPIONS
Men

	Individual	Team
1972	John Williams (US)	-
1976	Darrell Pace (US)	-
1980	Tomi Poikolainen (Fin)	-
1984	Darrell Pace (US)	-
1988	Jay Barrs (US)	South Korea

Women

	Individual	Team
1972	Doreen Wilber (US)	-
1976	Luann Ryan (US)	-
1980	Keto Lossaberidze (USSR)	-
1984	Seo Hyang-Soon (SKo)	-
1988	Soo Nyang-Kim (SKo)	South Korea

——— 1991 ———

Mar 12-16 World Indoor Championships (Norway); Jun 8-9 UK Masters (Lilleshall); Jul 3-5 Grand National Archery Society meeting (Lilleshall); Aug 10-11 British Target Championships (Lichfield); Aug 20-24 World Target Championships (Poland).

ASSOCIATION FOOTBALL

n a seething evening in Rome, West Germany beat the previous champions Argentina 1-0 to win the World Cup for the third time. It was the sort of result many people might have predicted before the tournament began. But very few of the other ingredients in Italia '90 were remotely predictable. From the opening game, in which Cameroon - finishing with nine men - beat Argentina, to the moments after the final when Argentine players were berating the referee, soccer's great festival produced a succession of amazing events.

In the process, it caught the imagination of the planet. From almost all corners of the globe came reports of quite unprecedented TV viewing figures. Eighty per cent of Czechoslovaks were reported to be watching their country's games; half of Singapore was said to be sitting up all night; there was a riot in Calcutta when the electricity failed during a match; when Italy played, petty crime in Italian cities ceased; and whenever Cameroon scored, the roars could be heard all over the cities of Africa. Only two groups of people appeared immune to this sickness. One, unfortunately, was the population of the United States, which is staging the next Cup in 1994. The other was the smaller clique of footballing experts and purists who pronounced it quite the least skilful, most boring and most defensive World Cup ever staged. Statistics backed them up. The average number of goals per game slumped to 2.21, the lowest-ever.

The final was the embodiment of this. Argentina's main aim was to survive both normal and extra time and win in a penalty shoot-out, as they had done in their previous two games. The game became increasingly foul-tempered and after 64 minutes Pedro Monzon became the only player to be sent off in a World Cup final. This record remained unique for only 22 minutes before this team-mate Gustavo Dezotti joined him. Two minutes before that, Argentina's strategy collapsed when the Germans were awarded a penalty, hit home by Andreas Brehme. The legitimacy of the penalty remained in dispute though the consensus outside Argentina was that justice had been done, if only roughly: Argentina deserved to lose and the Germans were not unworthy champions of the world.

The Italians also found it hard to share this view. The World Cup cost the country more than £3 billion, double the original estimate. The rush to finish the stadiums also cost the lives of 16 construction workers. The least Italy expected in return was to win. With their defence impenetrable and the attack bolstered by the emergence of a new goal-scoring hero, Salvatore "Toto" Schillaci, a crew-cut Sicilian with wild, inventor's eyes, the Italians progressed serenely to the semi-finals and remained as favourites, even though the Germans played with more élan. Germany played poorly only once, against Czechoslovakia. Their team physician said this was because they had eaten too much meat and not enough pasta beforehand.

The other two semi-finalists reached there anything but serenely. Argentina, after their initial disaster, did not progress so much as slither towards the final. Diego Maradona spent much of the tournament either arguing or horizontal (he was fouled 53 times) and produced only the briefest twinkles of his 1986 form. His team only scraped into the last 16 in third place in their group, knocked out Brazil against the run of play and beat both Yugoslavia and Italy on penalties. All Italy went quiet. The nation later consoled itself with Schillaci's victory in both the Golden Boot award for top scorer and the Golden Ball as best player, and tables in the sports papers which showed Italy would have won had the Cup been decided on points. In his home town, Palermo, a special mass was held to celebrate Schillaci's goals.

The English World Cup campaign had begun in a manner only possible in England. The war between the tabloid press and the England manager Bobby Robson had gone cold through a season in which the team established a run of 17 unbeaten matches. The week before England left for Italy, it went nuclear again. The newspaper *Today* ran a story saying that Robson was resigning as manager because a former lover of his was about to tell all. The story was partially true - Robson was indeed quitting, to take over as manager of the Dutch club PSV Eindhoven. There was no corroboration for the second part and Robson was livid. *Today* responded by calling him "a liar, a cheat and a traitor".

For the first fortnight, there appeared to be two World Cups: the main tournament, which was going rather well, and a sour-tempered sideshow in Sardinia, where the England team and the press on the one hand stared sullenly at each other - as did the England fans and the thousands of Italian police brought in to control them. The atmosphere worsened after a dreadful performance in the opening game against Ireland. "Bring them Home!" screamed *The Sun*. Though alcohol bans and fierce policing reduced the trouble amongst supporters, there were still two serious riots in Cagliari. There was a widespread feeling that the sooner England departed from the World Cup, the better.

Then suddenly the mood changed. After drawing with Holland and beating Egypt 1-0, England qualified as group winners. They beat Belgium with a goal in the 119th minute from the substitute David Platt and then came back from 2-1 down to beat Cameroon and earn a semi-final against the Germans. The nation suddenly rediscovered cheap patriotism (WE BEAT THEM IN 1945. NOW THE BATTLE OF 1990. HERR WE GO AGAIN - *The Sun*). Offices closed early so people could get home to watch the Germany game. And England played magnificently, dominating for long periods. But the teams were still level after two hours. The dreaded shoot-out came into effect - and then Stuart Pearce missed the most important shot of his life.

RAPTUROUS RETURN

Nonetheless, the team had done better than England had ever done overseas and returned home amidst general rapture, which Robson's long-standing press critics were forced to join in. The team also won the Fair Play award, because they fouled slightly less regularly than any of the other teams. A massive crowd met them at Luton Airport. Paul Gascoigne, whose skill and personality had dominated the team after Bryan Robson had observed personal tradition and gone home early through injury, put on a pair of false women's breasts and no one minded terribly much. Umbro, makers of the England strip, put on extra shifts to cope with the demand and Gascoigne applied to register the nickname "Gazza" as a trade mark.

In this extraordinary atmosphere, the politicians suddenly changed tack. Only ten days earlier, Colin Moynihan, the Sports Minister and pint-sized scourge of the football hooligans, had praised the Italian police for rounding up and deporting 246 English supporters in Rimini after fighting there - even though most of them had clearly not been involved. Suddenly, Moynihan pronounced himself satisfied with the fans and agreed with UEFA that English clubs should be re-admitted to European competition, five years after the Heysel Stadium disaster led to their exile.

There had indeed been little trouble in Italy at England's last two matches. The trouble had come in England instead. After the Cameroon game, 600 people were arrested in towns all over the country. In Brighton, 300 foreign students had to be locked in a nightclub for their own safety and Mrs Jackie Penfold, a 63-year-old publican, died of a heart attack as rioters tried to kick in her pub windows. In Totton, Hants, Ronald Goodwin, 33, died after being knocked to the ground as he tried to stop a gang damaging a garden fence. In Grantham the windows of Mrs Thatcher's former corner-shop home were smashed.

Two other teams provided major diversions during the World Cup. One was the Republic of Ireland, who reached the quarter-finals, losing to Italy, having been wafted all the way on a wave of Celtic romanticism - even though the manager and three-quarters of his squad had only marginal Irish connections and their football ranged between clod-hopping and crass. The other was Cameroon, who posed problems from the start both for spectators, uncertain where the country actually was, and their opponents. Cameroon's style was also based on muscularity rather than finesse but it was combined with speed and a vibrancy which suggested that Africa's long-awaited emergence from the footballing shadows was at last happening. FIFA announced that Africa would have three representatives instead of two in the 1994 Cup. President Biya of Cameroon was cheered at his party congress when he promised democracy; he was reportedly cheered twice as loud when he praised the football team. The Cameroon star was Roger Milla, the most improbable player in the whole World Cup. He had actually retired and was playing amateur soccer on the French island of Reunion when he was recalled to the team. A bit too ancient at 38 to play a full game, he kept coming on as substitute, scoring the crucial goals and then rushing to the corner flag to do a wiggle and shimmy.

Among other World Cup personalities were Isabella Ciaravolo, a Sardinian liaison officer attached to the England team, who was "re-assigned" after unsubstantiated press reports that she was liaising more closely than was intended. Bobby Robson denied the rumours, according to *Private Eye*, on the grounds that "None of my lads has scored in years". There was her outraged brother who was alleged to be on his way down from the mountains with a shotgun to settle his grievance with the press in the customary Sardinian fashion. There was Olga Stringfellow, Bryan Robson's faith healer, who was flown out to join the party but failed to prevent him being invalided out of his third successive World Cup. There was Chris Wright who organised the march in Sardinia which led to the worst rioting; he turned out to have been a Labour candidate at the past two general elections. There were also players like the Germans Matthäus and Klinsmann who simply played good, effective football. And of course there were the Scots who followed their own strange World Cup logic by losing to Costa Rica and threatening to beat Brazil. They failed to qualify.

Two English fans were killed in Italy: Robert Hawkins, 20, died in a bus crash in Sardinia which injured 33 other spectators. David Monaghan, 26, died when he was hit by a car as he ran away from two Italian fans in Bologna. Four people died in traffic accidents during Germany's victory celebrations. Thirty-one people died in Petrozavodsk, Soviet Union, when a bus driven by a man rushing home to watch the final was hit by a train.

DOMESTIC DISARRAY

The euphoria produced enormous expectations at the start of the 1990-91 season. However, two weeks before it began, the Football League remained unsure which teams would be where. Swindon Town, originally promoted to the First Division, were sensationally demoted to the Third instead by the League after pleading guilty to 35 charges of illegal payments to players. On appeal, the FA halved this punishment and left them in the Second. This all led to despair in Swindon and utter confusion elsewhere, as there was no procedure to decide who should go up instead. The League decided to promote Sunderland and Tranmere, the beaten play-off finalists, rather than reprieve Sheffield Wednesday and Bournemouth, the teams most narrowly relegated. Wednesday threatened to sue the League for "wrongful relegation" and Tranmere were embittered when the FA ruling left them back in the Third. Further chaos was caused by Aldershot who surpassed all previous acts of brinkmanship by bankrupt clubs. The company was wound up in the High Court owing £490,000. The argument was raging about who should replace them in the Fourth Division when a 19-year-old public schoolboy turned property speculator, Spencer Trethewy, appeared with £200,000. He was taken seriously.

The 1989-90 season finished in more usual fashion with Liverpool winning the Championship for the tenth time in 15 years. They were troubled for a long while by Aston Villa, whose manager Graham Taylor was rewarded - if that is the word - with Bobby Robson's bed of nails as England manager. Liverpool interspersed some great performances (like their wins at Maine Road and Stamford Bridge) with some much sleepier ones. The greatest of all came early on, when they blew away Crystal Palace 9-0, the biggest First Division win since 1963 when Fulham, of all teams, beat Ipswich 10-1. It was the first time in League history that eight different players on the same side had scored. But Villa managed to harry Liverpool until April Fool's Day when they lost a big televised game at home to Manchester City who had gone 42 First Division away games without winning. "We played like schoolboys," moaned Graham Taylor. Thereafter Villa forgot how to score goals and finished nine points adrift.

Charlton's term of office as the First Division's resident escapologists finally concluded and they went down without a whimper along with Millwall, who had three managers and just five wins. They looked like being joined by Luton - who had four chairmen in the year - until the final day, when an unexpected set of results propelled them ahead of Ron Atkinson's Sheffield Wednesday. Earlier in the season, a hypnotherapist offered to rid Wednesday's players of their subconscious feelings of inferiority.

For much of the season, Manchester United looked like relegation candidates too. They enlivened the early weeks of the season when Martin Edwards, the chief executive, sold his controlling stake for £20 million to a property developer and ego-tripper named Michael Knighton who went on to the field on the opening day and did ball-juggling tricks. The deal was criticised by everyone including the Takeover Panel and later unravelled. Eventually, Edwards relinquished overall control by selling some shares but remained in day-to-day charge of the club. His manager Alex Ferguson took his overall expenditure past £13 million but appeared to be getting nowhere. When United lost 5-1 to Manchester City, local humorists called it a snooker result - the blues worth five, and the reds one. When United kept losing to just about everyone else, it was suggested Ferguson was due for the OBE: Out By Easter.

It appeared that Ferguson might be sacked as soon as United went out of the FA Cup. But United never did go out of the Cup. The first all-seater final at Wembley, between United and Crystal Palace, produced the highest scoring since 1953, the first-ever 3-3 draw and extra time for the seventh time in ten years. Two goals by the substitute Ian Wright, injured since March, put Palace ahead but Mark Hughes scored his second goal to send the game to a replay. "I was born for this day," said Wright. The replay was dreadful. Palace concentrated on niggling and were beaten by two men who cost Ferguson not one penny of his 13 million. The only goal came from Lee Martin, who was signed on the YTS scheme. Palace's forwards were blunted by Les Sealey, on loan from Luton Reserves, who was preferred for the replay to Scotland's first-choice goalkeeper Jim Leighton. Sealey played perfectly then offered his winners' medal to Leighton (who was entitled to one anyway) and slipped quietly away without joining the celebrations. United equalled Villa and Spurs with seven wins, Bryan Robson became the first captain to lift the Cup three times, Ferguson kept his job.

PALACE COUP

If United's participation in the final was improbable, Palace's was little short of miraculous. They were drawn against Liverpool in the semi-final just seven months after their 9-0 horror. Liverpool were stunned by an equaliser seconds after the restart and, as David Lacey put it in *The Guardian*, "the season's most foregone conclusion became a classic cup-tie". After 19 minutes of extra time, Alan Pardew headed the winner to give Palace a 4-3 win; Pardew's only previous Cup goal was for Corinthian-Casuals in 1985. The last comparable shock in a semi-final was Leicester's win over Portsmouth in 1949.

United were almost shocked themselves by Second Division Oldham, who held them 3-3 in the first game before going down in extra time of the replay. The 13 goals in the two original semi-finals were scored by 13 different players. Other teams to make a mark on the Cup included Aylesbury, who beat Fourth Division Southend while the crowd in the Chicken Run chanted "There's only one Allan Pluckrose"; Blackpool, who won the re-run of 1953 against Bolton, (in the First Round this time, not the final) with a goal made by Matthews (Neil this time, not Stanley); and Fourth Division Cambridge United. Their players were ordered to take cold showers by the new manager John Beck. They promptly knocked out First Division Millwall 1-0 and the Third Division leaders Bristol City 5-1. In the sixth round, against Palace, they marched out to the anthem "Fanfare to the Common Man" before going out 1-0.

However, Oldham were the real giant-killers. They produced a succession of sensational results, particularly on their own plastic pitch. Their first semi-final in 77 years came after wins over Everton and Aston Villa. However, that was hardly a shock. They also had an amazing run in the Littlewoods Cup, beating Leeds, Scarborough 7-0 (Frankie Bunn scoring six), Arsenal, Southampton and, in the semi-finals, West Ham with a 6-0 win in the first leg. In the final, they lost narrowly to Nottingham Forest. All this distracted them from their main aim of winning promotion and Oldham faded to finish eighth. Nonetheless, a more imaginative jury would have chosen Joe Royle rather than Kenny Dalglish as manager of the year.

The teams who did go up to the First Division were Leeds, Sheffield United and - thanks to Swindon's shenanigans - Sunderland. Sheffield United were sold, before the deal was cancelled, to an Iraqi-born businessman, Sam Hashimi, apparently fronting a mysterious Saudi-based consortium. Hashimi claimed there were a million Blades supporters in the Middle East. The Watford chairman Elton John did sell out, after 14 years; Jack Petchey, vice-chairman of West Ham, bought his shares and took control. At Portsmouth, the goalposts were several inches too low for the first three months of the season but no one noticed; one of their supporters, however, was enthusiastic enough to change his name to John Anthony Portsmouth Football Club Westwood. Stoke City were among the clubs consigned to the Third Division, for the first time since 1927. One Mick Farebrother was jailed in California for grand theft after receiving a $2000 advance from the San Francisco Blackhawks on the basis that he had scored 17 goals for Stoke last season. The team only scored 35 between them. The two Bristol clubs were both promoted from the Third, along with Notts County. Exeter led the parade up from the Fourth.

Major League transfers included the sale of Gary Pallister from Middlesbrough to Manchester United for £2.3m and Tony Cascarino from Millwall to Aston Villa for £1.5m. Cascarino was originally bought by Gillingham from an amateur club in return for 12 tracksuits, two footballs and some corrugated iron. Three goalkeepers were transferred for over £1m: Nigel Martyn (Bristol Rovers to Crystal Palace), David Seaman (QPR to Arsenal) and John Lukic (Arsenal to Leeds). Seaman's fee equalled the world record for a goalkeeper of £1.3m; Rovers intend to replace Martyn with a new ground.

The Fulham goalkeeper Jim Stannard, in keeping with the club's long tradition of eccentricity, scored the winner against Crewe with a drop kick that bounced over the head of the opposing keeper. A promising teenager, Chaz Hodges turned down the chance of signing for Manchester United because they wanted him to have a hair cut. "I won't cut my hair for anyone except for my mum," he said. Ian Bowyer, the Hereford player-manager, went on to join his son Gary during the game at Scunthorpe. This was only the second time father and son have played together in the League, after Alec and David Herd, for Stockport against Hartlepool in 1950. Bowyer snr was later sacked for failing to secure Bowyer jnr's contract.

He was one of 36 League managers to go the way of all managerial flesh. Eighteen of the casualties were overtly sacked, two of them by Millwall. The rate of departure was slightly above the post-war mean: the average manager is supposed to last 3.3 years. The casualties included Mel Machin of Manchester City (replaced by Howard Kendall), Trevor Francis of QPR (replaced by Don Howe), Colin Appleton of Hull (after 14 games and no wins), Mick Mills of Stoke (after two wins in 30 games) and Lou Macari of West Ham. Macari had been appointed to change the club's good-natured image but revelations emanating from Swindon, Macari's previous club, included his involvement in a betting scandal-ette and he resigned amid a feeling that he was changing the image too well. Macari had lasted eight months against a club average of 15 years. He was

A WORD FROM THE MANAGEMENT

"I honestly hate spending club money."
Alex Ferguson, Manchester United

"Every time somebody looks at me I feel I have betrayed that man."
Alex Ferguson after losing 5-1 to Manchester City

"I'll have a large arsenic."
Terry Venables, Spurs, after losing 4-1 at home to Chelsea

"We cannot fall into the trap of committing practical haplography. It is also a dangerous feeling to consider that where we are in the league is of acceptable standard because standard is relevant to the standards we have set, which thereby may well indicate that we have not aspired to the standard we set ourselves. We must be the harbingers and nothing less than this can be acceptable."
Colin Murphy, Lincoln, winner of Golden Ball statuette presented by the Plain English campaign

"The last time we got a penalty away from home, Christ was a carpenter."
Lennie Lawrence, Charlton

"I hope you were as delighted as I was last weekend when Nelson Mandela was freed from a South African jail. But what I hadn't bargained for was the fact that his release was going to cut across the start of our Littlewoods Cup semi-final against Coventry."
Brian Clough, Nottingham Forest, in his programme notes

"Of course I won't say no – there's 15 games left – but if I said yes, you'd think 'what a prat'."
John Barnwell, Walsall, asked if they could avoid relegation

"I learn a little bit from all managers I got in football. Even some manager who maybe wasn't so good, I picked things up. As a player I always feel I was learning things – from players around, bad players, opposition.' What did he learn from Menotti? 'Smoke.' Burkinshaw? 'Play golf.'"
Interview with Ossie Ardiles, Swindon, in You magazine

"The management of the hotel we lodged in in Lagos kept my boys awake all night by deliberately showing endless pornography films on video."
Momar Thioune of the Senegalese club Diaraf, explaining defeat in Nigeria

"If you're a football manager, you don't have fitted carpets."
John Barnwell

"At least I haven't had a vote of confidence."
Lennie Lawrence

"Horrible as it sounds, passion and determination are more important than skill."
Steve Coppell, Crystal Palace

"I should be paid a million pounds a year for this job."
Alex Ferguson, Manchester United

"Football management these days is like nuclear warfare, there are no winners, just survivors."
Tommy Docherty

succeeded by an Upton Park family member, Billy Bonds, who improved the results. Graham Taylor, who was emphatically not sacked, was replaced by the manager of the Czechoslovak national team Dr Jozef Venglos, causing some initial consternation among the players. "You don't know where you are with a foreigner," Gordon Cowans was reported as saying.

Two League grounds were sold to developers: Walsall found a new stadium to replace Fellows Park; Chester City rendered themselves homeless by selling Sealand Road and were briefly in danger of extinction before the League grudgingly gave them permission to share with Macclesfield for a season. Charlton supporters took their campaign for a return from exile at Selhurst Park into the council elections at Greenwich. The Valley Party (no other policies) received 14,358 votes, ten per cent of the poll and ahead of both the Liberals and Charlton's average home gate. Most of the other 90 clubs thought about moving, including Liverpool who "reluctantly" decided not to join Everton in a 67,000-seat stadium at Aintree and instead went on with the hopeless task of improving Anfield.

THE HILLSBOROUGH LEGACY

The activity was forced on clubs by Lord Justice Taylor, whose full report into the Hillsborough Disaster demanded changes which the clubs costed at £666 million for the whole package, or £329 million for the essentials. He added 33 further recommendations to those made in his interim report, including an insistence on all-seater stadiums, for major clubs by 1994, the rest by 1999. He also strongly criticised the hated scheme to force football supporters to carry ID cards and the Government, embarrassed, finally dropped it. To try and raise money for improvements, the League voted to increase the population of the First Division in 1991 from 20 back to 22 - just when fixture congestion was about to increase again because of the end of the European ban. "Plain daft," said Graham Kelly, the FA secretary.

There was some limited optimism during the season that English football grounds were getting safer. "Without wishing to tempt providence," said John Stalker, the former police chief now advising Millwall, "things are better than for 20 years. It's almost as if hooliganism isn't fashionable any more." He was speaking just before the May Bank Holiday, when Leeds were at Bournemouth in a vital end-of-season game. There were 102 arrests, 12 serious injuries to the police and £40,000 worth of damage. There was trouble the same day at Chesterfield, Leicester and Birmingham. Police had warned the League to switch the Leeds fixture away from a holiday weekend, and the Home Secretary had his revenge for the ID defeat by forcing League officials to agree to give police a veto in future. There were 66 arrests after Sunderland went 2-0 up in their promotion play-off and Newcastle fans invaded the pitch in an obvious attempt to get the game abandoned. It was revealed that Arsenal's game against Chelsea required 360 police constables, 40 sergeants, 20 senior officers including a commander, 20 horses, 20 German shepherd dogs and a helicopter. Two Crystal Palace fans, on the way to the Cup final replay, saved a blind man who fell off the packed platform at East Croydon station in front of a train.

Soccer in Scotland was again dominated by Rangers, who were unchallenged at the top of the Premier Division from just before Christmas. They first went top on November 4 when Mo Johnston scored the only goal of the game against his former club Celtic; and they consolidated after winning the New Year Old Firm game as well. The manager Graeme Souness took his spending up to £13m and the club announced plans to bring out its own range of wines: Blue Nun, someone suggested. Souness's touchline ban was extended until 1992. Rangers' nearest rivals Aberdeen won both the Scottish Cup (beating Celtic 9-8 on penalties) and the Skol Cup. Celtic, meanwhile, lost more games than they won for the first time since the foundation of the Premier Division and the fans demonstrated against the Board after a defeat against Motherwell. Wallace Mercer, chairman of Hearts, tried to take over their Edinburgh rivals Hibernian before being deafened by the cries of dismay. Two Dublin businessmen, Colm McCarthy and Jonathan Irwin, announced a plan to form a Dublin club to compete in the Scottish League. "Is it April the first?" asked the League secretary Peter Donald. At Firs Park, East Stirlingshire's ground, only 18 people were in the ground at 2.45 so, rather than the team names, the Tannoy man announced their names instead. In a Skol Cup tie against Hearts, Falkirk equalled the British record of three men sent off.

In English non-League soccer, Darlington followed Lincoln by winning the GM-Vauxhall Conference and escaping back to the Fourth Division at the first attempt. Barnet were runners-up for the third time in four years. Crowds in the Conference were a record 659,835 - 83,000 up on the previous best. Two of its members left famous, sloping grounds to move to new stadiums: Yeovil sold The Huish, where they knocked Sunderland out of the Cup in 1949, to Tesco and sods of turf to supporters at £5 a time. Wycombe Wanderers moved from Loakes Park after 95 years. Newport AFC, successors to the club which went out of the League and business in 1989, played a season 75 miles from home in Moreton-in-Marsh, and won both the Federated Homes League and the right to move back to Somerton Park.

Dunstable were another club who had three men sent off: in an FA Cup tie at Staines; the remaining eight players walked off in protest and the club withdrew from the competition. They had not been expected to win it. Farnborough Town players had a whipround towards expenses of supporters who travelled to Northwich. Colin Revel, refereeing Langley Park v Northallerton in the Northern League Second Division, sent off both goalkeepers for swearing at their own players. The game ended 0-0. Martin McGuckin, a builders' labourer, was ordered to pay £12,681 damages to Trefor Parry, a policeman he injured in a "crude and reckless" tackle in a game between Holyhead Town and Treaddur Bay in 1984. The centre-half for the Tunisian Embassy, playing in the Middlesex Amateur League, refused to be sent off, claiming diplomatic immunity.

Goalkeeper Mike Bennett, playing for St Philips of Bristol, failed to move when a ball was punted over his head into the goal and was found to be immobilised by hypothermia. The Eton Manor left-back Neil Carlstrom scored a hat-trick of own goals in the Essex Senior League match against Canvey Island. John Varney, 58, scored a hat-trick for Heyford Athletic in the Oxfordshire League. Tony Hunt of Brampton Dynamoes in Rotherham had a goal disallowed after it was headed in by a small mongrel using the post for other purposes. Hook Advertising of London, playing a rival company BIPS of Cambridge, smuggled George Best - a friend of the managing director - into the ground to come on as a surprise substitute at half-time when Hook were losing 2-0. They finished losing 7-0. Impact United of the Matlock and District League finished the season with a record of Played 21, Won 0, Drawn 1, Lost 20. Unfortunately, they failed to fulfil their last fixture, had three points deducted and thus finished with minus two.

ITALIAN TREBLE

Italian clubs won all three European tournaments, the first time any country has done this. AC Milan won the European Cup thanks to their three Dutchmen: van Basten made the goal for Rijkaard in the 1-0 win over Benfica and Gullit played marvellously; none of them did anything of the kind in the World Cup. Sampdoria won the Cup-Winners Cup and Juventus won the UEFA Cup; their manager Dino Zoff was still fired. Nine of the 11 British clubs competing were knocked out at the first attempt, including Rangers, who lost their first game 3-1 at home to Bayern. Derry City were beaten 2-1 at home by Benfica; their captain, Felix Healy who doubles as a rock singer, returned straight after the game to his role as Teen Angel in Grease at the Derry Rialto.

Milan had been aiming to win every tournament they entered but lost the league to Naples and were beaten in the cup final by Juventus. Roberto Baggio was transferred from Fiorentina to Juventus for 16 billion lire (£7.7 million), easily beating Gullit's world record. Fernando D'Ercoli, playing for Pianta against Arpax in an Italian amateur game, was shown the red card by the referee, snatched it and ate it.

Three people died in the celebrations marking Naples' League title and 170 people were arrested across Europe that same weekend suggesting a trend towards European unity. Football hooliganism continued to spread round the globe, a triumph in some degree for British exports. Long before the World Cup, there was trouble at England matches in Sweden and Poland and 16 Swansea fans were jailed in Athens. But a good deal was indigenous. There was regular violence in many European countries, especially Holland which had eight serious injuries when a home-made bomb exploded at an Ajax v Feyenoord game. And it spread to many more improbable places: Bangladesh, where

100 people were injured in fighting between fans at Chittagong; India, where the final of the Dr BC Roy tournament between Meghalaya and Indian Railways was abandoned after a crowd of 50,000 invaded the field; Uzbekistan in the Soviet Union where fans angry about the cancellation of a game damaged 100 buildings; and Australia, where soccer authorities banned flags other than the national one because of ethnic clashes. Even placid Switzerland and Belgium reported problems: FC Bruges won the Belgian League and their fans celebrated by hurling billiard balls at the police along with crosses stolen from a cemetery. In Somalia, after President Siad Barre had made a speech at a football match, his bodyguard shot dead at least seven protesters, maybe many more.

There was a scandal in Greece when international referee Kostas Dimitriades alleged

---

"Let's stop playing football for half a year. We are paying the price of our own tolerance. It has become more than a soccer problem. It is a problem of society."
Arie van Eijden, Ajax director

"Those who cause the trouble are basically terrorists. I don't even want to mention soccer in the same breath because the situation is ridiculous."
Terry Venables, Spurs manager

"I kicked the boy in the face in the same way you would kick a football."
Gary Walker, England fan, in a Stockholm court

"I get a strange swell of pride when I hear of our football hooligans causing trouble abroad. It disgusts me when I read the papers talking as if they were animals or something... There were jewellers' shops in Stockholm that didn't have bars on the windows. To people who have got nothing that is provocation."
Joe Strummer, former lead singer with The Clash

"Don't call me a yob or I'll come over there and kick your face in."
Geoffrey Patten (Conservative) at Wolverhampton Council police committee debate on football hooliganism

"The police commander, a football man, posed a rhetorical question: 'Six of my men are in hospital and what are we talking about? A game. Is it all worth it?' The answer, of course, must be no. Some 700 police, 200 of them in full riot gear, fighting pitched battles to allow one Second Division match to go ahead. Madness."
Joe Lovejoy, The Independent, on Bournemouth v Leeds

---

that games were fixed by a group of managers, referees and journalists. The affair became an election issue with the Conservatives claiming the Socialists had been responsible. Franco Baresi, Italy's former World Cup captain, was jailed for 10 months and fined six million lire (£3,000) for failing to declare unofficial payments to the tax authorities. Nineteen other players were also convicted. A Colombian linesman, Alvaro Ortega, was murdered by two gunmen after running the line in a game between Independiente Medellin and America de Cali. The crowd had become angry because Ortega had allegedly favoured Cali. The Colombian season was eventually scrapped because of continual scandals involving the drug cartels. In an attempt to revive interest, Chile abolished offside, the throw-in, defensive walls and points for goalless draws. A Uruguayan programme of First Division fixtures contained seven games which produced seven red cards, and three goals. A player banned from a game in Beirut shot his coach dead and was then executed by local militia. Four players from the Tongogara club in Zimbabwe were banned for life for urinating on the field; a witchdoctor had told them that would ensure victory.

Meanwhile, the fashion designer John Galliano put tiny, shiny football shorts on his woman models. This suggested that, in spite of everything, football was becoming modish again. The World Cup viewing figures said the same.

THE WORLD CUP 1990

GROUP A

Rome, Jun 9, Att: 72,303

Italy	1	Austria	0

Schillaci 78

Schillaci scored less than four minutes after coming on as substitute. Italian TV audience highest in history.

Florence, Jun 10, Att: 33,266

Czechoslovakia	5	United States	1

Skuhravy 25, 79   Caligiuri
Bilek (Pen) 38
Hasek 51
Luhovy 90

Wynalda (US) sent off after 52 minutes. US TV audience measured at 1.2% of homes with cable

Rome, Jun 14, Att: 73,423

Italy	1	United States	0

Giannini 11

US victory quoted at 50-1 by William Hill, believed to be a record for any sports match.

Florence, Jun 15, Att: 38,962

Czechoslovakia	1	Austria	0

Bilek (pen) 29

Rome, Jun 19, Att: 73,303

Italy	2	Czechoslovakia	0

Schillaci 9
Baggio 77

Baggio beat two defenders before scoring brilliant goal.

Florence, Jun 19, Att: 34,857

Austria	2	United States	1

Ogris 49, Rodax 63   Murray 83

Artner (Austria) sent off after 33 minutes. Yellow cards: Austria 5; US 4.

Final Table

	P	W	D	L	F	A	PTS
ITALY	3	3	0	0	4	0	6
Czechoslovakia	3	2	0	1	6	3	4
Austria	3	1	0	2	2	3	2
United States	3	0	0	3	2	8	0

GROUP B

Milan, Jun 8, Att: 73,780

Cameroon	1	Argentina	0

Omam Biyik 67

Cameroon 14-1 with some London bookmakers. Massing and Kana-Biyik (Cameroon) sent off, 61 and 88 minutes. Sun headline: "Loony Roons Bargy Argie." Clarin (Buenos Aires) headline: "We Lost?"

Naples, Jun 13, Att: 55,759

Argentina	2	Soviet Union	0

Troglio 27
Buruchaga 79

Argentine goalkeeper Pumpido, broke leg colliding with team-mate Olarticoechea. Maradona saved a goal with his hand: no penalty. Bessonov (USSR) sent off, 48 minutes. Six yellow cards (five Argentine). Referee Fredriksson of Sweden threatened with being sent home.

Bari, Jun, Att: 38,687

Cameroon	2	Romania	1

Milla 76, 86   Balint 88

Milla came on as substitute after 58 minutes.

Bari, Jun 18, Att: 37,307

Soviet Union	4	Cameroon	0

Protasov 20, Zygantovich 29

Zavarov 52, Dobrovolsky 63

Cameroon had already qualified for the next round.

Naples, Jun 18, Att: 52,733

Argentina	1	Romania	1

Monzon 61   Balint 68

Final Table

	P	W	D	L	F	A	PTS
CAMEROON	3	2	0	1	3	5	4
Romania	3	1	1	1	4	3	3
Argentina	3	1	1	1	3	2	3
Soviet Union	3	1	0	2	4	4	2

GROUP C

Turin, Jun 10, Att: 62,628

Brazil	2	Sweden	1

Careca 40, 62   Brolin 78

Genoa, Jun 11, Att: 30,867

Costa Rica	1	Scotland	0

Cayaso 49

Turin, Jun 16, Att: 58,007

Brazil	1	Costa Rica	0

Muller 33

Costa Rica had no shots at goal and no corners.

Genoa, Jun 16, Att: 31.823

Scotland	2	Sweden	1

McCall 10, Johnston 81 (Pen)   Strömberg 85

Genoa, Jun 20, Att: 30,223

Costa Rica	2	Sweden	1

Flores 74, Medford 86   Ekström 31

Costa Rica were the only side in first round matches to come from behind to win.

Turin, Jun 20, Att: 62,502

Brazil	1	Scotland	0

Muller 81

Final Table

	P	W	D	L	F	A	PTS
BRAZIL	3	3	0	0	4	1	6
Costa Rica	3	2	0	1	3	2	4
Scotland	3	1	0	2	2	3	2
Sweden	3	0	0	3	3	6	0

GROUP D

Bologna, Jun 9, Att: 30,791

Colombia	2	United Arab Emirates	0

Redin 50, Valderrama 85

Milan, Jun 10, Att: 74,765

West Germany	4	Yugoslavia	1

Matthaus 28, 63, Völler 69   Jozic 54
Klinsmann 39

Riot after game led to deportation of 52 German supporters

Bologna, Jun 14, Att: 32,257

Yugoslavia	1	Colombia	0

Jozic 73

Higuita (Col) saved penalty by Hadzibejic, 76 mins

Milan, Jun 15, Att: 71,167

West Germany	5	United Arab Emirates	1

Völler 35, 74, Klinsmann 37   Khalid Ismail
Matthäus 47, Bein 58   Mubarak 46

Milan, Jun 19, Att: 72.510

| Colombia | 1 | West Germany | 1 |
| Rincon 90 | | Littbarski 88 | |

Colombian equaliser came in second minute of injury time.

Bologna, June 19, Att: 27,833

Yugoslavia	4	United Arab Emirates	1
Susic 4, Pancev 8, 46		Ali Thani Jumaa 21	
Prosinecki 90			

Mabarak (UAE 76 minutes) became 50th man in World Cup history to be sent off.

Final Table

	P	W	D	L	F	A	PTS
WEST GERMANY	3	2	1	0	10	3	5
Yugoslavia	3	2	0	1	6	5	4
Colombia	3	1	1	1	3	2	3
United Arab Emirates	3	0	0	3	2	11	0

GROUP E

Verona, Jun 12, Att: 32,486

| Belgium | 2 | South Korea | 0 |
| Dargrijse 52, De Wolf 63 | | | |

Udine, Jun 13, Att: 35,713

| Spain | 0 | Uruguay | 0 |

Sosa (Spa) missed penalty, 71 mins

Udine, June 17, Att: 32,733

| Spain | 3 | South Korea | 1 |
| Michel 23, 60, 80 | | Hwang Bo-Kwan 43 | |

Verona, Jun 17, Att: 33,759

Belgium	3	Uruguay	1
Clijsters 14, Scifo 23		Bengoechea 71	
Ceulemans 46			

Garets (Bel) sent off, 41 mins

Verona, Jun 21, Att: 35,950

Spain	2	Belgium	1
Michel 26 (pen),		Vervoort 29	
Gorriz 38			

Scifo (Bel) hit bar with penalty, 59 mins.

Udine, Jun 21, Att: 29,039

| Uruguay | 1 | South Korea | 0 |
| Fonseca 90. | | | |

Yoon Deuk-Yeo (SKo) sent off, 70 mins.
Uruguay's goal came two minutes into injury time to keep them in the tournament

Final Table

	P	W	D	L	F	A	PTS
SPAIN	3	2	1	0	5	2	5
Belgium	3	2	0	1	6	3	4
Uruguay	3	1	1	1	2	3	3
South Korea	3	0	0	3	1	6	0

GROUP F

Cagliari, Jun 11, Att: 35,238

| England | 1 | Rep of Ireland | 1 |
| Lineker 8 | | Sheedy 73 | |

Played in gale and second-half electric storm. "Artless, charmless, worthless" -The Guardian; "Return to the Planet of the Apes" -Daily Mail.

Palermo, Jun 12, Att: 33,288

| Egypt | 1 | Holland | 1 |
| Abdel Ghani 82(pen) | | Kieft 58 | |

Cagliari, Jun 16, Att: 35,267

| England | 0 | Holland | 0 |

Bobby Robson played a sweeper (Wright) for the first time as England manager. England had two goals disallowed. Shilton's 120th cap, beating Pat Jennings's record.

Palermo, Jun 17, Att: 33,288

| Egypt | 0 | Rep of Ireland | 0 |

Group F's fourth consecutive draw left all sides with identical records. Gunmen in Beirut fired machine-gun bursts into the sky to celebrate Egypt's performance.

Cagliari, Jun 21, 34,959

| England | 1 | Egypt | 0 |
| Wright 58 | | | |

Wright's first goal for England, from a Gascoigne free-kick

Palermo, Jun 21, 33,288

| Holland | 1 | Rep of Ireland | 1 |
| Gullit 11 | | Quinn 71 | |

Ireland and Holland finished with identical records. Ireland placed second after the drawing of lots.

Final Table

	P	W	D	L	F	A	PTS
ENGLAND	3	1	2	0	2	1	4
Rep of Ireland	3	0	3	0	2	2	3
Holland	3	0	3	0	2	2	3
Egypt	3	0	2	1	1	2	2

SECOND ROUND

Naples, Jun 23, Att: 50,026

| Cameroon | 2 | Colombia | 1 |
| Milla 106, 108 | | Redin 115 | |

Milla came on as sub after 52 mins. The second goal came after the keeper Higuita had tried to dribble upfield.

Bari, Jun 23, Att: 47,673

| Czechoslovakia | 4 | Costa Rica | 1 |
| Skuhravy 11, 62, 81 | | Kubic 72 | |

All Skuhravy's goals were headers.

Turin, Jun 24, Att: 61,381

| Argentina | 1 | Brazil | 0 |
| Caniggia 81 | | | |

Gomes (Bra) sent off, 80 mins.

Milan, Jun 24, Att: 74,559

| West Germany | 2 | Holland | 1 |
| Klinsmann 49, Brehme 84 | | R Koeman 88 (pen) | |

Widely regarded as the best game of the tournament, dominated by Klinsmann. Marred by the sending-off (after 21 mins) of Völler for fouling, and Rijkaard for spitting at him.

Genoa, Jun 25, Att: 31,818

| Rep of Ireland | 0 | Romania | 0 |

Rep of Ireland won 5-4 on penalties after extra time. Timofte missed for Romania and O'Leary scored the winner.

Rome, Jun 25, Att: 73,303

| Italy | 2 | Uruguay | 0 |
| Schillaci 65, Serena 83 | | | |

Verona, Jun 26, Att: 35,500

Yugoslavia	2	Spain	1
Stojkovic 78, 93		Salinas 84	

After extra time

Bologna, Jun 26, Att: 34,520

England	1	Belgium	0
Platt 119			

After extra time. England's winner scored 30 seconds from the end.

QUARTER-FINALS

Florence, Jun 30, Att: 38,971

Argentina	0	Yugoslavia	0

Argentina won 3-2 on penalties after extra time. Sabandzovic (Yug) sent off after 31 minutes. Five players missed penalties in shoot-out, including Maradona.

Rome, Jun 30, Att: 73,303

Italy	1	Rep of Ireland	0
Schillaci 37			

Milan, Jul 1, Att: 73,347

West Germany	1	Czechoslovakia 0
Matthäus 24 (pen)		

Germany reached a record ninth semi-final. Moravcik (Cze) sent off, 70 mins, two yellow cards.

Naples, Jul 1, Att: 55,205

England	3	Cameroon	2
Lineker 83, 105 (pens);		Kunde 61	
(pen); Platt 25;		Ekeke 65	

After extra time England's two penalties equalled their total in Robson's 92 previous games as manager.

SEMI-FINALS

Naples, Jul 3, Att: 59,978

Argentina	1	Italy	1
Caniggia 67		Schillaci 17	

Argentina won 4-3 on penalties after extra time.
Penalty sequence: (Italy first)
Baresi 1-0, Serrizuela 1-1; Baggio 2-1, Burruchaga 2-2; De Agostini 3-2, Olarticoechea 3-3; Donadoni saved 3-3, Maradona 3-4; Serena saved 3-4
Argentina: Goycochea; Serrizuela, Ruggeri, Simon, Basualdo (Batista), Burruchaga, Maradona, Giusti, Olartocoechea, Caniggia, Calderon (Troglio)
Italy: Zenga; Barese, Bergomi, Ferri, Maldini, De Agostini, De Napoli, Giannini (Baggio), Vialli (Serena), Donadoni, Schillaci
Referee: Michel Vautrot (France)
Zenga beat Shilton's record of 499 scoreless minutes in the world cup by 18. Giusti (Arg) sent off, 109 mins.

Turin, Jul 4, Att: 62,628

West Germany	1	England	1
Brehme 59		Lineker 80	

West Germany won 4-3 after extra time on penalties.
Penalty sequence: (England first)
Lineker 1-0, Brehme 1-1; Beardsley 2-1, Matthäus 2-2; Platt 3-2, Riedle 3-3; Pearce saved 3-3, Thön 3-4; Waddle over the bar 3-4
West Germany: Illgner; Brehme, Kohler, Augenthaler, Buchwald, Berthold, Matthäus, Hassler (Reuter), Thön, Völler (Riedle), Klinsmann
England: Shilton; Pearce, Walker, Parker, Wright, Waddle, Butcher (Steven), Platt, Gascoigne, Beardsley, Lineker
Referee: José Ramiz Wright (Brazil)
Gascoigne given yellow card which would have kept him out of the final had England qualified.

THIRD PLACE PLAY-OFF

Bari, Jul 7, Att: 51,426

Italy	2	England	1

Baggio 70,		Platt 80
Schillaci 85 (pen)		

Schillaci became the tournament's outright top scorer with his sixth in seven games. Shilton finished England career after 125 games with one of his worst mistakes.
Italy: Zenga; Baresi, Bergomi, De Agostini (Berti), Ferrara, Maldini, Vierchowod, Ancelotti, Giannini (Ferri), Baggio, Schillaci
England: Shilton; Stevens, Walker, Parker, Wright (Waddle), Dorigo, McMahon (Webb), Platt, Steven, Beardsley, Lineker
Referee: Joël Quiniou (France)

FINAL

Rome, Jul 8, Att: 73,603

West Germany	1	Argentina	0
Brehme 84 (pen)			

West Germany: Illgner; Brehme, Kohler, Augenthaler, Buchwald, Berthold (Reuter), Matthäus, Hassler, Littbarski, Völler, Klinsmann
Argentina: Goycochea; Lorenzo, Sensini, Serrizuela, Ruggeri (Monzon), Simón, Basualdo, Burruchaga (Calderón), Maradona, Troglio, Dezotti
Referee: Edgardo Codesal Mendez (Mexico)
First repeat World Cup Final and lowest scoring. Four Argentine players (Olarticoechea, Giusti, Caniggia and Batista) barred from the game because they had two yellow cards. Monzon first man sent off in World Cup Final, 64 mins; Dezotti second 82 mins.
Yellow cards: Dezotti, 5, Voeller, 52, Troglio, 83, Maradona 87.

Leading Scorers

6	Salvatore Schillaci (Italy)
5	Thomas Skuhravy (Czechoslovakia)
4	Michel (Spain); Roger Milla (Cameroon); Gary Lineker (England); Lothar Matthäus (West Germany)
3	David Platt (England); Andreas Brehme, Rudi Völler, Jürgen Klinsmann (all West Germany)
2	Davor Jozic, Dragan Stojkovic, Darko Pancev (all Yugoslavia); Bernardo Redin (Colombia); Careca, Muller (both Brazil); Marius Lăcătus, Gavril Balint (both Romania); Michal Bilek (Czechoslovakia); Roberto Baggio (Italy); Claudio Caniggia (Argentina)

Hat Tricks

Michel, Spain v South Korea
Thomás Skuhravy, Czechoslovakia v Costa Rica

Fastest Goal

4 mins: Safet Susic, Yugoslavia v United Arab Emirates
Total Goals Scored: 115 (Average 2.21)
Top scorers: West Germany, 15

Highest attendances

74,765 West Germany v Yugoslavia
74,559 West Germany v Holland
73,780 Cameroon v Argentina

Lowest attendances

27,833 Yugoslavia v United Arab Emirates
29,039 Uruguay v South Korea
30,223 Costa Rica v Sweden

Note: All attendance figures refer to tickets sold. Actual crowds were often significantly lower.

ITALIA '90 TEAM RECORDS

	P	W	D	L	F	A	Shots	Yellow Cards	Red Cards	Fouls	Mins per foul commited	Fouls suffered	Mins per foul suffered
West Germany	7	5	2	0	15	5	114	8	1	114	5.77	129	5.11
Argentina	7	2	3	2	5	4	57	22	3	177	3.89	165	4.18
Italy	7	6	1	0	10	2	96	6	_	115	5.74	185	3.57
England	7	3	3	1	8	6	71	6	_	106	6.79	124	5.81
Cameroon	5	3	0	2	7	9	60	15	2	136	3.75	93	5.48
Czechoslovakia	5	3	0	2	10	5	76	13	1	120	3.75	94	4.79
Ireland	5	0	4	1	2	3	44	4	_	112	4.29	81	5.93
Yugoslavia	5	3	1	1	8	6	57	9	1	89	5.73	121	4.21
Belgium	4	2	0	2	6	4	48	2	1	74	5.27	46	8.48
Brazil	4	3	0	1	4	2	52	7	1	71	5.07	78	4.62
Colombia	4	1	1	2	4	4	40	5	_	88	4.43	99	3.94
Costa Rica	4	2	0	2	4	6	27	6	_	59	6.10	58	6.21
Holland	4	0	3	1	3	4	49	5	1	72	5.00	55	6.55
Romania	4	1	2	1	4	3	62	7	_	76	5.13	88	4.43
Spain	4	2	1	1	6	4	39	4	_	85	4.59	83	4.70
Uruguay	4	1	1	2	2	5	54	9	_	82	4.39	113	3.19
Austria	3	1	0	2	2	3	26	11	1	60	4.50	60	4.50
Egypt	3	0	2	1	1	2	23	4	_	52	5.19	53	5.09
Scotland	3	1	0	2	2	3	30	3	_	51	5.29	37	7.30
South Korea	3	0	0	3	1	6	17	8	1	88	3.07	50	5.40
Soviet Union	3	1	0	2	4	4	32	3	1	59	4.58	64	4.22
Sweden	3	0	0	3	3	6	36	4	_	55	4.91	62	4.35
UAE	3	0	0	3	2	11	23	7	1	49	5.51	50	5.40
United States	3	0	0	3	2	8	29	7	1	62	4.35	61	4.43

THE 1990 WORLD CUP

ENGLAND

❝I find it's very important to win every match because if you don't all kinds of terrible things happen.❞
Bobby Robson, before the World Cup

"No Football, We're English"
Headline in La Gazzetta dello Sport *after England - Ireland*

"YOU'RE BONKERS, BOBBY
The Sun speaks its mind: Bring them Home!"
Headline in The Sun *after England-Ireland*

"Platt Saves The Queen"
Headline in La Gazzetta dello Sport *after England-Belgium*

"We never seriously doubted England's chances of clawing their way through the World Cup field."
The Sun, *after England-Belgium*

"Bobby Robson has something, though I'm not sure what. Perhaps there is some truth in the growing theory that he is simply the luckiest man in the world."
John Sadler, The Sun *after England-Belgium*

"Around Gazza and his young gang we can build a team to win the world. Four years on, remember you read it first in The Sun."
Leader in The Sun

"My little daughter could write what they write."
Chris Waddle on the tabloids

GAZZA

"To have called him, as England manager Bobby Robson once did, 'as daft as a brush', severely maligns brushes. Who else could fly into a hair-raising tackle, get penalised and then pat the referee on the head as though he were an old-aged pensioner complaining about the noise on the street?"
Stan Hey, Sunday Correspondent

"He was a highly charged figure on the field of play: fierce and comic, formidable and vulnerable, urchin-like and waif-like, a strong head and torso with comparatively frail-looking, breakable legs, strange-eyed, pink-faced, fair-haired, tense and upright, a priapic monolith in the Mediterranean sun."
Karl Miller, London Review of Books

"I'm extremely grateful to him and all he's done because at last people are going to be able to spell my name properly."
Bamber Gascoigne

THE FANS

"It does something to the human spirit when you are hit by a police officer after you have pleaded with him not to."
John Tummon, England fan

"I was sitting in a pub a mile away from where the trouble started and just got rounded up by the police. We were thrown into a room at the police station, about 90 of us, and all we got to eat in 17 hours was a ham roll each. We've been treated terribly. If they did this to Italian fans in England, there would be an outcry."
Terry Gardener, England fan deported from Rimini

"We're mega here. It's like being a film star."
"Raff from Coventry", England fan

"The violence this time was schoolyard stuff compared with the tightly and coldly organised aggression in West Germany, even though the provocation here was more intense. . .the ethos was wholly different from Germany; at last the thug seems to have been superseded by the scallywag."
Ed Vulliamy, The Guardian

IRELAND

"The way Ireland plays forces you to play badly. No team manages to escape their contagious crap".
Ahmed El-Mokadem, Egypt's sponsor

"I felt embarrassed for soccer, embarrassed for the country and for all the good players and great tradition we have in soccer."
Eamonn Dunphy on the Irish team

"We've got an effective way of stopping people. If we tried to play the way they played we'd get into a lot of trouble."
Jack Charlton

"Ah, the boss."
The Pope greeting Jack Charlton

"It was small wonder that not a single journalist covering this tournament felt he or she had done justice to Monday's events. Never mind the journalists' own considerable limitations, the English language itself, the glorious vehicle of *Hamlet* and *Paradise Lost*, of *Middlemarch* and *Ulysses*, is not up to the task."
Kevin Myers, Irish Times *on Ireland reaching the quarter-finals*

".. Actually, the story of Ireland's World Cup was more Barbara Cartland: romantic but not particularly well-written....when intellect takes over from emotion, the Irish look less attractive, playing some tedious, ugly football which failed to yield a win and produced a goal on average every four hours."
Ian Ridley, The Guardian

"He has created a labouring team for a labouring race. There's no problem with that. He's made them proud to be Irish."
Drinker in the Submarine bar, Dublin

SCOTLAND

"It wouldn't have been so bad, but when I asked Stuart McCall he wasn't sure either."
Murdo McCloud, concussed against Brazil, trying to find out which direction Scotland were playing

"Just one thing. Don't say we were as bad as England."
Stuart McCall, after the Costa Rica game

CAMEROON

"I read in a paper that Cameroon used black magic to beat Argentina. But if this is so, explain to me why we didn't win 5-0? I admit that many Cameroonians practise black magic. I admit that. But it is top-class black magic – better than 1-0."
Crécy Tawah, chargé d'affaires at the Cameroon Embassy in London

BRAZIL

"Players are being asked to play as if they are not Brazilian. Our national tradition means nothing. Winning is supposed to be everything but can anyone be really satisfied by such victories?"
Pele on Brazil's tactics

"They should come to us for a few lessons in sharp shooting."
Romeu Tuma, Brazilian federal police chief

"I feel like a delinquent who has just committed a crime. Everybody speaks about Lazaroni with anger, forgetting that I am a man like any other citizen."
Sebastiao Lazaroni, Brazilian manager, after defeat

THE HOSTS

" He makes me feel young again."
Zico on Roberto Baggio

"Baggio..Baaggio...Baaagggiiioo...Goooooooi .....Baaagggg-giiiliooooo."
Rough transcription of Italian TV commentary

"Italia No!"
Headline in La Gazzetta dello Sport after semi-final

"Basta. Stop. Chiuso. Finito. Amen. Requiem."
Start of leading article in La Stampa, Turin, after semi-final

ARGENTINA

"Maradona? He is a pygmy."
Careca, Brazilian striker

"The Argentina team is a fat lady. We are ready to abandon her for an affair with another."
Buenos Aires newspaper before the Brazil game

"Argentina's whole team cheats. It tries to hide age and inadequacy by suffocating games. Its players kick maliciously at selected opponents.
Rob Hughes, International Herald Tribune

"I will have to tell my elder daughter that the Mafia exists also in soccer. The penalty which defeated us did not exist and was given to award victory to West Germany and punish Argentina. The black hand of this man expelled Pedro Monzon for a normal action. Later he called a penalty against us from his imagination."
Diego Maradona after the final

"Champions arrive."
Buenos Aires headline on return of Argentine team

CHAMPIONS

We're already on the Brenner, we're going wild, yes, it will be great, here the frustration of unbridled desire will be put on the shade. Believe what we say in the Italian sun, there on the boot of the world."
German World Cup Song

"There were no doubts whatsoever who was going to win. For 90 minutes we attacked Argentina and there was no feeling of any danger at all that a goal would be scored against us."
Franz Beckenbauer, West German manager

"The choice will become even bigger and nobody will be able to beat us for years. I'm sorry for the rest of the world, but that's the truth."
Beckenbauer on German unification

SUMMING UP

"This has been the dream World Cup."
Joao Havelange, president of FIFA

"A World Cup encapsulated by the final: Uninspiring, untidy, instantly forgettable. The worst ever."
Ken Jones, The Independent

"It was not good, it was not nice, it was not beautiful. But we have to live with that."
Guido Tognoni, FIFA spokesman on the final

HERE'S TO THE NEXT TIME

"They're going to bring this thing to the United States of America and charge money for people to see it? Listen, if this thing were a Broadway show, it would have closed in one night.

Frank Deford, The National (US)

ENGLAND

Player	Games Played	Minutes Played	Substitutions Off	Substitutions On	Goals	Shots	Fouls Committed	Fouls Suffered
Peter Shilton	7	720	-	-	-	-	1	2
Des Walker	7	720	-	-	-	-	13	9
Gary Lineker	7	712	1	-	4	12	7	14
Paul Gascoigne	6	630	-	-	-	6	11	27
Paul Parker	6	630	-	-	-	3	12	9
Stuart Pearce	6	630	-	-	-	8	10	7
Chris Waddle	7	612	2	1	-	6	1	14
Mark Wright	6	610	1	-	1	7	9	2
Terry Butcher	5	441	2	-	-	1	3	1
David Platt	6	412	-	3	3	10	7	6
John Barnes	5	388	2	-	-	2	10	14
Peter Beardsley	5	360	1	2	-	3	7	1
Steve McMahon	4	252	2	1	-	1	4	3
Trevor Steven	3	189	-	2	-	1	1	3
Gary Stevens	2	180	-	-	-	1	2	-
Steve Bull	4	171	1	3	-	5	3	3
Bryan Robson	2	153	1	-	-	3	3	3
Tony Dorigo	1	90	-	-	-	1	1	-
Neil Webb	1	20	-	1	-	1	1	-
David Beasant	-	-	-	-	-	-	-	-
Steve Hodge	-	-	-	-	-	-	-	-
David Seaman	-	-	-	-	-	-	-	-
Chris Woods	-	-	-	-	-	-	-	-

Seaman was injured and, by special FIFA dispensation, was replaced in the squad by Beasant.

"...IT'S NOTHING BOSS REALLY"
Bryan Robson's injuries

1976	October	Broken right leg	Out 11 weeks	1986	March	Dislocated shoulder	Out 8 weeks
1977	April	Broken right leg	Out 5 weeks		World Cup	Dislocated shoulder	Out 7 weeks
1978	January	Broken right leg	Out 6 weeks	1987	August	Broken nose	Out 2 weeks
1982	World Cup	Groin injury	Missed 1 game	1988	January	Concussion	Out 2 weeks
1983	February	Torn ankle		1989	January	Concussion	Out 2 weeks
		ligaments	Out 11 weeks		August	Damaged ribs	Out 2 weeks
1984	June	Broken nose	Close season		September	Hairline fracture	
	December	Bruised foot	Out six weeks			of left leg	Out 2 weeks
1985	January	Dislocated		1990	February	Groin operation	Out 8 weeks
		shoulder	Out 7 weeks		World Cup	Achilles tendon	Invalided home
	October	Torn hamstring	Out 4 weeks				*Source: The Guardian*
	November	Torn hamstring	Out 11 weeks				

IRELAND

Player	Games Played	Minutes Played	Substitutions Off	Substitutions On	Goals	Shots	Fouls Committed	Fouls Suffered
Pat Bonner	5	480	-	-	-	-	-	5
Ray Houghton	5	480	-	-	-	3	5	5
Mick McCarthy	5	480	-	-	-	1	23	4
Paul McGrath	5	480	-	-	-	7	17	3
Kevin Moran	5	480	-	-	-	-	8	11
Chris Morris	5	480	-	-	-	1	12	6
Andy Townsend	5	480	-	-	-	2	6	7
Steve Staunton	5	453	1	-	-	6	6	4
Kevin Sheedy	5	451	1	-	1	10	8	8
Tony Cascarino	5	339	1	3	-	5	7	9
John Aldridge	5	285	5	-	-	2	6	4
Niall Quinn	4	269	1	1	1	6	13	7
Alan McLoughlin	2	54	-	2	-	1	-	-
Ronnie Whelan	1	29	-	1	-	-	1	-
David O'Leary	1	27	-	1	-	-	-	1
John Sheridan	1	13	-	1	-	-	-	-
John Byrne	-	-	-	-	-	-	-	-
Chris Hughton	-	-	-	-	-	-	-	-
David Kelly	-	-	-	-	-	-	-	-
Gerry Peyton	-	-	-	-	-	-	-	-
Bernie Slaven	-	-	-	-	-	-	-	-
Frank Stapleton	-	-	-	-	-	-	-	-

SCOTLAND

Player	Games Played	Minutes Played	Substitutions Off	Substitutions On	Goals	Shots	Fouls Committed	Fouls Suffered
Roy Aitken	3	270	-	-	-	6	5	3
Mo Johnston	3	270	-	-	1	7	8	5
Jim Leighton	3	270	-	-	-	-	-	2
Maurice Malpas	3	270	-	-	-	1	4	5
Stuart McCall	3	270	-	-	1	2	4	-
Alex McLeish	3	270	-	-	-	-	2	2
David McPherson	3	270	-	-	-	4	11	3
Paul McStay	3	196	-	1	-	2	4	3
Stewart McKimmie	2	135	-	1	-	2	1	2
Murdo McLeod	2	128	1	-	-	1	2	2
Ally McCoist	3	102	1	2	-	-	-	3
Robert Fleck	2	95	1	1	-	2	2	1
Craig Levein	1	90	-	-	-	-	-	4
Alan McInally	1	90	-	-	-	1	1	2
Gordon Durie	1	74	1	-	-	-	3	3
Jim Bett	1	73	1	-	-	1	-	-
Gary Gillespie	1	52	-	1	-	-	-	-
Richard Gough	1	45	1	-	-	1	-	-
John Collins	-	-	-	-	-	-	-	-
Andy Goram	-	-	-	-	-	-	-	-
Bryan Gunn	-	-	-	-	-	-	-	-
Gary McAllister	-	-	-	-	-	-	-	-

INDIVIDUAL RECORDS

MOST SHOTS

Total		Games Played	Goals
20	Salvatore Schillachi (Italy)	7	6
19	Tomás Skuhravy (Czechoslovakia)	5	2
	Juergen Klinsman (W Germany)	7	3
18	Gheorghe Hagi (Romania)	3	-
17	Rudi Voeller (W Germany)	6	4
16	Lothar Matthäus (W Germany)	7	4
15	Francois Omam Biyik (Cameroon)	5	1
14	Careca (Brazil)	4	2
	Pierre Littbarski (W Germany)	6	1
13	Jorge Burruchaga (Argentina)	7	1
	Luigi de Agostini (Italy)	6	-
12	Marius Lacatus (Romania)	3	2
	Ronald Koeman (Holland)	4	1

MOST FOULS COMMITTED

Total		Games Played	Fouls/ Games	Fouls Suffered
23	Mick McCarthy (Ireland)	5	4.60	4
21	Josef Chovaneck (Czechoslovakia)	5	4.20	5
	Guido Buchwald (W Germany)	7	3.00	9
19	Cyrille Makanaky (Cameroon)	5	3.80	9
18	Oscar Ruggeri (Argentina)	5	3.60	10
	Jose Serrizuela (Argentina)	5	3.60	6
17	Kim Joo Sung (S Korea)	3	5.67	9
	Diego Maradona (Argentina)	7	2.43	53
	Paul McGrath (Ireland)	5	3.40	3
	Stephen Tataw (Cameroon)	5	3.40	8
16	Gabriel Jaime Gomez (Colombia)	4	4.00	4
	Claudio Caniggia (Argentina)	6	2,67	19

WORLD CUP GOALS

Year	Nations Entered	In final stages	Matches	Goals	Average per games
1930	13	13	18	70	3.88
1934	32	16	17	70	4.11
1938	36	15	18	84	4.66
1950	34	13	22	88	4.00
1954	38	16	26	140	5.38
1958	51	16	35	126	3.60
1962	56	16	32	89	2.78
1966	70	16	32	89	2.78
1970	71	16	32	95	2.96
1974	95	16	38	97	2.55
1978	103	16	38	102	2.68
1982	109	24	52	146	2.81
1986	114	24	52	132	2.54
1990	112	24	52	115	2.21

MOST FOULS SUFFERED

Fouls		Games Played	Fouls/ Games	Fouls Committed
53	Diego Maradona (Argentina)	7	7.57	17
27	Paul Gascoigne (England)	6	4.50	11
22	Roberto Donadoni (Italy)	5	4.40	8
	Dragan Stojkovic (Yugoslavia)	5	4.40	8
	Salvatore Schillaci (Italy)	7	3.14	13
21	Carlos Valderrama (Colombia)	4	5.25	5
19	Tomas Skuhravy (Czechoslovakia)	5	3.80	11
	Claudio Caniggia (Argentina)	6	3.17	16
	Lothar Matthäus (W Germany)	7	2.71	7
18	Roberto Baggio (Italy)	5	3.60	5
	Juergen Klinsmann (W Germany)	7	2.57	9

WORLD CUP WINNERS

Year	Winners		Runners-up	Venue	3rd Place Play-off		
1930	Uruguay	4-2	Argentina	Montevideo	United States & Yugoslavia §		
1934	Italy	2-1†	Czechoslovakia	Rome	Germany	3-2	Austria
1938	Italy	4-2	Hungary	Paris	Brazil	4-2	Sweden
1950	Uruguay	2-1*	Brazil	Rio de Janeiro	Sweden		
1954	West Germany	3-2	Hungary	Berne	Austria	3-1	Uruguay
1958	Brazil	5-2	Sweden	Stockholm	France	6-3	West Germany
1962	Brazil	3-1	Czechoslovakia	Santiago	Chile	1-0	Yugoslavia
1966	England	4-2†	West Germany	London	Portugal	2-1	USSR
1970	Brazil	4-1	Italy	Mexico City	West Germany	1-0	Uruguay
1974	West Germany	2-1	Holland	Munich	Poland	1-0	Brazil
1978	Argentina	3-1†	Holland	Buenos Aires	Brazil	2-1	Italy
1982	Italy	3-1	West Germany	Madrid	Poland	3-2	France
1986	Argentina	3-2	West Germany	Mexico City	France	4-2	Belgium
1990	West Germany	1-0	Argentina	Rome	Italy	2-1	England

† After extra time
* Last four teams engaged in a final pool, Uruguay played Brazil in the deciding match, Sweden finished in third place
§ No play-off match

ENGLAND'S INTERNATIONAL MATCHES 1989-90

5 Sep v. SWEDEN *Stockholm*, World Cup qual., drew 0-0
Shilton Stevens Pearce Webb (Gascoigne) Walker Butcher Beardsley McMahon Waddle Lineker Barnes (Rocastle)
Terry Butcher needed seven stitches in his head at half-time and played on oozing blood. Bobby Robson said people get VC for less, and was forced to apologise by angry war veterans.

11 Oct v. POLAND *Chorzow*, World Cup qual., drew 0-0
Shilton Stevens Walker Butcher Pearce Rocastle McMahon Robson Waddle Lineker Beardsley
England make certain of qualifying for the finals.

15 Nov v. ITALY *Wembley*, Friendly, drew 0-0
Shilton (Beasant) Stevens Pearce (Winterburn) McMahon (Hodge) Walker Butcher Robson (Phelan) Waddle Beardsley (Platt) Lineker Barnes
Waddle in dazzling form. Four new caps: Beasant, Platt, Winterburn and Phelan.

13 Dec v. YUGOSLAVIA Wembley, Friendly, won 2-1
Shilton (Beasant) Parker Pearce (Dorigo) Thomas (Platt) Walker Butcher Robson[2] (McMahon) Rocastle (Hodge) Bull Lineker Waddle
England's 100th win at Wembley; Robson scored after 38 seconds, the fastest goal in a major game on the ground.

28 Mar v. BRAZIL Wembley, Friendly, won 1-0
Shilton (Woods) Stevens Pearce McMahon Butcher Walker Platt Barnes Waddle Lineker[1] Beardsley (Gascoigne)
Lineker's 30th England Goal. Pearce handled on line to save Muller shot.

25 Apr v. CZECHOSLOVAKIA *Wembley*, Friendly, won 4-2
Shilton (Seaman) Dixon Pearce[1] (Dorigo) Steven Walker (Wright) Butcher Robson (McMahon) Gascoigne[1] Bull[2] Lineker Hodge
Gascoigne played himself into the World Cup party.

15 May v. DENMARK *Wembley*, Friendly, won 1-0
Shilton (Woods) Stevens Walker Butcher Pearce (Dorigo) Waddle (Rocastle) Gascoigne MacMahon (Platt) Hodge Lineker[2] (Bull) Barnes
England's 17th successive unbeaten game.

22 May v. URUGUAY *Wembley*, Friendly, Lost 1-2
Shilton Parker Walker Butcher Pearce Waddle Gascoigne Robson Hodge (Beardsley) Lineker (Bull) Barnes[1]
Englands first home defeat for six years despite brilliant goal by Barnes.

2 Jun v. TUNISIA *Tunis*, Friendly, drew 1-1
Shilton Stevens Walker Butcher (Wright) Pearce Waddle (Platt) Gascoigne Robson Hodge (Beardsley) Lineker (Bull[1]) Barnes
Bull scored in last minute to save England from first-ever defeat by African country.

11 Jun v. REPUBLIC OF IRELAND *Cagliari*, World Cup, drew 1-1
Shilton Stevens Pearce Walker Butcher Robson Waddle Gascoigne Barnes Lineker[1] (Bull) Beardsley (McMahon)

16 Jun v. HOLLAND *Cagliari*, World Cup, drew 0-0
Shilton Pearce Walker Butcher Parker Wright Robson (Platt) Waddle (Bull) Gascoigne Lineker Barnes

21 Jun v. EGYPT *Cagliari*, World Cup, won 1-0
Shilton Parker Walker Wright[1] Waddle (Platt) McMahon Gascoigne Barnes Pearce Bull (Beardsley) Lineker

26 Jun v. BELGIUM, *Bologna* World Cup, won 1-0 aet
Shilton Parker Walker Butcher Pearce Wright Waddle McMahon (Platt[1]) Gascoigne Lineker Barnes (Bull)

1 Jul v. CAMEROON *Naples*, World Cup, won 3-2 aet
Shilton Parker Walker Butcher (Steven) Parker Wright Waddle Platt[1] Gascoigne Lineker[2] Barnes (Beardsley)

4 Jul v. WEST GERMANY, *Turin*, World Cup, drew 1-1 (lost 4-3 pens)

Shilton Pearce Walker Parker Wright Waddle Butcher (Steven) Platt Gascoigne Beardsley Lineker[1]

7 Jul v. ITALY *Bari* World Cup, lost 1-2
Shilton Stevens Walker Parker Wright (Waddle) Dorigo McMahon (Webb) Platt[1] Steven Beardsley Lineker

(Numbers after names refer to goals scored)

THE ROBSON YEARS

Bobby Robson's Record as England Manager

P	W	D	L	F	A
95	47	29	19	154	60

First match: 22 Sep 1982 v. Denmark, drew 2-2
Last match: 7 Jul 1990 v. Italy, lost 1-2
Biggest win: 9-0 v. Luxembourg, 15 Dec 1982, Wembley
Most goals against: 1-3 by West Germany, 9 Sep 1987, Düsseldorf
1-3 by Holland, 15 Jun 1988, Düsseldorf
1-3 by Soviet Union, 18 Jun 1988, Frankfurt
Robson's Captains: Bryan Robson (63 games), Peter Shilton (13), Ray Wilkins (10), Terry Butcher (3), Peter Beardsley (1)

ENGLAND PLAYERS 1989-90

	Appearances		Goals	
	1989-90	Career	1989-90	Career
John BARNES	11	58	1	10
Peter BEARDSLEY	11	45	-	7
Dave BEASANT	2	2	-	-
Steve BULL	9	1	3	4
Terry BUTCHER	14	77	-	3
Kerry DIXON †	1	9	-	4
Tony DORIGO	4	4	-	-
Paul GASCOIGNE	12	17	1	2
Steve HODGE	6	22	-	-
Gary LINEKER	16	58	6	35
Steve McMAHON	11	16	-	-
Paul PARKER	8	11	-	-
Stuart PEARCE	15	30	1	1
Michael PHELAN †	1	1	-	-
David PLATT	11	11	3	3
Bryan ROBSON	8	87	2	26
David ROCASTLE †	4	11	-	-
David SEAMAN	1	3	-	-
Peter SHILTON	16	125	-	-
Trevor STEVEN	4	29	-	3
Gary STEVENS	8	41	-	-
Michael THOMAS †	1	2	-	-
Chris WADDLE	15	59	-	6
Des WALKER	16	25	-	-
Neil WEBB	2	20	-	3
Nigel WINTERBURN †	1	1	-	-
Chris WOODS	2	16	-	-
Mark WRIGHT	8	30	1	1

(†) Indicates not included in World Cup squads

WORLD CUP TABLE 1930-1990

		Tournaments	P	W	D	L	F	A
1	Brazil	14	66	44	11	11	148	65
2	Germany/West Germany	12	68	39	15	14	145	90
3	Italy	12	54	31	12	11	89	54
4	Argentina	10	48	24	9	15	82	59
5	England	9	41	18	12	11	55	38
6	Uruguay	9	37	15	8	14	61	52
7	Soviet Union	7	31	15	6	10	53	34
8	France	9	34	15	5	14	71	56
9	Hungary	9	32	15	3	14	87	57
10	Yugoslavia	8	33	14	7	12	55	42
11	Spain	8	32	13	7	12	43	38
12	Poland	5	25	13	5	7	39	29
13	Austria	6	26	12	2	12	40	41
14	Sweden	8	31	11	6	14	51	52
15	Czechoslovakia	8	30	11	5	14	44	45
16	Holland	5	20	8	6	6	35	23
17	Belgium	8	25	7	4	14	33	49
18	Chile	6	21	7	3	11	26	32
19	Mexico	9	29	6	6	17	27	64
20	Portugal	2	9	6	0	3	19	12
21	Switzerland	6	18	5	2	11	28	44
22	Scotland	7	20	4	6	10	23	35
23	Peru	4	15	4	3	8	19	31
24	Northern Ireland	3	13	3	5	5	13	23
25	Paraguay	4	11	3	4	4	16	25
26	Cameroon	2	8	3	3	2	8	10
27	Romania	5	12	3	3	6	16	20
28	Denmark	1	4	3	0	4	10	6
29	United States	4	10	3	0	7	14	29
30	East Germany	1	6	2	2	2	5	5
31	Algeria	2	6	2	1	3	6	10
32	Costa Rica	1	4	2	0	2	4	5
33	Wales	1	5	1	3	1	4	4
34	Morocco	2	7	1	3	3	5	8
35	Colombia	2	7	1	2	4	9	15
36	Tunisia	1	3	1	1	1	3	2
37	North Korea	1	3	1	1	1	5	12
38	Cuba	1	4	1	1	2	5	9
39	Turkey	1	3	1	0	2	10	11
40	Bulgaria	5	16	0	6	10	11	35
41	Republic of Ireland	1	5	0	4	1	2	3
42	Honduras	1	3	0	2	1	2	3
43	Israel	1	3	0	2	1	1	3
44	Egypt	2	4	0	2	2	3	6
45	Kuwait	1	3	0	1	2	2	6
46	Australia	1	3	0	1	2	0	5
47	Iran	1	3	0	1	2	2	8
48	South Korea	3	8	0	1	7	5	29
49	Norway	1	1	0	0	1	1	2
50	Iraq	1	3	0	0	3	1	4
51	Canada	1	3	0	0	3	0	5
52	Dutch East Indies	1	1	0	0	1	0	6
53	United Arab Emirates	1	3	0	0	3	2	11
54	New Zealand	1	3	0	0	3	2	12
55	Haiti	1	3	0	0	3	2	14
56	Zaire	1	3	0	0	3	0	14
57	Bolivia	2	3	0	0	3	0	16
58	El Salvador	2	6	0	0	6	1	22

THE ENGLAND MANAGERS

	P	W	D	L	Years	New players used
WALTER WINTERBOTTOM	137	78	32	27	1946-62	152
ALF RAMSEY	113	68	28	17	1962-74	83
JOE MERCER	7	3	3	1	1974	3
DON REVIE	29	14	8	7	1974-77	29
RON GREENWOOD	55	33	12	10	1977-82	27
BOBBY ROBSON	95	47	29	19	1982-90	64

NORTHERN IRELAND 1989-90
5 Sep v. Hungary (h)	World Cup qualifier	lost 1-2	Whiteside
11 Oct v. Eire (a)	World Cup qualifier	lost 0-3	
27 Mar v. Norway (h)	Friendly	lost 2-3	Quinn, K. Wilson
18 May v. Uruguay (h)	Friendly	won 1-0	K. Wilson

SCOTLAND 1989-90
5 Sep v. Yugoslavia (a)	World Cup qualifier	lost 1-3	Durie
11 Oct v. France (a)	World Cup qualifier	lost 0-3	
15 Nov v. Norway (h)	World Cup qualifier	drew 1-1	McCoist
28 Mar v. Argentina (h)	Friendly	won 1-0	McKimmie
25 Apr v. East Germany (h)	Friendly	lost 0-1	
16 May v. Egypt (h)	Friendly	lost 1-3	McCoist
19 May v. Poland	Friendly	drew 1-1	Johnston
28 May v. Malta (a)	Friendly	won 2-1	McInally (2)
11 Jun v. Costa Rica (n)	World Cup	lost 0-1	
16 Jun v. Sweden (n)	World Cup	won 2-1	McCall, Johnston
20 Jun v. Brazil (n)	World Cup	lost 0-1	

WALES 1989-90
5 Sep v. Finland (a)	World Cup qualifier	lost 0-1	
11 Oct v. Holland (h)	World Cup qualifier	lost 1-2	Pascoe
15 Nov v. West Germany (a)	World Cup qualifier	lost 1-2	Allen
28 Mar v. Eire (a)	Friendly	lost 0-1	
25 Apr v. Sweden (a)	Friendly	lost 2-4	Saunders (2)
20 May v. Costa Rica (h)	Friendly	won 1-0	Saunders

REPUBLIC OF IRELAND 1989-90
5 Sep v. West Germany (h)	Friendly	drew 1-1	Stapleton
11 Oct v. N. Ireland (h)	World Cup qualifier	won 3-0	Whelan, Cascarino, Houghton
15 Nov v. Malta (a)	World Cup qualifier	won 2-0	Aldridge (2)
28 Mar v. Wales (h)	Friendly	won 1-0	Slaven
25 Apr Soviet Union (h)	Friendly	won 1-0	Staunton
16 May v. Finland (h)	Friendly	drew 1-1	Sheedy
27 May v. Turkey (a)	Friendly	drew 0-0	
11 Jun v. England (n)	World Cup	drew 1-1	Sheedy
17 Jun v. Egypt (n)	World Cup	drew 0-0	
21 Jun v. Holland (n)	World Cup	drew 1-1	Quinn
25 Jun v. Romania (n)	World Cup	drew 0-0 (Won 5-4 pens)	
30 Jun v. Italy (n)	World Cup	lost 0-1	

THE SHILTON YEARS
PETER SHILTON'S RECORD AS ENGLAND GOALKEEPER

Total England appearances: 125

World Cup final stages	*17*
World Cup qualifiers	*20*
European Championship finals	*3*
European Championship qualifiers	*13*
Friendlies/British Championship etc	*72*

Debut: 25 Nov 1970 v. East Germany, Wembley (won 3-1)
Matches missed since debut:91
50th cap: 1 Jun 1983 v. Scotland, Wembley (won 2-0)
100th cap: 15 Jun 1988 v. Holland, Düsseldorf (lost 1-3)

Goals conceded: 80

Clean sheets	*65*
Conceded one goal	*43 times*
Conceded two goals	*14 times*
Conceded three goals	*3 times*

England lost 4-3 to Austria in June 1979 but Shilton was replaced by Clemence at half-time with England trailing 3-1.

The only man to score a hat-trick past Shilton was Marco Van Basten (Holland) in 1988.

FOOTBALL LEAGUE
(1988-89 positions in brackets. Promoted clubs in bold. Relegated clubs in italics)

FIRST DIVISION

In Div Since					HOME P	W	D	L	F	A	AWAY W	D	L	F	A	Pts	Average Home Gate	Sent Off
1962	1	(2)	LIVERPOOL		38	13	5	1	38	15	10	5	4	40	22	79	36,589	1
1988	2	(17)	Aston Villa		38	13	3	3	36	20	8	4	7	21	18	70	25,554	1
1978	3	(6)	Tottenham H		38	12	1	6	35	24	7	5	7	24	23	63	26,588	2
1919	4	(1)	Arsenal		38	14	3	2	38	11	4	5	10	16	27	62	33,713	-
1989	5	(P)	Chelsea		38	8	7	4	31	24	8	5	6	27	26	60	21,531	-
1954	6	(8)	Everton		38	14	3	2	40	16	3	5	11	17	30	59	26,280	1
1978	7	(13)	Southampton		38	10	5	4	40	27	5	5	9	31	36	55	16,463	3
1986	8	(12)	Wimbledon		38	5	8	6	22	23	8	8	3	25	17	55	7,756	3
1977	9	(3)	Nottingham		38	9	4	6	31	21	6	5	8	24	26	54	20,606	-
1986	10	(4)	Norwich City		38	7	10	2	24	14	6	4	9	20	28	53	16,737	1
1983	11	(9)	QPR		38	9	4	6	27	22	4	7	8	18	22	50	13,218	1
1967	12	(7)	Coventry City		38	11	2	6	24	25	3	5	11	15	34	49	14,312	3
1975	13	(11)	Manchester U		38	8	6	5	26	14	5	3	11	20	33	48	39,077	1
1989	14	(P)	Manchester C		38	9	4	6	26	21	3	8	8	17	31	48	27,975	3
1989	15	(P)	Crystal Palace		38	8	7	4	27	23	5	2	12	15	43	48	17,105	3
1987	16	(5)	Derby County		38	9	1	9	29	21	4	6	9	14	19	46	17,426	1
1982	17	(16)	Luton Town		38	8	8	3	24	18	2	5	12	19	39	43	9,886	4
1984	18	(15)	*Sheffield Wed*		38	8	6	5	21	17	3	4	12	14	34	43	20,930	-
1986	19	(14)	*Charlton Ath*		38	4	6	9	18	25	3	3	13	13	32	30	10,748	-
1988	20	(10)	*Millwall*		38	4	6	9	23	25	1	5	13	16	40	26	12,413	2

Highest attendance: 47,245 Manchester U v. Arsenal Sep 19, 1989

Lowest attendance: 3,618 Wimbledon v. Luton Feb 14, 1990

TOP SCORERS (LEAGUE AND CUP)
28 John Barnes (Liverpool)
26 Gary Lineker (Tottenham)
26 Ian Rush (Liverpool)
25 Kerry Dixon (Chelsea)
24 Matthew Le Tissier (Southampton)
24 David Platt (Aston Villa)

FIRST DIVISION HAT-TRICKS
Mark Hughes, Manchester U v. Millwall, Sep 16;
Trevor Francis, QPR v. Aston Villa, Sep 23;
Gary Lineker, Tottenham v. QPR, Sep 30;
Gary Lineker, Tottenham v. Norwich, Feb 4;
Matthew Le Tissier, Southampton v. Norwich, Feb 27;
Matthew Le Tissier, Southampton v. Wimbledon, Mar 17;
Ronnie Rosenthal, Liverpool v. Charlton, Apr 11;
John Barnes, Liverpool v. Coventry, May 5;
Kerry Dixon, Chelsea v. Millwall, May 5.

HOW THE LEAD CHANGED HANDS
Aug 29 Millwall; Aug 30 Coventry; Sep 9 Millwall; Sep 12 Liverpool; Sep 16 Everton; Sep 23 Liverpool; Oct 21 Everton; Oct 29 Liverpool; Nov 4 Chelsea; Nov 18 Arsenal; Nov 26 Liverpool; Dec 9 Arsenal; Dec 26 Liverpool; Feb 21 Aston Villa; Mar 3 Liverpool; Mar 10 Aston Villa; Mar 31 LIVERPOOL.

SECOND DIVISION

In Div Since				P	HOME					AWAY					Pts	Average Home Gate	Sent Off
					W	D	L	F	A	W	D	L	F	A			
1982	1	(10)	**LEEDS UNITED**	46	16	6	1	46	18	8	7	8	33	34	85	28,210	-
1989	2	(P)	**Sheffield U**	46	14	5	4	43	27	10	8	5	35	31	85	16,989	-
1989	3	(R)	Newcastle U	46	17	4	2	51	26	5	10	8	29	29	80	21,590	-
1987	4	(6)	Swindon Town	46	12	6	5	49	29	8	8	7	30	30	74	9,394	4
1980	5	(5)	Blackburn Rovers	46	10	9	4	43	30	9	8	6	31	29	74	9,624	2
1988	6	(11)	**Sunderland**	46	10	8	5	41	32	10	6	7	29	32	74	17,728	4
1989	7	(R)	West Ham U	46	14	5	4	50	22	6	7	10	30	35	72	20,311	3
1974	8	(16)	Oldham Athletic	46	15	7	1	50	23	4	7	12	20	34	71	9,727	1
1986	9	(8)	Ipswich Town	46	13	7	3	38	22	6	5	12	29	44	69	12,913	-
1989	10	(P)	Wolves	46	12	5	6	37	20	6	8	9	30	40	67	17,045	3
1989	11	(P)	PortVale	46	11	9	3	37	20	4	7	12	25	37	61	8.978	-
1988	12	(20)	Portsmouth	46	9	8	6	40	34	6	8	9	22	31	61	8.959	3
1987	13	(15)	Leicester City	46	10	8	5	34	29	5	6	12	33	50	59	11,716	3
1985	14	(21)	Hull City	47	7	8	8	27	31	7	8	8	31	34	58	6,518	4
1988	15	(4)	Watford	46	11	6	6	41	28	3	9	11	17	32	57	10,353	3
1986	16	(18)	Plymouth Arg	46	9	8	6	30	23	5	5	13	28	40	55	8,749	3
1988	17	(17)	Oxford United	46	8	7	8	35	31	7	2	14	22	35	54	5,820	-
1988	18	(19)	Brighton	46	10	6	7	28	27	5	3	15	28	45	54	8,679	1
1981	19	(7)	Barnsley	46	7	9	7	22	23	6	6	11	27	48	54	9,033	5
1986	20	(9)	West Bromwich A	46	6	8	9	35	37	6	7	10	32	34	51	11,308	-
1989	21	(R)	Middlesbrough	46	10	3	10	33	29	3	8	12	19	34	50	16,269	-
1987	22	(12)	*Bournemouth*	46	8	6	9	30	31	4	6	13	27	45	48	7,454	-
1985	23	(14)	*Bradford City*	46	9	6	8	26	24	0	8	15	18	44	41	8,777	4
1985	24	(13)	*Stoke City*	46	4	11	8	20	24	2	8	13	15	39	37	12,449	2

Highest attendance: 37,697 Leeds v. Sheffield United , Apr 16
Lowest attendance: 3,863 Oxford v. Barnsley, Oct 21

PLAY-OFFS
Blackburn 1 1 SWINDON 2 2; SUNDERLAND 0 2 Newcastle 0 0

FINAL
Wembley, May 28
SWINDON 1 Sunderland 0 *Attendance: 72,873*

HOW THE LEAD CHANGED HANDS
Sep 2 West Ham; Sep 9 Sheffield U; Dec 16 LEEDS.

TOP SCORERS (LEAGUE AND CUP)
36 Mick Quinn (Newcastle)
32 Bernie Slaven (Middlesbrough)
28 Andy Ritchie (Oldham)
27 Steve Bull (Wolverhampton)
26 Duncan Shearer (Swindon)
25 Marco Gabbiadini (Sunderland)
25 Mark McGhee (Newcastle)
25 Steve White (Swindon)

THIRD DIVISION

In Div Since				P	HOME					AWAY					Pts	Average Home Gate	Sent Off
					W	D	L	F	A	W	D	L	F	A			
1981	1	(5)	**BRISTOL ROVERS**	46	15	8	0	43	14	11	7	5	28	21	93	6,202	5
1984	2	(11)	**Bristol City**	46	15	5	3	40	16	12	5	6	36	24	91	11,544	2
1985	3	(9)	**Notts County**	46	17	4	2	40	18	8	8	7	33	35	87	6,151	3
1989	4	(P)	Tranmere Rovers	46	15	5	3	54	22	8	6	9	32	27	80	7,449	3
1985	5	(13)	Bury	46	11	7	5	35	19	10	4	9	35	30	74	3,450	2
1988	6	(10)	Bolton Wanderers	46	12	7	4	32	19	6	8	9	27	29	69	7,286	-
1989	7	(R)	Birmingham City	46	10	7	6	33	19	8	5	10	27	40	66	8,558	1
1988	8	(14)	Huddersfield Town	46	11	5	7	30	23	6	9	8	31	39	65	5,630	-
1989	9	(P)	Rotherham United	46	12	6	5	48	28	5	7	11	23	34	64	5,612	1
1988	10	(18)	Reading	46	10	9	4	33	21	5	10	8	24	32	64	4,060	2
1989	11	(R)	Shrewsbury Town	46	10	9	4	38	24	6	6	11	21	30	63	3,521	2
1989	12	(P)	Crewe Alexandra	46	10	8	5	32	24	5	9	9	24	29	62	4,008	2
1978	13	(7)	Brentford	46	11	4	8	41	31	7	3	13	25	35	61	5,662	4
1989	14	(P)	Leyton Orient	46	9	6	8	28	24	7	4	12	24	32	58	4,365	-
1986	15	(15)	Mansfield Town	46	13	2	8	34	25	3	5	15	16	40	55	3,129	4
1986	16	(8)	Chester City	46	11	7	5	30	23	2	8	13	13	32	54	2,506	-
1988	17	(12)	Swansea City	46	10	6	7	25	27	4	6	13	20	36	54	4,223	1
1982	18	(17)	Wigan Athletic	46	10	6	7	29	22	3	8	12	19	42	53	2,758	-
1987	19	(6)	Preston North End	46	10	7	6	42	30	4	3	16	23	49	52	6,313	2
1986	20	(4)	Fulham	46	8	8	7	33	27	4	7	12	22	39	51	4,484	4
1988	21	(16)	*Cardiff City*	46	6	9	8	30	35	6	5	12	21	35	50	3,642	-
1987	22	(20)	*Northampton*	46	7	7	9	27	31	4	7	12	24	37	47	3,187	2
1985	23	(19)	*Blackpool*	46	8	6	9	29	33	2	10	11	20	40	46	4,075	2
1989	24	(R)	*Walsall*	46	6	8	9	23	30	6		14	17	42	41	4,077	1

Highest attendance: 19,483 Bristol C v. Walsall, May 5

Lowest attendance: 1,730 Chester v. Leyton O, Jan 6

PLAY-OFFS
Bolton 1 0 NOTTS COUNTY 1 2; Bury 0 0 TRANMERE 0 2

FINAL
Wembley, May 27
NOTTS COUNTY 2 Tranmere 0
Attendance: 29,252

TOP SCORERS (LEAGUE AND CUP)
34 Bob Taylor (Bristol City)
33 Ian Muir (Tranmere)
29 Dean Holdsworth (Brentford)
   (Including one for Watford)
26 John McGinlay (Shrewsbury)
24 Tony Philliskirk (Bolton)
23 Chris Malkin (Tranmere)
22 Bobby Williamson (Rotherham)

HOW THE LEAD CHANGED HANDS
Sep 2 Bristol R; Sep 9 Shrewsbury; Sep 16 Bristol R; Sep 22 Tranmere; Sep 23 Shrewsbury; Sep 26 Bristol R; Sep 29 Tranmere; Oct 21 Bristol R; Nov 4 Bristol C; Nov 10 Tranmere; Nov 11 Bristol R; Dec 26 Notts C; Jan 13 Bristol C; Mar 6 Tranmere; Mar 13 Bristol C; Mar 19 Tranmere; Mar 20 Bristol C; May 2 BRISTOL R.

FOURTH DIVISION

In Div Since				P	W	D	L	F	A	W	D	L	F	A	Pts	Average Home Att	Sent Off
						HOME						AWAY					
1984	1	(13)	EXETER CITY	46	20	3	0	50	14	8	2	13	33	34	89	4,859	4
1988	2	(9)	Grimsby Town	46	14	4	5	41	20	8	9	6	29	27	79	5,984	2
1989	3	(R)	Southend United	46	15	3	5	35	14	7	6	10	26	34	75	3,836	3
1970	4	(20)	Stockport County	46	13	6	4	45	27	8	5	10	23	35	74	3,899	1
1989	5	(P)	Maidstone United	46	14	4	5	49	21	8	3	12	28	40	73	2,427	3
1985	6	(8)	Cambridge United	46	14	3	6	45	30	7	7	9	31	36	73	3,359	3
1989	7	(R)	Chesterfield	46	12	9	2	41	19	7	5	11	22	31	71	4,181	3
1987	8	(12)	Carlisle United	46	15	4	4	38	20	6	4	13	23	40	71	4,740	4
1979	9	(17)	Peterborough United	46	10	8	5	35	23	7	9	7	24	23	68	4,804	1
1988	10	(10)	Lincoln City	46	11	6	6	30	27	7	8	8	18	21	68	4,071	3
1984	11	(4)	Scunthorpe United	46	9	9	5	42	25	8	6	9	27	29	66	3,524	6
1974	12	(18)	Rochdale	46	11	4	8	28	23	9	2	12	24	32	66	2,027	4
1988	13	(11)	York City	46	10	5	8	19	24	6	11	6	26	29	64	2,615	1
1989	14	(R)	Gillingham	46	9	8	6	28	21	8	3	12	18	27	62	3,887	1
1972	15	(14)	Torquay United	46	12	2	9	33	29	3	10	10	20	37	57	2,147	6
1985	16	(16)	Burnley	46	6	10	7	19	18	8	4	11	26	37	56	6,222	5
1978	17	(15)	Hereford United	46	7	4	12	31	32	8	6	9	25	30	55	2,676	2
1987	18	(5)	Scarborough	46	10	5	8	35	28	5	5	13	25	45	55	2,325	3
1969	19	(19)	Hartlepool	46	12	4	7	45	33	3	6	14	21	55	55	2,503	2
1988	20	(23)	Doncaster Rovers	46	7	7	9	29	29	7	2	14	24	31	51	2,706	5
1983	21	(7)	Wrexham	46	8	8	7	28	28	5	4	14	23	39	51	2,368	6
1989	22	(R)	Aldershot	46	8	7	8	28	26	4	7	12	21	43	50	2,022	5
1976	23	(21)	Halifax Town	46	5	9	9	31	29	7	4	12	26	36	49	1,895	1
1981	24	(22)	*Colchester United*	46	9	3	11	26	25	2	7	14	22	50	43	3,150	2

Highest Attendance : 12,277 Burnley v. Carlisle U, Dec 26

Lowest Attendance: 1,139 Aldershot v. Peterborough U, Feb 27

PLAY-OFFS
CAMBRIDGE 1 2 Maidstone 1 0;
CHESTERFIELD 4 2 Stockport 0 0

FINAL
Wembley, May 26
Cambridge 1 Chesterfield 0 *Attendance: 26,404*

TOP SCORERS (LEAGUE AND CUP)
30 Darren Rowbotham (Exeter)
28 Brett Angell (Stockport)
26 Steve Butler (Maidstone)
26 Mark Gall (Maidstone)
23 David Crown (Southend)
22 David Puckett (Aldershot)

Sendings-off include all competitive First-Team games.

HOW THE LEAD CHANGED HANDS
Sep 2 Lincoln; Sep 15 Southend; Sep 26 Lincoln; Oct 1 Southend; Oct 28 Stockport; Nov 1 Southend; Dec 17 Carlisle; Dec 26 Exeter; Jan 6 Carlisle; Jan 13 Exeter; Jan 20 Carlisle; Mar 3 Exeter; Mar 23 Southend; Mar 24 EXETER.

THE TURNAROUND

"I didn't feel embarrassed. I didn't feel humiliated. I just felt numb like my players."
Steve Coppell, Crystal Palace Manager, on losing 9-0 to Liverpool

"Give that title to Kenny NOW "
The Sun, September 13

"The way they play, Liverpool would have a hell of a chance of winning the World Cup - and I don't jest."
Bobby Campbell, Chelsea manager, after losing 5-2 at home

"I only plucked up courage yesterday to sit through the video of that awful night and we were even worse than I thought we'd been at the time."
Steve Coppell before the FA Cup semi-final

"3pm. MATCH OF THE DAY The Road to Wembley... Highlights (ie. the Liverpool goals)"
TV Listings, Sunday Correspondent

"The fact that the FA Cup semi-finals should produce 13 goals was remarkable enough. That four of them should be scored by Crystal Palace strained credulity to breaking point. That they should be placed in Liverpool's net is still almost beyond belief."
David Lacey, The Guardian

"We're forever blowing Doubles."
Alan Hansen, Liverpool captain

FA CUP

Winners are capitals. Underlined teams beat a team from a higher division.

FIRST ROUND
Aldershot 0 CAMBRIDGE 1; AYLESBURY 1 Southend United 0; BASINGSTOKE 3 Bromsgrove 0; Bath 2 1. FULHAM 2,2; BISHOP AUCKLAND 2 Tow Law 0; BLACKPOOL 2 Bolton 1; Brentford 0 COLCHESTER 1; BRISTOL CITY 2 Barnet 0; Bristol Rovers 1 1 0 READING 1 1 1; BURNLEY 1 2 Stockport 1 1; CARDIFF 1 Halesowen 0; CARLISLE 3 Wrexham 0; CREWE 2 Congleton 0; DARLINGTON 6 Northwich Victoria 2; Dartford 1,1 EXETER 1 4; DONCASTER 1 Notts County 0; Farnborough 0 HEREFORD 1; Gillingham 0 0 WELLING 1,1; GLOUCESTER 1 Dorchester 0; Hartlepool 0 HUDDERSFIELD 2; Kettering 0 NORTHAMPTON 1; Kidderminster Harriers 2 SWANSEA 3; Leyton Orient 0 BIRMINGHAM 1; LINCOLN 1 Billingham Synthonia 0; Macclesfield 1 2 CHESTER 1 3; MAIDSTONE 2 Yeovil 1;

Marine 0 ROCHDALE 1; PETERBOROUGH 1 1 Hayes 1,0; PRESTON 1 Tranmere 0; Redditch 1 MERTHYR 3; ROTHERHAM 0 2 Bury 0,1; Scarborough 0 WHITLEY BAY 1; SCUNTHORPE 4 Matlock 1; Shrewsbury 2 CHESTERFIELD 3; Slough 1 WOKING 2; Stafford Rangers 2 HALIFAX 3; Sutton 1,0 TORQUAY 1 4; Telford 0 WALSALL 3; WIGAN 2 Mansfield 0; York 1 GRIMSBY 2

SECOND ROUND
Basingstoke 2 TORQUAY 3; BLACKPOOL 3 Chester 0; BRISTOL CITY 2 Fulham 1; CAMBRIDGE 3 Woking 1; CARDIFF 2,1 Gloucester 2 0; Chesterfield 0 HUDDERSFIELD 2; Colchester 0 BIRMINGHAM 2; CREWE 1,2 Bishop Auckland 1 1; DARLINGTON 3 Halifax 1; GRIMSBY 1 Doncaster 0; HEREFORD U 3 Merthyr 2; Maidstone 1 2 EXETER C 1 3; NORTHAMPTON 0,1 Aylesbury 0,0; READING 0 1 0 2 Welling 0 1 0 1; ROCHDALE 3 Lincoln C 0; Scunthorpe 2 1 0 BURNLEY 2 1 5; SWANSEA 3 Peterborough 1; WALSALL 1 Rotherham 0; WHITLEY BAY 2 Preston 0; WIGAN 2 Carlisle 0

THIRD ROUND
Birmingham 1 0 OLDHAM 1 1; Blackburn 2 1 ASTON VILLA 2 3; BLACKPOOL 1 Burnley 0; BRIGHTON 4 Luton 1; BRISTOL CITY 2 Swindon 1; CAMBRIDGE U 0 3 Darlington 0 1; Cardiff 0 0 QPR 0 2; CHARLTON 1 3 Bradford City 1 0; CHELSEA 1 2 Crewe 1 0; CRYSTAL PALACE 2 Portsmouth 1; Exeter 1 0 NORWICH 1 2; HEREFORD 2 Walsall 1; HUDDERSFIELD 3 Grimsby 1; Hull 0 NEWCASTLE 1; Leeds 0 IPSWICH 1; Leicester 1 BARNSLEY 2; Manchester City 0 1 MILLWALL 0 3; Middlesbrough 0 1 0 EVERTON 0 1 1; NORTHAMPTON 1 Coventry 0; Nottingham Forest 0 MANCHESTER UNITED 1; Plymouth 0 OXFORD 1 1 PORT VALE 1 3 Derby 1 2; READING 2 Sunderland 1; ROCHDALE 1 Whitley Bay 0; SHEFFIELD UNITED 2 Bournemouth 0; Stoke 0 ARSENAL 1; Swansea C 0 0 LIVERPOOL 0 8; TORQUAY 1 West Ham U 0; Tottenham H 1 SOUTHAMPTON 3; WATFORD 2 Wigan A 0; WEST BROMWICH 2 Wimbledon 0; Wolverhampton 1 SHEFFIELD WEDNESDAY 2

FOURTH ROUND
Arsenal 0 0 QPR 0 2; ASTON VILLA 6 Port Vale 0; BARNSLEY 2 Ipswich 0; BLACKPOOL 1 Torquay 0; BRISTOL CITY 3 Chelsea 1; CRYSTAL PALACE 4 Huddersfield 0; Hereford 0 MANCHESTER UNITED 1; Millwall 1 0 CAMBRIDGE U 1 1; Norwich 0 1 LIVERPOOL 0 3; OLDHAM 2 Brighton 1; Reading 3 1 NEWCASTLE 3 4; ROCHDALE 3 Northampton 0; SHEFFIELD UNITED 1 2 Watford 1 1; Sheffield Wednesday 1 EVERTON 2; SOUTHAMPTON 1 Oxford 0; WEST BROMWICH 1 Charlton A 0

FIFTH ROUND

Blackpool 2 0 0 QPR 2 0 3; Bristol City 0 1 1 CAMBRIDGE U 0 1 5; CRYSTAL PALACE 1 Rochdale 0; LIVERPOOL 3 Southampton 0; Newcastle 2 MANCHESTER UNITED 3; OLDHAM 2 1 2 Everton 2 1 1; SHEFFIELD UNITED 2 0 1 Barnsley 2 0 1; West Bromwich 0 ASTON VILLA 2

FOURTH DIVISION CLUBS IN THE FA CUP SIXTH ROUND

1963-64 Oxford United
Round
1:      beat Folkestone (NL) 2-0
2:      beat Kettering (NL) 2-1
3:      beat Chesterfield(4) 1-0
4:      beat Brentford (3) 2-2,2-1
5:      beat Blackburn (1) 3-1
6:      lost to Preston (2) 1-2

1975-76 Bradford City
1:      beat Chesterfield (3) 1-0
2:      beat Rotherham (3) 3-0
3:      beat Shrewsbury (3) 2-1
4:      beat Tooting & M (NL) 3-1
5:      beat Norwich (1) 2-1
6:      lost to Southampton (2) 0-1

1970-71 Colchester United
1:      beat Ringmer (NL) 3-0
2:      beat Cambridge U (NL) 3-0
3:      beat Barnet (NL) 1-0
4:      beat Rochdale (3) 3-3, 5-0
5:      beat Leeds (1) 3-2
6:      lost to Everton (1) 0-5

1989-90 Cambridge United
1:      beat Aldershot (4) 1-0
2:      beat Woking (NL) 3-1
3:      beat Darlington (NL) 0-0,3-1
4:      beat Millwall (1) 1-1, 1-0
5:      beatBristol City (3) 0-0, 1-1, 5-1
6:      lost to Crystal Palace (1) 0-1

Figures in brackets indicate division opponents were in at the time.

SIXTH ROUND
Cambridge U 0 CRYSTAL PALACE 1; Sheffield United 0 MANCHESTER UNITED 1; QPR 2 0 LIVERPOOL 2 1; OLDHAM 3 Aston Villa 0

SEMI-FINALS
CRYSTAL PALACE 4 Liverpool 3; MANCHESTER UNITED 3 2 Oldham 3 1

FINAL
Wembley, May 12
Manchester United: 3 Crystal Palace 3 (after extra time)
Robson 35   O'Reilly 19
Hughes 62, 113   Wright 73, 92
United: Leighton, Ince, Martin (Blackmore), Bruce, Phelan, Pallister (Robins), Robson, Webb, McClair, Hughes, Wallace
Palace: Martyn, Pemberton, Shaw, Gray (Madden), O'Reilly, Thorn, Barber (Wright), Thomas, Bright, Salako, Pardew

Referee: A Gunn, Sussex
Attendance: 80,000
REPLAY
Wembley, May 17
MANCHESTER UNITED 1 Crystal Palace 0
Martin 61
United: Sealey, Ince, Martin, Bruce, Phelan, Pallister, Robson, Webb, McClair, Hughes, Wallace
Palace: Martyn, Pemberton, Shaw, Gray, O'Reilly, Thorn, Barber (Wright), Thomas, Bright, Salako (Madden), Pardew
Referee: A Gunn, Sussex
Attendance: 80,000

HIGHEST SCORING FA CUP SEMI-FINALS
17 goals 1891-92:
    West Brom v Nottingham Forest 1-1, 1-1, 6-2: Aston Villa v Sunderland 4-1
17 goals 1898-99:
    Sheffield United Liverpool 2-2, 4-4, 0-0, 0-1: Derby v Stoke 3-1
16 goals 1989-90:
    Crystal Palace v Liverpool 4-3
    Manchester U v Oldham A 3-3, 2-1
15 goals 1957-58:
    Bolton v Blackburn 2-1
    Manchester U v Fulham 2-2, 5-3

HIGHEST SCORING FA CUP FINALS
8:   1901 Tottenham v Sheffield United 2-2, 3-1
8:   1983 Manchester United v Brighton United 2-2, 4-0
7:   1890 Blackburn v Sheffield Wednesday 6-1
7:   1953 Blackpool v Bolton 4-3
7:   1970 Chelsea v Leeds 2-2, 2-1
7:   1981 Tottenham v Manchester City 1-1, 3-2
7:   1990 Manchester United v Crystal Palace 3-3, 1-0

LITTLEWOODS CUP
Winners are in capitals. Underlined teams beat a team from a higher division.

FIRST ROUND
STOCKPORT 1 1 Bury 0 1; BIRMINGHAM 2 1 Chesterfield 1 1; BLACKPOOL 2 1 Burnley 2 0; Bristol City 2 2 READING 3 2; CAMBRIDGE 3 1 Maidstone 1 0; Cardiff 0 2 PLYMOUTH 3 0; Colchester 3 1 SOUTHEND 4 2; CREWE 4 2 Chester 0 0; Gillingham 1 0 LEYTON ORIENT 4 3; HALIFAX 3 0 Carlisle 1 1; HUDDERSFIELD 1 2 Doncaster 1 1; Hull 1 0 GRIMSBY 0 2; MANSFIELD 1 2 Northampton T 1 0; Preston 3 1 TRANMERE 4 3; Rochdale 2 1 BOLTON 1 5; Sheffield United 1 0 ROTHERHAM 1 1; SHREWSBURY 3 1 Notts County 0 3; Torquay 0 0 HEREFORD 1 3; Walsall 1 0 PORT VALE 2 1; WOLVERHAMPTON 1 2 Lincoln 0 0;

Wrexham 0 0 WIGAN 0 5; Brighton 0 1 BRENTFORD 3 1; Bristol Rovers 1 0 PORTSMOUTH 0 2; EXETER 3 1 Swansea 0 1; FULHAM 0 5 Oxford 1 3; Hartlepool 3 1 YORK 3 4; Peterborough 2 2 ALDERSHOT 0 6; SCARBOROUGH 2 1 Scunthorpe 0 1

SECOND ROUND

Port Vale 1 0 WIMBLEDON 2 3; ARSENAL 2 6 Plymouth 0 1; Barnsley 1 1 BLACKPOOL 1 1 (won on pens); Birmingham C 1 1 WEST HAM 2 1; BOLTON 2 1 Watford 1 1; Brentford 2 1 MANCHESTER CITY 1 4; Cambridge 2 0 DERBY 1 5; Chelsea 1 2 SCARBOROUGH 1 3; Crewe 0 0 BOURNEMOUTH 1 0; CRYSTAL PALACE 1 3 Leicester C 2 2 (away goals); Grimsby 3 0 COVENTRY 1 3; Ipswich 0 0 TRANMERE 1 1; Leyton Orient 0 2 EVERTON 2 2; LIVERPOOL 5 3 Wigan 2 0; Mansfield 3 2 LUTON 4 7; OLDHAM 2 2 Leeds U 1 1; Reading 3 0 NEWCASTLE 1 4; Shrewsbury 0 1 SWINDON 3 3; Stoke 1 0 MILLWALL 0 2; SUNDERLAND 1 3 Fulham 1 0; ASTON VILLA 1 1 Wolverhampton 1 1; CHARLTON 3 1 Hereford 1 0; EXETER 3 1 Blackburn 0 2; MIDDLESBOROUGH 4 1 Halifax 0 0; NORWICH 1 1 Rotherham 1 0; NOTTINGHAM FOREST 1 3 Huddersfield T 1 3 (away goals); Portsmouth 2 0 MANCHESTER UNITED 3 0; QPR 1 0 Stockport 1 0; SHEFFIELD WEDNESDAY 0 8 Aldershot 0 0; TOTTENHAM 1 2 Southend 0 3 (away goals); WEST BROMWICH 1 5 Bradford City 3 3 (away goals); York 0 0 SOUTHAMPTON 1 2

THIRD ROUND

TRANMERE 3 Millwall 2; Crystal Palace 0 0 NOTTINGHAM FOREST 0 5; EVERTON 3 Luton 0; SOUTHAMPTON 1 Charlton 0;

SUNDERLAND 1 1 Bournemouth 1 0; SWINDON 3 1 1 2 Bolton 3 1 1 1; ARSENAL 1 Liverpool 0; Aston Villa 0 0 WEST HAM 0 1; DERBY 2 Sheffield Wednesday 1; EXETER 3 Blackpool 0; MANCHESTER CITY 3 Norwich 1; Manchester United 0 TOTTENHAM 3; Middlesborough 1 0 WIMBLEDON 1 1; Newcastle U WEST BROMWICH 1; OLDHAM 7 Scarborough 0; QPR 1 COVENTRY 2

FOURTH ROUND

DERBY 2 West Bromwich 0; Manchester City 0 COVENTRY 1; NOTTINGHAM FOREST 1 Everton 0; OLDHAM 3 Arsenal 1; Tranmere 2 0 TOTTENHAM 2 4; WEST HAM 1 Wimbledon 0; Exeter 2 2 SUNDERLAND 2 5; Swindon 0 2 SOUTHAMPTON 0 4

FIFTH ROUND

Southampton 2 0 OLDHAM 2 2; WEST HAM 1 0 2 Derby 1 0 1; Sunderland 0 0 COVENTRY 0 5; NOTTINGHAM FOREST 2 3 Tottenham 2 2

SEMI FINALS

NOTTINGHAM FOREST 2 0 Coventry 1 0; OLDHAM 6 0 West Ham 0 3

FINAL

Wembley, Apr 29
NOTTINGHAM FOREST 1 Oldham Athletic 0
Jemson 48
Forest: Sutton, Laws, Pearce, Walker, Chettle, Hodge, Crosby, Parker, Clough, Jemson, Carr
Oldham: Rhodes, Irwin, Barlow, Henry, Barrett, Warhurst, Adams, Ritchie, Bunn (Palmer), Milligan, Holden
Referee: J E Martin, Alton
Attendance: 74,343

RECORD FINES IMPOSED BY THE FA ON INDIVIDUALS

£8,500   Paul McGrath (Aston Villa, for newspaper article about Alex Ferguson, Nov 1989)

£5,000   Brian Clough (Nottm Forest manager, for striking spectators, Feb 1989)

£5,000   (£2,000 suspended) Mick Kennedy (Portsmouth, newspaper article claiming he 'was the hardest', Aug 1987)

£3,000   Allan Clarke (Barnsley manager, for comments about Vinny Jones, Sep 1988)

£3,000   Paul Davis (Arsenal, for breaking jaw of Southampton's Glenn Cockerell, Sep 1988)

£2,000   Graeme Hogg (Portsmouth, for comments about Manchester United, Nov 1988)

£2,000   John Fashanu (Wimbledon, for after-match incident against Manchester United, Dec 1988)

SCOTTISH SOCCER

SCOTTISH LEAGUE

Promoted clubs in bold. Relegated clubs in italics.
1988-89 positions in brackets.

PREMIER DIVISION

			P	W	D	L	F	A	W	D	L	F	A	Pts	Average Home Att
1	(1)	RANGERS	36	14	2	2	32	7	6	9	3	16	12	51	38,436
2	(2)	Aberdeen	36	12	4	2	33	13	5	6	7	23	20	44	15,448
3	(6)	Hearts	36	8	6	4	28	17	8	6	4	26	18	44	15,694
4	(4)	Dundee U	36	8	8	2	21	12	3	5	10	15	27	35	10,719
5	(3)	Celtic	36	6	6	6	21	20	4	8	6	16	17	34	28,616
6	(9)	Motherwell	36	7	6	5	23	21	4	6	8	20	26	34	8,362
7	(4)	Hibernian	36	8	5	5	25	23	4	5	9	9	18	34	10,705
8	(P)	Dunfermline	36	5	6	7	17	23	6	2	10	20	27	30	10,989
9	(7)	St Mirren	36	6	6	6	14	15	4	4	10	14	33	30	7,646
10	(8)	*Dundee*	36	4	4	6	23	26	1	6	11	18	39	24	8,884

HOW THE LEAD CHANGED HANDS

Sep 2 Celtic; Sep 16 Hearts; Sep 23 Aberdeen;Oct 3 Motherwell;Oct 4 Celtic; Nov 4 Rangers; Nov 8 Dunfermline; Nov 11 Hearts;Nov 22 Aberdeen; Dec 16 Rangers; Dec 20 Aberdeen;Dec 23 RANGERS

FIRST DIVISION

			P	W	D	L	F	A	W	D	L	F	A	Pts	Average Home Att
1	(6)	ST JOHNSTONE	39	13	3	4	40	16	12	5	2	41	23	58	5,866
2	(4)	Airdrieonians	39	12	6	2	45	23	11	2	6	32	22	54	2,295
3	(3)	Clydebank	39	10	4	5	39	29	7	6	7	35	35	44	1,117
4	(2)	Falkirk	39	11	5	3	38	17	3	10	7	21	29	43	3,062
5	(7)	Raith Rovers	39	10	4	5	30	22	5	6	7	27	28	42	1,683
6	(R)	Hamilton	39	9	5	5	33	27	5	8	7	19	26	41	1,739
7	(10)	Meadowbank Thistle	39	7	6	7	22	25	6	7	6	19	21	39	691
8	(8)	Partick Thistle	39	9	5	6	33	22	3	9	7	29	31	38	3,778
9	(12)	Clyde	39	5	9	5	18	20	5	6	9	21	26	35	1,050
10	(11)	Ayr United	39	6	8	5	24	23	5	5	10	17	39	35	2,677
11	(5)	Morton	39	4	10	6	21	20	5	6	8	17	26	34	1,572
12	(9)	Forfar Athletic*	39	5	7	7	29	33	3	8	9	22	32	29	1,009
13	(P)	*Albion Rovers*	39	4	8	8	31	38	4	3	12	19	40	27	1,191
14	(P)	*Alloa*	39	4	8	8	18	27	2	5	12	23	43	25	1,057

*2 pts deducted by the Scottish League

HOW THE LEAD CHANGED HANDS

Sep 2 St Johnstone; Jan 6 Airdrie; Jan 13 St Johnstone; Feb 10 Airdrie;Mar 31 ST JOHNSTONE

SECOND DIVISION

			P	W	D	L	F	A	W	D	L	F	A	Pts	Average Home Att
1	(3)	BRECHIN CITY	39	12	5	3	33	20	7	6	6	26	24	49	613
2	(R)	Kilmarnock	39	14	3	3	35	11	8	1	10	32	28	48	3,097
3	(4)	Stirling Albion	39	13	3	4	44	20	7	4	8	29	30	47	708
4	(14)	Stenhousemuir	39	10	2	7	30	29	8	6	6	30	24	44	556
5	(13)	Berwick Rangers	39	13	4	3	36	19	5	1	13	30	38	41	495
6	(12)	Dumbarton	39	9	5	5	33	29	6	5	9	37	44	40	607
7	(8)	Cowdenbeath	39	7	6	6	35	30	6	7	7	23	24	39	290
8	(11)	Stranraer	39	8	4	8	32	31	7	4	8	25	28	38	789
9	(5)	East Fife	39	7	7	5	37	30	5	5	10	23	34	36	696
10	(R)	Queen of the South	39	8	8	3	40	34	3	6	11	18	35	36	737
11	(7)	Queens Park	39	10	5	5	26	23	3	5	11	14	28	36	591
12	(10)	Arbroath	39	9	5	5	26	18	3	5	12	22	43	34	526
13	(6)	Montrose	39	5	7	8	28	29	5	5	9	25	34	32	400
14	(9)	East Stirling	39	8	3	8	20	25	0	7	13	14	41	26	315

HOW THE LEAD CHANGED HANDS

Sep 2 Brechin; Sep 9 Stirling A; Sep 16 Brechin;Sep 23 Queen's Park; Oct 7 Kilmarnock; Nov 11 Brechin; Jan 6 Stirling A ; Jan 13 BRECHIN

——SCOTTISH CUP——

Winners are in capitals. Underlined teams beat a
team from a higher division.

FIRST ROUND
Berwick 1 0 STENHOUSEMUIR 1 1; BRECHIN
3 Montrose 1; ELGIN 2 Arbroath 1; Queen's
Park 1 DUMBARTON 2; QUEEN OF THE
SOUTH 2 Cove R 1; STIRLING A 4
Coldstream 0

SECOND ROUND
Dumbarton 0 COWDENBEATH 2; Elgin 2 0
BRECHIN 2 8; Gala Fairydean 2 1
INVERNESS CALEDONIAN 2 4;
Stenhousemuir 0 QUEEN OF THE SOUTH 1;
STIRLING ALBION 3 Whitehill 0;
STRANRAER 1 0 Kilmarnock 1 0 (pens); Vale
of Leven 1 EAST STIRLING 3; EAST FIFE 4
Ross County 1

THIRD ROUND
Airdrie 2 1 INVERNESS CALEDONIAN 2 1
(pens); Albion R 0 CLYDEBANK 2; Ayr 0 1
ST MIRREN 0 2; Brechin 0 HIBERNIAN 2;
COWDENBEATH 3 Stranraer 1;
DUNFERMLINE 0 1 Hamilton 0 0; Dundee 0 0
DUNDEE UNITED 0 1; EAST FIFE 3
Meadowbank 1; East Stirling 0 STIRLING
ALBION 1; Forfar 1 CELTIC 2; HEARTS 2
Falkirk 0; MORTON 2 3 Raith 2 1;
MOTHERWELL 7 Clyde 0; Partick Thistle 2
ABERDEEN 6; QUEEN OF THE SOUTH 0 3
Alloa 0 2; RANGERS 3 St Johnstone 0

FOURTH ROUND
ABERDEEN 2 Morton 1; Cowdenbeath 1
DUNFERMLINE 2; DUNDEE UNITED 2
Queen of the South 1; HEARTS 4 Motherwell
0; HIBERNIAN 5 East Fife 1; St Mirren 1 2
CLYDEBANK 1 3; STIRLING ALBION 6
Inverness Caledonian 2; CELTIC 1 Rangers 0

FIFTH ROUND
ABERDEEN 4 Hearts 1; CLYDEBANK 1 1
Stirling Albion 1 0; Dunfermline A 0 0 CELTIC
0 3; DUNDEE UNITED 1 Hibernian 0

SEMI-FINALS
ABERDEEN 4 Dundee United 0; Clydebank 0
CELTIC 2

FINAL
Hampden Park, May 12
Aberdeen 0 Celtic 0
ABERDEEN won 9-8 on penalties after extra time
Aberdeen: Snelders, McKimmie, Robertson, B
Grant, McLeish, Irvine, Nicholas, Bett, Mason
(Watson), Connor, Gilhaus
Celtic: Bonner, Wdowczyk, Rogan, P Grant,
Elliott, Whyte, Stark (Galloway), McStay,
Dziekanowski, Walker (Coyne), Miller
Referee: G Smith (Edinburgh)
Att: 60,493

SCOTTISH LEAGUE (SKOL) CUP

FIRST ROUND
DUMBARTON 3 Stenhousemuir 0;
ARBROATH 1 East Stirling 0; Cowdenbeath 0
MONTROSE 4; East Fife 2 QUEEN'S PARK 2
(pens); Stirling Albion 0 BERWICK 3; Stranraer
3 BRECHIN 4

SECOND ROUND
AIRDRIE 4 Forfar 0; Ayr 0 HAMILTON 1;
Berwick 0 ST MIRREN 2; Dumbarton 0
CELTIC 3; DUNDEE 5 Clyde 1;
DUNFERMLINE 3 Raith 0; HIBERNIAN 2
Alloa 0; Kilmarnock 1 MOTHERWELL 4;
Queen's Park 0 MORTON 1; RANGERS 4
Arbroath 0; Albion 0 ABERDEEN 2; Brechin C
0 FALKIRK 3; CLYDEBANK 3 Meadowbank
1; DUNDEE UNITED 1 Partick Thistle 0;
HEARTS 3 Montrose 0; QUEEN OF THE
SOUTH 1 St Johnstone 0

THIRD ROUND
CELTIC 2 Queen of the South 0; HIBERNIAN
0 Clydebank 0 (pens); ABERDEEN 4 Airdrie 0;
DUNFERMLINE 1 Dundee 0; Falkirk 1
HEARTS 4; HAMILTON 2 Dundee U 1;
Morton 1 RANGERS 2; ST MIRREN 1
Motherwell 0

FOURTH ROUND
Hibernian 1 DUNFERMLINE 3; ABERDEEN
3 St Mirren 1; Hamilton 0 RANGERS 3; Hearts
2 CELTIC 2 (pens)

SEMI-FINALS
RANGERS 5 Dunfermline A 0; ABERDEEN 1
Celtic 0

FINAL
Hampden Park, Oct 22
ABERDEEN 2 Rangers 1
(After extra time)
Mason 22, 102   Walters 34
Aberdeen: Snelders, McKimmie, McLeish,
Miller, Robertson, D Mason, Bett, Grant (Van der
Ark), Connor, Nicholas, Jess (Irvine)
Rangers: Woods, Stevens,Gough, Butcher,
Munro, Steven, I Ferguson, Wilkins, Walters
(McCall), McCoist, Johnston
Referee: G Smith (Edinburgh)
Att: 61,190

NON-LEAGUE SOCCER

GM VAUXHALL CONFERENCE

				HOME					AWAY						Average
			P	W	D	L	F	A	W	D	L	F	A	Pts	Home Att
1	(R)	DARLINGTON	42	13	6	2	43	12	13	3	5	33	13	87	3,588
2	(8)	Barnet	42	15	4	2	46	14	11	3	7	35	27	85	2,869
3	(6)	Runcorn	42	16	3	2	52	20	3	10	8	27	42	70	809
4	(7)	Macclesfield	42	11	6	4	35	16	6	9	6	21	25	66	1,422
5	(2)	Kettering T	42	13	5	3	35	15	5	7	9	31	38	66	2,208
6	(11)	Welling U	42	11	6	4	36	16	7	4	10	26	34	64	1,108
7	(9)	Yeovil T	42	9	8	4	32	25	8	4	9	30	29	63	2,253
8	(12)	Sutton Utd	42	14	2	5	42	24	5	4	12	26	40	63	915
9	(P)	Merthyr T	42	9	9	3	41	30	7	5	9	26	33	62	1,645
10	(4)	Wycombe W	42	11	6	4	42	24	6	4	11	22	32	61	1,980
11	(15)	Cheltenham T	42	9	6	6	30	22	7	5	9	28	38	59	1,423
12	(16)	Telford U	42	8	7	6	31	29	7	6	8	25	34	58	1,219
13	(5)	Kidderminster H	42	7	6	8	37	33	8	3	10	27	34	54	1,415
14	(P)	Barrow	42	11	8	2	33	25	1	8	12	18	42	52	1,292
15	(10)	Northwich V	42	9	3	9	29	30	6	2	13	22	37	50	726
16	(14)	Altrincham	42	8	5	8	31	20	4	8	9	18	28	49	789
17	(19)	Stafford R	42	9	6	6	25	23	3	6	12	25	39	48	1,188
18	(3)	Boston Utd	42	10	3	8	36	30	3	5	13	12	37	47	1,579
19	(18)	Fisher A	42	9	1	11	34	34	4	6	11	21	44	46	552
20	(17)	Chorley	42	9	5	7	26	26	4	1	16	16	41	45	764
21	(P)	Farnborough T	42	7	5	9	33	30	3	7	11	27	43	42	937
22	(13)	Enfield	42	9	3	9	36	34	1	3	17	16	55	36	840

Runcorn's 9-0 win over Enfield (March 3) was the biggest ever in the Alliance Conference.

OTHER LEAGUE CHAMPIONS

Beazer Homes League (Premier)   DOVER
(Runners-up BATH CITY promoted to GM-Vauxhall Conference because Dover's ground considered sub-standard.)

HFS Loans League (Premier)   COLNE DYNAMOES
(Runners-up GATESHEAD promoted to Conference because Colne's ground considered sub-standard. The Colne club was then disbanded.)

Vauxhall League (Fremier)   SLOUGH

HFS Loans League (Div. 1)   LEEK TOWN

Beazer Homes League (Midland)   HALESOWEN

Beazer Homes League (Southern)   BASHLEY
(Bashley is a village near Bournemouth with no pub. The club is now two divisions away from the Football League.)

Vauxhall Opel League (First)   WIVENHOE

Ovenden Papers Football Combination   ARSENAL

Central League (Div.1)   LIVERPOOL

Skol Northern League (Div.1)   BILLINGHAM SYNTHONIA

Great Mills League   TAUNTON TOWN

Jewson South-Western League   FALMOUTH TOWN

Abacus Welsh Football League   HAVERFORDWEST COUNTY

Highland League   ELGIN CITY

OTHER RESULTS

TENNENTS CHARITY SHIELD
Wembley, Aug 12
LIVERPOOL   1   Arsenal   0
Beardsley 31

ZENITH DATA SYSTEMS CUP FINAL
Wembley, Mar 25
CHELSEA   1   Middlesbrough   0
Dorigo 35
Att: 76,369

LEYLAND DAF CUP FINAL
Wembley, May 20
TRANMERE ROVERS   2   Bristol Rovers   1
Muir 10, Steel 73   *White 51*
Att: 48,402

FA CHALLENGE TROPHY FINAL
Wembley, May 19
BARROW   3   Leek Town   0
Gordon 45, 58
Cowperthwaite 56
Att: 19,011

FA VASE FINAL
Wembley, May 5
Bridlington Town   0   Yeading   0
Replay, Elland Road, Leeds, May 14
YEADING   1   Bridlington Town   0

FA YOUTH CUP
1st Leg, May 8
Middlesbrough   1   Tottenham H   2

2nd Leg, May 13

| Tottenham H | 1 | Middlesbrough | 1 |

TOTTENHAM HOTSPUR won 3-2 on aggregate

WOMEN'S FA CUP

Derby, Apr 28

| DONCASTER BELLES | 1 | Friends of Fulham | 0 |

Coultard 60

Att: 3,000

IF WINTER COMES

❝When Upton Park roars its approval after one of its home defenders has apparently done his utmost to send a player of the quality of Gordon Strachan halfway towards Hackney Marshes, then football has indeed reached a fresh nadir."

David Lacey, The Guardian

"How bad is British football? The question is prompted by the wretched quality of this season's English First Division, the absolute desert of talentless, negative play."

Brian Glanville, Sunday Times

"Danny Blanchflower always said football...was about glory. It was about doing things in style, with a flourish. Danny Blanchflower never played for Aldershot."

Michael Hurd, Evening Standard

"Footballers are not wordy people, they are movement people. I recall Freddie Ayer being asked about football and he sounded as moronic as anyone else talking about the game, using phrases like 'tight at the back'."

Dr Desmond Morris

"We love it. We love being allocated 22 standing places behind a floodlight in The Den's Stalag Alcatraz away corner; holding the world record for the number of misspelt names in one season; not having got an away penalty since 1986; opening games of the season described as relegation battles; attracting attendances lower than Palace's goal difference. We're used to it.

Keith Hollins, Charlton supporter, in When Saturday Comes

"It's like trying to describe Disneyland to someone who hasn't been there."

Bobby Campbell, Chelsea manager after winning the Zenith Data Systems Cup

"It must have been on such an afternoon that Webb Ellis picked up the ball, shouted 'to hell with this' and invented rugby.❞

Stephen Bierley, The Guardian, on Leeds v Sheffield United

EUROPEAN SOCCER

EUROPEAN CUP

FIRST ROUND

Dynamo Dresden (GDR) 1 3 AEK ATHENS (Gre) 0 5 ; Rangers (Sco) 1 0 BAYERN MUNICH (FRG) 3 0; Derry C (NI) 1 0 BENFICA (Por) 2 4; MARSEILLE (Fra) 3 1 Brondby (Den) 0 1; Ruch Chorzow (Pol) 1 1 CFKA SREDETS (Bul) 1 5; Linfield (Ire) 1 0 DNEPR (USSR) 2 1; SPARTA PRAGUE (Cze) 3 2 Fenerbahce (Tur) 1 1; STEAUA BUCHAREST (Rom) 4 1 Reykjavik (Ice) 0 0; AC MILAN (Ita) 4 1 HJK Helsinki (Fin) 0 0; MALMO (Swe) 1 1 Inter Milan (Ita) 0 1; PSV EINDHOVEN (Hol) 3 2 Lucerne (Swi) 0 0; Rosenborg (Nor) 0 0 MECHELEN (Bel) 0 5; Sliema W (Mal) 1 0 NENTORI TIRANA (Alb) 0 5; FC TIROL (Aut) 6 3 Omonia Nicosia (Cyp) 0 2; Spora (Lux) 0 0 REAL MADRID (Spa) 3 6; HONVED (Hun) 1 1 Vojvidina Novi Sad (Yug) 0 2 (won on away goals)

SECOND ROUND

BAYERN MUNICH 3 3 Nentori Tirana 1 0; DNEPR 2 2 FC Tirol 0 2; Honved 0 0 BENFICA 2 7; Malmo 0 1 MECHELEN 0 4; MARSEILLE 2 1 AEK Athens 0 1; AC MILAN 2 0 Real Madrid 0 1; Sparta Prague 2 0 CFKA SREDETS 2 3; Steaua Bucharest 1 1 PSV EINDHOVEN 0 5

QUARTER-FINALS

BAYERN MUNICH 2 1 PSV Eindhoven 1 0; BENFICA 1 3 Dnepr 0 0; CFKA Sredets 0 1 MARSEILLE 1 3; Mechelen 0 0 AC MILAN 0 2

SEMI-FINALS

AC MILAN 1 1 Bayern Munich 0 2 (Milan won on away goals); Marseille 2 0 BENFICA 1 1 (Benfica won on away goals)

FINAL

Vienna, May 23

| AC MILAN | 1 | Benfica | 0 |

Rijkaard 67

AC Milan: Galli, Tassotti, Maldini, Colombo, Costacurta, Baresi, Ancelotti (Massaro), Rijkaard, Van Basten, Gullit, Evani

Benfica: Silvino, Jose Carlos, Ricardo, Samuel, Aldair, Thern, Paneira (Vata), Pacheco (Brito), Hernani, Valdo, Magnusson

Att: 57,000

EUROPEAN CUP-WINNERS' CUP FINAL

QUARTER-FINALS

ANDERLECHT 2 1 Admira Wacker 0 1; DINAMO BUCHAREST 2 2 Partizan Belgrade 1 0; Valladolid 0 0 MONACO 0 0 (Monaco wo 3-1 on pens); SAMPDORIA 2 2 Grasshoppers 0 1

SEMI-FINALS

ANDERLECHT 1 1 Dinamo Bucharest 1 0; Monaco 2 0 SAMPDORIA 2 2

FINAL

Gothenburg, May 9

| SAMPDORIA | 2 | Anderlecht | 0 |

Valli 105, 107

Sampdoria: Pagliuca, Mannini, Pellegrini, Vierchowod, Carboni, Invernizzi (Lombardo), Pari, Katanec (Salsano), Mancini, Vialli, Dossena

Anderlecht: De Wilde, Grun, Marchoul, Keshi, Kooiman, Gudjohnsen, Musonda, Vervoort, Jankovic, Degryse (Nilis), Van der Linden

Att: 20,103

How the British Isles teams fared:

FIRST ROUND
PARTIZAN BELGRADE 2 4 Celtic 1 5 (won on away goals); ANDERLECHT 6 4 Ballymena 0 0; PANATHINAIKOS 3 3 Swansea C 2 3; TORPEDO MOSCOW 5 1 Cork C 0 0

UEFA CUP FINAL

QUARTER-FINALS
Hamburg 0 2 JUVENTUS 2 1; COLOGNE 2 0 Antwerp 0 0; FC Liège 1 2 WERDER BREMEN 4 0; FIORENTINA 1 1 Auxerre 0 0

SEMI-FINALS
JUVENTUS 3 0 Cologne 2 0; Werder Bremen 1 0 FIORENTINA 1 0 (won on away goals)

FINAL
First Leg, May 2

Juventus	3	Fiorentina	1
Galia	3	Buso	10
Casiraghi	59		
De Agostini	73		

Juventus: Tacconi, Napoli, de Agostini, Galia, Brio , Bonetti, Aleinikov, Rui Barros, Casiraghi, Barocchi, Schillaci
Fiorentina: Landucci, Dell'Oglio, Volpecina, Dunga, Pin, Battistini, Nappi, Kubik, Baggio, Buso, Di Chiara
Att: 55,000
Juve's last match in the old Comunale Stadium

Second Leg, May 16

Fiorentina	0	Juventus	0

Fiorentina: Landucci, Dell'Oglio, Volpecina,Dunga, Pin, Battistini, Nappi, Kubik, Baggio, Buso, Di Chiara
Juventus: Tacconi, Napoli, de Agostini, Galia, Brio, Bonetti, Aleinikov, Rui Barros, Casirgahi, Barocchi, Schillaci
Att: 41,000

JUVENTUS won 3-1 on aggregate

How the British Isles teams fared:

FIRST ROUND
HIBERNIAN 1 3 Videoton 0 0; Aberdeen 2 0 RAPID VIENNA 1 1 (won on away goals); Glentoran 1 0 DUNDEE U 3 2; WETTINGEN 3 2 Dundalk 0 0

SECOND ROUND
ANTWERP 4 2 Dundee U 0 3; Hibernian 0 0 FC LIEGE 0 1

EUROPEAN SUPER CUP
First Leg, Nov 23

Barcelona	1	AC Milan	1
Amor 67		Van Basten (Pen) 44	

Second Leg, Dec 7

AC Milan	1	Barcelona	0
Evani 55			

AC MILAN won 2-1 on aggregate

WORLD CLUB CHAMPIONSHIP
(for the Toyota Cup)
Tokyo, Dec 16

AC MILAN	1	Atletico Nacional (Colombia)	0
Evani 118			

Att: 62,000

EUROPEAN TREBLE

In 1990 Italy became the first country to provide the winners of all three major European competitions. The following have provided two winners:

1958	SPAIN
1960	SPAIN
1961	ITALY
1962	SPAIN
1966	SPAIN
1968	ENGLAND
1970	ENGLAND
1971	ENGLAND
1975	WEST GERMANY
1981	ENGLAND
1984	ENGLAND
1989	ITALY

ACROSS EUROPE

Country	League Champions	Cup Winners
Albania	Dinamo Tirana	Dinamo Tirana
Austria	FCA Tirol	Austria Vienna
Belgium	FC Bruges	FC Liege
Bulgaria	CSKA Sofia	CFKA Sredets
Cyprus	Apoel	Salamina
Czechoslovakia	Sparta Prague	Dukla Prague
Denmark	Odense	Brondby
Finland	Kuusysi	Kupio Palloesura
France	Marseille	Montpellier
Germany, East	Dynamo Dresden	Dynamo Dresden
Germany, West	Bayern Munich	Kaiserlautern
Greece	Panathinaikos	Olympiakos
Holland	Ajax	PSV Eindhoven
Hungary	MTK-VM	Pecs
Iceland	KA Akureyri	Fram
Ireland, Northern	Portadown	Glentoran
Ireland, Rep of	St Patrick's	Bray Wanderers
Italy	Napoli	Juventus
Luxembourg	Union	Hesperange
Malta	Valetta	Sliema Wanderers
Norway	Lillestrom	Viking
Poland	Lech Poznan	Legia Warsaw
Portugal	Oporto	Estrela da Amadora
Romania	Dinamo	Dinamo
Spain	Real Madrid	Barcelona
Soviet Union	Spartak Moscow	Dnepr
Sweden	Malmo	Djurgaarden
Switzerland	Grasshoppers	Grasshoppers
Turkey	Besiktas	Besiktas
Wales	not applicable	Hereford United
Yugoslavia	Red Star Belgrade	Red Star Belgrade

AWARDS 1990

EUROPEAN FOOTBALLER OF THE YEAR
1 Marco Van Basten (AC Milan) 119 pts
2 Franco Baresi (AC Milan) 80 pts
3 Frank Rijkaard (AC Milan) 43 pts
4 Lothar Matthäus (Inter Milan) 24 pts
5 Peter Shilton (Derby County) 22 pts
6 Dragan Stojkovic (Red Star Belgrade) 19 pts

PFA AWARDS

Player of the Year
1   David Platt (Aston Villa)
2   John Barnes (Liverpool)
3   Des Walker (Nottingham Forest)

Young Player of the Year
1   Matthew Le Tissier (Southampton)
2   Rod Wallace (Southampton)
3   Tony Daley (Aston Villa)

Merit Award
Peter Shilton

FOOTBALL WRITERS' FOOTBALLER OF THE YEAR

1   John Barnes (Liverpool)
2   Alan Hansen (Liverpool)
3   Gary Lineker (Tottenham Hotspur)

Barnes won by one vote, closest poll since Stanley Matthews beat Dave Mackay in 1963

DUAL WINNERS OF THE FWA AWARD

Tom Finney (Preston NE)   1954/57
Danny Blanchflower (Tottenham H)   1958/61
Stanley Matthews (Blackpool/Stoke C)   1948/63
Kenny Dalglish (Liverpool)   1979/83
John Barnes (Liverpool)   1988/90

SCOTTISH FWA PLAYER OF THE YEAR

Alex McLeish (Aberdeen)

MANAGER OF THE YEAR

Kenny Dalglish (Liverpool)
Divisional Awards
Div.2: Howard Wilkinson (Leeds United)
Div.3: Gerry Francis (Bristol Rovers)
Div.4: Terry Cooper (Exeter City)
Silver Eagle: (Special presentation): Joe Royle (Oldham A)
Young Eagle: Matthew Le Tissier (Southampton)

ADIDAS GOLDEN BOOT AWARD

38 Goals: Hugo Sanchez (Real Madrid) and Jristo Stoikov (CSKA Sofia) shared title

——— CHAMPIONS ———

WORLD CUP

Year	Winners		Runners-up	Venue
1930	Uruguay	4-2	Argentina	Montevideo
1934	Italy	2-1†	Czechoslovakia	Rome
1938	Italy	4-2	Hungary	Paris
1950	Uruguay	2-1*	Brazil	Rio de Janeiro
1954	W Ger	3-2	Hungary	Berne
1958	Brazil	5-2	Sweden	Stockholm
1962	Brazil	3-1	Czechoslovakia	Santiago
1966	England	4-2†	West Germany	London
1970	Brazil	4-1	Italy	Mexico City
1974	W Ger	2-1	Holland	Munich
1978	Argentina	3-1†	Holland	Buenos Aires
1982	Italy	3-1	West Germany	Madrid
1986	Argentina	3-2	West Germany	Mexico City
1990	W Ger	1-0	Argentina	Rome

† After extra time
* Last four teams engaged in a final pool, Uruguay played Brazil in the deciding match, Sweden finished in third place
§ No play-off match

EUROPEAN CHAMPIONSHIP

Year	Winners		Runners-up	Venue
1960	USSR	2-1†	Yugoslavia	Paris
1964	Spain	2-1	USSR	Madrid
1968	Italy	1-1	Yugoslavia	Rome
	Italy	2-0	Yugoslavia	Rome
1972	W. Germany	3-0	USSR	Brussels
1976	Czechoslovakia	2-2†	W. Germany	Belgrade
	(Czechoslovakia won 5-3 on penalties)			
1980	West Germany	2-1	Belgium	Rome
1984	France	2-0	Spain	Paris
1988	Holland	2-0	USSR	Munich

EUROPEAN CUP

Year	Winners		Runners-up
1956	Real Madrid	4-3	Rheims
1957	Real Madrid	2-0	Fiorentina
1958	Real Madrid	3-2†	AC Milan
1959	Real Madrid	2-0	Rheims
1960	Real Madrid	7-3	Eintracht Frankfurt
1961	Benfica	3-2	Barcelona
1962	Benfica	5-3	Real Madrid
1963	AC Milan	2-1	Benfica
1964	Inter-Milan	3-1	Real Madrid
1965	Inter-Milan	1-0	Benfica
1966	Real Madrid	2-1	Partizan Belgrade
1967	Celtic	2-1	Inter-Milan
1968	Man Utd.	4-1†	Benfica
1969	AC Milan	4-1	Ajax
1970	Feyenoord	2-1†	Celtic
1971	Ajax	2-0	Panathinaikos
1972	Ajax	2-0	Inter-Milan
1973	Ajax	1-0	Juventus
1974	Bayern Munich	1-1	Atletico Madrid
	Bayern Munich	4-0	Atletico Madrid
1975	Bayern Munich	2-0	Leeds United
1976	Bayern Munich	1-0	St. Etienne
1977	Liverpool	3-1	Borussia Moenchengladbach
1978	Liverpool	1-0	FC Bruges
1979	Nottingham F	1-0	Malmo
1980	Nottingham F	1-0	SV Hamburg

WORLD RECORD TRANSFERS

Fee	Player	From	To	Date
£7.7m	Roberto Baggio	Fiorentina	Juventus	May 1990
£5.5m	Ruud Gullit	PSV Eindhoven	AC Milan	Jun 1987
£5.5m	Karl-Heinz Reidle	Weder Bremen	Lazio	Jun 1990
£5m	Diego Maradona	Barcelona	Napoli	Jun 1984
£5m	Thomas Hässler	Cologne	Juventus	Jun 1990
£4.8m	Dragan Stojkovic	Red Star Belgrade	Marseille	Jun 1990
£4.5m	Chris Waddle	Tottenham Hotspur	Marseille	Jul 1989

1981	Liverpool	1-0	Real Madrid
1982	Aston Villa	1-0	Bayern Munich
1983	SV Hamburg	1-0	Juventus
1984	Liverpool	1-1†	AS Roma

(Liverpool won 4-2 on penalties)

1985	Juventus	1-0	Liverpool
1986	Steaua Bucharest	0-0†	Barcelona

(Steaua won 2-0 on penalties)

1987	FC Porto	2-1	Bayern Munich
1988	PSV Eindhoven	0-0†	Benfica

(Eindhoven won 6-5 on penalties)

1989	AC Milan	4-0	Steaua Bucharest
1990	AC Milan	1-0	Benfica

EUROPEAN CUP-WINNERS' CUP

Year	Winners		Runners-up
1961	Rangers	0-2	Fiorentina
	Fiorentina	2-1	Rangers

(Fiorentina won 4-1 on aggregate)

1962	At. Madrid	1-1	Fiorentina
	At. Madrid	3-0	Fiorentina
1963	Tottenham H	5-1	Atletico Madrid
1964	Sporting Lisbon	3-3	MTK Budapest
	Sporting Lisbon	1-0	MTK Budapest
1965	West Ham U	2-0	Munich 1860
1966	B. Dortmund	2-1†	Liverpool
1967	Bayern Munich	1-0†	Rangers
1968	AC Milan	2-0	SV Hamburg
1969	Slovan Brat.	3-2	Barcelona
1970	Man City	2-1	Gornik Zabrze
1971	Chelsea	1-1	Real Madrid
	Chelsea	2-1	Real Madrid
1972	Rangers	3-2	Moscow Dynamo
1973	AC Milan	1-0	Leeds United
1974	FC Magdeburg	2-0	AC Milan
1975	Dynamo Kiev	3-0	Ferencvaros
1976	Anderlecht	4-2	West Ham United
1977	SV Hamburg	2-0	Anderlecht
1978	Anderlecht	4-0	Austria/WAC
1979	Barcelona	4-3†	Fortuna Dusseldorf
1980	Valencia	0-0†	Arsenal

(Valencia won 5-4 on penalties)

1981	Dynamo Tbilisi	2-1	Carl Zeiss Jena
1982	Barcelona	2-1	Standard Liège
1983	Aberdeen	2-1	Real Madrid
1984	Juventus	2-1	FC Porto
1985	Everton	3-1	R. Vienna
1986	Dynamo Kiev	3-0	Atletico Madrid
1987	Ajax	1-0	Lokomotiv Leipzig
1988	Mechelen	1-0	Ajax
1989	Barcelona	2-0	Sampdoria
1990	Sampdoria	2-0	Anderlecht

† after extra time

UEFA CUP

Known as the International Industries Fairs
Inter-Cities Cup 1958-65 and European Fairs Cup 1966-70

Year	Winners			Runners-up
1958	Barcelona	6-0,	2-2‡	London
1960	Barcelona	4-1,	0-0	Birmingham City
1961	AS Roma	2-0,	2-2	Birmingham City
1962	Valencia	6-2,	1-1	Barcelona
1963	Valencia	2-1,	2-0	Dynamo Zagreb
1964	Real Zaragoza	2-1		Valencia
1965	Ferencvaros	1-0		Juventus
1966	Barcelona	4-2,	0-1	Real Zaragoza
1967	Dynamo Zagreb	2-0,	0-0	Leeds United
1968	Leeds United	1-0,	0-0	Ferencvaros
1969	Newcastle Utd.	3-0,	3-2	Ujpest Dozsa
1970	Arsenal	3-0,	1-3	Anderlecht
1971	Leeds United	1-1,	2-2*	Juventus

1972	Tottenham H	2-1,	1-1	Wolverhampton W
1973	Liverpool	3-0,	0-2	Borussia M/bach
1974	Feyenoord	2-0,	2-2	Tottenham H
1975	Borussia M/bach	5-1,	0-0	Twente Enschede
1976	Liverpool	3-2,	1-1	FC Bruges
1977	Juventus	1-0,	1-2*	Ath. Bilbao
1978	PSV Eindhoven	3-0,	0-0	Bastia
1979	Borussia M/bach	1-0,	1-1	Red Star B'grade
1980	Eintracht F/furt	1-0,	2-3*	Borussia M/bach
1981	Ipswich Town	3-0,	2-4	AZ 67 Alkmaar
1982	IFK Gothenburg	1-0,	3-0	SV Hamburg
1983	Anderlecht	1-0,	1-1	Benfica
1984	Tottenham H	1-1,	1-1§	Anderlecht
1985	Real Madrid	3-0,	0-1	Videoton
1986	Real Madrid	5-1,	0-2	Cologne
1987	IFK Gothenburg	1-0,	1-1	Dundee United
1988	Bayer Leverkusen	0-3,	3-0§	Espanol
1989	Napoli	2-1,	3-3	VFB Stuttgart
1990	Juventus	3-1,	0-0	Fiorentina

* Won on away goals rule
§ Won on penalties
‡ Contested between cities, not clubs

EUROPE'S MOST SUCCESSFUL TEAMS

Wins	Total	EC	ECWC	UEFA
Real Madrid	8	6	-	2
Liverpool	6	4	-	2
Barcelona	6	-	3	3
AC Milan	6	4	2	-
Ajax	4	3	1	-
Bayern Munich	4	3	1	-
Juventus	4	1	1	2
Anderlecht	3	-	2	1
Tottenham Hotspur	3	-	1	2
Valencia	3	-	1	2

EUROPE'S MOST SUCCESSFUL NATIONS

Wins	Total	EC	ECWC	UEFA
England	22	8	5	9
Spain	19	6	5	8
Italy	16	7	5	4
West Germany	11	4	3	4
Holland	8	5	1	2
Portugal	4	3	1	-
Belgium	4	-	3	1
Scotland	3	1	2	-
USSR	3	-	3	-
Sweden	2	-	-	2

The following countries have each produced one winner:
Romania, Czechoslovakia, East Germany, Hungary,
Yugoslavia.

EUROPEAN SUPER CUP

Winners (aggregate scores)

1973	Ajax	6-3	Rangers
1974	Ajax	6-1	AC Milan
1975	Dynamo Kiev	3-0	Bayern Munich
1976	Anderlecht	5-3	Bayern Munich
1977	Liverpool	7-1	SV Hamburg
1978	Anderlecht	4-3	Liverpool
1979	Nottingham F	2-1	Barcelona
1980	Valencia	2-2	Nottingham F

(Valencia won on away goals)

1981	Not held		
1982	Aston Villa	3-1	Barcelona
1983	Aberdeen	2-0	SV Hamburg
1984	Juventus	2-0	Liverpool

(one game; played in Turin)

1985	Not held			1987	FC Porto	2-0	Ajax
1986	Steaua Bucharest	1-0	Dynamo Kiev	1988	Mechelen	3-1	PSV Eindhoven
(one game; played in Monaco)				1989	AC Milan	2-1	Barcelona

WORLD CLUB CHAMPIONSHIP

(1960-79 played over two games (except 1973). Not held 1975 and 1978. Scores are aggregates. Since 1980 a single game played in Tokyo for the Toyota Cup.)

Year	Winners		Runners-up
1960	Real Madrid (Spa)	5-1	Penarol (Uru)
1961	Penarol (Uru)	7-2*	Benfica (Por)
1962	Santos (Bra)	8-4	Benfica (Por)
1963	Santos (Bra)	7-6*	AC Milan (Ita)
1964	Inter Milan (Ita)	3-1*	Independiente (Arg)
1965	Inter Milan (Ita)	3-0	Independiente (Arg)
1966	Penarol (Uru)	4-0	Real Madrid (Spa)
1967	Racing Club (Arg)	3-2*	Celtic (Sco)
1968	Estudiantes (Arg)	2-1	Man Utd (Eng)
1969	AC Milan (Ita)	4-2	Estudiantes (Arg)
1970	Feyenoord (Hol)	3-2	Estudiantes (Arg)
1971	Nacional (Uru)	3-2	Panathinaikos (Gre)
1972	Ajax (Hol)	4-1	Independiente (Arg)
1973	Independiente (Arg)	1-0	Juventus (Ita)
1974	At. Madrid (Spa)	2-1	Independiente (Arg)
1976	Bayern Munich (FRG)	2-0	Cruzeiro (Bra)
1977	Boca Juniors (Arg)	5-2	B. M/gladbach (FRG)
1979	Olimpia (Par)	3-1	Malmo (Swe)
1980	Nacional (Uru)	1-0	Nottingham F (Eng)
1981	Flamengo (Bra)	3-0	Liverpool (Eng)
1982	Penarol (Uru)	2-0	Aston Villa (Eng)
1983	Gremio (Bra)	2-1	SV Hamburg (FRG)
1984	Independiente (Arg)	1-0	Liverpool (Eng)
1985	Juventus (Ita)	2-2	Argentinos Jr (Arg)
	(Juventus won 4-2 on penalties)		
1986	River Plate (Arg)	1-0	Steaua Buch. (Rom)
1987	FC Porto (Por)	2-1	Penarol (Uru)
1988	Nacional (Uru)	2-2	PSV Eindhoven (Hol)
	(Nacional won 7-6 on penalties)		
1989	AC Milan (Ita)	1-0	Atletico Nacional (Col)

* Including a play-off match

Most Wins *Clubs:* 3 Penarol, Nacional; 2 Inter Milan, Santos, AC Milan, Independiente *Countries:* 6 Argentina, Uruguay; 5 Italy; 4 Brazil, *Continents:* 17 South America; 11 Europe

FOOTBALL LEAGUE

Double Winners in capitals

FA CUP

	Winners	Pts	Runners-up	Pts	Winners	Score	Runners-up
1871-72	-				Wanderers	1-0	Royal Engineers
1872-73	-				Wanderers	2-0	Oxford University
1873-74	-				Oxford Univ	2-0	Royal Engineers
1874-75	-				Royal Engineers	1-1 2-0	Old Etonians
1875-76	-				Wanderers	1-1 3-0	Old Etonians
1876-77	-				Wanderers	2-1	Oxford University
1877-78	-				Wanderers	3-1	Royal Engineers
1878-79	-				Old Etonians	1-0	Clapham Rovers
1879-80	-				Clapham Rovers	1-0	Oxford University
1880-81	-				Old Carthusians	3-0	Old Etonians
1881-82	-				Old Etonians	1-0	Blackburn Rovers
1882-83	-				Blackburn Olympic	2-1	Old Etonians
1883-84	-				Blackburn Rovers	2-1	Queen's Park
1884-85	-				Blackburn Rovers	2-0	Queen's Park
1885-86	-				Blackburn Rovers	0-0 2-0	West Bromich A
1886-87	-				Aston Villa	2-0	West Bromich
1888-89	PRESTON NE	40	Aston Villa	29	PRESTON NE	3-0	Wolverhampton W
1889-90	Preston NE	33	Everton	31	Blackburn R	6-1	Sheffield W
1890-91	Everton	29	Preston NE	27	Blackburn R	3-1	Notts County
1891-92	Sunderland	42	Preston NE	37	West Bromwich A	3-0	Aston Villa
1892-93	Sunderland	48	Preston NE	37	Wolverhampton W	1-0	Everton
1893-94	Aston Villa	44	Sunderland	38	Notts County	4-1	Bolton County
1894-95	Sunderland	47	Everton	42	Aston Villa	1-0	West Bromwich A

FOOTBALL LEAGUE

This is how membership of the Football League has changed over the years.

Year	Total Clubs	1	2	3S	3N	3	4
1888	12	-	-	-	-	-	-
1891	14	-	-	-	-	-	-
1892	28	16	12	-	-	-	-
1893	31	16	15	-	-	-	-
1894	32	16	16	-	-	-	-
1898	36	18	18	-	-	-	-
1905	40	20	20	-	-	-	-
1919	44	22	22	-	-	-	-
1920	66	22	22	-	-	22	-
1921	86	22	22	22	20	-	-
1923	88	22	22	22	22	-	-
1950	92	22	22	24	24	-	-
1958	92	22	22	-	-	24	24
1987	92	21	23	-	-	24	24
1988	92	20	24	-	-	24	24
Proposed							
1991	93	22	24	-	-	24	23
1992	94	22	24	-	-	24	24

THE FOLLOWING CLUBS HAVE JOINED OR LEFT THE FOOTBALL LEAGUE SINCE 1923

Year	Joined	Left
1923	Bournemouth	Stalybridge Celtic
	Doncaster Rovers	
	New Brighton	
1927	Torquay United	Aberdare Athletic
1928	Carlisle United	Durham City
1929	York City	Ashington
1930	Thames	Merthyr Tydfil
1931	Mansfield Town	Newport County
	Chester	Nelson
1932	Aldershot	Thames
	Newport County	Wigan Borough
1938	Ipswich Town	Gillingham
1950	Colchester United	
	Gillingham	
	Scunthorpe United	
	Shrewsbury Town	
1951	Workington	New Brighton
1960	Peterborough United	Gateshead
1962	Oxford United	Accrington Stanley
1970	Cambridge United	Bradford PA
1972	Hereford United	Barrow
1977	Wimbledon	Workington
1978	Wigan Athletic	Southport
1987	Scarborough	Lincoln City
1988	Lincoln City	Newport County
1989	Maidstone United	Darlington
1990	Darlington	Colchester United

Football League

	Winners	Pts	Runners-up	Pts
1895-96	Aston Villa	45	Derby C	41
1896-97	ASTON VILLA	47	Sheffield U	36
1897-98	Sheffield U	42	Sunderland	37
1898-99	Aston Villa	45	Liverpool	43
1899-00	Aston Villa	50	Sheffield U	48
1900-01	Liverpool	45	Sunderland	43
1901-02	Sunderland	44	Everton	41
1902-03	Sheffield W	42	Aston Villa	41
1903-04	Sheffield W	47	Man City	44
1904-05	Newcastle U	48	Everton	47
1905-06	Liverpool	51	Preston NE	47
1906-07	Newcastle U	51	Bristol C	48
1907-08	Man Utd	52	Aston Villa	43
1908-09	Newcastle U	53	Everton	46
1909-10	Aston Villa	53	Liverpool	48
1910-11	Man Utd	52	Aston Villa	51
1911-12	Blackburn R	49	Everton	46
1912-13	Sunderland	54	Aston Villa	50
1913-14	Blackburn R	51	Aston Villa	44
1914-15	Everton	46	Oldham A	45
1919-20	West Brom. A	60	Burnley	51
1920-21	Burnley	59	Man City	54
1921-22	Liverpool	57	Tottenham	51
1922-23	Liverpool	60	Sunderland	54
1923-24	Huddersfield T	57	Cardiff C	57
1924-25	Huddersfield T	58	West Brom. A	56
1925-26	Huddersfield T	57	Arsenal	52
1926-27	Newcastle U	56	Huddersfield T	51
1927-28	Everton	53	Huddersfield T	51

FA Cup

Winners	Score	Runners-up
Sheffield W	2-1	Wolverhampton W
ASTON VILLA	3-2	Everton
Nottingham Forest	3-1	Derby County
Sheffield U	4-1	Derby County
Bury	4-0	Southampton
Tottenham H	2-2 3-1	Sheffield U
Sheffield U	1-1 2-1	Southampton
Bury	6-0	Derby County
Man City	1-0	Bolton Wanderers
Aston Villa	2-0	Newcastle U
Everton	1-0	Newcastle U
Sheffield W	2-1	Everton
Wolverhampton W	3-1	Newcastle U
Man Utd	1-0	Bristol City
Newcastle U	1-1 2-0	Barnsley
Bradford City	0-0 1-0	Newcastle
Barnsley	0-0 1-0	West Bromwich A
Aston Villa	1-0	Sunderland
Burnley	1-0	Liverpool
Sheffield United	3-0	Chelsea
Aston Villa	1-0	Huddersfield Town
Tottenham H	1-0	Wolverhampton W
Huddersfield Town	1-0	Preston NE
Bolton Wanderers	2-0	West Ham U
Newcastle United	2-0	Aston Villa
Sheffield United	1-0	Cardiff City
Bolton Wanderers	1-0	Man City
Cardiff City	1-0	Arsenal
Blackburn R	3-1	Huddersfield Town

	Football League				FA Cup		
	Winners	*Pts*	*Runners-up*	*Pts*	*Winners*	*Score*	*Runners-up*
1928-29	Sheffield W	52	Leicester City	51	Bolton Wanderers	2-0	Portsmouth
1929-30	Sheffield W	60	Derby County	50	Arsenal	2-0	Huddersfield Town
1930-31	Arsenal	66	Aston Villa	59	West Bromwich A	2-1	Birmingham
1931-32	Everton	56	Arsenal	54	Newcastle United	2-1	Arsenal
1932-33	Arsenal	58	Aston Villa	54	Everton	3-0	Man City
1933-34	Arsenal	59	Huddersfield T	56	Man City	2-1	Portsmouth
1934-35	Arsenal	58	Sunderland	54	Sheffield W	4-2	West Bromwich A
1935-36	Sunderland	56	Derby County	48	Arsenal	1-0	Sheffield United
1936-37	Man City	57	Charlton A	54	Sunderland	3-1	Preston NE
1937-38	Arsenal	52	W'hampton W	51	Preston NE	1-0	Huddersfield Town
1938-39	Everton	59	W'hampton W	55	Portsmouth	4-1	Wolverhampton W
1945-46	-				Derby County	4-1	Charlton Athletic
1946-47	Liverpool	57	Man Utd	56	Charlton Athletic	1-0	Burnley
1947-48	Arsenal	59	Man Utd	52	Man Utd	4-2	Blackpool
1948-49	Portsmouth	58	Man Utd	53	Wolverhampton W	3-1	Leicester City
1949-50	Portsmouth	53	W'hampton W	53	Arsenal	2-0	Liverpool
1950-51	Tottenham H	60	Man Utd	56	Newcastle United	2-0	Blackpool
1951-52	Man Utd	57	Tottenham H	53	Newcastle United	1-0	Arsenal
1952-53	Arsenal	54	Preston NE	54	Blackpool	4-3	Bolton Wanderers
1953-54	Wolverhampton	57	West Brom. A	53	West Bromwich A	3-2	Preston NE
1954-55	Chelsea	52	Wolverhampton	48	Newcastle United	3-1	Man City
1955-56	Man Utd	60	Blackpool	49	Man City	3-1	Birmingham C
1956-57	Man Utd	64	Tottenham	56	Aston Villa	2-1	Man Utd
1957-58	Wolverhampton	64	Preston NE	59	Bolton W	2-0	Man Utd
1958-59	Wolverhampton	61	Man Utd	55	Nottingham Forest	2-1	Luton Town
1959-60	Burnley	55	Wolverhampton	54	Wolverhampton W	3-0	Blackburn R
1960-61	TOTTENHAM H	66	Sheffield W	58	TOTTENHAM H	2-0	Leicester City
1961-62	Ipswich Town	56	Burnley	53	Tottenham H	3-1	Burnley
1962-63	Everton	61	Tottenham	55	Man Utd	3-1	Leicester City
1963-64	Liverpool	57	Man Utd	53	West Ham U	3-2	Preston NE
1964-65	Man Utd	61	Leeds United	61	Liverpool	2-1	Leeds United
1965-66	Liverpool	61	Leeds United	55	Everton	3-2	Sheffield W
1966-67	Man Utd	60	Nottingham F	56	Tottenham H	2-1	Chelsea
1967-68	Man City	58	Man Utd	56	West Bromwich A	1-0	Everton
1968-69	Leeds United	67	Liverpool	61	Man City	1-0	Leicester City
1969-70	Everton	66	Leeds United	57	Chelsea	2-2 2-1	Leeds United
1970-71	ARSENAL	65	Leeds United	64	ARSENAL	2-1	Liverpool
1971-72	Derby County	58	Leeds United	57	Leeds United	1-0	Arsenal
1972-73	Liverpool	60	Arsenal	57	Sunderland	1-0	Leeds United
1973-74	Leeds United	62	Liverpool	57	Liverpool	3-0	Newcastle United
1974-75	Derby County	53	Liverpool	51	West Ham U	2-0	Fulham
1975-76	Liverpool	60	QPR	59	Southampton	1-0	Man Utd
1976-77	Liverpool	57	Man City	56	Man Utd	2-1	Liverpool
1977-78	Nottingham F	64	Liverpool	57	Ipswich Town	1-0	Arsenal
1978-79	Liverpool	68	Nottingham F	60	Arsenal	3-2	Man Utd
1979-80	Liverpool	60	Man Utd	58	West Ham U	1-0	Arsenal
1980-81	Aston Villa	60	Ipswich Town	56	Tottenham H	1-1 3-2	Man City
1981-82	Liverpool	87	Ipswich Town	83	Tottenham H	1-1 1-0	Queens Park R
1982-83	Liverpool	82	Watford	71	Man Utd	2-2 4-0	Brighton & Hove A
1983-84	Liverpool	80	Southampton	77	Everton	2-0	Watford
1984-85	Everton	90	Liverpool	77	Man Utd	1-0	Everton
1985-86	LIVERPOOL	88	Everton	86	LIVERPOOL	3-1	Everton
1986-87	Everton	86	Liverpool	77	Coventry City	3-2	Tottenham Hotspur
1987-88	Liverpool	90	Man Utd	81	Wimbledon	1-0	Liverpool
1988-89	Arsenal	76	Liverpool	76	Liverpool	3-2	Everton
1989-90	Liverpool	79	Aston Villa	70	Man Utd	3-3 1-0	Crystal Palace

FOOTBALL LEAGUE

Most titles
Div 1: 18 Liverpool; 9 Arsenal, Everton; 7 Manchester United, Aston Villa; 6 Sunderland

Div 2: 6 Leicester, Man City; 5 Sheffield Wednesday; 4 Derby, Liverpool, Birmingham; 3 Notts C, Preston NE, Middlesbrough, Leeds United

Div 3: 2 Portsmouth, Oxford United

Div 4: 2 Chesterfield, Doncaster, Peterborough

Div 3(S): 3 Bristol City; 2 Charlton, Ipswich, Millwall, Notts County, Plymouth, Swansea

Div 3(N): 3 Barnsley, Doncaster, Lincoln; 2 Chesterfield, Grimsby, Hull , Port Vale, Stockport

FA CUP

Venues (Excluding replays)
62 times Wembley 1923-39, 1946-90; 20 Kennington Oval 1872, 1874-92, Crystal Palace 1895-1914; 3 Stamford Bridge 1920-22; 1 Lillie Bridge 1873, Fallowfield 1893, Goodison Park 1894, Old Trafford 1915

Replay Venues
Kennington Oval 1875, 1876;
Derby 1886;
Burnden Park 1901;
Crystal Palace 1902;
Goodison Park 1910;
Old Trafford 1911, 1970;
Bramall Lane 1912;
Wembley 1981, 1982, 1983, 1990.

THE TOP TEAMS: FA CUP

	Wins	Finals	SF
Manchester United	7	11	18
Aston Villa	7	9	17
Tottenham Hotspur	7	8	12
Newcastle United	6	11	13
Blackburn Rovers	6	8	16
Arsenal	5	11	16
West Bromwich Albion	5	10	19
The Wanderers	5	5	5
Everton	4	11	22
Liverpool	4	9	18
Wolverhampton Wanderers	4	8	13
Manchester City	4	8	10
Bolton Wanderers	4	7	12
Sheffield United	4	6	10
Sheffield Wednesday	3	5	15
West Ham United	3	4	5
Preston North End	2	7	10
Old Etonians	2	6	6
Sunderland	2	3	10
Nottingham Forest	2	2	10
Bury	2	2	2

Most wins at Wembley
5 Arsenal, Newcastle, Tottenham; 4 Bolton, Liverpool, Manchester United; 3 Everton, Manchester City, West Bromwich, West Ham

Most appearances at Wembley
11 Arsenal; 10 Manchester United; 8 Liverpool; 7 Everton, Manchester City

FOOTBALL LEAGUE CUP
Known as the Milk Cup 1982-85, Littlewoods Cup 1986-90, Rumbelows League Cup 1991. All finals 1961-66 were over two legs; since then they have been single games at Wembley.

Finals

1961	Aston Villa	3-0† 0-2	Rotherham U
1962	Norwich City	3-0 1-0	Rochdale
1963	Birmingham City	3-1 0-0	Aston Villa
1964	Leicester City	1-1 3-2	Stoke City
1965	Chelsea	3-2 0-0	Leicester City
1966	West Bromwich A	1-2 4-1	West Ham U
1967	Queen's Park R	3-2	West Brom. A
1968	Leeds United	1-0	Arsenal
1969	Swindon Town	3-1	Arsenal
1970	Man City	2-1	West Brom. A
1971	Tottenham Hotspur	2-0	Aston Villa
1972	Stoke City	2-1	Chelsea
1973	Tottenham Hotspur	1-0	Norwich City
1974	Wolverhampton W	2-1	Man City
1975	Aston Villa	1-0	Norwich City
1976	Man City	2-1	Newcastle U
1977	Aston Villa	0-0. 1-1† 3-2	Everton
1978	Nottingham Forest	0-0† 1-0	Liverpool
1979	Nottingham Forest	3-2	Southampton
1980	Wolverhampton W	1-0	Nottingham F
1981	Liverpool	1-1† 2-1	West Ham U
1982	Liverpool	3-1†	Tottenham H
1983	Liverpool	2-1†	Man Utd
1984	Liverpool	0-0† 1-0	Everton
1985	Norwich City	1-0	Sunderland
1986	Oxford United	3-0	QPR
1987	Arsenal	2-1	Liverpool
1988	Luton Town	3-2	Arsenal
1989	Nottingham Forest	3-1	Luton Town
1990	Nottingham Forest	1-0	Oldham Athletic

† after extra time

Most wins:
4 Liverpool, Nottingham Forest; 3 Aston Villa

Most finals:
6 Liverpool; 5 Aston Villa, Nottingham Forest; 4 Arsenal, Norwich C; 3 Manchester C, Tottenham H

MOST SUCCESSFUL ENGLISH CLUBS
(All Major Tournaments)

Total	FL	FAC	FLC	Eur.
32 Liverpool	18	4	4	6
18 Aston Villa	7	7	3	1
16 Arsenal	9	5	1	1
15 Manchester United	7	7	-	1
14 Everton	9	4	-	1
13 Tottenham Hotspur	2	7	2	2
11 Newcastle United	4	6	-	1
9 Wolverhampton W	3	4	2	-
9 Manchester City	2	4	2	1
9 Nottingham Forest	1	2	4	2
8 Sunderland	6	2	-	-
8 Blackburn Rovers	2	6	-	-
7 Sheffield Wednesday	4	3	-	-
7 West Bromwich Albion	1	5	1	-
6 Leeds United	2	1	1	2

SCOTLAND

	LEAGUE Winners	Pts	Runners-up	Pts	CUP Winners	Score	Runners-up
1873-74	-				Queen's Park	2-0	Clydesdale
1874-75	-				Queen's Park	3-0	Renton
1875-76	-				Queen's Park	1-1 2-0	Third Lanark
1876-77	-				Vale of Leven	1-1 1-1 3-2	Rangers
1877-78	-				Vale of Leven	1-0	Third Lanark
1878-79	-				(a)		
1879-80	-				Queen's Park	3-0	Thornlibank
1880-81	-				Queen's Park	3-1	Dumbarton
1881-82	-				Queen's Park	2-2 4-1	Dumbarton
1882-83	-				Dumbarton	2-2 2-1	Vale of Leven
1883-84	-				(b)		
1884-85	-				Renton	0-0 3-1	Vale of Leven
1885-86	-				Queen's Park	3-1	Renton
1886-87	-				Hibernian	2-1	Dumbarton
1887-88	-				Renton	6-1	Cambuslang
1888-89	-				Third Lanark	2-1	Celtic
1889-90	-				Queen's Park	1-1 2-1	Vale of Leven
1890-91	Dumbarton/ Rangers	29	-		Hearts	1-0	Dumbarton
1891-92	Dumbarton	37	Celtic	35	Celtic	5-1	Queen's Park
1892-93	Celtic	29	Rangers	28	Queen's Park	2-1	Celtic
	Division 1						
1893-94	Celtic	29	Hearts	26	Rangers	3-1	Celtic
1894-95	Hearts	31	Celtic	26	St. Bernard's	2-1	Renton
1895-96	Celtic	30	Rangers	26	Hearts	3-1	Hibernian
1896-97	Hearts	28	Hibernian	26	Rangers	5-1	Dumbarton
1897-98	Celtic	33	Rangers	29	Rangers	2-0	Kilmarnock
1898-99	Rangers	36	Hearts	26	Celtic	2-0	Rangers
1899-00	Rangers	32	Celtic	25	Celtic	4-3	Queen's Park
1900-01	Rangers	35	Celtic	29	Hearts	4-3	Celtic
1901-02	Rangers	28	Celtic	26	Hibernian	1-0	Celtic
1902-03	Hibernian	37	Dundee	31	Rangers	1-1 0-0 2-0	Hearts
1903-04	Third Lanark	43	Hearts	39	Celtic	3-2	Rangers
1904-05	Celtic	41	Rangers	41	Third Lanark	0-0 3-1	Rangers
1905-06	Celtic	49	Hearts	43	Hearts	1-0	Third Lanark
1906-07	Celtic	55	Dundee	48	Celtic	3-0	Hearts
1907-08	Celtic	55	Falkirk	51	Celtic	5-1	St. Mirren
1908-09	Celtic	51	Dundee	50	(c)		
1909-10	Celtic	54	Falkirk	52	Dundee	2-2 0-0 2-1	Clyde
1910-11	Rangers	52	Aberdeen	48	Celtic	0-0 2-0	Hamilton A
1911-12	Rangers	51	Celtic	45	Celtic	2-0	Clyde
1912-13	Rangers	53	Celtic	49	Falkirk	2-0	Raith R
1913-14	Celtic	65	Rangers	59	Celtic	0-0 4-1	Hibernian
1914-15	Celtic	65	Hearts	61	-		
1915-16	Celtic	67	Rangers	56	-		
1916-17	Celtic	64	Morton	54	-		
1917-18	Rangers	56	Celtic	55	-		
1918-19	Celtic	58	Rangers	57	-		
1919-20	Rangers	71	Celtic	68	Kilmarnock	3-2	Albion R
1920-21	Rangers	76	Celtic	66	Partick T	1-0	Rangers
1921-22	Celtic	67	Rangers	66	Morton	1-0	Rangers
1922-23	Rangers	55	Airdrieonians	50	Celtic	1-0	Hibernian
1923-24	Rangers	59	Airdrieonians	50	Airdrieonians	2-0	Hibernian
1924-25	Rangers	60	Airdrieonians	57	Celtic	2-1	Dundee
1925-26	Celtic	58	Airdrieonians	50	St. Mirren	2-0	Celtic
1926-27	Rangers	56	Motherwell	51	Celtic	3-1	East Fife
1927-28	Rangers	60	Celtic	55	Rangers	4-0	Celtic
1928-29	Rangers	67	Celtic	51	Kilmarnock	2-0	Rangers
1929-30	Rangers	60	Motherwell	55	Rangers	0-0 2-1	Partick T
1930-31	Rangers	60	Celtic	58	Celtic	2-2 4-2	Motherwell
1931-32	Motherwell	66	Rangers	61	Rangers	1-1 3-0	Kilmarnock
1932-33	Rangers	62	Motherwell	59	Celtic	1-0	Motherwell
1933-34	Rangers	66	Motherwell	62	Rangers	5-0	St. Mirren
1934-35	Rangers	55	Celtic	52	Rangers	2-1	Hamilton A
1935-36	Celtic	66	Rangers	61	Rangers	1-0	Third Lanark
1936-37	Rangers	61	Aberdeen	54	Celtic	2-1	Aberdeen
1937-38	Celtic	61	Hearts	58	East Fife	1-1 4-2	Kilmarnock
1938-39	Rangers	59	Celtic	48	Clyde	4-0	Motherwell

	League				FA Cup		
	Winners	Pts	Runners-up	Pts	Winners	Score	Runners-up
1946-47	Rangers	46	Hibernian	44	Aberdeen	2-1	Hibernian
1947-48	Hibernian	48	Rangers	46	Rangers	1-1 1-0	Morton
1948-49	Rangers	46	Dundee	45	Rangers	4-1	Clyde
1949-50	Rangers	50	Hibernian	49	Rangers	3-0	East Fife
1950-51	Hibernian	48	Rangers	38	Celtic	1-0	Motherwell
1951-52	Hibernian	45	Rangers	41	Motherwell	4-0	Dundee
1952-53	Rangers	43	Hibernian	43	Rangers	1-1 1-0	Aberdeen
1953-54	Celtic	43	Hearts	38	Celtic	2-1	Aberdeen
1954-55	Aberdeen	49	Celtic	46	Clyde	1-1 1-0	Celtic
1955-56	Rangers	52	Aberdeen	46	Hearts	3-1	Celtic
1956-57	Rangers	55	Hearts	53	Falkirk	1-1 2-1	Kilmarnock
1957-58	Hearts	62	Rangers	49	Clyde	1-0	Hibernian
1958-59	Rangers	50	Hearts	48	St. Mirren	3-1	Aberdeen
1959-60	Hearts	54	Kilmarnock	50	Rangers	2-0	Kilmarnock
1960-61	Rangers	51	Kilmarnock	50	Dunfermline A	0-0 2-0	Celtic
1961-62	Dundee	54	Rangers	51	Rangers	2-0	St. Mirren
1962-63	Rangers	57	Kilmarnock	48	Rangers	1-1 3-0	Celtic
1963-64	Rangers	55	Kilmarnock	49	Rangers	3-1	Dundee
1964-65	Kilmarnock	50	Hearts	50	Celtic	3-2	Dunfermline A
1965-66	Celtic	57	Rangers	55	Rangers	0-0 1-0	Celtic
1966-67	Celtic	58	Rangers	55	Celtic	2-0	Aberdeen
1967-68	Celtic	63	Rangers	61	Dunfermline A	3-1	Hearts
1968-69	Celtic	54	Rangers	49	Celtic	4-0	Rangers
1969-70	Celtic	57	Rangers	45	Aberdeen	3-1	Celtic
1970-71	Celtic	56	Aberdeen	54	Celtic	1-1 2-1	Rangers
1971-72	Celtic	60	Aberdeen	50	Celtic	6-1	Hibernian
1972-73	Celtic	57	Rangers	56	Rangers	3-2	Celtic
1973-74	Celtic	53	Hibernian	49	Celtic	3-0	Dundee United
1974-75	Rangers	56	Hibernian	49	Celtic	3-1	Airdrieonians
	Premier Division						
1975-76	Rangers	54	Celtic	48	Rangers	3-1	Hearts
1976-77	Celtic	55	Rangers	46	Celtic	1-0	Rangers
1977-78	Rangers	55	Aberdeen	53	Rangers	2-1	Aberdeen
1978-79	Celtic	48	Rangers	45	Rangers	0-0 0-0 3-2	Hibernian
1979-80	Aberdeen	48	Celtic	47	Celtic	1-0	Rangers
1980-81	Celtic	56	Aberdeen	49	Rangers	0-0 4-1	Dundee United
1981-82	Celtic	55	Aberdeen	53	Aberdeen	4-1	Rangers
1982-83	Dundee U	56	Celtic	55	Aberdeen	1-0	Rangers
1983-84	Aberdeen	57	Celtic	50	Aberdeen	2-1	Celtic
1984-85	Aberdeen	59	Celtic	52	Celtic	2-1	Dundee United
1985-86	Celtic	50	Hearts	50	Aberdeen	3-0	Hearts
1986-87	Rangers	69	Celtic	63	St. Mirren	1-0	Dundee United
1987-88	Celtic	72	Hearts	62	Celtic	2-1	Dundee United
1988-89	Rangers	56	Aberdeen	50	Celtic	1-0	Rangers
1989-90	Rangers	51	Aberdeen	44	Aberdeen	0-0 (d)	Celtic

(a) Cup awarded to Vale of Leven, Rangers failed to appear for replay after 1-1 draw
(b) Cup awarded to Queen's Park, Vale of Leven failed to appear for the final
(c) After two drawn games (2-2 and 1-1) between Celtic and Rangers, the Cup was withdrawn following a riot
(d) Aberdeen won 9-8 on penalties.

LEAGUE

Most titles:
Premier/1st Division:
40 Rangers; **35** Celtic; **4** Aberdeen, Hearts, Hibernian;
1st/2nd Division:
6 Ayr United, Morton; **5** Clyde, St Johnstone; **4** Hibernian, Motherwell, Partick Thistle, Raith Rovers, Stirling Albion
(New) 2nd Division: **2** Clyde, Brechin City

CUP

Most wins:
29 Celtic; **24** Rangers; **10** Queen's Park; **7** Aberdeen; **5** Hearts; **3** Clyde, St. Mirren, Vale of Leven

Most finals:
46 Celtic; **40** Rangers; **13** Aberdeen, Queen's Park; **10** Hearts, Hibernian; **7** Kilmarnock, Vale of Leven; **6** Clyde, Dumbarton, St. Mirren, Third Lanark

Venues (excluding replays)
Matches played at various Glasgow venues until 1924, except Logie Green, Edinburgh 1896. Current Hampden Park first used 1904 and every year since 1925. All replays have been in Glasgow and at Hampden Park regularly since 1930

SCOTTISH LEAGUE CUP

Skol Cup since 1984-85

1946-47	Rangers	4-0	Aberdeen
1947-48	East Fife	1-1† 4-1	Falkirk
1948-49	Rangers	2-0	Raith Rovers
1949-50	East Fife	3-0	Dunfermline
1950-51	Motherwell	3-0	Hibernian
1951-52	Dundee	3-2	Rangers
1952-53	Dundee	2-0	Kilmarnock
1953-54	East Fife	3-2	Partick Thistle
1954-55	Hearts	4-2	Motherwell
1955-56	Aberdeen	2-1	St. Mirren
1956-57	Celtic	0-0† 3-0	Partick Thistle
1957-58	Celtic	7-1	Rangers
1958-59	Hearts	5-1	Partick Thistle
1959-60	Hearts	2-1	Third Lanark
1960-61	Rangers	2-0	Kilmarnock

1961-62	Rangers	1-1† 3-1	Hearts
1962-63	Hearts	1-0	Kilmarnock
1963-64	Rangers	5-0	Morton
1964-65	Rangers	2-1	Celtic
1965-66	Celtic	2-1	Rangers
1966-67	Celtic	1-0	Rangers
1967-68	Celtic	5-3	Dundee
1968-69	Celtic	6-2	Hibernian
1969-70	Celtic	1-0	St. Johnstone
1970-71	Rangers	1-0	Celtic
1971-72	Partick Thistle	4-1	Celtic
1972-73	Hibernian	2-1	Celtic
1973-74	Dundee United	1-0	Celtic
1974-75	Celtic	6-3	Hibernian
1975-76	Rangers	1-0	Celtic
1976-77	Aberdeen	2-1	Celtic
1977-78	Rangers	2-1	Celtic
1978-79	Rangers	2-1	Aberdeen
1979-80	Dundee United	0-0 †3-0	Aberdeen
1980-81	Dundee United	3-0	
1981-82	Rangers	2-1	Dundee
1982-83	Celtic	2-1	Rangers
1983-84	Rangers	3-2†	Celtic
1984-85	Rangers	1-0	Dundee United
1985-86	Aberdeen	3-0	Hibernian
1986-87	Rangers	2-1	Celtic
1987-88	Rangers	3-3	Aberdeen
	(Rangers won 5-3 on penalties)		
1988-89	Rangers	3-2	Aberdeen
1989-90	Aberdeen	2-1	Rangers

Venues:
All finals and replays at Hampden Park except 1980 replay and 1981 final, which were played at Dens Park, Dundee

Most wins:
16 Rangers; **9** Celtic; **4** Hearts, Aberdeen, 3 Dundee, East Fife

Most finals:
22 Rangers; **19** Celtic; **9** Aberdeen; **5** Dundee, Hearts, Hibernian; **4** Dundee U, Partick T

NON-LEAGUE
(since 1970)

Northern Premier		Southern League		FA Challenge Trophy			
1969-70	Macclesfield Town	Cambridge United		Macclesfield Town	2-0		Telford United
1970-71	Wigan Athletic	Yeovil Town		Telford United	3-2		Hillingdon Borough
1971-72	Stafford Rangers	Chelmsford City		Stafford Rangers	3-0		Barnet
1972-73	Boston United	Kettering Town		Scarborough	2-1†		Wigan Athletic
1973-74	Boston United	Dartford		Morecambe	2-1		Dartford
1974-75	Wigan Athletic	Wimbledon		Matlock Town	4-0		Scarborough
1975-76	Runcorn	Wimbledon		Scarborough	3-2†		Stafford Rangers
1976-77	Boston United	Wimbledon		Scarborough	2-1		Dagenham
1977-78	Boston United	Bath City		Altrincham	3-1		Leatherhead
1978-79	Mossley	Worcester City		Stafford Rangers	2-0		Kettering Town

Alliance Premier League							
1979-80	Altrincham	56	Weymouth	54	Dagenham	2-1		Mossley
1980-81	Altrincham	54	Kettering Town	51	Bishop's Stortford	1-0		Sutton United
1981-82	Runcorn	93	Enfield	86	Enfield	1-0†		Altrincham
1982-83	Enfield	84	Maidstone United	83	Telford United	2-1		Northwich Vic
1983-84	Maidstone Utd	70	Nuneaton Borough	69	Northwich Vic	1-1† 2-1		Bangor City
1984-85	Wealdstone	62	Nuneaton Borough	58	Wealdstone	2-1		Boston United
1985-86	Enfield	76	Frickley Athletic	69	Altrincham	1-0		Runcorn
1986-87	Scarborough	91	Barnet	85	Kidderminster H	0-0† 2-1		Burton Albion
1987-88	Lincoln City	82	Barnet	80	Enfield	0-0† 3-2		Telford U
1988-89	Maidstone Utd	84	Kettering Town	76	Telford U	1-0†		Macclesfield
1989-90	Darlington	87	Barnet	85	Barrow	3-0		Leek Town

† after extra time
Alliance Premier League 1979-83, Gola League 1984-85, GM Vauxhall Conference 1986-

ENGLISH HONOURS BOARD - QUICK REFERENCE GUIDE

	Football League	FA Cup	Football League Cup
Arsenal	1931, 1933, 1934, 1935, 1938, 1948, 1953, 1971, 1989	1930, 1936, 1950, 1971, 1979	1987
Aston Villa	1894, 1896, 1897, 1899,1900, 1910, 1981	1887, 1895, 1897, 1905, 1913, 1920,1957	1961, 1975, 1977
Barnsley		1912	
Birmingham City			1963
Blackburn Olympic		1883	
Blackburn Rovers	1912, 1914	1884, 1885, 1886, 1890, 1891, 1928	
Blackpool		1953	
Bolton Wanderers		1923, 1926,1929, 1958	
Bradford City		1911	
Burnley	1921, 1960	1914	
Bury		1900, 1903	
Cardiff City		1927	
Charlton Athletic		1947	
Chelsea	1955	1970	1965
Clapham Rovers		1880	
Coventry City		1987	
Derby County	1972, 1975	1946	
Everton	1891, 1915, 1928, 1932, 1939, 1963, 1970, 1985, 1987	1906, 1933,1966, 1984	
Huddersfield Town	1924, 1925, 1926	1922	
Ipswich Town	1962	1978	
Leeds United	1969, 1974	1972	1968
Leicester City			1964
Liverpool	1901, 1906, 1922, 1923, 1947, 1964, 1966, 1973, 1976, 1977, 1979, 1980, 1982, 1983, 1984, 1986, 1988, 1990	1965, 1974, 1986, 1989	1981, 1982, 1983, 1984
Luton Town			1988
Manchester City	1937, 1968	1904, 1934,1956, 1969	1970, 1976
Manchester United	1908, 1911, 1952, 1956, 1957, 1965, 1967	1909, 1948, 1963, 1977, 1983, 1985, 1990	
Newcastle United	1905, 1907, 1909, 1927	1910, 1924, 1932, 1951, 1952, 1955	
Norwich City			1962, 1985
Nottingham Forest	1978	1898, 1959	1978, 1979, 1989, 1990
Notts County		1894	
Old Carthusians		1881	
Old Etonians		1879, 1882	
Oxford United			1986
Oxford University		1874	
Portsmouth	1949, 1950	1939	
Preston North End	1889, 1890	1889, 1938	
Queen's Park Rangers			1967
Royal Engineers		1875	
Sheffield United	1898	1899, 1902, 1915, 1925	
Sheffield Wednesday	1903, 1904, 1929, 1930	1896, 1907, 1935	
Southampton		1976	
Stoke City			1972
Sunderland	1892, 1893, 1895, 1902, 1913,	1937, 1973	1936
Swindon Town			1969
Tottenham Hotspur	1951, 1961	1901, 1921, 1961, 1962, 1967, 1981, 1982	1971, 1973
Wanderers		1872, 1873, 1876, 1877, 1878	
West Bromwich A	1920	1888, 1892, 1931, 1954, 1968	1966
West Ham United		1964, 1975, 1980	
Wimbledon		1988	
Wolverhampton W	1954, 1958, 1959	1893, 1908, 1949, 1960	1974, 1980

RECORDS

(to end of 1989-90 season)

APPEARANCES
Football League

PLAYERS WITH 760 OR MORE APPEARANCES:
899 Peter Shilton (Leicester C, Stoke C, Nottingham F, Southampton, Derby C) 1966-
824 Terry Paine (Southampton and Hereford U) 1957-77
777 Alan Oakes (Manchester C, Chester, Port Vale) 1959-84
770 John Trollope (Swindon T) 1960-80
764 Jimmy Dickinson (Portsmouth) 1946-65
762 Roy Sproson (Port Vale) 1950-72
Trollope's 770 games for Swindon T are a record for one club.

The most appearances in the Scottish League:
626 by Bob Ferrier (Motherwell) 1918-37

International Matches

BRITISH ISLES PLAYERS WITH OVER 100 CAPS:
125 Peter Shilton (England) 1970-90
119 Pat Jennings (Northern Ireland) 1964-86
108 Bobby Moore (England) 1962-73
106 Bobby Charlton (England) 1958-70
105 Billy Wright (England) 1946-59
102 Kenny Dalglish (Scotland) 1971-86
The most caps won by the other two nations:
Most for Wales: 72 Joey Jones 1972-86
Most for Republic of Ireland: 72 Liam Brady 1974-90

OTHER LEADING CAPPED PLAYERS:
150 Hector Chumpitaz (Peru) 1963-82
120 Rivelino (Brazil) 1968-79
115 Bjorn Nordqvist (Sweden) 1963-78
112 Dino Zoff (Italy) 1968-83
111 Pele (Brazil) 1957-71

ENGLAND'S CENTURIONS

125   Peter Shilton
First match: 25 Nov 1970 v E Germany
Last match: 7 Jul 1990 v Italy
108   Bobby Moore
First match: 20 May 1962 v Peru
Last match: 14 Nov 1973 v Italy
106   Bobby Charlton
First match: 19 Apr 1958 v Scotland
Last match: 14 Jun 1970 v W Germany
105   Billy Wright
First match: 28 Sep 1946 v N Ireland
Last match: 28 May 1959 v United States

ATTENDANCES
Record Attendances

World Cup
199,854 Brazil v Uruguay, 1950 Maracara Stadium, Rio de Janeiro
European Championship: 103,000 USSR v Hungary 1968, Moscow
International (Britain): 149,547 Scotland v England, 1937 Hampden Park
Club match (World): 177,656 Flamengo v Fluminese, 1963 (Brazilian League) Maracana Stadium, Rio de Janeiro
Club match (Europe): 146,433 Celtic v Aberdeen 1937, (Scottish Cup Final), Hampden Park
European Cup: 136,505 Celtic v Leeds U, 1970, Hampden Park
FA Cup Final: 126,047 Bolton W v West Ham U, 1923, Wembley Stadium
FA Cup (other than final): 84,569 Manchester C v Stoke C, 1934 (6th Round), Maine Road
Football League Cup (other than final): 63,418 Manchester U v Manchester C, 1969 (Semi-final), Old Trafford
Football League:
Div 1: 83,260 Man Utd v Arsenal, 1948, Maine Road
Div 2: 68, 029 Aston Villa v Coventry C, 1937, Villa Park
Div 3: 49,309 Sheffield W v Sheffield U, 1979, Hillsborough
Div 4: 37,774 Crystal P v Millwall, 1961, Selhurst Park
Div 3 (S): 51,621 Cardiff C v Bristol C, 1947, Ninian Park
Div 3 (N): 49,655 Hull C v Rotherham U, 1948, Boothferry Park
Highest Post-War Average: 57,552 Manchester U 1967-68
Scottish League
Div 1/Premier: 118,567 Rangers v Celtic, 1939, Ibrox Stadium
Lower Divisions: 27,205 Queen's Park v Kilmarnock, 1961, Hampden Park
Scottish FA Cup: 146,433 Celtic v Aberdeen (as above)
Scottish League Cup: 107,647 Celtic v Rangers, 1965, Hampden Park
GM Vauxhall Conference: 7,522 Lincoln C v Boston U, 1988, Sincil Bank

Lowest attendances
(Excluding matches played behind closed doors)
Football League: 13 Stockport C v Leicester C (Div 2), 1921, Old Trafford (*); 450 Rochdale v Cambridge U (Div 3), 1974, Spotland
Football League Div 1: 3,618 Wimbledon v Luton Town, 1990, Plough Lane
Scottish League: 80 Meadowbank T v Stenhousemuir (Div 2), 1979 Meadowbank Stadium
Major European Cup match: 483 Rapid Vienna v Juventus, (UEFA Cup), 1971
Home International: 2,315 Wales v Northern Ireland, 1982, Wrexham

England International at Wembley: 15,628 v Chile, 1989

(*)Disputed. Up to 2,000 believed present despite official figure

WINS
Most in a season
33(42) Doncaster R, Div 3(N), 1946-47
Div 1 record: 31(42) Tottenham H, 1960-61
Scottish record: 35(42) Rangers, 1920-21
Fewest in a season
1(34) Loughborough T, Div 2, 1899-1900
Div 1 record: 3(38) Woolwich Arsenal, 1912-13; 3(42) Stoke City, 1984-85
Scottish record: 0(22) Vale of Leven, 1891-92; post-war 1(34) Ayr U, Div 1, 1966-67.

DEFEATS
Most in a season
33(40) Rochdale, Div 3(N), 1931-32
33(46) Cambridge U, Div 3, 1984-85
33(46) Newport C, Div 4, 1987-88
Div 1 record: 31(42) Stoke C, 1984-85
Scottish record: 31(42) St Mirren, Div 1, 1920-21
Fewest in a season
0(22) Preston NE, Football League, 1888-89
0(28) Liverpool, Div 2, 1893-94
0(18) Celtic, Scottish Div 1, 1897-98
0(18) Rangers, Scottish Div 1, 1898-99
0(18) Kilmarnock, Scottish Div 2 1898-99

Post-war record: 2(42) Leeds U, Div 1, 1968-69; 2(40) Liverpool, Div 1, 1987-88; 2(39) St Mirren, Scottish Div 1, 1976-77; 2(38) Morton, Scottish Div 2, 1966-67
Figures in brackets indicate matches played

DRAWS
Most in a season
Football League
23(42) Norwich C, Div 1, 1978-79
23(46) Exeter C, Div 4, 1986-87

Scottish record:21(44) East Fife, Div 1, 1986-87
Figures in bracket indicate matches played

In August 1990 the longest serving football league managers were:

		Date Apptd.
Brian Clough	Nottingham F	Jan 1975
Joe Royle	Oldham A	Jul 1982
Lennie Lawrence	Charlton A	Nov 1982
Frank Clark	Leyton O	May 1983
Dario Gradi	Crewe A	Jun 1983
Harry Redknapp	Bournemouth	Oct 1983
John Rudge	Port Vale	Dec 1983

POINTS
Most points in a season
(Points available in brackets)
Football League (2pts for a win): 74(92) Lincoln C, Div 4, 1975-76
Div 1: 68(84) Liverpool, 1978-79

Football League (3 pts for a win): 102(138) Swindon T, Div 4, 1985-86
Div 1: 90(120) Liverpool, 1987-88; 90(126) Everton, 1984-85

Scottish League (2pts for a win): 76(84) Rangers, Div 1, 1920-21
Premier Division: 72(88) Celtic, 1987-88
Fewest points in a season
(Since expansion in 1898)
Football League: 8(68) Loughborough T, Div 2, 1899-1900; Doncaster R, Div 2, 1904-05
Div 1: 17(126) Stoke C, 1984-85 (since expansion in 1905)
Scottish League: 6(60) Stirling A, Div 1, 1954-55
Premier Division: 11(72) St Johnstone, 1975-76
In 1896-97 Abercorn collected just 3 points in the Scottish 1st Division from their 18 games, an all-time low for a British League side.

GOALSCORING
Fast Scoring
Fastest Football League Goals
(From kick-off): all 6 secs: Albert Mundy, Aldershot v Hartlepool U, 1958, Div 4; Barrie Jones, Notts C v Torquay U, 1962, Div 3; Keith Smith, Crystal P v Derby C, 1964, Div 2; Tommy Langley, Queen's Park R v Bolton W, 1980, Div 2
Fastest FA Cup Goal:
8 secs; Vic Lambden, Bristol R v Aldershot, 1951, 3rd Round
Fastest Goal for England:
27 secs; Bryan Robson, v France, 1982 World Cup
Fastest hat-trick:
2½ mins; Jimmy Scarth, Gillingham v Leyton O, 1952, Div 3(S)
Fastest International hat-trick:
3½ mins: Willie Hall, England v Ireland, 1938
Fastest own goal:
6 secs: Pat Kruse, Torquay U v Cambridge U, 1977, Div 4

Individual Scoring Records
Most Goals in a Single Game:
First Class Match: 16 Stephan Stanis, Racing Club Lens v Aubry-Asturies, (French Cup) 1942
Internationals: 10 Sofus Nielsen, Denmark v France, 1908 Olympics; 10 Gottfried Fuchs, Germany v Russia, 1912 Olympics
British International Football: 6 Joe Bambrick, N. Ireland v Wales, 1930
The record for England is: 5 Oliver Vaughton, v Ireland, 1882, 5 Steve Bloomer, v Wales, 1896; 5 Gilbert Smith, v Ireland, 1899; 5 Willie Hall, v Ireland, 1938; 5 Malcolm Macdonald, v Cyprus, 1975
European Club Competition: 6 Lothar Emmerich, Borussia Dortmund v Floriana, Cup-winners' Cup, 1965
British Record in Europe: 5 Ray Crawford, Ipswich T v Floriana (European Cup), 1962; 5 Peter Osgood, Chelsea v Jeunesse Hautcharage (Cup-winners' Cup), 1971
Football League: 10 Joe Payne, Luton T v Bristol R, Div 3(S), 1936
Div 1 record: 7 Jimmy Ross, Preston NE v Stoke, 1888; 7 Ted Drake, Arsenal v Aston Villa, 1935
FA Cup: *Preliminary competition:* 10 Chris Marron, South Shields v Radcliffe Borough, 1947
Competition proper: 9 Ted MacDougall, Bournemouth v Margate, 1st round, 1971
Scottish League: 8 Owen McNally, Arthurlie v Armadale, Div 2, 1927; 8 Jimmy McGrory, Celtic v Dumferline A, Div 1, 1928; 8 Jim Dyet, King's Park v Forfar A, Div 2, 1930; 8 John Calder, Morton v Raith R, Div 2, 1936; 8 Norman Haywood, Raith R v Brechin C, Div 2, 20 Aug 1937

Scottish Cup: 13 John Petrie, Arbroath v Bon Accord, 1885

Most Goals in a season
World Record: 127 Pele (Santos, Brazil) 1959
European Cup: 14 Jose Altafini (AC Milan) 1962-63
European Cup-winners' Cup:
14 Lothar Emmerich (Borussia Dortmund) 1965-66
Football League:
60 Dixie Dean (Everton), Div 1, 1927-28
The leading scorers in the other divisions have been:
Div 2: 59 George Camsell (Middlesbrough), 1927-28; Div 3: 39 Derek Reeves (Southampton), 1959-60; Div 4: 52 Terry Bly (Peterborough U), 1960-61; Div 3(S): 55 Joe Payne (Luton T), 1936-37; Div 3(N): 55 Ted Harston (Mansfield T), 1936-37
Scottish League: 66 Jim Smith (Ayr U), Div 2, 1927-28
FA Cup: 15 Albert Brown (Tottenham H), 1900-01
Football League Cup: 12 Clive Allen (Tottenham H), 1986-87

Most Goals in a Career
World Record: 1329 Artur Friedenreich (Germanio, CA Ipiranga, Americano, CA Paulistano, Sao Paulo, Flamengo, Brazil) 1909-35
Two other players have scored more than 1000 first class goals: 1280 Pele 1956-77; 1006 Franz Binder 1930-50
Internationals: 97 Pele (Brazil), 1957-70
British Internationals: 49 Bobby Charlton (England); 44 Jimmy Greaves (England); 35 Gary Lineker (England); 30 Tom Finney (England); 30 Nat Lofthouse (England); 30 Denis Law (Scotland); 30 Kenny Dalglish (Scotland); 29 Vivian Woodward (England); 26 Steve Bloomer (England)
The records for the other countries are:
Northern Ireland: 12 Joe Bambrick, Billy Gillespie, Gerry Armstrong; *Wales:* 23 Ivor Allchurch, Trevor Ford; *Republic of Ireland:* 19 Don Givens
European Cup: 49 Alfredo de Stefano (Real Madrid) 1955-64
British Record: 30 Peter Lorimer (Leeds U), 1965-77
Football League: 434 Arthur Rowley (West Bromwich A, Fulham, Leicester C, Shrewsbury T), 1946-65
Scottish League: 410 Jimmy McGrory (Celtic, Clydebank), 1922-38
FA Cup: 41 Denis Law (Huddersfield T, Man City, Man Utd)

Hat Tricks
Football League
Most in a career: 37 Dixie Dean (Tranmere R, Everton, Notts C), 1923-37
Most in one season: 9 George Camsell (Middlesbrough), Div 2, 1926-27
Hat tricks in FA Cup finals: William Townley, Blackburn R v Sheffield W, 1890; Jimmy Logan, Notts C v Bolton W, 1894; Stanley Mortensen, Blackpool v Bolton W, 1953

Team Records

Most goals scored in a season
Football League: 134 Peterborough U, Div 4, 1960-61
Div 1 record: 128 Aston Villa, 1930-31
Scottish League: 142 Raith R, Div 2, 1937-38
Div 1/Premier Division record: 132 Hearts, Div 1, 1957-58

Fewest goals scored in a season
Football League *(since expansion in 1905):*
24 Watford, Div 2, 1971-72; 24 Stoke C, Div 1, 1984-85
Scottish League: 18 Stirling A, Div 1, 1980-81

Most goals conceded in a season
Football League: 141 Darwen, Div 2, 1898-99
Div 1 record: 125 Blackpool, 1930-31
Scottish League: 146 Edinburgh C, Div 2 1931-32
Div 1/Premier Division record: 137 Leith A, Div 1, 1931-32

Fewest goals conceded in a season
(since expansion in 1905)
Football League: 16 Liverpool, Div 1, 1978-79
Scottish League: 14 Celtic, Div 1, 1913-14

Record Scores
Football League:
13-0 Stockport C v Halifax T, Div 3(N), 1933-34; 13-0 Newcastle U v Newport C 1946-47; 13-4 Tranmere R v Oldham A, Div 3(N), 1935-36;
Div 1 record: 12-0 West Bromwich v Darwen, 1891-92; 12-0 Nottingham F v Leicester F, 1908-09
Record Away Win: 10-0 Sheffield U at Burslem Port Vale, Div 2, 1892-93
Scottish League:
15-1 Airdrieonians v Dundee W, Div 2, 1894-95
Div 1/Premier Division: 11-0 Celtic v Dundee, 1895-95

TOP 10 EUROPEAN CLUBS BY INCOME

1	AC Milan	29.8m
2	Barcelona	21m
3	Napoli	20.8m
4	Inter-Milan	19m
5	Juventus	17m
6	Real Madrid	16m
7	Roma	14m
8	Bordeaux	12m
9	Fiorentina	11.9m
10	Marseille	11.8m

Source: Sunday Telegraph

━━━━━━EUROPEAN CHAMPIONSHIP 1990-1991 FIXTURES━━━━━

GROUP ONE
1990
Iceland v. Albania 2-0; Iceland v. France 1-2; Czechoslavakia v. Iceland, Sep 26; Spain v. Iceland, Oct 10; France v. Czechoslavakia, Oct 13; Czechoslavakia v. Spain, Nov 14; Albania v. France, Nov 17; Spain v. Albania, Dec 19
!991
France v. Spain, Feb 20; France v. Albania, Mar 30; Albania v. Czechoslavakia, May 1; Albania v. Iceland, May 26; Iceland v. Czechoslavakia, Jun 5; Czechoslavakia v. France, Sep 4;
Iceland v. Spain, Sep 25; Spain v. France, Oct 12; Czechoslavakia v. Albania, Oct 16; Spain v. Czechoslavakia, Nov 13; France v. Iceland, Nov 13 or 20; Albania v. Spain, Dec 18

GROUP TWO
1990
Switzerland v. Bulgaria 2-0; Scotland v. Romania 2-1; Romania v. Bulgaria, Oct 17; Scotland v. Switzerland, Oct 17; Bulgaria v. Scotland, Nov 14; San Marino v. Switzerland, Nov 14; Romania v. San Marino, Dec 5
1991
Scotland v. Bulgaria, Mar 27; San Marino v. Romania, Mar 27; Switzerland v. Romania, Apr 3; Bulgaria v. Switzerland, May 1; San Marino v. Scotland, May 1; San Marino v. Bulgaria, May 22; Switzerland v. San Marino, Jun 5; Switzerland v. Scotland, Sep 11; Bulgaria v. San Marino, Oct 16; Romania v. Switzerland, Nov 13; Bulgaria v. Romania, Nov 20

GROUP THREE
1990
Soviet Union v. Norway 2-0; Norway v. Hungary, Oct 10; Hungary v. Italy, Oct 17; Hungary v. Cyprus, Oct 31; Italy v. Soviet Union, Nov 3; Cyprus v. Norway, Nov 14; Cyprus v. Italy, Dec 22
1991
Cyprus v. Hungary, Apr 3; Hungary v. Soviet Union, Apr 17; Italy v. Hungary, May 1; Norway v. Cyprus, May 1; Soviet Union v. Cyprus, May 22 or 29; Norway v. Italy, Jun 5; Norway v. Soviet Union, Aug 28; Soviet Union v. Hungary, Sep 25; Soviet Union v. Italy, Oct 12; Hungary v. Norway, Ovt 30; Italy v. Norway, Nov 13; Cyprus v. Soviet Union, Nov 13; Italy v. Cyprus, Dec 21

GROUP FOUR
1990
Northern Ireland v. Yugoslavia 0-2; Faroe Islands v. Austria 1-0; Denmark v. Faroe Islands, Oct 10; Northern Ireland v. Denmark, Oct 17; Yugoslavia v. Austria, Oct 31; Denmark v. Yugoslavia, Nov 14; Austria v. Northern Ireland, Nov 14
1991
Yugoslavia v. Northern Ireland, Mar 27; Yugoslavia v. Denmark, May 1; Northern Ireland v. Faroe Islands, May 1; Yugoslavia v. Faroe Islands, May 14 or 15; Austria v. Faroe Islands, May 22; Denmark v. Austria, Jun 5; Faroe Islands v. Northern Ireland, Sep 11; Faroe Islands v. Denmark, Sep 25; Austria v. Denmark, Oct 9; Faroe Islands v. Yugoslavia, Oct 16; Northern Ireland v. Austria, Oct 16; Denmark v. Northern Ireland, Nov 13; Austria v. Yugoslavia, Nov 13

GROUP FIVE
1990
Belgium v. East Germany; Wales v. Belgium, Oct 17; East Germany v. Luxembourg, Oct 17; Luxembourg v. West Germany, Oct 31; Luxembourg v. Wales, Nov 14; East Germany v. West Germany, Nov 21
1991
Belgium v. Luxembourg, Feb 27; Luxembourg v. East Germany, Mar 13; Belgium v. Wales, Mar 27; West Germany, v. Belgium, May 1; East Germany v. Wales, May 1; Wales v. West Germany, Jun 5; Luxembourg v. Belgium, Sep 11; Wales v. East Germany, Sep 11; West Germany v. Wales, Oct 16; East Germany v. Belgium, Oct 16; Wales v. Luxembourg, Nov 13; Belgium v. Wesr Germany, Nov 20; West Germany v. Luxembourg, Dec 17; West Germany v. East Germany, Dec 21. **East Germany withdrawn**

GROUP SIX
1990
Finland v. Portugal 0-0; Portugal v. Holland, Oct 17; Greece v. Malta, Oct 31; Holland v. Greece, Nov 21; Malta v. Finland, Nov 25; Malta v. Holland, Dec 19 or 23
1991
Greece v. Portugal, Jan 23; Malta v. Portugal, Feb 9; Portugal v. Malta, Feb 20; Holland v. Malta, Mar 13; Holland v. Finland, Apr 17; Finland v. Malta, May 16; Finland v. Holland, Jun 5; Portugal v. Finland, Sep 11; Finland v. Greece, Oct 9; Holland v. Portugal, Oct 16; Greece v. Finland, Oct 30; Portugal v. Greece, Nov 20; Greece v. Holland, Dec 4; Malta v. Greece, Dec 22

GROUP SEVEN
1990
England v. Poland, Oct 17; Republic of Ireland v. Turkey, Oct 17; Republic of Ireland v. England, Nov 14; Turkey v. Poland, Nov 14
1991
England v. Republic of Ireland, Mar 27; Poland v. Turkey, Apr 17; Turkey v. England, May 1; Republic of Ireland v. Poland, May 1; Poland v. Republic of Ireland, Oct 16; England v. Turkey, Oct 16; Turkey v. Republic of Ireland, Nov 13; Poland v. England, Nov 13

1991

GENERAL FIXTURES

Jan 6 FA Cup third round; *Jan 16* League Cup quarter-finals; *Jan 26* FA Cup fourth round, Scottish Cup third round

Feb 6 England v Cameroon (Wembley); *Feb 13* League Cup semi-finals (first legs); *Feb 23* Scottish Cup fourth round; *Feb 26* England v Ireland (European under-21 championship).

Mar 9 Cup sixth round, Scottish Cup fifth round; *Mar 27* England v Ireland (European Championship, Wembley); Scotland v Bulgaria (European Championship, Hampden); Yugoslavia v Northern Ireland (European Championship).

Apr 6 Scottish Cup semi-finals (or Apr 20); *Apr 13* FA Cup semi-finals; *Apr 21* League Cup final (Wembley).

May 1 Ireland v Poland (European Championship, Dublin); San Marino v Scotland (European Championship); Northern Ireland v Faroe Islands (European Championship, Belfast); Turkey v England (European Championship).

May 4 FA Vase final (Wembley); *May 5* FA Sunday Cup final; *May 8* UEFA Cup final (first leg); *May 11* FA Trophy final (Wembley); *May 12* FA of Ireland Cup final; *May 15* European Cup-winners' Cup final; *May 18* FA CUP FINAL (Wembley), SCOTTISH CUP FINAL (Glasgow); *May 21* England v Argentina (Wembley); *May 22* UEFA Cup final (second leg); *May 25 or 26* England v USSR (Wembley); *May 29* European Cup final; *May 30* Turkey v England (European under-21 Championship).

Jun 6 Wales v West Germany (European Championship, Cardiff) *Jun 8* England v West Germany (schoolboys, Wembley).

FIRST DIVISION FIXTURES 1990-91

Away Team

Home Team	Arsenal	Aston V	Chelsea	Coventry	Crystal P.	Derby C	Everton	Leeds U	Liverpool	Luton T	Man C	Man. U	Norwich	Nottingham	QPR	Sheff W	Southampt.	Sunderland	Tottenham	Wimbledon
Arsenal	-	Apr 2	Sep 15	May 11	Feb 23	Dec 26	Jan 19	Mar 16	Dec 1	Aug 29	Apr 13	Apr 20	Oct 6	Feb 9	Mar 9	Dec 29	Nov 17	Oct 27	Sep 1	Dec 15
Aston Villa	Dec 22	-	May 11	Sep 8	Jan 1	Feb 2	Mar 30	Oct 27	Jan 12	Mar 9	Dec 8	Apr 6	Feb 16	Nov 10	Sep 22	Dec 1	Aug 25	Oct 6	Mar 16	Apr 20
Chelsea	Feb 2	Nov 3	-	Dec 22	Dec 8	Aug 25	Jan 1	Mar 20	May 4	Apr 6	Sep 22	Mar 9	Nov 10	Oct 20	Sep 29	Sep 29	Mar 23	Sep 8	Dec 1	Feb 16
Coventry C	Nov 3	Jan 19	Apr.1	-	Mar 2	Apr 13	Aug 29	Nov 24	Nov 17	Feb 9	Mar 23	Dec 15	Dec 29	Oct 20	May 4	Sep 1	Oct 20	Feb 23	Dec 26	Sep 15
Crystal Palace	Nov 10	Apr 13	Aug 28	Dec 1	-	Mar 16	Apr 20	Oct 6	Dec 29	Dec 16	Apr 1	May 11	Jan 19	Sep 1	Feb 16	Sep 1	Mar 9	Dec 26	Feb 9	Oct 27
Derby C	Mar 30	Sep 15	Dec 15	Jan 1	Sep 29	-	Apr 6	Feb 16	Mar 23	Nov 3	Oct 20	Nov 10	Feb 9	Nov 24	Dec 23	Aug 29	May 4	Mar 2	Jan 19	Sep 1
Everton	Sep 8	Dec 26	Apr 13	Dec 8	Oct 20	Dec 29	-	Aug 25	Sep 22	May 4	Jan 12	Dec 1	Apr 1	Mar 23	Jan 31	Feb 23	Sep 29	Feb 2	Nov 17	Mar 9
Leeds U	Sep 29	May 4	Dec 26	Mar 9	Mar 23	Nov 17	Dec 15	-	Apr 13	Jan 19	Feb 23	Aug 28	Sep 1	Nov 3	Oct 20	Feb 9	Dec 1	Apr 2	Sep 15	Dec 29
Liverpool	Mar 2	Sep 1	Oct 27	Feb 16	Apr 6	Oct 6	Feb 9	Jan 1	-	Nov 10	Nov 24	Sep 15	Apr 20	Aug 28	Mar 30	Dec 15	Dec 22	Mar 16	May 11	Jan 19
Luton T	Dec 8	Nov 24	Dec 29	Sep 22	Aug 25	May 11	Oct 27	Sep 8	Feb 23	-	Nov 17	Sep 4	Mar 16	Mar 2	Feb 2	Dec 26	Jan 12	Apr 20	Apr 1	Apr 13
Manchester C	Jan 1	Sep 5	Feb 9	Oct 6	Dec 22	Apr 20	Sep 1	Nov 10	Mar 9	Feb 16	-	Oct 27	Sep 15	Apr 6	Dec 1	Jan 19	Mar 30	May 11	Dec 15	Mar 16
Manchester U	Oct 20	Dec 29	Nov 24	Aug 25	Nov 3	Feb 23	Mar 2	Sep 23	Feb 2	Sep 29	May 4	-	Dec 26	Sep 29	Sep 8	Nov 17	Sep 22	Nov 12	Apr 13	Apr 2
Norwich C	Mar 23	Nov 17	Feb 23	Apr 6	Nov 3	Sep 22	Dec 8	Jan 12	Oct 20	Sep 29	Feb 2	Mar 30	-	Jan 2	May 4	Nov 3	Dec 8	Aug 25	Mar 9	Dec 1
Nottingham F	Sep 22	Feb 23	Apr 20	Jan 12	Feb 2	Mar 9	Oct 7	May 11	Dec 8	Dec 1	Dec 29	Mar 16	Apr 13	-	Aug 25	Apr 1	Sep 8	Nov 17	Oct 27	Dec 26
QPR	Nov 24	Feb 9	Sep 1	Mar 16	Nov 17	Apr 1	May 11	Apr 17	Dec 26	Sep 15	Mar 2	Jan 19	Oct 27	Dec 15	-	Apr 13	Feb 23	Dec 29	Oct 6	Aug 29
Sheffield U	Apr 6	Mar 2	Mar 16	Oct 27	Jan 12	Dec 8	Nov 10	Sep 23	Aug 25	Mar 30	Sep 8	Feb 16	May 11	Dec 22	Jan 1	-	Feb 2	Nov 24	Apr 20	Oct 6
Southampton	Feb 16	Dec 15	Oct 6	Apr 20	Nov 24	Oct 27	Mar 16	Mar 2	Apr 1	Sep 1	Dec 26	Feb 9	Aug 28	Jan 19	Nov 10	Sep 15	-	Apr 13	Dec 29	May 11
Sunderland	May 4	Mar 23	Jan 19	Nov 10	Mar 30	Dec 1	Sep 15	Dec 23	Sep 29	Oct 20	Nov 3	Sep 1	Dec 15	Feb 16	Apr 6	Mar 9	Jan 1	-	Aug 28	Feb 9
Tottenham H	Jan 12	Sep 29	Mar 2	Mar 30	Sep 22	Sep 8	Feb 16	Feb 2	Nov 3	Dec 22	Aug 25	Jan 1	Nov 24	May 4	Mar 23	Oct 20	Apr 6	Dec 8	-	Nov 10
Wimbledon	Aug 25	Oct 20	Nov 17	Feb 2	May 4	Jan 12	Nov 24	Apr 6	Sep 8	Jan 1	Sep 29	Dec 22	Mar 2	Mar 30	Dec 8	Mar 23	Nov 3	Sep 22	Feb 23	-

ATHLETICS

THE CLEANSING PROCESS

Athletics appeared to be entering a new era in 1990 as two of the dark forces that had dominated it for years began to fade into the background. One was East Germany, the nation that succeeded at sport but nothing else, and so decided to abolish itself. The other (not entirely unrelated) was drugs, whose demise was far less complete and less certain but every bit as welcome.

The indications that drugs were playing less of a part in the sport were patchy. Nonetheless, the system of random dope-testing — any time, any place — began to bite and there was a noticeable decline in the incidence of record-breaking. There were no new world records at the star-studded Weltklasse meeting in Zurich and only one at the European Championships (by the male French sprint relay team). Athletes everywhere seemed to be turning away from destroying their innards in pursuit of success and concentrating instead on the healthy business of simply making money.

These factors helped many wholesome British athletes and at the European Championships in Split, Yugoslavia, Britain came through triumphantly, winning nine gold medals, more than everyone except, of course, East Germany who, in spite of everything, still dominated the women's events. All but two of Britain's gold-winners were in the men's shorter distance track events. The exceptions were the remarkable javelin-thrower Steve Backley and the women's 3,000 metres runner Yvonne Murray. However, it was uncertain whether any of these successes would translate on to the global stage; only Backley and the hurdler Colin Jackson looked long-range favourites to win at the World Championships in Tokyo in August 1991.

Many of the other wins represented some kind of triumph over adversity, especially that of Roger Black who successfully defended his 400 metres title despite having spent most of the intervening period out with a foot injury. However, Britain failed to get any medal in the event it regards as its own, the 1,500 metres, in which Peter Elliott and Steve Cram were beaten into fourth and fifth places. Elliott, the pre-race favourite, was thumped to the ground in his heat by the East German Hauke Fuhlbrugge and appeared to be out of the event. Fuhlbrugge was disqualified; then to widespread astonishment the Jury of Appeal reinstated Elliott and allowed him into the final, citing IAAF rule 141 (1). Elliott himself felt a little sheepish; others were more strongly critical, suggesting it would lead to an epidemic of appeals from hard-done-by runners.

Jens-Peter Herold gave the East German men a rare success in the 1,500. But in other events the dying nation proved extraordinarily resilient, winning almost half the women's golds. They were able to do so as human beings rather than automata. Their parents were able to travel to watch them and the new track star Katrin Krabbe, 20, not only won both women's sprints but managed to look feminine in the process. The British women were much less happy. Their team manager Joan Allison heard as the Games ended that women's matches were being kept off TV in 1991. "Basically, they are saying 'Let's push the women under the carpet because they are an embarrassment" she said. "It is no wonder that our girls go into world-class competition without experience and get beaten."

Other ex-Communist countries such as Poland and Czechoslovakia sent only token teams to the Championships while the hosts used the event largely as a demonstration of Croatian nationalism, to the irritation of the Yugoslav government. Two condoms were handed out to all competitors and officials, including Maria Hartman, the 70-year-old British chef de mission. "Anyone else can come up and use mine if they need to," she said. Some of the new form-fitting leotards used by female athletes proved not to provide full covering at high-speed, to the horror of the wearers and the delight of some spectators. Steve Backley's girlfriend Kerry Shacklock seriously injured her back playing cards in his room, reportedly after leaping in the air because she had a good hand.

The East Germans held their 41st and last domestic championships in Dresden and prepared for athletic unity with the West early in 1991. Barely ten weeks after the fall of the Berlin Wall, Grundig and Volvo began sponsoring the East's athletic squad and competitors were soon able to keep 60% of their appearance money, 60% more than ever before. The changes may have been wonderful news for the athletes but not for the 592 state coaches, nearly all of whom were expected to become jobless.

Eastern bloc athletes joined all the others in chasing cash and there were a number of embarrassing set-piece attempts at record-breaking. Khalid Skah, the world cross-country champion, and Julius Kariuki persuaded organisers of a meeting in Brussels to remove the main opposition so they could make record attempts. Both failed and Kariuki was actually beaten. The only event in which new marks were set regularly was the javelin, a discipline complicated by arguments over design of the implement. The record was broken four times, on two occasions by Backley who passed the 90-metre mark on July 20, borrowing one of the Nemeth javelins which were banned at the European Championships,

SPLIT ENDS

❝I don't know what hurts most, my hand, my shoulder, my shin or my pride.❞
Peter Elliott, after being knocked headlong in the 1,500 metres heat

"In my hearts of hearts I don't think it's right that I'm in the race."
Elliott on being reinstated

"Officials have opened a can of worms. Protests will be coming in by the cartload."
Steve Ovett

"At least I made the sods run for it."
Steve Cram, in defeat

"I ran the race like a plonker but I'm a plonker with a gold medal around his neck."
Roger Black, in triumph

"When I sprinted across the line, all I could think of was "Thank you, Lord."
Kriss Akabusi, ditto

"I love being written off. I stuffed it down your effing throats.❞
Linford Christie, ditto

Among the sprinters, Leroy Burrell, Carl Lewis's protégé and training partner, emerged as the world leader, beating Lewis at the Goodwill Games by .03 of a second, his 12th successive win. Nonetheless, commercial interest centred on plans for a Lewis-Ben Johnson rematch after Johnson's return. His ban ended in September 1990. Johnson boasted about his ability but admitted he was bench pressing 70 lb less than in his pill-popping days; he said he intended to delay his comeback until January 1991. The Dubin Report into drugs in Canadian sport — released more than a year after Johnson admitted his guilt — recommended that sports organisations not politicians should decide when Johnson be allowed to run again: the Government had banned him from ever competing for Canada, the athletics organisation only for the two years and they got their way.

Sebastian Coe, the *Sportspages* British Sportsman of the decade, retired to become prospective Conservative party candidate for Falmouth and Camborne (C. maj 5,039). His possible heir as a British middle-distance champion, Peter Elliott, finally gave up his job as a joiner at the Rotherham steelworks to become a full-time athlete. Simon Mugglestone ran the 3,030th sub-four-minute mile but the first at Iffley Road, Oxford since British athletics', most famous day 36 years before. Sir Roger Bannister was there to see his track record beaten by half a second. "I'm just glad they're still a little breathless when they do it," he said. The report into the bizarre case of the Steve Ovett call concluded that Ovett did receive a phone-call offering him money before the 1989

AAA championships but declined to be definite whether it came from British athletics' promotions officer Andy Norman, as Ovett alleged, or from someone purporting to be Norman.

MARATHON MAN

Allister Hutton, 35, of Scotland won a surprising victory in the London Marathon. It was his first marathon victory in ten years of trying. Wanda Panfil of Poland, second last year, won a more expected victory in the women's race; she was promptly sick. One competitor died during the race: Robert Ward, 39, from Hampshire, who had a heart attack after 11 miles, and one shortly afterwards: Cyril Sharpe, 57, from Marylebone drowned in his bath after having an epileptic fit. Three of the 44,100 entrants in the 14-kilometre City-to-Surf race in Sydney died in the middle of it.

The Los Angeles Marathon introduced a digital tag, worn like a wristwatch, enabling the 20,000 competitors to be timed accurately. Madge Sharples, a 73-year-old marathon runner, outran a sex attacker who leapt on her while she was jogging at Twyford, Hampshire. A 42-year-old Ohio woman, Georgene Johnson, ran her first marathon by mistake. She thought she was competing in a 10km race. On discovering her error, she started to cry but saw another runner in a T-shirt saying "Just do it". So she did. Three psychiatrists from the University of Arizona said the compulsion to run marathons was analogous to anorexia nervosa.

Thirty athletes competing in the Rowntree Athletic Club's ten-mile road race hurdled a railway level-crossing moments before the Liverpool to Scarborough express came through. "There could have been a mass slaughter on the line," said a police officer. "I was 20 yards ahead," said Dr Peter McDaid, "and could not afford to let anyone catch up." The offenders were charged but given an absolute discharge by magistrates. It emerged that the race had been timed to avoid trains but that the express was running ten minutes early. Ted Adcock, 58, pleaded guilty to indecent assault at Bedlington Magistrates' court after he fondled Véronique Marot's breasts before the start of a road race at Morpeth. Adcock had previously tried to grab the Princess of Wales. Organisers of the 18th annual Round the Bays run in Auckland, New Zealand said that nearly half the 85,000 competitors cheated the Auckland Children's Hospital — the charity which the event supported — by running without paying the small entry fee.

Among the year's glamorous sponsorships was the "Post Office Counters Pole Vaulting Residential Weekend" at Stoke-on-Trent. Linford Christie was awarded five-figure damages against the Metropolitan Police for libel and unlawful arrest after he was alleged to have stolen a car. Don Thompson, walking gold medallist at the 1960 Olympics, returned to the sport aged 57 and came second in the national 100-mile championship. The 121-year-old Powderhall Sprint, held in Edinburgh every New Year for professionals, was abandoned because of the absence of a sponsor. A Martian might assume that this represented the final triumph of amateur athletics.

1990

Note: Goodwill and Commonwealth Games results can be found in their respective sections

EUROPEAN CHAMPIONSHIPS

Split, Yugoslavia, Aug 27-Sep 1

Men

100 Metres
1 Linford Christie (GB) 10.0s
2 Daniel Sangouma (Fra)10.04s
3 John Regis (GB) 10.07s

200 Metres
1 John Regis (GB) 20.11s
2 Jean-Charles Trouabal (Fra) 20.31s
3 Linford Christie (GB) 20.33s

400 Metres
1 Roger Black (GB) 45.08s
2 Thomas Schönlebe (GDR) 45.13s
3 Jens Carlowitz (GDR) 45.27s

800 Metres
1 Tom McKean (GB) 1m 44.76s
2 David Sharpe (GB) 1m 45.59s
3 Piotr Pierkarski (Pol) 1m 45.76s

1500 Metres
1 Jens-Peter Herold (GDR) 3m 38.25s
2 Gennaro Di Napoli (Ita) 3m 38.60s
3 Mario Silva (Por) 3m 38.73s

5000 Metres
1 Salvatore Antibo (Ita) 13m 22.00s
2 Gary Staines (GB) 13m 22.45s
3 Slawomir Majusak (Pol) 13m 22.92s

10,000 Metres
1 Salvatore Antibo (Ita) 27m 41.27s
2 Ari Nakkim (Nor) 28m 04.04s
3 Stefano Mei (Ita) 28m 04.46s

Marathon
1 Gelindo Bordin (Ita) 2h 14m 02s
2 Giovanni Poli (Ita) 2h 14m 55s
3 Dominique Chauvelier (Fra) 2h 15m 20s

110 Metres Hurdles
1 Colin Jackson (GB) 13.18s
2 Tony Jarrett (GB) 13.21s
3 Dietmar Koszewski (FRG) 13.50s

400 Metres Hurdles
1 Kriss Akabusi (GB) 47.92s
2 Sven Nylander (Swe) 48.43s
3 Niklas Wallenlind (Swe) 48.52s

3000 Metres Steeplechase
1 Francesco Panetta (Ita) 8m 12.66s
2 Mark Rowland (GB) 8m 13.27s
3 Alessandro Lambruschini (Ita) 8m 15.82s

20km Walk
1 Pavol Blazek (Cze) 1h 22m 05s
2 Daniel Plaza (Spa) 1h 22m 22s
3 Thierry Toutain (Fra) 1h 23m 22s

50km Walk
1 Andrey Perlov (USSR) 3h 54m 36s
2 Bernd Gummelt (GDR) 3h 56m 03s
3 Hartwig Gauder (GDR) 4h 00m 48s

4 x 100 Metres Relay
1 France 37.79s (world record)
2 Britain 37.98s
3 Italy 38.39s

4 x 400 Metres Relay
1 Britain 2m 58.22s
2 West Germany 3m 00.64s
3 East Germany 3m 01.51s

High Jump
1 Dragutin Topic (Yug) 2.34m
2 Alexsei Yemelin (USSR) 2.34m
3 Georgi Dakov (Bul) 2.34m

Long Jump
1 Dietmar Haaf (FRG) 8.25m
2 Angel Hernandez (Spa) 8.15m
3 Borut Bilac (Yug) 8.09m*
Bilac was disqualified after failing a drugs test. Frans Maas (Hol) promoted to third.

Triple Jump
1 Leonid Voloshin (USSR) 17.74m
2 Khristo Markov (Bul) 1743m
3 Igor Lapshin (USSR) 17.34m

Pole Vault
1 Rodion Gataulin (USSR) 5.85m
2 Grigory Yegorov (USSR) 5.75m
3 Hermann Fehringer (Aut) 5.75m

Shot
1 Ulf Timmermann (GDR) 21.32m
2 Sven-Oliver Buder (GDR) 21.03m
3 Viacheslav Lykho (USSR) 20.81m*
Lykho was disqualified after failing a drugs test. Georg Andersen (Nor) promoted to third.

Discus
1 Jürgen Schult (GDR) 64.58m
2 Erik de Bruin (Hol) 64.46m
3 Wolfgang Schmidt (FRG) 64.10m

Javelin
1 Steve Backley (GB) 87.30m
2 Viktor Zaitsez (USSR) 83.30m
3 Patrik Boden (Swe) 82.66

Hammer
1 Igor Astapkovitch (USSR) 84.14m
2 Tibor Gecsek (Hun) 80.14m
3 Igor Nikulin (USSR) 80.02m

Decathlon
1 Christian Plaziat (Fra) 8.574pts
2 Dexso Szabo (Hun) 8.436pts
3 Christian Schenk (GDR) 8.433pts

THE JAVELIN — TOWARDS 100 METRES....AGAIN

In 1986, after the men's world record had been pushed to 104.80 metres, the IAAF modified the rules of the javelin throw by moving the javelin's centre of gravity to reduce distances. Since then the record has gradually crept back up....

85.74m **Klaus Tafelmeier** (FRG), Cime, Italy, 21 Sep 1986
87.66m **Jan Zelezny** (Cze) Nitra, Czechoslovakia, 31 May 1987
89.10m **Patrik Boden** (Swe), Austin, Texas, 24 Mar 1990
89.58 m **Steve Backley** (GB), Stockholm, 2 Jul 1990
89.66m **Jan Zelezny** (Cze), Oslo, 14 Jul 1990
90.98m **Steve Backley** (GB), London, 20 Jul 1990

Women
100 Metres
1 Katrin Krabbe (GDR) 10.89s
2 Silke Moeller (GDR) 11.10s
3 Kerstin Behrendt (GDR) 11.17s

200 Metres
1 Katrin Krabbe (GDR) 21.95s
2 Heike Drechsler (GDR) 22.19s
3 Galina Malchugina (USSR) 22.23s

400 Metres
1 Grit Breuer (GDR) 49.50s
2 Petra Schersing (GDR) 50.51s
3 Marie-Josee Perec (Fra) 50.84s

800 Metres
1 Sigrun Wodars (GDR) 1m 55.87s
2 Christine Wachtel (GDR) 1m 56.11s
3 Lilia Nurutdinova (USSR) 1m 57.39s

1500 Metres
1 Snezana Pajkic (Yug) 4m 08.13s
2 Ellen Kiessling (GDR) 4m 08.67s
3 Sandra Gasser (Swi) 4m 08.89s

3000 Metres
1 Yvonne Murray (GB) 8m 43.06s
2 Yelena Romanova (USSR) 8m 43.68s
3 Roberta Brunet (Ita) 8m 46.19s

10,000 Metres
1 Elena Romanova (USSR) 31m 46.83s
2 Kathrin Ullrich (GDR) 31m 47.70s
3 Annette Sergent (Fra) 31m 51.68s

Marathon
1 Rosa Mota (Por) 2h 31m 27s
2 Valentina Yegorova (USSR) 2h 31m 32s
3 Maria Rebello-Lelut (Fra) 2h 35m 51s

100 Metres Hurdles
1 Monique Ewanje-Epée (Fra) 12.79s
2 Gloria Siebert (GDR) 12.91s
3 Lydia Iurkova (USSR) 12.92s

400 Metres Hurdles
1 Tatyana Ledovskaya (USSR) 53.62s
2 Anita Protti (Swi) 54.36s
3 Monica Westen (Swe) 54.75s

10km Walk
1 Anna-Rita Sidotti (Ita) 44m 00s
2 Olga Kardapoltseva (USSR) 44m 06s
3 Ileana Salvador (Ita) 44m 38s

4 x 100 Metres Relay
1 East Germany 41.68s
2 West Germany 43.02s
3 Britain 43.32s

4 x 400 Metres Relay
1 East Germany 3m 21.02s
2 Soviet Union 3m 23.34s
3 Britain 3m 24.78s

High Jump
1 Heike Henkel (GDR) 1.99m
2 Biljana Petrovic (Yug) 1.96m
3 Yelena Yelesina (USSR) 1.96m

Long Jump
1 Heike Drechsler (GDR) 7.30m
2 Marieta Ilcu (Rom) 7.02m
3 Helga Radtke (GDR) 6.94m

Shot
1 Astrid Kumbernuss (GDR) 20.38m
2 Natalya Lisovskaya 20.06m
3 Katrin Neimke (GDR) 19.96m

Discus
1 Ilke Wyludda (GDR) 68.46m
2 Olga Burova (USSR) 66.72m
3 Martina Hellmann (GDR) 66.66m

Javelin
1 Paivoi Alafrantti (Fin) 67.68m
2 Karen Forkel (GDR) 67.56m
3 Petra Felke (GDR) 66.56m

Heptathlon
1 Sabine Braun (FRG) 6.688pts
2 Heike Tischler (GDR) 6.572pts
3 Peggy Beer (GDR) 6.531pts

Medal Table

	G	S	B
34 East Germany	12	12	10
18 Britain	9	5	4
22 Soviet Union	6	9	7
12 Italy	5	2	5
10 France	3	2	5
7 West Germany	3	2	2
4 Yugoslavia	2	1	1
2 Portugal	1	0	1
1 Czechoslovakia	1	0	0
1 Finland	1	0	0
2 Spain	0	2	0
2 Hungary	0	2	0
4 Sweden	0	1	3
2 Switzerland	0	1	1
2 Bulgaria	0	1	1
1 Romania	0	1	0
1 Norway	0	1	0
1 Holland	0	1	0
2 Poland	0	0	2
1 Austria	0	0	1

MOBIL GRAND PRIX
Final Standings
N.B. Some events not held

Men
100 Metres
1 Leroy Burrell (US) 63pts
2 Mark Witherspoon (US) 50pts
3 Calvin Smith (US) 46pts

800 Metres
1 Nixon Kiprotich (Ken) 54pts
2 Reda Abdenouz (Alg) 45pts
3 William Tanui (Ken) 41pts

Mile
1 Nourredine Morceli (Alg) 61pts
2 Jens-Peter Herold (GDR) 46pts
3 Joe Falcon (US) 42pts

5000 Metres
1 Khalid Skah (Mor) 59pts
2 Brahim Boutayeb (Mor) 47pts
3 Yobes Ondieki (Ken) 46pts

400 Metres Hurdles
1 Danny Harris (US) 59pts
2 Samuel Matete (Zam) 56pts
3 Winthrop Graham (Jam) 50pts

3000 Metres Steeplechase
1 Julius Kariuki (Ken) 56pts
2 Patrick Sang (Ken) 49pts
3 Julius Korir (Ken) 40pts

CHEMICAL CORNER

"With or without doping, I'm the fastest sprinter in the world."

Ben Johnson

"The athletes who cheat must bear their full share of responsibility for the damage they have done to themselves and to sport, but they must not be held solely responsible. Until now, the focus has been only on the athletes. It is obvious that a broader net of responsibility will need to be cast. Coaches, physicians, therapists and others involved in the care and training of athletes cannot escape responsibility for the sorry state of sport today."

The Dubin Report into the Johnson affair

"I'll make it back in 1991 and 1992. All of the $25 million."

Ben Johnson

"Carl does not need the money, but whatever he gets he deserves more than Johnson, because he has done everything fair and square and if anyone has different ideas they can take a flying leap."
Joe Douglas, Lewis's agent, negotiating for the showdown

"If you take out the doped athletes, I'm probably in the top three."
Christian Plaziat, French decathlete, on joining the all-time top ten

"It was a common belief on the track circuit that Florence had used drugs."
Carl Lewis on Griffith-Joyner

"I'm ready as an athlete and serene as a lamb."
Johnson anticipating his comeback

High Jump
1 Hollis Conway (US) 56pts
2 Georgi Dakov (Bul) 49pts
3 Sergey Malchenko (USSR) 48.5pts

Triple Jump
1 Mike Conley (US) 59pts
2 Jan Cado (US) 49pts
3 Oleg Protsenko (USSR) 48pts

Shot
1 Ulf Timmermann (GDR) 54pts
2 Georg Andersen (Nor) 50pts
3 Ron Backes (US) 42pts

Hammer
1 Yuriy Sedykh (USSR) 59pts
2 Tibor Gecsek (Hun) 49pts
3 Henz Weiss (FRG) 48pts

Overall
1 Leroy Burrell (US) 63pts
2 Nourredine Morceli (Alg) 61pts
3 Danny Harris (US) 59pts
4 Mike Conley (US) 59pts
5 Yuriy Sedykh (USSR) 59pts
6 Khalid Skah (Mor) 59pts

Women
200 Metres
1 Merlene Ottey (Jam) 63pts
2 Grace Jackson (Jam) 53pts
3 Galina Malchugina (USSR) 49pts

400 Metres
1 Ana Quirot (Cub) 63pts
2 Grace Jackson (Jam) 53pts
3 Fatima Yusuf (Nig) 46pts

1500 Metres
1 Doina Melinte (Rom) 51pts
2 Svetlana Kitova (USSR) 46pts
3 Margareta Keszeg (Rom) 40pts

5000 Metres
1 PattiSue Plumer (US) 63pts
2 Vicrica Ghican (Rom) 45pts
3 Nadia Dandolo (Ita) 37pts

100 Metres Hurdles
1 Monique Ewanje-Epée (Fra) 57pts
2 Gloria Siebert (GDR) 52pts
3 Lydia Iurkova (USSR) 47pts

Long Jump
1 Heike Drechsler (GDR) 63pts
2 Ineisa Kravets (USSR) 55pts
3 Marieta Ilcu (Rom) 49pts

Discus
1 Ilke Wyludda (GDR) 63pts
2 Martina Hellmann (GDR) 28pts
3 Tsvetanka Khristova (Bul) 26pts

Javelin
1 Petra Felke (GDR) 63pts
2 Dulce Garcia (Cub) 46pts
3 Brigitte Graune (FRG) 43pts

Overall
1 Merlene Ottey (Jam) 63pts
2 Heike Drechsler (GDR) 63pts
3 Petra Felke (GDR) 63pts
4 Ilke Wyludda (GDR) 63pts
5 Ana Quirot (Cub) 63pts
6 PattiSue Plumer (US) 63pts

AAA/WAAA CHAMPIONSHIPS
Birmingham, Aug 3-5
Men

100 Metres:	Calvin Smith (US) 10.21s
200 Metres:	John Regis (Belgrave) 20.28s
400 Metres:	Howard Burnett (Jam) 45.52s
800 Metres:	William Tanui (Ken) 1m 44.14s
1500 Metres:	Neil Horsfield (Newport) 3m 44.70s
3000 Metres:	John Walker (NZ) 8m 05.01s
5000 Metres:	Eamonn Martin (Basildon) 13m 32.07s
110 Metres Hurdles:	Colin Jackson (Cardiff) 13.23s
400 Metres Hurdles:	Nat Page (US) 50.06s
3000 Metres Chase:	Phillip Barkutwo (Ken) 8m 22.22s
10,000 Metres Walk:	Mark Easton (Surrey) 41m 32.80s
High Jump:	Dalton Grant (Haringey) 2.28m
Long Jump:	Stewart Faulkner (Birchfield) 8.05m
Triple Jump:	John Herbert (Haringey) 16.61m
Pole Vault:	Paul Benavides (US) 5.30m

Shot:	Paul Edwards (RAF) 19.00m
Discus:	Abi Ekoku (Belgrave) 57.58m
Javelin:	Mick Hill (Leeds) 81.22m
Hammer:	Paul Head (Newham) 72.68m

Women

100 Metres:	Stephanie Douglas (Milton Keynes) 11.38s
200 Metres:	Jennifer Stoute (Essex) 23.07s
400 Metres:	Lillie Leatherwood (US) 51.62s
800 Metres:	Ann Williams (Sale) 2m 03.45s
1500 Metres:	Christine Cahill (Gateshead) 4m 12.54s
3000 Metres:	Yvonne Murray (Edinburgh) 8m 48.21s
100 Metres Hurdles:	Lesley-Ann Skeete (Swindon) 13.03s
400 Metres Hurdles:	Gowry Retchakan (Thurrock) 57.14s
5000 Metres Walk:	Betty Sworowski (Sheffield) 22m 23.25s
High Jump:	Lea Haggett (Croydon) 1.88m
Long Jump:	Fiona May (Derby) 6.66m
Shot:	Judy Oakes (Croydon) 18.63m
Discus:	Lisa-Marie Vizaniari (Aus) 57.22m
Javelin:	Tessa Sanderson (Hounslow) 58.42m

PEARL ASSURANCE UK CHAMPIONSHIPS

Cardiff, Jun 2-3
Men

100 Metres:	Linford Christie (Thames Valley) 10.13s
200 Metres:	Ade Mafe (London Irish) 21.13s
400 Metres:	Roger Black (Team Solent) 45.63s
800 Metres:	David Sharpe (Jarrow) 1m 51.46s
1500 Metres:	Neil Horsfield (Newport) 3m 48.39s
3000 Metres:	Geoff Turnbull (Valli) 8m 11.35s
5000 Metres:	Simon Mugglestone (Oxford University) 13m 34.70s
110 Metres Hurdles:	Colin Jackson (Cardiff) 13.10s
400 Metres Hurdles:	Kriss Akabusi (Team Solent) 51,50s
3000 Metres Chase:	Kenneth Penney (Haringey) 8m 50.90s
10,000 Metres Walk:	Ian McCombie (Cambridge) 41m 16.00s
High Jump:	Dalton Grant (Haringey) 2.25m
Long Jump:	Kevin Liddington (Birchfield) 7.62m
Triple Jump:	Francis Agyepong (Shaftesbury) 16.06m

Pole Vault:	Andrew Ashurst (Sale) 5.30m
Shot:	Paul Edwards (RAF) 18.57m
Discus:	Paul Mardle (Wolverhampton) 57.02m
Javelin:	Steve Backley (Cambridge) 88.46m
Hammer:	Paul Head (Newham) 71.64m

Women

100 Metres:	Sallyanne Short (Torfaen) 11.36s
200 Metres:	Phyllis Smith (Wolverhampton) 23.97s
400 Metres:	Diane Edwards (Sale) 54.32s
800 Metres:	Helen Thorpe (Cambridge) 2m 05.52s
1500 Metres:	Alison Wyeth (Parkside) 4m 20.40s
3000 Metres:	Andrea Wallace (Torbay) 9m 08.10s
100 Metres Hurdles:	Kay Morley (Cardiff) 13.16s
400 Metres Hurdles:	Claire Sugden (Stretford) 57.52s
5000 Metres Walk:	Betty Sworowski (Sheffield United) 22m 31.59s
High Jump:	Julia Bennett (Epsom) 1.84m
Long Jump:	Mary Berkeley (Shaftesbury) 6.17m
Triple Jump:	Michelle Griffith (Windsor) 12.94m
Shot:	Myrtle Augee (Bromley) 19.03m
Discus:	Jacqueline McKernan (Lisburn) 55.36m
Javelin:	Sharon Gibson (Notts) 58.32m

IAAF WORLD CROSS COUNTRY CHAMPIONSHIPS
Aix-les-Bains, France, Mar 24
Men- Individual
1 Khalid Skah (Mor) 34m 21s
2 Moses Tanui (Ken) 34m 21s
3 Julius Korir (Ken) 34m 22s
Men-Team
1 Kenya 42pts
2 Ethiopia 96pts
3 Spain 176pts
Women-Individual
1 Lynn Jennings (US) 19m 21s
2 Albertina Dias (Por) 19m 33s
3 Elena Romanova (USSR) 19m 33s
Women-Team
1 USSR 37pts
2 Ethiopia 75pts
3 Portugal 80pts

GRE BRITISH LEAGUE
Men
Division 1
1 Haringey 32pts
2 Birchfield 25pts
3 Belgrave 23.5pts

Division 2
1 Wolverhampton & Bilston 20pts
2 Woodford Green 20pts
3 Caledon Park 20pts
Division 3
1 Enfield 21pts
2 Cardiff 19pts
3 Sheffield 18pts
Division 4
1 Crawley 19pts (disqualified)
2 Hercules Wimbledon 17pts
3 Swansea 16pts
Division 5
1 London Irish 22pts
2 Croydon 19pts
3 GEC Avionics 14pts
Women
Division 1
1 Sale 18pts
2 Essex Ladies 13pts
3 Stretford 10pts
Division 2
1 Wigan 17pts
2 Glasgow 14pts
3 Shaftesbury Barnet 13pts
Division 3
1 City of Hull 18pts
2 Coventry 13.5pts
3 Notts 9.5pts
Division 4
1 Cardiff 16pts
2 Bromley 13pts
3 Wolverhampton & Bilston 12pts

GRE GOLD CUP (Men)
Birmingham, Aug 19
1 Haringey   122pts
2 Birchfield   111.5pts
3 Wolverhampton & Bilston   97.5pts
4 Belgrave   95pts
5 Shaftesbury Barnet   89.5pts
6 Thames Valley   81pts
7 Woodford Green   73pts
8 Newham & Essex   69.5pts

GRE JUBILEE CUP (Women)
Birmingham, Aug 19
1 Essex Ladies   105pts
2 Hounslow   77pts
3 Birchfield   73pts
4 Stretford   66.5pts
5 Croydon   64pts
6 Shaftesbury Barnet   59.5pts
7 Bromley   57pts
8 Sale   52pts

BOSTON MARATHON
Apr 16
Men
1 Gelindo Bordin (Ita) 2h 08m 19s
2 Juma Ikangaa (Tan) 2h 09m 52s
3 Rolando Vera (Ecu) 2h 10m 46s
Bordin was the first Olympic champion to win the race.
Women
1 Rosa Mota (Por) 2h 25m 24s
2 Uta Pippig (FRG) 2h 28m 03s
3 Maria Truhjillo (US) 2h 28m 53s
Mota was the first woman to win the race three times.

LONDON MARATHON
Apr 22
Men
1 Allister Hutton (GB) 2h 10m 10s
2 Salvatore Bettiol (Ita) 2h 10m 48s
3 Juan Romera (Spa) 2h 11m 04s
Women
1 Wanda Panfil (Pol) 2h 26m 31s
2 Frannie Larrieu-Smith (US) 2h 28m 01s
3 Lisa Weidenbach (US) 2h 28m 16s

EMSLEY CARR MILE
Gateshead, Aug 17
1 Peter Elliott (Eng) 3m 55.51s
2 Steve Crabb (Eng) 3m 56.28s
3 David Kibet (Ken) 3m 56.45s

EUROPEAN INDOOR CHAMPIONSHIPS
Glasgow, Mar 3-4
Men

60 metres:	Linford Christie (GB) 6.56s
200 metres:	Sandro Floris (Ita) 21.01s
400 metres:	Norbert Dobeleit (FRG) 46.08s
800 metres:	Tom McKean (GB) 1m 46.22s
1500 metres:	Jens-Peter Herold (GDR) 3m 44/39s
3000 metres:	Eric Dubus (Fra) 7m 53.94s
60 metres hurdles:	Igor Kazanov (USSR) 7.52s
5km walk:	Mikhail Schennikov (USSR) 19m 00.62s
High jump:	Artur Partyka (Pol) 2.33m
Long jump:	Dietmar Haaf (FRG) 8.11m
Triple jump:	Igor Lapshin (USSR) 17.14m
Pole vault:	Rodion Gataulin (USSR) 5.80m
Shot:	Klaus Bodenmüller (Aut) 21.03m

Women

60 metres:	Ulrike Sarvari (FRG) 7.10s
200 metres:	Ulrike Sarvari (FRG) 22.96s
400 metres:	Marina Shmonina (USSR) 51.22s
800 metres:	Lioubov Gurina (USSR) 2m 01.63s
1500 metres:	Doina Melinte (Rom) 4m 09.73s
3000 metres:	Elly van Hulst (Hol) 8m 57.28s
60 metres hurdles:	Lyudmila Narozhilenko (USSR) 7.74s
3km walk:	Beate Anders (GDR) 11m 59.36s
High jump:	Heike Henkel (FRG) 2.00m
Long jump:	Galina Chistiakova (USSR) 6.85m
Shot:	Claudia Losch (FRG) 20,64m
Triple Jump:+	Galina Chistiakova (USSR 14.14m

(+) Demonstration event only

> **❝❝I don't want to be remembered."**
> *Zola Pieterse, née Budd*
> **"The best thing about the revolution is that now I can keep all the money."**
> *Doina Melinte, Romanian runner*
> **"What's a nigger like you doing in an England tracksuit?"**
> *Policeman to Linford Christie*
> **"I've just got down to a good run once a day. I actually feel 20 times healthier than I did when I was racing and in supreme fitness. There is a difference between being fit and being healthy."**
> *Sebastian Coe, in retirement*
> **"Confidence isn't a problem for me. I haven't got any.❞❞**
> *Linda Keough, 400 metres runner*

CHAMPIONS

EUROPEAN CHAMPIONSHIPS

Year	Venue		Leading Gold Medal Winners	
1934	Turin	7 Germany	5 Finland	3 Holland
1938	Paris	12 Germany	5 Finland	4 Britain
1946	Oslo	11 Sweden	6 Soviet Union	4 Finland
1950	Brussels	8 Britain	6 Soviet Union	4 France, Holland
1954	Berne	16 Soviet Union	4 Czechoslovakia	4 Hungary
1958	Stockholm	11 Soviet Union	8 Poland	7 Britain
1962	Belgrade	13 Soviet Union	5 Britain	4 Germany
1966	Budapest	8 East Germany	7 Poland	6 Soviet Union
1969	Athens	11 East Germany	9 Soviet Union	6 Britain
1971	Helsinki	12 East Germany	9 Soviet Union	5 West Germany
1974	Rome	10 East Germany	9 Soviet Union	4 Finland, Poland, Britain
1978	Prague	13 Soviet Union	12 East Germany	4 Italy, West Germany
1982	Athens	12 East Germany	9 West Germany	6 Soviet Union
1986	Stuttgart	11 East Germany	11 Soviet Union	8 Britain
1990	Split	12 East Germany	9 Britain	6 Soviet Union

BRITISH CHAMPIONS

Men

1934 None
1938 (4)   Godfrey Brown (400m), Sydney Wooderson (1500m), Donald Finlay (110m hurdles), Harold Whitlock (50km walk)
1946 (2)   John Archer (100m), Sydney Wooderson (5000m)
1950 (6)   Brian Shenton (200m), Derek Pugh (400m), John Parlett (800m), Jack Holden (Marathon), 4x400m relay, Alan Paterson (high jump)
1954 (1)   Roger Bannister (1500m)
1958 (6)   John Wrighton (400m), Mike Rawson (800m), Brian Hewson (1500m), 4x400m relay, Arthur Rowe (shot), Stan Vickers (20km walk)
1962 (4)   Robbie Brightwell (400m), Bruce Tulloh (500m), Brian Kilby (Marathon), Ken Matthews (20km walk)
1966 (2)   Jim Hogan (Marathon), Lynn Davies (long jump)
1969 (4)   John Whetton (1500m), Ian Stewart (5000m), Ron Hill (Marathon), Paul Nihill (20km walk)
1971 (1)   David Jenkins (400m)
1974 (4)   Brendan Foster (5000m), Ian Thompson (Marathon), Alan Pascoe (400m hurdles), 4x400m relay
1978 (1)   Steve Ovett (1500m)
1982 (3)   Steve Cram (1500m), Keith Connor (triple jump), Daley Thompson (decathlon)
1986 (7)   Linford Christie (100m), Roger Black (400m), Sebastian Coe (800m), Steve Cram (1500m), Daley Thompson (decathlon), Jack Buckner (5000m), 4x400m relay
1990 (8)   Linford Christie (100m), John Regis (200m), Roger Black (400m), Tom McKean (800m), Colin Jackson (110m hurdles), Kriss Akabusi (400m hurdles), 4x400m relay, Steve Backley (javelin)

Women

1938 None
1946 None
1950 (2)   4x100m relay, Sheila Alexander (high jump)
1954 (2)   Thelma Hopkins (high jump), Jean Desforges (long jump)
1958 (1)   Heather Young (100m)
1962 (1)   Dorothy Hyman (100m)
1966 None
1969 (2)   Lillian Board (800m), 4x400m relay
1971 None
1974 None
1978 None
1982 None
1986 (1)   Fatima Whitbread (javelin)
1990 (1)   Yvonne Murray (3000m)

The Gold Medal Winners

121 Soviet Union	15 Czechoslovakia
88 East Germany	14 Holland
63 Britain	12 Hungary
31 Germany (1934-62), Poland	10 Finland
28 France	7 Bulgaria
27 Italy	6 Yugoslavia
26 West Germany	3 Norway, Switzerland, Romania, Iceland
20 Sweden	2 Portugal, Spain, Denmark, Belgium, Austria, Estonia
17 Finland	1 Greece, Latvia

SEBASTIAN COE'S CAREER

1971	Yorkshire Colts Cross Country champion
1973	AAA Youth 1500m champion
	English Schools Intermediate 3000m champion
1975	AAA Junior 1500m champion
1977	European Indoor 800m champion
1978	AAA Indoor 3000m champion
	European Championship, bronze 800m
1979	European Cup 800m winner
	World Record (800m): 1m 42.33s (Oslo)
	World Record (Mile): 3m 49.00s (Oslo)
	World Record (1500m): 3m 32.10s (Zurich)
1980	Olympic Games, gold 1500m, silver 800m
	World Record (1000m): 2m 13.40s (Oslo)
1981	AAA Indoor 3000m champion
	AAA 800m champion
	European Cup 800m winner
	World Cup 800m winner
	World Record (800m): 1m 41.73s (Florence)

World Record (1000m): 2m 12.18s (Oslo)
World Record (Mile): 3m 48.53s (Zurich)
World Record (Mile): 3m 47.33s (Brussels)
World Indoor Record (800m): 1m 46.00s (Cosford)

1982	European Championship, silver 800m
	World Record (4x800m relay): 7m 03.89s (London)
	Awarded MBE
1983	World Indoor Record (800m): 1m 44.91s (Cosford)
	World Indoor Record (1000m): 2m 18.58s (Oslo)
1984	Olympic Games, gold 1500m, silver 800m
1986	European Championship, gold 800m, silver 1500m
1989	AAA 1500m champion
1990	Awarded OBE
1991/2	Conservative MP??

OLYMPIC GAMES
Men
100 Metres

1896	Thomas Burke (US) 12.0s
1900	Francis Jarvis (US) 11.0s
1904	Archie Hahn (US) 11.0s
1908	Reginald Walker (SA) 10.8s
1912	Ralph Craig (US) 10.8s
1920	Charles Paddock (US) 10.8s
1924	Harold Abrahams (GB) 10.6s
1928	Percy Williams (Can) 10.8s
1932	Eddie Tolan (US) 10.38s
1936	Jesse Owens (US) 10.3s
1948	Harrison Dillard (US) 10.3s
1952	Lindy Remigino (US) 10.79s
1956	Bobby Morrow (US) 10.62s
1960	Armin Hary (FRG) 10.32s
1964	Robert Hayes (US) 10.06s
1968	James Hines (US) 9.95s
1972	Valeriy Borzov (USSR) 10.14s
1976	Hasely Crawford (Tri) 10.06s
1980	Allan Wells (GB) 10.25s
1984	Carl Lewis (US) 9.99s
1988	Carl Lewis (US) 9.92s

200 Metres

1900	Walter Tewksbury (US) 22.2s
1904	Archie Hahn (US) 21.6s
1908	Robert Kerr (Can) 22.6s
1912	Ralph Craig (US) 21.7s
1920	Allen Woodring (US) 22.0s
1924	Jackson Scholz (US) 21.6s
1928	Percy Williams (Can) 21.8s
1932	Eddie Tolan (US) 21.12s
1936	Jesse Owens (US) 20.7s
1948	Melvin Patton (US) 21.1s
1952	Andrew Stanfield (US) 20.81s
1956	Bobby Morrow (US) 20.75s
1960	Livio Berrutti (Ita) 20.62s
1964	Henry Carr (US) 20.36s
1968	Tommie Smith (US) 19.83s
1972	Valeriy Borzov (USSR) 20.00s
1976	Donald Quarrie (Jam) 20.22s
1980	Pietro Mennea (Ita) 20.19s
1984	Carl Lewis (US) 19.80s
1988	Joe DeLoach (US) 19.75s

400 Metres

1896	Thomas Burke (US) 54.2s
1900	Maxie Long (US) 49.4s
1904	Harry Hillman (US) 49.2s
1908	Wyndham Halswelle (GB) 50.0s
1912	Charles Reidpath (US) 48.2s
1920	Bevil Rudd (SA) 49.6s
1924	Eric Liddell (GB) 47.6s
1928	Ray Barbuti (US) 47.8s
1932	Bill Carr (US) 46.28s
1936	Archie Williams (US) 46.66s
1948	Arthur Wint (Jam) 46.2s
1952	George Rhoden (Jam) 46.09s
1956	Charles Jenkins (US) 46.86s
1960	Otis Davis (US) 45.07s
1964	Michael Larrabee (US) 45.15s
1968	Lee Evans (US) 43.86s
1972	Vincent Matthews (US) 44.66s
1976	Alberto Juantorena (Cub) 44.26s
1980	Viktor Markin (USSR) 44.60s
1984	Alonzo Babers (US) 44.27s
1988	Steve Lewis (US) 43.87s

800 Metres

1896	Edwin Flack (Aus) 2m 11.0s
1900	Alfred Tysoe (GB) 2m 01.2s
1904	James Lightbody (US) 1m 56.0s
1908	Mel Sheppard (US) 1m 52.8s
1912	James Meredith (US) 1m 51.9s
1920	Albert Hill (GB) 1m 53.4s
1924	Douglas Lowe (GB) 1m 52.4s
1928	Douglas Lowe (GB) 1m 51.8s
1932	Tom Hampson (GB) 1m 49.70s
1936	John Woodruff (US) 1m 52.9s
1948	Malvin Whitfield (US) 1m 49.2s
1952	Malvin Whitfield (US) 1m 49.34s
1956	Thomas Courtney (US) 1m 47.75s
1960	Peter Snell (NZ) 1m 46.48s
1964	Peter Snell (NZ) 1m 45.1s
1968	Ralph Doubell (Aus) 1m 44.40s
1972	David Wottle (US) 1m 45.86s
1976	Alberto Juantorena (Cub) 1m 43.50s
1980	Steve Ovett (GB) 1m 45.40s
1984	Joaquim Cruz (Bra) 1m 43.00s
1988	Paul Ereng (Ken) 1m 44.06s

1500 Metres

1896	Edwin Flack (Aus) 4m 33.2s
1900	Charles Bennett (GB) 4m 06.2s
1904	James Lightbody (US) 4m 05.4s
1908	Mel Sheppard (US) 4m 03.4s
1912	Arnold Jackson (GB) 3m 56.8s
1920	Albert Hill (GB) 4m 01.8s
1924	Paavo Nurmi (Fin) 3m 53.6s
1928	Harri Larva (Fin) 3m 53.2s
1932	Luigi Beccali (Ita) 3m 51.20s
1936	Jack Lovelock (NZ) 3m 47.8s
1948	Henry Eriksson (Swe) 3m 49.8s
1952	Josef Barthel (Lux) 3m 45.28s
1956	Ron Delany (Ire) 3m 41.49s
1960	Herbert Elliott (Aus) 3m 35.6s
1964	Peter Snell (NZ) 3m 38.1s
1968	Kipchoge Keino (Ken) 3m 34.91s
1972	Pekka Vasala (Fin) 3m 36.33s
1976	John Walker (NZ) 3m 39.17s
1980	Sebastian Coe (GB) 3m 38.40s
1984	Sebastian Coe (GB) 3m 32.53s
1988	Peter Rono (Ken) 3m 36.21s

5000 Metres

1912	Hannes Kolehmainen (Fin) 14m 36.6s
1920	Joseph Guillemot (Fra) 14m 55.6s
1924	Paavo Nurmi (Fin) 14m 31.2s
1928	Ville Ritola (Fin) 14m 38.0s
1932	Lauri Lehtinen (Fin) 14m 30.0s
1936	Gunnar Hockert (Fin) 14m 22.2s
1948	Gaston Reiff (Bel) 14m 17.6s
1952	Emil Zatopek (Cze) 14m 06.72s
1956	Vladimir Kuts (USSR) 13m 39.86s
1960	Murray Halberg (NZ) 13m 43.4s
1964	Robert Schul (US) 13m 48.8s
1968	Mohamed Gammoudi (Tun) 14m 05.0s
1972	Lasse Viren (Fin) 13m 26.42s
1976	Lasse Viren (Fin) 13m 24.76s
1980	Miruts Yifter (Eth) 13m 20.91s
1984	Said Aouita (Mor) 13m 05.59s
1988	John Ngugi (Ken) 13m 11.70s

10,000 Metres

1912	Hannes Kolehmainen (Fin) 31m 20.8s
1920	Paavo Nurmi (Fin) 31m 45.8s
1924	Ville Ritola (Fin) 30m 23.2s
1928	Paavo Nurmi (Fin) 30m 18.8s
1932	Janusz Kushocinski (Pol) 30m 11.4s
1936	Ilmari Salminen (Fin) 30m 15.4s
1948	Emil Zatopek (Cze) 29m 59.6s
1952	Emil Zatopek (Cze) 29m 17.0s
1956	Vladimir Kuts (USSR) 28m 45.60s
1960	Pyotr Bolotnikov (USSR) 28m 32.18s
1964	William Mills (US) 28m 24.4s
1968	Naftali Temu (Ken) 29m 27.4s
1972	Lasse Viren (Fin) 27m 38.35s
1976	Lasse Viren (Fin) 27m 40.38s
1980	Miruts Yifter (Eth) 27m 42.69s
1984	Alberto Cova (Ita) 27m 47.54s
1988	Moulay Brahim Boutaib (Mor) 27m 21.46s

Marathon

1896	Spyridon Louis (Gre) 2h 58m 50.0s
1900	Michel Theato (Fra) 2h 59m 45.0s
1904	Thomas Hicks (US) 3h 28m 35.0s
1908	John Hayes (US) 2h 55m 18.4s
1912	Kenneth McArthur (SA) 2h 36m 54.8s
1920	Hannes Kolehmainen (Fin) 2h 32m 35.8s
1924	Albin Stenroos (Fin) 2h 41m 22.6s
1928	Mohamed El Ouafi (Fra) 2h 32m 57.0s
1932	Juan Zabala (Arg) 2h 31m 36.0s
1936	Kitei Son (Jap) 2h 29m 19.2s
1948	Delfo Cabrera (Arg) 2h 34m 51.6s
1952	Emil Zatopek (Cze) 2h 23m 03.2s
1956	Alain Mimoun (Fra) 2h 25m 00.0s
1960	Abebe Bikila (Eth) 2h 15m 16.2s
1964	Abebe Bikila (Eth) 2h 12m 11.2s
1968	Mamo Wolde (Eth) 2h 20m 26.4s
1972	Frank Shorter (US) 2h 12m 19.8s
1976	Waldemar Cierpinski (GDR) 2h 09m 55s
1980	Waldemar Cierpinski (GDR) 2h 11m 03s
1984	Carlos Lopes (Por) 2h 09m 21s
1988	Gelindo Bordin (Ita) 2h 10m 32s

110 Metres Hurdles

1896	Thomas Curtis (US) 17.6s
1900	Alvin Kraenzlein (US) 15.4s
1904	Fred Schule (US) 16.0s
1908	Forrest Smithson (US) 15.0s
1912	Fred Kelly (US) 15.1s
1920	Earl Thomson (Can) 14.8s
1924	Daniel Kinsey (US) 15.0s
1928	Sydney Atkinson (SA) 14.8s
1932	George Saling (US) 14.56s
1936	Forrest Towns (US) 14.2s
1948	William Porter (US) 13.9s
1952	Harrison Dillard (US) 13.91s
1956	Lee Calhoun (US) 13.70s
1960	Lee Calhoun (US) 13.98s
1964	Hayes Jones (US) 13.67s
1968	Willie Davenport (US) 13.33s
1972	Rodney Milburn (US) 13.24s
1976	Guy Drut (Fra) 13.30s
1980	Thomas Munkelt (GDR) 13.39s
1984	Roger Kingdom (US) 13.20s
1988	Roger Kingdom (US) 12.98s

400 Metres Hurdles

1900	Walter Tewksbury (US) 57.6s
1904	Harry Hillman (US) 53.0s
1908	Charles Bacon (US) 55.0s
1920	Frank Loomis (US) 54.0s
1924	Morgan Taylor (US) 52.6s
1928	Lord Burghley (GB) 53.4s
1932	Robert Tisdall (Ire) 51.67s
1936	Glenn Hardin (US) 52.4s
1948	Roy Cochran (US) 51.1s
1952	Charles Moore (US) 51.06s
1956	Glenn Davis (US) 50.29s
1960	Glenn Davis (US) 49.51s
1964	Rex Cawley (US) 49.69s
1968	David Hemery (GB) 48.12s
1972	John Akii-Bua (Uga) 47.82s
1976	Edwin Moses (US) 47.63s
1980	Volker Beck (GDR) 48.70s
1984	Edwin Moses (US) 47.75s
1988	Andre Phillips (US) 47.19s

3000 Metres Steeplechase

1920	Percy Hodge (GB) 10m 00.4s
1924	Ville Ritola (Fin) 9m 33.6s
1928	Toivo Loukola (Fin) 9m 21.8s
1932	Volmari Iso-Hollo (Fin) 10m 33.4s*
1936	Volmari Iso-Hollo (Fin) 9m 03.8s
1948	Tore Sjöstrand (Swe) 9m 04.6s
1952	Horace Ashenfelter (US) 8m 45.68s
1956	Christopher Brasher (GB) 8m 41.35s
1960	Zdzislaw Kryszkowiak (Pol) 8m 34.31s
1964	Gaston Roelants (Bel) 8m 30.8s
1968	Amos Biwott (Ken) 8m 51.0s
1972	Kipchoge Keino (Ken) 8m 23.64s
1976	Anders Gärderud (Swe) 8m 08.02s
1980	Bronislaw Malinowski (Pol) 8m 09.70s
1984	Julius Korir (Ken) 8m 11.80s
1988	Julius Kariuki (Ken) 8m 05.51s

Competitors ran an extra lap in error.

20,000 Metres Walk
1956 Leonid Spirin (USSR) 1h 31m 27.4s
1960 Vladimir Golubnichiy (USSR) 1h 34m 07.2s
1964 Kenneth Matthews (GB) 1h 29m 34.0s
1968 Vladimir Golubnichiy (USSR) 1h 33m 58.4s
1972 Peter Frenkel (GDR) 1h 26m 42.4s
1976 Daniel Bautista (Mex) 1h 24m 40.6s
1980 Maurizio Damilano (Ita) 1h 23m 35.5s
1984 Ernesto Canto (Mex) 1h 23m 13s
1988 Jozef Pribilinec (Cze) 1h 19m 57s

50,000 Metres Walk
1932 Thomas Green (GB) 4h 50m 10.0s
1936 Harold Whitlock (GB) 4h 30m 41.1s
1948 John Ljunggren (Swe) 4h 41m 52.0s
1952 Giuseppe Dordoni (Ita) 4h 28m 07.8s
1956 Norman Read (NZ) 4h 30m 42.8s
1960 Don Thompson (GB) 4h 25m 30.0s
1964 Abdon Pamich (Ita) 4h 11m 12.4s
1968 Christophe Höhne (GDR) 4h 20m 13.6s
1972 Bernd Kannenberg (GDR) 3h 56m 11.6s
1980 Hartwig Gauder (GDR) 3h 49m 24s
1984 Raul Gonzales (Mex) 3h 47m 26s
1988 Viacheslav Ivanenko (USSR) 3h 38m 29s

4 x 100 Metres Relay
1912 Great Britain 42.4s
1920 United States 42.2s
1924 United States 41.0s
1928 United States 41.0s
1932 United States 40.0s
1936 United States 39.8s
1948 United States 40.6s
1952 United States 40.26s
1956 United States 39.59s
1960 West Germany 39.66s
1964 United States 39.06s
1968 United States 38.23s
1972 United States 38.19s
1976 United States 38.83s
1980 USSR 38.26s
1984 United States 37.83s
1988 USSR 38.19s

4 x 400 Metres Relay
1912 United States 3m 16.6s
1920 Great Britain 3m 22.2s
1924 United States 3m 16.0s
1928 United States 3m 14.2s
1932 United States 3m 08.2s
1936 Great Britain 3m 09.0s
1948 United States 3m 10.4s
1952 Jamaica 3m 04.04s
1956 United States 3m 04.80s
1960 United States 3m 02.37s
1964 United States 3m 00.71s
1968 United States 2m 56.16s
1972 Kenya 2m 59.83s
1976 United States 2m 58.66s
1980 USSR 3m 01.08s
1984 United States 2m 57.91s
1988 United States 2m 56.16s

High Jump
1896 Ellery Clark (US) 1.81m
1900 Irving Baxter (US) 1.90m
1904 Samuel Jones (US) 1.80m
1908 Harry Porter (US) 1.90m
1912 Alma Richards (US) 1.93m
1920 Richard Landon (US) 1.94m
1924 Harold Osborn (US) 1.98m
1928 Robert King (US) 1.94m
1932 Duncan McNaughton (Can) 1.97m

1936 Cornelius Johnson (US) 2.03m
1948 John Winter (Aus) 1.98m
1952 Walter Davis (US) 2.04m
1956 Charles Dumas (US) 2.12m
1960 Robert Shavlakadze (USSR) 2.16m
1964 Valeriy Brumel (USSR) 2.18m
1968 Dick Fosbury (US) 2.24m
1972 Yuriy Tarmak (USSR) 2.23m
1976 Jacek Wszola (Pol) 2.25m
1980 Gerd Wessig (GDR) 2.36m
1984 Dietmar Mögenburg (FRG) 2.35m
1988 Gennady Avdeyenko (USSR) 2.38m

Pole Vault
1896 William Hoyt (US) 3.30m
1900 Irving Baxter (US) 3.30m
1904 Charles Dvorak (US) 3.50m
1908 Edward Cooke & Alfred Gilbert (US) 3.71m
1912 Harry Babcock (US) 3.95m
1920 Frank Foss (US) 4.09m
1924 Lee Barnes (US) 3.95m
1928 Sabin Carr (US) 4.20m
1932 Bill Miller (US) 4.31m
1936 Earle Meadows (US) 4.35m
1948 Guinn Smith (US) 4.30m
1952 Robert Richards (US) 4.55m
1956 Robert Richards (US) 4.56m
1960 Dinald Bragg (US) 4.70m
1964 Frederick Hansen (US) 5.10m
1968 Bob Seagren (US) 5.40m
1972 Wolfgang Nordwig (GDR) 5.50m
1976 Tadeusz Slusarski (Pol) 5.50m
1980 Wladyslaw Kozakiewicz (Pol) 5.78m
1984 Pierre Quinon (Fra) 5.75m
1988 Sergey Bubka (USSR) 5.90m

Long Jump
1896 Ellery Clark (US) 6.35m
1900 Alvin Kraenzlein (US) 7.18m
1904 Myer Prinstein (US) 7.34m
1908 Francis Irons (US) 7.48m
1912 Albert Gutterson (US) 7.60m
1920 William Pettersson (Swe) 7.15m
1924 William De Hart Hubbard (US) 7.44m
1928 Edward Hamm (US) 7.73m
1932 Edward Gordon (US) 7.64m
1936 Jesse Owens (US) 8.06m
1948 William Steele (US) 7.82m
1952 Jerome Biffle (US) 7.57m
1956 Gregory Bell (US) 7.83m
1960 Ralph Boston (US) 8.12m
1964 Lynn Davies (GB) 8.07m
1968 Bob Beamon (US) 8.90m
1972 Randy Williams (US) 8.24m
1976 Arnie Robinson (US) 8.35m
1980 Lutz Dombrowski (GDR) 8.54m
1984 Carl Lewis (US) 8.54m
1988 Carl Lewis (US) 8.72m

Triple Jump
1896 James Connolly (US) 13.71m
1900 Myer Prinstein (US) 14.47m
1904 Myer Prinstein (US) 14.35m
1908 Tim Ahearne (GB) 14.91m
1912 Gustaf Lindblom (Swe) 14.76m
1920 Vilho Tuulos (Fin) 14.50m
1924 Anthony Winter (Aus) 15.52m
1928 Mikio Oda (Jap) 15.21m
1932 Chuhei Nambu (Jap) 15.72m
1936 Naoto Tajima (Jap) 16.00m
1948 Arne Ahman (Swe) 15.40m
1952 Adhemar Ferreira da Silva (Bra) 16.22m
1956 Adhemar Ferreira da Silva (Bra) 16.35m

1960	Jozef Schmidt (Pol) 16.81m
1964	Jozef Schmidt (Pol) 16.85m
1968	Viktor Saneyev (USSR) 17.39m
1972	Viktor Saneyev (USSR) 17.35m
1976	Viktor Saneyev (USSR) 17.29m
1980	Jaak Uudmae (USSR) 17.35m
1984	Al Joyner (US) 17.26m
1988	Hristo Markov (Bul) 17.61m

Shot

1896	Robert Garrett (US) 11.22m
1900	Richard Sheldon (US) 14.10m
1904	Ralph Rose (US) 14.80m
1908	Ralph Rose (US) 14.21m
1912	Patrick McDonald (US) 15.34m
1920	Ville Porhola (Fin) 14.81m
1924	Clarence Houser (US) 14.99m
1928	John Kuck (US) 15.87m
1932	Leo Sexton (US) 16.00m
1936	Hans Woellke (Ger) 16.20m
1948	Wilbur Thompson (US) 17.12m
1952	Parry O'Brien (US) 17.41m
1956	Parry O'Brien (US) 18.57m
1960	William Nieder (US) 19.68m
1964	Dallas Long (US) 20.33m
1968	Randy Matson (US) 20.54m
1972	Wladyslaw Komar (Pol) 21.18m
1976	Udo Beyer (GDR) 21.05m
1980	Vladimir Kiselyov (USSR) 21.35m
1984	Alessandro Andrei (Ita) 21.26m
1988	Ulf Timmermann (GDR) 22.47m

Discus

1896	Robert Garrett (US) 29.15m
1900	Rudolf Bauer (Hun) 36.04m
1904	Martin Sheridan (US) 39.28m
1908	Martin Sheridan (US) 40.89m
1912	Armas Taipale (Fin) 45.21m
1920	Elmer Niklander (Fin) 44.68m
1924	Clarence Houser (US) 46.15m
1928	Clarence Houser (US) 47.32m
1932	John Anderson (US) 49.49m
1936	Ken Carpenter (US) 50.48m
1948	Adolfo Consolini (Ita) 52.78m
1952	Sim Iness (US) 55.03m
1956	Al Oerter (US) 56.36m
1960	Al Oerter (US) 59.18m
1964	Al Oerter (US) 61.00m
1968	Al Oerter (US) 64.78m
1972	Ludvik Danek (Cze) 64.40m
1976	Mac Wilkins (US) 67.50m
1980	Viktor Rashchupkin (USSR) 66.64m
1984	Rolf Danneberg (FRG) 66.60m
1988	Jürgen Schult (GDR) 68.82m

Javelin

1908	Erik Lemming (Swe) 54.82m
1912	Erik Lemming (Swe) 60.64m
1920	Jonni Myyrä (Fin) 65.78m
1924	Jonni Myyrä (Fin) 62.96m
1928	Erik Lundkvist (Swe) 66.60m
1932	Matti Järvinen (Fin) 72.71m
1936	Gerhard Stöck (Ger) 71.84m
1948	Tapio Rautavaara (Fin) 69.77m
1952	Cyrus Young (US) 73.78m
1956	Egil Danielsen (Nor) 85.71
1960	Viktor Tsibulenko (USSR) 84.64m
1964	Pauli Nevala (Fin) 82.66m
1968	Janis Lusis (USSR) 90.10m
1972	Klaus Wolfermann (FRG) 90.48m
1976	Miklos Nemeth (Hun) 94.58m
1980	Dainis Kula (USSR) 91.20m

1984	Arto Harkönen (Fin) 86.76m
1988	Tapio Korjus (Fin) 84.28m

Hammer

1900	John Flanagan (US) 49.73m
1904	John Flanagan (US) 51.23m
1908	John Flanagan (US) 51.92m
1912	Matt McGrath (US) 54.74m
1920	Patrick Ryan (US) 52.87m
1924	Fred Tootell (US) 53.29m
1928	Patrick O'Callaghan (Ire) 51.39m
1932	Patrick O'Callaghan (Ire) 53.92m
1936	Karl Hein (Ger) 56.49m
1948	Imre Nemeth (Hun) 56.07m
1952	Jozsef Csermak (Hun) 60.34m
1956	Harold Connolly (US) 63.19m
1960	Vasiliy Rudenkov (USSR) 67.10m
1964	Romuald Klim (USSR) 69.74m
1968	Gyula Zsivotzky (Hun) 73.36m
1972	Anatoliy Bondarchuk (USSR) 75.50m
1976	Yuriy Sedykh (USSR) 77.52m
1980	Yuriy Sedykh (USSR) 81.80m
1984	Juha Tiainen (Fin) 78.08m
1988	Sergey Litvinov (USSR) 84.80m

Decathlon

Points converted to 1984 tables.

1904	Thomas Kiely (Ire) 6036pts
1912	Jim Thorpe (US) 6564pts†
1920	Helge Løvland (Nor) 5804pts
1924	Harold Osborn (US) 6476pts
1928	Paavo Yrjola (Fin) 6607pts
1932	James Bausch (US) 6735pts
1936	Glenn Morris (US) 7254pts
1948	Robert Mathias (US) 6628pts
1952	Robert Mathias (US) 7580pts
1956	Milton Campbell (US) 7565 pts
1960	Rafer Johnson (US) 7901pts
1964	Willi Holdorf (FRG) 7726pts est
1968	Bill Toomey (US) 8158pts
1972	Nikolai Avilov (USSR) 8466pts
1976	Bruce Jenner (US) 8634pts
1980	Daley Thompson (GB) 8522pts
1984	Daley Thompson (GB) 8847pts
1988	Christian Schenk (GDR) 8488pts

† *Thorpe disqualified for professionalism, and gold medal awarded to Hugo Weislander (Swe). Thorpe was posthumously re-instated in 1982.*

Women

100 Metres

1928	Elizabeth Robinson (US) 12.2s
1932	Stanislawa Walasiewicz (Pol) 11.9s
1936	Helen Stephens (US) 11.5s
1948	Fanny Blankers-Koen (Hol) 11.9s
1952	Marjorie Jackson (Aus) 11.65s
1956	Betty Cuthbert (Aus) 11.82s
1960	Wilma Rudolph (US) 11.08s
1964	Wyomia Tyus (US) 11.49s
1968	Wyomia Tyus (US) 11.08s
1972	Renate Stecher (GDR) 11.07s
1976	Annegret Richter (FRG) 11.08s
1980	Lyudmila Kondratyeva (USSR) 11.06s
1984	Evelyn Ashford (US) 10.97s
1988	Florence Griffith-Joyner (US) 10.54s

200 Metres

1948	Fanny Blankers-Koen (Hol) 24.4s
1952	Marjorie Jackson (Aus) 23.89s
1956	Betty Cuthbert (Aus) 23.55s
1960	Wilma Rudoph (US) 24.03s
1964	Edith Maguire (US) 23.05s
1968	Irena Szewinska (Pol) 22.58s

1972	Renate Stecher (GDR) 22.40s
1976	Barbel Eckert (GDR) 22.37s
1980	Barbel Wockel (née Eckert) (GDR) 22.03s
1984	Valerie Brisco-Hooks (US) 21.81s
1988	Florence Griffith-Joyner (US) 21.34s

400 Metres
1964	Betty Cuthbert (Aus) 52.01s
1968	Colette Besson (Fra) 52.03s
1972	Monika Zehrt (GDR) 51.08s
1976	Irena Szewinska (Pol) 49.29s
1980	Marita Koch (GDR) 48.88s
1984	Valerie Brisco-Hooks (US) 48.83s
1988	Olga Bryzgina (USSR) 48.65s

800 Metres
1928	Lina Radke (Ger) 2m 16.8s
1960	Lyudmila Shevtsova (USSR) 2m 04.50s
1964	Ann Packer (GB) 2m 01.1s
1968	Madeline Manning (US) 2m 00.92s
1972	Hildegard Falck (FRG) 1m 58.55s
1976	Tatyana Kazankina (USSR) 1m 54.94s
1980	Nadezhda Olizarenko (USSR) 1m 53.43s
1984	Doina Melinte (Rom) 1m 57.60s
1988	Sigrun Wodars (GDR) 1m 56.10s

1500 Metres
1972	Lyudmila Bragina (USSR) 4m 01.38s
1976	Tatyana Kazankina (USSR) 4m 05.48s
1980	Tatyana Kazankina (USSR) 3m 56.56s
1984	Gabriella Doria (Ita) 4m 03.25s
1988	Paula Ivan (Rom) 3m 53.96s

3000 Metres
| 1984 | Maricica Puica (Rom) 8m 35.96s |
| 1988 | Tatyana Samolenko (USSR) 8m 26.53s |

10,000 Metres
| 1988 | Olga Bondarenko (USSR) 31m 05.21s |

Marathon
| 1984 | Joan Benoit (US) 2h 24m 52s |
| 1988 | Rosa Mota (Por) 2h 25m 40s |

100 Metres Hurdles
(80 metres 1936-68)
1932	Mildred Didrikson (US) 11.7s
1936	Trebisonda Valla (Ita) 11.74s
1948	Fanny Blankers-Koen (Hol) 11.2s
1952	Shirley Strickland (Aus) 11.03s
1956	Shirley Strickland (Aus) 10.96s
1960	Irina Press (USSR) 10.94s
1964	Karin Balzar (GDR) 10.54s
1968	Maureen Caird (Aus) 10.39s
1972	Annelie Ehrhardt (GDR) 12.59s
1976	Johanna Schaller (GDR) 12.77s
1980	Vera Komisova (USSR) 12.56s
1984	Benita Fitzgerald-Brown (US) 12.84s
1988	Jordanka Donkova (Bul) 12.38s

400 Metres Hurdles
| 1984 | Nawal el Moutawakil (Mor) 54.61s |
| 1988 | Debbie Flintoff-King (Aus) 53.17s |

4 x 100 Metres Relay
1928	Canada 48.4s
1932	United States 47.0s
1936	United States 46.9s
1948	Netherlands 47.5s
1952	United States 46.14s
1956	Australia 44.65s
1960	United States 44.72s
1964	Poland 43.69s
1968	United States 42.87s
1972	West Germany 42.81s
1976	East Germany 42.55s
1980	East Germany 41.60s

| 1984 | United States 41.65s |
| 1988 | United States 41.98s |

4 x 400 Metres Relay
1972	East Germany 3m 22.95s
1976	East Germany 3m 19.23s
1980	USSR 3m 20.12s
1984	United States 3m 18.29s
1988	USSR 3m 15.18s

High Jump
1928	Ethel Catherwood (Can) 1.59m
1932	Jean Shiley (US) 1.65m
1936	Ibolya Csak (Hun) 1.60m
1948	Alice Coachman (US) 1.68m
1952	Esther Brand (SA) 1.67m
1956	Mildred McDaniel (US) 1.76m
1960	Iolanda Balas (Rom) 1.85m
1964	Iolanda Balas (Rom) 1.90m
1968	Miloslava Rezkova (Cze) 1.82m
1972	Ulrike Meyfarth (FRG) 1.92m
1976	Rosi Ackermann (GDR) 1.93m
1980	Sara Simeoni (Ita) 1.97m
1984	Ulrike Meyfarth (FRG) 2.02m
1988	Louise Ritter (US) 2.03m

Long Jump
1948	Olga Gyarmati (Hun) 5.69m
1952	Yvette Williams (NZ) 6.24m
1956	Elzbieta Krzesinska (Pol) 6.35m
1960	Vyera Krepkina (USSR) 6.37m
1964	Mary Rand (GB) 6.76m
1968	Viorica Viscopoleanu (Rom) 6.82m
1972	Heide Rosendahl (FRG) 6.78m
1976	Angela Voigt (GDR) 6.72m
1980	Tatyana Kolpakova (USSR) 7.06m
1984	Anisora Stanciu (Rom) 6.96m
1988	Jackie Joyner-Kersee (US) 7.40m

Shot
1948	Micheline Ostermeyer (Fra) 13.75m
1952	Galina Zybina (USSR) 15.28m
1956	Tamara Tishkyevich (USSR) 16.59m
1960	Tamara Press (USSR) 17.32m
1964	Tamara Press (USSR) 18.14m
1968	Margitta Gummel (GDR) 19.61m
1972	Nadezhda Chizhova (USSR) 21.03m
1976	Ivanka Khristova (Bul) 21.16m
1980	Ilona Slupianek (GDR) 22.41m
1984	Claudia Losch (FRG) 20.48m
1988	Natalya Lisovskaya (USSR) 22.24m

Discus
1928	Helena Konopacka (Pol) 39.62m
1932	Lillian Copeland (US) 40.58m
1936	Gisela Mauermayer (Ger) 47.63m
1948	Micheline Ostermeyer (Fra) 41.92m
1952	Nina Ponomaryeva (USSR) 51.42m
1956	Olga Fikotova (Cze) 53.69m
1960	Nina Ponomaryeva (USSR) 55.10m
1964	Tamara Press (USSR) 57.27m
1968	Lia Manoliu (Rom) 58.28m
1972	Faina Melnik (USSR) 66.62m
1976	Evelin Schlaak (GDR) 69.00m
1980	Evelin Jahl (née Schlaak) (GDR) 69.96m
1984	Ria Stalmach (Hol) 65.36m
1988	Martina Hellman (GDR) 72.30m

Javelin
1932	Mildred Didrikson (US) 43.68m
1936	Tilly Fleischer (Ger) 45.18m
1948	Herma Bauma (Aut) 45.57m
1952	Dana Zatopkova (Cze) 50.47m
1956	Inese Jaunzeme (USSR) 53.86m
1960	Elvira Ozolina (USSR) 55.98m

1964	Mihaela Penes (Rom) 60.54m
1968	Angela Nemeth (Hun) 60.36m
1972	Ruth Fuchs (GDR) 63.88m
1976	Ruth Fuchs (GDR) 65.94m
1980	Maria Colon (Cub) 68.40m
1984	Tessa Sanderson (GB) 69.56m
1988	Petra Felke (GDR) 74.68m

Pentathlon
1964	Irina Press (USSR) 5246pts
1968	Ingrid Becker (FRG) 5098pts
1972	Mary Peters (GB) 4801pts
1976	Sigrun Siegl (GDR) 4745pts
1980	Nadezhda Tkachenko (USSR) 5083pts

Heptathlon
| 1984 | Glynis Nunn (Aus) 6390pts |
| 1988 | Jackie Joyner-Kersee (US) 7291pts |

WORLD CHAMPIONSHIPS
Inaugurated 1983

Men	1983, Helsinki	1987, Rome
100m:	Carl Lewis (US) 10.07s	Ben Johnson (Can) 9.83s
200m:	Calvin Smith (US) 20.14s	Calvin Smith (US) 20.16s
400m:	Bert Cameron (Jam) 43.05s	Thomas Schoenlebe (GDR) 44.33s
800m:	Willi Wullbeck (FRG) 1m 43.65s	Billy Konchellah (Ken) 1m 43.06s
1500m:	Steve Cram (GB) 3m 41.59s	Abdi Bile (Som) 3m 36.80s
5000m:	Eamonn Coghlan (Ire) 13m 28.53s	Said Aouita (Mor) 13m 26.44s
10,000m:	Alberto Cova (Ita) 28m 01.04s	Paul Kipkoech (Ken) 27m 38.63s
Marathon:	Rob de Castella (Aus) 2h 10m 03s	Douglas Wakiihuri (Ken) 2h 11m 48s
3000m S/chase:	Patriz Ilg (FRG) 8m 15.06s	Francesco Panetta (Ita) 8m 08.57s
110m Hurdles:	Greg Foster (US) 13.42s	Greg Foster (US) 13.21s
400m Hurdles:	Edwin Moses (US) 47.50s	Edwin Moses (US) 47.46s
20km Walk:	Ernesto Canto (Mex) 1h 20m 49s	Maurizio Damilano (Ita) 1h 20m 45s
50km Walk:	Ronald Weigel (GDR) 3h 43m 08s	Hartwig Gauder (GDR) 3h 40m 53m
4 x 100m Relay:	United States 37.86s	United States 37.90s
4 x 400m Relay:	USSR 3m 00.79s	United States 2m 57.29s
High Jump:	Gennadiy Avdeyenko (USSR) 2.32m	Patrik Sjoberg (Swe) 2.38m
Long Jump:	Carl Lewis (US) 8.55m	Carl Lewis (US) 8.67m
Triple Jump:	Zdzislaw Hoffmann (Pol) 17.42m	Hristo Markov (Bul) 17.92m
Pole Vault:	Sergey Bubka (USSR) 5.70m	Sergey Bubka (USSR) 5.85m
Shot:	Edward Sarul (Pol) 21.29m	Werner Guenthoer (Swi) 22.23m
Javelin:	Detlef Michel (GDR) 89.48m	Seppo Raty (Fin) 83.54m
Discus:	Imrich Bugar (Cze) 67.72m	Jurgen Schult (GDR) 68.74m
Hammer:	Sergey Litvinov (USSR) 82.68m	Sergey Litvinov (USSR) 83.06m
Decathlon:	Daley Thompson (GB) 8714pts	Torsten Voss (GDR) 8680pts

Women	1983, Helsinki	1987, Rome
100m:	Marlies Gohr (GDR) 10.97s	Silke Gladisch (GDR) 10.90s
200m:	Marita Koch (GDR) 22.13s	Silke Gladisch (GDR) 21.74s
400m:	Jarmila Kratochvilova (Cze) 47.99s	Olga Bryzgina (USSR) 49.38s
800m:	Jarmila Kratochvilova (Cze) 1m 54.68s	Sigrun Wodars (GDR) 1m 55.26s
1500m:	Mary Decker (US) 4m 00.90s	Tatyana Samolenko (USSR) 3m 58.56s
3000m:	Mary Decker (US) 8m 34.62s	Tatyana Samolenko (USSR) 8m 38.73s
Marathon:	Greta Waitz (Nor) 2h 28m 09s	Rosa Mota (Por) 2h 25m 17s
100m Hurdles:	Bettina Jahn (GDR) 12.35s	Ginka Zagorcheva (Bul) 12.34s
400m Hurdles:	Ekaterina Fesenko (USSR) 54.14s	Sabine Busche (GDR) 53.62s
4 x 100m Relay:	East Germany 41.76s	United States 41.58s
4 x 400m Relay:	East Germany 3m 19.73s	East Germany 3m 18.63s
High Jump:	Tamara Bykova (USSR) 2.01m	Stefka Kostadinova (Bul) 2.09m
Long Jump:	Heike Daute (GDR) 7.27m	Jackie Joyner-Kersee (US) 7.36m
Shot:	Helena Fibingerova (Cze) 21.05m	Natalya Lisovskaya (USSR) 21.24m
Discus:	Martina Opitz (GDR) 68.94m	Martina Hellman (GDR) 71.62m
Javelin:	Tiina Lillak (Fin) 70.82m	Fatima Whitbread (GB) 76.64m
Heptathlon:	Ramona Neubert (GDR) 6770pts	Jackie Joyner-Kersee (US) 7128pts

WORLD CUP

Men

1977 Düsseldorf		Women	
1 East Germany	127pts	Europe	107pts
2 United States	120pts	East Germany	102pts
3 West Germany	112pts	USSR	89pts

1979 Montreal			
1 United States	119pts	East Germany	106pts
2 Europe	112pts	USSR	98pts
3 East Germany	108pts	Europe	88pts

1981 Rome			
1 Europe	147pts	East Germany	120.5pts

Men		Women	
2 East Germany	130pts	Europe	110pts
3 United States	127pts	USSR	98pts
1985 Canberra			
1 United States	123pts	East Germany	121pts
2 USSR	115pts	USSR	105.5pts
3 East Germany	114pts	Europe	86pts
1989 Barcelona			
1 United States	133pts	East Germany	124pts
2 Europe	127pts	USSR	106pts
3 Great Britain	119pts	Americas	94pts

EUROPEAN CUP
Winners

	Men	Women
1965	USSR	USSR
1967	USSR	USSR
1970	East Germany	East Germany
1973	USSR	East Germany
1975	East Germany	East Germany
1977	East Germany	East Germany
1979	East Germany	East Germany
1981	East Germany	East Germany
1983	East Germany	East Germany
1985	USSR	USSR
1987	USSR	East Germany
1989	Great Britain	East Germany

IAAF/MOBIL GRAND PRIX

	Men	Women
1985	Doug Padilla (US)	Mary Slaney (US)
1986	Said Aouita (Mor)	Yordanka Donkova (Bul)
1987	Tonie Campbell (US)	Merlene Ottey (Jam)
1988	Said Aouita (Mor)	Paula Ivan (Rom)
1989	Said Aouita (Mor)	Paula Ivan (Rom)
1990	Leroy Burrell (US)	Merlene Ottey (Jam)

MARATHON WORLD CUP
Inaugurated 1985
Men

	Individual	Team
1985	Ahmed Saleh (Dji)	Djibouti
1987	Ahmed Saleh (Dji)	Italy
1989	Keleke Metafeira (Eth)	Ethiopia

Women

	Individual	Team
1985	Katrine Dorre (GDR)	Italy
1987	Zoya Ivanova (USSR)	USSR
1989	Sue Marchiano (US)	USSR

LONDON MARATHON
Men

1981	Dick Beardsley (US) & Inge Simonsen (Nor)	2h 11m 48s
1982	Hugh Jones (GB)	2h 09m 24s
1983	Mike Gratton (GB)	2h 09m 43s
1984	Charlie Spedding (GB)	2h 09m 57s
1985	Steve Jones (GB)	2h 08m 16s
1986	Toshihiko Seko (Jap)	2h 10m 02s
1987	Hiromi Taniguchi (Jap)	2h 09m 50s
1988	Henryk Jorgensen (Den)	2h 10m 20s
1989	Douglas Wakiihuri (Ken)	2h 09m 03s
1990	Allister Hutton (GB)	2h 10m 10s

Women

1981	Joyce Smith (GB)	2h 29m 57s
1982	Joyce Smith (GB)	2h 29m 43s
1983	Greta Waitz (Nor)	2h 25m 29s
1984	Ingrid Kristiansen (Nor)	2h 24m 26s
1985	Ingrid Kristiansen (Nor)	2h 21m 06s
1986	Greta Waitz (Nor)	2h 24m 54s
1987	Ingrid Kristiansen (Nor)	2h 22m 48s
1988	Ingrid Kristiansen (Nor)	2h 25m 41s
1989	Veronique Marot (GB)	2h 25m 56s
1990	Wanda Panfil (Pol)	2h 26m 31s

WORLD CROSS COUNTRY CHAMPIONS
Winners since 1981
Men

	Individual	Team
1981	Craig Virgin (US)	Ethiopia
1982	Mohamed Kedir (Eth)	Ethiopia
1983	Bekele Debele (Eth)	Ethiopia
1984	Carlos Lopes (Por)	Ethiopia
1985	Carlos Lopes (Por)	Ethiopia
1986	John Ngugi (Ken)	Kenya
1987	John Ngugi (Ken)	Kenya
1988	John Ngugi (Ken)	Kenya
1989	John Ngugi (Ken)	Kenya
1990	Khalid Skah (Mor)	Kenya

Women

	Individual	Team
1981	Greta Waitz (Nor)	USSR
1982	Maricica Puica (Rom)	USSR
1983	Greta Waitz (Nor)	United States
1984	Maricica Puica (Rom)	United States
1985	Zola Budd (Eng)	United States
1986	Zola Budd (Eng)	England
1987	Annette Sergent (Fra)	United States
1988	Ingrid Kristiansen (Nor)	USSR
1989	Annette Sergent (Fra)	USSR
1990	Lynn Jennings (US)	USSR

RECORDS

WORLD OUTDOOR RECORDS
(September 1990)

Men

100m:	9.92s Carl Lewis (US); Seoul, Sep 24 1988
200m:	19.72s Pietro Mennea (Ita); Mexico City, Sep 12, 1979
400m:	43.29s Harry Reynolds (US); Zürich, Aug 17, 1988
800m:	1m 41.73s Sebastian Coe (GB); Florence, Jun 10, 1981
1000m:	2m 12.18s Sebastian Coe (GB); Oslo, Jul 11, 1981
1500m:	3m 29.46s Said Aouita (Mor); Berlin, Aug 23, 1985
Mile:	3m 46.32s Steve Cram (GB); Oslo, Jul 27, 1985
2000m:	4m 50.81s Said Aouita (Mor); Paris, Jul 16, 1987
3000m:	7m 29.45s Said Aouita (Mor); Cologne, Aug 20, 1989
5000m:	12m 58.39s Said Aouita (Mor); Rome, Jul 27, 1987
10,000m:	27m 08.23s Arturo Barrios (Mex); Berlin, Aug 18, 1989
20,000m:	57m 18.4s Dionisio Castro (Por); Flêche, France, Mar 31, 1990
1 Hour:	20,994 metres Jos Hermens (Hol); Papendal, Holland, May 1, 1976
25,000m:	1h 13m 55.8s Toshihiko Seko (Jap); Christchurch, NZ, Mar 22, 1981
30,000m:	1h 29m 18.8s Toshihiko Seko (Jap); Christchurch, NZ, Mar 22, 1981
110m Hdles:	12.92s Roger Kingdom (US); Zürich, Aug 16, 1989
400m Hdles:	47.02s Edwin Moses (US); Koblenz, Aug 31, 1983
3000m S/chase:	8m 05.35s Peter Koech (Ken); Stockholm, Jul 3, 1989
4 x 100m Relay:	37.79s France; Split, Sep 1, 1990
4 x 400m Relay:	2m 56.16s United States; Mexico City, Oct 20, 1968
	2m 56.16s United States; Seoul, Oct 1 1988

4 x 800m Relay:	7m 03.89s Great Britain; London, Aug 30, 1982
4 x 1500m Relay:	West Germany; Cologne, Aug 17, 1977
High Jump:	2.44m Javier Sotomayor (Cub); San Juan, Puerto Rico, Jul 30 1989
Pole Vault:	6.06m Sergey Bubka (USSR); Nice, Jul 10, 1988
Long Jump:	8.90m Bob Beamon (US); Mexico City, Oct 18, 1968
Triple Jump:	17.97m Willie Banks (US); Indianapolis, Jun 16, 1985
Shot:	23.12m Randy Barnes (US); Los Angeles, May 20, 1990
Discus:	74.08m Jürgen Schult (GDR); Neubrandenburg, GDR, Jun 6, 1986
Hammer:	86.74m Yuriy Sedykh (USSR); Stuttgart, Aug 30, 1986
Javelin:	90.98m Steven Backley (GB); London, Jul 20, 1990*
Decathlon:	8847pts Daley Thompson (GB); Los Angeles, Aug 8/9, 1984
Marathon (†):	2h 06m 50s Belayneh Dinsamo (Eth); Rotterdam, Apr 17, 1988

Women

100m:	10.49s Florence Griffith-Joyner (US); Indianapolis, Jul 16, 1988
200m:	21.34s Florence Griffith-Joyner (US); Seoul, Sep 29, 1988
400m:	47.60s Marita Koch (GDR); Canberra, Oct 6, 1985
800m:	1m 53.28s Jarmila Kratochvilova (Cze); Munich, Jul 26, 1983
1500m:	3m 52.47s Tatyana Kazankina (USSR); Zürich, Aug 13, 1980
Mile:	4m 15.61s Paula Ivan (Rom); Nice, Jul 10, 1989
2000m:	5m 28.69s Maricica Puica (Rom); London, Jul 11, 1986
3000m:	8m 22.62s Tatyana Kazankini (USSR); Leningrad, Aug 26, 1984
5000m:	14m 37.33s Ingrid Kristiansen (Nor); Stockholm, Aug 5, 1986
10,000m:	30m 13.74s Ingrid Kristiansen (Nor); Oslo, Jul 5, 1986
20,000m:	1h 29m 29.2s Karolina Szabo (Hun); Budapest, Apr 22, 1988
30,000m:	1h 49m 05.6s Karolina Szabo (Hun); Budapest, Apr 22, 1988
100m Hurdles:	12.21s Yordanka Donkova (Bul); Stara Zagora, Bul, Aug 20, 1988
400m Hurdles:	52.94s Marina Stepanova (USSR); Tashkent, Sep 17, 1986
4 x 100m Relay:	41.37s East Germany; Canberra, Oct 6, 1985
4 x 200m Relay:	1m 28.15s East Germany; Jena, GDR, Aug 9, 1980
4 x 400m Relay:	3m 15.17s USSR; Seoul, Oct 1, 1988
4 x 800m Relay:	7m 50.17s USSR; Moscow, Aug 5, 1984
High Jump:	2.09m Stefka Kostadinova (Bul); Rome, Aug 30, 1987
Long Jump:	7.52m Galina Chistyakova (USSR); Leningrad, Jun 11, 1988
Shot:	22.63m Natalya Lisovskaya (USSR); Moscow, Jun 7, 1987
Discus:	76.80m Gabriele Reinsch (GDR); Neubrandenburg, GDR, Jul 9, 1988
Javelin:	80.00m Petra Felke (GDR); Potsdam, GDR, Sep 9, 1988
Heptathlon:	7,291pts Jackie Joyner-Kersee (US); Seoul, Sep 23/24, 1988
Marathon (†):	2h 21m 06s Ingrid Kristiansen (Nor); London, Apr 21, 1985

† *World records not recognised for the Marathon, only best time*
* *(Subject to IAAF ratification)*

1991

3RD IAAF WORLD CHAMPIONSHIPS, TOKYO, JAPAN, AUG 24-SEP 1
Schedule (All Times BST)

SATURDAY, AUG 24-Day 1

00.30	20km Walk	M	Final (start)
01.00	100m	M	1st round
01.30	Shot	W	Qualifying
01.50	20km Walk	M	Final (finish)
02.25	10km Walk	W	Final (start)
02.30	Hammer Throw	M	Qualifying
03.05	10km Walk	W	Final (finish)
04.00	Hammer Throw	M	Qualifying
08.00	400m	W	1st round
08.50	100m	M	2nd round
09.30	800m	M	1st round
10.20	Long Jump	W	Qualifying
10.30	800m	W	1st round
10.40	Shot	W	Final
11.20	3,000m	W	1st round
12.05	10,000m	M	1st round

SUNDAY, AUG 25-Day 2

23.00 (Sat)	Marathon	W	Final (start)
01.00	Javelin	M	Qualifying
01.25	Marathon	W	Final (finish)
02.00	400m	M	1st round
02.30	Javelin	M	Qualifying
07.00	Hammer	M	Final

09.00	100m	M	Semi-finals
09.00	Triple Jump	M	Qualifying
09.30	400m Hurdles	M	1st round
10.20	400m	W	2nd round
10.30	Long Jump	W	Final
11.05	100m	M	Final
11.20	800m	M	Semi-final
11.50	800m	M	2nd round

MONDAY, AUG 26-Day 3

02.00	100m Hurdles	W	Heptathlon
02.00	Discus	M	Qualifying
02.45	100m	W	1st round
03.00	High Jump	W	Heptathlon
03.35	200m	M	1st round
03.40	Discus	M	Qualifying
07.30	400m Hurdles	W	1st round
08.00	Shot	W	Heptathlon
08.20	100m	W	2nd round
08.40	Triple Jump	M	Final
08.50	200m	M	2nd round
09.20	400m	M	2nd round
09.55	400m	M	Semi-finals
10.10	Javelin	M	Final
10.15	800m	M	Semi-finals
10.45	400m Hurdles	M	Semi-finals
11.10	800m	W	Final
11.25	3,000m	W	Final
11.45	200m	W	Heptathlon
12.10	10,000m	M	Final

TUESDAY, AUG 27-Day 4

02.00	110m Hurdles	M	1st round
02.10	Long Jump	W	Heptathlon
03.00	3000 Steeple	M	1st round
08.00	Javelin	W	Heptathlon
08.05	100m	W	Semi-finals
08.25	200m	M	Semi-finals
08.40	Pole Vault	M	Qualifying
09.00	110m Hurdles	M	Semi-finals
09.20	Javelin	W	Heptathlon
09.30	400m Hurdles	W	Semi-finals
10.00	400m Hurdles	M	Final
10.20	100m	W	Final
10.40	400m	M	Semi-finals
11.00	Discus	M	Final
11.10	200m	M	Final
11.30	400m	W	Final
11.50	800m	M	Final
12.05	800m	W	Heptathlon
12.25	10,000m	W	1st round

WEDNESDAY, AUG 28-Day 5-Rest Day
THURSDAY, AUG 29-Day 6

02.00	100m	M	Decathlon
02.20	High Jump	W	Qualifying
02.40	200m	W	1st round
02.50	Long Jump	M	Decathlon
03.40	100m Hurdles	W	1st round
04.30	Shot	M	Decathlon
08.00	Pole Vault	M	Final
08.10	Long Jump	M	Qualifying
08.10	High Jump	M	Decathlon
08.15	1,500m	W	1st round
08.55	1,500m	M	1st round
09.35	200m	W	2nd round
10.00	Discus	W	Qualifying
10.10	100m Hurdles	W	Semi-finals
10.40	110m Hurdles	M	Final
11.00	400m Hurdles	W	Final
11.20	3000 Steeple	M	Semi-finals
11.30	Discus	W	Qualifying
12.00	400m	M	Decathlon
12.20	400m	M	Final
12.35	5,000m	M	1st round

FRIDAY, AUG 30-Day 7

01.00	110m	M	Decathlon
01.45	Discus	M	Decathlon
02.00	4x400m	M	1st round
02.30	Shot	M	Qualifying
03.00	Discus	M	Decathlon
04.30	Pole Vault	M	Decathlon
08.30	Javelin	M	Decathlon (1)
08.40	High Jump	M	Qualifying
09.00	200m	W	Semi-finals
09.30	Long Jump	M	Final
09.30	1,500m	M	Semi-finals
09.50	100m Hurdles	W	Final
10.00	Javelin	M	Decathlon (2)
10.15	5,000m	M	Semi-finals
11.05	10,000m	W	Final
11.55	200m	W	Final
12.15	1,500m	M	Decathlon

SATURDAY, AUG 1-Day 8

23.00 (Fri)	50km Walk	M	Final (start)
02.00	Javelin	W	Qualifying (1)
02.45	50km Walk	M	Final (finish)
03.20	Javelin	W	Qualifying (2)
08.00	4x100m	W	1st round
08.30	High Jump	W	Final
08.50	4x100m	M	1st round
09.30	800m	W	Final
09.50	1,500m	M	Final
10.10	Discus	W	Final
10.20	4x100m	W	Semi-finals
10.30	Shot	M	Final
10.40	4x100m	M	Semi-finals
11.00	1,500m	W	Final
11.20	3000 Steeple	M	Final
11.45	4x400m	W	1st round
12.20	4x400m	M	Semi-finals

SUNDAY, SEP 1-Day 9

23.00 (Sat)	Marathon	M	Final (start)
01.10	Marathon	M	Final (finish)
07.00	High Jump	M	Final
07.40	1,500m	M	Final
08.00	Javelin	W	Final
08.15	4x100m	W	Final
08.50	4x100m	M	Final
09.10	5,000m	M	Final
09.50	4x400m	W	Final
10.10	4x400m	M	Final
11.00	Closing Ceremony		

Source: IAAF Newsletter

OTHER FIXTURES

Mar 8-10: World indoor championships (Seville); *Mar 24*: World cross-country championships (Antwerp); *Apr 21*: ADT London Marathon including World Marathon Cup; *Jun 1-2*: World Race Walking Cup (San José, California); *Jun 22-23*: European Cup B Final (Barcelona) and C, C1 and C2 (Athens and Portugal); *Jun 29-30:* European Cup A Final (Frankfurt); *Jul 6-7*: European Cup for combined events-A final (Helmond, Holland), B final (Stoke) and C final (Denmark); *Sep 20*: IAAF/Mobil Grand Prix finals.

AUSTRALIAN RULES FOOTBALL

1990

AUSTRALIAN FOOTBALL LEAGUE

		P	W	L	Goal %	Pts
1	(2) Essendon	22	17	5	139.2	68
2	(5) Collingwood	22	16	6	130.2	64
3	(11) West Coast Eagles	22	16	6	118.4	64
4	(4) Melbourne	22	14	8	113.2	56
5	(1) Hawthorn	22	14	8	120.6	56
6	(9) North Melbourne	22	12	10	114.0	48
7	(13) Footscray	22	12	10	99.3	48
8	(8) Carlton	22	11	11	104.1	44
9	(12) St Kilda	22	9	13	100.6	36
10	(3) Geelong	22	8	14	93.7	32
11	(14) Richmond	22	7	15	78.6	28
12	(6) Fitzroy	22	7	15	78.4	28
13	(7) Sydney Swans	22	5	17	70.4	20
14	(10) Brisbane Bears	22	4	18	71.4	16

Play-offs
Elimination Final
Melbourne beat Hawthorn 73-64
Qualifying Final
Collingwood beat West Coast 126-67 (after 90-90 draw)
Semi-finals
West Coast beat Melbourne 130-100; Collingwood beat
Essendon 117-54
Preliminary Final
Essendon beat West Coast 121-58
Grand Final
Melbourne Cricket Ground, Oct 7
COLLINGWOOD beat Essendon 89-41

**"There's a bit of a worry with O'Dwyer.
Whether he's got a groin or not."**
Crackers Keenan, Radio 3LO, Melbourne

CHAMPIONS

GRAND FINAL WINNERS
*(Victorian Football League 1897-1989; Australian
Football League 1990)*

1897	Essendon
1898	Fitzroy
1899	Fitzroy
1900	Melbourne
1901	Essendon
1902	Collingwood
1903	Collingwood
1904	Fitzroy
1905	Fitzroy
1906	Charlton
1907	Charlton
1908	Charlton
1909	South Melbourne
1910	Collingwood
1911	Essendon
1912	Essendon
1913	Fitzroy
1914	Carlton
1915	Carlton
1916	Fitzroy
1917	Collingwood
1918	South Melbourne
1919	Collingwood
1920	Richmond
1921	Richmond
1922	Fitzroy
1923	Essendon
1924	Essendon
1925	Geelong
1926	Melbourne
1927	Collingwood
1928	Collingwood
1929	Collingwood
1930	Collingwood
1931	Geelong
1932	Richmond
1933	South Melbourne
1934	Richmond
1935	Collingwood
1936	Collingwood
1937	Geelong
1938	Carlton
1939	Melbourne
1940	Melbourne
1941	Melbourne
1942	Essendon
1943	Richmond
1944	Fitzroy
1945	Carlton
1946	Essendon
1947	Carlton
1948	Melbourne
1949	Essendon
1950	Essendon
1951	Geelong
1952	Geelong
1953	Collingwood
1954	Footscray
1955	Melbourne
1956	Melbourne
1957	Melbourne
1958	Collingwood
1959	Melbourne
1960	Melbourne
1961	Hawthorn
1962	Essendon
1963	Geelong
1964	Melbourne
1965	Essendon
1966	St Kilda
1967	Richmond
1968	Carlton
1969	Richmond
1970	Carlton
1971	Hawthorn
1972	Carlton
1973	Richmond
1974	Richmond
1975	North Melbourne
1976	Hawthorn
1977	North Melbourne
1978	Hawthorn
1979	Carlton
1980	Richmond
1981	Carlton
1982	Carlton
1983	Hawthorn
1984	Essendon
1985	Essendon
1986	Hawthorn
1987	Carlton
1988	Hawthorn
1989	Hawthorn
1990	Collingwood

Most Wins:
15 Carlton; **14** Essendon; **13** Collingwood; **12** Melbourne

BADMINTON

THOMAS CUP

(Men's World Team Championships)
Nagoya, Japan, May 30-Jun 3

SEMI-FINALS
CHINA 5 Denmark 0; MALAYSIA 3 Indonesia 2\

FINAL
CHINA 4 Malaysia 1

UBER CUP

(Women's World Team Championships)
Nagoya, Japan, May 30 -June 3

SEMI-FINALS
CHINA 5 Indonesia 0; SOUTH KOREA 4 Japan 1

FINAL
CHINA 3 South Korea 2
China became first nation to win trophy four times in succession

EUROPEAN CHAMPIONSHIPS

Moscow, Apr 8-14

Men's singles

QUARTER-FINALS
DARREN HALL (Eng) beat Pontus Jantii (Fin) 15-10 10-15 15-16; STEVE BUTLER (Eng) beat Jens Olsson (Swe) 1-15 17-14 15-12; STEVE BADDELEY (Eng) beat Andrei Antropov (USSR) 15-8 15-8; POUL-ERIK HOYER-LARSEN (Den) beat Peter Axelsson (Swe) 15-5 15-8

SEMI-FINALS
HALL beat Butler 15-7 15-8; BADDELEY beat Hoyer-Larsen 15-10 0-15 15-11

FINAL
BADDELEY beat Hall 11-15 15-13 15-7

Women's singles

QUARTER-FINALS
PERNILLE NEDERGAARD (Den) beat Elena Rybkina (USSR) 11-4 6-11 12-10; HELEN TROKE (Eng) beat Vlada Chernyavskaya (USSR) 11-3 11-5; FIONA SMITH (Eng) beat Irina Serova (USSR) 11-3 11-3; CHRISTINE MAGNUSSON (Swe) beat Kirsten Larsen (Den) 2-11 11-4 11-0

SEMI-FINALS
NEDERGAARD beat Troke 11-2 11-6; SMITH beat Magnusson 11-3 11-1

FINAL
NEDERGAARD beat Smith 5-11 12-11 4-0 (Smith retired hurt)

MEN'S DOUBLES FINAL
HENRIK SVARRER & JAN PAULSEN (Den) beat Max Grandrup & Thomas Lund (Den) 17-16 15-5

WOMEN'S DOUBLES FINAL
DORTE KJAER & NETTIE NIELSEN (Den) beat Eline Coene & EricaVan Dijck (Hol) 15-5 15-6

MIXED DOUBLES FINAL
JOHN HOLST-CHRISTIANSEN & GRETE MOGENSEN (Den) beat Jan-Erik Antonsson & Maria Bengtsson (Swe) 15-7 15-8

ALL-ENGLAND CHAMPIONSHIPS

Wembley, Mar14-17

Men's singles

QUARTER-FINALS
ZHAO JIANHUA (Chn) beat Allan Budi Kusuma (Ina) 17-18 15-6 15-9; JOKO SUPRIANTO (Ina) beat Foo Kok Keong (Mal) 15-1 15-4; RASHID SIDEK (Mal) beat Morten Frost (Den) 15-6 15-6; EDDIE KURNIAWAN (Ina) beat Haryanto Arbi (Ina) 15-5 16-17 15-12

SEMI-FINALS
ZHAO JIANHUA beat Sidek 18-16 15-6; SUPRIANTO beat Kurniawan 15-4 15-10

FINAL
ZHAO JIANHUA beat Suprianto 15-4 15-1

Women's singles

QUARTER-FINALS
SUSI SUSANTI (Ina) beat Elena Rybkina (USSR) 11-8 11-1; HUANG HUA (Cha) beat Lee Yung-suk (SKo) 10-12 11-9 11-7; ZHOU LEI (Chn) beat Kirsten Larsen (Den) 11-7 11-3; LEE HEUNG-SOON (SKo) beat Pernille Nedergaard (Den) 6-11 11-4 12-10

SEMI-FINALS
SUSANTI beat Zhou Lei 2-11 11-5 11-9 HUANG HUA beat Lee Heung-Soon 11-0 11-0

FINAL
SUSANTI beat Huang 12-11 11-1

MEN'S DOUBLES FINAL
KIM MOON-SOO & PARK JOO-BONG (SKo) beat Li Yongbo & Tian Bingyi (Chn) 17-14 15-9

WOMEN'S DOUBLES FINAL
CHUNG MYUNG-HEE & HWANG HYE-YOUNG (SKo) beat Gillian Clark & Gillian Gowers (Eng) 6-15 15-4 15-4

MIXED DOUBLES FINAL
PARK JOO-BONG & CHUNG MYUNG-HEE (SKo) beat John Holst-Christiansen & Grete Mogensen (Den) 15-6 15-3

CHAMPIONS

THOMAS CUP

(Men's World Team Championship)

1949	Malaya
1952	Malaya
1955	Malaya
1958	Indonesia
1961	Indonesia
1964	Indonesia
1967	Malaysia
1970	Indonesia
1973	Indonesia
1976	Indonesia
1979	Indonesia
1982	China
1984	Indonesia
1986	China
1988	China
1990	China

Most wins: 8 Indonesia

UBER CUP
(Women's world team Championship)
1957	United States
1960	United States
1963	United States
1966	Japan
1969	Japan
1972	Japan
1975	Indonesia
1978	Japan
1981	Japan
1984	China
1986	China
1988	China
1990	China

Most wins: 5 Japan

WORLD CHAMPIONSHIPS
Men's singles
1977	Flemming Delfs (Den)
1980	Rudy Hartono (Ina)
1983	Icuk Sugiarto (Ina)
1985	Han Jian (Chn)
1987	Yang Yang (Chn)
1989	Yang Yang (Chn)

Women's singles
1977	Lene Koppen (Den)
1980	Wiharjo Verawaty (Ina)
1983	Li Lingwei (Chn)
1985	Han Aiping (Chn)
1987	Han Aiping (Chn)
1989	Li Lingwei (Chn)

Men's doubles
1977	Tjun Tjun & Johan Wahjudi (Ina)
1980	Ade Chandra & Hadinata Christian (Ina)
1983	Steen Fladberg & Jesper Helledie (Den)
1985	Park Joo Bong & Kim Moon Soo (SKo)
1987	Tian Bingyi & Li Yongbo (Chn)
1989	Tian Bingyi & Li Yongbo (Chn)

Women's doubles
1977	Etsuko Tuganoo & Emiko Vero (Jap)
1980	Nora Perry & Jane Webster (GB)
1983	Wu Dixi & Lin Ying (Chn)
1985	Han Aiping & Li Lingwei (Chn)
1987	Guan Weizhan & Lin Ying (Chn)
1989	Guan Weizhan & Lin Ying (Chn)

Mixed doubles
1977	Steen Stovgaard & Lene Koppen (Den)
1980	Hadinata Christian & Imelda Wigoeno (Ina)
1983	Thomas Kihlstrom (Swe) & Nora Perry (GB)
1985	Park Joo Bong & Yoo Sang Hee (SKo)
1987	Wang Pengrin & Shi Fangjing (Chn)
1989	Park Joo Bong & Chung Myung Hee (SKo)

Most titles: 3 Han Aiping, Li Lingwei, Lin Ying, Parc Joo Bong

ALL-ENGLAND CHAMPIONSHIPS
Inaugurated 1899 for doubles only. Singles first held 1900.
Post-war winners

Men's singles
1947	Conny Jepsen (Swe)
1948	Jörn Skaarup (Den)
1949	Dave Freeman (US)
1950	Wong Pcng Soon (Mal)
1951	Wong Peng Soon (Mal)
1952	Wong Peng Soon (Mal)
1953	Eddie Choong (Mal)
1954	Eddie Choong (Mal)
1955	Wong Peng Soon (Mal)
1956	Eddie Choong (Mal)
1957	Eddie Choong (Mal)
1958	Erland Kops (Den)
1959	Tan Joe Hok (Ina)
1960	Erland Kops (Den)
1961	Erland Kops (Den)
1962	Erland Kops (Den)
1963	Erland Kops (Den)
1964	Knud Nielsen (Den)
1965	Erland Kops (Den)
1966	Tan Aik Huang (Mal)
1967	Erland Kops (Den)
1968	Rudy Hartono (Ina)
1969	Rudy Hartono (Ina)
1970	Rudy Hartono (Ina)
1971	Rudy Hartono (Ina)
1972	Rudy Hartono (Ina)
1973	Rudy Hartono (Ina)
1974	Rudy Hartono (Ina)
1975	Sven Pri (Den)
1976	Rudy Hartono (Ina)
1977	Flemming Delfs (Den)
1978	Liem Swie King (Ina)
1979	Liem Swie King (Ina)
1980	Prakash Padukone (Ind)
1981	Liem Swie King (Ina)
1982	Morten Frost (Den)
1983	Luan Jin (Chn)
1984	Morten Frost (Den)
1985	Zhao Jianhua (Chn)
1986	Morten Frost (Den)
1987	Morten Frost (Den)
1988	Ib Frederiksen (Den)
1989	Yang Yang (Chn)
1990	Zhao Jianhua (Chn)

Most wins:
8 Rudy Hartono; 6 Frank Devlin (Ire) 1925-29, 1931, Erland Kops; 5 Ralph Nicholls (Eng) 1932, 1934, 1936-38; 4 George Thomas (Eng) 1920-23, Wong Peng Soon, Eddie Choong, Morten Frost

Women's singles
1947	Marie Ussing (Den)
1948	Kirsten Thorndahl (Den)
1949	Aase Jacobsen (Den)
1950	Tonny Olsen-Ahm (Den)
1951	Aase Jacobsen (Den)
1952	Tonny Olsen-Ahm (Den)
1953	Marie Ussing (Den)
1954	Judy Devlin (US)
1955	Margaret Varner (US)
1956	Margaret Varner (US)
1957	Judy Devlin (US)
1958	Judy Devlin (US)
1959	Heather Ward (Eng)
1960	Judy Devlin (US)
1961	Judy Hashman (née Devlin) (US)
1962	Judy Hashman (US)
1963	Judy Hashman (US)
1964	Judy Hashman (US)
1965	Ursula Smith (Eng)
1966	Judy Hashman (US)
1967	Judy Hashman (US)
1968	Eva Twedberg (Swe)
1969	Hiroe Yuki (Jap)
1970	Etsuko Takenaka (Jap)
1971	Eva Twedberg (Swe)
1972	Noriko Nakayama (Jap)
1973	Margaret Beck (Eng)
1974	Hiroe Yuki (Jap)
1975	Hiroe Yuki (Jap)

1976	Gillian Gilks (Eng)
1977	Hiroe Yuki (Jap)
1978	Gillian Gilks (Eng)
1979	Lene Köppen (Den)
1980	Lene Köppen (Den)
1981	Sun Ai Hwang (SKo)
1982	Zang Ailing (Chn)
1983	Zang Ailing (Chn)
1984	Li Lingwei (Chn)
1985	Han Aiping (Chn)
1986	Kim Yun-Ja (SKo)
1987	Kirsten Larsen (Den)
1988	Gu Jiaming (Chn)
1989	Li Lingwei (Chn)
1990	Susi Susanti (Ina)

Most wins:
10 Judy Hashman (née Devlin); 6 Meriel Lucas (Eng) 1902, 1905, 1907-10; 5 Ethel Thomson (Eng) 1900-01, 1903-04, 1906, Marjorie Barrett (Eng) 1926-27, 1929-31; **4** Kitty McKane (Eng) 1920-22, 1924.

Men's doubles
Winners since 1981

1981	Hariamanto Kartono & Rudy Heryanto (Ina)
1982	Razif Sidek & Jalaini Sidek (Mal)
1983	Stefan Karisson & Thomas Kihlstrom (Swe)
1984	Hariamanto Kartono & Rudy Heryanto (Ina)
1985	Kim Moon-Soo & Park Joo-Bong (SKo)
1986	Kim Moon-Soo & Park Joo-Bong (SKo)
1987	Li Yongbo & Tian Bingyi (Chn)
1988	Li Yongbo & Tian Bingyi (Chn)
1989	Lee-Sang Bok & Park Joo-Bong (SKo)
1990	Kim Moon-Soo & Park Joo-Bong (SKo)

Women's doubles

1981	Nora Perry & Jane Webster (Eng)
1982	Lin Ying & Wu Dixi (Chn)
1983	Xu Rong & Wu Jiangiu (Chn)
1984	Lin Ying & Wu Dixi (Chn)
1985	Li Lingwei & Han Aiping (Chn)
1986	Chung Myung-Hee & Hwang Hye-Young (SKo)
1987	Chung Myung-Hee & Hwang Hye-Young (SKo)
1988	Chung So-Young & Kim Yun-Ja (SKo)
1989	Chung Myung-Hee & Chung So-Young (SKo)
1990	Chung Myung-Hee & Hwang Hye-Young (SKo)

Mixed doubles

1981	Mike Tredgett & Nora Perry (Eng)
1982	Martin Dew & Gillian Gilks (Eng)
1983	Thomas Kihlstrom (Swe) & Nora Perry (Eng)
1984	Martin Dew & Gillian Gilks (Eng)
1985	Billy Gilliland & Nora Perry (Eng)
1986	Park Joo-Bong & Chung Myung-Hee (SKo)
1987	Lee Deuk-Choon & Chung Myung-Hee (SKo)
1988	Wang Pengrin & Shi Fangjiing (Chn)
1989	Park Joo-Bong & Chung Myung-Hee (SKo)
1990	Park Joo-Bong & Chung Myung-Hee (SKo)

Most Overall All-England titles:
21 George Thomas 1903-28; 18 Frank Devlin 1922-31; 17 Meriel Lucas 1899-1910, Judy Hashman (née Devlin) 1954-67

1991

Mar 11-16 All England Championships (Wembley); Apr 29 - May 5 World Championships/Sudirman Cup (Copenhagen)

BASEBALL

GOODBYE, GEORGE

There were moments in 1990 when everyone in baseball stood and cheered. Some reflected on-field landmarks, like 43-year-old Nolan Ryan's 300th career victory. But the loudest came at what should have been a solemn moment when the New York Yankees' principal owner George Steinbrenner - cable TV tycoon, egoist and chronic interferer - was banned from baseball.

Fay Vincent, the baseball commissioner, made the decision after an obscure and messy case involving a gambler called Howard Spira. Steinbrenner was found to have paid Spira $40,000. Spira alleged this was for information to discredit Dave Winfield, a player with whom Steinbrenner was feuding; Steinbrenner, after changing his story, said he was being blackmailed. Vincent said his behaviour bordered on the bizarre.

The ban delighted Yankee fans who chanted "No more George!" when the news came through to the stadium during a game, not because of the Spira case, but because of Steinbrenner's eccentric and disastrous stewardship. Since taking over baseball's most famous and successful club he had made 17 managerial changes in 17 years and the Yankees finished the season rock bottom of the American League East with the second-worst record in the major leagues.

Steinbrenner's nemesis was the lawyer John Dowd, whose previous report for the commissioner, in 1989, had led to the banning of the great Peter Rose for betting. Rose fell further in 1990 when he was jailed for five months for filing false income tax returns. Inmates gave varying accounts as to whether he was welcome on the prison softball team.

The season itself was delayed for a week because the owners locked the players out of spring training for 32 days during a contractual dispute. Nothing stopped the leading players' surge towards stratospheric salaries: José Canseco of Oakland Athletics became the game's best-paid player when he signed a five-year deal giving him an average salary of $4.76 million a year (about £2.5 million). Nolan Ryan, fifth on the list at just under $4 million, bought his own bank - the Danbury State Bank in Texas, to deposit his money.

The most exciting pennant race came in the American League East where the Boston Red Sox and the Toronto Blue Jays - two teams famous for folding late in the season - fought it out until the Red Sox clinched the division on the last night of the regular season. The 1990 world champions, the Oakland Athletics, easily won the American League West for the third consecutive year. The Cincinnati Reds, leaning heavily on a bullpen of relief pitchers known as the "Nasty Boys", won the National League West without ever being headed. The Pittsburgh Pirates just held off the New York Mets in the eastern division; the Mets improved after they sacked their manager Davey Johnson, who had won more games in the past six years than anyone else.

There were nine no-hitters during the season, two more than ever before. Cecil Fielder of the Detroit Tigers hit 51 home runs; he was the first player to get 50 in a season since 1977. The Minnesota Twins became the first team ever to execute two triple plays in a game but still lost 1-0 to the Red Sox. Ken Griffey sr and Ken Griffey jr of the Seattle Mariners became the first father and son to play together for the same major league team. Baseball's oldest stadium, Comiskey Park, home of the Chicago White Sox, closed.

Readers of USA Today, asked which of two alternative ways of spending an afternoon off they would prefer, voted: 34% sex, 66% baseball. A couple staying in the hotel built into the Toronto Skydome attempted to combine both options, forgetting that with the curtains open, their room was illuminated by the stadium lights; 49,000 people were able to watch.

1990

MAJOR LEAGUE BASEBALL

FINAL STANDINGS

American League - East

		W	L	%	GB
1 (3)	Boston Red Sox	88	74	.543	-
2 (1)	Toronto Blue Jays	86	76	.531	2
3 (7)	Detroit Tigers	79	83	.488	9
4 (6)	Cleveland Indians	77	85	.475	11
5 (2)	Baltimore Orioles	76	85	.472	$11^{1}/_{2}$
6 (4)	Milwaukee Brewers	74	88	.457	14
7 (5)	New York Yankees	67	95	.414	21

American League - West

		W	L	%	GB
1 (1)	Oakland Athletics	103	59	.636	-
2 (7)	Chicago White Sox	94	68	.580	9
3 (4)	Texas Rangers	83	79	.512	20
4 (3)	California Angels	80	82	.494	23
5 (6)	Seattle Mariners	77	85	.475	26
6 (2)	Kansas City Royals	75	86	.462	$27^{1}/_{2}$
7 (5)	Minnesota Twins	74	88	.457	29

Batting Champion
George Brett (Kansas City) .329

National League-East

		W	L	%	GB
1 (5)	Pittsburgh Pirates	95	67	.586	-
2 (2)	New York Mets	91	71	.562	4
3 (4)	Montreal Expos	85	77	.525	10
4 (1)	Chicago Cubs	77	85	.475	18
5 (6)	Philadelphia Phillies	77	85	.475	18
6 (3)	St Louis Cardinals	70	92	.432	25

National League-West

		W	L	%	GB
1 (5)	Cincinnati Reds	91	71	.562	-
2 (4)	Los Angeles Dodgers	86	76	.531	5
3 (1)	San Francisco Giants	85	77	.525	6
4 (3)	Houston Astros	75	87	.463	16
5 (2)	San Diago Padres	75	87	.463	16
6 (6)	Atlanta Braves	65	97	.401	26

Batting Champion
Willie McGee (St Louis) .335
Last season's positions in brackets. GB = Games behind leader.

Leading salaries (Summer 1990)	$M per year
José Canseco (Oakland Athletics)	4.76
Don Mattingly (New York Yankees)	3.86
Will Clark (San Francisco Giants)	3.75
Dave Stewart (Oakland Athletics)	3.50

Average salaries of Major League players
1967 $19,900
1975 $44,676
1978 $99,976
1990 $500,000 ++

61st ALL-STAR GAME
Wrigley Field, Chicago, Jul 10
AMERICAN LEAGUE 0 0 0 0 0 2 0 0-2
NATIONAL LEAGUE 0 0 0 0 0 0 0 0 0-0
MVP: Julio Franco (AL)
Attendance: 39,071
American League lead series 38-22 (one ties)

BRITISH CLUBS CHAMPIONSHIP
Sutton, Surrey, Sep 29
ENFIELD SPARTANS beat Hull Mets 22-2

WORLD AMATEUR CHAMPIONSHIP
Edmonton, Canada, Aug 20
Final
CUBA beat Nicaragua 14-0 and 11-5 (best-of-three).

1989

WORLD SERIES
Game 1 *Oct 14*: OAKLAND 5 San Francisco 0
Game 2 *Oct 15*: OAKLAND 5 San Francisco 1
Game 3 *Oct 27*: San Francisco 7 OAKLAND 13
Game 4 *Oct 28*: San Francisco 6 OAKLAND 9
Oakland won series 4-0
Series interrupted by San Francisco earthquake, which struck just before Game 3 was due to start.

❝Let me get this straight. The owners are about to shut down baseball when it's more prosperous than it's ever been, and that players are the ones who have to get their urine tested?❞
Ron Darling, Mets pitcher, on the pre-season lockout

"It's just billionaires v millionaires."
Tom LeMieux, Cubs fan, ditto

"People think we make three and four million dollars a year. They don't realise that most of us only make 500,000."
Pete Incaviglia, Texas Rangers outfielder

"Hell, man, it doesn't take much to please me. Give me my truck, 10 or 20 bucks in my pocket, a tankful of gas and my music and let me play baseball. Then I'm happy."
Kirby Puckett, Minneapolis Twins, on his $3 million salary

"We must recognise that there are two people here. Pete Rose, the living legend, the all-time hit leader and the idol of millions; and Pete Rose, the individual who appears today convicted of two counts of cheating on his taxes. Today we are not dealing with the legend."
US District Court Judge Arthur Spiegel

"The win won't turn Ryan's head. When the game ended, he embraced his teammates, returned to the clubhouse, jumped on an exercise bike and began pedalling. Toward no. 301.❞
New York Times on 43-year-old pitcher Nolan Ryan's 300th win

CHAMPIONS

WORLD SERIES

Year	Team	
1903	Boston Red Sox (AL)	5
	Pittsburgh Pirates (NL)	3
1904	Not held	
1905	New York Giants (NL)	4
	Philadelphia Athletics (AL)	1
1906	Chicago White Sox (AL)	4
	Chicago Cubs (NL)	2
1907	Chicago Cubs (NL)	4(*)
	Detroit Tigers (AL)	0
1908	Chicago Cubs (NL)	4
	Detroit Tigers (AL)	1
1909	Pittsburgh Pirates (NL)	4
	Detroit Tigers (AL)	3
1910	Philadelphia Athletics (AL)	4
	Chicago Cubs (NL)	1
1911	Philadelphia Athletics (AL)	4
	New York Giants (NL)	2
1912	Boston Red Sox (AL)	4
	New York Giants (NL)	3(*)
1913	Philadelphia Athletics (AL)	4
	New York Giants (NL)	1
1914	Boston Braves (NL)	4
	Philadelphia Athletics (AL)	0
1915	Boston Red Sox (AL)	4
	Philadelphia Phillies (NL)	1
1916	Boston Red Sox (AL)	4
	Brooklyn Dodgers (NL)	1
1917	Chicago White Sox (AL)	4
	New York Giants (NL)	2
1918	Boston Red Sox (AL)	4
	Chicago Cubs (NL)	2
1919	Cincinnati Reds (NL)	5
	Chicago White Sox (AL)	3
1920	Cleveland Indians (AL)	5
	Brooklyn Dodgers (NL)	2
1921	New York Giants (NL)	4
	New York Yankees (AL)	3
1922	New York Giants (NL)	4
	New York Yankees (AL)	0(*)
1923	New York Yankees (AL)	4
	New York Giants (NL)	2
1924	Washington Senators (AL)	4
	New York Giants (NL)	3
1925	Pittsburgh Pirates (NL)	4
	Washington Senators (AL)	3
1926	St Louis Cardinals (NL)	4
	New York Yankees (AL)	3
1927	New York Yankees (AL)	4
	Pittsburgh Pirates (NL)	0
1928	New York Yankees (AL)	4
	St Louis Cardinals (NL)	0
1929	Philadelphia Athletics (AL)	4
	Chicago Cubs (NL)	1
1930	Philadelphia Athletics (AL)	4
	St Louis Cardinals (NL)	2
1931	St Louis Cardinals (NL)	4
	Philadelphia Athletics (AL)	3
1932	New York Yankees (AL)	4
	Chicago Cubs (NL)	0
1933	New York Giants (NL)	4
	Washington Senators (AL)	1
1934	St Louis Cardinals (NL)	4
	Detroit Tigers (AL)	3
1935	Detroit Tigers (AL)	4
	Chicago Cubs (NL)	2
1936	New York Yankees (AL)	4
	New York Giants (NL)	2
1937	New York Yankees (AL)	4
	New York Giants (NL)	1
1938	New York Yankees (AL)	4
	Chicago Cubs (NL)	0
1939	New York Yankees (AL)	4
	Cincinnati Reds (NL)	0
1940	Cincinnati Reds (NL)	4
	Detroit Tigers (AL)	3
1941	New York Yankees (AL)	4
	Brooklyn Dodgers (NL)	1
1942	St Louis Cardinals (NL)	4
	New York Yankees (AL)	1
1943	New York Yankees (AL)	4
	St Louis Cardinals (NL)	1
1944	St Louis Cardinals (NL)	4
	St Louis Browns (AL)	2
1945	Detroit Tigers (AL)	4
	Chicago Cubs (NL)	3
1946	St Louis Cardinals (NL)	4
	Boston Red Sox (AL)	3
1947	New York Yankees (AL)	4
	Brooklyn Dodgers (NL)	3
1948	Cleveland Indians (AL)	4
	Boston Braves (NL)	2
1949	New York Yankees (AL)	4
	Brooklyn Dodgers (NL)	1
1950	New York Yankees (AL)	4
	Philadelphia Phillies (NL)	0
1951	New York Yankees (AL)	4
	New York Giants (NL)	2
1952	New York Yankees (AL)	4
	Brooklyn Dodgers (NL)	3
1953	New York Yankees (AL)	4
	Brooklyn Dodgers (NL)	2
1954	New York Giants (NL)	4
	Cleveland Indians (AL)	0
1955	Brooklyn Dodgers (NL)	4
	New York Yankees (AL)	3
1956	New York Yankees (AL)	4
	Brooklyn Dodgers (NL)	3
1957	Milwaukee Braves (NL)	4
	New York Yankees (AL)	3
1958	New York Yankees (AL)	4
	Milwaukee Braves (NL)	3
1959	Los Angeles Dodgers (NL)	4
	Chicago White Sox (AL)	2
1960	Pittsburgh Pirates (NL)	4
	New York Yankees (AL)	3
1961	New York Yankees (AL)	4
	Cincinnati Reds (NL)	1
1962	New York Yankees (AL)	4
	San Francisco Giants (NL)	3
1963	Los Angeles Dodgers (NL)	4
	New York Yankees (AL)	0
1964	St Louis Cardinals (NL)	4
	New York Yankees (AL)	3
1965	Los Angeles Dodgers (NL)	4
	Minnesota Twins (AL)	3
1966	Baltimore Orioles (AL)	4
	Los Angeles Dodgers (NL)	0
1967	St Louis Cardinals (NL)	4
	Boston Red Sox (AL)	3
1968	Detroit Tigers (AL)	4
	St Louis Cardinals (NL)	3
1969	New York Mets (NL)	4
	Baltimore Orioles (AL)	1
1970	Baltimore Orioles (AL)	4
	Cincinnati Reds (NL)	1
1971	Pittsburgh Pirates (NL)	4
	Baltimore Orioles (AL)	3

Year	Team	
1972	Oakland A's (AL)	4
	Cincinnati Reds (NL)	3
1973	Oakland A's (AL)	4
	New York Mets (NL)	3
1974	Oakland A's (AL)	4
	Los Angeles Dodgers (NL)	1
1975	Cincinnati Reds (NL)	4
	Boston Red Sox (AL)	3
1976	Cincinnati Reds (NL)	4
	New York Yankees (AL)	0
1977	New York Yankees (AL)	4
	Los Angeles Dodgers (NL)	3
1978	New York Yankees (AL)	4
	Los Angeles Dodgers (NL)	2
1979	Pittsburgh Pirates (NL)	4
	Baltimore Orioles (AL)	3
1980	Philadelphia Phillies (NL)	4
	Kansas City Royals (AL)	2
1981	Los Angeles Dodgers (NL)	4
	New York Yankees (AL)	2
1982	St Louis Cardinals (NL)	4
	Milwaukee Brewers (AL)	3
1983	Baltimore Orioles (AL)	4
	Philadelphia Phillies (NL)	1
1984	Detroit Tigers (AL)	4
	San Diego Padres (NL)	1
1985	Kansas City Royals (AL)	4
	St Louis Cardinals (NL)	3
1986	New York Mets (NL)	4
	Boston Red Sox (AL)	3
1987	Minnesota Twins (AL)	4
	St Louis Cardinals (NL)	3
1988	Los Angeles Dodgers (NL)	4
	Oakland Athletics (AL)	1
1989	Oakland Athletics (AL)	4
	San Francisco Giants (NL)	0

(*) Included one tied game
(AL) American League (NL) National Leaugue
Most Wins
22 New York Yankees; **9** St Louis Cardinals; **5** Boston Red Sox, Pittsburgh Pirates, Philadelphia Athletics, Los Angeles Dodgers, New York Giants; **4** Cincinnati Reds, Detroit Tigers, Oakland Athletics

PLAY-OFFS (Since 1981)

(Between winners of East division and West division)

American League

1981	Kansas City (W) beat New York (E)	3-0
1982	Milwaukee (E) beat California (W)	3-2
1983	Baltimore (E) beat Chicago (W)	3-1
1984	Detroit (E) beat Kansas City (W)	3-0
1985	Kansas City (W) beat Toronto (E)	4-3
1986	Boston (E) beat California (W)	4-3
1987	Minnesota (W) beat Detroit (E)	4-1
1988	Oakland (W) beat Boston (E)	4-0
1989	Oakland (W) beat Toronto (E)	4-1
1990	Oakland (W) beat Boston (E)	4-0

National League

1981	Los Angeles (W) beat Montreal (E)	3-2
1982	St Louis (E) beat Atlanta (W)	3-0
1983	Philadelphia (E) beat Los Angeles (W)	3-1
1984	San Diego (W) beat Chicago (E)	3-2
1985	St Louis (E) beat Los Angeles (W)	4-2
1986	New York (E) beat Houston (W)	4-2
1987	St Louis (E) beat San Francisco (W)	4-3
1988	Los Angeles (W) beat New York (E)	4-3
1989	San Francisco (W) beat Chicago (E)	4-1
1990	Cincinnati (W) beat Pittsburgh (E)	4-2

——— RECORDS ———

MOST HITS
4256 Pete Rose
4191 Ty Cobb
3771 Hank Aaron
3630 Stan Musial
3515 Tris Speaker

MOST HOME RUNS
755 Hank Aaron
714 Babe Ruth
660 Willie Mays
586 Frank Robinson
573 Harmon Killibrew
563 Reggie Jackson

MOST NO-HITTERS
6 Nolan Ryan
4 Sandy Koufax
3 Cy Young
  Bob Feller

BASKETBALL

DETROIT MOTOR ON

The Detroit Pistons joined the great teams of basketball history when they won their second successive NBA Championship, beating the Portland Trail Blazers 4-1. Only the Boston Celtics and the Lakers (first in their old Minneapolis home, then in Los Angeles) had previously won two years running.

It was a triumph, however, that tarnished very quickly. The city's celebration of the victory turned into carnage with seven people killed (six hit by cars), hundreds injured by gunfire and stabbings and 141 arrested. Detroit's mayor, Coleman Young, said he was disappointed but not surprised: "There sure wasn't any wild explosion of killings," he said. And two days after the victory, Isiah Thomas, the Most Valuable Player of the Championship series, was reported to be the target of a federal gambling investigation after allegations that he ran high-stakes dice games at his home.

Detroit's success was achieved with three victories in Portland, the last by 92 points to 90 in a game the Pistons had been losing 90-83 with two minutes left. The Los Angeles Lakers, the dominant team of recent seasons, were beaten in the Western Conference semi-finals, their earliest exit since 1981. During the regular season, the Milwaukee Bucks beat the Seattle SuperSonics 155-154 after five periods of overtime, the longest NBA game since 1951. Streatham-born Steve Bucknall, 22, became the first Briton in the NBA when he signed for the Los Angeles Lakers.

In Britain, the extraordinary wanderings of the country's leading club continued. The 1989 champions Glasgow Rangers migrated south again, reverted to their old name, Kingston, and their old home at Tolworth in Surrey and won all three main competitions.

Hank Gathers, a leading US college player, collapsed on court and died on March 3, five days after a British player, Tony Penny of Manchester Giants. Both were 23, both were 6ft 7in, both wore no.44 and both had a history of heart trouble.

The demand for designer sportswear in the US reached insane proportions with several teenagers reported killed in "sports-apparel murders". Their murderers were anxious to get hold of the $120 Nike Air Jordan shoes, heavily promoted in commercials featuring Michael Jordan and directed by Spike Lee. "Parents around the country are watching their children get mugged or even killed over the same sneakers Lee and Jordan are promoting," wrote Phil Mushnick in the *New York Post*. "Gentlemen, it's murder."

Lisa Leslie, 17, was four points away from the US single-game schools record of 105 points at half-time in a contest between Morningside High and South Torrance High in California. Her opponents then walked out.

1989

NBA FINAL STANDINGS
Eastern Conference

CENTRAL			W	L	%
1	(1)	Detroit Pistons	59	23	.720
2	(5)	Chicago Bulls	55	27	.671
3	(4)	Milwaukee Bucks	44	38	.537
4	(2)	Cleveland Cavaliers	42	40	.512
5	(6)	Indiana Pacers	42	40	.512
6	(3)	Atlanta Hawks	41	41	.500
7	(-)	Orlando Magic	18	65	.220

ATLANTIC			W	L	%
1	(2)	Philadelphia 76ers	53	29	.646
2	(3)	Boston Celtics	52	30	.634
3	(1)	New York Knicks	45	37	.549
4	(4)	Washington Bullets	31	51	.378

5	(6*)	Miami Heat	18	64	.220
6	(5)	New Jersey Nets	17	65	.207

(*) 6th in Western Conference, Mid West Division in 1989

Western Conference

MID WEST			W	L	%
1	(5)	San Antonio Spurs	56	26	.683
2	(1)	Utah Jazz	55	27	.671
3	(4)	Dallas Mavericks	47	35	.573
4	(3)	Denver Nuggets	43	39	.524
5	(2)	Houston Rockets	41	41	.500
6	(-)	Minnesota Timberwolves	22	60	.268
7	(6†)	Charlotte Hornets	19	63	.232

(†) 6th in Eastern Confernce Atlantic Division in 1989

PACIFIC		W	L	%
1	(1) Los Angeles Lakers	63	19	.768
2	(5) Portland Trail Blazers	59	23	.720
3	(2) Phoenix Suns	54	28	.659
4	(3) Seattle SuperSonics	41	41	.500
5	(4) Golden State Warriors	37	45	.451
6	(7) Los Angeles Clippers	30	52	.366
7	(6) Sacramento Kings	23	59	.280

Last season's position in brackets

PLAY-OFFS

EASTERN CONFERENCE
First Round
DETROIT 3 Indiana 0; NEW YORK 3 Boston 2;
CHICAGO 3 Milwaukee 1; PHILADELPHIA 3 Cleveland 2

Semi-finals
DETROIT 4 New York 1; CHICAGO 4 Philadelphia 1

Conference Final
DETROIT 4 Chicago 3

WESTERN CONFERENCE
First Round
LOS ANGELES LAKERS 3 Houston 1; PHOENIX 3
Utah 2; PORTLAND 3 Dallas 0; SAN ANTONIO 3
Denver 0

Semi-finals
PHOENIX 4 Los Angeles Lakers 1; PORTLAND 4 San Antonio 3

Conference Fina
PORTLAND 4 Phoenix 2

NBA CHAMPIONSHIP
Game 1: DETROIT 105 Portland 99
Game 2: Detroit 105 PORTLAND 106 (Overtime)
Game 3: Portland 106 DETROIT 121
Game 4: Portland 109 DETROIT 112
Game 5: DETROIT 92 Portland 90
DETROIT won best-of-seven series 4-1
Series MVP: Isiah Thomas (Detroit)

MEN'S WORLD CHAMPIONSHIP
Argentina, Aug 8-19
Group A
YUGOSLAVIA 92 Venezuela 84; PUERTO RICO 78
Angola 75; PUERTO RICO 88 Venezuela 74;
YUGOSLAVIA 92 Angola 79; VENEZUELA 83 Angola
77; PUERTO RICO 82 Yugoslavia 75

Group B
AUSTRALIA 106 China 85; BRAZIL 125 Italy 109;
ITALY 94 Australia 89; BRAZIL 138 China 95; ITALY
115 China 76; AUSTRALIA 69 Brazil 68

Group C
UNITED STATES 103 Greece 95; SPAIN 130 South
Korea 101; UNITED STATES 146 South Korea 67;
GREECE 103 Spain 93; GREECE 119 South Korea 76;
UNITED STATES 95 Spain 85

Group D
SOVIET UNION 97 Argentina 77; CANADA 83 Egypt
68; ARGENTINA 96 Canada 88; SOVIET UNION 102
Egypt 76; ARGENTINA 82 Egypt 65; SOVIET UNION
90 Canada 81

Quarter-finals
Group One
UNITED STATES 104 Argentina 100; PUERTO RICO 83
Australia 79; UNITED STATES 79 Australia 78; PUERTO
RICO 92 Argentina 76; PUERTO RICO 81 United States
79; Australia 95 Argentina 91

Group Two
SOVIET UNION 75 Greece 57; YUGOSLAVIA 105
Brazil 86; YUGOSLAVIA 100 Soviet Union 77; GREECE
103 Brazil 88; YUGOSLAVIA 77 Greece 67; SOVIET
UNION 110 Brazil 100

Semi-finals
YUGOSLAVIA 99 United States 91; SOVIET UNION 98
Puerto Rico 82

Third Place Play-off
UNITED STATES 107 Puerto Rico 105

Final
YUGOSLAVIA 92 Soviet Union 75

Final clasification:
1 Yugoslavia; 2 Soviet Union; 3 United States; 4 Puerto
Rico; 5 Brazil; 6 Greece; 7 Australia; 8 Argentina; 9 Italy;
10 Spain; 11 Venezuela; 12 Canada; 13 Angola; 14 China;
15 South Korea; 16 Egypt

WOMEN'S WORLD CHAMPIONSHIP
Malaysia, Jul 11-18
Group A
BULGARIA 65 Canada 61; UNITED STATES 87 Cuba 78;
CUBA 83 Bulgaria 81; UNITED STATES 95 Canada 71;
CUBA 75 Canada 69; UNITED STATES 93 Bulgaria 72

Group B
YUGOSLAVIA 81 Czechoslovakia 66; SOVIET UNION 70
Australia 60; CZECHOSLOVAKIA 82 Soviet Union 79;
YUGOSLAVIA 80 Australia 70; CZECHOSLOVAKIA 83
Australia 54; YUGOSLAVIA 64 Soviet Union 63

Semi-finals
UNITED STATES 87 Czechoslovakia 59; YUGOSLAVIA
74 Cuba 66

Third Place Play-off
CUBA 83 Czechoslovakia 61

Final
UNITED STATES 88 Yugoslavia 78

Final Classification:
1 United States; 2 Yugoslavia; 3 Cuba; 4 Czechoslovakia;
5 Soviet Union; 6 Australia; 7 Canada; 8 Bulgaria

ENGLISH BASKETBALL ASSOCIATION
Carlsberg Premier League

		P	W	L	F	A	Pts
1	(*) Kingston	28	25	3	2852	2406	50
2	(5) Manchester	28	21	7	2758	2437	42
3	(6) Sunderland	28	20	8	2752	2592	40
4	(3) Bracknell	28	20	8	2850	2577	40
5	(10) Derby	28	10	18	2385	2562	20
6	(4) Leicester	28	7	21	2437	2476	14
7	(9) Solent	28	7	21	2558	2823	14
8	(-) London	28	2	26	2128	2847	4

Player of the Year: Clyde Vaughan (Sunderland)
(*) As Glasgow 1989

National League - Men's Division One

		P	W	L	F	A	Pts
1	(1) Oldham	22	20	2	2139	1727	40
2	(4) Worthing	22	19	3	2307	1949	38
3	(2) Brixton	22	19	3	2258	1814	38
4	(R) Hemel Hemp	22	14	8	1983	1818	28
5	(P) Bury	22	11	11	1916	1895	22
6	(8) Cheshire	22	10	12	1915	1989	20
7	(R) Crystal Palace	22	9	13	1859	2140	18
8	(3) Birmingham	22	8	14	2031	2007	16
9	(P) Plymouth	22	8	14	1999	2120	16
10	(P) Stevenage	22	5	17	1997	2209	10
11	(5) Gateshead	22	5	17	1933	2177	9*
12	(9) Corby	22	4	18	1854	2346	8

Gateshead one point deducted for fielding ineligible player

Play-off
Oldham beat Brixton 200-197 agg

National League - Women's Division One

		P	W	L	F	A	Pts
1	(1) Northampton	22	22	0	1729	1139	44
2	(7) Sheffield	22	20	2	1570	1098	40
3	(5) Nottingham	22	15	7	1347	1142	30
4	(2) London YMCA	22	14	8	1566	1446	28
5	(9) Brixton	22	12	10	1474	1396	24
6	(6) Crystal Palace	22	11	11	1381	1400	22
7	(8) Ipswich	22	9	13	1423	1518	18
8	(-) Gateshead	22	8	14	1354	1394	16
9	(10) Cardiff	22	8	14	1294	1517	16
10	(11) Kingston	22	7	15	1396	1704	14
11	(3) Stockport	22	4	18	1184	1592	8
12	(-) Leicester	22	2	20	1349	1721	4

In above tables last season's positions are given in brackets

Carlsberg Championship Play-Offs
NEC, Birmingham, Apr 13-14

Semi-finals
KINGSTON 83 Bracknell 72; SUNDERLAND 111 Manchester 106 (overtime)

Third Place Play-off
MANCHESTER 110 Bracknell 103

Final
KINGSTON 87 Sunderland 82

Women's Final
NORTHAMPTON 70 Sheffield 68 (overtime)

COCA-COLA NATIONAL CUP FINALS
London Arena, Mar 25
Men

Semi-finals
SUNDERLAND 83 Derby 79; KINGSTON 87 Bracknel 68

Final
KINGSTON 103 Sunderland 78
Women

Semi-finals
BRIXTON 68 Northampton 64; SHEFFIELD 48 Nottingham 43

Final
SHEFFIELD 64 Brixton 46

EUROPEAN CUP-WINNERS' CUP FINAL
Florence, Italy, Mar 14
VIRTUS BOLOGNA 79 Real Madrid 74

EUROPEAN KORAC CUP FINAL
1st Leg, Mar 22
Scavolini Pesaro (Ita) 98 Joventut Badalona (Spa) 97
2nd Leg, Mar 29
Joventut Badalona (Spa) 98 Scavolini Pesaro (Ita) 86
JOVENTUT BADALONA won 195-184 on agg

MEN'S EUROPEAN CUP CHAMPIONSHIP FINAL
Zaragoza, Apr 17-19
JUGOPLASTIKA SPLIT (Yug) 72 Barcelona 67

WOMEN'S RONCHETTI CUP FINAL
Munich, Mar 22
PARMA PRIMIZIE (Ita) 150 Jedinstvo Aida (Yug) 131
Aggregate scores over two legs

——— CHAMPIONS ———

OLYMPIC GAMES

Men		Women	
1936	United States		
1948	United States		
1952	United States		
1956	United States		
1960	United States		
1964	United States		
1968	United States		
1972	USSR		
1976	United States	1976	USSR
1980	Yugoslavia	1980	USSR
1984	United States	1984	United States
1988	USSR	1988	United States

WORLD CHAMPIONSHIPS

Men		Women	
1950	Argentina	1953	United States
1954	United States	1957	United States
1959	Brazil	1959	USSR
1963	Brazil	1964	USSR
1967	USSR	1967	USSR
1970	Yugoslavia	1971	USSR
1974	USSR	1975	USSR
1978	Yugoslavia	1979	United States
1982	USSR	1983	USSR
1986	United States	1987	United States
1990	Yugoslavia	1990	United States

EUROPEAN CHAMPIONSHIPS

Men		Women	
1935	Latvia		
1937	Lithuania	1938	Italy
1939	Lithuania		
1946	Czechoslovakia		
1947	USSR		
1949	Egypt	1950	USSR
1951	USSR	1952	USSR
1953	USSR	1954	USSR
1955	Hungary	1956	USSR
1957	USSR	1958	Bulgaria
1959	USSR	1960	USSR
1961	USSR	1962	USSR
1963	USSR	1964	USSR
1965	USSR	1966	USSR
1967	USSR	1968	USSR
1969	USSR	1970	USSR
1971	USSR	1972	USSR
1973	Yugoslavia	1974	USSR
1975	Yugoslavia	1976	USSR

1977	Yugoslavia	1978	USSR
1979	USSR	1980	USSR
1981	USSR	1981	USSR
1983	Italy	1983	USSR
1985	USSR	1985	USSR
1987	Greece	1987	USSR
1989	Yugoslavia	1989	USSR

NBA

1947	Philadelphia Warriors
1948	Baltimore Bullets
1949	Minneapolis Lakers
1950	Minneapolis Lakers
1951	Rochester Royals
1952	Minneapolis Lakers
1953	Minneapolis Lakers
1954	Minneapolis Lakers
1955	Syracuse Nationals
1956	Philadelphia Warriors
1957	Boston Celtics
1958	St Louis Hawks
1959	Boston Celtics
1960	Boston Celtics
1961	Boston Celtics
1962	Boston Celtics
1963	Boston Celtics
1964	Boston Celtics
1965	Boston Celtics
1966	Boston Celtics
1967	Philadelphia 76ers
1968	Boston Celtics
1969	Boston Celtics
1970	New York Knicks
1971	Milwaukee Bucks
1972	Los Angeles Lakers
1973	New York Knicks
1974	Boston Celtics
1975	Golden State Warriors
1976	Boston Celtics
1977	Portland Trail Blazers
1978	Washington Bullets
1979	Seattle Supersonics
1980	Los Angeles Lakers
1981	Boston Celtics
1982	Los Angeles Lakers
1983	Philadelphia 76ers
1984	Boston Celtics
1985	Los Angeles Lakers
1986	Boston Celtics
1987	Los Angeles Lakers
1988	Los Angeles Lakers
1989	Detroit Pistons
1990	Detroit Pistons

ENGLISH BASKETBALL ASSOCIATION
National Champions

Men

1936	Hoylake YMCA
1937	Hoylake YMCA
1938	Catford Saints
1939	Catford Saints
1940	Birmingham Athletic Inst.
1947	Carpathians
1948	Latter Day Saints
1949	Latter Day Saints
1950	Latter Day Saints
1951	Birmingham Dolobran
1952	London Polytechnic
1953	London Polytechnic
1954	London Polytechnic
1955	London Polytechnic
1956	-
1957	Central YMCA
1958	Central YMCA
1959	Aspley O.B.
1960	Central YMCA
1961	London University
1962	Central YMCA
1963	Central YMCA
1964	Central YMCA
1965	Aldershot Warriors
1966	Oxford University
1967	Central YMCA
1968	Oxford University
1969	Central YMCA
1970	Liverpool Police
1971	Mancester University
1972	Avenue (Leyton)
1973	London Latvian SK
1974	Sutton & C. Palace
1975	Embassy All Stars
1976	Crystal Palace
1977	Crystal Palace
1978	Crystal Palace
1979	Crystal Palace
1980	Crystal Palace
1981	Sunderland
1982	Crystal Palace
1983	Sunderland
1984	Solent
1985	Manchester Untied
1986	Kingston
1987	BCP London
1988	Murray Livingston
1989	Glasgow Rangers
1990	Kingston

Women

1981	Southgate
1982	Southgate
1983	Southgate
1984	A.C. Northampton
1985	A.C. Northampton
1986	Crystal Palace
1987	A.C. Northampton
1988	Stockport
1989	Northampton
1990	Northampton

1991

Mar 2-3 Coca-Cola National Cup Finals (London Arena); *Mar 26* European Cup Winners' Cup Final, women (Barcelona); *Apr 12-13* Carlsberg Championships (NEC, Birmingham); *Apr 18* European Champions' Cup final (Paris); *Jun 12-17* European Championships, women; *Jun 25-30* European Championships, men.

BILLIARDS

━━━━1990━━━━

STRACHAN UK PROFESSIONAL CHAMPIONSHIP
Middlesbrough, Mar 4-8

FIRST ROUND
MIKE RUSSELL (Eng) beat Mark Wildman (Eng) 679-511; EDDIE CHARLTON (Aus) beat Eugene Hughes (Ire) 633-235; PETER GILCHRIST (Eng) beat Geoffrey Thompson (Eng) 640-487; CLIVE EVERTON (Wal) beat Robby Foldvari (Aus) 365-337; IAN WILLIAMSON (Eng) beat Fred Davis (Eng) 533-252; RAY EDMONDS (Eng) beat Hugh Nimmo (Sco) 673-463; BOB CLOSE (Eng) beat David Edwards (Wal) 680-455; JOHN MURPHY (Eng) beat Norman Dagley (Eng) 693-531

QUARTER-FINALS
EDMONDS beat Williamson 457-390; MURPHY beat Close 492-455; GILCHRIST beat Everton 863-264; RUSSELL beat Charlton 750-417

SEMI-FINALS
RUSSELL beat Gilchrist 1973-1014; MURPHY beat Edmonds 1149-1073

FINAL
RUSSELL beat Murphy 1478-1058
Highest Break: 268 Mike Russell (v. Gilchrist)

ENGLISH AMATEUR CHAMPIONSHIP FINAL
Leamington Spa, May 13
MARTIN GOODWILL (Wiltshire) beat Peter Shelley (Stoke-on-Trent) 2380-1350

━━━━ CHAMPIONS ━━━━

WORLD PROFESSIONAL CHAMPIONSHIP
1870–1909 operated on a challenge system and again 1951-71. Since 1980 it has been held on a knockout basis All winners British unless otherwise stated

1870	William Cook	1924	Tom Newman
1870	John Roberts, Jnr	1925	Tom Newman
1870	Joseph Bennett	1926	Tom Newman
1871	John Roberts, Jnr	1927	Tom Newman
1871	William Cook	1928	Joe Davis
1875	John Roberts, Jnr	1929	Joe Davis
1880	Joseph Bennett	1930	Joe Davis
1885	John Roberts, Jnr	1931	Not held
1889	Charles Dawson	1932	Joe Davis
1901	H. W. Stevenson	1933	Walter Lindrum (Aus)
1901	Charles Dawson	1934	Walter Lindrum (Aus)
1901	H. W. Stevenson	1951	Clark McConachy (NZ)
1903	Charles Dawson	1968	Rex Williams
1908	Melbourne Inman	1971	Leslie Driffield
1909	H. W. Stevenson	1971	Rex Williams
1910	H. W. Stevenson	1980	Fred Davis
1911	H. W. Stevenson	1982	Rex Williams
1912	Melbourne Inman	1983	Rex Williams
1913	Melbourne Inman	1984	Mark Wildman
1914	Melbourne Inman	1985	Ray Edmonds
1919	Melbourne Inman	1986	Robbie Foldvari (Aus)
1920	Willie Smith	1987	Norman Dagley
1921	Tom Newman	1988	Norman Dagley
1922	Tom Newman	1989	Mike Russell
1923	Willie Smith		

WORLD AMATEUR CHAMPIONSHIP
1926	Joe Earlham (Eng)
1927	Allan Prior (SA)
1929	Les Hayes (Aus)
1931	Laurie Steeples (Eng)
1933	Sydney Lee (Eng)
1935	Horace Coles (Wal)
1936	Robert Marshall (Aus)
1938	Robert Marshall (Aus)
1951	Robert Marshall (Aus)
1952	Leslie Driffield (Eng)
1954	Tom Cleary (Aus)
1958	Wilson Jones (Ind)
1960	Herbert Beetham (Eng)
1962	Robert Marshall (Aus)
1964	Wilson Jones (Ind)
1967	Leslie Driffield (Eng)
1969	Jack Karnehm (Eng)
1971	Norman Dagley (Eng)
1973	Mohammed Lafir (Sri)
1975	Norman Dagley (Eng)
1977	Michael Ferreira (Ind)
1979	Paul Mifsud (Malta)
1981	Michael Ferreira (Ind)
1983	Michael Ferreira (Ind)
1985	Geet Sethi (Ind)
1987	Geet Sethi (Ind)

U K PROFESSIONAL CHAMPIONSHIP
(Not held 1952-1978)
1934	Joe Davis
1935	Joe Davis
1936	Joe Davis
1937	Joe Davis
1938	Joe Davis
1939	Joe Davis
1946	John Barrie
1947	Joe Davis
1948	Sidney Smith
1950	John Barrie
1951	Fred Davis
1979	Rex Williams
1980	Jack Karnehm
1981	Rex Williams
1983	Mark Wildman
1987	Norman Dagley
1988	Ian Williamson
1989	Mike Russell
1990	Mike Russell

━━━━ RECORDS ━━━━

Highest break: 499,135 Tom Reece 3 Jun – 6 Jul 1907 (this incorporated the cradle cannon which is no longer allowed)

Highest break since introduction of 25-hazard rule (1926): 4,137 Walter Lindrum 1932

Highest break under current 'two pot' rule: 962 (unfinished) Michael Ferreira 29 Apr 1986

BOWLS

After 23 unsuccessful attempts over the past two decades, the England international Tony Allcock finally won his first title at the EBA National Championships, and his second as well. Allcock skipped his Cheltenham triple to victory and then won the singles, beating Kirk Smith of Buckinghamshire 25-12. "He was absolutely brilliant," said Smith. The triple from the Cheltenham club which Allcock skipped to victory also included Andy Wills, 20, and Jack Drummond-Henderson, 79, who is a karate black belt.

There was further proof of the game's ability to span the ages. Robert Newman from Reading, 15, together with his father Mike, reached the semi-finals in the pairs and the quarter-finals in the triples. Oliver Ovett from Brighton, the 14-year-old cousin of the runner Steve, narrowly lost in the first round of the triples. Ovett began playing as a 12-year-old. He joined Preston Manor because his father's previous club refused to admit youngsters. In Huddersfield, the Thongsbridge team in the local over-65 league lost the title for fielding a 61-year-old.

1991

MEN - OUTDOOR
WOOLWICH EBA NATIONAL CHAMPIONSHIPS
Worthing, Aug 13-24
Singles
Semi-finals
TONY ALLCOCK (Cheltenham) beat Brett Morley (GPT Beeston) 25-12; KIRK SMITH (Denham, Bucks) beat Terry James (Thrapston, Northants) 25-20
Final
ALLCOCK beat Smith 25-12
Pairs
Semi-finals
JOHN OTTAWAY & ROGER GUY (Wymondham Dell, Norfolk) beat Robert & Mike Newman (Reading) 20-18; COLIN HARMAN & PAUL CATER (West Ealing) beat Geoff Roll & John George (County Arts, Norwich) 18-16
Final
OTTAWAY & GUY beat Harman & Cater 18-16
Triples
Semi-finals
CHELTENHAM 17 Poole Park 13; WELFORD-ON-AVON 17 Walker 8
Final
CHELTENHAM 18 Welford-on-Avon 16
Fours
Semi-finals
MANSFIELD COLLIERY (Notts) 27 Topsham (Devon) 18; BATH (Somerset) 23 GPT Beeston (Notts) 17
Final
BATH 20 Mansfield Colliery 13

NATWEST MIDDLETON CUP
Worthing, Aug 25
Semi-finals
YORKSHIRE 107 Buckinghamshire 104; DORSET 121 Essex 104
Final
YORKSHIRE 136 Dorset 113

NATWEST BRITISH ISLES CHAMPIONSHIPS
Methilhill, Fife, Jul 3-6

International Series
1 ENGLAND; 2 Scotland; 3 Wales; 4 Ireland
Singles
JOHN OTTAWAY (Eng) beat Jim Baker (Ire) 25-22
Pairs
WALES 21 Ireland 16
Triples
IRELAND 17 England 6
Fours
ENGLAND 23 Wales 21

MEN - INDOOR
EMBASSY WORLD INDOOR CHAMPIONSHIPS
Preston, Feb 21-Mar 4
Singles
Quarter-finals
JOHN PRICE (Wal) beat Mark McMahon (HK) 2-7 7-3 7-6 0-7 7-2; IAN SCHUBACK (Aus) beat Willie Wood (Sco) 7-3 2-7 7-0 7-4; TONY ALLCOCK (Eng) beat Hugh Duff (Sco) 7-5 7-1 7-1; GARY SMITH (Eng) beat Andy Thomson (Eng) 2-7 7-3 7-3 2-7 7-2 7-6
Semi-finals
PRICE beat Allcock 7-6 4-7 7-1 3-7 7-2; SCHUBACK beat Smith 7-5 4-7 7-5 7-0
Final
PRICE beat Schuback 4-7 7-4 7-2 3-7 7-0
Pairs
Semi-finals
DAVID BRYANT & TONY ALLCOCK (Eng) beat Stephen Rees & John Price (Wal) 7-6 7-3 4-7 7-5; JIM YATES & IAN SCHUBACK beat Gerry Smyth & Steve Halmai (Eng) 6-7 7-5 7-1 7-1
Final
BRYANT & ALLCOCK beat Yates & Schuback 3-7 7-4 3-7 7-3 7-2

ENGLISH CHAMPIONSHIPS
Melton Mowbray, Mar 10-17
Singles
ANDY THOMSON (Cyphers, Beckenham) beat Tony Allcock (Bentham) 21-7

Pairs
GATESHEAD (Terry Scott & David Webb) 22 Thamesdown (David Snell & Mel Briggs) 10
Triples
SUNDERLAND 23 Bentham 17
Fours
CYPHERS 26 Preston Club, Brighton 6
Inter County Championship (Liberty Trophy)
MIDDLESEX beat Norfolk 128-102

BRITISH CHAMPIONSHIPS
Prestwick, Apr 2-6
Singles
GRAHAM ROBERTSON (Sco) beat Geoff McMullan (Ire) 21-7
Pairs
IRELAND (Marcus Craig & Jim Baker) 17 England (Martin & Mick Tomlin) 12
Triples
WALES 27 Scotland 16
Fours
ENGLAND 19 Ireland 13
Home International Championship (Hilton Trophy)
1 ENGLAND; 2 Scotland; 3 Wales; 4 Ireland

WOMEN - OUTDOOR

BRITISH ISLES CHAMPIONSHIPS
Saundersfoot, Wales, Jun 25-28
Singles
LIZ WREN (Sco) beat Jean Baker (Eng) 25-14
Pairs
ENGLAND 19 Ireland 16
Triples
WALES 15 England 13
Fours
WALES 19 Ireland 18
Home Internationals
1 ENGLAND; 2 Scotland; 3 Wales; 4 Ireland
COUNTY CHAMPIONSHIP
Leamington Spa, Jul 30
Semi-finals
KENT 124 Devon 107; NOTTINGHAMSHIRE 118 Norfolk 115
Final
KENT 101 Nottinghamshire 90

ENGLISH NATIONAL CHAMPIONSHIPS
Leamington Spa, Aug 1-11
Singles
BARBARA TILL (Milton Park, Portsmouth) beat Joan Howlett (West Bridgford, Notts) 21-15
Two-wood Singles
GILLIAN FITZGERALD (Kettering) beat Beryl Noble (Luton Town) 18-8
Champion of Champions
GILLIAN FITZGERALD (Kettering) beat Mavis Steele (Sunbury Sports) 21-17
Pairs
MAUREEN CHRISTMAS & JENNY TUNBRIDGE

(Chesterton, Cambridge) beat Margaret Bonsor & Jean Baker (Alfreton) 24-12
Both pairs of finalists were mother/daughter combinations
Triples
BALDOCK 20 North Scarle, Lincoln 17
Fours
STARCROSS DEVON 20 Kettering Lodge 14

WOMEN - INDOOR
ENGLISH CHAMPIONSHIPS
Luton, Mar 5-9
Singles
GILL SMITH (Bentham) beat Sally Franklin (Wisbech) 21-18
Pairs
DI WILSON & JEAN CAMMACK (Boston) beat Jane Rowntree & Gloria Thomas (West Cornwall) 22-12
Triples
BOSTON 26 Egerton Park 11
Fours
TEESIDE 26 Dartford 12
Yetton Trophy
ESSEX COUNTY 79 Torbay 70

BRITISH CHAMPIONSHIPS
Margate, Mar 19-22
Singles
MARGARET JOHNSTON (NI) beat Gill Smith (Eng) 21-12
Pairs
SCOTLAND (Anne McFarlane & Margaret Spink) 21 England (Jane Rowntree & Gloria Thomas) 19
Triples
ENGLAND 23 Scotland 11
Fours
ENGLAND 24 Scotland 16

HOME INTERNATIONALS
1 ENGLAND; 2 Wales; 3 Scotland; 4 Ireland

MIXED - INDOOR

CARLING INTERNATIONAL PAIRS
Llanelli, Apr 8-9
MARY PRICE & TONY ALLCOCK (Eng) beat Norma Shaw & David Bryant (Eng) 7-6 7-5 4-9 6-3

MACKESON MIXED PAIRS
Gedling, Mar 23-25
NOTTINGHAM (Norma Wilson & Brett Morley) 19 Spalding (Kath Inglis & Rick Collins) 15

MACKESON MIXED FOURS
Luton, Apr 20-22
MARCH 17 Isis 15

CROWN GREEN BOWLS

WATERLOO HANDICAP
Waterloo Hotel, Blackpool, completed Sep 12
Quarter-finals
ROBERT CRAWSHAW (Wilmslow) beat Steve Bennett (Coventry) 21-19; CHRIS MACDONALD (Wilmslow) beat Bill Green (Stockport) 21-15; JOHN HODSON (Preston) beat Tommy Johnstone (Warrington) 21-18; JOHN BANCROFT (Hyde) beat Mike Leach (Warley) 21-18

Semi-finals
MACDONALD beat Crawshaw 21-16; BANCROFT beat
Hodson 21-15
Final
BANCROFT beat Macdonald 21-12
Womens Finals
JANE JONES (Wirral) beat Pat Davis (Wirral) 21-16
The two finalists were sisters

——— CHAMPIONS ———

WORLD CHAMPIONSHIPS

Men-Outdoors
Singles
1966	David Bryant (Eng)
1972	Malwyn Evans (Wal)
1976	Doug Watson (SA)
1980	David Bryant (Eng)
1984	Peter Belliss (NZ)
1988	David Bryant (Eng)

Pairs
1966	Geoff Kelly & Bert Palm (Aus)
1972	Clementi Delgado & Eric Liddell (HK)
1976	Doug Watson & William Moseley (SA)
1980	Alf Sandercock & Peter Rheuben (Aus)
1984	George Adrain & Skippy Arculli (US)
1988	Rowan Brassey & Peter Belliss (NZ)

Triples / Fours
Triples		Fours	
1966	Australia	1966	New Zealand
1972	United States	1972	England
1976	South Africa	1976	South Africa
1980	England	1980	Hong Kong
1984	Ireland	1984	England
1988	New Zealand	1988	Ireland

Team
(Leonard Trophy)
1966	Australia
1972	Scotland
1976	South Africa
1980	England
1984	England
1988	England

Men-Indoors
Singles
1979	David Bryant (Eng)
1980	David Bryant (Eng)
1981	David Bryant (Eng)
1982	John Watson (Sco)
1983	Bob Sutherland (Sco)
1984	Jim Baker (Ire)
1985	Terry Sullivan (Wal)
1986	Tony Allcock (Eng)
1987	Tony Allcock (Eng)
1988	Hugh Duff (Sco)
1989	Richard Coursie (Sco)
1990	John Price (Wal)

Women-Outdoors
Singles
1969	Gladys Doyle (PNG)
1973	Elsie Wilke (NZ)
1977	Elsie Wilke (NZ)
1981	Norma Shaw (Eng)

1985	Merle Richardson (Aus)
1988	Janet Ackland (Wal)

Pairs
1969	E McDonald & M Cridlan (SA)
1973	Lorna Lucas & Dot Jenkinson (Aus)
1977	Helen Wong & Elvie Chok (HK)
1981	Eileen Bell & Nan Allely (Ire)
1985	Merle Richardson & Fay Craig (Aus)
1988	Margaret Johnston & Phyllis Nolan (Ire)

Triples / Fours
Triples		Fours	
1969	South Africa	1969	South Africa
1973	New Zealand	1973	New Zealand
1977	Wales	1977	Australia
1981	Hong Kong	1981	England
1985	Australia	1985	Scotland
1988	Australia	1988	Australia

Team
1969	South Africa
1973	New Zealand
1977	Australia
1981	England
1985	Australia
1988	England

Women-Indoors
Singles
1988	Margaret Johnston (Ire)
1989	Margaret Johnston (Ire)

EBA CHAMPIONSHIPS
Inaugurated 1903. Winners since 1981:
Singles
1981	Andy Thomson, Kent
1982	Chris Ward, Norfolk
1983	John Bell, Cumbria
1984	Wynne Richards, Surrey
1985	Roy Keating, Devon
1986	Wynne Richards, Surrey
1987	David Holt, Lancs
1988	Richard Bray, Cornwall
1989	John Ottaway, Norfolk
1990	Tony Allcock, Cheltenham

Pairs
1981	Burton House, Lincs
1982	Bedford Borough
1983	Eldon Grove, Durham
1984	Lenham, Kent
1985	Haxby Road, Yorks
1986	Owton Lodge, Durham
1987	Bolton, Lancs
1988	Leicester
1989	Essex County
1990	Wymondham Dell, Norfolk

Triples
1981	St Peter's, Hampshire
1982	Lenham, Kent
1983	Marlborough, Suffolk
1984	Clevedon, Somerset
1985	Clevedon, Somerset
1986	Poole Park, Dorset
1987	Worcester County
1988	Belgrave, Leicester
1989	Southbourne, Sussex
1990	Cheltenham

Fours
1981	Owton Lodge, Durham
1982	Castle, Nottinghamshire
1983	Bolton, Lancs

1984	Boscombe Cliff, Hampshire
1985	Aldershot, Essex
1986	Stony Stratford, Bucks
1987	Aylesbury Town, Bucks
1988	Summertown, Oxon
1989	Blackheath & Greenwich, Kent
1990	Bath

MIDDLETON CUP
Inaugurated 1911. Winners since 1981:

1981	Somerset
1982	Berkshire
1983	Surrey
1984	Somerset
1985	Northumberland
1986	Wiltshire
1987	Kent
1988	Northumberland
1989	Kent
1990	Yorkshire

CROWN GREEN BOWLS

WATERLOO CUP
Inaugurated 1907. Played at Waterloo Hotel, Blackpool.
Winners since 1981:

Men

1981	Roy Nicholson
1982	Dennis Mercer
1983	Stan Frith
1984	Steve Ellis
1985	Tommy Johnstone
1986	Brian Duncan
1987	Brian Duncan
1988	Ingham Gregory
1989	Brian Duncan
1990	John Bancroft

Most wins: 4 Brian Duncan

Women
(Inaugurated 1988)

1988	Barbara Rawcliffe
1989	Diane Hunt
1990	Jane Jones

—— 1991 ——

March 18-22 British Isles Indoor Championship
(Aberdeen); Mar 24-25 Champion of Champions
(Wellingborough); Apr 5-13 English Indoor National
Championships (Melton Mowbray); Jul 1-6 British Isles
Outdoor Championships (Wales); Aug 11-23 English
National Championships (Worthing); Aug 24 Middleton
Cup Final (Worthing).

BOXING

THE DOWNFALL OF IRON MIKE

In a half-full baseball dome during a Sunday lunchtime in Tokyo, the apparently invincible Mike Tyson was dethroned as world heavyweight champion by his utterly unconsidered opponent, James "Buster' Douglas. Tyson was knocked out in the 10th round. Most of the boxing writers had not troubled to attend and only one Las Vegas bookmaker bothered to take bets - with Tyson as a 42-1 on favourite. On that basis, it is quite accurate to describe Douglas's win as the greatest upset in boxing history.

It was not the last shock of a bizarre day. Douglas's moment was soured because the boxing establishment refused to believe their eyes. At the instigation of the promoter Don King, the presidents of the WBC and WBA, Jose Sulaiman and Gilberto Mendoza, initially rejected the result because the referee admitted he had made a mistake when Douglas had himself been knocked down for 12 to 13 seconds in the eighth round, but not counted out.

Douglas's handlers pointed out that their man was watching the referee and could have got up if he wanted. This view was widely shared and as world reaction intensified, Sulaiman and Mendoza retreated. Douglas had, in any case, dominated the fight in the opinion of everyone except two of the judges, one of whom scored the fight equal while the other had Tyson ahead.

How did it happen? Experts later thought Tyson may have lost too much weight too quickly. The endless upheavals in his turbulent personal life (private life is hardly the phrase) may have had their effect too. Tyson's corner - without sacked trainer Kevin Rooney - made elementary mistakes. There was no Endswell, the metal device used to press away any puffiness from a boxer's eyes; they even forgot to drain the icebag and so ended up holding a bag of iced water to his cut.

The ensuing months were given over to endless legal wrangles and name-calling between the various managements. The contracts for the fight had not encompassed the possibility that Tyson could lose. Eventually, Douglas bought his way out of his contract with King for $7m clearing the way for him to defend the title against Evander Holyfield, who was supposed to be Tyson's next opponent. Tyson began his rehabilitation with one of his familiar old quick kills, beating Henry Tillman in two minutes 47 seconds, but then his sparring partner Greg Page sliced open a gash over Tyson's eye that needed 48 stitches and a long lay-off. Douglas, meanwhile, stayed out of the ring and conducted himself with a quiet dignity that seemed out of place in this murky world.

The most talked-about heavyweight contender, bizarrely enough, was almost twice Tyson's age. The former champion George Foreman, 42, came to London in September and won his 24th fight since his comeback started in 1987 and began to be taken seriously again by the sport's increasingly desperate followers even though he now weighed almost 19 stone and looked more like a sumo wrestler. His presence merely served to emphasise the boxing's slide into disrepute. His fight against Gerry Cooney, who had not fought for $2^1/_2$ years ("the two geezers at Caesar's") was summed up by Peters, the cartoonist of the *Dayton Daily News* in Ohio, who had the referee warning: "Now remember, no hitting below the pacemaker or above the dentures."

THE TOKYO EARTHQUAKE

❝The biggest shocker in boxing - if not in all of sports - history
Bert Randolph Sugar, Boxing Illustrated

"I'll just hit him, I guess."
Buster Douglas, explaining his strategy in advance

"Two knock-outs took place but the first knock-out obliterates the second. Buster Douglas was knocked out and the referee did not do his job and panicked. As the promoter of both fighters, I am only seeking fair play."
Don King, after the fight

"As of today, there is no heavyweight champion."
Jose Sulaiman, WBC president.

"You guys know me. I never cried or bitched about anything, forgive my French. I'm just asking for a fair chance. I can handle a loss. I just want to lose fairly."
Mike Tyson, crying and bitching

"Now I'll be able to get the car fixed with a new coat of paint."
Douglas, on the plane home

"We must warn the WBA and the WBC that if they persist in not recognising Buster Douglas as the legitimate winner...we will petition the United States Justice Department and the Senate Anti-Trust Committee to investigate them (and their dishonest ventriloquist Don King) on charges of monopoly and racketeering for stealing from all right-thinking boxing fans *their* history and *their* trust.
Bert Randolph Sugar, Boxing Illustrated

"The WBC never stated that we would not recognise him as champion."
Jose Sulaiman, president of the WBC, one day later

"I never asked anybody to change the decision. I recognise Buster Douglas as heavyweight champion of the world. We just want the first shot at a rematch."
Don King, ditto

"No court in the land would say that Don King acted in James Douglas's best interests. We try to be forgiving, but we don't forget."
Johnny Johnson, Douglas's manager

"Johnson is a guy who used to ring me 24 hours a day, begging me for fights for Buster. The problem with Johnny is that he's suffering from amnesia, which is the dreaded disease of those who climb the ladder of success. I know, however, that Johnny is a man of God, and I pray he will soon recover from his shell-shock."
Don King

"I was arrogant when I was poor and I'm going to be arrogant when I'm wealthy."
Johnny Johnson

"We're dealing with a cuckoo bird."
Al Braverman, Don King aide, on Johnson

"Sometimes your greatest strength can be your greatest weakness. Michael was some-what deluded because he thought he could just go in there and use power...As a champion, you can't allow yourself to be content. If you're content, you lose your desire."
Jay Bright, Tyson's trainer

"I don't know what I was doing. I thought 'If I get up, I got to have the mouthpiece.' I couldn't grab it. I kept trying to. I kept saying 'Well, it was right here'."
Mike Tyson

"Tyson is over the hill, he's burned out"
George Foreman

"You're the greatest, man. But I'm still the greatest ever."
Muhammad Ali to Douglas

"Well, what do you know about that? We won. You and me and Buster Douglas. The good guys. We won because we stood up and hollered we were mad as hell and we weren't going to take it any more. We won because we told Don King he was a no-good, phoney, fast-talking, four-flusher and if he thought he was going to get away with this latest scam, he had another think coming. We won because when Don King saw that it wasn't going to work, he did what bullies everywhere do when their victims unite and face them down. He chickened out. He backed off. He showed himself for the coward he really is."
Ron Rapport, Boxing Illustrated

"Even Hollywood wouldn't have touched Stallone's script if he'd made it *that* implausible.❞
Steve Wulf, Sports Illustrated

In the absence of any young boxers whose names meant anything, the contest between the sport's ancients became the most bankable fights outside the heavyweight division as well. Nine years after Roberto Duran's famous cry of "No mas" against Sugar Ray Leonard, the two men met again for the WBC super-middleweight title. Leonard

THREE WISE MEN

Scores of the three judges of the Tyson-Douglas fight

	Larry Rozadilla (US)		Ken Morita (US)		Masakazu Ochida (Japan)	
1	Douglas	10-9		10-10	Douglas	10-9
2	Douglas	10-9	Douglas	10-9	Douglas	10-9
3	Douglas	10-9	Tyson	10-9	Tyson	10-9
4	Douglas	10-9		10-10		10-10
5	Douglas	10-9	Douglas	10-9	Douglas	10-9
6	Douglas	10-9		10-10	Tyson	10-9
7		10-10	Tyson	10-9		10-10
8	Tyson	10-8	Tyson	10-8	Tyson	10-8
9	Douglas	10-8	Douglas	10-9	Douglas	10-9
Totals:	Douglas	88	Tyson	87	Douglas	86
	Tyson	82	Douglas	86	Tyson	86

outpointed Duran though many spectators would have scored it about 1-0. "Please, guys, give us No Mas" said the *Vancouver Sun*. However, boxing appeared to be turning into an old man's game. Dr Harold "Hackie" Reitman, a 39-year-old orthopaedic surgeon who fights for charity, won his first three professional heavyweight bouts; and a light-heavyweight calling himself Lord Sir Anthony (formerly Tony Anthony) made a comeback in Oklahoma City aged 48, after a 26-year absence.

One of the few championship fights to create genuine controversy was between Julio Cesar Chavez and Meldrick Taylor in the junior-welterweight division. Taylor was stopped with two seconds of the last round to go, though he would have won on points. Taylor had just been knocked down and twice failed to respond to the question "Are you OK?" Some of the best entertainment came from Jorge "Maromero" Paez of Mexico, the IBF featherweight champion, who, among other antics, did aerial flips and break dancing before his fights. Paez spent his first 20 years in a circus.

BEST OF BRITISH

British boxers managed to maintain a share of the vast number of world titles now available. Dennis Andries regained his WBC light-heavyweight title from the Australian Jeff Harding after 13 months; Harding was ahead on points before Andries pummelled him. "It was pay-back time," said Andries. A member of Harding's entourage blamed the defeat on a huge piece of carrot cake his man had eaten before the fight. No one took much notice of Dave McAuley but he held on to his IBF flyweight title with successful defences against the Filipino Dodie Penalosa, the American Louis Curtis and Rodolfo Blanco of Colombia. At the Penalosa fight, the British judge Dave Parris gave McAuley 11 rounds out of 12; the Filipino judge Pascual Ingusol gave Penalosa five and McAuley three with four even. The IBF began to consider neutral judges. Glenn McCrory lost his IBF cruiserweight title on a knock-out to Jeff Lampkin of the US.

Meanwhile, Nigel Benn became a sort-of world champion when he won the middleweight title organised by the particularly ludicrous World Boxing Organisation. He broke a hand in beating Doug DeWitt but impressed US TV executives and signed to defend in Britain against Iran Barkley. The first was banned by the British Board because Barkley had recently undergone surgery for a detached retina. A furious Benn found more compliant hosts and stopped Barkley in the first round, apparently having so much pent-up energy that he hit him twice when he was on the canvas. Later, the two men threatened to punch each other at the post-fight press conference. "Now you would think," wrote Patrick Collins in the *Mail on Sunday*, "that no civilised city would allow a human wreck like Barkley within ten miles of a boxing ring. And you would be right because the fight took place in Las Vegas." Derek Williams lost his European heavyweight title to Jean Chanet of France, complaining of paralysis and dizziness. His manager Mike Barrett suspected that some substance had been administered, perhaps via Chanet's gloves. The best-known current British boxer remained Frank Bruno, and 600 well-wishers turned up at his wedding. His manager Terry Lawless said Bruno should retire; since he had not fought since February 1989 everyone else assumed he already had.

UPSETS IN BOXING HISTORY

1990 James 'Buster' Douglas beat Mike Tyson, ko-10th (Tokyo) heavyweight bout

1936 Max Schmeling beat Joe Louis, ko-12th (New York) non-title fight

1935 James J Braddock beat Max Baer, pts-15 (New York) world heavyweight bout

1964 Cassius Clay beat Sonny Liston, tko-7th (Miami) world heavyweight bout

1892 James J Corbett beat John L Sullivan, ko-21st (New Orleans) world heavyweight bout

1940 Fritzie Zivic beat Henry Armstrong, pts-15 (New York), world welterweight bout

1908 Billy Papke beat Stanley Ketchel, ko-12th (Los Angeles) world middleweight bout

1951 Randolph Turpin beat Sugar Ray Robinson, pts-15 (London) world middleweight bout

1915 Jess Willard beat Jack Johnson, ko-26th, (Havana, Cuba) world heavyweight bout

1922 Battling Siki beat Georges Carpentier ko-6th (Paris) world light-heavyweight bout

Source:*Boxing Illustrated*

THE GREATEST SHOCK OF ALL

US BETTING ON WORLD HEAVYWEIGHT BOXING UPSETS

1892 John L Sullivan 5-1 on. Lost to James J Corbett, ko 21st

1926 Jack Dempsey 5-1 on. Lost to Gene Tunney, pts

1935 Max Baer 10-1 on. Lost to James J Braddock, pts

1964 Sonny Liston 7-1 on. Lost to Cassius Clay, tko 7th

1978 Muhammad Ali 8-1 on. Lost to Leon Spinks, pts.

1990 Mike Tyson 42-1 on. Lost to James Douglas, ko 10th.

Source: *The Ring*

The British promoter Frank Warren was shot and wounded in a London street by a masked gunman. Two months later, Terry Marsh, the former world light welterweight champion, was sensationally charged with attempting to murder him. Rod Douglas had emergency brain surgery after losing a British middleweight title fight to Herol Graham; so did Mark Goult after winning the Southern Area bantamweight title. The Scottish-based promoter Alex Morrison, already banned for a year for helping a fighter with cataracts fight under another name, was alleged to have switched X-rays and brain scans to enable injured boxers to keep fighting. In America, Aaron Pryor, suspended from boxing in three states because of a detached retina, was granted a licence by Wisconsin. Officials said barring him would be discrimination against the handicapped. The heavyweight fight between the British-based boxer Lennox Lewis and Proud Kilimanjaro was called off because Kilimanjaro refused to hand over the result of an AIDS test. It was reported that among Kilimanjaro's previous opponents had been Captain Marvel, Ringo Starr, Mary Konate, The Bonyongo Destroyer and Juke Box Time Bomb. In Melbourne Jimmy Thunder knocked out Lee Lighting.

In Southampton, Mrs Minna Wilson stopped her son Tony's light-heavyweight title eliminator against Steve McCarthy by jumping into the ring and beating McCarthy with the heel of her shoe. McCarthy suffered a cut head. The fight was at first awarded to Wilson because McCarthy, who was winning easily, refused to continue. "I never want to be in the ring with a woman again," he said. "I'd rather take on Tyson." Mrs Wilson later explained that she became enraged because the crowd were calling her son a black bastard. The British Board eventually ordered a rematch. The amateur welterweight Geoff McCreash reversed the process by leaving the ring during the ABA quarter-finals in Birmingham to join a punch-up in the crowd after he saw his father being attacked. He was disqualified. The Hawaii Golden Gloves tournament was cancelled after a fight erupted between 75 boxers, coaches and spectators.

A Dorset school teacher, Richard Foley, devised an electronic helmet and breast-plate to protect fighters and simultaneously record the blows. He was supported by the ABA: "Some see it as poofy but things move on," said the former senior coach Kevin Hickey. A New York cable TV channel introduced a system to measure the power of the punches by sewing half-ounce transmitters into gloves.

Two South African welterweights, Norman Zwilibi and Zolani Sirunhu, landed simultaneous left-hooks to each other's jaw in a bout in East London to record the 14th double-ko in boxing history. The fight was ruled a draw. Roy Jones Jr thought he had knocked out the Texas junior middleweight champion, Derwin Richards, in the first round of a fight in Pensacola, Florida. Unfortunately, Richards was elsewhere at the time. The mystery fighter turned out to be one Tony Waddles, a car salesman from Oklahoma. Five Soviet boxers signed with the US promoter Lou Fracigno. Iran lifted its ban on boxing, imposed in 1979. Greenwich Council in London banned boxing on council premises: "Ratepayers' money shouldn't be put into beating people senseless," said Councillor David Clark. William Rose, a New Hampshire legislator, proposed a bill to make his state the first to ban boxing.

The former world heavyweight champion Larry Holmes did a song-and-dance act at The Sands, Las Vegas with a six-piece band; he was said to be a better singer than Joe Frazier. Charles Duncan, a 93-year-old ex-Navy boxer, punched a youth who tried to break into his house in Palmers Green, North London posing as a water board official. The youth fled. In Brighton, Kid Milo was arrested as he left the ring after losing a middleweight contest in Brighton to Chris Eubank for failing to answer charges of theft and criminal damage in the Midlands. In an Adelaide court Jason Abnett, 22, was convicted of blinding a man in one eye with a glass during a pub brawl. His lawyer said: "He might be given some allowance for the fact that he is a boxer."

——— 1989-90 ———

——— WORLD TITLE FIGHTS ———

(new champions underlined)

Heavyweight
Champions as at Aug 25 1989; WBC/WBA/IBF Mike Tyson, (US); WBO Francesco Damiani (Ita)
WBO: Dec 16, Cesena, Italy: Francesco Damiani beat Daniel Eduardo Netto (Arg) rtd 2nd
WBC/WBA/IBF Feb 10, Tokyo:James 'Buster' Douglas (US) beat MIke Tyson ko 10th

Cruiserweight
Champions as at Aug 25, 1989: WBC Carlos de Leon (PR) WBA Taoufik Belbouli (Fra) IBF Glenn McCrory (GB) WBO Vacant
IBF Oct 21, Middlesbrough: Glenn McCrory beat Siza Makhatini (SA) ko 11th
WBA Nov 28, Paris Robert Daniels (US) beat Dwight Qawi (US) pts
WBO Dec 3, Copenhagen; Richard 'Boone' Pultz (US) beat Magne Havnaa (Nor) pts
WBC Jan 27, Sheffield: Carlos De Leon and Johnny Nelson (GB) drew
IBF Mar 22, Gateshead: Jeff Lampkin (US) beat Glenn McCrory ko 3rd
WBO May 18, Aars, Denmark: Magne Havnaa (Nor) beat Richard Pultz rsf 5th
Havnaa became Norway's first world champion
WBA Jul 19, Seattle: Robert Daniels beat Craig Bodzianowski (US) pts
Bodzianowski had his right foot amputated in a road accident in 1984
WBC Jul 27, Capo D'Orlando, Sicily: Massimilio Duran (Ita) beat Carlos de Leon disq, 11th
IBF Jul 29, St Petersburg, Florida: Jeff Lampkin beat Siza Makhathini (SA) ko 8th

Light-heavyweight
Champions as at Aug 25, 1989: WBC Jeff Harding (Aus) WBC Virgil Hill (US); IBF Prince Charles Williams (US); WBO Michael Moorer (US)
WBC Oct 24, Brisbane: Jeff Harding beat Tom Collins (GB) tko 2nd
Collins refused to come out for 3rd round - purse withheld pending enquiry
WBA Oct 24, Bismarck, North Dakota: Virgil Hill beat James Kinchen (US) rsf 1st
WBO Nov 16, Atlantic City: Michael Moorer beat Jeff Thompson (US) rsf 1st
The fight lasted 106 seconds
WBO Dec 22, Auburn Hills, Michigan: Michael Moorer beat Mike Sedillo (US) rsf 6th
IBF Jan 7, Atlantic City: Prince Charles Williams beat Frankie Swindell (US) rsf 8th
WBO Feb 3, Atlantic City: Michael Moorer beat Marcellus Allen (US) tko 9th
WBA Feb 26, Bismarck, North Dakota: Virgil Hill beat David Vedder (US) pts
WBC Mar 18 Atlantic City: Jeff Harding beat Nestor Giovannini (Arg) rsf 11th
WBO Apr 28, Atlantic City: Michael Moorer beat Mario Melo (Arg) rsf 1st
WBA Jul 7, Bismarck, North Dakota: Virgil Hill beat Tyrone Frazier (US) pts
WBC Jul 28, Melbourne: Dennis Andries (GB) beat Jeff Harding ko 7th

Super-middleweight
Champions as at Aug 25, 1989: WBC: Sugar Ray Leonard (US); WBA: In-chul Baek (Sko); IBF: Graciano Rocchigiani (FRG); WBO: Thomas Hearns (US)
WBA Oct 8, Seoul: In-chul Baek beat Ron Esset (US) rsf 11th
WBC Dec 7, Las Vegas: Sugar Ray Leonard beat Roberto Duran (Pan) pts
Fight attracted a crowd of 16,000 who paid world record $9 million
WBA Jan 13, Ulsan, S.Korea: In-chul Baek beat Yoshiaki Tajima (Jap) rtd 7th
IBF Jan 27, New Orleans: Lindell Holmes (US) beat Frank Tate (US) pts
WBA Mar 30, Lyons: Christophe Tiozzo (Fra) beat In-chul Baek rsf 10th
WBO Apr 28, Atlantic City: Thomas Hearns beat Michael Olijade (Can) pts
WBA Jul 20 Arles, France: Christophe Tiozzo beat Paul Whitaker (US) rsf 8th
IBF Jul 20, Seattle: Lindell Homes beat Carl Sullivan (US) tko 9th

Middleweight
Champions as at Aug 25, 1989: WBC Roberto Duran (Pan); WBA: Mike McCallum (Jam); IBF: Michael Nunn (US); WBO Doug De Witt (US)
WBO Jan 15, Atlantic City: Doug De Witt beat Matthew Hilton (Can) rtd 11th
WBA Feb 3, Boston: Mike McCallum beat Steve Collins (US) pts
WBA Apr 14, London: Mike McCallum beat Michael Watson (GB) rsf 11th
IBF Apr 14, Las Vegas: Michael Nunn beat Marlon Starling (US) pts
WBO Apr 29, Atlantic City: Nigel Benn (GB) beat Doug De Witt rsf 8th
WBO Aug 18, Las Vegas: Nigel Benn beat Iran Barkley (US) rsf 1st.

Junior-middleweight
Champions as at Aug 25, 1989: WBC: John Mugabi (Uga) WBA: Julian Jackson (VI) IBF: Gianfranco Rosi (Ita) WBO: John David Jackson (US)
IBF Oct 27, St.Vincent: Gianfranco Rosi beat Troy Waters (Aus) pts
WBO Dec 1, Tucson, Arizona: John David Jackson beat Ruben Villamen (US) ko 2nd
WBO Feb 17, Deauville, France: John David Jackson v Martin Camara (Fra) No Contest
Fight declared void, Camara knocked down Jackson in 11th round. Before the referee could finish the count the ring was filled with jubilant fans.
WBC Mar 31, Tampa, Flarida: Terry Norris (US) beat John Mugabi ko 1st
IBF Apr 14, Monte Carlo: Gianfranco Rosi beat Kevin Daigle (US) rsf 7th
WBC Jul 13, Annecy, France: Terry Norris beat Rene Jacquot (Fra) pts
IBF Jul 21, Marino, Italy: Gianfranco Rosi beat Darrin Van Horn (US) pts

Welterweight
Champions as at Aug 25, 1989: WBC Marlon Starling (US) WBA Mark Breland (US) IBF Simon Brown (Jam) WBO: Genaro Leon (Mex)
WBC Sep 15, Hartford, Connecticut: Marlon Starling beat Yung-kil Chung (SKo) pts
IBF Sep 20, Rochester, New York: Simon Brown beat Bobby Joe Young (US) rsf 2nd
WBA Oct 13, Geneva: Mark Breland beat Mauro Martelli (Swi) rsf 2nd

OLD SOLDIERS NEVER DIE

❝It was one of the very few championship fights where the fans were unanimous in their sentiments. When the decision was announced they booed both fighters. If they had wanted to see dancing à la Sugar Ray they could have gone to the Lido at the Stardust. If they had wanted to support Duran they could have waited for a peace march.❞
Archie McDonald, Vancouver Sun, on Leonard-Duran

"Why play all these games? I think that George Foreman and Mike Tyson should meet and the winner of that fight would then fight for the world title. It's time for us to get together right now."
George Foreman

"Foreman is now a mountain of flab...Any prospect of him in the same ring as Tyson should be referred to some Human Rights Council."
Shirley Povich, Washington Post

"The old man is back. King Kong is back. Let me tell you one thing. I'm old, I'm fat, I'm out of shape. But one thing you can't take away: here I is."
George Foreman

"As you can see, I'm no hungry fighter."
George Foreman, while eating chocolate cake and chocolate-chip cookies

"Foreman fits a well-established advertising strategy: he reminds people fondly of their childhood.
Jonathan Rendall, Independent on Sunday

"This entire geezer circus is, in fact, quite wonderful, raising the sport to quite unprecedented levels of safety. I can even imagine Leonard one day meeting antique mooseweight George Foreman. It is a natural evolution. No matter the difference in size, they could do no more harm to each other than a spaniel circling a hydrant.❞
Bernie Lincicome, Chicago Tribune

IBF Nov 9, Springfield, Massachusetts: Simon Brown beat Luis Santana (US) pts
WBA Dec 10, Tokyo: Mark Breland beat Fujio Ozaki (Jap) rsf 4th
WBO Dec 15, Yabucua, Puerto Rico: Manning Galloway (US) beat Al Hamza (PR) pts
WBA Mar 3, London: Mark Breland beat Lloyd Honeyghan (GB) rsf 3rd
IBF Apr 1, Washington: Simon Brown beat Tyrone Price (US) Tko 10th
WBA Jul 9, Reno, Nevada: Aaron Davies (US) beat Mark Breland ko 9th
WBC Aug 19, Reno, Nevada: Maurice Blocker (US) beat Marlon Starling pts

Junior-welterweight
Champions as at Aug 25, 1989; WBC Julio Cesar Chavez (Mex) WBA Juan Martin Coggi (Arg); IBf Meldrick Taylor (US); WBO: Hector Camacho (PR)
IBF Sep 11 Atlantic City: Meldrick Taylor beat Courtney Hooper (US) pts

WBC Nov 18, Las Vegas: Julio Cesar Chavez beat Sammy Fuentes (PR) rsf 10th
WBC Dec 16, Mexico City: Julio Cesar Chavez beat Alberto Cortes (Arg) ko 3rd
Chavez and Cortes had a total of 112 wins between them before the contest without a single defeat
WBO Feb 3, Atlantic City: Hector Camacho beat Vinnie Pazienza (US) pts
WBC/IBF Mar 17, Las Vegas: Julio Cesar Chavez beat Meldrick Taylor rsf 12th
WBA Mar 24, Ajaccio, Corsica: Juan Martin Coggi beat Jose Luis Ramirez (Mex) pts
WBO Aug 11, Lake Tahoe, Nevada: Hector Camacho beat Tony Baltazar (US) pts
IBF Aug 11, Lake Tahoe, Nevada: Meldrick Taylor beat Primo Ramos (Mex) pts
WBA Aug 17, Nice: Loreto Garza (US) beat Juan Martin Coggi pts

Lightweight
Champions as at Aug 25, 1989: WBC/IBF: Pernell Whitaker (US) WBA: Edwin Rosario (US) WBO: Mauricio Aceves (Mex)
WBO Aug 30, Los Angeles: Mauricio Aceves beat Oscar Bejines (Mex) rsf 10th
WBC/IBF Feb 3, Atlantic City: Pernell Whitaker beat Freddie Pendleton (US) pts
WBA Apr 6, New York: Juan Nazario (PR) beat Edwin Rosario rsf 8th
WBC/IBF May 19, Las Vegas: Pernell Whitaker beat Azumah Nelson (Gha) pts
Nelson was attempting to become the first African to win world titles at three different weights
WBC/WBA/IBF Aug 11, Lake Tahoe, Nevada: Pernell Whitaker (US) beat Juan Nazario ko 1st

Super-featherweight/Junior lightweight
Champions as at Aug 25, 1989: WBC: Azumah Nelson (Gha); WBA: Brian Mitchell (SAF); IBF: Tony Lopez (US); WBO: Juan 'John-John' Molina (PR)
WBA Sep 28, Lewiston, Maine: Brian Mitchell beat Irving Mitchell (US) rsf 7th
IBF Oct 7, Sacramento: Juan 'John-John' Molina (PR) beat Tony Lopez rsf 10th
WBC Nov 5, London: Azumah Nelson beat Jim McDonnell (GB) rsf 12th
WBO Dec 9, Teramo, Italy: Kamel Bou Ali (Tun) beat Antonio Rivera (PR) ko 8th
IBF Jan 27, Atlantic City: Juan 'John-John' Molina beat Lupe Suarez (US) rsf 6th
WBA Mar 14, Grosetto, Italy: Brian Mitchell beat Jackie Beard (US) pts
IBF May 20, Reno: Tony Lopez (US) beat Juan 'John-John' Molina pts

Featherweight
Champions as at Aug 25, 1989: WBC: Jeff Fenech (Aus); WBA: Antonio Esparragoza (Ven); IBF: Jorge Paez (Mex); WBO: Maurizio Stecca (Ita)
IBF Sep 16, Mexico City: Jorge Paez beat Jose Mario Lopez (Arg) rsf 2nd
WBA Sep 22, Mexicali, Mexico: Antonio Esparragoza beat Eduardo Montoyo (Mex) ko 5th
WBO Nov 11, Rimini, Italy: Louie Espinoza (US) beat Maurizio Stecca rsf 7th
IBF Dec 9, Reno: Jorge Paez beat Lupe Gutierrez (US) rsf 6th
IBF Feb 4, Las Vegas: Jorge Paez beat Troy Dorsey (US) pts
IBF/WBO Apr 7, Las Vegas: Jorge Paez beat Louie Espinoza (US) pts
WBA May 13, Seoul: Antonio Esparragoza beat Chanmok Park (SKo) pts
WBC Jun 2, Manchester: Marcos Villasana (Mex) beat

Paul Hodkinson (GB) rsf 8th
Villasana won a world title at the fifth attempt
IBF Jul 8, Las Vegas: Jorge Paez drew with Troy Dorsey (US)
Dorsey came close to becoming the first kick-boxing champion to win a world title

Super-bantamweight/Junior-featherweight

Champions as at Aug 25, 1989: WBC: Daniel Zaragoza (Mex); WBA: Juan Jose Estrada (Mex); IBF: Fabrice Benichou (Fra); WBO: Kenny Mitchell (US)
WBC Aug 31, Los Angeles: Daniel Zaragoza beat Frankie Duarte (US) rsf 10th
WBO Sep 9, San Juan, Puerto Rico: Kenny Mitchell beat Simon Skosana (SA) pts
IBF Oct 7, Bordeaux: Fabrice Benichou beat Ramon Cruz (Dom) pts
WBC Dec 3, Seoul: Daniel Zaragoza beat Chan-Young Park (SKo) pts
WBO Dec 9, Teramo, Italy: Valerio Nati (Ita) beat Kenny Mitchell disq 4th
WBA Dec 11, Los Angeles: Jesus Salud (US) beat Juan Jose Estrada disq 9th
IBF Mar 10, Tel Aviv,: Welcome Ncita (SA) beat Fabrice Benichou pts
The first world title fight in Israel
WBC Apr 23, Los Angeles: Paul Banke (US) beat Daniel Zaragoza rsf 9th
WBA May 26, Cartagena, Colombia: Luis Mendoza (Col) drew with Ruben Palacios (Col)
For vacant title, title still vacant
WBO May 12, Sassari, Italy: Orlando Fernandez (PR) beat Valerio Nati rsf 10th
IBF Jun 2, Rome: Welcome Ncita beat Ramon Cruz (Dom) rsf 7th
WBC Aug 17, Seoul: Paul Banke beat Lee Ki-jun (SKo) rsf 12th

Bantamweight

Champions as at Aug 25, 1989: WBC: Raul Perez (Mex); WBA: Khaokor Galaxy (Tha); IBF: Orlando Canizales (US); WBO: Israel Contreras (Ven)
WBC Aug 26, Talcahuano, Chile: Raul Perez beat Cerdenio Ulloa (Chi) tko 8th
WBA Oct 18, Bangkok: Luisito Espinosa (Phi) beat Khaokor Galaxy rsf 1st
WBC Oct 23, Los Angeles: Raul Perez beat Diego Avilar (Mex) pts
WBC Jan 22, Los Angeles: Raul Perez beat Gaby Canizales (US) pts
IBF Jan 27, Sunderland: Orlando Canizales beat Billy Hardy (GB) pts
WBC May 7, Los Angeles: Raul Perez beat Gerardo Martinez (US) rsf 9th
WBA May 30, Bangkok: Luisito Espinosa beat Hurley Snead (US) rtd 9th
IBF Jun 10, El Paso: Orlando Canizales beat Paul Gonzalez (US) rsf 2nd
IBF Aug 14, New York: Orlando Canizales beat Eddie Rangel (US) rsf 5th

Super-flyweight/Junior bantamweight

Champions as at Aug 25, 1989: WBC: Gilberto Roman (Mex); WBA: Khaosai Galaxy (Tha); IBF: Ellyas Pical (Ina); WBO: Jose Ruiz (PR)
WBO Sep 9, San Juan, Puerto Rico: Jose Ruiz beat Juan Caroza (PR) rsf 1st
WBC Sep 12, Los Angeles: Gilberto Roman beat Santos Laciar (Arg) pts
IBF Oct 14, Roanoke, Virginia: Juan Polo Perez (Col) beat Ellyas Pical pts
WBO Oct 21, San Juan, Puerto Rico: Jose Ruiz beat Angel Rosario (PR) rsf 12th

WBA Oct 31, Kobe, Japan: Khaosai Galaxy beat Keji Matsumura (Jap) rsf 12th
WBC Nov 7, Mexico City: Nana Yaw Konadu (Gha) beat Gilberto Roman pts
WBC Jan 20, Seoul: Moon Sung-kil (SKo) beat Nana Yaw Konadu TD 9th
WBA Mar 29, Bangkok: Khaosai Galaxy beat Ari Blanca (Phi) ko 5th
IBF Apr 21, Sunderland: Roberto Quiroga (US) beat Juan Polo Perez pts
WBC Jun 9, Seoul: Moon Sung-kil beat Gilberto Roman (Mex) rtd 8th
WBA Jun 30, Chiangmai, Thailand: Khaosai Galaxy beat Shunichi Nakajima (Jap) rsf 8th

Flyweight

Champions as at Aug 25, 1989: WBC: Sot Chitalada (Tha); WBA: Fidel Bassa (Col); IBF: Dave McAuley (GB); WBO: Elvis Alvarez (Col)
WBA Sep 30, Baranquilla, Colombia: Jesus Rojas (Ven) beat Fidel Bassa pts
IBF Nov 8, London: Dave McAuley beat Dodie Penalosa (Phi) pts
WBC Jan 30, Bangkok: Sot Chitalada beat Ric Siodoro (Phi) pts
WBA Mar 10, Taejon City, South Korea: Lee Yul-woo (SKo) beat Jesus Rojas pts
IBF Mar 17, Belfast: Dave McAuley beat Louis Curtis (US) pts
WBC May 1, Bangkok: Sot Chitalada beat Carlos Salazar (Arg) pts
WBA Jul 28, Mito, Japan: Leopard Tamakuma (Jap) beat Lee Yul-woo (SKo) rsf 10th
WBO Aug 18, Ponce, Puerto Rico: Isidiro Perez (Mex) beat Angel Rosario (PR) ko 1st

---

❝Does Senor Samaranch really need 12 medical research centres to look into boxing's damaging effects? How much evidence does he need?... The very aim of the sport is to knock your opponent senseless.❞

Letter to The Guardian *from Dr John Dawson of the BMA*

"The face of courage they called it, before summoning an ambulance. Jim McDonnell looked more like a rabbit infected with myxomatosis than a young man in the prime of life."

Michael Calvin, Daily Telegraph

"You always think: It's never going to happen. Not with YOUR opponent...I keep thinking: What have I done? What have I done."

Herol Graham after brain surgery on his opponent Rod Douglas

❝I suppose people who deplore boxing will be up in arms again, but there is more danger in motor racing and American football.❞

Mickey Duff after the Graham-Douglas fight

"It's a sport whose day has come and gone. I don't think it should be sanctioned any more.❞

Gene Tunney jr, son of the champ

Light-flyweight

*Champions as at Aug 25, 1989: **WBC**: Humberto Gonzalez (Mex); **WBA**: Yuh Myung-woo (SKo); **IBF**: Muangchai Kittikasem (Tha); **WBO**: Jose de Jesus (PR)*

WBA Sep 24, Suanbo, South Korea: Yuh Myung-woo beat Kenbun Taiho (Jap) ko 11th

IBF Oct 6, Bangkok: Muangchai Kittikasem beat Tacy Macalos (Phi) rsf 7th

WBO Oct 21, San Juan, Puerto Rico: Jose de Jesus beat Isidro Perez (Mex) pts

WBC Dec 9, Seoul: Humberto Gonzalez beat Jung-Koo Chang (SKo) pts

WBA Jan 14, Seoul: Yuh Myung-woo beat Hisashi Takashima (Jap) rsf 7th

IBF Jan 19, Bangkok: Muangchai Kittikasem beat Lee Jeung-jai (SKo) ko 3rd

WBC Mar 24, Mexico City: Humberto Gonzalez beat Francisco Tejedor (Col) ko 3rd

IBF Apr 10, Bangkok: Muangchai Kittikasem beat Abdy Pohan (Ina) pts

WBA Apr 29, Seoul: Yuh Myung-woo beat Leo Gamez (Ven) pts

WBO May 5, Talcahuano, Chile: Jose de Jesus beat Alli Galvez (Chi) ko 5th

WBC Jun 4, Inglewood, California: Humberto Gonzalez beat Luis Monzote (Cub) rsf 3rd

WBC Jul 23, Inglewood, California: Humberto Gonzalez beat Lim Jeung-keun (SKo) rsf 5th

IBF Jul 29, Phoenix, Arizona: Michael Garbajal (US) beat Muangchai Kittikasem rsf 7th

Straw-weight

*Champions as at Aug 25, 1989: **WBC**: Napa Kiatwanchai (Tha); **WBA**: Kim Bong-jun (SKo); **IBF**: Nico Thomas (Ina); **WBO**: Vacant*

IBF Sep 21, Jakarta,: Eric Chavez (Phi) beat Nico Thomas ko 5th

WBO Sep 1, Santo Domingo, Costa Rica,: Rafael Torres (Dom) beat Yamil Caraballo (Col) pts

WBA Oct 22, Pohang, South Korea: Kim Bong-Jun beat John Arief (Ina) rsf 9th

WBC Nov 12, Seoul: Choi Jeum-hwan (SKo) beat Napa Kiatwanchai rsf 12th

WBC Feb 7, Tokyo: Hideyuki Ohashi (Jap) beat Choi Jeum-hwan (SKo) ko 9th

WBA Feb 10, Seoul: Kim-bong Jun beat Petthal Chuvatana (Tha) ko 4th

IBF Feb 21, Bangkok: Falan Lookmingkwan (Tha) beat Eric Chavez rsf 7th

WBA May 13, Seoul: Kim-bong Jun beat Silverio Barcenas (Pan) pts

WBC Jun 8, Tokyo: Hideyuki Ohashi beat Napa Kiatwanchai (Tha) pts

IBF Jun 15, Bangkok: Falan Lookmingkwan beat Joe Constantino (Phi) pts

WBO Jul 31, Jakarta: Rafael Torres beat Hunsi Ray (Ina) pts

IBF Aug 15, Bangkok: Falan Lookmingkwan beat Eric Chavez (Phi) pts

BRITISH TITLE FIGHTS 1989-90
Heavyweight

Champion as at Sep 20, 1989: Gary Mason (Chatham)
No fights

Cruiserweight

Champion as at Sep 20, 1989: Johnny Nelson (Sheffield)
Oct 2, Hanley: Johnny Nelson beat Ian Bulloch (Bolsover) ko 2nd
Mar 28, Bethnal Green: Johnny Nelson beat Lou Gent (Streatham) ko 4th
Nelson won Lonsdale Belt outright

Light-heavyweight

Champion as at Sep 20, 1989: Tom Collins (Leeds)
No fights

Super-heavyweight

Champion as at Sep 20, 1989: Sam Storey (Belfast)
Nov 29, Belfast: Sam Storey beat Noel Magee (Belfast) rsf 9th

Middleweight

Champion as at Sep 20, 1989: Herol Graham (Sheffield)
Oct 25, Wembley Arena: Herol Graham beat Rod Douglas (Bow) rsf 11th
In a support bout for the Graham-Douglas contest, Victor Egorov became the first Soviet boxer to fight professionally in the West. He stopped Mustapha Cole (US) in the fifth round

Light-middleweight

Champion as at Sep 20, 1989: Gary Stretch (St Helens)
Oct 11, London Arena: Gary Stretch beat Derek Wormald (Rochdale) rsf 1st
Stretch relinquished title Sep 6 1990

Welterweight

Champion as at Sep 20, 1989: Kirkland Laing (Nottingham)
Nov 15, Reading: Kirkland Laing beat George Collins (Yateley) rsf 5th
Mar 27, Grosvenor House Hotel, London: Kirkland Laing beat Trevor Smith (Harlow) rsf 6th

Light-welterweight

Champion as at Sep 20, 1989: Pat Barrett (Manchester)
Oct 24, Wolverhampton: Pat Barrett beat Robert Harkin (Helensburgh) pts
Barrett gave up his title Aug 28, to concentrate on world title bid

Lightweight

Champion as at Sep 20, 1989: Steve Boyle (Glasgow)
No fights

Super-featherweight

Champion as at Sep 20, 1989: John Doherty (Bradford)
Feb 6, Oldham: Joey Jacobs (Oldham) beat John Doherty pts

Featherweight

Champion as at Sep 20, 1989: Paul Hodkinson (Kirkby)
Hodkinson vacated title March 1990 to concentrate on European & World title bids
May 25, St Albans: Sean Murphy (St Albans) beat John Doherty (Bradford) ko 3rd

Bantamweight

Champion as at Sep 20, 1989: Billy Hardy (Sunderland)
Oct 10, Sunderland: Billy Hardy beat Brian Holmes (Glasgow) ko 1st
Fight lasted 160 seconds

Flyweight

Champion as at Sep 20, 1989: Pat Clinton (Glasgow)
Oct 24, Watford: Pat Clinton beat Danny Porter (Hitchin) rsf 5th
Dec 19, Gorleston: Pat Clinton beat David Afan-Jones (Port Talbot) rsf 6th
Clinton won Lonsdale belt outright

COMMONWEALTH CHAMPIONS 1989-90

Weight	Champion on Sep 17, 1989	New champion(s) since then
HEAVYWEIGHT	Derek Williams (Eng)	None
CRUISERWEIGHT	Apollo Sweet (Aus)	Derek Angol (Eng)
LIGHT-HEAVYWEIGHT	Guy Waters (Aus)	None
SUPER-MIDDLEWEIGHT	Vacent	Rodney Carr (Aus)
MIDDLEWEIGHT	Michael Watson (Eng)	None
LIGHT-MIDDLEWEIGHT	Troy Waters (Aus)	None
WELTERWEIGHT	Gary Jacobs (Sco)	Donovan Boucher (Can)
LIGHT-WELTERWEIGHT	Steve Larramore (Bah)	Tony Ekubia (Eng)
LIGHTWEIGHT	Najib Daho (Eng)	Carl Crook (Eng)
SUPER-FEATHERWEIGHT	John Sichula (Zam)	Mark Reefer (Eng)
FEATHERWEIGHT	Percy Oblitey Commey (Gha)	Modest Napunyi (Ken)
BANTAMWEIGHT	Ray Minus, Jnr (Bah)	None
FLYWEIGHT	Vacant	Alfred Kotey (Gha)

❝ I'm the thoroughbred of heavyweight boxing. It's just that I've been starting from the wrong gate.❞
Tyrrell Biggs

"Boxing's a great soap opera but at the moment it's Coronation Street with balls and I want it to be Dallas with balls."
Barry Hearn, aspiring promoter

"World champion boxing promoter? Give me ten years. Yeah, ten years. Sweet as a nut."
Barry Hearn

"I see myself as a bank manager. He jumps in his car and goes to work. I do the same."
Lennox Lewis, heavyweight

"My girlfriend boos me when we make love because she knows it turns me on."
Hector Camacho

"He is such a nice guy. It's a shame I have to beat him up."
Lloyd Honeyghan before losing to Mark Breland

Question: "What do you consider the most over-rated virtue?"
Answer: "All of them."
Interview with Frank Warren, Sunday Correspondent

"I'm fixing to be the world heavyweight champion in Nineteen Ninety-four. And talk no more. ❞
Larry Donald, Goodwill Games super-heavyweight champion and Ali's heir-presumptive

EUROPEAN CHAMPIONS 1989-90

Weight	Champion on Sep 17, 1989	New champion(s) since then
HEAVYWEIGHT		Derek Williams (Eng)
	Vacant	Jean-Maurice Chanet (Fra)

Chanet was 35 when he won his title. He turned pro only four years earlier. He was one of 17 children and worked as an itinerant fairground stallholder

Weight	Champion on Sep 17, 1989	New champion(s) since then
CRUISERWEIGHT	Angelo Rottoli (Ita)	Anaclet Wamba (Fra)
LIGHT-HEAVYWEIGHT	Jan Lefeber (Hol)	Eric Nicoletta (Fra)
		Tom Collins (GB)
SUPER-MIDDLEWEIGHT	First contested 1990	Mauro Galvano (Ita)
MIDDLEWEIGHT	Francesco Dell'Aquila (Ita)	Sumbu Kalambay (Ita)
LIGHT-MIDDLEWEIGHT	Giuseppe Leto (Ita)	Gilbert Dele (Fra)
WELTERWEIGHT	Nino La Rocca (Ita)	Antoine Fernandez (Fra)
		Kirkland Laing (GB)
LIGHT-WELTERWEIGHT	Efrem Calamati (Ita)	Pat Barrett (GB)
LIGHTWEIGHT	Policarpo Diaz (Spa)	None
SUPER-FEATHERWEIGHT	Daniel Londas (Fra)	None
FEATHERWEIGHT	Paul Hodkinson (GB)	None
BANTAMWEIGHT	Vincenzo Balcastro (Ita)	None
FLYWEIGHT	Eyup Can (Den)	Pat Clinton (GB)

AMATEUR
ABA FINALS 1990

LIGHT-FLYWEIGHT:	Nick Tooley (Dawlish) beat Paul Weir (Springside) pts
FLYWEIGHT:	John Armour (St Mary's) beat Paul Ingle (Scarborough) pts
BANTAMWEIGHT:	Paul Lloyd (Vauxhall Motors) beat Partick Mullings (Harrow) rsf 2nd
FEATHERWEIGHT:	Brian Carr (Auchengeich) beat John Williams (Pontypool & Panteg) pts
LIGHTWEIGHT:	Patrick Gallagher (Angel) beat Billy Schwer (Luton Irish) pts
LIGHT-WELTERWEIGHT:	Jim Pender (St Francis) beat Adrian Stone (Empire Bristol) pts
WELTERWEIGHT:	Adrian Carew (Lynn) beat Peter Waudby (St Pauls) rsf 2nd
LIGHT-MIDDLEWEIGHT:	Tim Taylor (Newco-Repton) beat John Culwick (Army) pts
MIDDLEWEIGHT:	Steve Wilson (Haddington) beat Darron Griffiths (Rhondda) pts
LIGHT-HEAVYWEIGHT:	Joe McCluskey (Croy Miners) beat Mark Baker (Newco-Repton) rsf 2nd
HEAVYWEIGHT:	Keith Inglis (Tunbridge Wells) beat Paul Lawson (Newco-Repton) rsf 2nd
SUPER-HEAVYWEIGHT:	Kevin McCormack (Coed-Eva) beat Tom Cherubin (Newco-Repton) pts

WORLD HEAVYWEIGHT CHAMPIONS

How the title changed hands (undisputed champions only)

Date	Fight	Successful Defences
Sep 7 1892	James J Corbett (US) beat John L Sullivan (US), ko 21st	1
Mar 17 1897	Bob Fitzsimmons (GB) beat Corbett ko 14th	0
Jun 9 1899	James J Jefferies (US) beat Fitzsimmons, ko 11th	6
Jefferies relinquished title		
Jul 3 1905	Mervin Hart (US) beat Jack Root (US), tko 12th	0
Feb 23 1906	Tommy Burns (Can) beat Hart, pts 20th	11
Dec 26 1908	Jack Jackson (US) beat Burns, tko 14th	9
Apr 5 1914	Jess Willard (US) beat Johnson, ko 26th	1
Jul 4 1919	Jack Dempsey (US) beat Willard, ko 3rd	5
Sep 23 1926	Gene Tunney (US) beat Dempsey, pts 10	2
Tunney relinquished title		
Jun 12 1930	Max Schmeling (Ger) beat Jack Sharkey (US), disq	1
Jun 21 1932	Sharkey beat Schmeling, pts 15	0
Jun 29 1933	Primo Carnera (Ita) beat Sharkey, ko 6th	2
Jun 14 1934	Max Baer (US) beat Carnera, ko 11th	0
Jun 13 1935	James J Braddock (US) beat Baer, pts 15	0
Jun 22 1937	Joe Louis (US) beat Braddock, ko 8th	25
Louis relinquished title		
Jun 22 1949	Ezzard Charles (US) beat Jersey Joe Walcott (US), pts 15	8
Jul 18 1951	Walcott beat Charles, ko 7th	1
Sep 23 1952	Rocky Marciano (US) beat Walcott, ko 3rd	6
Marciano relinquished title		
Nov 30 1956	Floyd Patterson (US) beat Archie Moore (US), ko 5th	4
Jun 26 1959	Ingemar Johansson (Swe) beat Patterson, tko 3rd	0
Jun 20 1960	Patterson beat Johansson, ko 5th	2
Sep 25 1962	Sonny Liston (US) beat Patterson, ko 1st	1
Feb 25 1964	Cassius Clay (US) beat Liston, tko 7th	9
Clay/Ali stripped of title		
Feb 16 1970	Joe Frazier (US) beat Jimmy Ellis (US), ko 5th	4
Jan 22 1973	George Foreman (US) beat Frazier, ko 2nd	2
Oct 30 1974	Muhammad Ali beat Foreman, ko 8th	10
Feb 15 1978	Leon Spinks (US) beat Muhammad Ali, pts 15	0
The division became split because Spinks was not recognised as champion by the WBC		
Aug 1 1987	Mike Tyson (US) beat Tony Tucker (US) pts 12	6
Feb 10 1990	James 'Buster' Douglas beat Tyson ko 10th	-
The three main boxing organisations, WBC, WBA and IBF, all recognised Douglas.		

WORLD CHAMPIONS

Heavyweight

Year	Champion	Org
1882	John L. Sullivan (US)	
1892	James J. Corbett (US)	
1897	Bob Fitzsimmons (GB)	
1899	James J. Jefferies (US)	
1905	Marvin Hart (US)	
1906	Tommy Burns (Can)	
1908	Jack Johnson (US)	
1915	Jess Willard (US)	
1919	Jack Dempsey (US)	
1926	Gene Tunney (US)	
1930	Max Schmeling (Ger)	
1932	Jack Sharkey (US)	
1933	Primo Carnera (Ita)	
1934	Max Baer (US)	
1935	James J. Braddock (US)	
1937	Joe Louis (US)	
1949	Ezzard Charles (US)	
1951	Jersey Joe Walcott (US)	
1952	Rocky Marciano (US)	
1956	Floyd Patterson (US)	
1959	Ingemar Johansson (Swe)	
1960	Floyd Patterson (US)	
1962	Sonny Liston (US)	
1964	Cassius Clay (US)	
1965	Ernie Terrell (US)	(WBA)
1968	Jimmy Ellis (US)	(WBA)
1970	Joe Frazier (US)	
1973	George Foreman (US)	
1974	Muhammad Ali (US)	
1978	Leon Spinks (US)	
1978	Ken Norton (US)	(WBC)
1978	Muhammad Ali (US)	(WBA)
1978	Larry Holmes (US)	(WBC)
1979	John Tate (US)	(WBA)
1980	Mike Weaver (US)	(WBA)
1982	Mike Dokes (US)	(WBA)
1983	Gerrie Coetzee (SA)	(WBA)
1984	Larry Holmes (US)	(IBF)
1984	Tim Witherspoon (US)	(WBC)
1984	Pinklon Thomas (US)	(WBC)
1984	Greg Page (US)	(WBA)
1985	Michael Spinks (US)	(IBF)
1985	Tony Tubbs (US)	(WBA)
1986	Tim Witherspoon (US)	(WBA)
1986	Trevor Berbick (Jam)	(WBC)
1986	James Smith (US)	(WBA)
1987	Mike Tyson (US)	(WBA/WBC)

1987	Tony Tucker (US)	(IBF)
1987	Mike Tyson (US)	
1989	Francesco Damiani (Ita)	(WBO)
1989	Mike Tyson (US)	(WBA/WBC/IBF)
1990	James Douglas (US)	(WBA/WBC/IBF)

Cruiserweight

1979	Marvin Camel (US)	(WBC)
1980	Carlos de Leon (PR)	(WBC)
1982	Ossie Ocasio (PR)	(WBA)
1982	S.T. Gordon (US)	(WBC)
1983	Carlos de Leon (PR)	(WBC)
1983	Marvin Camel (US)	(IBF)
1984	Lee Roy Murphy (US)	(IBF)
1984	Piet Crous (SA)	(WBA)
1985	Alfonso Ratliff (US)	(WBC)
1985	Dwight Muhammad Qawi (US)	(WBA)
1985	Bernard Benton (US)	(WBC)
1986	Carlos de Leon (PR)	(WBC)
1986	Evander Holyfield (US)	(WBA)
1986	Rickey Parkey (US)	(IBF)
1987	Evander Holyfield (US)	(IBF)
1988	Evander Holyfield (US)	
1989	Taoufik Belbouli (Fra)	(WBA)
1989	Carlos de Leon (PR)	(WBC)
1989	Glenn McCrory (GB)	(IBF)
1989	Robert Daniels (US)	(WBA)
1989	Richard 'Boone' Pultz (US)	(WBO)
1990	Jeff Lampkin (US)	(IBF)
1990	Magne Havnaa (Nor)	(WBO)
1990	Massimilio Duran (Ita)	(WBC)

Light-heavyweight

1903	Jack Root (Aut)	
1903	George Gardner (Ire)	
1903	Bob Fitzsimmons (GB)	
1905	Jack O'Brien (US)	
1912	Jack Dillon (US)	
1916	Battling Levinsky (US)	
1920	Georges Carpentier (Fra)	
1922	Battling Siki (Sen)	
1923	Mike McTigue (Ire)	
1925	Paul Berlenbach (US)	
1926	Jack Delaney (Can)	
1927	Jim Slattery (US)	
1927	Tommy Loughran (US)	
1930	Jim Slattery (US)	
1930	Maxie Rosenbloom (US)	
1934	Bob Olin (US)	
1935	John Henry Lewis (US)	
1939	Melio Bettina (US)	
1939	Billy Conn (US)	
1941	Anton Christoforidis (Gre)	
1941	Gus Lesnevich (US)	
1948	Freddie Mills (GB)	
1950	Joey Maxim (US)	
1952	Archie Moore (US)	
1962	Harold Johnson (US)	
1963	Willie Pastrano (US)	
1965	Jose Torres (PR)	
1966	Dick Tiger (Nig)	
1968	Bob Foster (US)	
1971	Vicente Rondon (Ven)	(WBA)
1974	John Conteh (GB)	(WBC)
1974	Victor Galindez (Arg)	(WBA)
1977	Miguel Cuello (Arg)	(WBC)
1978	Mate Parlov (Yug)	(WBC)
1978	Mike Rossman (US)	(WBA)
1978	Marvin Johnson (US)	(WBC)
1979	Victor Galindez (Arg)	(WBA)
1979	Matthew Saad Muhammad (US)	(WBC)
1979	Marvin Johnson (US)	(WBA)
1980	Eddie Mustafa Muhammad (US)	(WBA)

1981	Michael Spinks (US)	(WBA)
1981	Dwight Muhammah Qawi (US)	(WBC)
1983	Michael Spinks (US)	
1985	J.B. Williamson (US)	(WBC)
1985	Slobodan Kacar (Yug)	(IBF)
1986	Marvin Johnson (US)	(WBA)
1986	Dennis Andries (GB)	(WBC)
1986	Bobby Czyz (US)	(IBF)
1987	Thomas Hearns (US)	(WBC)
1987	Leslie Stewart (Jam)	(WBA)
1987	Virgil Hill (US)	(WBA)
1987	Prince Charles Williams (US)	(IBF)
1988	Donny Lalonde (Can)	(WBC)
1988	Sugar Ray Leonard (US)	(WBC)
1988	Michael Moorer (US)	(WBO)
1989	Dennis Andries (GB)	(WBC)
1989	Jeff Harding (Aus)	(WBC)
1990	Dennis Andries (GB)	(WBC)

Super-middleweight

1984	Murray Sutherland (Can)	(IBF)
1984	Chong-Pal Park (SKo)	(WBA)
1988	Graciano Rocchigniani (FRG)	(IBF)
1988	Fulgencio Obelmejias (Ven)	(WBA)
1988	Sugar Ray Leonard (US)	(WBC)
1988	Thomas Hearns (US)	(WBO)
1989	In-Chul Baek (SKo)	(WBA)
1990	Lindell Holmes (US)	(IBF)
1990	Christophe Tiozzo (Fra)	(WBA)

Middleweight

1891	Nonpareil Jack Dempsey (Ire)	
1891	Bob Fitzsimmons (GB)	
1897	Kid McCoy (US)	
1898	Tommy Ryan (US)	
1908	Stanley Ketchel (US)	
1908	Billy Papke (US)	
1908	Stanley Ketchel (US)	
1910	Billy Papke (US)	
1911	Cyclone Thompson (US)	
1911	Billy Papke (US)	
1912	Frank Mantell (US)	
1912	Billy Papke (US)	
1913	Frank Klaus (US)	
1913	George Chip (US)	
1914	Al McCoy (US)	
1917	Mike O'Dowd (US)	
1920	Johnny Wilson (US)	
1923	Harry Greb (US)	
1926	Tiger Flowers (US)	
1926	Mickey Walker (US)	
1931	Gorilla Jones (US)	
1932	Marcel Thil (Fra)	
1937	Fred Apostoli (US)	
1939	Ceferino Garcia (Phi)	
1940	Ken Overlin (US)	
1941	Billy Soose (US)	
1941	Tony Zale (US)	
1947	Rocky Graziano (US)	
1948	Tony Zale (US)	
1948	Marcel Cerdan (Alg)	
1949	Jake la Motta (US)	
1951	Sugar Ray Robinson (US)	
1951	Randolph Turpin (GB)	
1951	Sugar Ray Robinson (US)	
1953	Carl Bobo Olsen (Haw)	
1955	Sugar Ray Robinson (US)	
1957	Gene Fullmer (US)	
1957	Sugar Ray Robinson (US)	
1957	Carmen Basilio (US)	
1958	Sugar Ray Robinson (US)	
1960	Paul Pender (US)	

1961	Terry Downes (GB)	
1962	Paul Pender (US)	
1962	Dick Tiger (Nig)	
1963	Joey Giardello (US)	
1965	Dick Tiger (Nig)	
1966	Emile Griffith (VI)	
1968	Nino Benvenuti (Ita)	
1970	Carlos Monzon (Arg)	
1974	Rodrigo Valdez (Col)	(WBC)
1976	Carlos Monzon (Arg)	
1977	Rodrigo Valdez (Col)	
1978	Hugo Corro (Arg)	
1979	Vito Antuofermo (Ita)	
1980	Alan Minter (GB)	
1980	Marvin Hagler (US)	
1987	Sugar Ray Leonard (US)	(WBC)
1987	Frank Tate (US)	(IBF)
1987	Sambu Kalambay (Zai)	(WBA)
1987	Thomas Hearns (US)	(WBC)
1988	Iran Barkley (US)	(WBC)
1988	Michael Nunn (US)	(IBF)
1989	Roberto Duran (Pan)	(WBC)
1989	Mike McCallum (US)	(WBA)
1989	Doug De Witt (US)	(WBO)
1990	Nigel Benn (GB)	(WBO)

Junior-middleweight

1962	Denny Moyer (US)	
1963	Ralph Dupas (US)	
1963	Sandro Mazzinghi (Ita)	
1965	Nino Benvenuti (Ita)	
1966	Ki-Soo Kim (SKo)	
1968	Sandro Mazzinghi (Ita)	
1969	Freddie Little (US)	
1970	Carmelo Bossi (Ita)	
1971	Koichi Wajima (Jap)	
1974	Oscar Albarado (US)	
1975	Koichi Wajima (Jap)	
1975	Miguel de Oliviera (Bra)	(WBC)
1975	Jae-Do Yuh (SKo)	(WBA)
1975	Elisha Obed (Bah)	(WBC)
1976	Koichi Wajima (Jap)	(WBA)
1976	Jose Duran (Spa)	(WBA)
1976	Eckhard Dagge (FRG)	(WBC)
1976	Angel Castellini (Arg)	(WBA)
1977	Eddie Gazo (Nic)	(WBA)
1977	Rocky Mattioli (Ita)	(WBC)
1978	Masashi Kudo (Jap)	(WBA)
1979	Maurice Hope (GB)	(WBC)
1979	Ayube Kalule (Uga)	(WBA)
1981	Wilfred Benitez (US)	(WBC)
1981	Sugar Ray Leonard (US)	(WBA)
1981	Tadashi Mihara (Jap)	(WBA)
1982	Davey Moore (US)	(WBA)
1982	Thomas Hearns (US)	(WBC)
1983	Roberto Duran (Pan)	(WBA)
1984	Mark Medal (US)	(IBF)
1984	Mike McCallum (Jam)	(WBA)
1984	Carlos Santos (PR)	(IBF)
1986	Buster Drayton (US)	(IBF)
1986	Duane Thomas (US)	(WBC)
1987	Matthew Hilton (Can)	(IBF)
1987	Lupe Aquino (Mex)	(WBC)
1988	Gianfranco Rossi (Ita)	(WBC)
1988	Don Curry (US)	(WBC)
1988	Julian Jackson (VI)	(WBA)
1988	Robert Hines (US)	(IBF)
1988	John David Jackson (US)	(WBO)
1989	Darrin Van Horn (US)	(IBF)
1989	René Jacquot (Fra)	(WBC)
1989	John Mugabi (Uga)	(WBC)

1989	Gianfranco Rosi (Ita)	(IBF)
1990	Terry Norris (US)	(WBC)

Welterweight

1892	Billy Smith (US)	
1894	Tommy Ryan (US)	
1898	Billy Smith (US)	
1900	Rube Ferns (US)	
1900	Matty Matthews (US)	
1901	Rube Ferns (US)	
1901	Joe Walcott (Bar)	
1904	Dixie Kid (US)	
1905	Joe Walcott (Bar)	
1906	Honey Mellody (US)	
1907	Mike Sullivan (US)	
1908	Harry Lewis (US)	
1914	Waldemar Holberg (Den)	
1914	Tom McCormick (Ire)	
1914	Matt Wells (GB)	
1915	Mike Glover (US)	
1915	Jack Britton (US)	
1915	Ted Kid Lewis (GB)	
1916	Jack Britton (US)	
1917	Ted Kid Lewis (GB)	
1919	Jack Britton (US)	
1922	Mickey Walker (US)	
1926	Pete Latzo (US)	
1927	Joe Dundee (Ita)	
1928	Jack Thompson (US)	
1929	Jackie Fields (US)	
1930	Jack Thompson (US)	
1930	Tommy Freeman (US)	
1931	Jack Thompson (US)	
1931	Lou Brouillard (Can)	
1932	Jackie Fields (US)	
1933	Young Corbett III (Ita)	
1933	Jimmy McLarnin (Ire)	
1934	Barney Ross (US)	
1934	Jimmy McLarnin (Ire)	
1935	Barney Ross (US)	
1938	Henry Armstrong (US)	
1940	Fritzie Zivic (US)	
1941	Red Cochrane (US)	
1946	Marty Servo (US)	
1946	Sugar Ray Robinson (US)	
1951	Johnny Bratton (US)	
1951	Kid Gavilan (Cub)	
1954	Johnny Saxton (US)	
1955	Tony de Marco (US)	
1955	Carmen Basilio (US)	
1956	Johnny Saxton (US)	
1956	Carmen Basilio (US)	
1958	Virgil Atkins (US)	
1958	Don Jordon (Dom)	
1960	Benny Kid Paret (Cub)	
1961	Emile Griffith (VI)	
1961	Benny Kid Paret (Cub)	
1962	Emile Griffith (VI)	
1963	Louis Rodriguez (Cub)	
1963	Emile Griffith (VI)	
1966	Curtis Cokes (US)	
1969	Jose Napoles (Cub)	
1970	Billy Backus (US)	
1971	Jose Napoles (Cub)	
1975	Angel Espada (PR)	(WBA)
1975	John H. Stracey (GB)	(WBC)
1976	Carlos Palomino (Mex)	(WBC)
1976	Pipino Cuevas (Mex)	(WBA)
1979	Wilfred Benitez (US)	(WBC)
1979	Sugar Ray Leonard (US)	(WBC)
1980	Roberto Duran (Pan)	(WBC)

1980	Thomas Hearns (US)	(WBA)
1980	Sugar Ray Leonard (US)	(WBC)
1981	Sugar Ray Leonard (US)	
1983	Don Curry (US)	(WBA)
1983	Milton McCrory (US)	(WBC)
1984	Don Curry (US)	(IBF)
1985	Don Curry (US)	
1986	Lloyd Honeyghan (GB)	
1987	Mark Breland (US)	(WBA)
1987	Lloyd Honeyghan (GB)	(WBC/IBF)
1987	Marlon Starling (US)	(WBA)
1987	Jorge Vaca (Mex)	(WBC)
1988	Simon Brown (Jam)	(IBF)
1988	Tomas Molinares (Col)	(WBA)
1988	Lloyd Honeyghan (GB)	(WBC)
1989	Mark Breland (US)	(WBA)
1989	Marlon Starling (US)	(WBC)
1989	Genaro Leon (Mex)	(WBO)
1989	Manning Galloway (US)	(WBO)
1990	Aaron Davis (US)	(WBA)
1990	Maurice Blocker (US)	(WBC)

Junior-welterweight

1922	Pinky Mitchell (US)	
1926	Mushy Callahan (US)	
1930	Jackie Kid Berg (GB)	
1931	Tony Canzoneri (US)	
1932	Johnny Jaddick (US)	
1933	Battling Shaw (Mex)	
1933	Tony Canzoneri (US)	
1933	Barney Ross (US)	
1946	Tippy Larkin (US)	
1959	Carlos Ortiz (PR)	
1969	Duilio Loi (Ita)	
1962	Eddie Perkins (US)	
1962	Duilio Loi (Ita)	
1963	Roberto Cruz (Phi)	
1963	Eddie Perkins (US)	
1965	Carlos Hernandez (Ven)	
1966	Sandro Lopoplo (Ita)	
1967	Paul Fujii (Haw)	
1968	Nicolino Loche (Arg)	(WBA)
1968	Pedro Adigue (Phi)	(WBC)
1970	Bruno Acari (Ita)	(WBC)
1972	Alfonso Frazer (Pan)	(WBA)
1972	Antonio Cervantes (Col)	(WBA)
1974	Perico Fernandez (Spa)	(WBC)
1975	Saensak Muangsurin (Tha)	(WBC)
1976	Wilfred Benitez (US)	(WBA)
1976	Miguel Velasquez (Spa)	(WBC)
1976	Saensak Muangsurin (Tha)	(WBC)
1977	Antonio Cervantes (Col)	(WBA)
1978	Sang-Hyun Kim (SKo)	(WBC)
1980	Saoul Mamby (US)	(WBC)
1980	Aaron Pryor (US)	(WBA)
1982	Leroy Haley (US)	(WBC)
1983	Aaron Pryor (US)	(IBF)
1983	Bruce Curry (US)	(WBC)
1984	Johnny Bumphus (US)	(WBA)
1984	Billy Costello (US)	(WBC)
1984	Gene Hatcher (US)	(WBA)
1985	Ubaldo Sacco (Arg)	(WBA)
1985	Lonnie Smith (US)	(WBC)
1986	Patrizio Oliva (Ita)	(WBA)
1986	Gary Hinton (US)	(IBF)
1986	Tsuyoshi Hamada (Jap)	(WBC)
1986	René Arredondo (Mex)	(WBC)
1986	Joe Louis Manley (US)	(IBF)
1987	Terry Marsh (GB)	(IBF)
1987	Juan Martin Coggi (Arg)	(WBA)
1987	René Arredondo (Mex)	(WBC)

1988	James Buddy McGirt (US)	(IBF)
1988	Roger Mayweather (US)	(WBC)
1988	Meldrick Taylor (US)	(IBF)
1989	Hector Camacho (PR)	(WBO)
1989	Julio Cesar Chavez (Mex)	(WBC)
1990	Loreto Garza (US)	(WBA)

Lightweight

1896	George Lavigne (US)	
1899	Frank Erne (Swi)	
1902	Joe Gans (US)	
1908	Battling Nelson (Den)	
1910	Ad Wolgast (US)	
1912	Willie Ritchie (US)	
1914	Freddie Welsh (GB)	
1917	Benny Leonard (US)	
1925	Jimmy Goodrich (US)	
1925	Rocky Kansas (US)	
1926	Sammy Mandell (US)	
1930	Al Singer (US)	
1930	Tony Canzeroni (US)	
1933	Barney Ross (US)	
1935	Tony Canzeroni (US)	
1936	Lou Ambers (US)	
1938	Henry Armstrong (US)	
1939	Lou Ambers (US)	
1940	Lew Jenkins (US)	
1941	Sammy Angott (US)	
1942	Beau Jack (US)	
1943	Bob Montgomery (US)	
1943	Sammy Angott (US)	
1944	Juan Zurita (Mex)	
1945	Ike Williams (US)	
1951	Jimmy Carter (US)	
1952	Lauro Salas (Mex)	
1952	Jimmy Carter (US)	
1954	Paddy de Marco (US)	
1954	Jimmy Carter (US)	
1955	Wallace Bud Smith (US)	
1956	Joe Brown (US)	
1962	Carlos Ortiz (PR)	
1965	Ismael Laguna (Pan)	
1965	Carlos Ortiz (PR)	
1968	Carlos Teo Cruz (Dom)	
1969	Mando Ramos (US)	
1970	Ismael Laguna (Pan)	
1970	Ken Buchanan (GB)	(WBA)
1971	Pedro Carrasco (Spa)	(WBC)
1972	Mando Ramos (US)	(WBC)
1972	Roberto Duran (Pan)	(WBA)
1972	Chango Carmona (Mex)	(WBC)
1972	Rodolfo Gonzalez (Mex)	(WBC)
1974	Guts Ishimatsu (Jap)	(WBC)
1976	Esteban de Jesus (PR)	(WBC)
1978	Roberto Duran (Pan)	
1979	Jim Watt (GB)	(WBC)
1979	Ernesto Espana (Ven)	(WBA)
1980	Hilmer Kenty (US)	(WBA)
1981	Sean O'Grady (US)	(WBA)
1981	Alexis Arguello (Nic)	(WBC)
1981	Claude Noel (Tri)	(WBA)
1981	Arturo Frias (US)	(WBA)
1982	Ray Mancini (US)	(WBA)
1983	Edwin Rosario (PR)	(WBC)
1984	Charlie Brown (US)	(IBF)
1984	Livingstone Bramble (US)	(WBA)
1984	Harry Arroyo (US)	(IBF)
1984	Jose Luis Ramirez (Mex)	(WBC)
1985	Jimmy Paul (US)	(IBF)
1985	Hector Camacho (PR)	(WBC)
1986	Edwin Rosario (PR)	(WBA)

1986	Greg Haugen (US)	(IBF)
1987	Vinny Pazienza (US)	(IBF)
1987	Jose Luis Ramirez (Mex)	(WBC)
1987	Julio Cesar Chavez (Mex)	(WBA)
1988	Greg Haugen (US)	(IBF)
1988	Julio Cesar Chavez (Mex)	(WBC/WBA)
1989	Amancio Castro (Col)	(WBO)
1989	Pernell Whitaker (US)	(IBF)
1989	Mauricio Aceves (Mex)	(WBO)
1989	Edwin Rosario (US)	(WBA)
1989	Pernell Whitaker (US)	(WBC/IBF)
1990	Juan Nazario (PR)	(WBC)
1990	Pernell Whitaker (US)	(WBC/WBA/IBF)

Super-featherweight

1921	Johnny Dundee (Ita)	
1923	Jack Bernstein (US)	
1923	Johnny Dundee (Ita)	
1924	Kid Sullivan (US)	
1925	Mike Ballerino (US)	
1925	Tod Morgan (US)	
1929	Benny Bass (US)	
1931	Kid Chocolate (Cub)	
1933	Frankie Klick (US)	
1959	Harold Gomes (US)	
1960	Flash Elorde (Phi)	
1967	Yoshiaki Numata (Jap)	
1967	Hiroshi Kobayashi (Jap)	
1969	Rene Barrientos (Phi)	(WBC)
1970	Yoshiaki Numata (Jap)	(WBC)
1971	Alfredo Marcano (Ven)	(WBA)
1971	Ricardo Arredondo (Mex)	(WBC)
1972	Ben Villaflor (Phi)	(WBA)
1973	Kuniaki Shibata (Jap)	(WBA)
1973	Ben Villaflor (Phi)	(WBA)
1974	Kuniaki Shibata (Jap)	(WBC)
1975	Alfredo Escalera (PR)	(WBC)
1976	Sam Serrano (PR)	(WBA)
1978	Alexis Arguello (Nic)	(WBC)
1980	Yasutsune Uehara (Jap)	(WBA)
1980	Rafael Limon (Mex)	(WBC)
1981	Cornelius Boza Edwards (Uga)	(WBC)
1981	Sam Serrano (PR)	(WBA)
1981	Rolando Navarette (Phi)	(WBC)
1982	Rafael Limon (Mex)	(WBC)
1982	Bobby Chacon (US)	(WBC)
1983	Roger Mayweather (US)	(WBA)
1983	Hector Camacho (PR)	(WBC)
1984	Rocky Lockridge (US)	(WBA)
1984	Hwan-Kil Yuh (SKo)	(IBF)
1984	Julio Cesar Chavez (Mex)	(WBC)
1985	Lester Ellis (Aus)	(IBF)
1985	Wilfredo Gomez (PR)	(WBA)
1985	Barry Michael (Aus)	(IBF)
1986	Alfredo Layne (Pan)	(WBA)
1986	Brian Mitchell (SA)	(WBA)
1987	Julio Cesar Chavez (Mex)	(WBC)
1987	Rocky Lockridge (US)	(IBF)
1988	Azumah Nelson (Gha)	(WBC)
1988	Tony Lopez (US)	(IBF)
1989	Juan Molina (PR)	(WBO)
1989	Juan Molina (PR)	(IBF)
1989	Kamel Bou Ali (Tun)	(WBO)
1990	Tony Lopez (US)	(IBF)

Featherweight

1891	Young Griffo (Aus)	
1892	George Dixon (Can)	
1897	Solly Smith (US)	
1898	Dave Sullivan (Ire)	

1898	George Dixon (Can)	
1900	Terry McGovern (US)	
1901	Young Corbett II (US)	
1904	Jimmy Britt (US)	
1904	Tommy Sullivan (US)	
1906	Abe Attell (US)	
1912	Johnny Kilbane (US)	
1923	Eugene Criqui (Fra)	
1923	Johnny Dundee (Ita)	
1925	Kid Kaplan (US)	
1927	Benny Bass (US)	
1928	Tony Canzoneri (US)	
1928	André Routis (Fra)	
1929	Battling Battalino (US)	
1932	Kid Chocolate (Cub)	
1933	Freddie Miller (US)	
1936	Petey Sarron (US)	
1937	Henry Armstrong (US)	
1938	Joey Archibald (US)	
1940	Harry Jeffra (US)	
1941	Joey Archibald (US)	
1941	Chalky Wright (Mex)	
1942	Willie Pep (US)	
1948	Sandy Saddler (US)	
1949	Willie Pep (US)	
1950	Sandy Saddler (US)	
1957	Hogan Kid Bassey (Nig)	
1959	Davey Moore (US)	
1963	Sugar Ramos (Cub)	
1964	Vicente Saldivar (Mex)	
1968	Howard Winstone (GB)	(WBC)
1968	Raul Rojas (US)	(WBA)
1968	Jose Legra (Cub)	(WBC)
1968	Shozo Saijyo (Jap)	(WBA)
1969	Johnny Famechon (Fra)	(WBC)
1970	Vicente Saldivar (Mex)	(WBC)
1970	Kuniaki Shibata (Jap)	(WBC)
1971	Antonio Gomez (Ven)	(WBA)
1972	Clemente Sanchez (Mex)	(WBC)
1972	Ernesto Marcel (Pan)	(WBA)
1972	Jose Legra (Cub)	(WBC)
1973	Eder Jofre (Bra)	(WBC)
1974	Ruben Olivares (Mex)	(WBA)
1974	Bobby Chacon (US)	(WBC)
1974	Alexis Arguello (Nic)	(WBA)
1975	Ruben Olivares (Mex)	(WBC)
1975	David Kotey (Gha)	(WBC)
1976	Danny Lopez (US)	(WBC)
1977	Rafael Ortega (Pan)	(WBA)
1977	Cecilio Lastra (Spa)	(WBA)
1978	Eusebio Pedroza (Pan)	(WBA)
1980	Salvador Sanchez (Mex)	(WBC)
1982	Juan Laporte (PR)	(WBC)
1984	Min-Keum Oh (SKo)	(IBF)
1984	Wilfredo Gomez (PR)	(WBC)
1984	Azumah Nelson (Gha)	(WBC)
1985	Barry McGuigan (Ire)	(WBA)
1985	Ki-Young Chung (SKo)	(IBF)
1986	Steve Cruz (US)	(WBA)
1986	Antonio Rivera (PR)	(IBF)
1987	Antonio Esparragoza (Ven)	(WBA)
1988	Calvin Grove (US)	(IBF)
1988	Jeff Fenech (Aus)	(WBC)
1988	Jorge Paez (Mex)	(IBF)
1989	Maurizio Stecca (Ita)	(WBO)
1989	Louie Espinoza (US)	(WBO)
1990	Marcos Villasana (Mex)	(WBC)

Junior-featherweight

1922	Jack Kid Wolfe (US)	
1923	Carl Duane (US)	
1976	Rigoberto Riasca (Pan)	(WBC)
1976	Royal Kobayashi (Jap)	(WBC)
1976	Dong-Kyun Yum (SKo)	(WBC)
1977	Wilfredo Gomez (PR)	(WBC)
1977	Soo-Hwan Hong (SKo)	(WBA)
1978	Ricardo Cardona (Col)	(WBA)
1980	Leo Randolph (US)	(WBA)
1980	Sergio Palma (Arg)	(WBA)
1982	Leo Cruz (Dom)	(WBA)
1983	Jaime Garza (US)	(WBC)
1983	Bobby Berna (Phi)	(IBF)
1984	Loris Stecca (Ita)	(WBA)
1984	Seung-Il Suh (SKo)	(IBF)
1984	Victor Callejas (PR)	(WBA)
1984	Juan Meza (Mex)	(WBC)
1985	Ji-Won Kim (SKo)	(IBF)
1985	Lupe Pintor (Mex)	(WBC)
1986	Samart Payakarun (Tha)	(WBC)
1987	Louis Espinoza (US)	(WBA)
1987	Seung-Hoon Lee (SKo)	(IBF)
1987	Jeff Fenech (Aus)	(WBC)
1987	Julio Gervacio (Dom)	(WBA)
1988	Bernardo Pinango (Ven)	(WBA)
1988	Daniel Zaragoza (Mex)	(WBC)
1988	Jose Sanabria (Ven)	(IBF)
1988	Juan Jose Estrada (Mex)	(WBA)
1989	Fabrice Benichou (Fra)	(IBF)
1989	Kenny Mitchell (US)	(WBO)
1989	Valerio Nati (Ita)	(WBO)
1989	Jesus Salud (US)	(WBA)
1990	Welcome Ncita (SA)	(IBF)
1990	Paul Banke (US)	(WBC)
1990	Orlando Fernandez (PR)	(WBO)

Bantamweight

1891	George Dixon (Can)	
1892	Billy Plimmer (GB)	
1895	Pedlar Palmer (GB)	
1899	Terry McGovern (US)	
1901	Harry Forbes (US)	
1903	Frankie Neil (US)	
1904	Joe Bowker (GB)	
1905	Jimmy Walsh (US)	
1907	Owen Moran (GB)	
1908	Johnny Coulon (Can)	
1914	Kid Williams (Den)	
1917	Pete Herman (US)	
1920	Joe Lynch (US)	
1921	Pete Herman (US)	
1921	Johnny Buff (US)	
1922	Joe Lynch (US)	
1924	Abe Goldstein (US)	
1924	Eddie Martin (US)	
1925	Charlie Rosenberg (US)	
1927	Bud Taylor (US)	
1928	Bushy Graham (Ita)	
1929	Al Brown (Pan)	
1935	Baltazar Sangchilli (Spa)	
1936	Tony Marino (US)	
1936	Sixto Escobar (Spa)	
1937	Harry Jeffra (US)	
1938	Sixto Escobar (Spa)	
1940	Lou Salica (US)	
1942	Manuel Ortiz (US)	
1947	Harold Dade (US)	
1947	Manuel Ortiz (US)	
1950	Vic Toweel (SA)	
1952	Jimmy Carruthers (Aus)	
1954	Robert Cohen (Alg)	
1956	Mario D'Agata (Ita)	
1957	Alphonse Halimi (Alg)	
1959	Joe Becerra (Mex)	
1960	Eder Jofre (Bra)	
1965	Fighting Harada (Jap)	
1968	Lionel Rose (Aus)	
1969	Ruben Olivares (Mex)	
1970	Chucho Castillo (Mex)	
1971	Ruben Olivares (Mex)	
1972	Rafael Herrera (Mex)	
1972	Enrique Pinder (Pan)	
1973	Romeo Anaya (Mex)	(WBA)
1973	Rafael Herrera (Mex)	(WBC)
1973	Arnold Taylor (SA)	(WBA)
1974	Soo-Hwan Hong (SKo)	(WBA)
1974	Rudolfo Martinez (Mex)	(WBC)
1975	Alfonso Zamora (Mex)	(WBA)
1976	Carlos Zarate (Mex)	(WBC)
1977	Jorge Lujan (Pan)	(WBA)
1979	Lupe Pintor (Mex)	(WBC)
1980	Julian Solis (PR)	(WBA)
1980	Jeff Chandler (US)	(WBA)
1983	Alberto Davila (US)	(WBC)
1984	Richard Sandoval (US)	(WBA)
1984	Satoshi Shingaki (Jap)	(IBF)
1985	Jeff Fenech (Aus)	(IBF)
1985	Daniel Zaragoza (Mex)	(WBC)
1985	Miguel Lora (Col)	(WBC)
1986	Gaby Canizales (US)	(WBA)
1986	Bernardo Pinanago (Ven)	(WBA)
1987	Takuya Muguruma (Jap)	(WBA)
1987	Kelvin Seabrooks (US)	(IBF)
1987	Chang-Young Park (SKo)	(WBA)
1987	Wilfredo Vasquez (PR)	(WBA)
1988	Kaokor Galaxy (Tha)	(WBA)
1988	Orlando Canizales (US)	(IBF)
1988	Sung-Kil Moon (SKo)	(WBA)
1988	Raul Perez (Mex)	(WBC)
1989	Israel Contreras (Ven)	(WBO)
1989	Khaokor Galaxy (Tha)	(WBA)
1989	Luisito Espinosa (Phi)	(WBA)

Super-flyweight

1980	Rafael Orono (Ven)	(WBC)
1981	Chul-Ho Kim (SKo)	(WBC)
1981	Gustavo Ballas (Arg)	(WBA)
1981	Rafael Pedroza (Pan)	(WBA)
1982	Jiro Watanabe (Jap)	(WBA)
1982	Rafael Orono (Ven)	(WBC)
1983	Payao Poontarat (Tha)	(WBC)
1983	Joo-Do Chun (SKo)	(IBF)
1984	Jiro Watanabe (Jap)	(WBC)
1984	Kaosai Galaxy (Tha)	(WBA)
1985	Ellyas Pical (Ina)	(IBF)
1986	Cesar Polanco (Dom)	(IBF)
1986	Gilberto Roman (Mex)	(WBC)
1986	Tae-Il Chang (SKo)	(IBF)
1987	Ellyas Pical (Ina)	(IBF)
1987	Santos Laciar (Arg)	(WBC)
1987	Jesus Rojas (Col)	(WBC)
1988	Gilberto Roman (Mex)	(WBC)
1989	Jose Ruiz (PR)	(WBO)
1989	Juan Polo Perez (Col)	(IBF)
1989	Nana Yaw Konadu (Gha)	(WBC)
1990	Moon Sung-Kil (SKo)	(WBC)
1990	Roberto Quiroga (US)	(IBF)

Flyweight

1913	Sid Smith (GB)	
1913	Bill Ladbury (GB)	
1914	Percy Jones (GB)	
1915	Joe Symonds (GB)	
1916	Jimmy Wilde (GB)	
1923	Pancho Villa (Phi)	
1925	Fidel la Barba (US)	
1928	Frankie Genaro (US)	
1929	Emile Pladner (Fra)	
1929	Frankie Genaro (US)	
1931	Young Perez (Tun)	
1932	Jackie Brown (Eng)	
1935	Benny Lynch (GB)	
1938	Peter Kane (GB)	
1943	Jackie Paterson (GB)	
1948	Rinty Monaghan (GB)	
1950	Terry Allen (GB)	
1950	Dado Marino (Haw)	
1952	Yoshio Shirai (Jap)	
1954	Pascual Perez (Arg)	
1960	Pone Kingpetch (Tha)	
1960	Fighting Harada (Jap)	
1963	Pone Kingpetch (Tha)	
1963	Hiroyuki Ebihara (Jap)	
1964	Pone Kingpetch (Tha)	
1965	Salvatore Burruni (Ita)	
1966	Horacio Accavallo (Arg)	(WBA)
1966	Walter McGowan (GB)	(WBC)
1966	Chartchai Chionoi (Tha)	(WBC)
1969	Efren Torres (Mex)	(WBC)
1969	Hiroyuki Ebihara (Jap)	(WBA)
1969	Bernabe Villacampo (Phi)	(WBA)
1970	Chartchai Chionoi (Tha)	(WBC)
1970	Berkrerk Chartvanchai (Tha)	(WBA)
1970	Masao Ohba (Jap)	(WBA)
1970	Erbito Salavarria (Phi)	(WBC)
1972	Venice Borkorsor (Tha)	(WBC)
1973	Chartchai Chionoi (Tha)	(WBA)
1973	Betulio Gonzalez (Ven)	(WBC)
1974	Shoji Oguma (Jap)	(WBC)
1974	Susumu Hanagata (Jap)	(WBA)
1975	Miguel Canto (Mex)	(WBC)
1975	Erbito Salavarria (Phi)	(WBA)
1976	Alfonso Lopez (Pan)	(WBA)
1976	Guty Espadas (Mex)	(WBA)
1978	Betulio Gonzalez (Ven)	(WBA)
1979	Chan-Hee Park (SKo)	(WBC)
1979	Luis Ibarra (Pan)	(WBA)
1980	Tae-Shik Kim (SKo)	(WBA)
1980	Shoji Oguma (Jap)	(WBA)
1980	Peter Mathebula (SA)	(WBA)
1981	Santos Laciar (Arg)	(WBA)
1981	Antonio Avelar (Mex)	(WBC)
1981	Luis Ibarra (Pan)	(WBA)
1981	Juan Herrera (Mex)	(WBA)
1982	Prudencio Cardona (Col)	(WBC)
1982	Santos Laciar (Arg)	(WBA)
1982	Freddie Castillo (Mex)	(WBC)
1982	Eleoncio Mercedes (Dom)	(WBC)
1983	Charlie Magri (GB)	(WBC)
1983	Frank Cedeno (Phi)	(WBC)
1983	Soon-Chun Kwon (SKo)	(IBF)
1984	Koji Kobayashi (Jap)	(WBC)
1984	Gabriel Bernal (Mex)	(WBC)
1984	Sot Chitalada (Tha)	(WBC)
1985	Hilario Zapata (Pan)	(WBA)
1985	Chong-Kwan Chung (SKo)	(IBF)
1986	Bi-Won Chung (SKo)	(IBF)
1986	Hi-Sup Shin (SKo)	(IBF)

1987	Fidel Bassa (Col)	(WBA)
1987	Dodie Penalosa (Phi)	(IBF)
1987	Chang-Ho Choi (SKo)	(IBF)
1988	Rolando Bohol (Phi)	(IBF)
1988	Yung-Kang Kim (SKo)	(WBC)
1988	Duke McKenzie (GB)	(IBF)
1989	Elvis Alvarez (Col)	(WBO)
1989	Sot Chitalda (Tha)	(WBC)
1989	Dave McAuley (GB)	(IBF)
1989	Jesus Rojas (Ven)	(WBA)
1990	Lee Yul-Woo (Sko)	(WBA)
1990	Leonard Tamakuma (Jap)	(WBA)
1990	Isidiro Perez (Mex)	(WBO)

Light-flyweight

1975	Franco Udella (Ita)	(WBC)
1975	Jaime Rios (Pan)	(WBA)
1975	Luis Estaba (Ven)	(WBC)
1976	Juan Jose Guzman (Dom)	(WBA)
1976	Yoko Gushiken (Jap)	(WBA)
1978	Freddie Castillo (Mex)	(WBC)
1978	Netrnoi Vorasingh (Tha)	(WBC)
1978	Sung-Jun Kim (SKo)	(WBC)
1980	Shigeo Nakajima (Jap)	(WBC)
1980	Hilario Zapata (Pan)	(WBC)
1981	Pedro Flores (Mex)	(WBA)
1981	Hwan-Jin KIm (SKo)	(WBA)
1981	Katsuo Takashiki (Jap)	(WBA)
1982	Amado Ursua (Mex)	(WBC)
1982	Tadashi Tomori (Jap)	(WBC)
1982	Hilario Zapata (Pan)	(WBC)
1983	Jung-Koo Chang (Kor)	(WBC)
1983	Lupe Madera (Mex)	(WBA)
1983	Dodie Penalosa (Phi)	(IBF)
1984	Francisco Quiroz (Dom)	(WBA)
1985	Joey Olivo (US)	(WBA)
1985	Myung-Woo Yuh (SKo)	(WBA)
1986	Chong-Hwan Choi (SKo)	(IBF)
1988	Tacy Macalos (Phi)	(IBF)
1988	German Torres (Mex)	(WBC)
1989	Yol-Woo Lee (SKo)	(WBC)
1989	Muancgchai Kittikasem (Tha)	(IBF)
1989	Jose de Jesus (PR)	(WBO)
1989	Humberto Gonzalez (Mex)	(WBC)
1990	Michael Carbajal (US)	(IBF)

Straw-weight

1987	Kyung-Yung Lee (SKo)	(WBC)
1988	Leo Gomez (Dom)	(WBA)
1988	Hiroki Ioka (Jap)	(WBC)
1988	Samuth Sithnaruepol (Tha)	(IBF)
1988	Napa Kiatwanchai (Tha)	(WBC)
1989	Kim Bong-Jun (SKo)	(WBA)
1989	Nico Thomas (Ina)	(IBF)
1989	Eric Chavez (Phi)	(IBF)
1989	Rafael Torres (Dom)	(WBO)
1989	Choi Jeum-Hwan (SKo)	(WBC)
1990	Hideyuki Ohashi (Jap)	(WBC)
1990	Falan Lookmingkwan (Tha)	(IBF)

HEAVYWEIGHT CHAMPIONS

British

1891	Ted Pritchard
1895	Jem Smith
1897	George Crisp
1903	Jack Palmer
1906	Gunner Jim Moir
1909	William 'Iron' Hague
1911	Bombardier Billy Wells
1919	Joe Beckett
1919	Frank Goddard
1919	Joe Beckett
1923	Frank Goddard
1926	Phil Scott
1931	Reggie Meen
1932	Jack Petersen
1933	Len Harvey
1934	Jack Petersen
1936	Ben Foord
1937	Tommy Farr
1938	Len Harvey
1944	Jack London
1945	Bruce Woodcock
1950	Jack Gardner
1952	Johnny Williams
1953	Don Cockell
1956	Jack Erskine
1958	Brian London
1959	Henry Cooper
1969	Jack Bodell
1970	Henry Cooper
1971	Joe Bugner
1971	Jack Bodell
1972	Danny McAlinden
1975	Bunny Johnson
1975	Richard Dunn
1976	Joe Bugner
1978	John L Gardner
1981	Gordon Ferris
1981	Neville Meade
1983	David Pearce
1985	Hughroy Currie
1986	Horace Notice
1989	Gary Mason

European

1906	Gunner Moir (GB)
1909	Iron Hague (GB)
1911	Bombardier Billy Wells (GB)
1913	Georges Carpentier (Fra)
1922	Battling Siki (Sen)
1923	Erminio Spalla (Ita)
1926	Paolino Uzcudin (Spa)
1929	Pierre Charles (Bel)
1931	Heinz Muller (Ger)
1932	Pierre Charles (Bel)
1933	Paolino Uzcudin (Spa)
1933	Primo Carnera (Ita)
1935	Pierre Charles (Bel)
1937	Arno Kollin (Ger)
1938	Heinz Lazek (Aut)
1939	Adolph Heuser (Ger)
1939	Max Schmeling (Ger)
1943	Olle Tandberg (Swe)
1943	Karel Sys (Bel)
1946	Bruce Woodcock (GB)
1950	Jo Weidin (Aus)
1951	Jack Gardner (GB)
1951	Hein Ten Hoff (Ger)
1952	Karel Sys (Bel)
1952	Heinz Neuhaus (Ger)
1955	Franco Cavicchi (Ita)
1956	Ingemar Johansson (Swe)
1960	Dick Richardson (GB)
1962	Ingemar Johansson (Swe)
1964	Henry Cooper (GB)
1964	Karl Mildenberger (Ger)
1968	Henry Cooper (GB)
1969	Peter Weiland (Ger)
1970	Jose Urtain (Spa)
1970	Henry Cooper (GB)
1971	Joe Bugner (GB)
1971	Jack Bodell (GB)
1971	Jose Urtain (Spa)
1972	Jurgen Blin (Ger)
1972	Joe Bugner (GB)
1976	Richard Dunn (GB)
1976	Joe Bugner (GB)
1977	Jean-Pierre Coopman (Bel)
1977	Lucien Rodriguez (Fra)
1977	Alfredo Evangelista (Spa)
1979	Lorenzo Zanon (Ita)
1980	John L Gardner (GB)
1981	Lucien Rodriguez (Fra)
1984	Steffen Tangstad (Nor)
1985	Anders Eklund (Swe)
1985	Frank Bruno (GB)
1986	Steffen Tangstad (Nor)
1987	Alfredo Evangelista (Spa)
1987	Anders Eklund (Swe)
1988	Francesco Damiani (Ita)
1989	Derek Williams (GB)
1990	Jean-Maurice Chanet (Fra)

Commonwealth

1910	Tommy Burns (Can)
1911	Matthew Curran (Eng)
1911	Bombardier Billy Wells (Eng)
1919	Joe Beckett (Eng)
1926	Phil Scott (Eng)
1931	Larry Gains (Can)
1934	Len Harvey (Eng)
1934	Jack Petersen (Wal)
1936	Ben Foord (SA)
1937	Tommy Farr (Wal)
1939	Len Harvey (Eng)
1944	Jack London (Eng)
1945	Bruce Woodcock (Eng)
1950	Jack Gardner (Eng)
1952	Johnny Williams (Wal)
1953	Don Cockell (Eng)
1956	Joe Bygraves (Jam)
1957	Joe Erskine (Wal)
1958	Brian London (Eng)
1959	Henry Cooper (Eng)
1971	Joe Bugner (Eng)
1971	Jack Bodell (Eng)
1972	Danny McAlinden (NI)
1975	Bunny Johnson (Eng)
1975	Richard Dunn (Eng)
1976	Joe Bugner (Eng)
1978	John L Gardner (Eng)
1981	Trevor Berbick (Can)
1986	Horace Notice (Eng)
1988	Derek Williams (Eng)

OLYMPIC CHAMPIONS

Super-heavyweight
1984　Tyrell Biggs (US)
1988　Lennox Lewis (Can)

Heavyweight
1904　Samuel Berger (US)
1908　A.L. Oldham (GB)
1912　Not held
1920　Ronald Rawson (GB)
1924　Otto von Porat (Nor)
1928　Arturo Rodriguez Jurado (Arg)
1932　Santiago Lovell (Arg)
1936　Herbert Runge (Ger)
1948　Rafael Iglesias (Arg)
1952　Edward Sanders (US)
1956　Peter Rademacher (US)
1960　Franco de Piccoli (Ita)
1964　Joe Frazier (US)
1968　George Foreman (US)
1972　Teofilio Stevenson (Cub)
1976　Teofilio Stevenson (Cub)
1980　Teofilio Stevenson (Cub)
1984　Henry Tillman (US)
1988　Ray Mercer (US)

Light-heavyweight
1920　Eddie Eagan (US)
1924　Harry Mitchell (GB)
1928　Victor Avendano (Arg)
1932　David Carstens (SA)
1936　Roger Michelot (Fra)
1948　George Hunter (SA)
1952　Norvel Lee (US)
1956　James Boyd (US)
1960　Cassius Clay (US)
1964　Cosimo Pinto (Ita)
1968　Dan Poznyak (USSR)
1972　Mate Parlov (Yug)
1976　Leon Spinks (US)
1980　Slobodan Kacar (Yug)
1984　Anton Jospovic (Yug)
1988　Andrew Maynard (US)

Middleweight
1904　Charles Mayer (US)
1908　John Douglas (GB)
1920　Harry Mallin (GB)
1924　Harry Mallin (GB)
1928　Piero Toscani (Ita)
1932　Carmen Barth (US)
1936　Jean Despeaux (Fra)
1948　Laszlo Papp (Hun)
1952　Floyd Patterson (US)
1956　Genaddy Schatkov (USSR)
1960　Edward Crook (US)
1964　Valery Popenchenko (USSR)
1968　Chris Finnegan (GB)
1972　Vyacheslav Lewechev (USSR)
1976　Michael Spinks (US)
1980　Jose Gomez (Cub)
1984　Sin-Joon Sup (SKo)
1988　Henry Maske (GDR)

Light-middleweight
1952　Laszlo Papp (Hun)
1956　Laszlo Papp (Hun)
1960　Wilbert McClure (US)
1964　Boris Lagutin (USSR)
1968　Boris Lagutin (USSR)
1972　Dieter Kottysch (FRG)
1976　Jerzy Rybicki (Pol)

1980　Armando Martinez (Cub)
1984　Frank Tate (US)
1988　Park Si-Hun (Kor)

Welterweight
1904　Albert Young (US)
1908　not held
1920　Albert Schneider (Can)
1924　Jean Delarge (Bel)
1928　Edward Morgan (NZ)
1932　Edward Flynn (US)
1936　Sten Suvio (Fin)
1948　Julius Torma (Cze)
1952　Zygmunt Chychia (Pol)
1956　Nicolae Linca (Rom)
1960　Giovanni Benvenuti (Ita)
1964　Marian Kasprzyk (Pol)
1968　Manfred Wolke (GDR)
1972　Emilio Correa (Cub)
1976　Jochen Bachfeld (GDR)
1980　Andres Aldama (Cub)
1984　Mark Breland (US)
1988　Robert Wangila (Ken)

Light-welterweight
1952　Charles Adkins (US)
1956　Vladimir Yengibaryan (USSR)
1960　Bohumil Nemecek (Cze)
1964　Jerzy Kulej (Pol)
1968　Jerzy Kulej (Pol)
1972　Ray Seales (US)
1976　Ray Leonard (US)
1980　Patrizio Oliva (Ita)
1984　Jerry Page (US)
1988　Viatcheslav Janovski (USSR)

Lightweight
1904　Harry Spanger (US)
1908　Frederick Grace (GB)
1920　Samuel Mosberg (US)
1924　Hans Neilsen (Den)
1928　Carlo Orlando (Ita)
1932　Lawrence Stevens (SA)
1936　Imre Harangi (Hun)
1948　Gerald Dreyer (SA)
1952　Aureliano Bolognesi (Ita)
1956　Dick McTaggart (GB)
1960　Kazimierz Pazdzior (Pol)
1964　Jozef Grudzien (Pol)
1968　Ron Harris (US)
1972　Jan Szczepanski (Pol)
1976　Howard Davis (US)
1980　Angel Herrera (Cub)
1984　Pernell Whitaker (US)
1988　Andreas Zuelow (GDR)

Featherweight
1904　Oliver Kirk (US)
1908　Richard Gunn (GB)
1920　Paul Fritsch (Fra)
1924　John Fields (US)
1928　Lambertus van Klavaren (Hol)
1932　Carmelo Robledo (Arg)
1936　Oscar Casanovas (Arg)
1948　Ernesto Formenti (Ita)
1952　Jan Zachara (Cze)
1956　Vladimir Safronov (USSR)
1960　Francesco Musso (Ita)
1964　Stanislav Stepashkin (USSR)
1968　Antonio Roldan (Mex)
1972　Boris Kousnetsov (USSR)
1976　Angel Herrera (Cub)
1980　Rudi Fink (GDR)

| 1984 | Meldrick Taylor (US) |
| 1988 | Giovanni Parisi (Ita) |

Bantamweight
1904	Oliver Kirk (US)
1908	Henry Thomas (GB)
1920	Clarence Walker (SA)
1924	William Smith (SA)
1928	Vittorio Tamagnini (Ita)
1932	Horace Gwynne (Can)
1936	Ulderico Sergo (Ita)
1948	Tibor Csik (Hun)
1952	Pentti Hamalainen (Fin)
1956	Wolfgang Behrendt (FRG)
1960	Oleg Grigoryev (USSR)
1964	Takao Sakurai (Jap)
1968	Valery Sokolov (USSR)
1972	Orlando Martinez (Cub)
1976	Yung-Jo Gu (NKo)
1980	Juan Hernandez (Cub)
1984	Maurizio Stecca (Ita)
1988	Kennedy McKinney (US)

Flyweight
1904	George Finnegan (US)
1908	not held
1920	Frank Di Gennara (US)
1924	Fidel La Barba (US)
1928	Antal Kocsis (Hun)
1932	Istvan Enekes (Hun)
1936	Willi Kaiser (Ger)
1948	Pascual Perez (Arg)
1952	Nathan Brooks (US)
1956	Terry Spinks (GB)
1960	Gyula Torok (Hun)
1964	Fernando Atzori (Ita)
1968	Ricardo Delgado (Mex)
1972	Georgi Kostadinov (Bul)
1976	Leo Randolph (US)
1980	Peter Lessov (Bul)
1984	Steve McCrory (US)
1988	Kim Kwang-Sun (Kor)

Light-flyweight
1968	Francisco Rodriguez (Ven)
1972	Gyorgy Gedo (Hun)
1976	Jorge Hernandez (Cub)
1980	Shamil Sabyrov (USSR)
1984	Paul Gonzales (US)
1988	Ivalio Hristov (Bul)

RECORDS

MOST WORLD TITLES
(at different weights)
5 Thomas Hearns; Sugar Ray Leonard.
4 Roberto Duran.
3 Terry McGovern; Bob Fitzsimmons; Stanley Ketchel; Tony Canzoneri; Barney Ross; Henry Armstrong; Emile Griffiths; Wilfred Benitez; Alexis Arguello; Wilfredo Gomez; Hector Camacho; Julio Cesar Chavez; Jeff Fenech

UNDEFEATED WORLD CHAMPIONS
Jimmy Barry (70 bouts); Jack McAuliffe (53 bouts); Rocky Marciano (49 bouts).

LONGEST REIGNING WORLD CHAMPION
11 years 252 days Joe Louis (heavyweight) 22 June 1937 to 1 March 1949.

MOST SUCCESSFUL WORLD TITLE DEFENCES
25 Joe Louis (heavyweight) 1937-48

MOST WORLD TITLE FIGHTS
27 Joe Louis (heavyweight) 1937-50

SHORTEST WORLD TITLE FIGHTS
45 seconds Al McCoy (US) v George Chip (US), middleweight 1914
45 seconds Lloyd Honeyghan (GB) v Gene Hatcher (US) welterweight 1987.

MOST KNOCKDOWNS IN WORLD TITLE FIGHT
14 – Vic Toweel (SA) knocked down Danny O'Sullivan (GB) 14 times during their bantamweight contest in 1950.

OLDEST WORLD CHAMPION
48 yr 59 dy Archie Moore (light-heavyweight). Moore may have been only 45. Either way, he is still the oldest world champion.

HEAVIEST WORLD CHAMPION
270 lb Primo Carnera (heavyweight)

1991

AMATEUR FIXTURES
Jan 17 Scotland v England (Dundee); Mar 30 Schoolboy finals (Derby); May 6-12 European Senior finals (Gothenburg); Jun 13 Golden Gloves (Cardiff).

CANOEING

1990

WORLD RACING CHAMPIONSHIPS
Poznan, Poland, Aug 15-19

Men

500m	Kayak Singles:	Sergey Kalesnik (USSR) 1m 43.58s
500m	Kayak Pairs:	Sergey Kalesnik & Anatoliy Tsizenko (USSR) 1m 33.82s
500m	Kayak Fours:	USSR 1m 25.20s
500m	Canadian Singles:	Mikhail Slivinsky (USSR) 1m 55.95s
500m	Canadian Pairs:	Viktor Raneysky & Nikolai Juravsky (USSR) 1m 46.01s
500m	Canadian Fours:	USSR 1m 37.00s
1000m	Kayak Singles:	Knut Holmann (Nor) 3m 33.18s
1000m	Kayak Pairs:	Kay Bluhm & Torsten Gutsche (GDR) 3m 15.7s
1000m	Kayak Fours:	Hungary 2m 57.89s
1000m	Canadian Singles:	Ivan Klementiev (USSR) 4m 01.06s
1000m	Canadian Pairs:	Ulrich Papke & Ingo Spelly (GDR) 3m 38.45s
1000m	Canadian Fours:	USSR 3m 24.74s
10,000m	Kayak Singles:	Philippe Boccara (Fra) 42m 24.03s
10,000m	Kayak Pairs:	Ivan Lawler & Grayson Bourne (GB) 39m 48.21s
10,000m	Kayak Fours:	USSR 35m 21.86s
10,000m	Canadian Singles:	Zsolt Bohacs (Hun) 48m 48.24s
10,000m	Canadian Pairs:	Arne Nielsson & Christian Fredriksen (Den) 43m 04,38s

Women

500m	Kayak Singles:	Josefa Idem (FRG) 1m 57.58s
500m	Kayak Pairs:	Anke von Seck & Ramona Portwich (GDR) 1m 46.92s
500m	Kayak Fours:	East Germany 1m 35.58s

CHAMPIONS

OLYMPIC GAMES
Men
500 Metres Kayak Singles
1976	Vasile Diba (Rom)
1980	Vladimir Parfenovich (USSR)
1984	Ian Ferguson (NZ)
1988	Zsolt Gyulay (Hun)

1000 Metres Kayak Singles
1936	Gregor Hradetzky (Aut)
1948	Gert Fredriksson (Swe)
1952	Gert Fredriksson (Swe)
1956	Gert Fredriksson (Swe)
1960	Erik Hansen (Den)
1964	Rolf Peterson (Swe)
1968	Mihaly Hesz (Hun)
1972	Alexandr Shaparenko (USSR)
1976	Rudiger Helm (GDR)
1980	Rudiger Helm (GDR)
1984	Alan Thompson (NZ)
1988	Greg Barton (US)

500 Metres Kayak Pairs
1976	East Germany
1980	USSR
1984	New Zealand
1988	New Zealand

1000 Metres Kayak Pairs
1936	Austria
1948	Sweden
1952	Finland
1956	West Germany
1960	Sweden
1964	Sweden
1968	USSR
1972	USSR
1976	USSR
1980	USSR
1984	Canada
1988	United States

1000 Metres Kayak Fours
1964	USSR
1968	Norway
1972	USSR
1976	USSR
1980	East Germany
1984	New Zealand
1988	Hungary

500 Metres Canadian Singles
1976	Alexandr Rogov (USSR)
1980	Sergey Postrekhin (USSR)
1984	Larry Cain (Can)
1988	Olaf Heukrodt (GDR)

1000 Metres Canadian Singles
1936	Francis Amyot (Can)
1948	Josef Holecek (Cze)
1952	Josef Holecek (Cze)
1956	Leon Rotman (Rom)
1960	Josef Parti (Hun)
1964	Jürgen Eschert (FRG)
1968	Tibor Tatai (Hun)
1972	Ivan Patzaichin (Rom)
1976	Matija Ljubek (Yug)
1980	Lubomir Lubenov (Bul)
1984	Ulrich Eicke (FRG)
1988	Ivan Klementiev (USSR)

500 Metres Canadian Pairs
1976	USSR
1980	Hungary
1984	Yugoslavia
1988	USSR

1000 Metres Canadian Pairs
1936	Czechoslovakia
1948	Czechoslovakia
1952	Denmark
1956	Romania
1960	USSR
1964	USSR

1968	Romania
1972	USSR
1976	USSR
1980	Romania
1984	Romania
1988	USSR

Women

500 Metres Kayak Singles
1948	Karen Hoff (Den)
1952	Sylvi Saimo (Fin)
1956	Elisaveta Dementyeva (USSR)
1960	Anatonina Seredina (USSR)
1964	Lyudmila Khvedosyuk (USSR)
1968	Lyudmila Pinayeva (USSR)
1972	Yulia Ryabchinskaya (USSR)
1976	Carola Zirzow (GDR)
1980	Birgit Fischer (GDR)
1984	Agneta Anderson (Swe)
1988	Vania Guecheva (USSR)

500 Metres Kayak Pairs
1960	USSR
1964	West Germany
1968	West Germany
1972	USSR
1976	USSR
1980	East Germany
1984	Sweden
1988	East Germany

500 Metres Kayak Fours
1984	Romania
1988	East Germany

WORLD CHAMPIONS
Inaugurated 1938. Not held in Olympic years
Winners since 1985

Men

500 Metres Kayak Singles
1985	Andreas Stahle (GDR)
1986	Jeremy West (GB)
1987	Peter MacDonald (NZ)
1989	Martin Hunter (Aus)
1990	Sergey Kalesnik (USSR)

1000 Metres Kayak Singles
1985	Ferenc Csipes (Hun)
1986	Jeremy West (GB)
1987	Greg Barton (US)
1989	Zsolt Gyulay (Hun)
1990	Knut Holmann (Nor)

10,000 Metres Kayak Singles
1985	Greg Barton (US)
1986	Ferenc Csipes (Hun)
1987	Greg Barton (US)
1989	Attila Szabo (Cze)
1990	Philippe Boccara (FRA)

500 Metres Kayak Pairs
1985	New Zealand
1986	West Germany
1987	Hungary
1989	East Germany
1990	USSR

1000 Metres Kayak Pairs
1985	France
1986	Romania
1987	New Zealand
1989	East Germany
1990	East Germany

10,000 Metres Kayak Pairs

1985	Sweden
1986	Hungary
1987	France
1989	Hungary
1990	Great Britain

500 Metres Kayak Fours
1985	Hungary
1986	East Germany
1987	USSR
1989	USSR
1990	USSR

1000 Metres Kayak Fours
1985	Sweden
1986	Hungary
1987	Hungary
1989	Hungary
1990	East Germany

10,000 Metres Kayak Fours
1985	Hungary
1986	USSR
1987	Norway
1989	USSR
1990	USSR

500 Metres Canadian Singles
1985	Olaf Heokrodt (GDR)
1986	Olaf Heokrodt (GDR)
1987	Olaf Heokrodt (GDR)
1989	Mikhail Slivinsky (USSR)
1990	Mikhail Slivinsky (USSR)

1000 Metres Canadian Singles
1985	Ivan Klementiev (USSR)
1986	Aurel Macarencu (Rom)
1987	Olaf Heokrodt (GDR)
1989	Ivan Klementiev (USSR)
1990	Ivan Klementiev (USSR)

10,000 Metres Canadian Singles
1985	Jiri Vrdlovec (Cze)
1986	Aurel Macarencu (Rom)
1987	Ivan Sabjan (Yug)
1989	Ivan Klementiev (USSR)
1990	Zssolt Bohacs (Hun)

500 Metres Canadian Pairs
1985	Hungary
1986	Hungary
1987	Poland
1989	USSR
1990	USSR

1000 Metres Canadian Pairs
1985	East Germany
1986	Hungary
1987	USSR
1989	Denmark
1990	USSR

10,000 Metres Canadian Pairs
1985	Yugoslavia
1986	Poland
1987	Denmark
1989	Denmark
1990	Denmark

500 Metres Canadian Fours
First held 1989
1989	USSR
1990	USSR

1000 Metres Canadian Fours
First held 1989
1989	USSR
1990	USSR

Women
500 Metres Kayak Singles
1985   Birgit Fischer (GDR)
1986   Vania Gesheva (Bul)
1987   Birgit Schmidt (GDR)
1989   Katrin Borchert (GDR)
1990   Josefa Iden (FRG)

5000 Metres Kayak Singles
First held 1989
1989   Katrin Borchert (GDR)

500 Metres Kayak Pairs
1985   East Germany
1986   Hungary
1987   East Germany
1989   East Germany
1990   East Germany

5000 Metres Kayak Pairs
First held 1989
1989   East Germany

500 Metres Kayak Fours
1985   East Germany
1986   Hungary
1987   East Germany
1989   East Germany
1990   East Germany

COMMONWEALTH GAMES

THE QUIET GAMES

The 1990 Commonwealth Games, held in Auckland, New Zealand, re-established the event as a worthwhile and (just about) viable exercise after the disaster of the boycotted 1986 Games in Edinburgh. A record 55 nations, quasi-nations, colonial leftovers and mircodots were represented and 29 of them won medals, including many of the most improbable.

The standards in most sports never matched the size of the event. No world records were broken and only one was equalled - by the English breast-stroker Adrian Moorhouse. Public interest remained patchy too, even in Auckland where only the opening and closing ceremonies filled the main stadium, though the Australians - egged on by commercial television and a large collection of early gold medals in the swimming - became very excited. Their entire squad was given a ticker-tape reception on their return to Sydney.

Most other countries were more sceptical. Even the expected climax proved disappointing when Sebastian Coe, planning a dramatic departure before retiring into politics, was beaten into sixth place in the 800 metres and withdrew from the 1500 through illness. The highspot of the track meet was an amazing 5000 metres when John Ngugi of Kenya fell, then raced through the field and looked certain to win until he was caught by an unlikely Australian, Andrew Lloyd.

The weightlifting provided excitement of a sort with a succession of drug-related disqualifications. Subratakumar Paul of India, winner of two silvers and a bronze in the lightweight division, was thrown out along with two Welshmen, Ricky Chaplin, winner of the 75kg snatch gold medal, and Gareth Hives.

Among the Games's surprises were defeats of two of England's hottest and best-known favourites: Malcolm Cooper, the double Olympic champion, who only won silver in the three-positions rifle shooting, and David Bryant, four-times Commonwealth champion, who was beaten into fourth in the men's singles bowls.

The shock winners included Marcus Stephen of Nauru (population 8,042 and a lot of bird-droppings) in the featherweight weightlifting - Nauru's first and only competitor; Marios Hadjiandreou of Cyprus who won the triple jump and Geau Tau of Papua New Guinea who won the women's singles bowls. Tau beat the New Zealander Millie Khan, who played before being told that her week-old grandson Brad had died. The Western Samoan entrant in the same event, Laufili Pativaine Ainuu, was ordered to make less noise because her shouts of encouragement to her woods were putting off other competitors.

The people of the New Zealand town of Wanganui brought Joseph Kibor of Kenya a goat to replace the one he had to sell to pay for his bus fare to the trials. Mike Tereui, a weightlifter from the Cook Islands, competed despite breaking his hand before the Games, punching a pig who raided his vegetable patch. The Falkland Islands sent two 10,000 metre-runners who, in the absence of a track, had trained on the airstrip. They were lapped after 2,000 metres and finished 12 minutes behind the winner. "If a man was meant to run ten kilometres he should have had four legs and a bigger set of lungs," said one, William Goss.

The Australian team, managed by the controversial authoritarian Arthur Tunstall, was involved in a row before the Games because two athletes were alleged to have streaked round the village while another two were alleged to have made an offensive suggestion (reportedly "show us your whizzer") to a female runner, Michelle Baumgartner.

Administrators informally agreed that after the 1994 Games - to be held in Victoria, British Columbia - a city in a developing country should be allowed to stage the event. New Delhi and Kuala Lumpur are applying for 1998. Journalists informally agreed that a shorter, tauter programme would be better to prevent the long, dreary gaps between events, especially at the athletics. The badminton finals were delayed three hours because contractors engaged to put up seats fell asleep.

14TH COMMONWEALTH GAMES

Auckland, New Zealand, Jan 24-Feb 3 1990

MEDALS TABLE

Total		G	S	B
162	Australia	52	54	56
129	England	47	40	42
112	Canada	35	41	36
58	New Zealand	17	14	27
32	India	13	8	11
25	Wales	10	3	12
25	Nigeria	5	13	7
22	Scotland	5	7	10
18	Kenya	6	9	3
9	N.Ireland	1	3	5
5	Hong Kong	1	1	3
4	Malaysia	2	2	0
4	Jamaica	2	0	2
4	Uganda	2	0	2
3	Nauru	1	2	0
3	Zimbabwe	0	2	1
3	Tanzania	0	1	2
3	Zambia	0	0	3
2	Cyprus	1	1	0
2	Bangladesh	1	0	1
2	Jersey	1	0	1
2	Ghana	0	2	0
2	Bahamas	0	0	2
2	W.Samoa	0	0	2
1	Bermuda	1	0	0
1	Guernsey	1	0	0
1	Papua New Guinea	1	0	0
1	Guyana	0	0	1
1	Malta	0	0	1

ATHLETICS

Men

100 Metres
1   Linford Christie (Eng) 9.93s
2   David Ezinwa (Nig) 10.05s
3   Bruny Surin (Can) 10.12s

200 Metres
1   Marcus Adam (Eng) 20.10s
2   John Regis (Eng) 20.16s
3   Ade Mafe (Eng) 20.26s

400 Metres
1   Darren Clark (Aus) 44.60s
2   Samson Kitur (Ken) 44.88s
3   Simon Kipkemboi (Ken) 44.93s

800 Metres
1   Sammy Tirop (Ken) 1m 45.98s
2   Nixon Kiprotich (Ken) 1m 46.00s
3   Matthew Yates (Eng) 1m 62s

1500 Metres
1   Peter Elliott (Eng) 3m 33.39s
2   Wilfred Kirochi (Ken) 3m 34.41s
3   Peter O'Donoghue (NZ) 3m 35.14s

5000 Metres
1   Andrew Lloyd (Aus) 13m 24.86s
2   John Ngugi (Ken) 13m 24.94s
3   Ian Hamer (Wal) 13m 25.63s

10000 Metres
1   Eamonn Martin (Eng) 28m 08.57s
2   Moses Tanui (Ken) 28m 11.56s
3   Paul Williams (Can) 28m 12.71s

110 Metres Hurdles
1   Colin Jackson (Wal) 13.08s
2   Tony Jarrett (Eng) 13.34s
3   David Nelson (Eng) 13.54s

400 Metres Hurdles
1   Kriss Akabusi (Eng) 48.89s
2   Gideon Yego (Ken) 49.25s
3   John Graham (Can) 50.24s

3000 Metres Steeplechase
1   Julius Kariuki (Ken) 8m 20.64s
2   Joshua Kipkemboi (Ken) 8m 24.26s
3   Colin Walker (Eng) 8m 26.50s

Marathon
1   Douglas Wakiihuri (Ken) 2h 10m 27s
2   Steve Moneghetti (Aus) 2h 10m 34s
3   Simon Naali (Tan) 2h 10m 38s

30km Walk
1   Guillaume Leblanc (Can) 2h 8m 28s
2   Andrew Jachno (Aus) 2h 09m 09s
3   Ian McCombie (Eng) 2h 09m 20s

4 x 100 Metres Relay
1   England 38.67s
2   Nigeria 38.85s
3   Jamaica 39.11s

4 x 400 Metres Relay
1   Kenya 3m 02.48s
2   Scotland 3m 04.68s
3   Jamaica 3m 04.96s

High Jump
1   Nick Saunders (Ber) 2.36m
2   Dalton Grant (Eng) 2.34m
3   Milt Ottey (Can) & (shared) Geoff Parsons (Sco) 2.23

Long Jump
1   Yusuf Alli (Nig) 8.39m
2   David Culbert (Aus) 8.20m
3   Festus Igbinoghene (Nig) 8.18m

Triple Jump
1   Marios Hadjiandreou (Cyp) 16.95m
2   Jon Edwards (Eng) 16.93m
3   Elkrick Floreal (Can) 16.89m

Pole Vault
1   Simon Arkell (Aus) 5.35m
2   Ian Tullett (Eng) 5.25m
3   Simon Poelman (NZ) 5.20m

Javelin
1 Steve Backley (Eng) 86.02m
2 Mick Hill (Eng) 83.32m
3 Gavin Lovegrove (NZ) 81.66m
Shot
1 Simon Williams (Eng) 18.54m
2 Adewale Olukoju (Nig) 18.48m
3 Paul Edwards (Wal) 18.17m
Hammer
1 Sean Carlin (Aus) 75.66m
2 David Smith (Eng) 73.52m
3 Angus Cooper (NZ) 71.26m
Discus
1 Adewale Olukoju (Nig) 62.62m
2 Werner Reiterer (Aus) 61.56m
3 Paul Nandapi (Aus) 59.94m
Decathlon
1 Mike Smith (Can) 8,525pts
2 Simon Poelman (NZ) 8,207pts
3 Eugene Gilkes (Eng) 7,705pts

Women
100 Metres
1 Merlene Ottey (Jam) 11.02s
2 Kerry Johnson (Aus) 11.17s
3 Pauline Davis (Bah) 11.20s
200 Metres
1 Merlene Ottey (Jam) 22.76s
2 Kerry Johnson (Aus) 22.88s
3 Pauline Davis (Bah) 23.15s
400 Metres
1 Fatima Jusuf (Nig) 51.08s
2 Linda Keough (Eng) 51.63s
3 Charity Opara (Nig) 52.01s
800 Metres
1 Diane Edwards (Eng) 2m 00.25s
2 Ann Williams (Eng) 2m 00.40s
3 Sharon Stewart (Aus) 2m 00.87s
1500 Metres
1 Angela Chalmers (Can) 4m 08.41s
2 Chris Cahill (Eng) 4m 08.75s
3 Bev Nicholson (Eng) 4m 09.00s
3000 Metres
1 Angela Chalmers (Can) 8m 38.38s
2 Yvonne Murray (Sco) 8m 39.46s
3 Liz McColgan (Sco) 8m 47.66s
10000 Metres
1 Liz McColgan (Sco) 32m 23.56s
2 Jill Hunter (Eng) 32m 33.21s
3 Barbara Moore (NZ) 32m 44.73s
100 Metres Hurdles
1 Kay Morley (Wal) 12.91s
2 Sally Gunnell (Eng) 13.12s
3 Lesley-Ann Skeete (Eng) 13.31s
400 Metres Hurdles
1 Sally Gunnell (Eng) 55.38s
2 Debbie Flintoff-King (Aus) 56.00s
3 Jenny Laurendet (Aus) 56.74s

Marathon
1 Lisa Martin (Aus) 2h 25m 28s
2 Tani Ruckle (Aus) 2h 33m 16s
3 Angela Pain (Eng) 2h 36m 35s
10km Walk
1 Kerry Saxby (Aus) 45m 03s
2 Anne Judkins (NZ) 47m 03s
3 Lisa Langford (Eng) 47m 23s
4 x 100 Metres Relay
1 Australia 43.87s
2 England 44.15s
3 Nigeria 44.67s
4 x 400 Metres Relay
1 England 3m 28.08s
2 Australia 3m 30.74s
3 Canada 3m 33.26s
High Jump
1 Tania Murray (NZ) 1.88m
2 Janet Boyle (NI) 1.88m
3 Tracy Phillips (NZ) 1.88m
Long Jump
1 Jane Flemming (Aus) 6.78m
2 Beatrice Otondu (Nig) 6.65m
3 Fiona May (Eng) 6.55m
Javelin
1 Tessa Sanderson (Eng) 65.72m
2 Sue Howland (Aus) 61.18m
3 Kate Farrow (Aus) 58.98m
Shot
1 Myrtle Augee (Eng) 18.48m
2 Judy Oakes (Eng) 18.43m
3 Yvonne Hanson-Nortey (Eng) 16.00m
Discus
1 Lisa Vizaniari (Aus) 56.38m
2 Jackie McKernan (NI) 54.86m
3 Astra Vitols (Aus) 53.84m
Heptathlon
1 Jane Flemming (Aus) 6,695pts
2 Sharon Jaklofsky-Smith (Aus) 6,115pts
3 Judy Simpson (Eng) 6,085pts

Medal Winners

Total		G	S	B
40	England	13	14	13
26	Australia	10	11	5
12	Kenya	4	7	1
10	Nigeria	3	4	3
9	Canada	4	0	5
9	New Zealand	1	2	6
5	Scotland	1	2	2
4	Jamaica	2	0	2
4	Wales	2	0	2
2	N.Ireland	0	2	0
2	Bahamas	0	0	2
1	Bermuda	1	0	0
1	Cyprus	1	0	0
1	Tanzania	0	0	1

BADMINTON
Team
1 England
2 Canada
3 Hong Kong

(England won final 5-0; Hong Kong beat New Zealand 5-0 in bronze medal match)

Men's Singles
1   Rashid Sidek (Mal)
2   Foo Kok Keong (Mal)
3   Darren Hall (Eng)

(Sidek won final 15-8 15-10)

Men's Doubles
1   Jalani & Razuf Sidek (Mal)
2   Rashid Sidek & Soon Kit Cheah (Mal)
3   Michael Bitten & Brian Blanchard (Can)

(J & R Sidek won final 15-4 15-5)

Women's Singles
1   Fiona Smith (Eng)
2   Denyse Julien (Can)
3   Helen Troke (Eng)

(Smith won final 11-7 12-9)

Women's Doubles
1   Fiona Smith & Sara Sankey (Eng)
2   Gillian Gowers & Gillian Clark (Eng)
3   Denyse Julien & Johanne Falardeau (Can)

(Smith & Sankey won final 18-4, 2-15, 15-9)

Mixed Doubles
1   Chi Choi Chan & Amy Chan (HK)
2   Miles Johnson and Sarah Sankey (Eng)
3   Andy goode & Gillian Clark (Eng)
(Chan & Chan won final 15-7 15-12)

Medal Winners

Total		G	S	B
8	England	3	2	3
4	Malaysia	2	2	0
4	Canada	0	2	2
2	Hong Kong	1	0	1

BOWLS
Men
Singles
1   Rob Parella (Aus)
2   Mark McMahon (HK)
3   Richard Corsie (Sco)

(Parella won final 25-14)

Pairs
1   Australia (Trevor Morris & Ian Schuback)
2   Canada (George Boxwell & Alf Wallace)
3   New Zealand (Rowan Brassey & Maurice Symes)

Fours
1   Scotland
2   Northern Ireland
3   New Zealand

(Scotland won final 19-14)

Women
Singles
1   Geau Tau (PNG)
2   Millie Khan (NZ)
3   Margaret Johnstone (NI)

(Tau won final 25-18)

Pairs
1   New Zealand (Marie Watson & Judy Howat)
2   Australia (Edda Bonutto & Maureen Hobbs)
3   England (Jayne Roylance & Mary Price)

Fours
1   Australia
2   New Zealand
3   Hong Kong

Medal Winners

Total		G	S	B
5	New Zealand	1	2	2
4	Australia	3	1	0
2	Scotland	1	0	1
2	Hong Kong	0	1	1
2	N.Ireland	0	1	1
1	Papua NG	1	0	0
1	Canada	0	1	0
1	England	0	0	1

BOXING
Light-flyweight
1   Justin Juko (Uga)
2   Abudrahaman Ramadhani (Ken)
3   Dharmender Yadav (Ind) & Domenic Figliomeni (Can)

Flyweight
1   Wayne McCulloch (NI)
2   Nokuthula Tshabangu (Zim)
3   Maurice Maina (Ken) & Born Siwakwi (Zim)

Bantamweight
1   Sabo Mohammed (Nig)
2   Geronimo Bie (Can)
3   Wesley Christmas (Guy) & Justine Chikwanda (Zam)

Featherweight
1   John Irwin (Eng)
2   Haji Ally (Tan)
3   David Gakuha (Ken) & James Nicholson (Aus)

Lightweight
1   Godfrey Nyakana (Uga)
2   Justin Rowsell (Aus)
3   Bakari Mambeya (Tan) & Dave Anderson (Sco)

Light-welterweight
1   Charles Kane (Sco)
2   Nicoddemus Odore (Ken)
3   Duke Chinyadza (Zim) & Stefan Scriggins (Aus)

Welterweight
1   David Defiagbon (Nig)
2   Greg Johnson (Can)
3   Antony Mwamba (Zam) & Graham Cheney (Aus)

Light-middleweight
1   Richie Woodhall (Eng)
2   Ray Downey (Can)
3   Sillilo Figota (W Sam) & Andy Creery (NZ)

Middleweight
1   Chris Johnson (Can)
2   Joseph Laryea (Gha)
3   Chris Matata (Uga) & Mark Edwards (Eng)

Light-heavyweight
1   Joseph Akhasamba (Ken)
2   Dale Brown (Can)
3   Abdu Kaddu (Uga) & Nigel Anderson (NZ)

Heavyweight
1   George Onyango (Ken)
2   Patrick Jordan (Can)
3   Emeric Fainuulua (W.Sam) & Kevin Onwuka (Nig)
Jordan and Fainuulua had byes into the semi-finals and were thus guaranteed medals before competition began

Super-heavyweight

1. Michael Kenny (NZ)
2. Liadi Alhassan (Gha)
3. Vernon Linklater (Can) & Paul Douglas (NI)

Medal Winners

Total		G	S	B
8	Canada	1	5	2
6	Kenya	2	2	2
4	Uganda	2	0	2
4	Australia	0	1	3
3	England	2	0	1
3	Nigeria	2	0	1
3	New Zealand	1	0	2
3	Zambia	0	0	3
2	N.Ireland	1	0	1
2	Scotland	1	0	1
2	Ghana	0	2	0
2	Tanzania	0	1	1
2	Zimbabwe	0	1	1
2	Western Samoa	0	0	2
1	Guyana	0	0	1
1	India	0	0	1

CYCLING
Men
100 km Team Time Trial

1. New Zealand 2h 06m 46.55s
2. Canada 2h 09m 19.59s
3. England 2h 09m 33.17s

1000m Individual Time Trial

1. Martin Vinnicombe (Aus) 1m 05.572s
2. Gary Anderson (NZ) 1m 06.196s
3. Jon Andrews (NZ) 1m 06.516s

4000m Individual Pursuit

1. Gary Anderson (NZ) 4m 44.610s
2. Mark Kingsland (Aus) 4m 52.750s
3. Darren Winter (Aus)

4000m Team Pursuit

1. New Zealand 4m 22.70s
2. Australia 4m 25.52s
3. England

1000m Sprint

1. Gary Neiwand (Aus)
2. Curtis Harnett (Can)
3. Jon Andrews (NZ)

50km Points Race

1. Robert Burns (Aus) 81,00pts
2. Craig Connell (NZ) 72,00pts
3. Alastair Irvine (NI) 39,00pts

10 Mile Race

1. Gary Anderson (NZ) 19m 44.20s
2. Shaun O'Brien (Aus) 19m 44.22s
3. Stephen McGlede (Aus) 19m 44.26s

Road Race

1. Graeme Miller (NZ) 4h 34m 00s
2. Brian Fowler (NZ) at 39.00s
3. Scotty Goguen (Can) at 3m 26.45s

Women
1000m Sprint

1. Louise Jones (Wal)
2. Julie Speight (Aus)
3. Susan Golder (NZ)

3000m Individual Pursuit

1. Madonna Harris (NZ) 3m 54.67s
2. Kathy Watt (Aus) 3m 54.78s
3. Kathy-Ann Way (Can)

Road Race

1. Kathy Watt (Aus) 1h 55m 11.60s
2. Lisa Brambini (Eng) at 0.28s
3. Kathleen Shannon (Aus) at 0.46s

Medal Winners

Total		G	S	B
12	New Zealand	6	3	3
12	Australia	4	5	3
4	Canada	0	2	2
3	England	0	1	2
1	Wales	1	0	0
1	N.Ireland	0	0	1

GYMNASTICS
Men
Team

1. Canada 171.800 pts
2. England 170.450 pts
3. Australia 169.500 pts

Individual All-Round

1. Curtis Hibbert (Can) 57,950pts
2. Alan Nolet (Can) 57,800pts
3. James May (Eng) 57,400pts

Floor

1. Neil Thomas (Eng) 9,750pts
2. Alan Nolet (Can) 9,675pts
3. Curtis Hibbert (Can) 9,600pts

Pommel Horse

1. Brennon Dowrick (Aus) 9,825pts
2. Tim Lees (Aus) 9,725pts
3. James May (Eng) 9,700pts

Rings

1. Curtis Hibbert (Can) 9.775pts
2. James May (Eng) 9,750pts
3. Ken Meredith (Aus) 9,725pts

Vault

1. James May (Eng)
2. Curtis Hibbert (Can) 9,570pts
3. Tim Lees (Aus) 9,250pts

Parallel Bars

1. Curtis Hibbert (Can) 9,8000pts
2. Kent Meredith (Aus) 9,975pts
3. Peter Hogan (Aus) 9,600pts

High Bar

1. Alan Nolet (Can) & Curtis Hibbert (Can) 9,850pts shared
3. Brennon Dowrick (Aus) 9,800pts

Women
Team

1. Canada 116,784 pts
2. Austalia 115.272 pts
3. England 114.046 pts

Individual All-Round

1. Lori Strong (Can) 38,912pts
2. Monique Allen (Aus) 38,687pts
3. Kylie Shadbolt (Aus) 38,499pts

Vault
1   Nicky Jenkins (NZ) 9,712pts
2   Lori Strong (Can) 9,643pts
3   Monique Allen (Aus) 9,506pts

Asymmetric Bars
1   Monique Allen (Aus) 9,875pts
2   Lori Strong (Can) 9,850pts
3   Michelle Telfer (Aus) 9,737pts

Beam
1   Lori Strong (Can) 9,850pts
2   Larissa Lowing (Can) 9,7602pts
3   Kylie Shadbolt (Aus) 9,700pts

Floor
1   Lori Strong (Can) 9,887pts
2   Larissa Lowing (Can) 9,837pts
3   Kylie Shadbolt (Aus) 9,675pts

Rhythmic-Overall Individual
1   Mary Fuzesi (Can) 37,650pts
2   Madonna Gimotea (Can) 37,250pts
3   Angela Walker (NZ) 36,900pts

Rhythmic-Individual Rope
1   Angela Walker (NZ) 9,300pts
2   Madonna Gimotea (Can) 9,275pts
3   Mary Fuzesi (Can) 9,250pts

Rhythmic-Individual Hoop
1   Mary Fuzesi (Can) 9,400pts
2   Madonna Gimotea (Can) 9,200pts
3   Raewyn Jack (NZ), Alitia Sands (Eng) &
      Viva Seifert (Eng) 9,100pts (shared)

Rhythmic-Individual Ribbon
1   Mary Fuzesi (Can) 9,400pts
2   Madonna Gimotea (Can) 9,300pts
3   Raewyn Jack (NZ), Viva Seifert (Eng)
      & Angela Walker (NZ) 9,200pts (shared)

Rhythmic-Individual Ball
1   Madonna Gimotea (Can) 9,450pts
2   Mary Fuzesi (Can) 9,400pts
3   Angela Walker (NZ) 9,250pts

Medal Winners

Total		G	S	B
28	Canada	14	12	2
16	Australia	2	4	10
10	England	2	2	6
7	New Zealand	2	0	5

Two golds and no silver medal awarded in men's High Bar competition; six bronze medals awarded in the Rhythmic Ribbons and Hoops competitions

JUDO
Men
Under 60kg
1   Carl Finney (Eng)
2   Kevin West (Can)
3   Jim Charles (Wal) & Narender Singh (Ind)

Under 65kg
1   Brent Cooper (NZ)
2   Mark Preston (Sco)
3   Mark Adshead (Eng) & Jean-Pierre Cantin (Can)

Under 71kg
1   Roy Stone (Eng)
2   Majemite Omagbaluwaje (Nig)
      Bill Cusack (Sco) & Colin Savage (N.Ire)

Under 78kg
1   David Southby (Eng)
2   Graeme Spinks (NZ)
3   Gavin Kelly (Aus) & Roger Cole (Can)

Under 86kg
1   Densign White (Eng)
2   Winston Sweatman (Sco)
3   Chris Bacon (Aus) & Rajender Dhanger (Ind)

Under 95kg
1   Ray Stevens (Eng)
2   Dean Lampkin (Aus)
3   Graham Campbell (Sco) & Jim Kendrick (Can)

Over 95kg
1   Elvis Gordon (Eng)
2   Tom Greenway (Can)
3   Wayne Watson (NZ)
No bronze medal awarded as there were too few competitors

Open
1   Elvis Gordon (Eng)
2   Mario Laroche (Can)
3   Graham Campbell (Sco) &
      Majemite Omagbaluwaje (Nig)

Women
Under 48kg
1   Karen Briggs (Eng)
2   Helen Duston (Wal)
3   Julie Reardon (Aus) & Donna Robertson (Sco)

Under 52kg
1   Sharron Rendle (Eng)
2   Claire Shiach (Sch)
3   Lisa Griffiths (Wal) & Catherine Grainger (Aus)

Under 56kg
1   Loretta Cusack (Sco)
2   Suzanne Williams (Aus)
3   Moira Sutton (Wal) & Ann Hughes (Eng)

Under 61kg
1   Diane Bell (Eng)
2   Donna Guy-Halkyard (NZ)
3   Mandy Clayton (Can) & Laurie Pace (Malta)

Under 66kg
1   Sharon Mills (Eng)
2   Karen Hayde (Can)
3   Narelle Hill (Aus) & Joyce Malley (N.Ire)

Under 72kg
1   Jane Morris (Eng)
2   Alison Webb (Can)
3   Cbristy Obekpa (Nig) & Phillipa Knowles (Wal)

Over 72kg
1   Sharon Lee (Eng)
2   Geraldine Dekker (Aus)
3   Ruth Vondy (IOM)
No bronze medal awarded as there were too few competitors

Open
1   Sharon Lee (Eng)
2   Jane Patterson (Can)
3   Geraldine Dekker (Aus) & Nicola Morris (NZ)

Medal Winners

Total		G	S	B
16	England	14	0	2
10	Canada	0	6	4
9	Australia	0	3	6
8	Scotland	1	3	4
5	Wales	0	1	4
4	New Zealand	1	2	1
3	Nigeria	0	1	2
2	India	0	0	2
2	N.Ireland	0	0	2
1	Malta	0	0	1

❝ Athletes want to be treated as professionals and I'm quite happy to treat them that way but if they're going to behave like children they will be treated like children and smacked on the bottom and sent home".
Rick Pannell, Australian athletics team manager

Journalist: "Have you considered resigning?" Myrddin John, Welsh team manager: "I'm amazed, sir".
Exchange after weightlifting drugs scandal

"Adams is a hard man. Nothing worries him. Warm beer, cold pies, whatever."
New Zealand shooter Julian Lawton on his Australian rival Phil Adams

"I would have liked to have been on top but I'm happy with the result. No, that's a lie. I would have loved to have been on top and I'm darn disappointed with the result."
Paul Kingsman, beaten New Zealand swimmer

"I thought 'bugger the silver' go for the gold".
Andrew Lloyd, victorious Australian runner

Philip Leishman, New Zealand TV anchorman: "And now we're about to cross to Doug Armstrong at the bowls where I'm told the action is enthralling."

Doug Armstrong: That's right, Philip, enthralling with a capital A.❞

SHOOTING
Small Bore Rifle - 3 Position (Individual)
1   Mart Klepp (Can) 1,157pts
2   Malcolm Cooper (Eng) 1,154pts
3   Soma Dutta (Ind) 1,143pts
Small Bore Rifle - 3 Position (Pairs)
1   Canada (Jean-François Sénéhal & Mart Klepp) 2,272pts
2   England (Malcolm Cooper & Rob Smith) 2,268pts
3   Scotland (Bill Murray & Bob Law) 2,258pts
Air Rifle (Individual)
1   Guy Lorian (Can) 583pts
2   Chris Hector (Eng) 578pts
3   Mart Klepp (Can) 577pts
Air Rifle (Pairs)
1   Canada (Guy Lorion & Mart Klepp) 1,163 pts
2   England (Chris Hector & Rob Smith) 1,155 pts
3   India (Soma Dutta & Samai Bhagirath) 1,148 pts
Full Bore Rifle (Individual)
1   Colin Mallett (Jer) 394pts
2   Andrew Tucker (Eng) 390pts

3   James Corbett (Aus) 390pts
Full Bore Rifle (Pairs)
1   England (Simon Belither & Andrew Tucker) 508 pts
2   Australia (James Corbett & Barry Wood) 565 pts
3   Jersey (Cliff Mallett & Colin Mallett) 564 pts
Smallbore Rifle - Prone (Individual)
1   Roger Harvey (NZ) 591pts
2   Stephen Pettersson (NZ) 590pts
3   Phil Scanlan (Eng) 590pts
Smallbore Rifle - Prone (Pairs)
1   New Zealand (Roger Harvey & Stephen Pettersson) 1,185pts
2   Canada (Barry Sutherland & Michael Ashcroft) 1,184pts
3   England (Bob Jarvis & Phil Scanlan) 1,180pts
Free Pistol (Individual)
1   Phillip Adams (Aus) 554pts
2   Bengt Sandstrom (Aus) 549pts
3   Gilbert U (HK) 549pts
Free Pistol (Pairs)
1   Australia (Phillip Adams & Bengt Sandstrom) 1,106pts
2   New Zealand (Brian Read & Greg Yelavich 1,084pts
3   Bangladesh (Attequur Rahman & Abdu Sattar) 1,078pts
Air Pistol (Individual)
1   Bengt Sandstrom (Aus) 580pts
2   Phillip Adams (Aus) 574pts
3   David Lowe (Eng) 574pts
Air Pistol (Pairs)
1   Bangladesh (Attequur Rahman & Abdu Sattar) 1,138pts
2   Australia (Phillip Adams & Bengt Sandstrom) 1,138pts
3   New Zealand (Julian Lawton & Greg Yelavich) 1,137
Shotgun Trench (Individual)
1   John Maxwell (Aus) 184pts
2   Kevin Gill (Eng) 183pts
3   Ian Peel (Eng) 179pts
Shotgun Trench (Pairs)
1   England (Kevin Gill & Ian Peel) 181pts
2   Wales (Colin Evans & Chris Birkett-Evans) 178pts
3   Australia (Russell Mark & John Maxwell) 178pts
Shotgun Skeet (Individual)
1   Ken Harman (Eng) 187pts
2   Georgios Sakellis (Cyp) 187pts
3   Austin Austin (Eng) 184
Shotgun Skeet (Pairs)
1   Scotland (Ian Marsden & James Dunlop) 189pts
2   England (Austin Austin & Ken Harman) 185pts
3   New Zealand (Tim Dodds & John Wooley) 183pts
Rapid Fire Pistol (Individual)
1   Adrian Breton (Gue) 583pts
2   Pat Murray (Aus) 582pts
3   Michael Jay (Wal) 579pts
Rapid Fire Pistol (Pairs)
1   Australia (Bruce Farrell & Pat Murray) 1,153pts
2   Canada (Stanley Wills & Mark Hawkins) 1,138pts

3   England (Brian Girling & John Wolfe) 1,133 pts

Centre Fire Pistol (Individual)
1   Ashot Pandit (Ind) 583pts
2   Surinder Marwah (Ind) 577pts
3   Bruce Quick (Aus) 576pts

Centre Fire Pistol (Pairs)
1   Australia (Phillip Adams & Bruce Quick) 1,155pts
2   New Zealand (Barry O'Neale & Greg Yelavich) 1,144pts
3   India (Ashot & Pandit & Surinder Marwah) 1,142pts

Running Target (Individual)
1   Colin Robertson (Aus) 539pts
2   John Madison (Eng) 539pts
3   Anthony Clarke (NZ) 536pts

Running Target (Pairs)
1   New Zealand (Paul Carmine & Anthony Clarke) 1,091pts
2   Canada (David Lee & Mark Bedlington) 1,070pts
3   England (David Chapman & John Madison) 1,064pts
No bronze medal awarded as there were too few competitors

Medal Winners

Total		G	S	B
17	England	3	8	6
15	Australia	7	5	3
9	New Zealand	3	3	3
8	Canada	4	3	1
5	India	1	1	3
2	Bangladesh	1	0	1
2	Jersey	1	0	1
2	Scotland	1	0	1
2	Wales	0	1	1
1	Guernsey	1	0	0
1	Cyprus	0	1	0
1	Hong Kong	0	0	1

SWIMMING
Men
50 Metres Freestyle
1   Andrew Baildon (Aus) 22.76s
2   Angus Waddell (Aus) 23.03s
3   Mark Foster (Eng) 23.16s

100 Metres Freestyle
1   Andrew Baildon (Aus) 49.80s
2   Chris Fydler (Aus) 50.59s
3   Mike Fibbens (Eng) 50.76s

200 Metres Freestyle
1   Martin Roberts (Aus) 1m 49.58s
2   Ian Brown (Aus) 1m 49.60s
3   Thomas Stachewicz (Aus) 1m 49.98s

400 Metres Freestyle
1   Ian Brown (Aus) 3m 49.91s
2   Glen Housman (Aus) 3m 53.90s
3   Chris Bowie (Can) 3m 54.04s

1500 Metres Freestyle
1   Glen Housman (Aus) 14m 55.25s
2   Kieren Perkins (Aus) 14m 58.08s
3   Mike McKenzie (Aus) 15m 09.95s

100 Metres Breaststroke
1   Adrian Moorhouse (Eng) 1m 01.49s
2   James Parrack (Eng) 1m 03.15s
3   Nick Gillingham (Eng) 1m 03.16s

200 Metres Breaststroke
1   John Cleveland (Can) 2m 14.96s
2   Rodney Lawson (Aus) 2m 15.68s
3   Nick Gillingham (Eng) 2m 16.02s

100 Metres Butterfly
1   Andrew Baildon (Aus) 53.98s
2   Marcel Gery (Can) 54.24s
3   Jason Cooper (Aus) 54.47s

200 Metres Butterfly
1   Anthony Mosse (NZ) 1m 57.33s
2   Martin Roberts (Aus) 1m 59.95s
3   Jon Kelly (Can) 2m 00.37s

100 Metres Backstroke
1   Mark Tewksbury (Can) 56.07s
2   Gary Anderson (Can) 56.84s
3   Paul Kingsman (NZ) 57.07s

200 Metres Backstroke
1   Gary Anderson (Can) 2m 01.69s
2   Paul Kingsman (NZ) 2m 01.86s
3   Kevin Draxinger (Can) 2m 02.02s

200 Metres Individual Medley
1   Gary Anderson (Can) 2m 02.94s
2   Rob Bruce (Aus) 2m 03.78s
3   Martin Roberts (Aus) 2m 04.03s

400 Metres Individual Medley
1   Rob Bruce (Aus) 4m 20.26s
2   Rob Woodhouse (Aus) 4m 21.79s
3   Jon Kelly (Can) 4m 23.96s

4 x 100 Metres Freestyle Relay
1   Australia 3m 20.05s
2   England 3m 22.61s
3   Canada 3m 22.79s

4 x 200 Metres Freestyle Relay
1   Australia 7m 21.17s
2   Canada 7m 25.53s
3   New Zealand 7m 30.10s

4 x 100 Metres Medley Relay
1   Canada 3m 42.45s
2   England 3m 43.88s
3   Australia 3m 43.91s

1 Metre Springboard Diving
1   Russell Butler (Aus) 583.65pts
2   David Beddard (Can) 547.35pts
3   Simon McCormack (Aus) 546.87pts

3 Metre Springboard Diving
1   Craig Rogerson (Aus) 594.84pts
2   Mark Rourke (Can) 569.97pts
3   Larry Flewwelling (Can) 569.79pts

Platform Diving
1   Bobby Morgan (Wal) 639.84pts
2   David Beddard (Can) 555.54pts
3   Bruno Fournier (Can) 544.50pts

Women
50 Metres Freestyle
1   Lisa Curry-Kenny (Aus) 25.80s
2   Karen Van Wirdum (Aus) 26.00s
3   Andrea Nugent (Can) 26.26s

100 Metres Freestyle
1 Karen Van Wirdum (Aus) 56.48s
2 Lisa Curry-Kenny (Aus) 56.61s
3 Patricia Noall (Can) 56.67s

200 Metres Freestyle
1 Hayley Lewis (Aus) 2m 00.79s
2 Jennifer McMahon (Aus) 2m 02.43s
3 Patricia Noall (Can) 2m 02.66s

400 Metres Freestyle
1 Hayley Lewis (Aus) 4m 08.89s
2 Julie McDoanld (Aus) 4m 09.72s
3 Janelle Elford (Aus) 4m 10.74s

800 Metres Freestyle
1 Julie McDonald (Aus) 8m 30.27s
2 Janelle Elford (Aus) 8m 30.47s
3 Sheridan Burge-Lopez (Aus) 8m 36.78s

100 Metres Butterfly
1 Lisa Curry-Kenny (Aus) 1m 00.66s
2 Susan O'Neill (Aus) 1m 01.34s
3 Madelaine Scarborough (Eng) 1m 01.33s

200 Metres Butterfly
1 Hayley Lewis (Aus) 2m 11.15s
2 Helen Morris (Aus) 2m 11.76s
3 Nicole Redford (Aus) 2m 13.53s

100 Metres Breaststroke
1 Keltie Duggan (Can) 1m 10.74s
2 Guylaine Cloutier (Can) 1m 11.22s
3 Sukie Brownsdon (Eng) 1m 11.54s

200 Metres Breaststroke
1 Nathalia Giguere (Can) 2m 32.16s
2 Guylaine Cloutier (Can) 2m 32.91s
3 Helen Morris (Aus) 2m 33.57s

100 Metres Backstroke
1 Nicole Livingstone (Aus) 1m 02.46s
2 Anna Simcic (NZ) 1m 02.55s
3 Johanna Griggs (Aus) 1m 03.69s

200 Metres Backstroke
1 Anna Simcic (NZ) 2m 12.32s
2 Nicole Livingstone (Aus) 2m 12.62s
3 Karen Lord (Aus) 2m 14.53s

200 Metres Individual Medley
1 Nancy Sweetnam (Can) 2m 15.61s
2 Jodie Clatworthy (Aus) 2m 17.10s
3 Hayley Lewis (Aus) 2m 17.31s

400 Metres Individual Medley
1 Hayley Lewis (Aus) 4m 42.65s
2 Jodie Clatworthy (Aus) 4m 45.76s
3 Diane Procter (Aus) 4m 47.38s

4 x 100 Metres Freestyle Relay
1 Australia 3m 46.85s
2 Canada 3m 48.69s
3 England 3m 51.26s

4 x 200 Metres Freestyle Relay
1 Australia 8m 08.95s
2 England 8m 16.31s
3 New Zealand 8m 22.60s

4 x 100 Metres Medley Relay
1 Australia 4m 10.87s
2 England 4m 11.88s
2 Canada 4m 12.20s

1 Metre Springboard Diving
1 Mary De Peiro (Can) 443.28pts
2 Tracy Linda Cox (Zim) 423.93pts
3 Peta Taylor (Aus) 418.71pts

3 Metre Springboard Diving
1 Jenny Donnet (Aus) 491.79pts
2 Barbara Bush (Can) 458.43pts
3 Nicky Cooney (NZ) 457.29pts

Highboard Diving
1 Anna Dacyshyn (Can) 391.68pts
2 April Adams (Aus) 380.49pts
3 Polige Gordon (Can) 380.43pts

Synchronised - Solo
1 Sylvie Frechette (Can) 195.560 pts
2 Kerry Shacklock (Eng) 183.550 pts
3 Semon Rohloff (Aus) 173,200pts
No bronze medal awarded as there were too few competitors

Synchronised -Duet
1 Canada (Christine Larsen & Kathy Glen) 191.230pts
2 England (Kerry Shacklock & Sarah Northey) 185.435pts
3 Australia (Lisa Lieschke & Semon Rohloff) 175.765pts

Medal Winners

Total		G	S	B
59	Australia	24	20	15
34	Canada	12	10	12
15	England	1	7	7
8	New Zealand	2	2	4
1	Wales	1	0	0
1	Zimbabwe	0	1	0

WEIGHTLIFTING
Three medals awarded for snatch, clean & jerk, and combined. First three given are for the overall competition, with winners of the snatch and clean & jerk competitions indicated in brackets.

52kg
1 Chandersekaran Raghavan (Ind) 232.5kg (S/C&J)
2 Velu Govindraj (Ind) 212.5kg
3 Greg Hayman (Aus) 207.5kg

56kg
1 Rangaswamy Punnuswamy (Ind) 247.5kg (S/C&J)
2 Alan Ogilvie (Sco) 230.0kg
3 Gopal Maruthachelam (Ind) 227.5kg

60kg
1 Parvesh Chandra Sharma (Ind) 257.5kg (C&J)
2 Marcus Stephen (Nauru) 255.0 (S)
3 Kymasesen Sudaimani (Ind) 252.5kg

67.5kg
1 Paramjit Sharma (Ind) 295.0kg (S/C&J)
2 Lawrence Iquaibom (Nig) 290.0kg
3 Malcolm Roach (Wal) 280.00kg
Subratakumar Paul (Ind) originally placed second with 292.5kg but subsequently disqualified following positive drug test

75kg
1 Ron Laycock (Aus) 310.0kg (C&J)
2 Karnadhar Mondal (Ind) 305.0kg (S)
3 Benoit Gagne (Can) 292.5kg

Ricky Chaplin (Wal) won gold in snatch but was later disqualified after failing a drugs test

82.5kg
1 David Morgan (Wal) 347.5kg (S/C&J)
2 Muyiwa Odusanya (Nig) 332.5kg
3 Andrew Callard (Eng) 317.5kg

90kg
1 Duncan Dawkins (Eng) 357.5kg (S/C&J)
2 Keith Boxell (Eng) 345.0kg
3 Harvey Goodman (Aus) 340.0kg

100kg
1 Andrew Saxton (Eng) 362.5kg (S/C&J)
2 Peter May (Eng) 320.0kg
3 Guy Greavette (Can) 315.00kg

Gareth Hives (Wal) won silver with 350.0kg but was later

disqualified following positive drug test

110kg
1 Mark Thomas (Eng) 357.5kg (S/C&J)
2 Jason Roberts (Aus) 345.0pts
3 Aled Arnold (Wal) 335.0kg

Medal Winners

Total		G	S	B
24	India	12	7	5
17	Australia	2	4	11
16	England	9	6	1
12	Wales	6	1	5
9	Nigeria	0	8	1
6	Canada	0	0	6
3	Nauru	1	2	0
3	Scotland	0	2	1

CHAMPIONS

VENUES

Year	Venue	Competing Nations
1930	Hamilton, Canada	11
1934	London, England	16
1938	Sydney, Australia	15
1950	Auckland, New Zealand	13
1954	Vancouver, Canada	24
1958	Cardiff, Wales	35
1962	Perth, Australia	35
1966	Kingston, Jamaica	34
1970	Edinburgh, Scotland	42
1974	Christchurch, New Zealand	38
1978	Edmonton, Canada	46
1982	Brisbane, Australia	46
1986	Edinburgh, Scotland	27
1990	Auckland, New Zealand	55

THE LEADING NATIONS

Most Gold Medals

420	**England**
397	**Australia**
287	**Canada**
94	**New Zealand**
60	**South Africa**
56	**Scotland**
32	**Wales**
37	**India**
35	**Kenya**
20	**Jamaica**
20	**Pakistan**

Most Medals

		G	S	B
1156	**England**	420	368	368
1093	**Australia**	397	374	322
887	**Canada**	287	301	299
376	**New Zealand**	94	121	161
239	**Scotland**	56	74	109
151	**South Africa**	60	44	47
131	**Wales**	32	39	60
104	**India**	37	36	31
93	**Kenya**	35	25	33
70	**Nigeria**	19	25	26

Most Individual Golds
**9 Bill Hoskins (Eng) Fencing 1958-70;
Michael Wenden (Aus) Swimming 1966-74**

Leading Gold Medal Winners

24	England	20	Canada	6	South Africa
29	England	17	Canada	8	Australia
24	Australia	15	England	13	Canada
34	Australia	19	England	10	New Zealand
23	England	20	Australia	16	South Africa
29	England	27	Australia	13	South Africa
38	Australia	29	England	10	New Zealand
34	England	23	Australia	14	Canada
36	Australia	27	England	18	Canada
32	Australia	28	England	23	Canada
44	Canada	27	England	25	Australia
39	Australia	38	England	26	Canada
52	England	51	Canada	40	Australia
52	Australia	47	England	35	Canada

ARCHERY

Men
1982   Mark Blenkarne (Eng)

Women
1982   Neroli Fairhall (NZ)

ATHLETICS
w - Wind Assisted

Men

100 Metres

(100 yards 1930-66)		time
1930	Percy Williams (Can)	9.9s
1934	Arthur Sweeney (Eng)	10.0s
1938	Cyril Holmes (Eng)	9.7s
1950	John Treloar (Aus)	9.7s
1954	Mike Agostini (Tri)	9.6s
1958	Keith Gardner (Jam)	9.66s
1962	Seraphino Antao (Ken)	9.50s
1966	Harry Jerome (Can)	9.41s
1970	Don Quarrie (Jam)	10.24s
1974	Don Quarrie (Jam)	10.38s
1978	Don Quarrie (Jam)	10.03s
1982	Allan Wells (Sco)	10.05s
1986	Ben Johnson (Can)	10.07s
1990	Linford Christie (Eng)	9.93s

200 Metres

(220 yards 1930-66)		
1930	Stanley Engelhart (Eng)	21.8s
1934	Arthur Sweeney (Eng)	21.9s
1938	Cyril Holmes (Eng)	21.2s
1950	John Treloar (Aus)	21.5s
1954	Donald Jowett (NZ)	21.5s
1958	Tom Robinson (Bah)	21.08s

1962	Seraphino Antao (Ken)	21.28s
1966	Stanley Allotey (Gha)	20.65s
1970	Don Quarrie (Jam)	20.56s
1974	Don Quarrie (Jam)	20.73s
1978	Allan Wells (Sco)	20.12s
1982	Allan Wells (Sco) & Mike Mc Farlane (Eng)	
		20.43s
1986	Atlee Mahorn (Can)	20.31s
1990	Marcus Adam (Eng)	20.10s

400 Metres
(440 yards 1930-66)

1930	Alex Wilson (Can)	48.8s
1934	Godfrey Rampling (Eng)	48.0s
1938	Bill Roberts (Eng)	47.9s
1950	Edwin Carr (Aus)	47.9s
1954	Kevin Gosper (Aus)	47.2s
1958	Mikha Singh (Ind)	46.71s
1962	George Kerr (Jam)	46.74s
1966	Wendell Mottley (Tri)	45.08s
1970	Charles Assati (Ken)	45.01s
1974	Charles Assati (Ken)	46.04s
1978	Rick Mitchell (Aus)	46.43s
1982	Bert Cameron (Jam)	45.89s
1986	Roger Black (Eng)	45.57s
1990	Darren Clark (Aus)	44.60s

800 Metres
(880 yards 1930-66)

1930	Thomas Hampson (Eng)	1m 52.4s
1934	Phil Edwards (Guy)	1m 54.2s
1938	Vernon Boot (NZ)	1m 51.2s
1950	John Parlett (Eng)	1m 53.1s
1954	Derek Johnson (Eng)	1m 50.7s
1958	Herb Elliott (Aus)	1m 49.32s
1962	Peter Snell (NZ)	1m 47.64s
1966	Noel Clough (Aus)	1m 46.9s
1970	Robert Ouko (Ken)	1m 46.89s
1974	John Kipkurgat (Ken)	1m 43.85s
1978	Mike Boit (Ken)	1m 46.39s
1982	Peter Bourke (Aus)	1m 45.18s
1986	Steve Cram (Eng)	1m 43.22s
1990	Sammy Tirop (Ken)	1m 45.98s

1500 Metres
(1 mile 1930-66)

1930	Reg Thomas (Eng)	4m 14.0s
1934	Jack Lovelock (NZ)	4m 12.8s
1938	Jim Alford (Wal)	4m 11.6s
1950	William Parnall (Can)	4m 11.0s
1954	Roger Bannister (Eng)	3m 58.8s
1958	Herb Elliott (Aus)	3m 59.03s
1962	Peter Snell (NZ)	4m 04.58s
1966	Kipchoge Keino (Ken)	3m 55.34s
1970	Kipchoge Keino (Ken)	3m 36.60s
1974	Filbert Bayi (Tan)	3m 32.16s
1978	David Moorcroft (Eng)	3m 35.48s
1982	Steve Cram (Eng)	3m 42.37s
1986	Steve Cram (Eng)	3m 50.87s
1990	Peter Elliott (Eng)	3m 33.39s

5000 Metres
(3 miles 1930-66)

1930	Stan Tomlin (Eng)	14m 27.4s
1934	Walter Beavers (Eng)	14m 32.6s
1938	Cecil Matthews (NZ)	13m 59.6s
1950	Len Eyre (Eng)	14m 23.6s
1954	Chris Chataway (Eng)	13m 35.2s
1958	Murray Halberg (NZ)	13m 14.96s
1962	Murray Halberg (NZ)	13m 34.15s
1966	Kipchoge Keino (Ken)	12m 57.4s
1970	Ian Stewart (Sco)	13m 22.8s
1974	Ben Jipcho (Ken)	13m 14.4s
1978	Henry Rono (Ken)	13m 23.04s
1982	David Moorcroft (Eng)	13m 33.00s
1986	Steve Ovett (Eng)	13m 24.11s
1990	Andrew Lloyd (Aus)	13m 24.86s

10,000 Metres
(6 miles 1930-66)

1930	John Savidan (NZ)	30m 49.6s
1934	Arthur Penny (Eng)	31m 00.6s
1938	Cecil Matthews (NZ)	30m 14.5s
1950	Harold Nelson (NZ)	30m 29.6s
1954	Peter Driver (Eng)	29m 09.4s
1958	David Power (Aus)	28m 48.16s
1962	Bruce Kidd (Can)	28m 26.13s
1966	Naftali Temu (Ken)	27m 14.21s
1970	Lachie Stewart (Sco)	28m 11.71s
1974	Richard Taylor (NZ)	27m 46.4s
1978	Brendan Foster (Eng)	28m 13.65s
1982	Gidamis Shahanga (Tan)	28m 10.15s
1986	Jonathan Solly (Eng)	27m 57.42s
1990	Eamonn Martin (Eng)	28m 08.57s

Marathon

1930	Duncan McL.Wright (Sco)	2h 43m 43s
1934	Harold Webster (Can)	2h 40m 36s
1938	Johannes Coleman (SA)	2h 30m 49.8s
1950	Jack Holden (Eng)	2m 32m 57s
1954	Joseph Mc Gee (Sco)	2h 39m 36s
1958	David Power (Aus)	2h 22m 45.6s
1962	Brian Kilby (Eng)	2h 21m 17s
1966	Jim Alder (Sco)	2h 22m 07.8s
1970	Ron Hill (Eng)	2h 09m 28s
1974	Ian Thompson (Eng)	2h 09m 12s
1978	Gidamis Shahanga (Tan)	2h 15m 39.8s
1982	Rob de Castella (Aus)	2h 09m 18s
1986	Rob de Castella (Aus)	2h 10m 15s
1990	Douglas Wakiihuri (Ken)	2h 10 m 27s

3000 Metres Steeplechase
(8 laps in 1930; 2 miles in 1934)

1930	George Bailey (Eng)	9m 52.0s
1934	Stanley Scarsbrook (Eng)	10m 23.4s
1962	Trevor Vincent (Aus)	8m 43.4s
1966	Peter Welsh (NZ)	8m 29.44s
1970	Tony Manning (Aus)	8m 26.2s
1974	Ben Jipcho (Ken)	8m 20.8s
1978	Henry Rono (Ken)	8m 26.54s
1982	Julius Korir (Ken)	8m 23.94s
1986	Graeme Fell (Can)	8m 24.49s
1990	Julius Kariuki (Ken)	8m 20.64s

110 Metres Hurdles
(120 yards 1930-66)

1930	Lord Burghley (Eng)	14.6s
1934	Don Finlay (Eng)	15.2s
1938	Tom Lavery (SA) w	14.0s
1950	Peter Gardner (Aus)	14.3s
1954	Keith Gardner (Jam)	14.2s
1958	Keith Gardner (Jam)	14.20s
1962	Ghulam Raziq (Pak)	14.34s
1966	David Hemery (Eng)	14.1s
1970	David Hemery (Eng)	13.66s
1974	Fatwel Kimaiyo (Ken)	13.69s
1978	Berwyn Price (Wal)	13.70s
1982	Mark McKoy (Can)	13.37s
1986	Mark McKoy (Can)	13.31s
1990	Colin Jackson (Wal)	13.08s

400 Metres Hurdles
(440 yards 1930-66)

1930	Lord Burghley (Eng)	54.4s
1934	Alan Hunter (Sco)	55.2s
1938	John Loaring (Can)	52.9s
1950	Duncan White (Ceylon)	52.5s
1954	David Lean (Aus)	52.4s
1958	Gerhardus Potgeiter (SA)	49.73s
1962	Ken Roche (Aus)	51.5s
1966	Ken Roche (Aus)	50.95s
1970	John Sherwood (Eng)	50.03s
1974	Alan Pascoe (Eng)	48.83s
1978	Daniel Kimaiyo (Ken)	49.48s

1982	Garry Brown (Aus)	49.37s
1986	Phil Beattie (NI)	49.60s
1990	Kriss Akabusi (Eng)	48.89s

4 x 100 Metres Relay
(4 x 110 yards 1930-66)

1930	Canada	42.2s
1934	England	42.2s
1938	Canada	41.6s
1950	Australia	42.2s
1954	Canada	41.3s
1958	England	40.72s
1962	England	40.62s
1966	Ghana	39.8s
1970	Jamaica	39.46s
1974	Australia	39.31s
1978	Scotland	39.24s
1982	Nigeria	39.15s
1986	Canada	39.15s
1990	England	38.67s

4 x 400 Metres Relay
(4 x 440 yards 1930-66)

1930	England	3m 19.4s
1934	England	3m 16.8s
1938	Canada	3:m 16.9s
1950	Australia	3m 17.8s
1954	England	3m 11.2s
1958	South Africa	3m 08.21s
1962	Jamaica	3m 10.2s
1966	Trinidad & Tobago	3m 02.8s
1970	Kenya	3m 03.63s
1974	Kenya	3m 04.4s
1978	Kenya	3m 03.54s
1982	England	3m 05.45s
1986	England	3m 07.19s
1990	Kenya	3m 02.48s

High Jump

		metres
1930	Johannes Viljoen (SA)	1.90m
1934	Edwin Thacker (SA)	1.90m
1938	Edwin Thacker (SA)	1.96m
1950	John Winter (Aus)	1.98m
1954	Emmanual Ifeajuna (Nig)	2.03m
1958	Ernest Haisley (Jam)	2.06m
1962	Percy Hobson (Aus)	2.11m
1966	Lawrie Peckham (Aus)	2.08m
1970	Lawrie Peckham (Aus)	2.14m
1974	Gordon Windeyer (Aus)	2.16m
1978	Claude Ferragne (Can)	2.20m
1982	Milt Ottey (Can)	2.31m
1986	Milt Ottey (Can)	2.30m
1990	Nick Saunders (Ber)	2.36m

Long Jump

1930	Leonard Hutton (Can)	7.20m
1934	Sam Richardson (Can)	7.17m
1938	Harold Brown (Can)	7.43m
1950	Neville Price (SA)	7.31m
1954	Ken Wilmshurst (Eng)	7.54m
1958	Paul Foreman (Jam)	7.47m
1962	Michael Ahey (Gha)w	8.05m
1966	Lynn Davies (Wales)	7.99m
1970	Lynn Davies (Wales)w	8.06m
1974	Alan Lerwill (Eng)	7.94m
1978	Roy Mitchell (Eng)	8.06m
1982	Gary Honey (Aus)	8.13m
1986	Gary Honey (Aus)	8.08m
1990	Yusuf Alli (Nig)	8.39m

Triple Jump

1930	Gordon Smallacombe (Can)	14.76m
1934	Jack Metcalfe (Aus)	15.63m
1938	Jack Metcalfe (Aus)	15.49m
˜50	Brian Oliver (Aus)	15.61m

1954	Ken Wilmshurst (Eng)	15.28m
1958	Ian Tomlinson (Aus)	15.74m
1962	Ian Tomlinson (Aus)	16.20m
1966	Samuel Igun (Nig)	16.40m
1970	Phil May (Aus)	16.72m
1974	Joshua Owusu (Gha)	16.50m
1978	Keith Connor (Eng)	17.21m
1982	Keith Connor (Eng)	17.81m
1986	John Herbert (Eng)	17.27m
1990	Marios Hadjiandreou (Cyp)	16.95m

Pole Vault

1930	Victor Pickard (Can)	3.73m
1934	Sylvanus Apps (Can)	3.88m
1938	Andries Du Plessis (SA)	4.11m
1950	Tim Anderson (Eng)	3.97m
1954	Geoff Elliott (Eng)	4.26m
1958	Geoff Elliott (Eng)	4.16m
1962	Trevor Bickle (Aus)	4.49m
1966	Trevor Bickle (Aus)	4.80m
1970	Mike Bull (NI)	5.10m
1974	Don Baird (Aus)	5.05m
1978	Bruce Simpson (Can)	5.10m
1982	Ray Boyd (Aus)	5.20m
1986	Andrew Ashurst (Eng)	5.20m
1990	Simon Arkell (Aus)	5.35m

Shot

1930	Henrick Hart (SA)	14.58m
1934	Henrick Hart (SA)	14.67m
1938	Louis Fouche (SA)	14.48m
1950	Maitaika Tuicakau (Fij)	14.64m
1954	John Savidge (Eng)	16.77m
1958	Arthur Rowe (Eng)	17.57m
1962	Martyn Lucking (Eng)	18.08m
1966	David Steen (Can)	18.79m
1970	David Steen (Can)	19.21m
1974	Geoff Capes (Eng)	20.74m
1978	Geoff Capes (Eng)	19.77m
1982	Bruno Pauletto (Can)	19.55m
1986	Billy Cole (Eng)	18.16m
1990	Simon Williams (Eng)	18.54m

Javelin

1930	Stanley Lay (NZ)	63.12m
1934	Robert Dixon (Can)	60.02m
1938	James Courtwright (Can)	62.80m
1950	Leo Roininen (Can)	57.10m
1954	James Achurch (Aus)	68.52m
1958	Colin Smith (Eng)	71.28m
1962	Alfred Mitchell (Aus)	78.10m
1966	John FitzSimons (Eng)	79.78m
1970	David Travis (Eng)	79.50m
1974	Charles Clover (Eng)	84.92m
1978	Phil Olsen (Can)	84.00m
1982	Michael O'Rourke (NZ)	89.48m
1986	David Ottley (Eng)	80.62m
1990	Steve Backley (Eng)	86.02m

Discus

1930	Hendrick Hart (SA)	41.44m
1934	Hendrick Hart (SA)	41.54m
1938	Eric Coy (Can)	44.76m
1950	Ian Reed (Aus)	47.72m
1954	Stephanus du Plessis (SA)	51.70m
1958	Stephanus du Plessis (SA)	55.94m
1962	Warwick Selvey (Aus)	56.48m
1966	Les Mills (NZ)	56.18m
1970	George Puce (Can)	59.02m
1974	Robin Tait (NZ)	63.08m
1978	Borys Chambul (Can)	59.70m
1982	Brad Cooper (Bah)	64.04m
1986	Raymond Lazdins (Can)	58.86m
1990	Adewale Olokoju (Nig)	62.62m

Hammer

1930	Malcolm Nokes (Eng)	47.12m
1934	Malcolm Nokes (Eng)	48.24m
1938	George Sutherland (Can)	48.70m
1950	Duncan Clark (Sco)	49.94m
1954	Muhammad Iqbal (Pak)	55.38m
1958	Mike Ellis (Eng)	62.90m
1962	Howard Payne (Eng)	61.64m
1966	Howard Payne (Eng)	61.98m
1970	Howard Payne (Eng)	67.80m
1974	Ian Chipchase (Eng)	69.56m
1978	Peter Farmer (Aus)	71.10m
1982	Robert Weir (Eng)	75.08m
1986	David Smith (Eng)	74.06m
1990	Sean Carlin (Aus)	75.66m

Decathlon
(Adjusted to 1984 tables)

1966	Roy Williams (NZ)	7133pts
1970	Geoff Smith (Aus)	7420pts
1974	Mike Bull (NI)	7363pts
1978	Daley Thompson (Eng)	8470pts
1982	Daley Thompson (Eng)	8424pts
1986	Daley Thompson (Eng)	8663pts
1990	Mike Smith (Can)	8525pts

30 km Walk
(20 miles/32.18 km 1966-74)

1966	Ron Wallwork (Eng)	2h 44m 42.8s
1970	Noel Freeman (Aus)	2h 33m 33s
1974	John Warhurst (Eng)	2h 35m 23.0s
1978	Ollie Flynn (Eng)	2h 22m 03.7s
1982	Steve Barry (Wales)	2h 10m 16s
1986	Simon Baker (Aus)	2h 07m 47s

Women

100 Metres
(100 yards 1934 - 66)

1934	Eileen Hiscock (Eng)	11.3s
1938	Decima Norman (Aus)	11.1s
1950	Marjorie Jackson (Aus)	10.8s
1954	Marjorie Nelson (née Jackson) (Aus)	10.7s
1958	Marlene Willard (Aus)	10.70s
1962	Dorothy Hyman (Eng)	11.2s
1966	Dianne Burge (Aus)	10.6s
1970	Raelene Boyle (Aus)	11.26s
1974	Raelene Boyle (Aus)	11.27s
1978	Sonia Lannaman (Eng)	11.27s
1982	Angella Taylor (Can)	11.00s
1986	Heather Oakes (Eng)	11.20s
1990	Merlene Ottey (Jam)	11.02s

200 Metres
(220 yards 1934-66)

1934	Eileen Hiscock (Eng)	25.0s
1938	Decima Norman (Aus)	24.7s
1950	Marjorie Jackson (Aus)	24.3s
1954	Marjorie Nelson (née Jackson)(Aus)	24.0s
1958	Marlene Willard (Aus)	23.65s
1962	Dorothy Hyman (Eng)	24.00s
1966	Dianne Burge (Aus)	23.73s
1970	Raelene Boyle (Aus)	22.75s
1974	Raelene Boyle (Aus)	22.50s
1978	Denise Boyd (Aus)	22.82s
1982	Merlene Ottey (Jam)	22.19s
1986	Angella Issajenko (née Taylor) (Can)	22.91s
1990	Merlene Ottey (Jam)	22.76s

400 Metres
(440 yards 1934-66)

1966	Judy Pollock (Aus)	53.0s
1970	Marilyn Neufville (Jam)	51.02s
1974	Yvonne Saunders (Can)	51.67s
1978	Donna Hartley (Eng)	51.69s
1982	Raelene Boyle (Aus)	51.26s
1986	Debbie Flintoff (Aus)	51.29s
1990	Fatima Yusuf (Nig)	51.08s

800 Metres
(880 yards 1934-66)

1934	Gladys Lunn (Eng)	2m19.4s
1962	Dixie Willis (Aus)	2m03.85s
1966	Abigail Hoffman (Can)	2m 04.3s
1970	Rosemary Stirling (Sco)	2m 06.24s
1974	Charlene Redina (Aus)	2m 01.1s
1978	Judy Peckham (Aus)	2m 02.82s
1982	Kirsty McDermott (Wales)	2m 01.31s
1986	Kirsty Wade (née McDermott) (Wales)	2m 00.94s
1990	Diane Edwards (Eng)	2m 00.25s

1500 Metres

1970	Rita Ridley (Eng)	4m 18.8s
1974	Glenda Reiser (Can)	4m 07.8s
1978	Mary Stewart (Eng)	4m 06.34s
1982	Christina Boxer (Eng)	4m 08.28s
1986	Kirsty Wade (Wales)	4m.10.91s
1990	Angela Chalmers (Can)	4m 08.41s

3000 Metres

1978	Paula Fudge (Eng)	9m 13.0s
1982	Anne Audain (NZ)	8m 45.53s
1986	Lynn Williams (Can)	8m 54.29s
1990	Angela Chalmers (Can)	8m 38.38s

10,000 Metres

1986	Liz Lynch (Sco)	31m 41.42s
1990	Liz McColgan (née Lynch) (Sco)	32m 23.56s

Marathon

1986	Lisa Martin (Aus)	2h 27m 07s
1990	Lisa Martin (Aus)	2h 25m 28s

80 Metres Hurdles

1934	Marjorie Clark (SA)	11.8s
1938	Barbara Burke (SA)	11.7s
1950	Shirley Strickland (Aus)	11.6s
1954	Edna Maskell (Zam)	10.9s
1958	Norma Thrower (Aus)	10.72s
1962	Pam Kilborn (Aus)	11.07s
1966	Pam Kilborn (Aus)	10.9s

100 Metres Hurdles

1970	Pam Kilborn (Aus)	13.27s
1974	Judy Vernon (Eng)	13.45s
1978	Lorna Boothe (Eng)	12.98s
1982	Shirley Strong (Eng)	12.78s
1986	Sally Gunnell (Eng)	13.29s
1990	Kay Morley (Wal)	12.91s

400 Metres Hurdles

1982	Debbie Flintoff (Aus)	55.89s
1986	Debbie Flintoff (Aus)	54.94s
1990	Sally Gunnell (Eng)	55.38s

4 x 100 Metres Relay
(4 x 110 yards 1934-66)

1954	Australia	46.8s
1958	England	45.37s
1962	Australia	46.71s
1966	Australia	45.3s
1970	Australia	44.14s
1974	Australia	43.51s
1978	England	43.70s
1982	England	43.15s
1986	England	43.39s
1990	Australia	43.87s

4 x 400 Metres Relay

1974	England	3m29.2s
1978	England	3m27.19s
1982	Canada	3m27.70s
1986	Canada	3m28.92s
1990	England	3m 28.08s

Discontinued Sprint Relays
2 x 110 yards 1 x 220 yards

1934	England	49.4s
1938	Australia	49.1s
1950	Australia	47.9s

2 x 220 yards 2 x 110 yards

1934	Canada	1:14.4s
1938	Australia	1:15.2s
1950	Australia	1:13.4s

10 Kilometres Walk

1990	Kerry Saxby (Aus)	45m 03s

High Jump

1934	Marjorie Clark (SA)	1.60m
1938	Dorothy Odam (Eng)	1.60m
1950	Dorothy Tyler (née Odam) (Eng)	1.60m
1954	Thelma Hopkins (NI)	1.67m
1958	Michele Mason (Aus)	1.70m
1962	Robyn Woodhouse (Aus)	1.78m
1966	Michele Brown (née Mason) (Aus)	1.73m
1970	Debbie Brill (Can)	1.78m
1974	Barbara Lawton (Eng)	1.84m
1978	Katrina Gibbs (Aus)	1.93m
1982	Debbie Brill (Can)	1.88m
1986	Christine Stanton (Aus)	1.92m
1990	Tania Murray (NZ)	1.88m

Long Jump

1934	Phyllis Bartholomew (Eng)	5.47m
1938	Decima Norman (Aus)	5.80m
1950	Yvette Williams (NZ)	5.90m
1954	Yvette Williams (NZ)	6.08m
1958	Sheila Hoskin (Eng)	6.02m
1962	Pam Kilborn (Aus)	6.27m
1966	Mary Rand (Eng)	6.36m
1970	Sheila Sherwood (Eng)	6.73m
1974	Modupe Oshikoya (Nig)	6.46m
1978	Sue Reeve (Eng)	6.59m
1982	Shonel Ferguson (Bah)w	6.91m
1986	Joyce Oladapo (Eng)	6.43m
1990	Jane Flemming (Aus)	6.78m

Shot

1954	Yvette Williams (NZ)	13.96m
1958	Valerie Sloper (NZ)	15.54m
1962	Valerie Young (née Sloper) (NZ)	15.23m
1966	Valerie Young (NZ)	16.50m
1970	Mary Peters (NI)	15.93m
1974	Jane Haist (Can)	16.12m
1978	Gael Mulhall (Aus)	17.31m
1982	Judy Oakes (Eng)	17.92m
1986	Gael Martin (née Mulhall) (Aus)	19.00m
1990	Myrtle Augee (Eng)	18.48m

Javelin

1934	Gladys Lunn (Eng)	32.18m
1938	Robina Higgins (Can)	38.28m
1950	Charlotte MacGibbon-Weeks (Aus)	38.84m
1954	Magdelena Swanepoel (SA)	43.82m
1958	Anna Pazera (Aus)	57.40m
1962	Susan Platt (Eng)	50.24m
1966	Margaret Parker (Aus)	51.38m
1970	Petra Rivers (Aus)	52.00m
1974	Petra Rivers (Aus)	55.48m
1978	Tessa Sanderson (Eng)	61.34m
1982	Suzanne Howland (Aus)	64.46m
1986	Tessa Sanderson (Eng)	69.80m
1990	Tessa Sanderson (Eng)	65.72m

Discus

1954	Yvette Williams (NZ)	45.02m
1958	Suzanne Allday (Eng)	45.91m
1962	Valerie Young (NZ)	50.20m
1966	Valerie Young (NZ)	49.78m
1970	Rosemary Payne (Sco)	54.46m
1974	Jane Haist (Can)	55.52m
1978	Carmen Ionescu (Can)	62.16m
1982	Margaret Ritchie (Sco)	62.98m
1986	Gael Martin (Aus)	56.42m
1990	Lisa-Marie Vizaniari (Aus)	56.38

Pentathlon
(Adjusted to 1971 tables)

1970	Mary Peters (NI)	4515pts
1974	Mary Peters (NI)	4455pts
1978	Diane Konihowski (Can)	4768pts

Heptathlon

1982	Glynis Nunn (Aus)	6254pts
1986	Judy Simpson (Eng)	6282pts
1990	Jane Flemming (Aus)	6695pts

Leading Gold Medal Countries in athletics:
Men - England 94, Australia 52, Canada 40, Kenya 23, New Zealand 18, South Africa 16, Jamaica 16, Scotland 11. *Women* - Australia 61, England 44, Canada 19, New Zealand 11

BADMINTON
Men
Singles

1966	Tan Aik Huang (Mal)
1970	Jamie Paulson (Can)
1974	Punch Gunalan (Mal)
1978	Padukone Prakash (Ind)
1982	Syed Modi (Ind)
1986	Steve Baddeley (Eng)
1990	Rashid Sidek (Mal)

Doubles

1966	Huang & Hoe (Mal)
1970	Bee & Gunalam (Mal)
1974	Talbot & Stuart (Eng)
1978	Stevens & Tredgett (Eng)
1982	Sidek & Ong (Mal)
1986	Gilliland & Travers (Sco)
1990	Sidek & Sidek (Mal)

Women
Singles

1966	Angela Bairstow (Eng)
1970	Margaret Beck (Eng)
1974	Gillian Gilks (Eng)
1978	Sylvia Ng (Mal)
1982	Helen Troke (Eng)
1986	Helen Troke (Eng)
1990	Fiona Smith (Eng)

Doubles

1966	Horton & Smith (Eng)
1970	Boxall & Whetnall (Eng)
1974	Beck & Gilks (Eng)
1978	Perry & Statt (Eng)
1982	Backhouse & Falardeau (Can)
1986	Clark & Gowers (Eng)
1990	Smith & Sankey (Eng)

Mixed Doubles

1966	Mills & Bairstow (Eng)
1970	Talbot & Boxall (Eng)
1974	Talbot & Gilks (Eng)
1978	Tredgett & Perry (Eng)
1982	Dew & Chapman (Eng)
1986	Scandolera & Tucket (Aus)
1990	Choi & Chan (HK)

Team
1978　England
1982　England
1986　England
1990　England

BOWLS
Men
Singles
1930　Robert Colquhoun (Eng)
1934　Robert Sprot (Sco)
1938　Horace Harvey (SA)
1950　James Pirret (NZ)
1954　Ralph Hodges (Zim)
1958　Phineas Danilowitz (SA)
1962　David Bryant (Eng)
1970　David Bryant (Eng)
1974　David Bryant (Eng)
1978　David Bryant (Eng)
1982　William Wood (Sco)
1986　Ian Dickison (NZ)
1990　Rob Parella (Aus)

Pairs
1930　Hills & Wright (Eng)
1934　Hills & Wright (Eng)
1938　Macey & Denison (NZ)
1950　Henry & Exelby (NZ)
1954　Rosbotham & Watson (NZ)
1958　Morris & Pilkington (NZ)
1962　McDonald & Robson (NZ)
1970　King & Line (Eng)
1974　Christie & McIntosh (Sco)
1978　Liddell & Delgado (HK)
1982　Watson & Gourlay (Sco)
1986　Adrain & Knox (Sco)
1990　Morris & Schuback (Aus)

Fours
1930　England
1934　England
1938　New Zealand
1950　South Africa
1954　South Africa
1958　England
1962　England
1970　Hong Kong
1974　New Zealand
1978　Hong Kong
1982　Australia
1986　Wales
1990　Scotland

Women
Singles
1986　Wendy Line (Eng)
1990　Geau Tau (PNG)

Pairs
1986　Freda Elliott & Margaret Johnstone (NI)
1990　Marie Watson & Judy Howat (NZ)

Triples
1982　Zimbabwe

Fours
1986　Wales
1990　Australia

BOXING
Super-heavyweight
1986　Lennox Lewis (Can)
1990　Michael Kenny (NZ)

Heavyweight
1930　Victor Stuart (Eng)
1934　Pat Floyd (Eng)
1938　Thomas Osborne (Can)
1950　Frank Creagh (NZ)
1954　Brian Harper (Eng)
1958　Daniel Bekker (SA)
1962　George Oywello (Uga)
1966　William Kini (NZ)
1970　Benson Masanda (Uga)
1974　Neville Meade (Eng)
1978　Julius Awome (Eng)
1982　Willie DeWit (Can)
1986　James Peau (NZ)
1990　George Onyango (Ken)

Light-heavyweight
1930　Joe Goyder (Eng)
1934　George Brennan (Eng)
1938　Nicholas Wolmarans (SA)
1950　Donald Scott (Eng)
1954　Piet Van Vuuren (SA)
1958　Tony Madigan (Aus)
1962　Tony Madigan (Aus)
1966　Roger Tighe (Eng)
1970　Fatai Ayinla (Nig)
1974　William Knight (Eng)
1978　Roger Fortin (Can)
1982　Fine Sani (Fiji)
1986　James Moran (Eng)
1990　Joseph Akhasamba (Nig)

Middleweight
1930　Frederick Mallin (Eng)
1934　Alf Shawyer (Eng)
1938　Denis Reardon (Wales)
1950　Theunis van Schalkwyk (SA)
1954　Johnannes van der Kolff (SA)
1958　Terry Milligan (NI)
1962　Cephas Coquhoun (Jam)
1966　Joe Darkey (Gha)
1970　John Conteh (Eng)
1974　Frankie Lucas (SVI)
1978　Philip McElwaine (Aus)
1982　Jimmy Price (Eng)
1986　Rod Douglas (Eng)
1990　Christopher Johnson (Can)

Light-middleweight
1954　Wilfred Greaves (Can)
1958　Grant Webster (SA)
1962　Harold Mann (Can)
1966　Mark Rowe (Eng)
1970　Tom Imrie (Sco)
1974　Lotti Mwale (Zam)
1978　Kelly Perlette (Can)
1982　Shawn O'Sullivan (Can)
1986　Dan Sherry (Can)
1990　Richie Woodhall (Eng)

Welterweight
1930　Leonard Hall (SA)
1934　David McCleave (Eng)
1938　Bill Smith (Aus)
1950　Terence Ratcliffe (Eng)
1954　Nicholas Gargano (Eng)
1958　Joseph Grayling (SA)
1962　Wallace Coe (NZ)
1966　Eddie Blay (Gha)
1970　Emma Ankudey (Gha)

1974	Muhamad Muruli (Uga)
1978	Michael McCallum (Jam)
1982	Christopher Pyatt (Eng)
1986	Darren Dyer (Eng)
1990	Dand Defiagbon (Nig)

Light-welterweight
1954	Mickey Bergin (Can)
1958	Henry Loubscher (SA)
1962	Clement Quartey (Gha)
1966	James McCourt (NI)
1970	Muhamad Muruli (Uga)
1974	Obisia Nwakpa (Nig)
1978	Winfield Braithwaite (Guy)
1982	Christopher Ossai (Nig)
1986	Howard Grant (Can)
1990	Charlie Kane (Sco)

Lightweight
1930	James Rolland (Sco)
1934	Leslie Cook (Aus)
1938	Harry Groves (Eng)
1950	Ronald Latham (Eng)
1954	Piet van Staden (Zim)
1958	Dick McTaggart (Sco)
1962	Eddie Blay (Gha)
1966	Anthony Andeh (Nig)
1970	Abayomi Adeyemi (Nig)
1974	Ayub Kalule (Uga)
1978	Gerard Hamil (NI)
1982	Hussein Khalili (Ken)
1986	Asif Dar (Can)
1990	Godfrey Nyakana (Uga)

Featherweight
1930	F.R. Meacham (Eng)
1934	Charles Catterall (SA)
1938	Anadale Henricus (Sri)
1950	Henry Gilliland (Sco)
1954	Leonard Leisching (SA)
1958	Wally Taylor (Aus)
1962	John McDermott (Sco)
1966	Philip Waruinge (Ken)
1970	Philip Waruinge (Ken)
1974	Edward Ndukwa (Nig)
1978	Nelson Azumah (Gha)
1982	Peter Knoyegwachie (Nig)
1986	Bill Downey (Can)
1990	John Irwin (Eng)

Bantamweight
1930	Hyman Mizler (Eng)
1934	Freddy Ryan (Eng)
1938	William Butler (Eng)
1950	Johannes van Rensburg (SA)
1954	John Smillie (Sco)
1958	Howard Winstone (Wales)
1962	Jeffery Dynevor (Aus)
1966	Edward Ndukwu (Nig)
1970	Sulley Shittu (Gha)
1974	Pat Cowdell (Eng)
1978	Barry McGuigan (NI)
1982	Joe Orewa (Nig)
1986	Sean Murphy (Eng)
1990	Sabo Mohammed (Nig)

Flyweight
1930	Jacob Smith (SA)
1934	Patrick Palmer (Eng)
1938	Johannes Joubert (SA)
1950	Hugh Riley (Sco)
1954	Richard Currie (Sco)
1958	Jackie Brown (Sco)
1962	Robert Mallon (Sco)
1966	Sulley Shittu (Gha)
1970	David Needham (Eng)
1974	David Lamour (NI)
1978	Michael Irungu (Ken)

1982	Michael Mutua (Ken)
1986	John Lyon (Eng)
1990	Wayne McCulloch

Light-flyweight
1970	James Odwori (Uga)
1974	Stephen Muchoki (Ken)
1978	Stephen Muchoki (Ken)
1982	Abraham Wachire (Ken)
1986	Scott Olson (Can)
1990	Justin Juko (Uga)

CYCLING
Sprint
1934	Ernest Higgins (Eng)
1938	Edgar Gray (Aus)
1950	Russell Mockridge (Aus)
1954	Cyril Peacock (Eng)
1958	Dick Ploog (Aus)
1962	Thomas Harrison (Aus)
1966	Roger Gibbon (Tri)
1970	John Nicholson (Aus)
1974	John Nicholson (Aus)
1978	Kenrick Tucker (Aus)
1982	Kenrick Tucker (Aus)
1986	Gary Neiwand (Aus)
1990	Gary Neiwand (Aus)

1000 Metres Time Trial
1934	Edgar Gray (Aus)
1938	Robert Porter (Aus)
1950	Russell Mockridge (Aus)
1954	Dick Ploog (Aus) & Alfred Swift (SA)
1958	Neville Tong (Eng)
1962	Peter Bartels (Aus)
1966	Roger Gibbon (Tri)
1970	Harry Kent (NZ)
1974	Dick Paris (Aus)
1978	Jocelyn Lovell (Can)
1982	Craig Adair (NZ)
1986	Martin Vinnicombe (Aus)
1990	Martin Vinnicombe (Aus)

4000 Metres Individual Pursuit
1950	Cyril Cartwright (Eng)
1954	Norman Sheil (Eng)
1958	Norman Sheil (Eng)
1962	Maxwell Langshaw (Aus)
1966	Hugh Porter (Eng)
1970	Ian Hallam (Eng)
1974	Ian Hallam (Eng)
1978	Michael Richards (NZ)
1982	Michael Turtur (Aus)
1986	Dean Woods (Aus)
1990	Garry Anderson (NZ)

4000 Metres Team Pursuit
1974	England
1978	Australia
1982	Australia
1986	Australia
1990	New Zealand

100 km Team Time Trial
1982	England
1986	England
1990	New Zealand

Tandem Sprint
1970	Johnson & Jonker (Aus)
1974	Cook & Crutchlow (Eng)
1978	Lovell & Singleton (Can)

10 Mile Track Race
1934	Robert McLeod (Can)
1938	William Maxfield (Eng)
1950	William Heseltine (Aus)
1954	Lindsay Cocks (Aus)

1958	Ian Browne (Aus)
1962	Douglas Adams (Aus)
1966	Ian Alsop (Eng)
1970	Jocelyn Lovell (Can)
1974	Stephen Heffernan (Eng)
1978	Jocelyn Lovell (Can)
1982	Kevin Nichols (Aus)
1986	Wayne McCarney (Aus)
1990	Garry Anderson (NZ)

Road Race

1938	Hendrick Binneman (SA)
1950	Hector Sutherland (Aus)
1954	Eric Thompson (Eng)
1958	Ray Booty (Eng)
1962	Wesley Mason (Eng)
1966	Peter Buckley (IOM)
1970	Bruce Biddle (NZ)
1974	Clyde Sefton (Aus)
1978	Philip Anderson (Aus)
1982	Malcolm Elliott (Eng)
1986	Paul Curran (Eng)
1990	Graeme Miller (NZ)

Women
Sprint

1990	Louise Jones (Wal)

3,000 Metres Individual Pursuit

1990	Madonna Harris (NZ)

Road Race

1990	Kathny Watt (Aus)

FENCING
(Discontinued 1970)

Men
Foil

	Individual	Team
1950	Rene Paul (Eng)	England
1954	Rene Paul (Eng)	England
1958	Raymond Paul (Eng)	England
1962	Alex Leckie (Sco)	England
1966	Allan Jay (Eng)	England
1970	Mike Breckin (Eng)	England

Epee

	Individual	Team
1950	Chas-L. de Beaumont (Eng)	Australia
1954	Ivan Lund (Aus)	England
1958	William Hoskyns (Eng)	England
1962	Ivan Lund (Aus)	England
1966	William Hoskyns (Eng)	England
1970	William Hoskyns (Eng)	England

Sabre

	Individual	Team
1950	Arthur Pilbrow (Eng)	England
1954	Michael Amberg (Eng)	Canada
1958	William Hoskyns (Eng)	England
1962	Ralph Cooperman (Eng)	England
1966	Ralph Cooperman (Eng)	England
1970	Alex Leckie (Sco)	England

Women
Foil

	Individual	Team
1950	Mary Glen-Haig (Eng)	-
1954	Mary Glen-Haig (Eng)	-
1958	Gillian Sheen (Eng)	-
1962	Melody Coleman (NZ)	-
1966	Janet Wardell-Yerburgh (Eng)	England
1970	Janet Wardell-Yerburgh (Eng)	England

GYMNASTICS
Men

	Individual	Team
1978	Philip Delesalle (Can)	Canada
1990	Curtis Hibbert (Can)	Canada

Women

	Individual	Team
1978	Elfi Schlegel (Can)	Canada
1990	Lori Strong (Can)	Canada

JUDO
Men

60kg	1990	Carl Finney (Eng)
65kg	1990	Brent Cooper (NZ)
71kg	1990	Roy Stone (Eng)
78kg	1990	David Southby (Eng)
86kg	1990	Densign White (Eng)
95kg	1990	Ray Stevens (Eng)
Over 95kg	1990	Elvis Gordon (Eng)
Open	1990	Elvis Gordon (Eng)

Women

48kg	1990	Karen Briggs (Eng)
52kg	1990	Sharon Rendle (Eng)
56kg	1990	Loretta Cusak (Sco)
61g	1990	Diane Bell (Eng)
66kg	1990	Sharon Mills (Eng)
72kg	1990	Jane Morris (Eng)
Over 72kg	1990	Sharon Lee (Eng)
Open	1990	Sharon Lee (Eng)

ROWING
Men
Single Sculls

1930	Bobby Pearce (Aus)
1938	Herbert Turner (Aus)
1950	Mervyn Wood (Aus)
1954	Donald Rowlands (NZ)
1958	Stuart Mackenzie (Aus)
1962	James Hill (NZ)
1986	Steven Redgrave (Eng)

Double Sculls

1930	Bole & Richards (Can)
1950	Wood & Riley (Aus)
1954	Wood & Riley (Aus)
1958	Spracklen & Baker (Eng)
1962	Justice & Birkmyre (Eng)
1986	Walter & Ford (Can)

Coxless Pairs

1950	Lambert & Webster (Aus)
1954	Parker & Douglas (NZ)
1958	Parker & Douglas (NZ)
1962	Farquharson & Lee-Nicholson (Eng)
1986	Redgrave & Holmes (Eng)

Coxless Fours

1930	England
1958	England
1962	England
1986	Canada

Coxed Fours

1930	New Zealand
1938	Australia
1950	New Zealand
1954	Australia
1958	England
1962	New Zealand
1986	England

Eights
1930   England
1938   England
1950   Australia
1954   Canada
1958   Canada
1962   Australia
1986   Australia

Lightweight Single Sculls
1986   Peter Antonie (Aus)

Lightweight Coxless Fours
1986   England

Women
(Only held 1986)

Single Sculls
1986   Stephanie Foster (NZ)

Double Sculls
1986   Foster & Clark (NZ)

Coxless Pairs
1986   Barr & Schreiner (Can)

Coxed Fours
1986   Canada

Eights
1986   Australia

Lightweight Single Sculls
1986   Adair Ferguson (Aus)

Lightweight Coxless Fours
1986   England

SHOOTING
Small Bore Rifle
1966   Gilmour Boa (Can)
1974   Yvonne Gowland (Aus)
1978   Alister Allan (Sco)

Small Bore Rifle - Prone
Individual
1982   Alan Smith (Aus)
1986   Alan Smith (Aus)
1990   Roger Harvey (NZ)
Pairs
1982   Cooper & Sullivan (Eng)
1986   Ashcroft & Stewart (Can)
1990   Pettersson & Harvey (NZ)

Small Bore Rifle - Three Positions
Individual
1982   Alister Allan (Sco)
1986   Malcolm Cooper (Eng)
1990   Mart Klepp (Can)
Pairs
1982   Cooper & Dagger (Eng)
1986   Cooper & Cooper (Eng)
1990   Senecal & Klepp (Can)

Full Bore Rifle
Individual
1966   Lord John Swansea (Wales)
1974   Maurice Gordon (NZ)
1978   Desmond Vamplew (Can)
1982   Arthur Clarke (Sco)
1986   Stan Golinski (Aus)
1990   Colin Mallet (Jersey)
Pairs
1982   Affleck & Ayling (Aus)
1986   Marion & Baldwin (Can)
1990   Belither & Tucker (Eng)

Free Pistol
Individual
1966   Charles Sexton (Eng)
1974   Jules Sobrian (Can)
1978   Yvon Trempe (Can)
1982   Tom Guinn (Can)
1986   Greg Yelavich (NZ)
1990   Phillip Adams (Aus)
Pairs
1982   Adams & Tremelling (Aus)
1986   Guinn & Beaulieu (Can)
1990   Adams & Sandstrom (Aus)

Centre Fire Pistol
Individual
1966   James Lee (Can)
1982   John Cooke (Eng)
1986   Robert Northover (Eng)
1990   Ashok Pandit (Ind)
Pairs
1982   Ryan & Taransky (Aus)
1986   Adams & Hack (Aus)
1990   Adams & Quick (Aus)

Rapid Fire Pistol
Individual
1966   Anthony Clark (Eng)
1974   William Hare (Can)
1978   Jules Sobrian (Can)
1982   Solomon Lee (HK)
1986   Pat Murray (Aus)
1990   Adrian Breton
Pairs
1982   Heuke & Taransky (Aus)
1986   Girling & Turner (Eng)
1990   Farrell & Murray (Aus)

Olympic Trap
Individual
1974   John Primrose (Can)
1978   John Primrose (Can)
1982   Peter Boden (Eng)
1986   Ian Peel (Eng)
1990   John Maxwell (Aus)
Pairs
1982   Ellis & Rumbel (Aus)
1986   Peel & Boden (Eng)
1990   Gill & Peel (Eng)

Skeet
Individual
1974   Harry Willsie (Can)
1978   John Woolley (NZ)
1982   John Woolley (NZ)
1986   Nigel Kelly (IOM)
1990   Ken Harman (Eng)
Pairs
1982   Gabriel & Altmann (Can)
1986   Neville & Harman (Eng)
1990   Marsden & Dunlop (Sco)

Air Pistol
Individual
1982   George Darling (Eng)
1986   Greg Yelavich (NZ)
1990   Bengt Sandstrom (Aus)
Pairs
1982   Adams & Colbert (Aus)
1986   Leatherdale & Reid (Eng)
1990   Rahman & Sattar (Ban)

Air Rifle
Individual
1982   Jean-Francois Senecal (Can)
1986   Guy Lorion (Can)
1990   Guy Lorion (Can)

Pairs

1982	Allan & McNeil (Sco)
1986	Lorion & Bowes (Can)
1990	Lorion & Klepp (Can)

Running Boar

1990	Colin Robertson (Aus)

SWIMMING
Men
50 Metres Freestyle

1990	Andrew Baildon (Aus)	22.76s

100 Metres Freestyle

(100 yards 1930-34; 110 yards 1938-66)   *time*

1930	Munroe Bourne (Can)	56.0s
1934	George Burleigh (Can)	55.0s
1938	Bob Pirie (Can)	59.6s
1950	Peter Salmon (Can)	1:00.4s
1954	Jon Henricks (Aus)	56.5s
1958	John Devitt (Aus)	56.6s
1962	Richard Pound (Can)	55.8s
1966	Mike Wenden (Aus)	54.0s
19~0	Mike Wenden (Aus)	53.06s
1974	Mike Wenden (Aus)	52.73s
1978	Mark Morgan (Aus)	52.70s
1982	Neil Brooks (Aus)	51.14s
1986	Greg Fasala (Aus)	50.95s
1990	Andrew Baildon (Aus)	49.80s

200 Metres Freestyle

(400 yards 1930; 440 yards 1934-66)

1970	Mike Wenden (Aus)	1m 56.69s
1974	Stephen Badger (Aus)	1m 56.72s
1978	Ron McKeon (Aus)	1m 52.06s
1982	Andrew Astbury (Eng)	1m 51.52s
1986	Robert Gleria (Aus)	1m 50.57s
1990	Martin Roberts (Aus)	1m 49.58s

400 Metres Freestyle

(400 yards 1930; 440 yards 1934-66)

1930	Noel Ryan (Aus)	4m 39.38s
1934	Noel Ryan (Aus)	5m 03.0s
1938	Bob Pirie (Can)	4m 54.6s
1950	Garrick Agnew (Aus)	4m 49.4s
1954	Gary Chapman (Aus)	4m 39.8s
1958	John Konrads (Aus)	4m 25.9s
1962	Murray Rose (Aus)	4m 20.0s
1966	Robert Windle (Aus)	4m 15.0s
1970	Graham White (Aus)	4m 08.48s
1974	John Kulasalu (Aus)	4m 01.44s
1978	Ron McKeon (Aus)	3m 54.43s
1982	Andrew Astbury (Eng)	3m 53.29s
1986	Duncan Armstrong (Aus)	3m 52.25s
1990	Ian Brown (Aus) 3m 49.91s	

1500 Metres Freestyle

(1,500 yards 1930-34; 1,650 yards 1938-66)

1930	Noel Ryan (Aus)	18m 55.4s
1934	Noel Ryan (Aus)	18m 25.4s
1938	Robert Leivers (Eng)	19m 46.4s
1950	Graham Johnston (SA)	19m 55.7s
1954	Graham Johnston (SA)	1m :01.4s
1958	John Konrads (Aus)	17m 45.4s
1962	Murray Rose (Aus)	17m 18.1s
1966	Ron Jackson (Aus)	17m 25.9s
1970	Graham Windeatt (Aus)	16m 23.82s
1974	Steve Holland (Aus)	15m 34.73s
1978	Max Metzker (Aus)	15m 31.92s
1982	Max Metzker (Aus)	15m 23.94
1986	Jason Plummer (Aus)	15m 12.62
1990	Glen Housman (Aus)	14m 55.25s

100 Metres Backstroke

(100 yards 1930-34; 110 yards 1938-66)

1930	John Trippett (Eng)	1m 05.4s
1934	Willie Francis (Sco)	1m 05.2s
1938	Percy Oliver (Aus)	1m 07.9s
1950	Jacobus Wiid (SA)	1m 07.7s
1954	John Brockway (Wales)	1m 06.5s
1958	John Monckton (Aus)	1m 01.7s
1962	Graham Sykes (Eng)	1m 04.5s
1966	Peter Reynolds (Aus)	1m 02.4s
1970	Bill Kennedy (Can)	1m 01.65s
1974	Mark Tonelli (Aus)	59.65s
1978	Glenn Patching (Aus)	57.90s
1982	Michael West (Can)	57.12s
1986	Mark Tewksbury (Can)	56.45s
1990	Mark Tewksbury (Can)	56.07s

200 Metres Backstroke

(200 yards 1962-66)

1962	Julian Carroll (Aus)	2m 20.9s
1966	Peter Reynolds (Aus)	2m 12.0s
1970	Mike Richards (Wales)	2m 14.53s
1974	Brad Cooper (Aus)	2m 06.31s
1978	Gary Hurring (NZ)	2m 04.37s
1982	Cameron Henning (Can)	2m 02.58s
1986	Sandy Goss (Can)	2m 02.55s
1990	Gary Anderson (Can)	2m 01.69s

100 Metres Breaststroke

(110 yards 1962-66)

1962	Ian O'Brien (Aus)	1m 11.4s
1966	Ian O'Brien (Aus)	1m 08.2s
1970	Bill Mahoney (Can)	1m 09.0ss
1974	David Leigh (Eng)	1m 06.52
1978	Graham Smith (Can)	1m 03.81s
1982	Adrian Moorhouse (Eng)	1m 02.93s
1986	Victor Davis (Can)	1m 03.01s
1990	Adrian Moorhouse (Eng)	1m 01.49s

200 Metres Breaststroke

(200 yards 1930-34)

1930	Jack Aubin (Can)	2m 38.4s
1934	Norman Hamilton (Sco)	2m 41.4s
1938	John Davies (Eng)	2m 51.9s
1950	David Hawkins (Aus)	2m 54.1s
1954	John Doms (NZ)	2m 52.6s
1958	Terry Gathercole (Aus)	2m 41.6s
1962	Ian O'Brien (Aus)	2m 38.2s
1966	Ian O'Brien (Aus)	2m 29.3s
1970	Bill Mahoney (Can)	2m 30.29s
1974	David Wilkie (Sco)	2m 24.42s
1978	Graham Smith (Can)	2m 20.86s
1982	Victor Davis (Can)	2m 16.25s
1986	Adrian Moorhouse (Eng)	2m 16.35s
1990	John Cleveland (Eng)	2m 14.96s

100 Metres Butterfly

(110 yards 1962-66)

1962	Kevin Berry (Aus)	59.5s
1966	Ron Jacks (Can)	1m 00.3s
1970	Byron MacDonald (Can)	58 44s
1974	Neil Rogers (Aus)	56 58s
1978	Dan Thompson (Can)	55 04s
1982	Dan Thompson (Can)	54 71s
1986	Andrew Jameson (Eng)	54 07s
1990	Andrew Baildon (Aus)	53.98s

200 Metres Butterfly

(220 yards 1958-66)

1958	Ian Black (Sco)	2m 22.6s
1962	Kevin Berry (Aus)	2m 10.8s
1966	David Gerrard (NZ)	2m 12.7s
1970	Tom Arusoo (Can)	2m 08.97s
1974	Brian Brinkley (Eng)	2m 04.51s
1978	George Nagy (Can)	2m 01.99s
1982	Phil Hubble (Eng)	2m 00.90s
1986	Anthony Mosse (NZ)	1m 57.27s
1990	Anthony Mosse (NZ)	1m 57.33s

200 Metres Individual Medley

1970	George Smith (Can)	2m 13.72s
1974	David Wilkie (Sco)	2m 10.11s

1978	Graham Smith (Can)	2m 05.25s
1982	Alex Baumann (Can)	2m 02.25s
1986	Alex Baumann (Can)	2m 01.80s
1990	Gary Anderson (Can)	2m 02.94s

400 Metres Individual Medley
(440 yards 1962-66)

1962	Alex Alexander (Aus)	5m 15.3s
1966	Peter Reynolds (Aus)	4m 50.8s
1970	George Smith (Can)	4m 48.87s
1974	Mark Treffers (NZ)	4m 35.90s
1978	Graham Smith (Can)	4m 27.34s
1982	Alex Baumann (Can)	4m 23.53s
1986	Alex Baumann (Can)	4m 18.29s
1990	Rob Bruce (Aus)	4m 20.26s

4 x 100 Metres Freestyle Relay
(4 x 110 yards 1962-66)

1962	Australia	3m 43.9s
1966	Australia	3m 35.6s
1970	Australia	3m 36.02s
1974	Canada	3m 33.79s
1978	Canada	3m 27.94s
1982	Australia	3m 24.17s
1986	Australia	3m 21.58s
1990	Australia	3m 20.05s

4 x 200 Metres Freestyle Relay
(4 x 200 yards 1930-34; 4 x 220 yards 1938-66)

1930	Canada	8m 42.4s
1934	Canada	8m 40.6s
1938	England	9m 19.0s
1950	New Zealand	9m 27.7s
1954	Australia	8m 47.6s
1958	Australia	8m 33.4s
1962	Australia	8m 13.4s
1966	Australia	7m 59.5s
1970	Australia	7m 50.77s
1974	Australia	7m 50.13s
1978	Australia	7m 34.83s
1982	Australia	7m 28.81s
1986	Australia	7m 23.49s
1990	Australia	7m 21.17s

4 x 100 Metres Medley Relay
(3 x 100 yards 1934; 3 x 110 yards 1938-54; 4 x 110 yards 1958-66. Butterfly included from 1958)

1934	Canada	3m 11.2s
1938	England	3m 28.2s
1950	England	3m 26.6s
1954	Australia	3m 22.0s
1958	Australia	4m 14.2s
1962	Australia	4m 12.4s
1966	Canada	4m 10.5s
1970	Canada	4m 01.10s
1974	Canada	3m 52.93s
1978	Canada	3m 49.76s
1982	Australia	3m 47.34s
1986	Canada	3m 44.00s
1990	Canada	3m 42.45s

Springboard Diving

1930	Alfred Phillips (Can)
1934	J. Briscoe Ray (Eng)
1938	Ron Masters (Aus)
1950	George Athans (Can)
1954	Peter Heatly (Sco)
1958	Keith Collin (Eng)
1962	Brian Phelps (Eng)
1966	Brian Phelps (Eng)
1970	Donald Wagstaff (Aus)
1974	Donald Wagstaff (Aus)
1978	Chris Snode (Eng)
1982	Chris Snode (Eng)
1986	Shaun Panayi (Aus)
1990	(1 metre) Russell Butler (Aus)
	(3 metres) Craig Rogerson (Aus)

Highboard Diving

1930	Alfred Phillips (Can)
1934	Tommy Mather (Eng)
1938	Doug Tomalin (Eng)
1950	Peter Heatly (Sco)
1954	William Patrick (Can)
1958	Peter Heatly (Sco)
1962	Brian Phelps (Eng)
1966	Brian Phelps (Eng)
1970	Donald Wagstaff (Aus)
1974	Donald Wagstaff (Aus)
1978	Chris Snode (Eng)
1982	Chris Snode (Eng)
1986	Craig Rogerson (Aus)
1990	Robert Morgan (Wal)

Water Polo

1950	Australia

Women

50 Metres Freestyle

1990	Lisa Curry-Kenny (Aus)	25.80s

100 Metres Freestyle
(100 yards 1930-34; 110 yards 1938-66)

1930	Joyce Cooper (Eng)	1m 07.0s
1934	Phyllis Dewar (Can)	1m 03.5s
1938	Evelyn de Lacy (Aus)	1m 10.1s
1950	Marjorie McQuade (Aus)	1m 09.0s
1954	Lorraine Crapp (Aus)	1m 05.8s
1958	Dawn Fraser (Aus)	1m 01.4s
1962	Dawn Fraser (Aus)	59.5s
1966	Marion Lay (Can)	1m 02.3s
1970	Angela Coughlan (Can)	1m 01.22s
1974	Sonya Gray (Aus)	59.13s
1978	Carol Klimpel (Can)	57.78s
1982	June Croft (Eng)	56.97s
1986	Jane Kerr (Can)	57.62s
1990	Karen Van Wirdum (Aus)	56.48s

200 Metres Freestyle

1970	Karen Moras (Aus)	2m 09.78s
1974	Sonya Gray (Aus)	2m 04.27s
1978	Rebecca Perrott (NZ)	2m 00.63s
1982	June Croft (Eng)	1m 59.74s
1986	Susie Baumer (Aus)	2m 00.61s
1990	Hayley Lewis (Aus)	2m 00.79s

400 Metres Freestyle
(400 yards 1930; 440 yards 1934 - 66)

1930	Joyce Cooper (Eng)	5m 25.4s
1934	Phyllis Dewar (Can)	5m 45.6s
1938	Dorothy Green (Aus)	5m 39.7s
1950	Joan Harrison (SA)	5m 26.4s
1954	Lorraine Crapp (Aus)	5m 11.4s
1958	Ilsa Konrads (Aus)	4m 49.4s
1962	Dawn Fraser (Aus)	4m 51.4s
1966	Kathy Wainwright (Aus)	4m 38.8s
1970	Karen Moras (Aus)	4m 27.38s
1974	Jenny Turrall (Aus)	4m 22.09s
1978	Tracey Wickham (Aus)	4m 08.45s
1982	Tracey Wickham (Aus)	4m 08.82s
1986	Sarah Hardcastle (Eng)	4m 07.68s
1990	Hayley Lewis (Aus)	4m 38.80s

800 Metres Freestyle

1970	Karen Moras (Aus)	9m 02.45s
1974	Jaynie Parkhouse (NZ)	8m 58.49s
1978	Tracey Wickham (Aus)	8m 24.62s
1982	Tracey Wickham (Aus)	8m 29.05s
1986	Sarah Hardcastle (Eng)	8m 24.77s
1990	Julie McDonald	8m 30.27s

100 Metres Backstroke
(100 yards 1930-34; 110 yards 1938-66)

1930	Joyce Cooper (Eng)	1m 15.0s
1934	Phyllis Harding (Eng)	1m 13.8s
1938	Pat Norton (Aus)	1m 19.5s

1950	Judy-Joy Davies (Aus)	1m 18.6s
1954	Joan Harrison (SA)	1m 15.2s
1958	Judy Grinham (Eng)	1m 11.9s
1962	Linda Ludgrove (Eng)	1m 11.1s
1966	Linda Ludgrove (Eng)	1m 09.2s
1970	Lynne Watson (Aus)	1m 07.10s
1974	Wendy Cook (Can)	1m 06.37s
1978	Debra Forster (Aus)	1m 03.97s
1982	Lisa Forrest (Aus)	1m 03.48s
1986	Sylvia Hume (NZ)	1m 04.00s
1990	Nicole Livingstone (Aus)	1m 02.46s

200 Metres Backstroke
(220 yards 1962-66)

1962	Linda Ludgrove (Eng)	2m 35.2s
1966	Linda Ludgrove (Eng)	2m 28.5s
1970	Lynne Watson (Aus)	2m 22.86s
1974	Wendy Cook (Can)	2m 20.37s
1978	Cheryl Gibson (Can)	2m 16.57s
1982	Lisa Forrest (Aus)	2m 13.36s
1986	Georgina Parkes (Aus)	2m 14.88s
1990	Anna Simcic (NZ)	2m 12.32s

100 Metres Breaststroke
(110 yards 1962-66)

1962	Anita Lonsbrough (Eng)	1m 21.3s
1966	Diana Harris (Eng)	1m 19.7s
1970	Beverley Whitfield (Aus)	1m 17.40s
1974	Catherine Gaskell (Eng)	1m 16.42s
1978	Robin Corsiglia (Can)	1m 13.56s
1982	Kathy Bald (Can)	1m 11.89s
1986	Alison Higson (Can)	1m 10.84s
1990	Keltie Duggan (Can)	1m 10.74s

200 Metres Breaststroke
(200 yards 1930-34; 220 yards 1938-66)

1930	Celia Wolstenholme (Eng)	2m 54.8s
1934	Claire Dennis (Aus)	2m 50.2s
1938	Doris Storey (Eng)	3m 06.3s
1950	Elenor Gordon (Sco)	3m 01.7s
1954	Elenor Gordon (Sco)	2m 59.2s
1958	Anita Lonsbrough (Eng)	2m 53.5s
1962	Anita Lonsbrough (Eng)	2m 51.7s
1966	Jill Slattery (Eng)	2m 50.3s
1970	Beverley Whitfield (Aus)	2m 44.12s
1974	Pat Beaan (Wales)	2m 43.11s
1978	Lisa Borsholt (Can)	2m 37.70s
1982	Anne Ottenbrite (Can)	2m 32.07s
1986	Allison Higson (Can)	2m 31.20s
1990	Nathalia Giguere (Can)	2m 32.16s

100 Metres Butterfly
(110 yards 1958-66)

1958	Beverley Bainbridge (Aus)	1m 13.5s
1962	Mary Stewart (Can)	1m 10.1s
1966	Elaine Tanner (Can)	1m 06.8s
1970	Diane Lansley (Eng)	1m 07.90s
1974	Patti Stenhouse (Can)	1m 05.38s
1978	Wendy Quirk (Can)	1m 01.92s
1982	Lisa Curry (Aus)	1m 01.22s
1986	Caroline Cooper (Eng)	1m 02.12s
1990	Lisa Curry-Kenny (Aus)	1m 00.66s

200 Metres Butterfly
(220 yards 1966)

1966	Elaine Tanner (Can)	2m 29.9s
1970	Maree Robinson (Aus)	2m 24.67s
1974	Sandra Yost (Aus)	2m 20.57s
1978	Michele Ford (Aus)	2m 11.29s
1982	Michele Ford (Aus)	2m 11.89s
1986	Donna McGinnis (Can)	2m 11.97s
1990	Hayley Lewis (Aus)	2m 11.15s

200 Metres Individual Medley

1970	Denise Langford (Aus)	2m 28.89s
1974	Leslie Cliff (Can)	2m 24.13s

1978	Sharron Davies (Eng)	2m 18.37s
1982	Lisa Curry (Aus)	2m 16.94s
1986	Suzanne Landells (Aus)	2m 17.02s
1990	Nancy Sweetnam (Can)	2m 15.61s

400 Metres Individual Medley
(440 yards 1962-66)

1962	Anita Lonsbrough (Eng)	5m 38.6s
1966	Elaine Tanner (Can)	5m 26.3s
1970	Denise Langford (Aus)	5m 10.74s
1974	Leslie Cliff (Can)	5m 01.35s
1978	Sharron Davies (Eng)	4m 52.44s
1982	Lisa Curry (Aus)	4m 51.95s
1986	Suzanne Landells (Aus)	4m 45.82s
1990	Hayley Lewis (Aus)	4m 42.65s

4 x 100 Metres Freestyle Relay
(4 x 100 yards 1930-34; 4 x 110 yards 1938-66)

1930	England	4m 32.8s
1934	Canada	4m 21.8s
1938	Canada	4m 48.3s
1950	Australia	4m 44.9s
1954	South Africa	4m 33.9s
1958	Australia	4m 17.4s
1962	Australia	4m 11.0s
1966	Canada	4m 10.8s
1970	Australia	4m 06.41s
1974	Canada	3m 57.14s
1978	Canada	3m 50.28s
1982	England	3m 50.28s
1986	Canada	3m 48.45s
1990	Australia	3m 46.85s

4 x 200 Metres Freestyle Relay

1986	Australia	8m 12.09s
1990	Australia	8m 08.95s

4 x 100 Metres Medley Relay
(3 x 100 yards 1934; 3 x 110 yards 1938-54; 4 x 110 yards 1958. Butterfly included from 1958)

1934	Canada	3m 42.0s
1938	England	3m 57.7s
1950	Australia	3m 53.8s
1954	Scotland	3m 51.0s
1958	England	4m 54.0s
1962	Australia	4m 45.9s
1966	England	4m 40.6s
1970	Australia	4m 30.66s
1974	Canada	4m 24.77s
1978	Canada	4m 15.26s
1982	Canada	4m 14.33s
1986	England	4m 13.48s
1990	Australia	4m 10.87s

Springboard Diving

1930	Oonagh Whitsett (SA)
1934	Judy Moss (Can)
1938	Irene Donnett (Aus)
1950	Edna Child (Eng)
1954	Ann Long (Eng)
1958	Charmain Welsh (Eng)
1962	Susan Knight (Aus)
1966	Kathy Rowlatt (Eng)
1970	Beverley Boys (Can)
1974	Cindy Shatto (Can)
1978	Janet Nutter (Can)
1982	Jenny Donnett (Aus)
1986	Debbie Fuller (Can)
1990	(1 metre) Mary de Piero (Can)
	(3 metre) Jenny Donnet (Aus)

Highboard Diving

1930	Pearl Stoneham (Can)
1934	Elizabeth Macready (Eng)
1938	Lurline Hook (Aus)
1950	Edna Child (Eng)
1954	Barbara McAulay (Aus)

1958	Charmain Welsh (Eng)
1962	Susan Knight (Aus)
1966	Joy Newman (Eng)
1970	Beverley Boys (Can)
1974	Beverley Boys (Can)
1978	Linda Cuthbert (Can)
1982	Valerie Beddoe (Aus)
1986	Debbie Fuller (Can)
1990	Anna Dacyshyn (Can)

Synchronised Swimming
Solo

1986	Sylvie Frechette (Can)
1990	Sylvie Frechette (Can)

Duet

1986	Waldo & Cameron (Can)
1990	Glen & Larsen (Can)

Leading Gold Medal countries in swimming.
Men Australia 88, Canada 51, England 28, Scotland 8, New Zealand 7. *Women* Australia 71, Canada 51, England 40, South Africa 4, Scotland and New Zealand 4.

WEIGHTLIFTING
Flyweight

1970	George Vasiliades (Aus)
1974	Precious McKenzie (Eng)
1978	Ekambaram Karunakaran (Ind)
1982	Nick Voukelatos (Aus)
1986	Greg Hayman (Aus)
1990	Chandersekaran Raghavan (Ind)

Bantamweight

1950	Tho Fook Hung (Mal)
1954	Maurice Magennis (Eng)
1958	Reginald Gaffley (SA)
1962	Chua Phung Kim (Sin)
1966	Precious McKenzie (Eng)
1970	Precious McKenzie (Eng)
1974	Michael Adams (Aus)
1978	Precious McKenzie (NZ)
1982	Geoffrey Laws (Eng)
1986	Nick Voukelatos (Aus)
1990	Rangaswamy Punnuswamy (Ind)

Featherweight

1950	Koh Eng Tong (Mal)
1954	Rodney Wilkes (Tri)
1958	Tan Ser Cher (Sin)
1962	George Newton (Eng)
1966	Kum Weng Chung (Wales)
1970	George Perrin (Eng)
1974	George Vasiliades (Aus)
1978	Michel Mercier (Can)
1982	Dean Willey (Eng)
1986	Raymond Williams (Wales)
1990	Chandra Sharma (Ind)

Lightweight

1950	James Halliday (Eng)
1954	Verdi Barberis (Aus)
1958	Tan Howe Liang (Sin)
1962	Carlton Goring (Eng)
1966	Hugo Gittens (Tri)
1970	George Newton (Eng)
1974	George Newton (Eng)
1978	Bill Stellios (Aus)
1982	David Morgan (Wales)
1986	Dean Willey (Eng)
1990	Paramjit Sharma (Ind)

Middleweight

1950	Gerard Gratton (Can)
1954	James Halliday (Eng)
1958	Blair Blenman (Bar)
1962	Tan Howe Laing (Sin)
1966	Pierre St Jean (Can)
1970	Russell Perry (Aus)
1974	Tony Ebert (NZ)

1978	Sam Castiglione (Aus)
1982	Stephen Pinsent (Eng)
1986	Bill Stellios (Aus)
1990	Ron Laycock (Aus)

Light-heavyweight

1950	James Varaleau (Can)
1954	Gerry Gratton (Can)
1958	Phil Caira (Sco)
1962	Phil Caira (Sco)
1966	George Vakakis (Aus)
1970	Nicolo Ciancio (Aus)
1974	Tony Ford (Eng)
1978	Robert Kabbas (Aus)
1982	Newton Burrowes (Eng)
1986	David Morgan (Wales)
1990	David Morgan (Wal)

Middle-heavyweight

1954	Keevil Daly (Can)
1958	Manoel Santos (Aus)
1962	Louis Martin (Eng)
1966	Louis Martin (Eng)
1970	Louis Martin (Eng)
1974	Nicolo Ciancio (Aus)
1978	Gary Langford (Eng)
1982	Robert Kabbas (Aus)
1986	Keith Boxell (Eng)
1990	Duncan Dawkins (Eng)

Sub-heavyweight

1978	John Burns (Wales)
1982	Oliver Orok (Nig)
1986	Denis Garon (Can)
1990	Andrew Saxton (Eng)

Heavyweight

1950	Harold Cleghorn (NZ)
1954	Doug Hepburn (Can)
1958	Ken McDonald (Eng)
1962	Arthur Shannos (Aus)
1966	Donald Oliver (NZ)
1970	Russell Prior (Can)
1974	Russell Prior (Can)
1978	Russell Prior (Can)
1982	John Burns (Wales)
1986	Kevin Roy (Can)
1990	Mark Thomas (Eng)

Super-heavyweight

1970	Ray Rigby (Aus)
1974	Graham May (NZ)
1978	Jean-Marc Cardinal (Can)
1982	Dean Lukin (Aus)
1986	Dean Lukin (Aus)
1990	Andrew Davies (Wal)

WRESTLING (Freestyle)
Light-flyweight

1970	Ved Prakash (Ind)
1974	Mitchell Kawasaki (Can)
1978	Ashok Kumar (Ind)
1982	Ram Cahnder Sarang (Ind)
1986	Ron Moncur (Can)

Flyweight

1950	Bert Harris (Aus)
1954	Louis Base (SA)
1958	Ian Epton (SA)
1962	Muhammad Niaz (Pak)
1966	Mohammad Nazir (Pak)
1970	Sudesh Kumar (Ind)
1974	Sudesh Kumar (Ind)
1978	Ray Takahashi (Can)
1982	Mahabir Singh (Ind)
1986	Chris Woodcroft (Can)

Bantamweight
1930	James Trifunov (Can)
1934	Edward Melrose (Sco)
1938	Ted Purcell (Aus)
1950	Douglas Mudgeway (NZ)
1954	Geoffrey Jameson (Aus)
1958	Mohammad Akhtar (Pak)
1962	Siraj-ud-Din (Pak)
1966	Bishambar Singh (Ind)
1970	Sadar Mohd (Pak)
1974	Premnath (Ind)
1978	Satbir Singh (Ind)
1982	Brian Aspen (Eng)
1986	Mitch Ostberg (Can)

Featherweight
1930	Clifford Chilcott (Can)
1934	Robert McNab (Can)
1938	Roy Purchase (Aus)
1950	John Armitt (NZ)
1954	Abraham Geldenhuys (SA)
1958	Abraham Geldenhuys (SA)
1962	Ala-ud-Din (Pak)
1966	Mohammad Akhtar (Pak)
1970	Mohammad Saeed (Pak)
1974	Egon Beiler (Can)
1978	Egon Beiler (Can
1982	Bob Robinson (Can)
1986	Paul Hughes (Can)

Lightweight
1930	Howard Thomas (Can)
1934	Richard Garrard (Aus)
1938	Richard Garrard (Aus)
1950	Richard Garrard (Aus)
1954	Godfrey Pienaar (SA)
1958	Muhammad Ashraf (Pak)
1962	Muhammad Akhtar (Pak)
1966	Mukhtiar Singh (Ind)
1970	Udey Chand (Ind)
1974	Jagrup Singh (Ind)
1978	Zsigmund Kelevitz (Aus)
1982	Jagminder Singh (Ind)
1986	David McKay (Can)

Welterweight
1930	Reg Priestley (Can)
1934	Joseph Schleimer (Can)
1938	Thomas Trevaskis (Aus)
1950	Henry Hudson (Can)
1954	Nicholas Laubscher (SA)
1958	Muhammad Bashir (Pak)
1962	Muhammad Bashir (Pak)
1966	Muhammad Bashir (Pak)
1970	Mukhtiar Singh (Ind)
1974	Raghunath Pawar (Ind)
1978	Rajinder Singh (Ind)
1982	Rajinder Singh (Ind)
1986	Gary Holmes (Can)

Middleweight
1930	Mike Chepwick (Can)
1934	Terry Evans (Can)
1938	Terry Evans (Can)
1950	Maurice Vachon (Can)
1954	Hermanus van Zyl (SA)
1958	Hermanus van Zyl (SA)
1962	Muhammad Faiz (Pak)
1966	Muhammad Faiz (Pak)
1970	Harish Rajindra (Ind)
1974	David Aspin (NZ)
1978	Richard Deschatelets (Can)
1982	Chris Rinke (Can)
1986	Chris Rinke (Can)

Light-heavyweight
1930	Bill McIntyre (Can)
1934	Mick Cubbin (SA)
1938	Edward Scarf (Aus)
1950	Patrick Morton (SA)
1954	Jacob Theron (SA)
1958	Jacob Theron (SA)
1962	Anthony Buck (Eng)
1966	Robert Chamberot (Can)
1970	Muhammad Faiz (Pak)
1974	Terry Paice (Can)
1978	Stephen Danier (Can)
1982	Clark Davis (Can)
1986	Noel Loban (Eng)

Heavyweight
1930	Earl McCready (Can)
1934	Jack Knight (Aus)
1938	Jack Knight (Aus)
1950	James Armstrong (Aus)
1954	Kenneth Richmond (Eng)
1958	Lila Ram (Ind)
1962	Muhammad Niaz (Pak)
1966	Bhim Singh (Ind)
1970	Edward Millard (Can)
1974	Claude Pilon (Can)
1978	Wyatt Wishart (Can)
1982	Richard Deschatelets (Can)
1986	Clark Davis (Can)

Super-heavyweight
1970	Ikram Ilahi (Pak)
1974	Bill Benko (Can)
1978	Robert Gibbons (Can)
1982	Wyatt Wishart (Can)
1986	Wayne Brightwell (Can)

CRICKET

THE YEAR OF THE BAT

On the first morning of England's first Test of 1990, the West Indies were cruising along at 62 for no wicket, England's bowlers were getting nowhere and the balance of power in world cricket looked to be exactly where it was throughout the 1980s.

Then Gordon Greenidge tucked the ball down to Devon Malcolm at long leg. The ball rebounded off Malcolm's knee; Greenidge underestimated his man and attempted to run a second. The throw zeroed in. Greenidge was out, West Indies collapsed to 164 all out and England won the Test match by nine wickets. It had been 16 years and 30 Tests since England had beaten the West Indies. A lot of people underestimated Devon Malcolm and his team-mates. They broke the sequence when no one expected it and the Kingston Test will be remembered as one of the greatest and most improbable victories of all time. The previous summer England had been humiliated by Australia. This was a new chapter.

It was a chapter that belonged to England's captain Graham Gooch. By the end of the summer, he had established himself beyond any doubt as the pre-eminent figure in English cricket with a stature both as player and leader unmatched by anyone for at least a generation. England still lost the series in West Indies; they lost the last two Tests when Gooch was absent injured. But they came back home, beat both New Zealand and India and set off for Australia with a confidence that would have been unthinkable a year earlier. Much of this was due to Gooch's leadership, which displayed a selflessness and a sureness of touch few people thought he possessed.

But Gooch led mainly by example: the victory against India came at Lord's in another extraordinary and wonderful Test match which represented the apogee of Gooch's career. He amassed 333 in the first innings, a performance that broke a whole stack of records and the Indian bowlers' hearts. Then he hit 123 in the second innings, giving him more runs than any cricketer has ever scored in a first-class match except when Hanif Mohammad took 499 for Karachi off the bowlers of Bahawalpur, in rather more obscure circumstances.

Gooch spent the summer rearranging the record books. He finished the English season with 2746 runs and an average of almost 102. But for getting injured again and missing Essex's last two matches, he could well have become the first man since Bill Alley in 1961 to pass 3,000. Considering that he played in all the Tests and so only batted in ten Championship matches, this was a phenomenal achievement.

MAN OF THE YEAR

Before the Lord's Test, Graham Gooch was no more than a cricketer, a bit special, but still a cricketer. Ten days later, he has become a legend."
Robin Marlar, Sunday Times

"It was OK."
Graham Gooch on his 333

"I know I look like a totally miserable sod on television. I wish I didn't. But there you are."
Gooch

Q "Is this the pinnacle of your career, Graham?"

A **"Well, it's nice to be asked."**
Gooch on being appointed captain in Australia.

"Gooch IS the leadership. This is the side he created in his own dedicated, charmless and spectacularly efficient image. He is the sun around which the team revolves."
Simon Barnes, The Times

"An authentically important phenomenon, the new Briton-forceful, plebeian, undeferential, a winner. He is cricket's Thatcher."
Sunday Telegraph on Gooch

But he was not alone. 1990 was the greatest summer for batsmen in modern times. Gooch's 333 was not even the highest score. In a freakish four-day Championship match at The Oval, Neil Fairbrother made 366 during a Lancashire innings of 863 (the second-highest total in Championship history) which was in reply to Surrey's 707 (the tenth-highest).

Jimmy Cook of Somerset also made a triple-century. There were 29 other double-centuries, a normal ration for five years and 428 centuries, the most ever. Almost every week new batting records fell, many of them ancient, some of them cherished. In the midst of Gooch's triumph at Lord's, Tom Moody, Warwickshire's Australian, knocked nine minutes off Percy Fender's famous fastest hundred, set in 35 dramatic minutes seventy years before; Moody was being fed donkey-drops by the Glamorgan batsmen to get a declaration. As one eye-witness, Edward Bevan of the *Daily Telegraph*, wrote: "It was a mockery of the national averages, the feats of great players of the past and the game of cricket."

But the same could be said of the whole season. 1990 saw probably the greatest change in the balance of power between bat and ball in the game's history. The counties, having rejected the idea of switching completely to four-day cricket, saw their three-day games become utterly untenable since results were almost always impossible without declarations. At The Oval, even seven-day games might not have been long enough.

DURING HIS 333 AT LORD'S GRAHAM GOOCH...

Batted 627 minutes, faced 485 balls, hit 43 fours and three sixes
Became the first man to score four Test centuries at Lord's
Took his career total past 30,000 runs
Made the record score by any Test captain
Hit the 12th triple-century in Test cricket
Made the highest score at Lord's
Made the highest score against India

AND FOR AN ENCORE...

Scored 123 in the second innings to become the first man to score five Test centuries at Lord's
Beat the England run-scoring record for a home series against India in one match
Made his aggregate in the game 456, the second-highest in any first-class match, behind Hanif Mohammad's 499 for Karachi v Bahawalpur, 1958-9.
Became the first man to score a triple century and a century in the same first-class match

---

How did it happen? There were at least four reasons, the first being another hot, dry and, for bowlers, punishing summer. Secondly, a new ball was introduced with a less prominent seam which made it far more difficult for ordinary medium-pace bowlers to take wickets. Thirdly, the threat of a 25-point deduction in the County Championship made it impossible for groundsmen to prepare fair pitches; they were terrified that a surface which gave any help to the bowlers would lead to the club being punished (though in the event, only Derbyshire copped it). Fourthly, and more arguably, the art and science of batting - in England anyway - does now seem to be better-developed than bowling. But by the end of the season, even Gooch, the chief beneficiary, was arguing that things had gone too far and that Lord's had to give the bowlers more chance.

ARISE, SIR RICHARD

The bat's dominance gradually spilled over into the summer's two Test series. The first, against New Zealand was played against the competition of the soccer World Cup and attracted little public attention. The main interest in the game at Lord's was whether the scorecard could cope with the change in the name of R J Hadlee, who became Sir Richard in the Queen's Birthday Honours. It did.

In February, Hadlee had become the first man to take 400 Test wickets when he bowled Sanjay Manjrekar of India in Christchurch; he was presented with a bouquet and the loudspeaker played My Way. Hadlee said he was retiring before the England tour. Then he changed his mind. He had Gooch lbw for nought with his first ball of the series (a most misleading indicator of what was to come) and Malcolm lbw for nought with his last, which gave him five wickets in a Test innings for the 36th time. Then, laden with the praise of the cricketing world, he really did retire. We think.

England won the last Test giving them their first home series win since 1985. John Wright, the New Zealand captain, had put them in to bat on a pitch which then deteriorated fast. Wright, very graciously, accepted the blame. At Lord's, Mohammed Azharuddin, the Indian captain, also decided to bowl first. Having had plenty of time to reflect during Gooch's 333, he insisted he had done the right thing. During the Indian series, Gooch's batting was matched - in quality if not in quantity - by Azharuddin himself and the 17-year-old prodigy Sachin Tendulkar who saved India from defeat at Old Trafford by becoming (after Mushtaq Mohammad) the second-youngest Test century-maker in history.

INDIAN SUMMER

" One of the beauties of cricket is how it lends itself to such diverse renderings...It is no good expecting an Englishman to bat like it. You might as well ask a greyhound to retrieve a pheasant or a labrador to win the greyhound derby."
John Woodcock, The Times, *on Mohammed Azharuddin*

"He must hold in the locket around his neck not only some verses of the Koran but also the secret of dazzling strokeplay, the key to cricket played by Trumper and McCabe and the other immortals, and by Worrell at his freest and Gower at his best."
Scyld Berry, Sunday Correspondent, *on Azharuddin*

"India could score anything with women, without a cricket ball. What female wouldn't be lifted spinning to well beyond her boundary by those dusky limbs, flashing teeth under sexy moustaches, and flying manes of blue-black hair? Even the exotic names of these latter-day Indian princes chime like temple bells at sunset reflected in the Ganges."
Jean Rook, Daily Express, *on Azharuddin's team*

"The Indian bowling attack is the worst I've seen in Test cricket."
Ray Illingworth, Daily Express

"As the greatest run-getter of all time you have undone all your deeds at one stroke by ridiculing the greatest institution of cricket in the world. You have proven that only the mighty can be petty. I feel personally quite disgusted and ashamed I ever played cricket with you."
Bishen Bedi's letter to Gavaskar

"Gavaskar is a patriot and has put the MCC in its place."
Editorial in Delhi Midday

"As our contribution to the UN's response to the Iraqi invasion of Kuwait, the Government is sending a detachment of MCC gatemen with instructions not to return until they have ejected President Saddam Hussein by the scruff of his neck. **"**
Ned Sherrin, Loose Ends, Radio Four

And then there was David Gower, who had a very curious year indeed. Having been deprived of the captaincy after the Australian debacle and left out of the West Indies tour, his life changed very dramatically. He split with both his fiancée Vicki Stewart, after many years, and his county Leicestershire, joining Hampshire instead. He narrowly escaped death when he tried to drive across a Swiss lake which was less frozen than he thought. He went out to the West Indies as a columnist for *The Times* but was brought in to play against Barbados after Gooch was injured. Gower thought he was going to play in the final Test in Antigua then was stood down just before the game - apparently at the insistence of the manager Micky Stewart.

In England, he was brought back for the one-day internationals against New Zealand, dropped again, recalled to play against India, kept failing and appeared to be on the brink of being dropped yet again. Then, at The Oval, with England needing to bat out the game, Gower saved both the team and himself by scoring 157 not out. It was noted that for this innings Gower had abandoned his frivolous blue socks for businesslike grey. Amid all his ups and downs, he still managed to become England's second most prolific Test batsman, overhauling Colin Cowdrey to be behind only Geoff Boycott.

The England management's handling of Gower was just one of the oddities of the West Indies tour. During the Bridgetown Test, which West Indies won to square the series, Vivian Richards charged towards umpire Lloyd Barker after appealing for a catch against Robert Bailey. To English eyes, this appeared to change Barker's mind. The English commentator Christopher Martin-Jenkins's description of the incident caused offence throughout the Caribbean and led to Barker issuing a writ. The cartoonist Nick Newman suggested a new line-up for Test Match Special: Johnners, Blowers, Jenkers and Lawyers. During the Antigua Test, Richards chose not to lead his team on to the field for the second day; instead he was in the press box threatening James Lawton of the *Daily Express*. Late in this game, a West Indian umpire - at long, long last - warned someone for intimidatory bowling: it was, to general disbelief and hilarity, the English medium-pacer David Capel. A Trinidad woman, Marilyn Williams, asked Gooch to adopt her baby.

New English players began to move into prominence. Devon Malcolm, the Jamaican-born Derbyshire fast bowler who was ridiculed when he first appeared for England in 1989, brilliantly established himself on tour. "If we could," said the West Indian commentator Tony Cozier, "we'd like him back please." Mike Atherton of Lancashire emerged, fresh from Cambridge, as Gooch's opening partner and England captain-in-waiting. Robin Smith, Angus Fraser and (to most eyes) Jack Russell continued to enhance their reputations.

NOISES OFF

Most of the major English cricketing figures of the 80s were far less prominent in the New Age. Ian Botham battled with injuries and the years at Worcester and mostly appeared to be losing. During a cup-tie at Bristol, he hit six sixes, one of which smashed a picture of Gilbert Jessop in the pavilion, and he played a memorable innings in a quarter-final at Northampton. But his county still lost, which never happened when he played like that in the old days. Botham was among the 43 players asked if he was available to tour Australia but was never likely to be among the final 16. He declined to reply. Having taken part in a number of pantomimes while playing for England, he signed to spend Christmas in Jack and the Beanstalk at the Alhambra Theatre, Bradford. It was a fair bet that the next time a Botham appeared for England it would be his son Liam. Playing in an under-13 game for Cundall Manor Prep School, Thirsk, against Red House, York, Botham jnr scored 161 not out in a total of 208 and then took ten wickets for three - seven bowled, three lbw. Dad was very proud.

Mike Gatting's alternative tour to South Africa turned into the biggest pantomime of them all. His team of malcontents were forced home after a succession of demonstrations outside the grounds, associated troubles in black townships and traditional South African police over-reaction. There was much farce: bewildered blacks were bribed and bussed into games while hotel workers refused to serve the players their meals. Gatting himself displayed considerable personal courage. It all could, however, have led to tragedy. Fortunately, before there was a fatality, the South African Cricket Union did a deal with the National Sports Congress, who arranged the protests, sending

...BUT NOT FORGOTTEN

" Form is temporary. Class is permanent."

Ian Botham's T-shirt

"He used to be included just because he was Ian Botham. Now he is being left out for the same reason. The two wrongs do not make a right."

Tim de Lisle, Independent on Sunday

"I'm very pleased to be still considered one of the best 43 cricketers in England."

Ian Botham on being asked by the TCCB if he was available for the Ashes tour

"Now there can be no way back for him...hopes of a Botham revival have been sustained largely by general nostalgia and tabloid imagination."

Alan Lee, The Times, when Botham refused to reply

"A fat has-been"

Dermot Reeve, Warwickshire cricketer, on Botham

"I would love to sit in a deckchair and watch Malcolm Marshall knock his block off. "

Ian Botham, asked if he would tour with Peter Roebuck

the team back early and cancelling the next tour. The seventh rebel tour of South Africa was almost certainly the last. The South African government's decision to begin negotiating with its black population led to talks between the rival cricket authorities as well and there were growing hopes that South Africa might be able to return to Test cricket, with a general welcome, in the mid-1990s. The welcome was not there yet: returning home, Gatting had a pint of beer poured over him in a Cambridge pub.

Gatting was then largely forgotten. But he achieved one triumph over Gooch when Middlesex saw off a late surge from Essex and won the County Championship for the 10th time. Essex were 15th in early June then briefly took the lead before Gooch was injured. Hampshire came third ahead of the deposed champions, Worcestershire, after making 446 to beat Gloucestershire in the final game. Gloucestershire and Leicestershire both imported distinguished overseas managers, Bobby Simpson and Eddie Barlow, to no obvious effect. Glamorgan imported Viv Richards to bat and came eighth, their highest position in 20 years. Sussex came bottom but won the Second XI Competition, often a harbinger of better days ahead.

Lancashire dominated one-day cricket and became the first county to win both Lord's finals in the same season. Both games were too one-sided to be exciting. They crushed Worcestershire in the Benson and Hedges and in the NatWest final their fast bowler Phil DeFreitas settled the game even more conclusively by taking five Northamptonshire wickets inside the first hour. Of the last 17 Cup finals in dewy September, 14 have been won by the team batting second.

The earlier rounds were affected by the same batting mania that afflicted the first-class season. Lancashire scored a competition record 352 for six in the B and H against Hampshire only to have it expunged when the game was abandoned through rain. But that total soon seemed puny. Against Gloucestershire in the NatWest, Lancashire scored 372 and won by 241 runs. They had hoped to get five players into the England party to tour Australia but managed one. A Lancastrian, Colin Snape, suggested in a letter to *The Times* that the north should take revenge, declare UDI and take on the south in Tests. Derbyshire won the Sunday League for the first time while Somerset destroyed the League batting record by scoring 360 for three against Glamorgan at Neath, 50 more than ever before; they also scored 413 for four in a NatWest game against the unfortunate part-timers of Devon. The Test and County Cricket Board, in its infinite dedication to the traditions and integrity of the game, began painting sponsors' names on outfields and announced plans to put them on England players' shirts. Satellite TV moved into cricket: Rupert Murdoch's channel Sky showed the series in the West Indies, complete with crass commentary from Tony Greig; both Sky and its rival BSB won a share of the domestic season as well and most viewers were unable to watch the Sunday

League or the Benson and Hedges Cup. Only 107,000 watched the three Tests against New Zealand, the lowest for a series in England since 1982. This was partly inevitable. Much of Lord's was unusable as the new Compton and Edrich stands, supposed to be finished for the start of the season, remained a construction site.

The last but one major ground to deny women access to the pavilion relented in the spring when Lancashire voted to give women full membership. It transpired that one woman was already in: Ms Stephanie Lloyd rose at the AGM to announce that she had joined the club before her operation when she was Mr K Hull. The last bastion remained impregnable. Mrs Pat Lloyd (no relation to Stephanie), a Glamorgan committee member, was barred from the Lord's pavilion during her team's NatWest quarter-final there. "I wasn't going to stand in my suspenders, knock on the pavilion door and demand to get in," she said. The former England women's captain Rachel Heyhoe-Flint applied to join, having discovered that no rule specifically forbade women from becoming members and Colonel John Stephenson, the MCC secretary, speculated that women would be allowed in the pavilion, perhaps in the 22nd century. It was unclear whether the new stands would be finished first. Meanwhile, MCC began a programme of conducted tours round Lord's for the public, aimed at Japanese tourists; a talking head of W G Grace was put in the museum. Two hundred seats from the Lord's pavilion were offered to MCC members and all snapped up in a week. "There's been a greater clamour for these seats than for Test match tickets," said a spokesman."It's been total chaos." David Pennington, a 46-year-old management consultant and MCC member, was given a suspended prison sentence after he admitted attacking his fiancée with his club tie.

NOT CRICKET

During Glamorgan's cup-tie at Lord's, there were fights between rival football supporters from Swansea and Cardiff. The Indoor Cricket Federation said it was worried by obscenities and taunting of players at their knock-out cup. "We didn't get fights or anything like that," said the ICF chairman Peter Robinson, "but I don't even like to see people stubbing out cigarettes on the carpet." The game between France and Germany in the European Cricketer Cup in Guernsey came close to fisticuffs when a German bowler Francis Stewart (really Australian) threw the ball in celebration at a dismissed French batsman Nigel Drummond (really English) and hit him on the legs. Drummond threw his bat at the bowler. "These are the Friendly Games," said Mike Burbridge of the Guernsey Tourist Board. In Bhopal, India, during the Nehru Cup, a boy killed his brother for predicting that Pakistan would win the competition. They did.

Curtly Ambrose of Northamptonshire was warned for bowling three beamers at Dermot Reeve of Warwickshire. Paul Smith of Warwickshire (size 10) took a hat-trick for Warwickshire at Eastbourne wearing a boot borrowed from his team-mate Tim Munton (size 12). Munton claimed a share in the feet if not the feat. Bob White and Alan Whitehead, the umpires at a Sunday match between Glamorgan and Surrey at Cardiff, watched a TV recording before deciding the result. Viv Richards had hit a four to win the game but as the fielders walked off they noticed that a bail had been dislodged. After seeing the recording, the umpires agreed it might have blown off. A deer ran across the outfield during a rain stoppage at The Parks, Oxford.

Among first-class cricketers to announce their retirements were Alvin Kallicharran (41), Geoff Cook (38), David Graveney (37), Brian Hardie (40), Grahame Clinton (37) and Jonathan Agnew (30). Cook took a job helping County Durham's campaign for first-class status; Agnew was appointed cricket correspondent of the newspaper *Today*. David Bairstow (38) was sacked by Yorkshire after 20 years but managed to climb into 14th place in the all-time wicket-keeping list, ahead of George Duckworth. Geoff Miller (38) left Derbyshire, for the second time.

Granada TV and the Australian network, Channel Nine, both experimented with mini-cameras inside the middle stump while televising a Roses match. Channel Nine were forced to give up plans to include one inside the umpires' hats. The Gloucester helmet-makers, WG Cricket, reported a 1000% rise in sales. Edgar Watts of Bungay, once Bradman's batmakers, announced their closure because gales had led to a shortage of mature willows. Callers ringing a TV phone-in on the future of Yorkshire cricket instead found themselves put through to a helpline on the problems of premature ejaculation. British Telecom said it was their engineers' fault.

FUN FOR ALL AGES

Cyril Hollinshead, an 88-year-old slow left-armer, took three wickets in five overs in a game in Gloucestershire. Dennis Bishop, a 77-year-old offspinner who plays for the Stanford-le-Hope club in Essex, took his 5,000th wicket since he began keeping records after the war; he first played in 1928 but did not bother counting then. Harold Stead, 69, who had played for Boconnoc in Cornwall since he was nine, left the club to play for its rivals Penharrow. Jack Green, 68, headed the winning four for the Co-op in Sheffield against Eastwoods. Sam Bardney, 15, asked to make up the numbers for Warmsworth in Doncaster, took all 10 wickets against Brecks.

Greg Fitzgerald of Old Brentwood hit 42 in an over (which included a no-ball) bowled by Ian Mundy of Hoddesdon. Simon Harrington, playing for Halstead against Hadleigh, took a hat-trick comprising three members of the same family: Steve Claireaux, his brother Vincent and his father Clive. Alton 2nd XI were bowled out by Bournemouth for nought. "It was just one of those days," said their captain Steve Goater. In Durham, Darlington beat Synthonia without a run coming off the bat. Only two Synthonia players turned up and one, Steven Eland, was bowled fourth ball for nought. He then bowled a wide when Darlington's openers batted with their team-mates acting as fielders. PC Steve Crouch, playing for Sudbury Police against Newton Green, had the apposite bowling figures of 9 for 9 in 9 overs. Edward Palmer, 15, playing for Winchester Junior Colts v Canford Junior Colts, scored 103 and took 10 for 13; the statistician Robert Brooke unearthed 45 similar cases. Bill Kingston of St Michaels bowled Peter Teckman of the Bold Dragoon at 4.17 am on June 21, at the start of a Longest Day charity match in Northampton.

John Whibley lost the captaincy of the GEC Alsthom team at Stafford after writing a letter to the local paper criticising his team-mates. He then poured sodium chlorate on the pitch, rendering it useless for weeks and was fined £150 for criminal damage. A motorist at Nuneaton drove on to the pitch and flattened the stumps after a six went through his windscreen. Andrew Mathewman of Penistone left a game to take his wife to hospital where she gave birth to a daughter. He returned to run out the last batsman. A swarm of bees stopped play during a Welsh cup tie between Brecon and Miskin Manor and a shower of wheat stalks forced suspension of play at Devizes, though there was no wind and no fields nearby. Ipplepen CC in Devon voted Holly the collie Fielder of the Year because of her skill finding lost balls. Roger and Tracey Weston of Worcester named their baby son Liam Bobby so he could have the initials LBW.

Further afield, New South Wales won the Sheffield Shield for the 40th time; the remarkably prolific Mark Taylor scored two centuries in the final. Geoff Marsh scored 355 for Western Australia against South Australia, the equal 21st highest score ever though not the highest in the past year (see Fairbrother, above). Darren Lehmann of South Australia, 20, became the youngest player to score 1,000 runs in an Australian season, beating Doug Walters' record (1965-66) by 25 days. Darren Berry, the South Australian wicket-keeper, set a world record by not conceding a bye while 2,133 runs were scored. Greg Shipperd scored the slowest first-class century ever - 449 minutes for Tasmania against Western Australia. In Sharjah, Simon O'Donnell scored the fastest 50 in a one-day international, in 18 balls against Sri Lanka.

Dr Donald Curran, writing in the *Australian Medical Journal*, said the tradition of Australian players drinking their way from Sydney to London before a tour could prove lethal. David Boon was said to have drunk 58 cans of beer en route to the 1989 tour of England, breaking Rod Marsh's record of 50; Boon, however, was helped by a longer stopover in Bahrain. The Association of Cricket Statisticians revealed that Sir Donald Bradman attended 1,713 committee meetings of the South Australian Cricket Association between September 1935 and June 1986. Lynette Batt met Jeremy Ball at an indoor school in Perth and subsequently married him.

ROBERT VANCE'S CRAZY OVER

The following took place in the space of one over between Canterbury and Wellington at Christchurch:
Vance to Germon: 0 4 4 4 6 6 4 6 1
Vance to Ford: 4 1
Vance to Germon: 0 6 6 6 6 6 0 0 4 0 1
Only balls 2, 18, 19, 21 and 22 were legitimate; the rest were deliberate no-balls. The over was completed after five balls because of an umpire's error.

In a Shell Trophy game in Christchurch, Canterbury scored a world first-class record 77 in an over off Robert Vance of Wellington. It was the penultimate over and Vance bowled 17 deliberate soft no-balls to keep Canterbury interested in victory and thus give themselves a chance of bowling them out. Lee Germon scored 69 in the over, including eight sixes. The umpires became so confused that only five legitimate balls were bowled. After 17 more off the last over, including further no-balls from Evan Gray, Canterbury only needed one to win off the last ball. The batsman made no attempt to hit it. Nearer home, the phrase "le cricket" was accepted by the Académie Française as being part of the French language along with le cowboy and la cover-girl. There is hope for them yet.

1990

WEST INDIES V ENGLAND

First Test *Kingston, Jamaica, Feb 24-Mar 1*

Compared to the team that lost to Australia at The Oval six months earlier, Larkins, Stewart, Lamb, Hussain, Fraser and Malcolm replaced Stephenson, Atherton, Gower, Pringle, Cook and Igglesden. Debuts: Stewart, Hussain (England).

West Indies won the toss.

WEST INDIES
First Innings

C G Greenidge run out	32
D L Haynes c & b Small	36
R B Richardson c Small b Capel	10
C A Best c Russell b Capel	4
C L Hooper c Capel b Fraser	20
* I V A Richards lbw b Malcolm	21
†P J L Dujon not out	19
M D Marshall b Fraser	0
I R Bishop c Larkins b Fraser	0
C A Walsh b Fraser	6
B P Patterson b Fraser	0
Extras (b9 nb4 lb3)	16
Total	**164**

Fall: 1-62 2-81 3-92 4-92 5-124 6-144 7-144 8-150 9-164

Bowling: Small 15-6-44-1 Malcolm 16-4-49-1 Fraser 20-8-28-5 Capel 13-4-31-2
West Indies' lowest score against England since 1969.

ENGLAND
First Innings

*G.A. Gooch c Dujon b Patterson	18
W Larkins lbw b Walsh	46
A J Stewart c Best b Bishop	13
A J Lamb c Hooper b Walsh	132
R A Smith c Best b Bishop	57
N Hussain c Dujon b Bishop	13
D J Capel c Richardson b Walsh	5
†R C Russell c Patterson b Walsh	26
G C Small lbw b Marshall	4
A R C Fraser not out	2
D E Malcolm lbw b Walsh	0
Extras (b23 lb12 w1 nb12)	48
Total	**364**

Fall: 1-40 2-60 3-116 4-288 5-315 6-315 7-325 8-339 9-364

Bowling : Patterson 18-2-74-1 Bishop 27-5-72-3 Marshall 18-3-46-1 Walsh 27.2-4-68-5 Hooper 6-0-28-0 Richards 9-1-22-0 Best 4-0-19-0
Lamb's 10th Test hundred but his first outside England. England's highest total against West Indies for 41 innings since The Oval 1980.

WEST INDIES
Second Innings

C G Greenidge c Hussain b Malcolm	36
D L Haynes b Malcolm	14
R B Richardson lbw b Fraser	25
C A Best c Gooch b Small	64
C L Hooper c Larkins b Small	8
* I V A Richards b Malcolm	37
† P J L Dujon b Malcolm	15
M D Marshall not out	8
I R Bishop c Larkins b Small	3
C A Walsh b Small	2
B P Patterson run out	2
Extras (b14 lb10 w1 nb1)	26

Total	**240**

Fall: 1-26 2-69 3-87 4-112 5-192 6-222 7-222 8-227 9-237

Bowling: Small 22-6-58-4 Malcolm 21.3-2-77-4 Capel 15-1-50-0 Fraser 14-5-31-1

ENGLAND
Second Innings

*G A Gooch c Greenidge b Bishop	8
W Larkins not out	29
A J Stewart not out	0
Extras (lb1 nb3)	4
Total (1 wkt)	**41**

Fall: 1-35

Did not bat: A J Lamb, R A Smith, N Hussain, D J Capel, R C Russell, G C Small, A R C Fraser, D E Malcolm
Bowling: Patterson 3-1-11-0 Bishop 7.3-3-17-1 Walsh 6-0-12-0

ENGLAND WON BY NINE WICKETS
England's first win against West Indies in 16 years and 30 Tests
Man of the match: Lamb

Second Test *Georgetown, Guyana, Mar 9-14*
ABANDONED WITHOUT A BALL BEING BOWLED

Third Test *Port of Spain, Trinidad, Mar 23-28*
Bailey replaced Hussain. Debut: Moseley (WI). England won toss.

WEST INDIES
First Innings

*D L Haynes c Lamb b Small	0
G C Greenidge c Stewart b Malcolm	5
R B Richardson c Russell b Fraser	8
C A Best c Lamb b Fraser	10
† P J Dujon lbw b Small	4
A L Logie c Lamb b Fraser	98
C L Hooper c Russell b Capel	32
E A Moseley c Russell b Malcolm	0
C E L Ambrose c Russell b Malcolm	7
I R Bishop b Malcolm	16
C A Walsh not out	8
Extras (4lb, 7nb)	11
Total	**199**

Fall: 1-5 2-5 3-22 4-27 5-29 6-92 7-93 8-103 9-177
Bowling: Small 17-4-41-2 Malcolm 20-2-60-4 Fraser 13.1-2-41-3 Capel 15-2-53-1

ENGLAND
First Innings

*G A Gooch c Dujon b Bishop	84
W Larkins c Dujon b Ambrose	54
A J Stewart c Dujon b Ambrose	9
A J Lamb b Bishop	32
R A Smith c Dujon b Moseley	5
R J Bailey c Logie b Moseley	0
D J Capel c Moseley b Ambrose	40
†R C Russell c Best b Walsh	15
G C Small lbw b Bishop	0
A R Fraser c Hooper b Ambrose	11
D E Malcolm not out	0
Extras (b6, lb13, w3, nb16)	38
Total	**288**

Fall: 1-112 2-152 3-195 4-214 5-214 6-214 7-243 8-244 9-284

Bowling: Ambrose 36.2-8-59-4 Bishop 31-6-69-3 Walsh 22-5-45-1 Hooper 18-5-26-0 Moseley 30-5-70-2

WEST INDIES
Second Innings
G C Greenidge lbw b Fraser.....................42
*D L Haynes c Lamb b Malcolm 45
R B Richardson c Gooch b Small 34
C A Best lbw b Malcolm...........................0
†P J Dujon b Malcolm...............................0
A L Logie c Larkins b Malcolm................20
C L Hooper run out 10
E A Moseley c Lamb b Malcolm 26
C E L Ambrose c Russell b Fraser 18
I R Bishop not out 15
C A Walsh lbw b Malcolm..........................1
Extras (b2, lb13, w1, nb12)......................28
Total **239**

Fall: 1-96 2-100 3-100 4-100 5-142 6-167 7-200 8-200
9-234
Bowling: Malcolm 26.2-5-77-6 Small 28-8-56-1 Capel
13-3-30-0 Fraser 24-4-61-2
*Malcolm was the first England bowler to take 10 in a
match against West Indies since Tony Greig, 1973-4.*

ENGLAND
Second Innings
*G A Gooch retired hurt 18
W Larkins c Dujon b Moseley 7
A J Stewart c Bishop b Walsh 31
A J Lamb lbw b Bishop............................25
R A Smith lbw b Walsh.............................2
R J Bailey b Walsh 0
D J Capel not out 17
†R C Russell not out 5
Extras (b2, lb7, nb6)................................15
Total (5 wkts).....................................**120**
Did not bat: G C Small, A R Fraser, D E Malcolm

Fall: 1-27 2-74 3-79 4-85 5-106
Bowling: Bishop 10-1-31-1 Ambrose 6-0-20-0 Moseley
10-2-33-1 Walsh 7-0-27-3
MATCH DRAWN
*England needed only 78 to win just after lunch on the last
day with nine wickets left. It then rained for three hours
and England were denied victory by bad light and a slow
over-rate. Gooch had his hand broken by Moseley.*
Man of the match: Malcolm

Fourth Test *Bridgetown, Barbados, Apr 5-10*
*Gooch missed a match through injury for the first time in
his career. Lamb England captain for the first time.*
Hussain for Gooch. DeFreitas for Fraser (injured).
England won toss.

WEST INDIES
First Innings
G C Greenidge c Russell b DeFreitas 41
D L Haynes c Stewart b Small 0
R B Richardson c Russell b Small 45
C A Best c Russell b Small.....................164
*I V A Richards c Russell b Capel............70
A L Logie c Russell b Capel 31
†P J L Dujon b Capel...............................31
M D Marshall c Lamb b Small....................4
C E L Ambrose not out 20
I R Bishop run out 10
E A Moseley b DeFreitas 4
Extras (lb8 nb18)....................................26
Total **446**

Fall: 1-6 2-69 3-108 4-227 5-291 6-395 7-406 8-411
9-431
Bowling: Malcolm 33-6-142-0 Small 35-5-109-4
DeFreitas 29.5-5-99-2 Capel 24-5-88-3

*Richards transformed the series psychologically on the
first day by hitting 19 in an over off Malcolm, including
two pulled sixes, both of which were nearly caught. This
overshadowed Best's maiden Test hundred.*

ENGLAND
First Innings
W Larkins c Richardson b Bishop 0
A J Stewart c Richards b Moseley 45
R J Bailey b Bishop.................................17
*A J Lamb lbw b Ambrose.....................119
R A Smith b Moseley..............................62
N Hussain lbw b Marshall........................18
D J Capel c Greenidge b Marshall 2
†R C Russell lbw b Bishop.........................7
P A J DeFreitas c & b Ambrose 24
C L Small not out 1
D E Malcolm b Bishop.............................12
Extras (b14, lb9, w3, nb25)......................51
Total **358**

Fall: 1-1 2-46 3-75 4-268 5-297 6-301 7-308 8-340 9-
340
Bowling: Bishop 24.3-8-70-4 Ambrose 25-2-82-2
Moseley 28-3-114-2 Marshall 23-6-55-2 Richards 9-4-14-0
*Lamb's sixth hundred against the West Indies, more than
anyone except Gavaskar.*

WEST INDIES
Second Innings
G C Greenidge lbw b Small 3
D L Haynes c Malcolm b Small...............109
R B Richardson lbw b DeFreitas...............39
*I V A Richards c Small b Capel 12
A L Logie lbw b DeFreitas........................48
E A Moseley b Small..................................5
M D Marshall c Smith b Small 7
†P J L Dujon not out 15
C E L Ambrose c Capel b DeFreitas...........1
I R Bishop not out 11
Extras (lb12, w1, nb4)..............................17
Total (8 wkts dec) **267**
 Did not bat: C A Best

Fall: 1-13 2-80 3-109 4-223 5-228 6-238 7-238 8-239
Bowling: Malcolm 10-0-46-0 Small 20-1-74-4 DeFreitas
to 22-2-69-3 Capel 16-1-66-1

ENGLAND
Second Innings
A J Stewart c Richards b Ambrose 37
W Larkins c Dujon b Bishop.......................0
R J Bailey c Dujon b Ambrose....................6
G C Small lbw b Ambrose 0
†R C Russell b Ambrose 55
*A J Lamb c Dujon b Moseley 10
R A Smith not out 40
N Hussain lbw b Ambrose 0
D J Capel lbw b Ambrose 6
P A J DeFreitas lbw b Ambrose 0
D E Malcolm lbw b Ambrose 4
Extras (b8, lb9, w1, nb15)........................33
Total **191**

Fall: 1-1 2-10 3-10 4-71 5-97 6-166 7-173 8-181
9-181
Bowling: Bishop 20-7-40-1 Ambrose 22.4-10-45-8
Marshall 18-8-31-0 Moseley 19-3-44-1 Richards 10-5-11-
0 Richardson 2-1-3-0
Man of the Match: Ambrose
His 8-45 were the best figures for West Indies v. England
WEST INDIES WON BY 164 RUNS

Fifth Test *St John's, Antigua, Apr 12-16*

England unchanged.
England won toss

ENGLAND
First Innings

A J Stewart c Richards b Walsh.....................27
W Larkins c Hooper b Ambrose...................30
R J Bailey c Dujon b Bishop 42
*A J Lamb c Richards b Ambrose.................37
R A Smith lbw b Walsh 12
N Hussain c Dujon b Bishop 35
D J Capel c Haynes b Bishop 10
†R C Russell c Dujon b Bishop..........................7
P A J DeFreitas lbw b Bishop.........................21
G C Small lbw b Walsh 8
D E Malcolm not out 0
Extras (b5, lb11, nb15) 31
Total **260**

Fall: 1-42 2-101 3-143 4-167 5-167 6-195 7-212
8-242 9-259

Bowling: Bishop 28.1-6-84-5 Ambrose 29-5-79-2 Walsh
21-4-51-3 Baptiste 13-4-30-0

WEST INDIES
First Innings

G C Greenidge run out 149
D L Haynes c Russell b Small 167
R B Richardson c Russell b Malcolm.............34
C L Hooper b Capel 1
*I V A Richards c Smith b Malcolm 1
A L Logie c Lamb b DeFreitas.......................15
†P J L Dujon run out 25
E A E Baptiste c Russell b Malcolm 9
C E L Ambrose c DeFreitas b Capel 5
I R Bishop not out..14
C A Walsh b Malcolm 8
Extras (lb5, nb13)..18
Total **446**

Fall: 1-298 2-357 3-358 4-359 5-382 6-384 7-415
8-417 9-433

Bowling: Small 31-3-123-1 Malcolm 34.5-3-126-4 Capel
28-1-118-2 DeFreitas 27-4-74-1
Record opening stand for West Indies

ENGLAND
Second Innings

A J Stewart c Richardson b Bishop 8
W Larkins b Ambrose 10
G C Small b Ambrose....................................4
R J Bailey c Dujon b Bishop 8
*A J Lamb b Baptiste 35
R A Smith retired hurt 8
N Hussain c Dujon b Bishop 34
D J Capel run out...1
†R C Russell c Richardson b Ambrose 24
P A J DeFreitas c Greenidge b Ambrose..........0
D E Malcolm not out 1
Extras (b1, lb8, w1, nb11) 21
Total **154**

Fall:1-16 2-20 3-33 4-37 5-86 6-96 7-148 8-148
9-154

Bowling: Bishop 14-2-36-3 Ambrose 13-7-22-4 Walsh
10-1-40-0 Baptiste 10-1-47-1

Man of the Match: Haynes

Man of the Series: Ambrose

WEST INDIES WON BY AN INNINGS AND 32

Leading Batting Averages

	M	I	NO	RUNS	HS	AVGE
1.Allan Lamb (E)	4	7	0	390	132	55.71
2.Desmond Haynes (WI)	4	7	0	371	167	53.00
3.Carlisle Best (WI)	3	5	0	242	164	48.40
4.Gordon Greenidge (WI)	4	7	0	308	149	44.00
5.Graham Gooch (E)	2	4	1	128	84	42.66
6. Gus Logie (WI)	3	5	0	212	98	42.40

Leading Bowling Averages

	M	BLS	RNS	WKS	AVGE	BEST
1.Angus Fraser (E)	2	427	161	11	14.63	5-28
2 .Curtly Ambrose (WI)	3	792	307	20	15.35	8-45
3.Ian Bishop (WI)	4	973	419	21	19.95	5-84
4.Courtney Walsh (WI)	3	560	243	12	20.25	5-68
5.Gladstone Small (E)	4	966	505	17	29.70	4-58
6.Devon Malcolm (E)	4	970	577	19	30.36	6-77

England's Other First-Class Matches in West Indies

Leeward Islands v England XI
Warner Park, St, Kitts, Feb 2-5
Match Drawn
ENGLAND 444-6dec (W Larkins 107, A J Stewart 125)
and 213-6dec; LEEWARD ISLANDS 256 & 301-5

Windward Island v England XI
Mindoo Phillip Park, St Lucia, Feb 8-11
Windward Islands won by 1 wicket
WINDWARD ISLANDS 317 & 139-9; ENGLAND 126
(M Durand 7-15) & 326

Jamaica v England XI
Sabina Park, Kingston, Feb 19-21
Match Drawn
ENGLAND 405 (G A Gooch 239) & 248-4dec (W Larkins
124 rtd hurt); JAMAICA 311 & 44-2

President''s XI v England XI
Guaracara Park, Point-a-Pierre, Mar 17-20
England XI won by 113 runs
ENGLAND 252 & 278 (R C Haynes 6-90);
PRESIDENT'S XI 294 (B C Lara 134) & 123

Barbados v England XI
Kensington Oval, Bridgetown, Mar 30-Apr 1
Match Drawn
BARBADOS 367 (C G Greenidge 183, E E Hemmings 5-
77) & 225-5dec; ENGLAND 158 & 126-1

Tour notes:
England's defeat against the Windward Islands came after
they were forced to follow on by the weakest first-class
team in the Caribbean. Their destroyer, Mervyn Durand, is
a left-arm spinner and (more regularly) an electrician.
The Middlesex fast bowler Ricky Ellcock left the tour
without playing a game due to a back injury. Chris Lewis
was brought from Zimbabwe as a replacement. After
Gooch broke his hand in the Trinidad Test, David Gower
(from the press box) and David Smith (from England) were
called in as replacements.
David Bairstow, who was on a friendly tour with Yorkshire,
was called away from a trip round a rum distillery to keep
wicket as substitute after Bailey was injured in the game
against Barbados. This was against Law 2.2, which
forbids substitute wicket-keepers.

THE HAPPY ISLES

I've collected many bruises about the body facing them, scored a few runs but never beaten them in a Test.
Graham Gooch

"Against the fiercest bowling side in the world it was never less than heavy odds-on that England's cricketers would all be nursing headaches during this tour, but not from celebration hangovers... If there has ever been a more remarkable result in the history of Test cricket, it is hard to call it to mind."
Martin Johnson, The Independent, on the Kingston Test

"For 20 years we have seen Kingsmen jerk back their heads as if hit an invisible uppercut, hop about wringing their fingers and throw down their bats as if the handle were red-hot. The difference this time was that they were wearing maroon helmets."
Peter Johnson, Daily Mail, on the Trinidad Test

"Both sides have cheated on the overs and yesterday a very good umpire cracked under pressure...It wasn't his mistake that was so sad. It was the fact that Lloyd Barker was pressurised into changing his initial decision. If that is gamesmanship or professionalism, I am not quite sure what cheating is."
Christopher Martin-Jenkins, BBC Radio, during the Barbados Test

"My little jig was very ceremonial."
Viv Richards

"Viv appeals that way all the time and no one coerces me."
Lloyd Barker

"I withdraw the word cheating, although everyone should ask themselves if the alternative words, professionalism and gamesmanship, are not in fact euphemisms."
Christopher Martin-Jenkins

"All the radio commentator is required to do is to tell his listeners what the umpire's decision is. That decision does not need his approval, and even when he suggests that he agrees with it, he is detracting from the authority of the judge from whose decision the laws of the game provide no appeal."
Editorial in Weekend Nation, Barbados

"CAPTAIN VIV BLOWS HIS TOP"
Headline in Daily Express

"Someone's going to sort you out and it may be me."
Viv Richards blowing his top to James Lawton of the Daily Express after seeing the headline

"Richards... a man always happy to change a kerfuffle into a first-class row."
Simon Barnes, The Times

"I don't think Viv entertains any animosity against anyone."
Clive Lloyd, West Indies manager

"Sir, At my level of cricket we have a solution to the problem of difficult fixtures. When there is a club which regularly beats us and against which no one really enjoys playing, we wait until we can inflict a rare defeat on them and then promptly drop the fixture. Given England's recent success and the resulting display of bad sportsmanship from the West Indies, perhaps the TCCB should consider adopting the same policy."
Letter to The Times from Oliver Gravell of London W12

"Forget the time-honoured phrase 'It's not cricket'. The fact is that Test cricket itself is not any longer cricket."
David Miller, The Times

"Russell set the highest possible standard behind the stumps."
Vic Marks, The Observer, after the West Indies tour

"The keeping in this series was abysmal.**
Robin Marlar, Sunday Times, ditto

CORNHILL TESTS

ENGLAND V NEW ZEALAND

First Test *Trent Bridge, Jun 7-12*
Compared to the previous Test in Antigua, Gooch (fit again), Atherton, Fairbrother and Hemmings returned instead of Larkins, Hussain (injured), Bailey and Capel (dropped). Debut: Priest (NZ)
NZ won the toss
NEW ZEALAND
First Innings
T J Franklin b Malcolm 33
J G Wright c Stewart b Small 8

A H Jones c Stewart b Malcolm....................39
M D Crowe b DeFreitas 59
M J Greatbatch b Hemmings..........................1
M W Priest c Russell b DeFreitas 26
M C Snedden c Gooch b DeFreitas.................0
J G Bracewell c Gooch b Small 28
R J Hadlee b DeFreitas....................................0
†I D Smith not out..2
D K Morrison lbw b DeFreitas 0
Extras (b1, lb10, w1).....................................12
Total **208**

Fall: 1-16 2-75 3-110 4-121 5-170 6-174 7-191 8-191 9-203

Bowling: Small 29-9-49-2   Malcolm 19-7-48-2
Hemmings 19-6-47-1 DeFreitas 22-6-53-5

ENGLAND

First Innings

*G A Gooch lbw b Hadlee	0
M A Atherton c Snedden b Priest	151
A J Stewart c Small b Hadlee	27
A J Lamb lbw b Hadlee	0
R A Smith c Smith b Bracewell	55
N H Fairbrother c Franklin b Snedden	19
†R C Russell c Snedden b Morrison	28
P A J DeFreitas lbw b Bracewell	14
G C Small c Crowe b Hadlee	26
E E Hemmings not out	13
D E Malcolm not out	4
Extras (2b, 3lb, 3nb)	8
Total (9 wkts dec)	345

Fall: 1-0 2-43 3-45 4-141 5-168 6-260 7-302 8-306 9-340

Bowling: Hadlee 33-6-89-4 Morrison 22-3-96-1 Snedden 36-17-54-1 Bracewell 35-8-75-2 Priest 12-4-26-1

Atherton, at 22yrs 81 days, became youngest Englishman to score Test 100 since Gower in 1978. He batted 501 minutes but hit only six fours. Gooch was out first ball.

NEW ZEALAND

Second Innings

T J Franklin not out	22
*J G Wright c Russell b Small	1
A H Jones c Russell b DeFreitas	13
D K Morrison not out	0
Total (2 wkts)	36

Fall: 1-8 2-36

Bowling: Malcolm 7-2-22-0 Small 6-2-14-1 DeFreitas 2-2-0-1 Hemmings 2-2-0-0

MATCH DRAWN

Only five overs bowled on the Friday, twelve on the Saturday. Hadlee's last game at Trent Bridge.

Man of the Match: Atherton

Second Test

Lord's, Jun 21-26
Hadlee knighted week before Test. England unchanged NZ won the toss

ENGLAND

First Innings

*G A Gooch c & b Bracewell	85
M A Atherton b Morrison	0
A J Stewart lbw b Hadlee	54
A J Lamb lbw b Snedden	9
R A Smith c Bracewell b Morrison	64
N H Fairbrother c Morrison b Bracewell	2
†R C Russell b Hadlee	13
P A J DeFreitas c Franklin b Morrison	38
G C Small b Morrison	3
E E Hemmings b Hadlee	0
D E Malcolm not out	0
Extras (lb13, w1, nb22)	36
Total	334

Fall: 1-3 2-151 3-178 4-216 5-226 6-255 7-319 8-322 9-332

Bowling: Hadlee 29-5-113-3 Morrison 18.4-4-64-4 Snedden 21-4-72-1 Bracewell 21-3-72-2

NEW ZEALAND

First Innings

T J Franklin c Russell b Malcolm	101
*J G Wright c Stewart b Small	98

A H Jones c Stewart b Malcolm	49
M D Crowe c Russell b Hemmings	1
M J Greatbach b Malcolm	47
K R Rutherford c Fairbrother b Malcolm	0
Sir Richard Hadlee b Hemmings	86
J G Bracewell run out	4
†I D Smith c Small b Malcolm	27
M C Snedden not out	13
D K Morrison not out	2
Extras (b12, lb15, w2, nb5)	34
Total (9 wkts dec)	462

Fall: 1-185 2-278 3-281 4-284 5-285 6-408 7-415 8-425 9-448

Bowling: Malcolm 43-14-94-5 Small 35-4-127-1 DeFreitas 35.4-1-122-0 Hemmings 30-13-67-2 Gooch 13-7-25-0 Atherton 1-1-0-0

Franklin's maiden Test century, and one of the slowest ever. He lasted seven hours 12 minutes. With Wright he put on a record first-wicket partnership for New Zealand against England.

ENGLAND

Second Innings

*G A Gooch b Hadlee	37
M A Atherton c Bracewell b Jones	54
A J Stewart c sub b Bracewell	42
A J Lamb not out	84
R A Smith hit wkt b Bracewell	0
N H Fairbrother not out	33
Extras (b8, lb8, nb6)	22
Total (4wkts)	272

Fall: 168 2-135 3-171 4-175

Bowling: Hadlee 12-2-32-1; Morrison 16-0-81-0; Bracewell 34-13-85-2; Jones 12-3-40-1; Rutherford 3-0-18-0

MATCH DRAWN

Man of the Match: Hadlee

Third Test

Edgbaston, Jul 5-10
Lewis replaced DeFreitas (fever). Debuts: Lewis (E) and Parore (NZ). NZ won the toss.

ENGLAND

First Innings

*G A Gooch c Hadlee b Morrison	154
M A Atherton lbw b Snedden	82
A J Stewart c Parore b Morrison	9
A J Lamb c Parore b Hadlee	2
R A Smith c Jones b Bracewell	19
N H Fairbrother lbw b Snedden	2
†R C Russell b Snedden	43
C C Lewis c Rutherford b Bracewell	32
G C Small not out	44
E E Hemmings c Parore b Hadlee	20
D E Malcolm b Hadlee	0
Extras (b4, lb15, nb9)	28
Total	435

Fall: 1-170 2-193 3-198 4-245 5-254 6-316 7-351 8-381 9-435

Bowling: Hadlee 37. 5-8-97-3; Morrison 26-7-81-2; Snedden 35-9-106-3; Bracewell 42-12-130-2; Jones 1-0-2-0

Gooch's first century as England captain, En route he passed 5000 runs in Tests.

NEW ZEALAND
First Innings

T J Franklin c Smith b Hemmings	66
*J G Wright c Russell b Malcolm	24
A H Jones c Russell b Malcolm	2
M D Crowe lbw b Lewis	11
M J Greatbatch b Malcolm	45
K R Rutherford c Stewart b Hemmings	29
Sir Richard Hadlee c Atherton b Hemmings	8
J G Bracewell b Hemmings	25
†A C Parore not out	12
M C Snedden lbw b Hemmings	2
D K Morrison b Hemmings	1
Extras (b9, lb11, w2, nb2)	24
Total	**249**

Fall: 1-45 2-67 3-90 4-161 5-163 6-185 7-223 8-230 9-243

Bowling: Small 18-7-44-0; Malcolm 25-7-59-3; Lewis 19-5-51-1; Hemmings 27 3-10-58-6; Atherton 9-5-17-0

ENGLAND
Second Innings

*G A Gooch b Snedden	30
M A Atherton c Rutherford b Bracewell	70
A J Stewart lbw b Bracewell	15
A J Lamb st Parore b Bracewell	4
R A Smith c & b Hadlee	14
N H Fairbrother lbw b Bracewell	3
†R C Russell c sub b Hadlee	0
C C Lewis c Parore b Hadlee	1
G C Small not out	11
E E Hemmings b Hadlee	0
D E Malcolm lbw b Hadlee	0
Extras (lb6, nb4)	10
Total	**158**

Fall: 1-50 2-87 3-99 4-129 5-136 6-141 7-146 8-157 9-158

Bowling: Hadlee 21-3-53-5; Morrison 3-1-29-0; Snedden 9-0-32-1; Bracewell 16-5-38-4

Hadlee took a wicket with his last ball in Test cricket.

NEW ZEALAND
Second Innings

T J Franklin lbw b Malcolm	5
*J G Wright c Smith b Lewis	46
A H Jones c Gooch b Small	40
M D Crowe lbw b Malcolm	25
M J Greatbatch c Atherton b Hemmings	22
K R Rutherford c Lamb b Lewis	18
Sir Richard Hadlee b Malcolm	13
†A C Parore c Lamb b Lewis	20
J G Bracewell c Atherton b Malcolm	0
M C Snedden not out	21
D K Morrison b Malcolm	6
Extras (lb9, w1, nb4)	14
Total	**230**

Fall: 1-25 2-85 3-111 4-125 5-155 6-163 7-180 8-180 9-203

Bowling: Malcolm 24 4-8-46-5; Small 16-5-56-1; Hemmings 29-13-43-1; Lewis 22-3-76-3

ENGLAND WON BY 114 RUNS

England's first home Test series win since 1985."I was wrong to put England in. No two ways about it, it was a bad decision."-Wright.

Man of the Match: Malcolm

Leading Batting Averages

	M	I	NO	RNS	HS	AVGE
1. Michael Atherton (E)	3	5	0	357	151	71.40
2. Graham Gooch (E)	3	5	0	306	154	61.20
3. Trevor Franklin (NZ)	3	5	1	227	101	56.75
4. Gladstone Small (E)	3	4	2	84	44*	42.00
5. John Wright (NZ)	3	5	0	177	98	35.40
6. Allan Lamb (E)	3	5	1	129	84*	32.25

Leading Bowling Averages

	M	BLS	RNS	WKS	AVGE	BST
1. Devon Malcolm (E)	3	712	269	15	17.93	5-46
2. Eddie Hemmings (E)	3	645	215	10	21.50	6-58
3. Richard Hadlee (NZ)	3	803	384	16	24.00	5-53
4. Mark Priest (NZ)	1	72	26	1	26.00	1-26
5. Phillip DeFreitas (E)	2	358	175	6	29.16	5-53
6. Chris Lewis (E)	1	246	127	4	31.75	3-76

CRICKET KNIGHTS

For services on the field:
Sir Donald Bradman (1949)
Sir Richard Hadlee (1990)
Sir Jack Hobbs (1953)
Sir Leonard Hutton (1956)
Sir Garfield Sobers (1975)
Sir Frank Worrell (1964)
For services on and off the field:
Sir George Allen (1986), player, selector, and administrator
Sir Neville Cardus (1967), writer
Sir Henry Leveson Gower (1953), player, selector and administrator
Sir Francis Lacey (1926), secretary of MCC
Sir Frederick Toone (1929), Yorkshire secretary and MCC tour manager
Sir Pelham Warner (1937), player, selector and administrator
Note: Sir Learie, later Lord, Constantine was honoured for non-cricketing services. So was the Maharajah of Vizianagram. The knighthood awarded by nickname to Sir Geoffrey Boycott was strictly unofficial.

ENGLAND V INDIA
First Test

Lord's , July 26-31
Morris (debut) and Gower for Stewart (injured) and Fairbrother (dropped). DeFreitas 12th man. India won toss.

ENGLAND
First Innings

*G A Gooch b Prabhakar	333
M A Atherton b Kapil Dev	8
D I Gower c Manjrekar b Hirwani	40
A J Lamb c Manjrekar b Sharma	139
R A Smith not out	100
J E Morris not out	4
Extras (b2, lb21, w2, nb4)	29
Total (4 wkts dec)	**653**

Fall: 1-14 2-141 3-449 4-641

Did not bat: †R C Russell, C C Lewis, E E Hemmings, A R C Fraser, D E Malcolm

Bowling: Kapil Dev 34-5-120-1; Prabhakar 43-6-187-1; Sharma 33-5-122-1; Shastri 22-0-99-0; Hirwani 30-1-102-1

Gooch became the first and Lamb the second men to compile four Test centuries at Lord's. Gooch's stand of 308 for the third wicket with Lamb was a record for any wicket against India. England's total was their highest against India and the highest in all Test matches by a side put in to bat.

INDIA

First Innings

R J Shastri c Gooch b Hemmings		100
N S Sidhu c Morris b Fraser		30
S V Manjrekar c Russell b Gooch		18
D B Vengsarkar c Russell b Fraser		52
*M Azharuddin b Hemmings		121
S R Tendulkar b Lewis		10
M Prabhakar c Lewis b Malcolm		25
Kapil Dev not out		77
†K S More c Morris b Fraser		8
S K Sharma c Russell b Fraser		0
N D Hirwani lbw b Fraser		0
Extras (lb1, w4, nb8)		13
Total		**454**

Fall: 1-62 2-102 3-191 4-241 5-288 6-348 7-393 8-430 9-430

Bowling: Malcolm 25-1-106-1; Fraser 39 1-9-104-5; Lewis 24-3-108-1; Gooch 6-3-26-1; Hemmings 20-3-109-2

Kapil Dev hit four successive sixes (emulating Walter Hammond and Sylvester Clarke in Tests) off Hemmings to take India past the follow-on target.

ENGLAND

Second Innings

*G A Gooch c Azharuddin b Sharma		123
M A Atherton c Vengsarkar b Sharma		72
D I Gower not out		32
A J Lamb c Tendulkar b Hirwani		19
R A Smith b Prabhakar		15
Extras (lb11)		11
Total (4 wkts dec)		**272**

Fall: 1-204 2-207 3-250 4-272

Bowling: Kapil Dev 10-0-53-0; Prabhakar 11 2-2-45-1; Shastri 7-0-38-0; Sharma 15-0-75-2; Hirwani 11-0-50-1

Gooch became the first man to hit five Test centuries at Lord's.

INDIA

Second Innings

R J Shastri c Russell b Malcolm		12
N S Sidhu c Morris b Fraser		1
S V Manjrekar c Russell b Malcolm		33
D B Vengsarkar c Russell b Hemmings		35
*M Azharuddin c Atherton b Lewis		37
S R Tendulkar c Gooch b Fraser		27
M Prabhakar lbw b Lewis		8
Kapil Dev c Lewis b Hemmings		7
†K S More lbw b Fraser		16
S K Sharma run out		38
N D Hirwani not out		0
Extras (b3, lb1, nb6)		10
Total		**224**

Fall: 1-9 2-23 3-63 4-114 5-127 6-140 7-158 8-181 9-206

Bowling: Fraser 22-7-39-3; Malcolm 10-0-65-2; Hemmings 21-2-79-2; Atherton 1-0-11-0; Lewis 8-1-26-2

ENGLAND WON BY 247 RUNS.

Gooch won the game by running out Sharma with a direct hit and won the man of the match award, obviously. The match aggregate of 1,603 runs was the second-highest for

a Test in England, behind the 1,723 at Headingley against Australia in 1948.

Second Test

Old Trafford, Aug 9-14

DeFreitas (injured) withdrew from 12. Williams brought in and became 12th man. Debut: Kumble (I).England won the toss.

ENGLAND

First Innings

*G A Gooch c More b Prabhakar		116
M A Atherton c More b Hirwani		131
D I Gower c Tendulkar b Kapil Dev		38
A J Lamb c Manjrekar b Kumble		38
†R C Russell c More b Hirwani		8
R A Smith not out		121
J E Morris b Kumble		13
C C Lewis b Hirwani		3
E E Hemmings lbw b Hirwani		19
A R C Fraser c Tendulkar b Hirwani		1
D E Malcolm lbw b Shastri		13
Extras (b2, lb9,w1, nb6)		18
Total		**519**

Fall: 1-225 2-292 3-312 4-324 5-366 6-392 7-404 8-434 9-459

Bowling: Kapil Dev 13-2-67-1; Prabhakar 25-2-112-1; Kumble 43-7-105-3; Hirwani 62-10-174-4; Shastri 17.5-2-50-1

Gooch became first Englishman since Geoff Boycott in 1971 to score three consecutive Test centuries. Opening stand of 225 a new record for England against India, beating the 204 set at Lord's in the last game. Atherton became only the second Lancastrian after Geoff Pullar in 1959 to score a Test century on his home ground. The first home ground 100 by any Englishman since Boycott in 1977. This was the first time India had bowled out a team all tour.

INDIA

First Innings

R J Shastri c Gooch b Fraser		25
N S Sidhu c Gooch b Fraser		13
S V Manjrekar c Smith b Hemmings		93
D B Vengsarkar c Russell b Fraser		6
*M Azharuddin c Atherton b Fraser		179
S R Tendulkar c Lewis b Hemmings		68
M Prabhakar c Russell b Malcolm		4
Kapil Dev lbw b Lewis		0
†K S More b Fraser		6
A Kumble run out		2
N D Hirwani not out		15
Extras (b5, lb4, nb12)		21
Total		**432**

Fall: 1-26 2-48 3-57 4-246 5-358 6-364 7-365 8-396 9-401

Bowling: Malcolm 26-3-96-1; Fraser 35-5-124-5; Hemmings 29 2-8-74-2; Lewis 13-1-61-1; Atherton 16-3-68-0

ENGLAND

Second Innings

*G A Gooch c More b Prabhakar		7
M A Atherton lbw b Kapil Dev		74
D I Gower b Hirwani		16
A J Lamb b Kapil Dev		109
R A Smith not out		61
J E Morris retired hurt		15
†R C Russell not out		16

Extras (lb15, nb7)..22
Total (for 4 wkts dec).................................**320**
Did not bat: C C Lewis, E E Hemmings, A R C Fraser, D E Malcolm
Fall: 1-15 2-46 3-180 4-248
Bowling: Kapil Dev 22-4-69-2; Prabhakar 18-1-80-1; Hirwani 15-0-52-1; Kumble 17-3-65-0; Shastri 9-0-39-0

INDIA
Second Innings
R J Shastri b Malcolm 12
N S Sidhu c sub (Adams) b Fraser 0
S V Manjrekar c sub (Adams) b Hemmings .50
D B Vengsarkar b Lewis.................................32
*M Azharuddin c Lewis b Hemmings 11
S R Tendulkar not out.....................................119
Kapil Dev b Hemmings...................................26
M Prabhakar not out.......................................67
Extras (b17, lb3, nb6)....................................26
Total (for 6 wkts) **343**
Did not bat: †K S More, A Kumble, N D Hirwani
Fall: 1-4 2-35 3-109 4-109 5-127 6-183
Bowling: Malcolm 14-5-59-1; Fraser 21-3-81-1; Hemmings 31-10-75-3; Atherton 4-0-22-0; Lewis 20-3-86-1

MATCH DRAWN
Tendulkar, at 17y 112d, became the second youngest person to score a Test century.
Man/boy of the match: Tendulkar

Third Test
The Oval, Aug 23-28
Williams (debut) replaced Lewis, ill. India won toss.

INDIA
First Innings
R J Shastri c Lamb b Malcolm 187
N S Sidhu c Russell b Fraser.........................12
S V Manjrekar c Russell b Malcolm 22
D B Vengsarkar c & b Atherton 33
*M Azharuddin c Russell b Williams 78
M Prabhakar lbw b Fraser 28
S R Tendulkar c Lamb b Williams 21
Kapil Dev st Russell b Hemming 110
†K S More not out...61
A Wasson b Hemmings 15
N D Hirwani not out 2
Extras (b7, lb8, w6, nb16)............................37
Total (9 wkts dec) **606**
Fall: 1-16 2-61 3-150 4-289 5-335 6-368 7-478 8-552 9-576

Bowling: Malcolm 35-7-110-2; Fraser 42-17-112-2; Williams 41-5-148-2; Gooch 12-1-44-0; Hemmings 36-3-117-2; Atherton 7-0-60-1
India's total was their highest against England, and their third-highest ever.

ENGLAND
First Innings
*G A Gooch c Shastri b Hirwani 85
M A Atherton c More b Prabhakar.................7
N F Williams lbw b Prabhakar 38
D I Gower lbw b Wasson 8
J E Morris c More b Wasson 7
A J Lamb b Kapil Dev.....................................7
R A Smith c Manjrekar b Shastri 57
†R C Russell run out 35
E E Hemmings c Vengsarkar b Prabhakar 51
A R C Fraser c More b Prabhakar 0
D E Malcolm not out 15
Extras (b8, lb9,w4, nb9)...........................30
Total **340**
Fall: 1-18 2-92 3-111 4-120 5-139 6-231 7-233 8-295 9-299
Bowling: Kapil Dev 25-7-70-1; Prabhakar 32 4-9-74-4; Wasson 19-3-79-2; Hirwani 35-12-71-1; Shastri 12-2-29-0

ENGLAND
Second Innings
*G A Gooch c Vengsarkar b Hirwani...........88
M A Atherton lbw b Kapil Dev....................86
D I Gower not out...157
J E Morris c More b Wasson 32
A J Lamb c Shastri b Kapil Dev.................52
R A Smith not out...7
Extras (b16, lb22,w6, nb11) 55
Total (4 wkts dec).......................................**477**
Fall: 1-176 2-251 3-334 4-463
Bowling: Prabhakar 25-8-56-0; Kapil Dev 24-5-66-2; Wasson 18-2-94-1; Hirwani 59-18-137-1; Shastri 28-2-86-0

MATCH DRAWN
Gooch took his total runs in the summer's six Test matches to 1,058, beating Bradman's record of 974 (1930) on Sir Don's 82nd birthday. Gower became England's second-highest rungetter in Tests, after Boycott. Hirwani bowled unchanged from the Vauxhall End between 3.06pm Monday and 4.30pm Tuesday (with a break for nightfall etc), 59 overs, beating the 51 overs bowled by Tom Veivers at Old Trafford 1964. Bill Frindall, BBC scorer, missed a no-ball signal and admitted that he had made a mistake.
Man of the match: Shastri

Leading Batting Averages

		M	I	NO	RUNS	HS	AVGE
1.	Robin Smith (E)	3	6	4	361	121*	180.50
2.	Graham Gooch (E)	3	6	0	752	333	125.33
3.	Mohammed Azharuddin (I)	3	5	0	426	179	85.20
4.	David Gower (E)	3	6	2	291	157*	72.75
5.	Ravi Shastri (I)	3	5	0	336	187	67.20
6.	Michael Atherton (E)	3	6	0	378	131	63.00

Leading Bowling Averages

		M	BALLS	RUNS	WKTS	AVGE	BEST
1.	Angus Fraser (E)	3	955	460	16	28.75	5-104
2.	Eddie Hemmings (E)	3	824	454	11	41.27	3-75
3.	Chris Lewis (E)	2	390	281	5	56.20	2-26
4.	Anil Kumble (I)	1	360	170	3	56.66	3-105
5.	Atul Wasson (I)	1	222	173	3	57.66	2-79
6.	Devon Malcolm (E)	3	660	436	7	62.28	2-65

TEST TRIPLE CENTURIES

365*   Gary Sobers, West Indies v Pakistan, 1957-58
364   Len Hutton, England v Australia, 1938
337   Hanif Mohammad, Pakistan v West Indies, 1957-58
336*   Walter Hammond, England v New Zealand, 1932-33
334   Don Bradman, Australia v England, 1930
333   GRAHAM GOOCH, ENGLAND v INDIA, 1990
325   Andy Sandham, England v West Indies, 1929-30
311   Bobby Simpson, Australia v England, 1964
310*   John Edrich, England v New Zealand, 1965
307   Bob Cowper, Australia v England, 1966
304   Don Bradman, Australia v England, 1934
302   Lawrence Rowe, West Indies v England, 1973-74

ENGLAND'S TESTS 1990

WEST INDIES V ENGLAND

Kingston, Feb 24	ENGLAND WON by nine wickets
Georgetown, Mar 9	ABANDONED
Port of Spain, Mar 23	DRAWN
Bridgetown, Apr 5	WEST INDIES WON by 164 runs
Antigua, Apr 12	WEST INDIES WON by an innings and 32

ENGLAND V NEW ZEALAND

Trent Bridge, Jun 7	DRAWN
Lord's, Jun 21	DRAWN
Edgbaston, Jul 5	ENGLAND WON by 114 runs

ENGLAND V INDIA

Lord's, Jul 26	ENGLAND WON by 247 runs
Old Trafford, Aug 9	DRAWN
The Oval, Aug 23	DRAWN

ENGLAND TEST AVERAGES 1990
(Composite figures from three series)
Batting

	M	I	NO	RUNS	HS	AVGE	M	I	NO	RUNS	HS	AVGE
							Updated career figures					
Graham Gooch	8	15	1	1186	333	84.71	81	147	5	5910	333	41.62
David Gower	3	6	2	291	157*	72.75	109	189	15	7674	215	44.10
Michael Atherton	6	11	0	735	151	66.82	8	15	0	808	151	53.87
Robin Smith	10	18	6	699	121*	58.25	18	34	8	1397	143	53.73
Allan Lamb	10	18	1	883	139	51.94	67	118	10	3981	139	36.86
Neil Williams	1	1	0	38	38	38.00	1	1	0	38	38	38.00
Alec Stewart	7	13	1	317	54	26.42	7	13	1	317	54	26.42
Wayne Larkins	4	8	1	176	54	25.14	10	19	1	352	54	19.56
Jack Russell	10	14	2	282	55	23.50	17	26	5	690	128*	32.85
Eddie Hemmings	6	6	1	103	51	20.60	15	20	4	383	95	23.94
Nasser Hussain	3	5	0	100	35	20.00	3	5	0	100	35	20.00
Phillip DeFreitas	4	6	0	103	32	17.17	17	25	1	301	40	12.54
Neil Fairbrother	3	5	1	59	33*	14.75	7	9	1	64	33*	8.00
Gladstone Small	7	10	3	101	44*	14.43	13	18	6	221	59	18.42
John Morris	3	5	0	71	32	14.20	3	5	0	71	32	14.20
David Capel	4	7	1	81	40	13.50	15	25	1	374	98	15.58
Robert Bailey	3	6	0	73	42	12.17	4	8	0	119	43	14.88
Chris Lewis	3	3	0	36	32	12.00	3	3	0	36	32	12.00
Devon Malcolm	10	12	6	49	15*	8.17	11	14	6	63	15*	7.87
Angus Fraser	5	4	1	14	11	4.67	8	9	1	61	29	7.63

Bowling

	BALLS	RUNS	WKTS	BEST	AVGE	BALLS	RUNS	WKTS	BEST	AVGE
						Updated career figures				
Fraser	1382	621	27	5-28	23.00	2248	944	36	5-28	26.22
Malcolm	2342	1282	41	6-77	31.27	2606	1448	42	6-77	34.48
Hemmings	1469	669	21	6-58	31.86	3999	1626	37	6-58	43.95
DeFreitas	831	417	12	5-53	34.75	3550	1713	38	5-53	45.08
Small	1590	795	22	4-58	36.14	3033	1447	46	5-48	31.46
Lewis	636	408	9	3-76	45.33	636	408	9	3-76	45.33
Capel	744	436	9	3-88	48.44	2000	1064	21	3-88	50.67
Williams	246	148	2	2-148	74.00	246	148	2	2-148	74.00
Gooch	174	95	1	1-26	95.00	1791	717	15	2-12	47.80
Atherton	228	178	1	1-60	178.00	276	212	1	1-60	212.00

GOOCH'S GOLDEN SUMMER

Graham Gooch's first-class scores 1990

Essex v Middlesex	137	39
Essex v Leicestershire	215	
Essex v Worcestershire	121	42*
Essex v Middlesex	0	120
England v New Zealand FIRST TEST	0	
Essex v Somerset	72	
England v New Zealand SECOND TEST	85	37
Essex v New Zealanders	102*	
England v New Zealand THIRD TEST	154	30
Essex v Lancashire	17	177
England v India FIRST TEST	333	123
Essex v Nottinghamshire	87	65*
England v India SECOND TEST	116	7
Essex v Surrey	9	53
England v India THIRD TEST	85	88
Essex v Northamptonshire	174	126
Essex v Northamptonshire	92	40

RECORD OF ENGLAND CAPTAINS

(Test matches since January 1, 1980)

	P	W	D	L	% of wins
Mike Brearley	7	4	1	2	57
Graham Gooch	10	4	5	1	40
Bob Willis	18	7	6	5	38
David Gower	32	5	9	18	15
Keith Fletcher	7	1	5	1	14
Mike Gatting	23	2	16	5	8
Ian Botham	12	0	8	4	0
Chris Cowdrey	1	0	0	1	0
John Emburey	2	0	0	2	0
Allan Lamb	2	0	0	2	0

— OTHER TEST MATCHES —

PAKISTAN V INDIA
First Test
Karachi, Nov 15-20
Drawn
PAKISTAN 409 (Imran Khan 109*, M Prabhakar 5-104) and 305-5 dec (Salim Malik 102*); INDIA 262 and 303-3 (S V Manjrekar 113*)
A Muslim fanatic invaded the pitch, attacked Kapil Dev and tore Srikkanth's shirt. Kapil, in his 100th Test, was man of the match for scoring 55 and taking seven wickets.

Second Test
Faisalbad, Nov 23-28
Drawn
INDIA 288 and 398-7 (M Azharuddin 109); PAKISTAN 423-9dec (Aamer Malik 107; M Prabhakar 6-132)

Third Test
Lahore, Dec 1-6
Drawn
INDIA 509 (S V Manjrekar 218); PAKISTAN 699-5 (Shoaib Mohammad 203*, Javed Miandad 145, Aamer Malik 113)
Javed, in his 100th Test, became the sixth-highest Test rungetter

Fourth Test
Sialkot, Dec 9-14
Drawn
INDIA 324 (Wasim Akram 5-101) and 234-7; PAKISTAN 250 (Vivek Razdan 5-79)
Imran became fifth player to take 350 Test wickets. English umpires John Holder and John Hampshire officiated throughout a series that was free of usual controversy about bias, or indeed any other excitement.
Series drawn 0-0

AUSTRALIA V NEW ZEALAND
Perth, Nov 24-28
Drawn
AUSTRALIA 521-9dec (D C Boon 200); NEW ZEALAND 231 and 322-7 (M J Greatbatch 146*)
Greatbatch batted 11 hours; his century (462mins) was the slowest-ever in Australian first-class cricket.

AUSTRALIA V SRI LANKA
First Test
Brisbane, Dec 8-12
Drawn
AUSTRALIA 367 (T Moody 106, G F Labrooy 5-133) and 375-6 (M A Taylor 164); SRI LANKA 418 (P A de Silva 167)

Second Test
Hobart, Dec 16-20
Australia won by 173 runs
AUSTRALIA 224 (R Ratnayake 6-66) and 513-5dec (S R Waugh 134*, D M Jones 118*, M A Taylor 108); SRI LANKA 216 and 348 (M Hughes 5-88)
Bellerive Oval became the world's 62nd Test ground. Taylor took total for 1989 past 1,200. Sri Lankans accused Australian team of "racist taunts". Aravinda da Silva man of the match for 75 and 72 and man of the series.

Australia won series 1-0

AUSTRALIA V PAKISTAN
First Test
Melbourne, Jan 9-13
Australia won by 92 runs
AUSTRALIA 223 (Wasim Akram 6-62) and 312-8dec (M A Taylor 101, Wasim Akram 5-98); PAKISTAN 107 and 336 (Ijaz Ahmed 121, T M Alderman 5-105)

Second Test
Adelaide, Jan 19-23
Drawn
PAKISTAN 257 and 387-9dec (Imran Khan 136, Wasim Akram 123, M G Hughes 5-111); AUSTRALIA 341 (D M Jones 116, Wasim Akram 5-100) and 233-6 (D M Jones 121*)

Third Test
Sydney, Feb 3-8
Drawn
PAKISTAN 199 (T Alderman 5-65); AUSTRALIA 176-2 (M A Taylor 101*)
Taylor's fourth hundred in six home Tests. Sydney was hit by a cyclone and, although an extra day was arranged, three were completely blank.

Australia won series 1-0

NEW ZEALAND V INDIA
First Test
Christchurch, Feb 2-5
New Zealand won by 10 wickets
NEW ZEALAND 459 (J G Wright 185) and 2-0; INDIA 164 (D K Morrison 5-75) and 296
Sanjay Manjrekar became Richard Hadlee's 400th Test victim.

Second Test
Napier, Feb 9-13
Drawn
INDIA 358-9dec (D K Morrison 5-98); NEW ZEALAND 178-1 (J G Wright 113*)

Third Test
Auckland, Feb 22-26

Drawn
NEW ZEALAND 391 (I D S Smith 173) and 483-5dec (A H Jones 170*, M D Crowe 113); INDIA 482 (M Azharuddin 192, D K Morrison 5-145) and 149-0
New Zealand won series 1-0

NEW ZEALAND V AUSTRALIA
Wellington, Mar 15-19
New Zealand won by 9 wickets
AUSTRALIA 110 (R J Hadlee 5-39) and 269 (J G Bracewell 6-85); NEW ZEALAND 202 and 181-1 (J G Wright 117*)
Martin Snedden was scoreless for 94 minutes (54 balls), a Test record. Hadlee's 100th five in an innings in first-class cricket. Australia's first defeat in 15 Tests.

COOPERS DELOITTE RATINGS
September 1990

(September 1989 in brackets)

BATTING				BOWLING			
1	(7)	Mark Taylor (Aus)	813	1	(1)	Sir Richard Hadlee (NZ)	868
2	(1)	Javed Miandad (Pak)	807	2	(2)	Malcolm Marshall (WI)	836
3	(28)	Graham Gooch (Eng)	793	3	(11)	Ian Bishop (WI)	766
4	(9)	Desmond Haynes (WI)	781	4	(40)	Angus Fraser (Eng)	755
5	(8)	Robin Smith (Eng)	778	5	(3)	Imran Khan (Pak)	753
6	(2)	Richie Richardson (WI)	774	6	(4)	Terry Alderman (Aus)	712
7	(6)	Allan Border (Aus)	758	7	(9)	Curtly Ambrose (WI)	688
8	(18)	Mohammed Azharuddin (Ind)	721	8	(–)	Wasim Akram (Pak)	688
9	(95)	Michael Atherton (Eng)	711	9	(22)	Merv Hughes (Aus)	680
10	(19)	Imran Khan (Pak)	703	10	(7)	Courtney Walsh (WI))	644

ENGLAND'S ONE-DAY INTERNATIONALS

NEHRU CUP
Feroz Shah Kotla, Delhi, Oct 15
England beat Sri Lanka by 5 wickets
SRI LANKA 193 (48.3 overs) (P A De Silva 80); ENGLAND 196-5 (48.4 overs) (R A Smith 81*, A J Lamb 52)

Lal Bahadur Shastri Stadium, Hyderabad, Oct 19
England beat Australia by 7 wickets
AUSTRALIA 242-3 (50 overs) (A R Border 84*, G R Marsh 54, D M Jones 50); ENGLAND 243-3 (47.3 overs) W Larkins 124, G A Gooch 56)

Baribati Stadium, Cuttack, Oct 22
England beat Pakistan by 4 wickets
PAKISTAN 148-9 (50 overs); ENGLAND 149-6 (43.2 overs)

Green Park, Kanpur, Oct 25
India beat England by 6 wickets
ENGLAND 255-7 (50 overs) (A J Lamb 91, A J Stewart 61); INDIA 259-4 (48.1 overs) (C Sharma 101*, N S Sidhu 61)
Roop Singh Stadium, Gwalior, Oct 27
West Indies beat England by 26 runs
WEST INDIES 265-5 (50 overs) (D L Haynes 138*); ENGLAND 239-8 (50 overs) (R A Smith 65, G A Gooch 59)

SEMI-FINAL
Vidharba C.A. Stadium, Nagpur, Oct 30
Pakistan beat England by 6 wickets
ENGLAND 194-7 (30 overs) (R A Smith 55); PAKISTAN 195-4 (28.3 overs) (Ramiz Raja 85*, Salim Malik 66)

IN WEST INDIES
Queen's Park Oval, Port of Spain, Feb 14
Match Abandoned
WEST INDIES 208-8 (50 overs) (R B Richardson 51); ENGLAND 26-1 (13 overs)
Queen's Park Oval, Port of Spain, Feb 17
Match Abandoned
WEST INDIES 13-0 (5.5 overs)

Sabina Park, Kingston, Mar 3
West Indies won by 3 wickets
ENGLAND 214-8 (50 overs) (A J Lamb 66, I R Bishop 4-28); WEST INDIES 216-7 (50 overs) (R B Richardson 108*)

Bourda, Georgetown, Mar 7
West Indies won by 6 wickets
ENGLAND 188-8 (48 overs); WEST INDIES 191-4 (45.2 overs) (C A Best 100, D L Haynes 50)

Bourda, Georgetown, Mar 15
(Extra game)
West Indies won by 7 wickets
ENGLAND 166-9 (49 overs) (C E L Ambrose 4-18); WEST INDIES 167-3 (40.2 overs) (C G Greenidge 77)

Kensington Oval, Bridgetown, Apr 3
West Indies won by 4 wickets
ENGLAND 214-3 (38 overs) (R A Smith 69, A J Lamb 55*); WEST INDIES 217-6 (37.3 overs) (R B Richardson 80, C A Best 51)

West Indies won the five match series 3-0 with two matches abandoned.

GATTING'S ODYSSEY

❝What are you going to get out of it, a second home, Mr Yachting?"
Demonstrator at pre-tour press conference

"If you do not consider money more important than the lives of our people, you should not come here."
Zingale Dingaan, protesters' leader, to Mike Gatting

"As far as I was concerned, there was a few people singing and dancing and that was it."
Gatting on the demonstration in Kimberley

"He said he was shot on the way back from a peaceful demonstration. That's bollocks."
Mike Gatting after meeting injured protester John Seganetco

"It was the most heroic sporting achievement off the field I have ever seen. You guys in the British press have vilified Mike. But he has come here with no knowledge of the country and has said nothing more stupid than a lot of white South Africans do every day."
Ali Bacher after Gatting walked through the line of demonstrators in Pietermaritzburg

"Mike Gatting, I think, is to be congratulated. It is rare that a man ignorant of politics devises such painstaking methods of self-education."
Letter in The Guardian *from Paul Heapy of Alfreton*

"I always wait in the same place for a job. Today they came along with this bus and said we should go along as they had work for us."
Black spectator in Johannesburg

"These were teenage girls who had been given the afternoon off school. They were ushered past a row of edgy security guards whose alsatians were barely able to contain themselves. The girls had been promised a free coachride, a free packed lunch and a free entry ticket. They had been hoping to go to the zoo."
Frank Partridge, BBC Radio, on the black spectators

"Mike Gatting and his jackals of cricket are coming home early with their bats between their legs. Having disgraced their country and their sport it is only fitting that they should be abandoned by the South Africa to which they sold their reputation. They went there for blood money, and that is what they are getting. Full pay for a short and despicable performance."
Daily Mirror

"Nelson Mandela can't bowl, can he?"
Bill Athey, asked about the implications for the tour of Mandela's release

"I've learned a lot more in probably two weeks about the country than I'll ever do about England...."
"Have you been an innocent abroad?"
"I've certainly been an innocent, a well-used innocent."
TV interview with Mike Gatting

"What good did that do?"
"Well, it made me feel a lot better. ❞
Exchange between Gatting and protester who poured beer over him

TEXACO TROPHY

Headingley, May 23
New Zealand won by 4 wickets
ENGLAND 295-6 (55 overs) (G A Gooch 55, R A Smith 128)
NEW ZEALAND 298-6 (54.5 overs) (J G Wright 52, A H Jones 51, M J Greatbatch 102*)
Man of the Match: Greatbatch (NZ)

The Oval, May 25
England won by 6 wickets
NEW ZEALAND 212-6 (55 overs) (M J Greatbatch 111)
ENGLAND 213-4 (49.3 overs) (G A Gooch 112*)
Man of the Match: Malcolm (Eng)
England won the two-match series on faster run rate

Headingley, Jul 18
India won by 6 wickets
ENGLAND 229 (54.3 overs) (A J Lamb 56, D I Gower 50)
INDIA 223-4 (53 overs) (S V Manjrekar 82, M Azharuddin 56)
Man of the Match: Kumble (I)

Trent Bridge, Jul 20
India won by 5 wickets
ENGLAND 281 (55 overs) (R A Smith 103, M A Atherton 59, R C Russell 50)
INDIA 282-5 (53 overs) (M Azharuddin 63*, S V Manjrekar 59, D B Vengsarkar 54)
Man of the Match: Smith (E)

India won the two-match series 2-0

"What about intimidatory batting?"
Simon Hughes, Middlesex bowler
"Bowling in county cricket has become a breeze, like cycling downhill with your feet on the handlebars, which is as easy for Eddie Edwards as it is for Eddy Merckx. The real test comes when the pedalling is uphill, and this year the mediocre bowlers were simply found out."
Mike Selvey, The Guardian
"There was nothing to suggest, I am afraid, that the bowling was noticeably more accurate now than it was this time last year. The idea that the combination of four-day cricket, a reduced seam and a fine summer would have the spinners wering their fingers to the bone was almost seen to have come to nothing."
John Woodcock, The Times
"Now the pitches are just too good. The balance has gone too far in favour of the batsmen."
Graham Gooch
"Just how many records had been broken in the summer, nobody could say for sure. But it was probably a record."
Tim de Lisle, Independent on Sunday

THE ENGLISH SEASON 1990

First-Class Averages

Batting

			Runs	Avge
1	(36)	Graham Gooch	2746	101.70
2	(7)	Graeme Hick	2347	90.26
3	(69)	Tom Moody	1163	89.46
4	(-)	Mohammed Azharuddin	770	77.00
5	(136)	David Ward	2072	76.74
5	(26)	Mark Waugh	2072	76.74
7	(3)	Jimmy Cook	2608	76.70
8	(90)	Brian Hardie	728	72.80
9	(92)	Michael Atherton	1924	71.25
10	(-)	Aravinda De Silva	563	70.37
11	(29)	Neil Fairbrother	1740	69.60
12	(61)	Darren Bicknell	1317	69.31
13	(171)	Mark Crawley	762	69.27
14	(21)	Desmond Haynes	2346	69.00
15	(4)	Robin Smith	1454	66.09

Others with 1750 runs

			Runs	Avge
17	(77)	Robert Bailey	1987	64.09
21	(30)	Neil Taylor	1979	61.84
22	(32)	Chris Smith	1886	60.83
24	(18)	Alan Butcher	2116	58.77
30	(49)	John Stephenson	1887	57.18
34	(80)	Hugh Morris	2276	55.51
37	(43)	Chris Broad	2226	54.29
46	(75)	Ashley Metcalfe	2047	51.17
50	(133)	Nigel Briers	1996	49.90
56	(74)	Andy Moles	1854	48.78
77	(47)	James Whitaker	1767	45.30
85	(83)	Alan Fordham	1767	44.17

Bowling

			Wkts	Avge
1	(29)	Ian Bishop	59	19.05
2	(5)	Malcolm Marshall	72	19.18
3	(-)	David Millns	31	21.35
4	(–)	Vince Wells	12	21.41
5	(17)	Ole Mortensen	35	22.42
6	(76)	Curtly Ambrose	61	23.16
7	(-)	Waqar Younis	57	23.80
8	(-)	Richard Hadlee	24	24.41
9	(–)	Mark Alleyne	16	24.43
10	(65)	Paul Smith	20	24.85
11	(23)	Neil Foster	94	26.61
12	(-)	Rangith Madurasinghe	21	26.66
13	(16)	Angus Fraser	57	26.89
14	(57)	Martin Bicknell	67	27.26
15	(-)	Graeme Labrooy	16	27.50

Others with 65 wickets

			Wkts	Avge
19	(18)	Courtney Walsh	72	28.08
20	(25)	Richard Illingworth	75	28.29
25	(55)	Tim Munton	78	28.89
58	(77)	Philip Tufnell	74	35.60
67	(106)	Rajesh Maru	66	36.66
88	(139)	Richard Davis	73	38.95
92	(46)	Steve Watkin	69	39.30

(1989 positions in brackets)

WICKET-KEEPERS: 1 Steven Rhodes 69 (61ct 8st); 2 Karl Krikken 63 (60ct 3st); 3 Peter Moores 63 (53ct 10st)
FIELDERS: 1 John Emburey, Damian D'Oliveira 33; 3 Keith Brown, Rajesh Maru, Monte Lynch 30
Source:TCCB/Bull

THE YEAR OF THE BAT

	300s	200s	100s	2,000 In Season	Totals Over 600	Over 500	Bowlers with 10 Wkts in a match
1980	-	10	201	3	-	-	23
1981	-	7	264	3	-	-	29
1982	1	16	281	1	1	6	23
1983	-	10	262	1	1	4	23
1984	-	16	328	5	1	8	20
1985	1	9	309	3	-	5	16
1986	1	10	255	2	-	4	34
1987	-	8	244	-	1	2	20
1988	1	9	235	2	3	8	35
1989	-	6	248	1	2	6	30
1990	3	32	428	10	8	25	13

Highest Totals

863	Lancs v Surrey	(The Oval)
761-6d	Essex v Leics	(Chelmsford)
707-9d	Surrey v Lancs	(The Oval)
653-4d	England v India	(Lord's)
648	Surrey v Kent	(Canterbury)
636-6d	Northants v Essex	(Chelmsford)
613-6d	Surrey v Essex	(The Oval)
606-9d	England v India	(The Oval)
600-8d	Hampshire v Sussex	(Southampton)
592-6d	Northants v Essex	(Northampton)
574	Gloucs v Yorks	(Cheltenham)
558-6d	Lancs v Oxford U	(The Parks)
551-8d	Gloucs v Worcs	(Bristol)
539	Essex v Surrey	(The Oval)
535-2d	Somerset v Glamorgan	(Cardiff)

Lowest Totals

50	Northants v Derby	(Northampton)
72	Derby v Gloucs	(Derby)
96	Warwicks v Worcs	(Worcester)
99	Middlesex v Derby	(Derby)
100	Notts v Surrey	(Trent Bridge)
106	Cambridge U v Derby	(Fenner's)
108	Sussex v Lancs	(Horsham)
110	Notts v Hampshire	(Portsmouth)
110	Cambridge U v Derby	(Fenner's)

Highest Individual Scores

366	Neil Fairbrother	Lancs v Surrey (The Oval)
333	Graham Gooch	England v India (Lord's)
313*	Jimmy Cook	Somerset v Glamorgan (Cardiff)
291	Ian Greig	Surrey v Lancs (The Oval)
263	David Ward	Surrey v Kent (Canterbury)
256	Mark Alleyne	Gloucs v Northants (Northampton)
255*	Desmond Haynes	Middlesex v Sussex (Lord's)
252*	Graeme Hick	Worcs v Glamorgan (Abergavenny)
245	Paul Prichard	Essex v Leics (Chelmsford)
235	Allan Lamb	Northants v Yorks (Headingley)
234	Simon Hinks	Kent v Middlesex (Canterbury)

Best Bowling

9-113	Garfield Harrison	Ireland v Scotland (Edinburgh)
8-58	Courtney Walsh	Gloucs v Northants (Cheltenham)
7-47	Malcolm Marshall	Hampshire v Derby (Portsmouth)
7-61	Neil Williams	Middlesex v Kent (Lord's)
7-73	Waqar Younis	Surrey v Warwicks (The Oval)
7-75	Greg Thomas	Northants v Glamorgan (Northampton)
7-89	Curtly Ambrose	Northants v Leics (Leicester)
7-92	Keith Medlycott	Surrey v Notts (Trent Bridge)
7-120	John Bracewell	New Zealand v Combined Univs (Fenner's)
7-128	Andy Pick	Notts v Leics (Leicester)

Most Centuries

12	Graham Gooch (Essex)
10	Hugh Morris (Glamorgan)
9	Chris Broad (Notts)
	Jimmy Cook (Somerset)
8	Desmond Haynes (Middlesex)
	Graeme Hick (Worcs)
	Mark Waugh (Essex)
7	Michael Atherton (Lancs)
	Robert Bailey (Northants)
	Tom Moody (Warwicks)
	Viv Richards (Glam)
	Neil Taylor (Kent)
	David Ward (Surrey)

Most One-day Centuries

6	Graham Gooch (Essex)
4	Jimmy Cook (Somerset)
	Paul Johnson (Notts)
	Robin Smith (Hants)

Fastest Centuries

36 balls*	Tom Moody, Warwicks v Glam (The Oval)
69 balls	Phil DeFreitas, Lancs v Oxford U (The Parks)
70 balls	Asif Din, Warwicks v Cambridge U (Fenner's)
71 balls	Graeme Hick, Worcs v Glamorgan (Abergavenny)
73 balls	Viv Richards, Glamorgan v Sussex (Hove)

*26 minutes. World record by time.

LANCASHIRE SCORECARD v SURREY, May 7, 1990

G D Mendis run out 102
G Fowler run out 20
M A Atherton c Greig b Kendrick............91
N H Fairbrother c Kendrick b Greig.......366
T E Jesty retired hurt............................18
M Watkinson b Greig..............................46
†W K Hegg c Ward b Bicknell 45
P A J DeFreitas b Murphy......................31
*D P Hughes not out...............................8
J D Fitton c Stewart b Murphy 3
B P Patterson c Greig b Medlycott 0
Extras (b8, lb15, w1, nb9)..........................33
Total...863
Fall: 1-45 2-184 3-548 4-745 5-774 6-844 7-848 8-862 9-863
Bowling: Murphy 44-6-160-2; Bicknell: 43-2-175-1; Kendrick 56-10-192-1; Medlycott 50 5-4-177-1; Lynch 5-2-17-0; Greig 19-3-73-2; Thorpe 7-1-46-0

THERE'LL ALWAYS BE A YORKSHIRE

"My husband and I were appalled by the constant stream of lewd and incredibly offensive remarks about coloured people, in particular, coloured women and Jewish men...Among these middle-aged louts was a man who had held high office in the cricketing world but could certainly not be described as a Yorkshire gentleman."

Lady Hill, wife of Sir James Hill Bt, complaining about the crowd at a Headingley one-day international.

"That's just the Yorkshire people trying to show the Asians that they care. Which they don't."

Talij Dutt, captain of Al-Faiah cricket club on Yorkshire's attempts to find Asian players.

"The biggest community in this area is the Asian community, the poorer people that hadn't got jobs over there, came over to come into the textile trade, low wages. Did you know that, over in Pakistan and India, the poorer people didn't know cricket even existed? There's a hundred years of bloody tradition on Yorkshire lads. As soon as a male's born, bloody
hell, the fellow says, good, I'm glad he was born in Yorkshire. By the time he's toddling, he's got a bat in his hand. Bloody Pakistanis-they didn't know the damn thing."

Brian Close

"After having a good deal to say for himself, Geoffrey was asked repeatedly by other committee members if he had any constructive rather than negative contributions to make. He decided to leave."

Brian Walsh QC on Boycott's behaviour at an emergency committee meeting

"I had beaten my brains out for 3 1/2 hours.Brian Close would not accept any measure of responsibility for the mess we are in. How can I serve on the cricket committee when I don't see eye to eye with them on any subject?"

Boycott on the same meeting

"Hello, it's God here,who's that?"

Boycott ringing the sports desk of The Sun about his column

Britannic Assurance Championship 1990

		P	W	L	D	BONUS BAT	BONUS BOWL	POINTS
1 (3)	MIDDLESEX	22	10	1	11	73	55	288
2 (2)	Essex	22	8	2	12	73	56	257
3 (6)	Hampshire	22	8	4	10	67	48	243
4 (1)	Worcestershire	22	7	1	14	70	58	240
5 (8)	Warwickshire	22	7	7	8	55	64	231
6 (4)	Lancashire	22	6	3	13	65	56	217
7 (13)	Leicestershire	22	6	7	9	61	53	210
8 (17)	Glamorgan	22	5	6	11	64	48	192
9 (12)	Surrey	22	4	3	15	54	64	190
10 (16)	Yorkshire	22	5	9	8	52	55	187
11 (5)	Northants	22	4	9	9	61	60	185
12 (6)	Derbyshire	22	6	7	9	58	52	181
13 (9)	Gloucestershire	22	4	7	11	51	58	173
13 (11)	Notts	22	4	8	10	51	58	173
15 (14)	Somerset	22	3	4	15	73	45	166
16 (15)	Kent	22	3	6	13	69	35	152
17 (10)	Sussex	22	3	9	10	51	44	143

Derbys:- 25pts deducted for sub-standard pitch. Surrey awarded eight points for batting last in drawn match with scores level. (1989 positions in brackets)
Top of the table: May 5 Warwickshire; May 19 Notts; May 23 Notts/Derbys; May 26 Derbys; Jun 2 Notts; Jun 9 Lancs; Jun 16 Warwicks; Jun 20 Middlesex; Aug 29 Essex; Sep 7 Middlesex; Sep 20 Middlesex became champions.
Bottom of the table: May 5 Yorkshire; May 23 Gloucs; Jun 2 Surrey; Jun 9 Gloucs; Aug 8 Sussex.

CHAMPIONSHIP RESULTS CHART

Home Team \ Away Team	Derby	Essex	Glam	Glos	Hants	Kent	Lancs	Leics	Middx	Northants	Notts	Somerset	Surrey	Sussex	Warwicks	Worcs	Yorks
Derbyshire	-	INN+94 A	X	D	X	10 wkts H	60 runs A	D	171 runs H	D	D	X	X	X	2 wkts A	D	144 runs H
Essex	9 wkts H	-	D	D	X	D	6 wkts H	D	D	276 runs A	10 wkts H	X	283 runs H	D	X	X	X
Glamorgan	D	X	-	D	8 wkts A	6 runs A	D	9 wkts A	X	X	X	D	D	X	5 wkts H	D	5 wkts A
Glos	X	X	145 runs A	-	D	D	X	111 runs A	X	INN+128 H	D	D	D	INN+86 A	66 runs H	D	D
Hants	48 runs H	D	4 wkts A	2 wkts H	-	D	X	X	D	INN+22 H	8 wkts H	D	9 wkts A	INN+157 A	X	X	X
Kent	X	4 wkts A	X	X	6 runs A	-	3 wkts A	7 wkts H	D	X	7 wkts H	D	D	5 wkts H	X	D	D
Lancs	D	X	X	5 wkts H	D	2 wkts H	-	D	5 wkts A	X	D	D	D	X	A	1 run A	X
Leics	140 runs H	X	X	X	D	8 wks H	X	-	103 runs A	X	5 wkts A	D	X	29 runs A	X	A	7 wks H
Middx	X	D	D	10 wkts H	X	8 wks H	X	D	-	X	10 wks A	4 wks H	D	D	D	D	D
Northants	INN+51 runs A	D	6 wkts A	157 runs A	X	D	D	D	79 runs A	-	H	X	D	D	INN+30 A	X	4 wks A
Notts	D	X	238 runs A	D	X	X	10 wkts A	D	D	8 wks H	-	X	D	D	X	173 runs A	X
Somerset	146 runs A	D	D	X	X	D	X	INN+5 H	D	7 wks A	D	-	D	7 wkts A	D	D	X
Surrey	D	D	170 runs H	10 wkts H	D	D	9 wkts A	X	INN+51 A	147 runs H	X	10 wkts H	-	X	168 runs H	D	INN+5 H
Sussex	18 runs A	X	D	X	6 wkts H	X	X	6 wkts A	X	X	5 runs A	X	5 wkts H	-	6 wkts H	X	7 wkts H
Warwicks	X	5 wkts H	D	X	D	D	D	X	D	D	D	X	X	X	-	D	INN+5 H
Worcs	X	10 wkts A	261 runs H	148 runs A	D	X	10 wkts A	X	X	INN+50 A	INN+6 H	D	X	D	322 runs H	-	D
Yorks	4 wkts H	INN+11 A	X	X	5 wkts A	X	X	8 wkts A	64 runs A	A	5 wkts A	D	D	X	2 wkts H	X	-

H = Home win   A = Away win   D = Draw   X = No fixture

ONE-DAY CRICKET
NatWest Bank Trophy
First Round
Marlow: NOTTINGHAMSHIRE beat Buckinghamshire by 192 runs; Chesterfield: DERBYSHIRE best Shropshire by 7 wkts; Torquay: SOMERSET beat Devon by 346 runs (Competition record); Chelmsford: ESSEX beat Scotland by 9 wkts; Gloucester: GLOUCESTERSHIRE beat Lincolnshire by 195 runs; St Albans: WARWICKSHIRE beat Hertfordshire by 128 runs; Old Trafford: LANCASHIRE beat Durham by 8 wkts; Leicester: HAMPSHIRE beat Leicestershire by 1 run; Lord's: MIDDLESEX beat Berkshire by 4 wkts; Northampton: NORTHAMPTONSHIRE beat Staffordshire by 216 runs; Christ Church: KENT beat Oxfordshire by 102 runs; Bury St Edmunds: WORCESTERSHIRE beat Suffolk by 8 wkts; Trowbridge: SURREY beat Wiltshire by 9 wkts; Headingley: YORKSHIRE beat Norfolk by 10 wkts; Downpatrick: SUSSEX beat Ireland by 9 wkts; Swansea: GLAMORGAN beat Dorset by 34 runs

Second Round
Bristol: GLOUCESTERSHIRE beat Kent by 6 wkts; Headingley: YORKSHIRE beat Warwickshire by 10 wkts; Taunton: WORCESTERSHIRE beat Somerset by 7 wkts; Northampton: NORTHAMPTONSHIRE beat Nottinghamshire by 24 runs; Cardiff: GLAMORGAN beat Sussex by 24 runs; Derby: LANCASHIRE beat Derbyshire by 3 wkts; Chelmsford: HAMPSHIRE beat Essex on fewer wickets lost after tied match; Uxbridge: MIDDLESEX beat Surrey by 5 wkts

Quarter-finals
Northampton: NORTHAMPTONSHIRE beat Worcestershire by 4 runs; Old Trafford: LANCASHIRE beat Gloucestershire by 241 runs; Southampton: HAMPSHIRE beat Yorkshire by 111 runs; Lord's: MIDDLESEX beat Glamorgan by 9 wkts

Semi-finals
Southampton: NORTHAMPTONSHIRE beat Hampshire by 1 run; Old Trafford: LANCASHIRE beat Middlesex by 5 wkts

Final
Lord's, Sep 1
NORTHAMPTONSHIRE
A Fordham lbw DeFreitas 5
N A Felton c Allott b DeFreitas 4
W Larkins c Hegg b DeFreitas 7
*A J Lamb lbw b DeFreitas 8
R J Bailey c Hegg b DeFreitas 7
D J Capel run out 36
R G Williams b Watkinson 9
†D Ripley b Watkinson 13
C E L Ambrose run out 48
N G B Cook b Austin 9
M A Robinson not out 3
Extras (b1, lb10, w9, nb2) 22
Total (60 overs) 171
Fall: 1-8 2-19 3-20 4-38 5-39 6-56 7-87 8-126 9-166
Bowling: Allott 12-3-29-0; DeFreitas 12-4-26-5; Wasim Akram 12-0-35-0; Watkinson 12-1-29-2; Austin 12-4-41-1

LANCASHIRE
G D Mendis c Ripley b Capel 14
G Fowler c Cook b Robinson 7
M A Atherton not out 38
N H Fairbrother c Ambrose b Williams 81
M Watkinson not out 24
Extras (lb4, w2, nb3) 9
Total (3 wkts, 45.4 overs) 173

Fall: 1-16 2-28 3-142
Did not bat: *D P Hughes, Wasim Akram, P A J DeFreitas, †W K Hegg, I D Austin, P J W Allott
Bowling: Ambrose 10-1-23-0; Robinson 9-2-26-1; Cook 10 4-2-50-0; Capel 9-0-44-1; Williams 7-0-26-1
Man of the Match: Phillip DeFreitas
Lancashire won by 7 wickets

APPEARED IN BOTH LORD'S FINALS IN ONE SEASON
1975 Middlesex (lost B&H, lost Gillette)
1985 Essex (lost B&H, won Natwest)
1987 Northamptonshire (lost B&H, lost Natwest)
1990 Lancashire (won B&H, won Natwest)

BEST PERFORMANCES
Highest Score – Team
413-4 Somerset v Devon (Competition record); 372-5 Lancashire v Gloucestershire (highest score between two first-class counties in a one day game); 360-2 Northamptonshire v Staffordshire; 336-7 Warwickshire v Hertfordshire; 325-4 Gloucestershire v Lincolnshire.
Highest Individual Innings
162* C J Tavaré (Somerset v Devon); 149* Desmond Haynes (Middlesex v Lancs); 144 G A Gooch (Essex v Hants); 130 A Fordham (Northants v Staffs); 127* A A Metcalfe (Yorks v Warwicks); 121* Gehan Mendis (Lancs v Middlesex)
Best Bowling
7-14 R Lefebvre (Somerset v Devon); 6-9 A I C Dodemaide (Sussex v Ireland); 6-21 C A Walsh (Gloucs v Kent); 5-22 S R Lampitt (Worcs v Suffolk); 5-30 M W Alleyne (Gloucs v Lincs); 5-40 Asif Din (Warwicks v Herts)

BENSON & HEDGES CUP
Group A
Edgbaston: GLAMORGAN beat Warwickshire by 3 runs; Bristol: WORCESTERSHIRE beat Gloucestershire by 3 wkts; Cardiff: GLAMORGAN beat Gloucestershire by 9 runs; Worcester: WORCESTERSHIRE beat Kent by 27 runs; Canterbury: KENT beat Warwickshire by 70 runs; Worcester: GLAMORGAN beat Worcestershire by 16 runs; Edgbaston: WORCESTERSHIRE beat Warwickshire by 32 runs; Canterbury: Kent v Gloucestershire, match abandoned; Swansea: KENT beat Glamorgan by 18 runs; Bristol: WARWICKSHIRE beat Gloucestershire by 6 wkts
WORCESTERSHIRE & GLAMORGAN qualified

Group B
Lord's: MIDDLESEX beat Minor Counties by 4 wkts; Derby: SUSSEX beat Derbyshire by 5 wkts; Marlow: SUSSEX beat Minor Counties by 5 wkts; Taunton: SOMERSET beat Derbyshire by 7 runs; Hove: MIDDLESEX beat Sussex on faster scoring rate; Taunton: SOMERSET beat Minor Counties by 6 wkts; Wellington: DERBYSHIRE beat Minor Counties by 43 runs; Lord's: MIDDLESEX beat Somerset by 8 runs; Derby: DERBYSHIRE beat Middlesex by 8 runs; Hove: SOMERSET beat Sussex by 107 runs
MIDDLESEX & SOMERSET qualified

Group C
Southampton: YORKSHIRE beat Hampshire by 7 wkts; Old Trafford: LANCASHIRE beat Surrey by 76 runs; Fenner's: LANCASHIRE beat Combined Universities by 22 runs; Oval: SURREY beat Hampshire by 87 runs; Headingley: COMBINED UNIVERSITIES beat Yorkshire by 2 wkts; Old Trafford: Lancashire v Hampshire, match

abandoned; Headingley: LANCASHIRE beat Yorkshire by 5 wkts; The Parks: SURREY beat Combined Universities by 6 wkts; Oval: YORKSHIRE beat Surrey by 6 wkts; Southampton: HAMPSHIRE beat Combined Universities by 99 runs
LANCASHIRE & SURREY qualified

Group D
Leicester: NORTHAMPTONSHIRE beat Leicestershire by 5 runs; Chelmsford: ESSEX beat Nottinghamshire by 4 wkts; Trent Bridge: NOTTINGHAMSHIRE beat Leicestershire by 4 wkts; Glasgow: ESSEX beat Scotland by 83 runs; Northampton: ESSEX beat Northamptonshire by 8 wkts; Glasgow: NOTTINGHAMSHIRE beat Scotland by 4 wkts; Northampton: SCOTLAND beat Northamptonshire by 2 runs; Chelmsford: Essex v Leicestershire, match abandoned; Trent Bridge: NOTTINGHAMSHIRE beat Northamptonshire by 3 wkts; Leicester: LEICESTERSHIRE beat Scotland by 7 wkts
ESSEX & NOTTINGHAMSHIRE qualified

Quarter-finals
Taunton: SOMERSET beat Middlesex by 22 runs; Chelmsford: NOTTINGHAMSHIRE beat Essex by 6 wkts; Worcester: WORCESTERSHIRE beat Glamorgan by 7 wkts; Old Trafford: LANCASHIRE beat Surrey by 46 runs

Semi-finals
Trent Bridge: WORCESTERSHIRE beat Nottinghamshire by 9 wkts; Old Trafford: LANCASHIRE beat Somerset by 6 wkts

Final
Lord's, Jul 14

LANCASHIRE
G D Mendis c Neale b Botham	9
G Fowler c Neale b Newport	11
M A Atherton run out	40
N H Fairbrother b Lampitt	11
M Watkinson c&b Botham	50
Wasim Akram c Radford b Newport	28
P A J DeFreitas b Lampitt	28
I D Austin run out	17
†W K Hegg not out	31
*D P Hughes not out	1

Did not bat: P J W Allott

Extras (lb4, nb1) 5
Total for 8 wkts (55 overs) 241
Fall: 1-25 2-33 3-47 4-135 5-136 6-191 7-199 8-231
Bowling: Newport 11-1-47-2; Botham 11-0-49-2; Lampitt 11-3-43-2; Radford 8-1-41-0; Illingworth 11-0-41-0; Hick 3-0-16-1

WORCESTERSHIRE
T S Curtis c Hegg b Wasim Akram	16
M J Weston b Watkinson	19
G A Hick c Hegg b Wasim Akram	1
D B D'Oliveira b Watkinson	23
I T Botham b DeFreitas	38
*P A Neale c Hegg b Austin	0
†S J Rhodes lbw b Allott	5
N V Radford not out	26
R K Illingworth lbw b DeFreitas	16
P J Newport b Wasim Akram	3
S R Lampitt b Austin	4

Extras (lb9, w8, nb4) 21
Total (54 overs) 172
Fall: 1-27 2-38 3-41 4-82 5-87 6-112 7-114 8-154 9-164
Bowling: Allott 10-1-22-1; DeFreitas 11-2-30-2; Wasim Akram 11-0-30-3; Watkinson 11-0-37-2; Austin 11-1-44-2
Lancashire won by 69 runs
Gold Award: Mike Watkinson

BEST PERFORMANCES
Highest Score-Team
331-5 Surrey v Hampshire; 321-5 Somerset v Sussex; 310-3 Somerset v Derbyshire
Lancashire scored a competition best 352-6 in the abandoned game against Hampshire. Their record does not stand.

Highest Individual Innings
177 S J Cook (Somerset v Sussex); 154* C L Smith (Hants v Combined Universities); 138* I T Botham (Worcs v Glamorgan, group match)
Neil Fairbrother scored 145 in Lancashire's abandoned match against Hampshire

Best Bowling
4-16 C L Parfitt (Scotland v Hants); 4-22 G C Small (Warwicks v Glamorgan); 4-25 M Frost (Glamorgan v Worcs, group match); P J Newport (Worcs v Kent); I D Austin (Lancs v Surrey, group match)

Refuge Assurance (Sunday) League

		P	W	L	T	NR	Pts
1 (5)	DERBYSHIRE	16	12	3	0	1	50
2 (1)	Lancashire	16	11	3	0	2	48
3 (9)	Middlesex	16	10	5	0	1	42
4 (4)	Nottinghamshire	16	10	5	0	1	42
5 (6)	Hampshire	16	9	5	0	2	40
6 (11)	Yorkshire	16	9	6	0	1	38
7 (7)	Surrey	16	9	6	0	1	38
8 (10)	Somerset	16	8	8	0	0	32
9 (16)	Gloucestershire	16	7	7	0	2	32
10 (2)	Worcestershire	16	7	8	0	1	30
11 (12)	Kent	16	7	8	0	1	30
12 (3)	Essex	16	6	9	0	1	26
13 (13)	Sussex	16	5	9	0	2	24
14 (15)	Warwickshire	16	5	10	0	1	22
15 (17)	Glamorgan	16	4	11	0	1	18
16 (14)	Leicestershire	16	4	11	0	1	18
17 (8)	Northamptonshire	16	3	12	0	1	14

Last season's positions in brackets

Refuge Assurance Cup
Semi-finals
Middlesex beat Lancashire by 45 runs; Derbyshire beat Nottinghamshire by 22 runs.
Final
Edgbaston, Sep 16
DERBYSHIRE 197-7 (40 overs); MIDDLESEX 201-5 (39.4 overs)
Middlesex won by 5 wickets
Man of the Match: Paul Downton (Middlesex)

MEN AND MATTERS

❝ It's a bit like the four-minute mile or climbing Mount Everest. Someone is going to do it eventually but nobody forgets the person who did it first."

Sir Richard Hadlee on his 400 Test wickets

"I feel I have lost my edge with the ball, I am not beating guys off a length now. I have lost that zip, that yard of pace. I am slow in the field now, a cart-horse. I am weary."

Sir Richard Hadlee

"Since I have never been one to dispute the umpire's decision, I accept with pleasure."

Sir Donald Bradman on agreeing to have a new stand named after him at Adelaide.

"When we lose we're a joke. When we win there are dubious decisions that went our way. We never get any kudos for just playing well and outplaying the opposition."

Allan Border on the Australian media

"Anyone with anything original to say about Mark Taylor should contact our sports desk immediately....Does it not dawn on the blessed fellow to do something idiotic or, better still, to hit a bad patch so that we scribes can start worrying about him? Batting is difficult , its movements being unnatural, and one error means ignominy. Has no one told him this?"

Peter Roebuck, Sydney Morning Herald

"My friend Imran Khan, who is a famous cricketer and a very popular man with the ladies, has bodyguards outside his room warding women off. I have guys warding them in."

Zia Mahmood, leading bridge player

"The gesture demonstrates the sublimated socially acceptable face of the homo-erotic impulse that makes sport possible."

Oliver James, clinical psychiatrist, analysing a picture of Alec Stewart and Chris Lewis embracing at the fall of a wicket

"I've started counting my teeth every morning because I've been kicked in them so often."

David Bairstow on being dropped by Yorkshire

"I wouldn't say I have reached the stage where I'm going to tell the selectors to stuff it but....I have got as far as saying sod 'em"

David Gower on being dropped by England again

"Most of the summer I have been at a different party to the others and it is nice to join the main one now. **❞**

Gower on his century at The Oval

A RECORD A DAY...

1 Three triple-centuries were hit in England in 1990 (by Gooch, Fairbrother and Cook), which has happened before only in 1899 (Abel, Poore and Trumper) and 1934 (Ashdown, Bradman and Hammond).

2 Gooch and Stephenson, for Essex against Northamptonshire, became the third pair to record two opening partnerships above 200 in the same match

3 Tom Moody of Warwickshire and Australia hit seven centuries in eight games and completed 1,000 runs in 12 innings, a record for a player in his debut season. Warwickshire promptly released him, preferring to keep the fast bowler Allan Donald as their overseas player; Moody joined Worcestershire instead.

4 Graeme Hick of Worcestershire narrowly missed the world record of 709 runs without being dismissed set by K C Ibrahim for Bombay in 1947-48. Hick reached 645, an English record. Hick also became the youngest man to score 50 centuries, aged 24 against Bradman's 26, though Bradman needed only 175 innings against Hick's 249. Hick was not given out lbw until September 14.

5 Jimmy Cook scored 902 runs in the Sunday League beating the record of 814 set by Clive Rice in 1977.

6 Northamptonshire beat their highest-ever twice in a week, both times against Essex: 592 for six then 632 for six declared.

7 Hugh Morris scored ten centuries for Glamorgan, beating Javed Miandad's record of eight.

8 David Ward became the first Surrey player to score 2,000 runs in a season since 1962.

9 Darren Bicknell and David Ward of Surrey put on 413 for the third wicket, the highest stand ever against Kent.

10 Mark Alleyne's 256 for Gloucestershire against Northamptonshire was the county's highest since 1939.

11 Desmond Haynes of Middlesex hit 1000 runs on Saturdays.

Refuge Assurance Results Chart

Team	Derbys	Ess	Gla	Glo	Han	Ke	Lan	Lei	Mx	Nor	Not	Som	Sur	Sus	War	Wor	Yor
Derbys	–	W	W	W	L	W	W	W	A	W	L	W	W	W	W	W	L
Essex	L	–	W	L	L	L	L	L	L	W	L	W	A	W	W	W	L
Glam	L	L	–	W	L	L	L	W	L	L	L	L	W	L	W	L	A
Glos	L	W	L	–	A	W	W	L	L	L	A	W	W	W	W	L	L
Hants	W	W	W	A	–	L	A	W	L	W	W	L	L	L	W	W	W
Kent	L	W	W	L	W	–	L	L	L	W	W	W	L	A	L	L	W
Lancs	L	W	W	L	A	W	–	W	L	W	W	W	A	W	W	W	W
Leics	L	W	L	W	L	W	L	–	L	L	L	L	L	W	A	L	L
Middx	A	W	W	W	W	W	W	W	–	W	L	L	L	L	W	W	L
Northants	L	L	W	W	L	L	L	W	L	–	L	L	L	L	L	A	L
Notts	W	W	W	A	L	L	L	W	W	W	–	L	W	W	W	L	W
Somerset	L	L	W	L	W	L	L	W	W	W	W	–	L	W	W	L	L
Surrey	L	A	L	L	W	W	L	W	W	W	L	W	–	L	W	W	W
Sussex	L	L	W	L	W	A	A	L	W	W	L	L	W	–	L	L	L
Warwicks	L	L	L	L	L	W	W	A	L	W	L	L	L	W	–	W	W
Worcs	L	L	W	W	L	W	L	W	L	A	W	W	L	W	L	–	L
Yorks	W	W	A	W	L	L	L	W	W	W	L	W	L	W	L	W	–

W = won L = lost T = tied A = abandoned

OTHER CRICKET 1990

NEHRU CUP FINAL
Eden Gardens, Calcutta, Nov 1
Pakistan won by four wickets
WEST INDIES 273-5 (50 overs) D L Haynes 107*
PAKISTAN 277-6 (49.5 overs) Ejaz Ahmed 56, Salim Malik 71, Imran Khan 55*

ICC Trophy Final
The Hague, Jun 23
Holland 197-9 (60 overs) (Ali Shah 4-56)
Zimbabwe 198-4 (54,2 overs) (A Flower 69no)
Zimbabwe won by 6 wickets and qualify for the 1992 World Cup.

Minor Counties Championship Final
Luton, Sep 9
BERKSHIRE 171-5 (55 overs) (G T Headley 50*)
HERTS 172-3 (52,5 overs) (N R C MacLaurin 52*)
Hertfordshire won by 7 wickets

National Village Championship
Lord's, Aug 25
Goatacre (Wiltshire) 267-5 (K M Iles 123, J P Turner 53); Dunstall (Staffs) 217-8 (P M Wallbank 51; J I Angell 4-18)
Goatacre won by 50 runs

Women's European Cup Final
Great Oakley, Northamptonshire, Jul 23
ENGLAND 224-3 (25 overs) (Watson 107*)
IRELAND 159-8 (25 overs) (Moore 44)
England won by 65 runs

ALL-TIME COUNTY CHAMPIONSHIP TABLE 1864-1990

		P	W	L	T	D	Titles	% Wins
1	Yorkshire	2650	1194	441	2	1013	31	45.05
2	Surrey	2629	1042	574	4	1009	18	39.63
3	Middlesex	2252	842	570	5	835	10	37.38
4	Lancashire	2550	951	517	3	1079	8	37.29
5	Kent	2472	895	751	4	822	6	36.21
6	Nottinghamshire	2381	723	624	-	1034	14	30.36
7	Gloucestershire	2350	694	867	2	787	3	29.53
8	Essex	2075	585	596	5	889	4	28.19
9	Sussex	2521	702	870	5	944	-	27.85
10	Hampshire	2184	572	752	4	856	2	26.19
11	Warwickshire	2056	535	603	1	917	3	26.02
12	Worcestershire	1997	493	703	1	800	5	24.69
13	Derbyshire	2112	517	769	1	825	1	24.47
14	Northants	1809	429	643	3	734	-	23.71
15	Somerset	2082	485	851	3	743	-	23.29
16	Leicestershire	2042	441	761	1	839	1	21.60
17	Glamorgan	1609	346	554	-	709	2	21.50

Figures based on *Wisden Cricketer's Almanack*. Titles include only outright wins.

ALL-TIME SUNDAY LEAGUE TABLE 1969-1990

		P	W	L	T	A	Titles	Pts
1	Essex	352	191	128	3	30	3	830
2	Kent	352	186	128	4	34	3	820
3	Hampshire	352	187	130	6	29	3	818
4	Lancashire	352	172	134	7	39	3	780
5	Somerset	352	175	141	2	34	1	772
6	Worcestershire	352	171	149	5	27	3	748
7	Middlesex	352	161	148	4	39	-	730
8	Leicestershire	352	158	146	2	46	2	728
9	Sussex	352	156	154	4	38	1	708
10	Yorkshire	352	151	157	2	42	1	692
11	Derbyshire	352	153	162	2	35	1	686
12	Surrey	352	147	163	4	38	-	672
13	Nottinghamshire	352	147	171	3	31	-	656
14	Warwickshire	352	132	177	6	37	1	614
15	Northamptonshire	352	128	185	4	35	-	590
16	Gloucestershire	352	123	184	5	40	-	582
17	Glamorgan	352	116	197	3	36	-	542

P: Played *W*: Won *L*: Lost *T*: Tied *A*: Abondoned *D*: Drawn

CHAMPIONS

WORLD CUP

1975	West Indies beat Australia by 17 runs
1979	West Indies beat England by 92 runs
1983	India beat West Indies by 43 runs
1987	Australia beat England by 7 runs

COUNTY CHAMPIONS

1864	Surrey	1905	Yorkshire	1955	Surrey
1865	Nottinghamshire	1906	Kent	1956	Surrey
1866	Middlesex	1907	Nottinghamshire	1957	Surrey
1867	Yorkshire	1908	Yorkshire	1958	Surrey
1868	Nottinghamshire	1909	Kent	1959	Yorkshire
1869	Notts & Yorks (shared)	1910	Kent	1960	Yorkshire
1870	Yorkshire	1911	Warwickshire	1961	Hampshire
1871	Notts	1912	Yorkshire	1962	Yorkshire
1872	Notts	1913	Kent	1963	Yorkshire
1873	Gloucs & Notts (shared)	1914	Surrey	1964	Worcestershire
1874	Gloucestershire	1915-18	Not held	1965	Worcestershire
1875	Nottinghamshire	1919	Yorkshire	1966	Yorkshire
1876	Gloucestershire	1920	Middlesex	1967	Yorkshire
1877	Gloucestershire	1921	Middlesex	1968	Yorkshire
1878	Undecided	1922	Yorkshire	1969	Glamorgan
1879	Lancs & Notts (shared)	1923	Yorkshire	1970	Kent
1880	Nottinghamshire	1924	Yorkshire	1971	Surrey
1881	Lancashire	1925	Yorkshire	1972	Warwickshire
1882	Lancs & Notts (shared)	1926	Lancashire	1973	Hampshire
1883	Nottinghamshire	1927	Lancashire	1974	Worcestershire
1884	Nottinghamshire	1928	Lancashire	1974	Worcestershire
1885	Nottinghamshire	1929	Nottinghamshire	1975	Leicestershire
1886	Nottinghamshire	1930	Lancashire	1976	Middlesex
1887	Surrey	1931	Yorkshire	1977	Kent & Middx (shared)
1888	Surrey	1932	Yorkshire	1978	Kent
1889	Lancs, Notts & Surrey	1933	Yorkshire	1979	Essex
	(shared)	1934	Lancashire	1980	Middlesex
1890	Surrey	1935	Yorkshire	1981	Nottinghamshire
1891	Surrey	1936	Derbyshire	1982	Middlesex
1892	Surrey	1937	Yorkshire	1983	Essex
1893	Yorkshire	1938	Yorkshire	1984	Essex
1894	Surrey	1939	Yorkshire	1985	Middlesex
1895	Surrey	1940-45	Not held	1986	Essex
1896	Yorkshire	1946	Yorkshire	1987	Nottinghamshire
1897	Lancashire	1947	Middlesex	1988	Worcestershire
1898	Yorkshire	1948	Glamorgan	1989	Worcestershire
1899	Surrey	1949	Middx & Yorks (shared)	1990	Middlesex
1900	Yorkshire	1950	Lancs & Surrey (shared)		
1901	Yorkshire	1951	Warwickshire		
1902	Yorkshire	1952	Surrey		
1903	Middlesex	1953	Surrey		
1904	Lancashire	1954	Surrey		

Most outright wins
31 Yorkshire; **18** Surrey; **14** Nottinghamshire; **10** Middlesex; **8** Lancashire; **6** Kent; **5** Worcestershire.

NATWEST BANK TROPHY

(Gillette Cup 1963-80)

1963	Sussex beat Worcestershire by 14 runs
1964	Sussex beat Warwickshire by 8 wickets
1965	Yorkshire beat Surrey by 175 runs
1966	Warwickshire beat Worcs by 5 wickets
1967	Kent beat Somerset by 32 runs
1968	Warwickshire beat Sussex by 4 wickets
1969	Yorkshire beat Derbyshire by 69 runs
1970	Lancashire beat Sussex by 6 wickets
1971	Lancashire beat Kent by 24 runs
1972	Lancashire beat Warwickshire by 4 wickets
1973	Gloucestershire beat Sussex by 40 runs
1974	Kent beat Lancashire by 4 wickets
1975	Lancashire beat Middlesex by 7 wickets
1976	Northants beat Lancashire by 4 wickets
1977	Middlesex beat Glamorgan by 5 wickets
1978	Sussex beat Somerset by 5 wickets
1979	Somerset beat Northants by 45 runs
1980	Middlesex beat Surrey by 7 wickets
1981	Derbyshire beat Northants fewer wickets lost (scores level)
1982	Surrey beat Warwickshire by 9 wickets
1983	Somerset beat Kent by 24 runs
1984	Middlesex beat Kent by 4 wickets
1985	Essex beat Nottinghamshire by 1 run
1986	Sussex beat Lancashire by 7 wickets
1987	Nottinghamshire beat Northants by 3 wickets
1988	Middlesex beat Worcestershire by 3 wickets
1989	Warwickshire beat Middlesex by 4 wickets
1990	Lancashire beat Northants by 7 wickets

Most wins
5 Lancashire, **4** Sussex, Middlesex

REFUGE ASSURANCE LEAGUE
(John Player League 1969-86)

		Pts
1969	Lancashire	49
1970	Lancashire	53
1971	Worcestershire	44
1972	Kent	45
1973	Kent	50
1974	Leicestershire	54
1975	Hampshire	52
1976	Kent	40
1977	Leicestershire	52
1978	Hampshire	48
1979	Somerset	50
1980	Warwickshire	46
1981	Essex	50
1982	Sussex	58
1983	Yorkshire	46
1984	Essex	50
1985	Essex	44
1986	Hampshire	50
1987	Worcestershire	46
1988	Worcestershire	50
1989	Lancashire	52
1990	Derbyshire	50

Most wins
3 Essex, Kent, Hampshire, Worcestershire, Lancashire

BENSON & HEDGES CUP

1972	Leicestershire beat Yorkshire by 5 wickets
1973	Kent beat Worcestershire by 39 runs
1974	Surrey beat Leicestershire by 27 runs
1975	Leicestershire beat Middlesex by 5 wickets
1976	Kent beat Worcestershire by 43 runs
1977	Gloucestershire beat Kent by 64 runs
1978	Kent beat Derbyshire by 6 wickets
1979	Essex beat Surrey by 35 runs
1980	Northants beat Essex by 6 runs
1981	Somerset beat Surrey by 7 wickets
1982	Somerset beat Nottinghamshire by 9 wickets
1983	Middlesex beat Essex by 4 runs
1984	Lancashire beat Warwickshire by 6 wickets
1985	Leicestershire beat Essex by 5 wickets
1986	Middlesex beat Kent by 2 runs
1987	Yorkshire beat Northants fewer wickets lost (scores level)
1988	Hampshire beat Derbyshire by 7 wickets
1989	Nottinghamshire beat Essex by 3 wickets
1990	Lancashire beat Worcestershire by 69 runs

Most wins
3 Leicestershire, Kent

ENGLAND AGAINST OTHER COUNTRIES
v Australia

	W	L	D
1876-77	1	1	0
1878-79	0	1	0
1880	1	0	0
1881-82	0	2	2
1882	0	1	0
1882-83	2	2	0
1884	1	0	2
1884-85	3	2	0
1886	3	0	0
1886-87	2	0	0
1887-88	1	0	0
1888	2	1	0
1890	2	0	0
1891-92	1	2	0
1893	1	0	2
1894-95	3	2	0
1896	2	1	0
1897-98	1	4	0
1899	0	1	4
1901-02	1	4	0
1902	1	2	2
1903-04	3	2	0
1905	2	0	3
1907-08	1	4	0
1909	1	2	2
1911-12	4	1	0
1912	1	0	2
1920-21	0	5	0
1921	0	3	2
1924-25	1	4	0
1926	1	0	4
1928-29	4	1	0
1930	1	2	2
1932-33	4	1	0
1934	1	2	2
1936-37	2	3	0
1938	1	1	2
1946-47	0	3	2
1948	0	4	1
1950-51	1	4	0
1953	1	0	4
1954-55	3	1	1
1956	2	1	2
1958-59	0	4	1
1961	1	2	2
1962-63	1	1	3
1964	0	1	4
1965-66	1	1	3
1968	1	1	3
1970-71	2	0	4
1972	2	2	1
1974-75	1	4	1
1975	0	1	3
1976-77	0	1	0
1977	3	0	2
1978-79	5	1	0
1979-80	0	3	0
1980	0	0	1
1981	3	1	2
1982-83	1	2	2
1985	3	1	2
1986-87	2	1	2
1987-88	0	0	1
1989	0	4	2
Total	*88*	*101*	*80*

v South Africa

	E	SA	D
1888-89	2	0	0
1891-92	1	0	0
1895-96	3	0	0
1898-99	2	0	0
1905-06	1	4	0
1907	1	0	2
1909-10	2	3	0
1912	3	0	0
1913-14	4	0	1
1922-23	2	1	2
1924	3	0	2
1927-28	2	2	1
1929	2	0	3
1930-31	0	1	4

1935	0	1	4
1938-39	1	0	4
1947	3	0	2
1948-49	2	0	3
1951	3	1	1
1955	3	2	0
1956-57	2	2	1
1960	3	0	2
1964-65	1	0	4
1965	0	1	2
Total	*46*	*18*	*38*

v West Indies

	E	WI	D
1928	3	0	0
1929-30	1	1	2
1933	2	0	1
1934-35	1	2	1
1939	1	0	2
1947-48	0	2	2
1950	1	3	0
1953-54	2	2	1
1957	3	0	2
1959-60	1	0	4
1963	1	3	1
1966	1	3	1
1967-68	1	0	4
1969	2	0	1
1973	0	2	1
1973-74	1	1	3
1976	0	3	2
1980	0	1	4
1980-81	0	2	2
1984	0	5	0
1985-86	0	5	0
1988	0	4	1
1989-90	1	2	1
Total	*22*	*41*	*36*

v New Zealand

	E	NZ	D
1929-30	1	0	3
1931	1	0	2
1932-33	0	0	2
1937	1	0	2
1946-47	0	0	1
1949	0	0	4
1950-51	1	0	1
1954-55	2	0	0
1958	4	0	1
1958-59	1	0	1
1962-63	3	0	0
1965	3	0	0
1965-66	0	0	3
1969	2	0	1
1970-71	1	0	1
1973	2	0	1
1974-75	1	0	1
1977-78	1	1	1
1978	3	0	0
1983	3	1	0
1983-84	0	1	2
1986	0	1	2
1987-88	0	0	3
1990	1	0	2
Total	*31*	*4*	*34*

v India

	E	I	D
1932	1	0	0
1933-34	2	0	1
1936	2	0	1
1946	1	0	2

1951-52	1	1	3
1952	3	0	1
1959	5	0	0
1961-62	0	2	3
1963-64	0	0	5
1967	3	0	0
1971	0	1	2
1972-73	1	2	2
1974	3	0	0
1976-77	3	1	1
1979	1	0	3
1979-80	1	0	0
1981-82	0	1	5
1982	1	0	2
1984-85	2	1	2
1986	0	2	1
1990	1	0	2
Total	*31*	*11*	*36*

v Pakistan

	E	P	D
1954	1	1	2
1961-62	1	0	2
1962	4	0	1
1967	2	0	1
1968-69	0	0	3
1971	1	0	2
1972-73	0	0	3
1974	0	0	3
1977-78	0	0	3
1978	2	0	1
1982	2	1	0
1983-84	0	1	2
1987	0	1	4
1987-88	0	1	2
Total	*13*	*5*	*29*

v Sri Lanka

	E	SL	D
1981-82	1	0	0
1984	0	0	1
1988	1	0	0
Total	*2*	*0*	*1*

——— RECORDS ———

BATTING RECORDS

Most Runs in a Career
61,237 J.B. Hobbs; 58,969 F.E. Woolley; 57,611 E.H. Hendren; 55,061 C.P. Mead; 54,896 W.G. Grace; 50,551 W.R. Hammond; 50,138 H. Sutcliffe

Highest Individual Scores
499 Hanif Mohammad, Karachi v Bahawalpur (Karachi) 1958-59; 452* D.G. Bradman NSW v Queensland (Sydney) 1929-30; 443* B.B. Nimbalkar, Maharashtra v Kathiawar (Poona) 1948-49

Most Runs in an Over
77: L K Germon and R M Ford off R H Vance, Canterbury v Wellington (Christchurch) 1989-90; Off a six-ball over –36: G.S. Sobers off M.A. Nash, Nottinghamshire v Glamorgan (Swansea) 1968; R.J. Shastri off Tilak Raj, Bombay v Baroda (Bombay) 1984-85

Most Sixes
In an innings: 15 J.R. Reid, Wellington v Northern Districts (Wellington) 1962-63
In a match: 17 W.J. Stewart, Warwickshire v Lancashire (Blackpool) 1959
In a season: 80 I.T. Botham, Somerset 1985

Separate Hundreds in a Match
Eight times: Zaheer Abbas; seven times: W.R. Hammond; six times: J.B. Hobbs, G.M. Turner

Most Consecutive Hundreds
Six: C.B. Fry 1901; D.G. Bradman 1938-39; M.J. Procter 1970-71. Five E.D. Weekes 1955-56

Most Hundreds in a Season
18 D.C.S. Compton 1947. 16 J.B. Hobbs 1925. 15 W.R. Hammond 1938. 14 H. Sutcliffe 1932

Most Runs in a Season
3816 D.C.S. Compton 1947; 3539 W.J. Edrich 1947; 3518 T.W. Hayward 1906

Most Hundreds in a Career
197 J.B.Hobbs; 170 E.H. Hendren; 167 W.R. Hammond; 153 C.P. Mead; 151 G. Boycott

Highest Average in an English Season
115.66 D.G. Bradman 1938; 102.53 G. Boycott 1979; 102.00 W.A. Johnston 1953; 101.70 G. A. Gooch 1990; 100.12 G. Boycott 1971

Fastest Fifty
Eight minutes: C.C. Inman (57), Leicestershire v Nottinghamshire (Nottingham) 1965

Fastest Hundred
26 minutes T. Moody, Warwicks v Glamorgan (Swansea),1990; 35 minutes P. G. H. Fender (113*), Surrey v Northamptonshire (Northampton), 1920; 35 minutes S. J. O'Shaughnessy (105), Lancashire v Leicestershire (Manchester), 1983

Highest Partnerships
577: V.S. Hazare (288) and Gul Mahomed (319), fourth wicket, Baroda v Holkar (Baroda) 1946-47; 574*: F.M. Worrell (255*) and C.L. Walcott (314*), fourth wicket, Barbados v Trinidad (Port of Spain) 1945-46; 561: Waheed Mirza (324) and Mansoor Akhtar (224*), first wicket, Karachi Whites v Quetta (Karachi) 1976-77

1,000 Runs before June
1,000 in May: W.G. Grace 1895; W.R. Hammond 1927; C. Hallows 1928
1,000 before June: T.W. Hayward 1900; D.G. Bradman 1930, 1938; W.J. Edrich 1938; G.M. Turner 1973; G.A. Hick 1988

SIR LEONARD HUTTON
YORKSHIRE AND ENGLAND
1916-1990
First-class record: 40,140 runs at an average of 55.51. 129 centuries. 173 wickets with leg-spin at an average of 29.42. 396 catches.
Test record: 79 Tests. 6,971 runs at an average of 56.67. 19 centuries. 3 wickets at an average of 77.33. 57 catches.

BOWLING RECORDS
Most Wickets in a Career
4,187 W. Rhodes, 1898-1930; 3,776 A.P. Freeman, 1914-36; 3,278 C.W.L. Parker, 1903-35; 3,061 J.T. Hearne, 1888-1923

Most Wickets in a Match
19-90 J.C. Laker, England v Australia (Manchester) 1956

Most Wickets in a Day
17-48 C. Blythe, Kent v Northamptonshire (Northampton) 1907; 17-91 H. Verity, Yorkshire v Essex (Leyton) 1933;

17-106 T.W. Goddard, Gloucestershire v Kent (Bristol) 1939

Most Hat-Tricks in a Career
Seven: D.V.P. Wright; six: T.W. Goddard, C.W.L. Parker; five: S. Haigh, V.W.C. Jupp, A.E.G. Rhodes, F.A. Tarrant

Most Wickets in a Season
304 A.P. Freeman 1928; 298 A.P. Freeman 1933; 290 T. Richardson 1895

100 Wickets in a Season Most Times
23 W. Rhodes; 20 D. Shackleton (in successive seasons 1949-68); 17 A.P. Freeman

The Double: 1,000 Runs and 100 Wickets in a Season
16 W. Rhodes; 14 G.H. Hirst; 10 V.W.C. Jupp

WICKETKEEPING RECORDS
Most Dismissals in an Innings
Eight (all ct): A.T.W. Grout, Queensland v Western Australia (Brisbane) 1959-60; D.E. East, Essex v Somerset (Taunton) 1985

Most Dismissals in a Match
12: (8ct 4st) E. Pooley, Surrey v Sussex (The Oval) 1868; (9ct 3st) D. Tallon, Queensland v New South Wales (Sydney) 1938-39; (9ct 3st) H.B. Taber, New South Wales v South Australia (Adelaide) 1968-69

Most Dismissals in a Season
128 (79ct 49st) L.E.G. Ames 1929; 122 (70ct 52st) L.E.G. Ames 1928; 110 (63ct 47st) H. Yarnold 1949

Most Dismissals in a Career
1,648 R.W. Taylor 1960-86; 1,527 J.T. Murray 1952-75; 1,497 H. Strudwick 1902-27; 1,344 A.P.E. Knott 1964-85; 1,310 F.H. Huish 1895-1914

FIELDING RECORDS
Most Catches in an Innings
Seven: M.J. Stewart, Surrey v Northamptonshire (Northampton) 1957; A.S. Brown, Gloucestershire v Nottinghamshire (Nottingham) 1966

Most Catches in a Match
Ten: W.R. Hammond, Gloucestershire v Surrey (Cheltenham) 1928

Most Catches in a Season
78 W.R. Hammond 1928; 77 M.J. Stewart 1957; 73 P.M. Walker 1961; 71 P.J. Sharpe 1962

Most Catches in a Career
1,018 F.E. Woolley 1906-38; 887 W.G. Grace 1865-1908; 831 G.A.R. Lock 1946-70; 819 W.R. Hammond 1920-51; 813 D.B. Close 1949-86

TEAM RECORDS
Highest Totals
1,107: Victoria v New South Wales (Melbourne) 1926-27; 1,059: Victoria v Tasmania (Melbourne) 1922-23
County Championship 887: Yorkshire v Warwickshire (Birmingham) 1896; 863 Lancashire v Surrey (The Oval) 1990

Lowest Totals
12: Oxford University v MCC and Ground (Oxford) 1877, Northamptonshire v Gloucestershire (Gloucester) 1907

Largest Victories
Inns and 851 runs: Railways (910-6 dec) v Dera Ismail Khan (Lahore) 1964-65; Inns and 666 runs: Victoria (1,059) v Tasmania (Melbourne) 1922-23; Inns and 656 runs: Victoria (1,107) v New South Wales (Melbourne) 1926-27

TEN HIGHEST COUNTY CHAMPIONSHIP SCORES

887 Yorks v Warwicks (Edgbaston) 1896
863 LANCS v SURREY (The Oval) 1990
811 Surrey v Somerset (The Oval) 1899
803-4d Kent v Essex (Brentwood) 1934
801 Lancashire v Somerset (Taunton) 1895
761-6d ESSEX v LEICS (Chelmsford) 1990
742 Surrey v Hampshire (The Oval) 1909
739-7d Notts v Sussex (Trent Bridge) 1903
726 Notts v Sussex (Trent Bridge) 1895
701-9d SURREY v LANCS (The Oval) 1990

TEST MATCH RECORDS
BATTING
Most Runs in a Career
10,122 S.M. Gavaskar 1971-87; 8701 A.R. Border 1974-90; 8114 G. Boycott 1964-82; 8032 G.S. Sobers 1954-74; 7990 I.V.A. Richards 1978-90; 7891 Javed Miandad 1976-90; 7674 D I Gower 1978-90; 7624 M.C. Cowdrey 1954-75; 7515 C.H. Lloyd 1966-85
Highest Individual Innings
365* G.S. Sobers, West Indies v Pakistan (Kingston) 1957-58; 364 L. Hutton, England v Australia (The Oval) 1938; 337 Hanif Mohammad, Pakistan v West Indies (Bridgetown) 1957-58; 336* W.R. Hammond, England v New Zealand (Auckland) 1932-33; 334 D.G. Bradman, Australia v England (Leeds) 1930; 333 G A.Gooch, England v India (Lord's) 1990
Most Runs in a Series
974 D.G. Bradman 1930; 905 W.R. Hammond 1928-29; 839 M.A. Taylor 1989
Highest Career Averages
99.94 D.G. Bradman; 60.97 R.G. Pollock; 60.83 G.A. Headley; 60.73 H. Sutcliffe
Most Hundreds
34 S.M. Gavaskar; 29 D.G. Bradman; 26 G.S. Sobers; 24 G.S. Chappell, I.V.A. Richards; 23 A.R. Border

YOUNGEST TEST CRICKETERS
Year	Days	
15	124	Mustaq Mohammed (Pak) 1958-59
16	189	Aaqib Javed (Pak) 1988-89
16	205	SACHIN TENDULKAR (Ind) 1989-90
16	221	Aftab Baloch (Pak) 1969-70
16	248	Nasim-ul-Ghani (Pak) 1957-58
16	352	Khalid Hassan (Pak) 1954

YOUNGEST TEST CENTURY MAKERS
Year	Days	
17	82	Mustaq Mohammed, Pakistan v India, 1960-61
17	112	SACHIN TENDULKAR, India v England, 1990
19	26	Mohammad Ilyas, Pakistan v New Zealand, 1965-66
19	119	Javed Miandad, Pakistan v New Zealand, 1976-77
19	121	Giff Vivian, New Zealand v South Africa, 1931-32
19	121	Neil Harvey, Australia v India, 1947-48

BOWLING
Most Wickets in a Career
431 R.J. Hadlee 1973-90; 376 I.T. Botham 1977-89; 371 Kapil Dev 1978-90; 358 Imran Khan 1971-90; 355 D.K. Lillee 1971-84; 329 M.D. Marshall 1978-90; 325 R.G.D. Willis 1971-84; 309 L.R. Gibbs 1958-76; 307 F.S. Trueman 1952-65
Most Wickets in an Innings
10-53 J.C. Laker, England v Australia (Manchester) 1956
Most Wickets in a Match
19-90 J.C. Laker, England v Australia (Manchester) 1956; 17-159 S.F. Barnes, England v South Africa (Johannesburg) 1913-14
Most Wickets in a Series
49 S.F. Barnes 1913-14; 46 J.C. Laker 1956; 44 C.V. Grimmett 1935-36; 42 T.M.Alderman 1981

THE LEADING TEST BOWLERS
The men with 300 wickets

	Test	Wkts	Avge	5wI	10wM
Sir Richard Hadlee	86	431	22.29	36	9
Ian Botham	97	376	28.27	27	4
Kapil Dev	109	371	30.19	21	2
Imran Khan	82	358	22.87	23	6
Dennis Lillee	70	355	23.92	23	7
Malcolm Marshall	68	329	20.76	22	4
Bob Willis	90	325	25.20	16	0
Lance Gibbs	79	309	29.09	18	2
Fred Trueman	67	307	21.57	17	3

WICKETKEEPING
Most Dismissals in a Career
355 R.W. Marsh; 269 A.P.E. Knott; 228 Wasim Bari; 223 P J Dujon; 219 T.G. Evans
Most Dismissals in One Test
10 R.W. Taylor, England v India (Bombay) 1979-80
Most Dismissals in an Innings
7: Wasim Bari, Pakistan v New Zealand (Auckland) 1978-79, R.W. Taylor, England v India (Bombay) 1979-80

FIELDING
Most Catches in an Innings
5: V.Y. Richardson, Australia v South Africa (Durban) 1935-36; Yajurvindra Singh, India v England (Bangalore) 1976-77; Mohammed Azharuddin, India v Pakistan (Karachi) 1989-90
Most Catches in a Career
125 A. R. Border 122 G.S. Chappell; 120 M.C. Cowdrey; 116 I.V.A. Richards, I.T. Botham; 110 R.B. Simpson; 110 W.R. Hammond

TEAM RECORDS
Highest Team Totals
903-7 dec England v Australia (The Oval) 1938; 849 England v West Indies (Kingston) 1929-30; 790-3 dec West Indies v Pakistan (Kingston) 1957-58; 758-8 dec Australia v West Indies (Kingston) 1954-55
Lowest Team Totals
26: New Zealand v England (Auckland) 1954-55; 30: South Africa v England (Port Elizabeth) 1895-96; South Africa v England (Birmingham) 1924; 35: South Africa v ngland (Cape Town) 1898-99

1990-91

England Test team in Australia
Graham Gooch (Essex), Allan Lamb (Northants, vice-capt), Michael Atherton (Lancs), Martin Bicknell (Surrey), Angus Fraser (Middlesex), David Gower (Hants), Eddie Hemmings (Notts), Wayne Larkins (Northants), Chris Lewis (Leics), Devon Malcolm (Derbys), John Morris (Derbys), Jack Russell (Gloucestershire), Robin Smith (Hants), Gladstone Small (Warwickshire), Alec Stewart (Surrey), Philip Tufnell (Middlesex).
Manager : Peter Lush; Team Manager: Micky Stewart; Physio: Laurie Brown (Lancs); Scorer: Clem Driver (Essex).

England A team in Pakistan
Hugh Morris (Glamorgan, capt), Neil Fairbrother (Lancs, vice-capt), Darren Bicknell (Surrey), Richard Blakey (Yorkshire), Phil DeFreitas (Lancs), Warren Hegg (Lancs), Nasser Hussain (Essex), Richard Illingworth (Worcs), Keith Medlycott (Middlesex), Tim Munton (Warwickshire), Phil Newport (Worcs), Andy Pick (Notts), Mark Ramprakash (Middlesex), Steve Rhodes (Worcs), Ian Salisbury (Sussex), Graham Thorpe (Surrey)
Manager: Bob Bennett (Lancs); Team Manager: Keith Fletcher (Essex)

England tour to Australia
Oct 25 Western Australia President's X1 (Lilac Hill); Oct 27 Western Australia Country X1 (Geraldton); Oct 30 Western Australia Invitation X1 (Perth, day-night); Nov 2-5 Western Australia (Perth); Nov 7 South Australia Country X1 (Port Pirie); Nov 9-12 South Australia (Adelaide); Nov 14 Tasmania (Hobart); Nov 16-19 Australian X1 (Hobart); Nov 23-27 FIRST TEST (Brisbane); Dec 4 Prime Minister's X1 (Canberra); Dec 7 New Zealand (WSC, Sydney, day-night); Dec 9 Australia (WSC, Perth); Dec 11 Bradman X1 (Bowral); Dec 13 New Zealand (WSC, Sydney, d-n); Dec 15 New Zealand (WSC, Brisbane); Dec 16 Australia (WSC, Brisbane); Dec 20-23 Victoria (Ballarat); Dec 26-30 SECOND TEST (Melbourne).
Jan 1 Australia (WSC, Sydney, d-n); Jan 4-8 THIRD TEST (Sydney); Jan 10 Australia (WSC, Melbourne, d-n);Jan 13 WSC First final (Sydney); Jan 15 WSC Second final (Melbourne, d n); Jan 17 Third final (Melbourne, d-n, if necessary); Jan 19-22 Queensland (Carrara); Jan 25-29 FOURTH TEST (Adelaide); Feb 1-6 FIFTH TEST (Perth). WSC=World Series Cup; d-n=day-night game

England mini-tour to New Zealand
All games one-day internationals against New Zealand Feb 9 Christchurch; Feb 13 Wellington; Feb 16 Auckland.

Australian Tour of West Indies
Mar 1-6 FIRST TEST (Kingston); Mar 23-28 SECOND TEST (Georgetown); Apr 5-10 THIRD TEST (Port of Spain); Apr 19-24 FOURTH TEST (Bridgetown); Apr 27-May 2 FIFTH TEST (St John's, Antigua).
One-day internationals: Feb 26 Kingston; Mar 9 and 10 Port of Spain; Mar 13 Bridgetown; Mar 20 Georgetown.

1991

ENGLISH SEASON 1991
The main touring team in 1991 are the West Indies, who will play five Tests; they will be followed by Sri Lanka who will play one Test at Lord's. For the first time since 1983 there will be Sunday play in the Tests and no rest day. The only exception will be the Third Test at Trent Bridge to avoid a clash with the men's final at Wimbledon.
There is a major change in the County Championship. After starting on Wednesdays and Saturdays since 1920, the three-day fixtures will start on Tuesdays and Fridays instead. This is to allow the England players two days preparation before each Test. The only new venue on the county list is Checkley (Staffordshire) where Derbyshire will play a Sunday League game.

Duration of Matches

Cornhill Insurance Test Series	5 days
Britannic Assurance County Championship	3 days unless stated
Tourist Matches	3 days unless stated
Universities v Counties	3 days
Texaco Trophy One Day Internationals	1 day
Benson & Hedges Cup	1 day
NatWest Bank Trophy	1 day
Refuge Assurance (Sunday) League/ Refuge Assurance Cup	1 day

Date	Venue	Match
APRIL		
13	Fenner's	*Cambridge University v Lancashire
	The Parks	Oxford University v Hampshire
16	Lord's	MCC v Middlesex (four days)
	Fenner's	Cambridge U v Northamptonshire
17	The Parks	Oxford University v Glamorgan
19	Fenner's	Cambridge University v Essex
21		**Refuge Assurance League**
	Cardiff	Glamorgan v Northamptonshire
	Bristol	Gloucestershire v Middlesex
	Southampton	Hampshire v Yorkshire
	Old Trafford	Lancashire v Nottinghamshire
	Leicester	Leicestershire v Derbyshire
	The Oval	Surrey v Somerset
	Edgbaston	Warwickshire v Sussex
	Worcester	Worcestershire v Kent
23		**Benson & Hedges Cup**
	Derby	Derbyshire v Nortamptonshire
	Bristol	Gloucestershire v Combined Univ
	Southampton	Hampshire v Nottinghamshire
	Canterbury	Kent v Leicestershire
	Taunton	Somerset v Middlesex
	The Oval	Surrey v Essex
	Trowbridge	Minor Counties v Glamorgan
	Forfar	Scotland v Lancashire
25		**Benson & Hedges Cup**
	Old Trafford	Lancashire v Kent
	Lord's	Middlesex v Surrey
	Trent Bridge	Nottinghamshire v Yorkshire
	Hove	Sussex v Leicestershire
	Edgbaston	Warwickshire v Essex
	Worcester	Worcestershire v Gloucestershire
	Fenner's/ The Parks	Combined Univ v Derbyshire
	Trowbridge	Minor Counties v Hampshire
27		**Britannic Assurance Championship** *(four days)*
	Derby	Derbyshire v Northamptonshire
	Chelmsford	Essex v Surrey
	Southampton	*Hampshire v Kent
	Leicester	Leicestershire v Glamorgan
	Lord's	Middlesex v Yorkshire
	Taunton	Somerset v Sussex
	Edgbaston	Warwickshire v Lancashire
	Worcester	*Worcestershire v Gloucestershire
		Other Match
	The Parks	Oxford University v Nottinghamshire
28		**Refuge Assurance League**
	Chelmsford	Essex v Yorkshire
	Old Trafford	Lancashire v Northamptonshire
	Leicester	Leicestershire v Glamorgan
	Lord's	Middlesex v Surrey
	Trent Bridge	Nottinghamshire v Warwickshire
	Taunton	Somerset v Sussex

MAY

2		**Benson & Hedges Cup**
	Chelmsford	Essex v Middlesex
	Bristol	Gloucestershire v Northamptonshire
	Southampton	Hampshire v Glamorgan
	Canterbury	Kent v Sussex
	Leicester	Leicestershire v Scotland
	Edgbaston	Warwickshire v Somerset
	Headingley	Yorkshire v Minor Counties
		Combined Univ v Worcestershire
4		**Benson & Hedges Cup**
	Cardiff	Glamorgan v Nottinghamshire
	Leicester	Leicestershire v Lancashire
	Lord's	Middlesex v Warwickshire
	Northampton	Northamptonshire v Combined Univ
	Taunton	Somerset v Surrey
	Worcester	Worcestershire v Derbyshire
	Headingley	Yorkshire v Hampshire
5		**Refuge Assurance League**
	Derby	Derbyshire v Hampshire
	Chelmsford	Essex v Leicestershire
	Cardiff	Glamorgan v Nottinghamshire
	Bristol	Gloucestershire v Worcestershire
	Canterbury	Kent v Warwickshire
	Lord's	Middlesex v Northamptonshire
7		**Benson & Hedges Cup**
	Lord's	Middlesex v Northamptonshire
	Derby	Derbyshire v Gloucestershire
	Chelmsford	Essex v Somerset
	Cardiff	Glamorgan v Yorkshire
	Old Trafford	Lancashire v Sussex
	Northampton	Northamptonshire v Worcestershire
	Trent Bridge	Nottinghamshire v Minor Counties
	The Oval	Surrey v Warwickshire
		Scotland v Kent
9		**Britannic Assurance Championship**
		(four days)
	Bristol	Gloucestershire v Hampshire
	Lord's	Middlesex v Sussex
	Northampton	Northamptonshire v Essex
	Trent Bridge	Nottinghamshire v Leicestershire
	Taunton	Somerset v Glamorgan
	The Oval	Surrey v Kent
	Worcester	Worcestershire v Lancashire
	Headingley	Yorkshire v Warwickshire
9		**Other Match**
	Fenner's	Cambridge University v Derbyshire
12		**Refuge Assurance League**
	Southampton	Hampshire v Kent
	Northampton	Northamptonshire v Leicestershire
	Trent Bridge	Nottinghamshire v Essex
	Taunton	Somerset v Glamorgan
	The Oval	Surrey v Gloucestershire
	Hove	Sussex v Middlesex
	Worcester	Worcestershire v Lancashire
	Headingley	Yorkshire v Warwickshire
12		**Tourist Match**
	Arundel	Lavinia, Duchess of Norfolk's XI
		v West Indies (one Day)
14		**Tourist Match**
	Bristol	Gloucestershire v West Indies
		(one day)
15		**Tourist Match**
	Worcester	Worcestershire v West Indies
		Other Matches
	Fenner's	Cambridge University v Middlesex
	The Parks	Oxford University v Gloucestershire
16		**Britannic Assurance Championship**
		(four days)
	Swansea	Glamorgan v Warwickshire

	Folkestone	Kent v Essex
	Old Trafford	Lancashire v Derbyshire
	Northampton	Northamptonshire v Leicestershire
	Hove	Sussex v Hampshire
	Headingley	Yorkshire v Nottinghamshire
18		**Tourist Match**
	Lord's	Middlesex v West Indies
		Other Match
	Fenner's	Cambridge University v Surrey
19		**Refuge Assurance League**
	Derby	Derbyshire v Lancashire
	Swansea	Glamorgan v Warwickshire
	Bournemouth	Hampshire v Somerset
	Folkestone	Kent v Essex
	Leicester	Leicestershire v Yorkshire
	Northampton	Northamptonshire v Worcestershire
	Hove	Sussex v Gloucestershire
22		**Britannic Assurance Championship**
	Derby	Derbyshire v Somerset
	Chelmsford	Glamorgan v Warwickshire
	Cardiff	Glamorgan v Northamptonshire
	Trent Bridge	Nottinghamshire v Kent
	The Oval	Surrey v Lancashire
	Hove	Sussex v Middlesex
	Sheffield	Yorkshire v Gloucestershire
		Other Match
	Fenner's	Cambridge Univ v Leicestershire
23		**Texaco Trophy**
	Edgbaston	ENGLAND v WEST INDIES
		(First One-day International)
25		**Texaco Trophy**
	Old Trafford	ENGLAND v WEST INDIES
		(Second One-day International)
		Britannic Assurance Championship
	Cardiff	Glamorgan v Sussex
	Bournemouth	Hampshire v Surrey
	Canterbury	Kent v Derbyshire
	Leicester	Leicestershire v Nottinghamshire
	Taunton	Somerset v Middlesex
	Edgbaston	Warwickshire v Gloucestershire
	Headingley	Yorkshire v Northamptonshire
		Other Match
	The Parks	Oxford University v Worcestershire
26		**Refuge Assurance League**
	Swansea	Glamorgan v Sussex
	Swindon	Gloucestershire v Hampshire
	Canterbury	Kent v Derbyshire
	Leicester	Leicestershire v Nottinghamshire
	Taunton	Somerset v Middlesex
	The Oval	Surrey v Essex
	Edgbaston	Warwickshire v Worcestershire
	Headingley	Yorkshire v Northamptonshire
27		**Texaco Trophy**
	Lord's	ENGLAND v WEST INDIES
		(Third One-day International)
29		**Benson & Hedges Cup**
		Quarter-finals
		Tourist Match
	Taunton/	
	The Oval	Somerset or Surrey v West Indies
31		**Britannic Assurance Championship**
	Bristol	Gloucestershire v Esex
	Old Trafford	Lancashire v Sussex
	Lord's	Middlesex v Kent
	Northampton	Northants v Derbyshire
	Trent Bridge	Nottinghamshire v Hampshire
	Edgbaston	Warwickshire v Yorkshire
	Worcester	Worcestershire v Glamorgan

JUNE

1		**Tourist Match**
	Leicester	Leicestershire v West Indies
2		**Refuge Assurance League**
	Chesterfield	Derbyshire v Yorkshire
	Pontypridd	Glamorgan v Essex
	Old Trafford	Lancashire v Sussex
		Middlesex v Kent
	Northampton	Northamptonshire vHampshire
	Edgbaston	Warwickshire v Somerset
		Worcestershire v Surrey
4		**Britannic Assurance Championship**
	Ilford	Essex v Leicestershire
	Swansea	Glamorgan v Somerset
	Bristol	Gloucestershire v Middlesex
	Basingstoke	Hampshire v Lancashire
	Tunbridge Wells	Kent v Warwickshire
	Northampton	Northamptonshire v Worcestershire
	The Oval	Surrey v Nottinghamshire
		Other Match
	The Parks	Oxford University v Yorkshire
6		**CORNHILL INSURANCE TEST MATCH**
	Headingley	ENGLAND v WEST INDIES
		(First Test Match)
7		**Britannic Assurance Championship**
	Chesterfield	Derbyshire v Glamorgan
	Ilford	Essex v Worcestershire
	Southampton	Hampshire v Gloucestershire
	Tunbridge Wells	Kent v Sussex
		Middlesex v Leicestershire
	Edgbaston	Warwickshire v Somerset
		Other Match
	The Parks	Oxford University v Lancashire
9		**Refuge Assurance League**
	Chesterfield	Derbyshire v Surrey
	Ilford	Essex v Worcestershire
	Moreton-in-Marsh	
		Gloucestershire v Northamptonshire
	Basingstoke	Hampshire v Sussex
	Old Trafford	Lancashire v Glamorgan
		Middlesex v Leicestershire
	Trent Bridge	Nottinghamshire v Somerset
12		**Benson & Hedges Cup**
		Semi-finals
		Tourist Match
	Derby/	
	Old Trafford	Derbyshire or Lancashire v West Indies
14		**Britannic Assurance Championship**
	Cardiff	Glamorgan v Middlesex
	Gloucester	Gloucestershire v Nottinghamshire
	Leicester	Leicestershire v Surrey
	Hove	Sussex v Worcestershire
	Harrogate	Yorkshire v Kent
15		**Tourist Match**
	Northampton	*Northamptonshire v West Indies
16		**Refuge Assurance League**
	Checkley (Staffs)	Derbyshire v Somerset
	Chelmsford	Essex v Hampshire
	Cardiff	Glamorgan v Middlesex
	Gloucester	Gloucestershire v Nottinghamshire
	Leicester	Leicestershire v Surrey
	Hove	Sussex v Worcestershire
	Edgbaston	Warwickshire v Lancashire
	Scarborough	Yorkshire v Kent
18		**Britannic Assurance Championship**
	Gloucester	Gloucestershire v Derbyshire
	Leicester	Leicestershire v Lancashire
	Bath	Somerset v Hampshire
	Coventry	Warwickshire v Sussex

	Worcester	Worcestershire v Nottinghamshire
		Other Matches
	Fenner's	Cambridge University v Glamorgan
	The Parks	Oxford University v Kent
20		**CORNHILL INSURANCE TEST MATCH**
	Lord's	*ENGLAND v WEST INDIES
		(Second Test Match)
21		**Britannic Assurance Championship**
	Derby	Derbyshire v Surrey
	Neath (Prov)	*Glamorgan v Leicestershire
	Old Trafford	Lancashire v Kent
	Northampton	*Northamptonshire v Hampshire
	Trent Bridge	Nottinghamshire vWarwickshire
	Bath	Somerset v Gloucestershire
	Horsham	Sussex v Essex
	Sheffield	Yorkshire v Middlesex
22		**Other Match**
		*Ireland v Scotland (Three days)
23		**Refuge Assurance League**
	Old Trafford	Lancashire v Kent
	Trent Bridge	Nottinghamshire v Middlesex
	Bath	Somerset v Gloucestershire
	Horsham	Sussex v Essex
	Edgbaston	Warwickshire v Surrey
	Sheffield	Yorkshire v Worcestershire
26		**NatWest Bank Trophy**
		First Round
		Tourist Match
	The Parks	Oxbridge v West Indies (Two days)
28		**Britannic Assurance Championship**
	Liverpool	Lancashire v Glamorgan
	Lord's	Middlesex v Essex
	Luton	Northamptonshire v Gloucestershire
	The Oval	Surrey v Somerset
	Edgbaston	Warwickshire v Derbyshire
	Worcester	Worcestershire v Leicestershire
		Tourist Match
		League Cricket Conference v West Indies (One day)
29		**Tourist Match**
	Southampton	*Hampshire v West Indies
		Other Match
	Hove	Sussex v Cambridge University
30		**Refuge Assurance League**
	Chelmsford	Essex v Derbyshire
	Canterbury	Kent v Gloucestershire
	Luton	Northamptonshire v Somerset
	The Oval	Surrey v Nottinghamshire
	Worcester	Worcestershire v Leicestershire
	Headingley	Yorkshire v Glamorgan

JULY

2		**Britannic Assurance Championship**
	Chelmsford	Essex v Hampshire
	Colwyn Bay (Prov)	Glamorgan v Nottinghamshire
	Maidstone	Kent v Northamptonshire
	Hinckley	Leicestershire v Gloucestershire
	Taunton	Somerset v Lancashire
	Arundel	Sussex v Surrey
	Edgbaston	Warwickshire v Middlesex
	Headingley	Yorkshire v Worcestershire
		Other Match
	Lord's	Oxford v Cambridge (Varsity Match)
4		**CORNHILL INSURANCE TEST MATCH**
	Trent Bridge	*ENGLAND v WEST INDIES
		(Third Test Match)
5		**Britannic Assurance Championship**
	Derby	Derbyshire v Sussex
	Southampton	Hampshire v Yorkshire
	Maidstone	Kent v Glamorgan
	Leicester	Leicestershire v Northamptonshire
	The Oval	Surrey v Essex

7		**Refuge Assurance League**
	Derby	Derbyshire v Sussex
	Chelmsford	Essex v Warwickshire
	Southampton	Hampshire v Worcestershire
	Maidstone	Kent v Glamorgan
	Leicester	Leicestershire v Lancashire
	Lord's	Middlesex v Yorkshire
	Tring	Northamptonshire v Surrey
10		**Tourist Match**
		Minor Counties v West Indies
		(Two days)
11		**NatWest Bank Trophy**
		Second Round
13	Lord's	**BENSON & HEDGES CUP FINAL**
		Tourist Match
		Ireland v West Indies (One-day)
14		**Refuge Assurance League**
	Canterbury	Kent v Leicestershire
	Trent Bridge	Nottinghamshire v Hampshire
	Taunton	Somerset v Lancashire
	The Oval	Surrey v Sussex
	Edgbaston	Warwickshire v Middlesex
	Worcester	Worcestershire v Derbyshire
	Scarborough	Yorkshire v Gloucestershire
15		**Tourist Match**
	Brecon	Wales v West Indies (One-day)
16		**Britannic Assurance Championship**
	Southend	Essex v Kent
	Portsmouth	Nottinghamshire v Hampshire
	Uxbridge	Middlesex v Northamptonshire
	Trent Bridge	Nottinghamshire v Lancashire
	Guildford	Surrey v Gloucestershire
	Hove	Sussex v Somerset
	Scarborough	Yorkshire v Derbyshire
		Tourist Match
	Swansea	Glamorgan v West Indies
19		**Britannic Assurance Championship**
	Southend	Essex v Somerset
	Cheltenham	Gloucestershire v Glamorgan
	Portsmouth	Hampshire v Warwickshire
	Uxbridge	Middlesex v Lancashire
	Wellingborough	Northamptonshire v Nottinghamshire
	Guildford	Surrey v Yorkshire
	Hove	Sussex v Leicestershire
	Kidderminster	Worcestershire v Derbyshire
20		**Tourist Match**
	Canterbury	*Kent v West Indies
21		**Refuge Assurance League**
	Southend	Essex v Somerset
	Cheltenham	Gloucestershire v Derbyshire
	Portsmouth	Hampshire v Warwickshire
	Uxbridge	Middlesex v Lancashire
	Northampton	Northamptonshire v Nottinghamshire
	The Oval	Surrey v Yorkshire
	Hove	Sussex v Leicestershire
	Worcester	Worcestershire v Glamorgan
23		**Britannic Assurance Championship**
	Chesterfield	Derbyshire v Hampshire
	Cardiff	Glamorgan v Essex
	Cheltenham	Gloucestershire v Sussex
	Old Trafford	Lancashire v Warwickshire
	Northampton	Northamptonshire v Somerset
	Worksop	Nottinghamshire v Yorkshire
	Worcester	Worcestershire v Kent
24		**Tourist Match**
		England Amateur X1 v Sri Lanka
		(One day)
25		**CORNHILL INSURANCE TEST MATCH**
	Edgbaston	*ENGLAND v WEST INDIES
		(Fourth Test Match)
		Tourist Match
		? v Sri Lanka (One day)

26		**Britannic Assurance Championship**
	Cheltenham	Gloucestershire v Worcestershire
	Leicester	*Leicestershire v Warwickshire
	Lord's	Middlesex v Nottinghamshire
	Taunton	Somerset v Kent
	The Oval	Surrey v Glamorgan
27		**Tourist Match**
	Headingley	*Yorkshire v Sri Lanka
28		**Refuge Assurance League**
	Derby	Derbyshire v Northamptonshire
	Cheltenham	Gloucestershire v Essex
	Southampton	Hampshire v Lancashire
	Taunton	Somerset v Kent
	The Oval	Surrey v Glamorgan
	Hove	Sussex v Nottinghamshire
30		**Tourist Match**
	Swansea/	
	Worcester	Glamorgan or Worcestershire v Sri Lanka
31		**NatWest Bank Trophy**
		Quarter-finals
		Tourist Match
		Nottinghamshire or Gloucestershire v West Indies
AUGUST		
2		**Britannic Assurance Championship**
	Canterbury	Kent v Surrey
	Old Trafford	Lancashire v Yorkshire
	Lord's	Middlesex v Hampshire
	Weston-super-Mare	Somerset v Leicestershire
	Eastbourne	Sussex v Northamptonshire
	Worcester	Worcestershire v Warwickshire
		Tourist Match
	Derby or Chesterfield	Derbyshire v Sri Lanka
3		**Tourist Match**
	Chelmsford	*Essex v West Indies
4		**Refuge Assurance League**
	Swansea	Glamorgan v Gloucestershire
	Canterbury	Kent v Surrey
	Old Trafford	Lancashire v Yorkshire
	Lord's	Middlesex v Hampshire
	Trent Bridge	Nottinghamshire v Worcestershire
	Weston-super-Mare	Somerset v Leicestershire
	Eastbourne	Sussex v Northamptonshire
	Edgbaston	Warwickshire v Derbyshire
6		**Britannic Assurance Championship**
	Derby	Derbyshire v Essex
	Canterbury	Kent v Hampshire
	Lytham	Lancashire v Northamptonshire
	Leicester	Leicestershire v Yorkshire
	Weston-super-Mare	Somerset v Worcestershire
	Eastbourne	Sussex v Nottinghamshire
	Edgbaston	Warwickshire v Surrey
		Tourist Match
	Bristol	Gloucestershire v Sri Lanka
8		**CORNHILL INSURANCE TEST MATCH**
	The Oval	*ENGLAND v WEST INDIES
		(Fifth Test Match)
9		**Britannic Assurance Championship**
	Swansea	Glamorgan v Hampshire
	Bristol	Gloucestershire v Lancashire
	Leicester	Leicestershire v Kent
	Lord's	Middlesex v Derbyshire
	Northampton	Northamptonshire v Warwickshire
	Trent Bridge	Nottinghamshire v Essex
	Middlesbrough	Yorkshire v Sussex
10		**Tourist Match**
	Taunton	*Somerset v Sri Lanka

11		**Refuge Assurance League**
	Ebbw Vale	Glamorgan v Hampshire
	Bristol	Gloucestershire v Lancashire
	Leicester	Leicestershire v Warwickshire
	Lord's	Middlesex v Derbyshire
	Peterborough	Northamptonshire v Essex
	Trent Bridge	Nottinghamshire v Kent
	Middlesbrough	Yorkshire v Sussex
14		**NatWest Bank Trophy**
		Semi-finals
		Tourist Match
	Old Trafford	England 'A' v Sri Lanka (One day)
15		**Tourist Match**
	Old Trafford	England 'A' v Sri Lanka (One day)
16		
	Derby	Derbyshire v Lancashire
	Colchester	Essex v Northamptonshire
	Bournemouth	Hampshire v Leicestershire
	Trent Bridge	Nottinghamshire v Somerset
	Worcester	Worcestershire v Surrey
	Headingley	Yorkshire v Glamorgan
17		**Tourist Match**
	Hove	*Sussex v Sri Lanka
18		**Refuge Assurance League**
	Derby	Derbyshire v Glamorgan
	Colchester	Essex v Middlesex
	Bournemouth	Hampshire v Leicestershire
	Canterbury	Kent v Northamptonshire
	Old Trafford	Lancashire v Surrey
	Edgbaston	Warwickshire v Gloucestershire
	Worcester	Worcestershire v Somerset
	Scarborough	Yorkshire v Nottinghamshire
20		**Britannic Assurance Championship**
	Derby	Derbyshire v Leicestershire
	Colchester	Essex v Yorkshire
	Bournemouth	Hampshire v Sussex
	Canterbury or Dartford	
		Kent v Gloucestershire
	Blackpool	Lancashire v Worcestershire
	The Oval	Surrey v Middlesex
	Edgbaston	Warwickshire v Glamorgan
22		**CORNHILL INSURANCE TEST MATCH**
	Lord's	*ENGLAND v SRI LANKA
23		**Britannic Assurance Championship**
	Old Trafford	Lancashire v Essex
	Northampton	Northamptonshire v Surrey
	Trent Bridge	Nottinghamshire v Derbyshire
	Taunton	Somerset v Yorkshire
	Worcester	Worcestershire v Middlesex
25		**Refuge Assurance Cup**
	Old Trafford	Lancashire v Essex
	Leicester	Leicestershire v Gloucestershire
	Northampton	Northamptonshire v Warwickshire
	Trent Bridge	Nottinghamshire v Derbyshire
	Taunton	Somerset v Yorkshire
	The Oval	Surrey v Hampshire
	Hove	Sussex v Kent
		Worcestershire v Middlesex
28		**Britannic Assurance Championship**
		(four days)
	Abergavenny	Glamorgan v Gloucestershire
	Southampton	Hampshire v Somerset
	Canterbury	Kent v Middlesex
	Old Trafford	Lancashire v Nottinghamshire
	Leicester	Leicestershire v Derbyshire
	Northampton	Northamptonshire v Yorkshire
	The Oval	Surrey v Sussex
	Edgbaston	Warwickshire v Worcestershire

SEPTEMBER		
1		**Refuge Assurance Cup**
		Semi-finals
3		**Britannic Assurance Championship**
		(four days)
	Chelmsford	Essex v Derbyshire
	Bristol	Gloucestershire v Northamptonshire
	Trent Bridge	Nottinghamshire v Middlesex
	The Oval	Surrey v Hampshire
	Hove	Sussex v Kent
	Worcester	Worcestershire v Somerset
	Scarborough	Yorkshire v Lancashire
7	Lord's	**NATWEST BANK TROPHY FINAL**
10		**Britannic Assurance Championship**
		(four days)
	Derby	Derbyshire v Nottinghamshire
	Cardiff	Glamorgan v Worcestershire
	Bristol	Gloucestershire v Somerset
	Leicester	Leicestershire v Essex
	Lord's	Middlesex v Surrey
	Edgbaston	Warwickshire v Northamptonshire
15		**REFUGE ASSURANCE CUP FINAL**
17		**Britannic Assurance Championship**
		(four days)
	Chesterfield	Derbyshire v Yorkshire
	Chelmsford	Essex v Middlesex
	Southampton	Hampshire v Glamorgan
	Canterbury	Kent v Leicestershire
	Old Trafford	Lancashire v Surrey
	Trent Bridge	Nottinghamshire v Worcestershire
	Taunton	Somerset v Warwickshire
22		**Britannic Assurance Challenge**
		(one day)
		Champion County v Sheffield Shield winners
23		**Britannic Assurance Challenge**
		(four days)
		Champion County v Sheffield Shield winners

*Includes Sunday play

CROQUET

WORLD CHAMPIONSHIPS
Hurlingham, Sep 2-9

SEMI-FINALS
ROBERT FULFORD (Eng) beat Robert Stark (US) 2-0
MARK SAURIN (Ire) beat Steve Mulliner (Eng) 2-1

FINAL
FULFORD beat Saurin 2-0

ATCO BRITISH OPEN CHAMPIONSHIPS
Hurlingham, Jul 15-22

SINGLES
STEVE MULLINER beat Robert Fulford 2-0

DOUBLES
ROBERT FULFORD & CHRIS CLARKE beat Steve
Comish & Duncan Reeve 2-0

BRITISH CHAMPIONSHIPS
Cheltenham, May 30-Jun 7

MEN
ROBERT FULFORD beat Steve Mulliner 3-1

WOMEN
FRANCES RANSOME beat Fiona McCoig 2-1

MIXED DOUBLES
MARK SAURIN & FIONA McCOIG beat Alan & Gill
Bogle 2-0

BRITISH RANKINGS
Issued Jul 26
Jt. 1 Robert Fulford & Steve Mulliner
   3 Colin Irwin
   4 David Openshaw
   5 Nigel Aspinall
   6 David Maugham
   7 Mark Avery
   8 Chris Clarke
   9 Martin Murray
Jt. 10 Michael Heap & Mark Saurin

CHAMPIONS

WORLD CHAMPIONSHIPS
Inaugurated 1989
1989   Joe Hogan (NZ)
1990   Robert Fulford (GB)

OPEN SINGLES
Inaugurated 1867
Winners since 1981 (British unless stated)
1981   David Openshaw
1982   Nigel Aspinall
1983   Nigel Aspinall
1984   Nigel Aspinall
1985   David Openshaw
1986   Joe Hogan (NZ)
1987   Mark Avery
1988   Steve Mulliner
1989   Joe Hogan (NZ)
1990   Robert Fulford
Most wins
10 John Solomon 1953, 1956, 1959, 1961, 1963-68; **8**
Nigel Aspinall 1969, 1974-76, 1978, 1982-84; **7**
Humphrey Hicks 1932, 1939, 1947-50, 1952; **5** Cyril
Corbally 1902-03, 1906, 1908, 1913

CURLING

WORLD CHAMPIONSHIPS
Vasteras, Sweden, Apr 2-8

Men
Final Round Robin Standings

		Won	Lost
1	Canada	7	2
2	Denmark	7	2
2	Scotland	7	2
4	Sweden	7	2
5	Norway	5	4
6	Switzerland	4	5
7	United States	4	5
8	Finland	2	7
9	Italy	2	7
10	West Germany	0	9

SEMI-FINALS
SCOTLAND 5 Sweden 3; CANADA 5 Denmark 4

FINAL
CANADA 3 Scotland 1
Winning Skip: Ed Werenich

Women
Final Round Robin Standings

		Won	Lost
1	Canada	8	1
2	Denmark	6	3
3	Norway	6	3
4	Scotland	6	3
5	Sweden	5	4
6	West Germany	5	4
7	Switzerland	4	5
8	France	2	7
9	United States	2	7
10	Japan	1	8

SEMI-FINALS
SCOTLAND 8 Denmark 3; NORWAY 7 Canada 4

FINAL
NORWAY 4 Scotland 2
Winning Skip: Dordi Nordby

CHAMPIONS

WORLD CHAMPIONS

	Men	Women
1959	Canada	-
1960	Canada	-
1961	Canada	-
1962	Canada	-
1963	Canada	-
1964	Canada	-
1965	United States	-
1966	Canada	-
1967	Scotland	-
1968	Canada	-
1969	Canada	-
1970	Canada	-
1971	Canada	-
1972	Canada	-
1973	Sweden	-
1974	United States	-
1975	Switzerland	-
1976	United States	-
1977	Sweden	-
1978	United States	-
1979	Norway	Switzerland
1980	Canada	Canada
1981	Switzerland	Sweden
1982	Canada	Denmark
1983	Canada	Switzerland
1984	Norway	Canada
1985	Canada	Canada
1986	Canada	Canada
1987	Canada	Canada
1988	Norway	West Germany
1989	Canada	Canada
1990	Canada	Norway
Most wins		**Most wins**
Canada 20		Canada 6

CYCLING

GREG AND THE EGG

Greg LeMond, well short of his best, was still good enough to win the Tour de France for the second successive year. LeMond became the first Tour winner in 14 years not to win a stage and by the time the race reached Paris he had a saddle sore as big as an egg, and pain that was allowing him barely four hours, sleep a night.

Lemond only acquired the yellow jersey on the penultimate day, during the individual time trial. But there was none of the last-minute excitement of his 1989 win. The man he beat that year, Laurent Fignon, withdrew from the race at a feeding station on the fifth stage. He covered his face with a paper like a criminal, and was taken away by a helicopter. For the first time since 1925 France had no rider in the top ten; their best, Fabrice Philipot, was 14th, a record low.

The race began with a "bizarre" (Stephen Roche's word) breakaway by four unconsidered riders, led by Steve Bauer of Canada who established a lead of over 10½ minutes. But as Bauer put it: "You know, ten minutes between Greg LeMond and me is a great deal. But ten minutes between me and Greg, it's really very little." And sure enough, LeMond slowly sliced into the deficit, sprinting up Luz Ardiden in the Pyrenees to go only seconds behind the then-leader, Claudio Chiappucci. Four people held the yellow jersey at various times, three members of the original breakaway: Bauer, Chiappucci and Ronan Pensec (the fourth, Frans Maassen, fell back in the mountains) plus LeMond. Chester Pyle, an amateur cyclist and student of aerodynamics, said that Fignon's ponytail would have cost him more than ten seconds in the 1989 Tour by adding to his wind resistance. Fignon lost by eight seconds.

LeMond failed to repeat his 1989 double when he lost the road race at the world championships in Japan. He finished fourth, eight seconds behind the unexpected winner Rudy Dhaenens of Belgium. LeMond had arrived late and apparently under-prepared. Dhaenens was fined $2000 for a piece of impromptu advertising stuck on his jersey as he stood on the winners' podium. The commercial was cheap at the price.

Shane Sutton became the first Australian to win the Milk Race, carrying on despite the death of his father in mid-race. Robert Millar lost his chance of winning the Kellogg's Tour of Britain for the second year running when he crashed on the finishing circuit. The Harpenden Sports Injury Clinic reported that a 27-year-old cyclist suffered eight months of impotence after a two-day race.

1990

WORLD TRACK CHAMPIONSHIPS
Maebashi, Japan, Aug 20-26
Men - Professional
Sprint
1 Michael Hubner (GDR) won 2-0
2 Claudio Golinelli (Ita)
3 Stephen Pate (Aus)
Individual Pursuit
1 Viatcheslav Ekimov (USSR) 5m 39.04s
2 Francis Moreau (Fra) 5m 42.95s
3 Armand de las Cuevas (Fra)
Kierin
1 Michael Hubner (GDR)
2 Michael Vaarten (Bel)
3 Claudio Golinelli (Ita)
Motor Paced
1 Walter Brugna (Ita)
2 Peter Steiger (Swi)
3 Danny Clark (Aus)

Points Race
1 Laurent Biondi (Fra) 38pts
2 Michael Marcussen (Den) 15pts
3 Danny Clark (Aus) at 1 lap
Men - Amateur
1km Individual Time Trial
1 Alexsandr Kirichenko (USSR) 1m 03.565s
2 Martin Vinnicombe (Aus) 1m 03.919s
3 Jens Gluecklich (GDR) 1m 04.210s
Individual Pursuit
1 Evgeni Berzin (USSR) 4m 33.015s
2 Valeri Baturo (USSR) 4m 42.912s
3 Mike McCarthy (US)
Team Pursuit
1 Soviet Union 4m 09.28s
2 West Germany 4m 15.01s
3 Australia
Sprint
1 Bill Huck (GDR) won 2-0
2 Curt Harnett (Can)
3 Jens Fiedler (GDR)

Points Race
1 Stephen McGlede (Aus) 42pts
2 Bruno Risi (Swi) 32pts
3 Jan Petersen (Den) 24pts

Tandem
1 Gianluca Capitano/Federico Paris (Ita) won 2-0
2 Toshinobu Saito/Narihiro Inamura (Jap)
3 Uwe Buchtmann/Markus Nagel (FRG)

Motor Paced
1 Roland Königshofer (Aut)
2 Davide Solari (Ita)
3 Andrea Bellati (Swi)

Women
Sprint
1 Connie Young (US)
2 Renee Duprel (US)
3 Rita Razmaite (USSR)

Individual Pursuit
1 Leontien van Moorsel (Hol) 3m 44.34s
2 Madonna Harris (NZ) 3m 46.98s
3 Barbara Erdin (Swi)

Points Race
1 Karen Holliday (NZ) 33pts
2 Svetlana Samokhvalova (USSR) 26pts
3 Kristell Werckx (Bel) 25pts

Leading Medal winners

	G	S	B	Total
Soviet Union	4	2	1	7
Australia	1	1	4	6
East Germany	3	-	2	5
Italy	2	2	1	5

WORLD ROAD RACE CHAMPIONSHIPS
Utsunomiya, Japan, Sep 1-2
Men - Professional (261km)
1 Rudy Dhaenens (Bel) 6h 51m 59s
2 Dirk de Wolf (Bel) same time
3 Gianni Bugno (Ita) at 8s
Men - Amateur (174m)
1 Mirko Gualdi (Ita) 4h 39m 17s
2 Roberto Caruso (Ita) at 54s
3 Jean-Philippe Dojwa (Fra) at 56s
Men's 100km Team Trial (Amateur)
1 Soviet Union 1h 56m 50s
2 East Germany 1h 57m 05s
3 West Germany 1h 57m 09s
Women (72.5km)
1 Catherine Marsal (Fra) 2h 00m 07s
2 Ruthie Matthes (US) at 3m 24s
3 Luisa Seghezzi (Ita) same time
Women's 50km Team Time Trial
1 Holland 1h 03m 51s
2 United States 1h 04m 07s
3 Soviet Union 1h 04m 21s

TOUR DE FRANCE
Start Futoroscope, nr Poitiers, Jun 30. Finish Paris, Jul 22
Individual
1 Greg LeMond (US/Z) 90h 43m 20s
2 Claudio Chiapucci (Ita/Carrera) at 2m 16s
3 Eric Breukink (Hol/PDM) at 2m 29s
4 Pedro Delgado (Spa/Banesto) at 5m 01s
5 Marino Lejaretta (Spa/ONCE) at 5m 05s
6 Eduardo Chozas (Spa/ONCE) at 9m 14s
7 Gianni Bugno (Ita/Château d'Ax) at 9m 39s
8 Raul Alcalá (Mex/PDM) at 11m 14s
9 Claude Criquielion (Bel/Lotto) at 12m 04s
10 Miguel Indurain (Spa/Banesto) at 12m 47s
11 Andy Hampsten (US/7-Eleven) at 12m 54s
12 Pelo-Ruiz Cabestany (Spa/ONCE) at 13m 39s
13 Fabio Parra (Col/Kelme) at 14m 35s
14 Fabrice Philipot (Fra/Castorama) at 15m 49s
15 Philippe Delion (Fra/Helvetia) at 16m 57s

Team
1 Z 272h 21m 23s; 2 ONCE at 14s; 3 Banesto at 23m 42s; 4 PDM at 33m 03s; 5 RMO at 56m 09s; 6 Postobon at 1m 09.34s.

Points
1 Olaf Ludwig (GDR/Panasonic) 256 pts; 2 Johan Museeuw (Bel/Lotto) 221 pts; 3 Eric Breukink (Hol/PDM) 118 pts.

King of the Mountains
1 Thierry Claveyrolat (Fra) 321 pts; 2 Claudio Chiappucci (Ita) 179 pts; 3 Roberto Conti (Ita/Ariostea) 160 pts.

Stage Winners

	Stage Details	Stage Winner	Yellow Jersey
Prologue:	Futuroscope (4)	Thierry Marie (Fra)	Marie
Stage 1:	Futuroscope-Poitiers (86)	Frans Maassen (Bel)	Steve Bauer (Can)
Stage 2:	Poitiers (28*)	Panasonic-Sportlife (Hol)	Bauer
Stage 3:	Poitiers-Nantes (148)	Moreno Argentin (Arg)	Bauer

Protesting sheep farmers blocked roads with burning straw and slurry. A local youth on a scooter led the race to safety through the back lanes.

Stage 4:	Nantes-Mont St.Michel (126)	Johan Museeuw (Bel)	Bauer
Stage 5:	Avranches-Rouen (187)	Gerrit Solleveld (Hol)	Bauer

Laurent Fignon withdrew, for the third year out of five.

Stage 6:	Sarrebourg-Vittel (126)	Jelle Nijdam (Hol)	Bauer

Nijdam has won a stage every year since 1987.

Stage 7:	Vittel-Epinal (38.5†)	Raul Alcalá (Mex)	Bauer
Stage 8:	Epinal-Besancon (113)	Olaf Ludwig (GDR)	Bauer

Ludwig became the first and last East German to win a stage in the Tour de France

Stage 9:	Besancon-Geneva (122)	Massimo Ghirotto (Ita)	Bauer
Stage 10:	Geneva-St Gervais Mont Blanc (74)	Thierry Claveyrolat (Fra)	Ronan Pensec (Fra)
Stage 11:	St Gervais Mont Blanc-L'Alpe D'Huez (114)	Gianni Bugno (Ita)	Pensec

Bugno became the first Italian to win the Alpe d'Huez climb since 1952

Stage 12:	Grenoble-Villard De-Lans (21†)	Eric Breukink (Hol)	Claudio Chiappucci (Ita)
Stage 13:	Villard De-Lans-St.Etienne (93)	Eduardo Chozas (Spa)	Chiappucci
Stage 14:	Le Puy-Millau (127)	Marino Lejaretta (Spa)	Chiappucci
Stage 15:	Millau-Revel (106)	Charly Mottet (Fra)	Chiappucci
Stage 16:	Blagnac-Luz Ardiden (134)	Miguel Indurain (Spa)	Chiappucci
Stage 17:	Lourdes-Pau (93)	Dmitri Konyshev (USSR)	Chiappucci

Konyshev was the first Soviet to win a stage in the Tour

| Stage 18: | Pau-Bordeaux (125) | Gianni Bugno (Ita) | Chiappucci |

Bugno became the first man to win the classic mountain and sprint stages - Alpe d'Huez and Bordeaux

Stage 19:	Castillon La Bataille-Limoges	Guido Bontempi (Ita)	Chiappucci
Stage 20:	Lac De Vassiviére (29†)	Eric Breukink (Hol)	Greg LeMond (US)
Stage 21:	Limoges-Paris (114)	Johan Museeuw (Bel)	LeMond

*Figures in brackets indicate stage distance in miles: *indicates Team Time Trial: † indicates Individual Time Trial*
Where the yellow jersey wearers eventually finished: Marie 121st; Bauer 27th; Pensec 20th; Chiappucci 2nd

❝❝All winter I had people throwing money at me. Hundreds of thousand of dollars. Would you have said no?"

Greg LeMond, explaining his lack of condition

"Greg is a very great racer, but he hasn't shown the panache of a Merkx or a Hinault."

Lucien van Impe, former Tour de France Winner

"Panache, panache! It's a race of tactics not panache."

Greg LeMond

"There's so much tackle that goes down, so many are charged to bloody Armageddon ...every professional rider walks around with an attaché case. What do you think they keep in them? Not their bleeding sandwiches, that's for sure.... You can't take your amphets before the start. You only get about three hours on them. So you want to take them just before the biggest hill. But, of course, other riders want to take them there as well. So at the start of this hill, you can suddenly feel the speed go whooosh. It's like going up a gear. Then suddenly you see all this silver foil coming fluttering down the bikes... Look where it gets you. Everybody knows about the famous riders who've won the Tour De France and then died prematurely. But how many down the pecking order have slipped off somewhere and died quietly?"

Paul Watson,professional cyclist interviewed in The Guardian

"I'm certain the use of drugs is not widespread. The truth is that drug controls nowadays are virtually impossible to cheat.❞❞

Malcolm Elliott, professional cyclist.

TOUR OF SPAIN
(Vuelta de Espana), Apr 21-May 15
1 Marco Giovanetti (Ita) 94h 36m 40s
2 Pedro Delgado (Spa) at 1m 28s
3 Anselmo Fuerto (Spa) at 1m 48s
4 Peio-Ruiz Cabestany (Spa) at 2m 16s
5 Fabio Parra (Col) at 3m 07s
6 Federico Echave (Spa) at 3m 52s

TOUR OF ITALY
(Giro d'Italia), May 18-Jun 6
1 Gianni Bugno (Ita) 91h 51m 8s
2 Charly Mottet (Fra) at 6m 33s
3 Marco Giovanetti (Ita) at 9m 01s
4 Vladimir Poulnikov (USSR) at 12m 19s
5 Federico Echave (Spa) at 12m 25s
6 Franco Chioccioli (Ita) at 12m 36s
Bugno equalled Eddy Merckx's record of leading the race from start to finish

WORLD CUP RACES
MILAN-SAN REMO
Mar 17 (184 miles)
1 Gianni Bugno (Ita) 6h 25m 6s
2 Rolf Golz (FRG) at 4s
3 Gilles Delion (Fra) at 23s

TOUR OF FLANDERS
Apr 1 (165 miles)
1 Moreno Argentin (Ita) 6h 47m 0s
2 Rudy Dhaemens (Bel) same time
3 Jon Talen (Hol) at 11s

PARIS-ROUBAIX
Apr 8 (165 miles)
1 Eddy Planckaert (Bel) 7h 23m 02s
2 Steve Bauer (Can) same time
3 Edwin Van Hooydonck (Bel) same time

LIÈGE-BASTOGNE-LIÈGE
Apr 15 (165 miles)
1 Eric van Lancker (Bel) 7h 10m 00s
2 Jean-Claude Leclerq (Fra) at 34s
3 Steven Rooks (Hol) same time

AMSTEL GOLD RACE
Holland, Apr 21 (155 miles)
1 Arie van der Poel (Hol) 6h 17m 17s
2 Luc Roosen (Bel) same time
3 Jelle Nijdam (Hol) same time

WINCANTON CLASSIC
Newcastle, Jul 29 (148 miles)
1   Gianni Bugno (Ita) 6h 09m 51s
2   Sean Kelly (Ire) at 13s
3   Rudy Dhaemens (Bel) at 13s

SAN SEBASTIAN CLASSIC
Spain, Aug 12 (154 miles)
1   Miguel Indurain (Spa) 6h 19m 59s
2   Laurent Jalabert (Fra) at 2m 34s
3   Sean Kelly (Ire) same time

CHAMPIONSHIP OF ZURICH
Aug 19 (149 miles)
1   Charly Mottet (Fra) 6h 07m 08s
2   Greg LeMond (US) same time
3   Claudio Chiappucci (Ita) same time

MAJOR BRITISH RACES
SCOTTISH PROVIDENT LEAGUE SERIES
Race winners
Round 1, Portsmouth: Chris Lillywhite (Banana-Falcon)
Round 2, Liverpool: Joey McLoughlin
                        (Ever Ready-Halfords)
Round 3, Belfast: Chris Lillywhite (Banana-Falcon)
Round 4, Leeds: Chris Walker (Banana-Falcon)
Round 5, Sheffield: Chris Walker (Banana-Falcon)
Round 6, Bradford: Dave Mann (PCA)
Round 7, Cardiff: Chris Walker (Banana-Falcon)
Round 8, Birmingham: Shane Sutton (Banana-Falcon)
Round 9, Edinburgh: Malcolm Elliott (Teka)

Final Standings:
1   Dave Rayner (Banana-Falcon) 192pts
2   Joey McLoughlin (Ever Ready-Halfords) 180pts
3   Chris Walker (Banana-Falcon) 169pts

MILK RACE
Start Land's End, May 27, Finish Liverpool Jun 9
Individual
1   Shane Sutton (Aus) 48h 26m 22s
2   Rob Holden (GB) at 2m 40s
3   Miloslav Vasicek (Cze) at 2m 41s
4   Didier Thueux (Fra) at 2m 53s
5   Chris Walker (GB) at 3m 28s
6   Ruud Poels (Hol) at 4m 02s
Team
1   Banana-Falcon 144h 46m 13s; 24th Tulip Computers
     at 5m 41s; 3 Czechoslovakia at 7m 59s.

KELLOGG'S PROFESSIONAL TOUR OF BRITAIN
Start Brighton July 31, Finish Manchester Aug 5
Individual
1   Michel Dernies (Bel) 29h 11m 20s
2   Robert Millar (GB) at 4s
3   Maurizio Fondriest (Ita) at 1m 38s
4   Federico Echave (Spa) at 1m 56s
5   Jorg Muller (Swi) at 2m 03s
6   Emanuelle Bombini (Ita) at 2m 03s
Team
1   Toshiba (Fra) 87h 44m 43s; 2 Weinmann SMM (Bel)
     87h 51m 24s; 3 Del Tongo (Ita) 87h 53m 10s.

WORLD CYCLO-CROSS CHAMPIONSHIPS
Getxo, Spain, Feb 3-4
PROFESSIONAL
1   Henk Baars (Hol) 1h 03m 14s
2   Adri Van der Poel (Hol) at 5s
3   Bruno Le Bras (Fra) same time

AMATEUR
Individual
1   Andreas Buesser (Swi) 48m 27s
2   Miroslav Kvasnicka (Cze) at 12s
3   Thomas Frishknecht (Swi) at 15s
Team
1   Switzerland 13pts
2   Holland 20pts
3   Czechoslovakia 28pts

————— 1989 —————

WORLD CUP
FINAL STANDINGS
1   Sean Kelly (Ire) 44pts
2   Toni Rominger (Swi) 32pts
3   Rolf Sorensen (Den) 27pts
4   Frans Maasen (Hol) 23pts
5   Steve Bauer (Can) 23pts
6   Edwig van Hooydonck (Bel) 20pts

————— CHAMPIONS —————

TOUR DE FRANCE

1903	Maurice Garin (Fra)	1914	Philippe Thys (Bel)	1929	Maurice de Waele (Bel)
1904	Henri Cornet (Fra)	1919	Firmin Lambot (Bel)	1930	André Leducq (Fra)
1905	Louis Trousselier (Fra)	1920	Philippe Thys (Bel)	1931	Antonin Magne (Fra)
1906	René Pottier (Fra)	1921	Leon Scieur (Bel)	1932	Andre Leducq (Fra)
1907	Lucien Petit-Breton (Fra)	1922	Firmin Lambot (Bel)	1933	Georges Speicher (Fra)
1908	Lucien Petit-Breton (Fra)	1923	Henri Pelissier (Fra)	1934	Antonin Magne (Fra)
1909	François Faber (Lux)	1924	Ottavio Bottecchia (Ita)	1935	Romain Maes (Bel)
1910	Octave Lapize (Fra)	1925	Ottavio Bottecchia (Ita)	1936	Sylvère Maes (Bel)
1911	Gustave Garrigou (Fra)	1926	Lucien Buysse (Bel)	1937	Roger Lapebie (Fra)
1912	Odile Defraye (Bel)	1927	Nicholas Frantz (Lux)	1938	Gino Bartali (Ita)
1913	Philippe Thys (Bel)	1928	Nicholas Frantz (Lux)	1939	Sylvère Maes (Bal)

POST-WAR WINNERS OF THE THREE MAJOR TOURS

	Tour de France	Tour of Italy	Tour of Spain
1947	Jean Robic (Fra)	Fausto Coppi (Ita)	E Van Dyck (Bel)
1948	Gino Bartali (Ita)	Fiorenzo Magni (Ita)	B Ruiz (Spa)
1949	Fausto Coppi (Ita)	Fausto Coppi (Ita)	–
1950	Ferdinand Kebler (Swi)	Hugo Koblet (Swi)	E Rodriquez (Spa)
1951	Hugo Koblet (Swi)	Fiorenzo Magni (Ita)	–
1952	Fausto Coppi (Ita)	Fausto Coppi (Ita)	–
1953	Louison Bobet (Fra)	Fausto Coppi (Ita)	–
1954	Louison Bobet (Fra)	Carlo Clerici (Swi)	–
1955	Louison Bobet (Fra)	Fiorenzo Magni (Ita)	J Dotto (Spa)
1956	Roger Walkowiak (Fra)	Charly Gaul (Lux)	A Contero (Ita)
1957	Jacques Anquetil (Fra)	Gastone Nencini (Ita)	J Lorono (Spa)
1958	Charly Gaul (Lux)	Ercole Baldani (Ita)	Jean Stablinski (Fra)
1959	Federico Bahamontès (Spa)	Charly Gaul (Lux)	A Suarez (Spa)
1960	Gastone Nencini (Ita)	Jacques Anquetil (Fra)	F de Mulder (Bel)
1961	Jacques Anquetil (Fra)	Arn Pambianco (Ita)	A Soler (Spa)
1962	Jacques Anquetil (Fra)	Franco Balmamion (Ita)	Rudi Altig (FRG)
1963	Jacques Anquetil (Fra)	Franco Balmamion (Ita)	Jacques Anquetil (Fra)
1964	Jacques Anquetil (Fra)	Jacques Anquetil (Fra)	Raymond Poulidor (Fra)
1965	Felice Gimondi (Ita)	Vittorio Ardoni (Ita)	R Wolfshohl (FRG)
1966	Lucien Aimar (Fra)	Gianni Motta (Ita)	F Gabicagogeascoa (Spa)
1967	Roger Pingeon (Fra)	Felice Gimondi (Ita)	Jan Janssen (Hol)
1968	Jan Janssen (Hol)	Eddy Merckx (Bel)	Felice Gimondi (Ita)
1969	Eddy Merckx (Bel)	Felice Gimondi (Ita)	Roger Pingeon (Fra)
1970	Eddy Merckx (Bel)	Eddy Merckx (Bel)	Luis Ocana (Spa)
1971	Eddy Merckx (Bel)	Gosta Petterson (Swe)	F Bracke (Bel)
1972	Eddy Merckx (Bel)	Eddy Merckx (Bel)	José-Manuel Fuente (Spa)
1973	Luis Ocana (Spa)	Eddy Merckx (Bel)	Eddy Merckx (Bel)
1974	Eddy Merckx (Bel)	Eddy Merckx (Bel)	José-Manuel Fuente (Spa)
1975	Bernard Thevenet (Fra)	F Bertoglio (Ita)	G Tamames (Spa)
1976	Lucien van Impe (Bel)	Felice Gimondi (Ita)	J Pesarrodona (Spa)
1977	Bernard Thevenet (Fra)	Michel Pollentier (Bel)	Freddie Maertens (Bel)
1978	Bernard Hinault (Fra)	Johan De Muynck (Bel)	Bernard Hinault (Fra)
1979	Bernard Hinault (Fra)	Giuseppe Saronni (Ita)	Joop Zoetemelk (Hol)
1980	Joop Zoetemelk (Hol)	Bernard Hinault (Fra)	Faustino Ruperez (Spa)
1981	Bernard Hinault (Fra)	Giovanni Bartaglin (Ita)	Giovanni Bartaglin (Ita)
1982	Bernard Hinault (Fra)	Bernard Hinault (Fra)	Marino Lejaretta (Spa)
1983	Laurent Fignon (Fra)	Giuseppe Saronni (Ita)	Bernard Hinault (Fra)
1984	Laurent Fignon (Fra)	Francesco Moser (Ita)	Eric Caritoux (Fra)
1985	Bernard Hinault (Fra)	Bernard Hinault (Fra)	Pedro Delgado (Spa)
1986	Greg LeMond (US)	Roberto Visentini (Ita)	Alvaro Pino (Spa)
1987	Stephen Roche (Ire)	Stephen Roche (Ire)	Luis Herrera (Col)
1988	Pedro Delgado (Spa)	Andy Hampsten (US)	Sean Kelly (Ire)
1989	Greg LeMond (US)	Laurent Fignon (Fra)	Pedro Delgado (Spa)
1990	Greg LeMond (US)	Gianni Bugno (Ita)	Marco Giovanetti (Ita)

Most Wins

Tour de France: 5 Jacques Anquetil, Eddy Merckx, Bernard Hinault
Tour of Italy: 5 Alfredo Binda (Ita) 1925, 1927-29, 1933;
Fausto Coppi 1940, 1947, 1949, 1952-53; Eddy Merckx
Tour of Spain: 2 Gustave Deloor (Bel) 1935-36; Julio Barrendero (Spa) 1941-42; José-Manuel Fuente; Bernard Hinault; Pedro Delgado.

WORLD PROFESSIONAL ROAD RACE CHAMPIONSHIP

(Post-war winners)

1946	Hans Knecht (Swi)
1947	Theo Middlekamp (Hol)
1948	Alberic Scotte (Bel)
1949	Rik van Steenbergen (Bel)
1950	Alberic Schotts (Bel)
1951	Ferdi Kubler (Swi)
1952	Heinz Muller (Ger)
1953	Fausto Coppi (Ita)
1954	Louison Bobet (Fra)
1955	Stan Ockers (Bel)
1956	Rik van Steenbergen (Bel)
1957	Rik van Steenbergen (Bel)
1958	Ercole Baldini (Ita)
1959	André Darrigade (Fra)
1960	Rik van Looy (Bel)
1961	Rik van Looy (Bel)
1962	Jean Stablinski (Fra)
1963	Renoni Beheyt (Bel)
1964	Jan Janssen (Hol)
1965	Tom Simpson (GB)
1966	Rudi Altig (FRG)
1967	Eddy Merckx (Bel)
1968	Vittorio Adorni (Ita)
1969	Harm Ottenbros (Hol)
1970	Jean-Pierre Monsère (Bel)
1971	Eddy Merckx (Bel)
1972	Marino Basso (Ita)
1973	Felice Gimondi (Ita)
1974	Eddy Merckx (Bel)

1975	Hennie Kuiper (Hol)
1976	Freddy Maertens (Bel)
1977	Francesco Moser (Ita)
1978	Gerrie Knetemann (Hol)
1979	Jan Raas (Hol)
1980	Bernard Hinault (Fra)
1981	Freddy Maertens (Bel)
1982	Giuseppe Saronni (Ita)
1983	Greg LeMond (US)
1984	Claude Criquielon (Bel)
1985	Joop Zoetemelk (Hol)
1986	Moreno Argentin (Ita)
1987	Stephen Roche (Ire)
1988	Maurizio Fondriest (Ita)
1989	Greg LeMond (US)
1990	Rudy Dhaemens (Bel)

Most Wins
3 Alfredo Binda (Ita) 1927, 1930, 1932;
Rik van Steenbergen, Eddy Merckx

TOUR OF BRITAIN (Milk Race)

1951	Ian Steel (GB)
1952	Ken Russell (GB)
1953	Gordon Thomas (GB)
1954	Eugène Tamburlini (Fra)
1955	Anthony Hewson (GB)
1958	Richard Durlacher (Aut)
1959	Bill Bradley (GB)
1960	Bill Bradley (GB)
1961	Billy Holmes (GB)
1962	Eugen Pokorny (Pol)
1963	Peter Chisman (GB)
1964	Arthur Metcalfe (GB)
1965	Les West (GB)
1966	Josef Gawliczek (Pol)
1967	Les West (GB)
1968	Gosta Pettersson (Swe)
1969	Fedor Den Hertog (Hol)
1970	Jiri Mainus (Cs)
1971	Fedor Den Hertog (Hol)
1972	Hennie Kuiper (Hol)
1973	Piet van Katwijk (Hol)
1974	Roy Schuiten (Hol)
1975	Bernt Johansson (Swe)
1976	Bill Nickson (GB)
1977	Said Gusseinov (USSR)
1978	Jan Brzezny (Pol)
1979	Yuriy Kashirin (USSR)
1980	Ivan Mitchtenko (USSR)
1981	Sergey Krivocheyev (USSR)
1982	Yuriy Kashirin (USSR)
1983	Matt Eaton (USA)
1984	Oleg Czougeda (USSR)
1985	Eric van Lancker (Bel)
1986	Joey McLoughlin (GB)
1987	Malcolm Elliott (GB)
1988	Vasiliy Zhdanov (USSR)
1989	Brian Walton (Can)
1990	Shane Sutton (Aus)

KELLOGG'S TOUR OF BRITAIN
(Inaugurated 1987)

1987	Joey McLoughlin (GB)
1988	Malcolm Elliott (GB)
1989	Robert Millar (GB)
1990	Michel Dernies (Bel)

OLYMPIC GAMES
Men
1000 Metres Sprint

1896	Paul Masson (Fra)
1900	Georges Taillandier (Fra)
1908	No gold medal awarded
1920	Maurice Peeters (Hol)
1924	Lucien Michard (Fra)
1928	René Beaufrand (Fra)
1932	Jacobus van Egmond (Hol)
1936	Toni Merkens (Ger)
1948	Mario Ghella (Ita)
1952	Enzo Sacchi (Ita)
1956	Michel Rousseau (Fra)
1960	Sante Gaiardoni (Ita)
1964	Giovanni Pettenella (Ita)
1968	Daniel Morelon (Fra)
1972	Daniel Morelon (Fra)
1976	Anton Tkac (Cze)
1980	Lutz Hesslich (GDR)
1984	Mark Gorski (US)
1988	Lutz Hesslich (GDR)

1000 Metres Time Trial

1896	Paul Masson (Fra)
1928	Willy Falck-Hansen (Den)
1932	Edgar Gray (Aus)
1936	Arie van Vliet (Hol)
1948	Jacques Dupont (Fra)
1952	Russell Mockridge (Aus)
1956	Leandro Faggin (Ita)
1960	Sante Gaiardoni (Ita)
1964	Patrick Sercu (Bel)
1968	Pierre Trentin (Fra)
1972	Niels-Christian Fredborg (Den)
1976	Klaus-Jürgen Grunke (GDR)
1980	Lothar Thoms (GDR)
1984	Freddy Schmidtke (FRG)
1988	Alexander Kirchenko (USSR)

100 km Team Time Trial

1912	Sweden
1920	France
1924	France
1928	Denmark
1932	Italy
1936	France
1948	Belgium
1952	Belgium
1956	France
1960	Italy
1964	Holland
1968	Holland
1972	USSR
1976	USSR
1980	USSR
1984	Italy
1988	East Germany

4000 Metres Individual Pursuit

1964	Jiri Daler (Cze)
1968	Daniel Rebillard (Fra)
1972	Knut Knudsen (Nor)
1976	Gregor Braun (GDR)
1980	Robert Dill-Bundi (Swi)
1984	Steve Hegg (US)
1988	Giantautus Umarus (USSR)

4000 Metres Team Pursuit

1908	Great Britain
1920	Italy
1924	Italy
1928	Italy
1932	Italy
1936	France
1948	France
1952	Italy
1956	Italy
1960	Italy

1964	West Germany
1968	Denmark
1972	West Germany
1976	West Germany
1980	USSR
1984	Australia
1988	USSR

Points Races
1984	Roger Ilegems (Bel)
1988	Dan Frost (Den)

Road Race
1896	Aristidis Konstantinidis (Gre)
1912	Rudolph Lewis (SAf)
1920	Harry Stenqvist (Swe)
1924	Armand Blanchonnet (Fra)
1928	Henry Hansen (Den)
1932	Attilio Pavesi (Ita)
1936	Robert Charpentier (Fra)
1948	José Beyaert (Fra)
1952	André Noyelle (Bel)
1956	Ercole Baldini (Ita)
1960	Viktor Kapitonov (USSR)
1964	Mario Zanin (Ita)
1968	Pierfranco Vianelli (Ita)
1972	Hennie Kuiper (Hol)
1976	Bernt Johansson (Swe)
1980	Sergey Sukhoruchenkov (USSR)
1984	Alexi Grewal (US)
1988	Olaf Ludwig (GDR)

Women
1000 Metres Sprint
1988	Erika Saloumiae (USSR)

Road Race
1984	Connie Carpenter-Phinney (US)
1988	Monique Knol (Hol)

WORLD CHAMPIONS
(Since 1981)
(In Olympic years, if an event is included at the Games then it is not contested at the World Championships)

Men – Professional
Sprint
1981	Koichi Nakano (Jap)
1982	Koichi Nakano (Jap)
1983	Koichi Nakano (Jap)
1984	Koichi Nakano (Jap)
1985	Koichi Nakano (Jap)
1986	Koichi Nakano (Jap)
1987	Nabuyuki Tawara (Jap)
1988	Stephen Pate (Aus)
1989	Claudio Golinelli (Ita)
1990	Michael Hubner (GDR)

Individual Pursuit
1981	Alain Bondue (Fra)
1982	Alain Bondue (Fra)
1983	Steele Bishop (Aus)
1984	Hans-Henrik Oersted (Den)
1985	Hans-Henrik Oersted (Den)
1986	Tony Doyle (GB)
1987	Hans-Henrik Oersted (Den)
1988	Lech Piasecki (Pol)
1989	Colin Sturgess (GB)
1990	Viatcheslav Ekimov (USSR)

Kierin
1981	Danny Clark (Aus)
1982	Gordon Singleton (Can)
1983	Urs Freuler (Swi)
1984	Robert Dill-Bundi (Swi)
1985	Urs Freuler (Swi)

1986	Michel Vaarten (Bel)
1987	Hazuni Honda (Jap)
1988	Claudio Golinelli (Ita)
1989	Claudio Golinelli (Ita)
1990	Michael Hubner (GDR)

Motor Paced
1981	Rene Kos (Hol)
1982	Martin Venix (Hol)
1983	Bruno Vicini (Ita)
1984	Horst Schutz (FRG)
1985	Bruno Vicini (Ita)
1986	Bruno Vicini (Ita)
1987	Max Hurzeler (Swi)
1988	Danny Clark (Aus)
1989	Giovanni Renosto (Ita)
1990	Walter Brugna (Ita)

Points Race
1981	Urs Freuler (Swi)
1982	Urs Freuler (Swi)
1983	Urs Freuler (Swi)
1984	Urs Freuler (Swi)
1985	Urs Freuler (Swi)
1986	Urs Freuler (Swi)
1987	Urs Freuler (Swi)
1988	Daniel Wyder (Swi)
1989	Urs Freuler (Swi)
1990	Laurent Biondi (Fra)

Men – Amateur
1 km Individual Time Trial
1981	Lothar Thoms (GDR)
1982	Fredy Schmidteke (FRG)
1983	Sergey Kopylov (USSR)
1985	Jens Glücklich (GDR)
1986	Maik Malchow (GDR)
1987	Martin Vinnicombe (Aus)
1989	Jens Glücklich (GDR)
1990	Alexsandr Kirichenko (USSR)

Individual Pursuit
1981	Detlef Macha (GDR)
1982	Detlef Macha (GDR)
1983	Viktor Kupovets (USSR)
1985	Vyacheslav Yekimov (USSR)
1986	Vyacheslav Yekimov (USSR)
1987	Guintautas Umaros (USSR)
1989	Vyacheslav Yekimov (USSR)
1990	Evgeni Berzin (USSR)

Team Pursuit
1981	East Germany
1982	USSR
1983	West Germany
1985	Italy
1986	Czechoslovakia
1987	USSR
1989	East Germany
1990	USSR

Sprint
1981	Sergey Kopylov (USSR)
1982	Sergey Kopylov (USSR)
1983	Lutz Hesslich (GDR)
1985	Lutz Hesslich (GDR)
1986	Michael Hubner (GDR)
1987	Lutz Hesslich (GDR)
1989	Bill Huck (GDR)
1990	Bill Huck (GDR)

Points Race
1981	Lutz Haueisen (GDR)
1982	Hans-Jaochim Pohl (GDR)
1983	Michael Marcussen (Den)

1985	Martin Penc (Cze)
1986	Dan Frost (Den)
1987	Marat Ganeev (USSR)
1989	Marat Satybaliev (USSR)
1990	Stephen McGlade (Aus)

Tandem

1981	Ivan Kucirek & Pavel Martinek (Cze)
1982	Ivan Kucirek & Pavel Martinek (Cze)
1983	Philippe Vernet & Frank Depine (Fra)
1984	Jürgen Greil & Frank Weber (FRG)
1985	Vitezlav Voboril & Roman Rekhousek (Cze)
1986	Vitezlav Voboril & Roman Rekhousek (Cze)
1987	Fabrice Colas & Frédéric Magne (Fra)
1988	Fabrice Colas & Frédéric Magne (Fra)
1989	Fabrice Colas & Frédéric Magne (Fra)
1990	Gianluca Capitano & Federico Paris (Ita)

Motor Paced

1981	Matthe Pronk (Hol)
1982	Gaby Minneboo (Hol)
1983	Rainer Podlesch (GDR)
1984	Jan de Nijs (Hol)
1985	Roberto Dotti (Ita)
1986	Mario Gentilo (Ita)
1987	Mario Gentilo (Ita)
1988	Vincenzo Colamartino (Ita)
1989	Roland Königshofer (Aut)
1990	Roland Königshofer (Aut)

Road Team Time Trial

1981	East Germany
1982	Netherlands
1983	USSR
1985	USSR
1986	Netherlands
1987	Italy
1989	East Germany
1990	USSR

Road Race

1981	Andrey Vedernikov (USSR)
1982	Bernd Drogan (GDR)
1983	Uwe Raab (GDR)
1985	Lech Piasecki (Pol)
1986	Uwe Ampler (GDR)
1987	Richard Vivean (Fra)
1989	Joachim Halupczok (Pol)
1990	Mirko Gualdi (Ita)

Women

Sprint

1981	Sheila Ochowitz (US)
1982	Connie Paraskevin (US)
1983	Connie Paraskevin (US)
1984	Connie Paraskevin (US)
1985	Isabelle Nicoloso (Fra)
1986	Christa Rothenburger (GDR)
1987	Erika Salumiae (USSR)
1989	Erika Salumiae (USSR)
1990	Connie Young (US)

Individual Pursuit

1981	Nadezhda Kibardina (USSR)
1982	Rebecca Twigg (US)
1983	Connie Carpenter (US)
1984	Rebecca Twigg (US)
1985	Rebecca Twigg (US)
1986	Jeannie Longo (Fra)
1987	Rebecca Twigg-Whitehead (US)
1988	Jeannie Longo (Fra)
1989	Jeannie Longo (Fra)
1990	Leontien van Moorsel (Hol)

Points Race

1988	Sally Hodge (GB)
1989	Jeannie Longo (Fra)
1990	Karen Holliday (NZ)

Road Team Time Trial

1987	USSR
1988	Italy
1989	USSR
1990	Holland

Road Race

1981	Ute Enzenauer (FRG)
1982	Mandy Jones (GB)
1983	Marianne Berglund (Swe)
1985	Jeannie Longo (Fra)
1986	Jeannie Longo (Fra)
1987	Jeannie Longo (Fra)
1989	Jeannie Longo (Fra)
1990	Catherine Marsal (Fra)

CYCLO CROSS
WORLD CHAMPIONS
(Since 1981)

Professional

1981	Johannes Stamsnidjer (Hol)
1982	Roland Liboton (Bel)
1983	Roland Liboton (Bel)
1984	Roland Liboton (Bel)
1985	Klaus-Peter Thaler (FRG)
1986	Albert Zweifel (Swi)
1987	Klaus-Peter Thaler (FRG)
1988	Pascal Richard (Swi)
1989	Danny De Bie (Bel)
1990	Henk Baars (Hol)

Most Wins:
7 Eric de Vlaeminck (Bel) 1966, 1968-73

Amateur

1981	Milos Fisera (Cze)
1982	Milos Fisera (Cze)
1983	Radomir Simunek (Cze)
1984	Radomir Simunek (Cze)
1985	Mike Kluge (FRG)
1986	Vito di Tano (Ita)
1987	Mike Kluge (FRG)
1988	Karal Camrda (Cze)
1989	Ondrej Glajza (Cze)
1990	Andreas Buesser (Swi)

Most Wins:
5 Robert Vermiere (Bel) 1970-71, 1974-75, 1977

1991

Apr 29-May 19 Tour of Spain; *May 26-Jun 8* Milk Race (start hill); *May 26-Jun 14* Tour of Italy; *Jun 30* National road race championships; *Jul 6-28* Tour de France; *Aug 6-11* Kellogg's Tour of Britain; *Aug 25* World road race championship (West Germany). Perrier World Cup *Mar 23* Milan to San Remo; *Apr 7* Tour of Flanders; *Apr 14* Paris to Roubaix; *Apr 21* Liège-Bastogne-Liège; *Apr 27* Amstel Gold Race (Holland); *Aug 4* Wincanton Classic (Brighton); *Aug 10* San Sebastian; *Sep 15* Grand Prix de la Libération (Holland); *Oct 6* Grand Prix of Americas (Canada); *Oct 13* Paris to Tours; *Oct 19* Tour of Lombardy; *Oct 26* Grand Prix des Nations (France).

DARTS

1989-90

EMBASSY WORLD PROFESSIONAL CHAMPIONSHIP
Frimley Green, Surrey, Jan 5-13

2ND ROUND
ERIC BRISTOW (Eng) beat Steve Gittins (Eng) 3-2;
MAGNUS CARIS (Swe) beat Brian Cairns (Wal) 3-1; JOCKY
WILSON (Sco) beat Chris Whiting (Eng) 3-2; MIKE
GREGORY (Eng) beat Leo Laurens (Bel) 3-1; CLIFF
LAZARENKO (Eng) beat Jann Hoffman (Den) 3-0; PAUL
LIM (US) beat Jack McKenna (Ire) 3-2; PHIL TAYLOR
(Eng) beat Dennis Hickling (Eng) 3-0; RONNIE SHARP
(Sco) beat John Lowe (Eng) 3-2

QUARTER-FINALS
BRISTOW beat Cairns 4-1; GREGORY beat Wilson 4-3;
LAZARENKO beat Lim 4-0; TAYLOR beat Sharp 4-2

SEMI-FINALS
BRISTOW beat Gregory 5-2; TAYLOR beat Lazarenko 5-0

FINAL
TAYLOR beat Bristow 6-1
Taylor was a 100-1 outsider at start of the tournament
Highest check-out: 170 Taylor, Evison

*PAUL LIM, a Singapore-born American won £52,000
bonus for completing the first ever nine-darter in World
Championship history. Playing Irishman Jack McKenna,
he completed his game of 501 as follows: 7 x treble 20, 1 x
treble 19, double 12*

BRITISH OPEN
Kensington, London, Dec 29-30

Men
ALAN WARRINER beat Wayne Jones 2-1

Women
SHARON COLCLOUGH beat Sandra Muir 3-0

NEWS OF THE WORLD CHAMPIONSHIP
London Arena, Jun 6

Men
PAUL COOK (Western Counties) beat Steve Hudson
(Yorkshire)

Women
(Inaugurated 1990)
LYNNE ORMOND (Eastern Counties) beat Jane Stubbs
(Lancashire/Cheshire)

BSB WORLD CHAMPIONS CHALLENGE
(Inaugurated 1990)
Lakeside Country Club, Apr 7-8

SEMI-FINALS
ERIC BRISTOW beat Keith Deller 3-2; BOB
ANDERSON beat John Lowe 3-1

FINAL
ANDERSON beat Bristow 3-0

WORLD CUP
Toronto, Oct 19-21

Men's Finals
OVERALL
1 ENGLAND 124 pts; 2 Canada 75 pts; 3 Republic of
Ireland 60 pts
INDIVIDUAL
ERIC BRISTOW (Eng) beat Jack McKenna (Ire) 4-2
PAIRS
ENGLAND (John Lowe & Eric Bristow) beat Belgium
(Leo Laurens & Stefan Eekelaert) 4-2

TEAM
CANADA beat Australia 9-7

Women's Finals
OVERALL
1 ENGLAND 76 pts; 2 United States 66 pts; 3 Australia 34
pts
INDIVIDUAL
1 EVA GRISBY (US) beat Sharon Colclough (Eng) 4-2
PAIRS
1 ENGLAND (Sharon Colclough & Sue Edwards) beat
Australia (Louise Bell & Eileen Morton) 4-0

CHAMPIONS
(All winners British unless otherwise stated)

EMBASSY WORLD PROFESSIONAL CHAMPIONSHIP
Venues: 1978 Heart of the Midlands Night Club,
Nottingham; 1979-85 Jollees, Longton, Stoke-on-Trent;
1986 Lakeside Country Club, Frimley Green, Surrey.

Year	Winner	Runner-up
1978	Leighton Rees	John Lowe
1979	John Lowe	Leighton Rees
1980	Eric Bristow	Bobby George
1981	Eric Bristow	John Lowe
1982	Jocky Wilson	John Lowe
1983	Keith Deller	Eric Bristow
1984	Eric Bristow	Dave Whitcombe
1985	Eric Bristow	John Lowe
1986	Eric Bristow	Dave Whitcombe
1987	John Lowe	Eric Bristow
1988	Bob Anderson	John Lowe
1989	Jocky Wilson	Eric Bristow
1990	Phil Taylor	Eric Bristow

BRITISH OPEN
1975	Alan Evans	
1976	Jack North	
1977	John Lowe	
1978	Eric Bristow	
1979	Tony Brown	
1980	Cliff Lazarenko	
1981	Eric Bristow	
1982	Jocky Wilson	
1983	Eric Bristow	
1984	John Cusnett	
1985	Eric Bristow	
1986	Eric Bristow	
1987	Bob Anderson	
1988	John Lowe	
1989	Brian Cairns	
1990	Alan Warriner	

NEWS OF THE WORLD CHAMPIONSHIP
Winners since 1981

1981	John Lowe	
1982	Roy Morgan	
1983	Eric Bristow	
1984	Eric Bristow	
1985	Dave Lee	
1986	Bobby George	
1987	Mike Gregory	
1988	Mike Gregory	
1989	Dave Whitcombe	
1990	Paul Cooke	

1991
Jan 4-12 Embassy World Professional Championship
(Lakeside Country Club)

EQUESTRIANISM

The year's events in equestrianism were overshadowed by the sudden emergence into the limelight of the sport's seamier side. Only a few days before the World Equestrian Games began in Sweden, the German Animal Protection Association accused the West German star Paul Schockemohle of cruelty for "rapping" — beating the legs of horses to make them jump higher. The sport's main German sponsors demanded a guarantee that rapping, de-nerving and doping cease at once or they would withdraw support. Schockemohle retired from international competition two days later and Princess Anne, president of the International Equestrian Federation, announced an independent inquiry.

However, the sport's big event was tarnished. It seemed less significant when the New Zealander Blyth Tait on the 12-year-old Messiah won the individual three-day event gold medal at the Games and led his team to victory as well, which confirmed that New Zealand had supplanted Britain as the leading nation in eventing.

Ian Stark, second at the Olympics, was unlucky again on Murphy Himself. However, for Stark, this was a comparatively minor misfortune. In March, he was banned for three months after a test on his horse Foxy V proved positive to the painkiller phenylbutazone ("bute") after the Werribee three-day event in Australia. The ban was lifted in May and a £3,000 fine substituted. But then, at Burghley, Stark was suspended for "excessive pressing of an exhausted horse" and given one of the sport's newly-introduced yellow warning cards.

Nicola McIrvine was the surprise winner of the Whitbread Trophy at Badminton on Middle Road,. Four months later she became Mrs Sebastian Coe. The brothers Whitaker, John and Michael, signed a £1.5 million sponsorship deal which means their horses all have to have the word "Henderson" in their names. The Whitakers themselves do not — yet.

1990

WORLD EQUESTRIAN GAMES
Stockholm, Jul 24-Aug 5

Show Jumping
Individual
1 Eric Navet (Fra) on Malesan Quito de Baussy
2 John Whitaker (GB) on Henderson Milton
3 Hubert Bourdy (Fra) on Morgat

Team
1 France	18.88pts
2 West Germany	28.56pts
3 Great Britain	29. 91pts

Three-Day Event
Individual
1 Blyth Tait (NZ) on Messiah
2 Ian Stark (GB) on Murphy Himself
3 Bruce Davidson (US) on Pirate Lion

Team
1 New Zealand	205.9pts
2 Great Britain	246.65pts
3 West Germany	259.85pts

Dressage
Individual
1 Nicole Uphoff (FRG) on Rembrandt
2 Kyra Kyrklund (Fin) on Matador
3 Monica Theodorescu (FRG) on Ganimedes

Team
1 West Germany	4.389pts
2 Soviet Union	4.124pts
3 Switzerland	4.091pts

Carriage Driving
Individual
1 Ad Aaarts (Hol)	131.2pts
2 Tomas Eriksson (Swe)	131.4pts
3 Jozsef Bozsik (Hun)	131.8pts

Team
1 Holland	264.2pts
2 Sweden	271.6pts
3 Hungary	292.8pts

Endurance
Individual
1 Becky Hart (US) on RO Grand Sultan
2 Jane Donovan (GB) on Ibriz
3 June Petersen (Aus) on Abbeline Lionel

Team
1 Great Britain
2 Belgium
3 Spain

Vaulting
Men - Individual
1 Micheal Lehner (FRG)
2 Christopher Lensing (FRG)
3 Dietmar Otto (FRG

Women - Individual
1 Silke Bernhard (FRG)
2 Silke Michelberger (FRG)
3 Ute Schonlan (FRG)

Teams
1 Switzerland
2 West Germany
3 United States

Medal Table

Total		G	S	B
12	West Germany	4	4	4
6	Great Britain	1	4	1
3	France	2	0	1
3	United States	1	0	2
2	Holland	2	0	0
2	New Zealand	2	0	0
2	Switzerland	1	0	1
2	Sweden	0	2	0
2	Hungary	0	0	2
1	Belgium	0	1	0
1	Finland	0	1	0
1	Soviet Union	0	1	0
1	Australia	0	0	1
1	Spain	0	0	1

SHOW JUMPING

VOLVO WORLD CUP FINAL
Dortmund, Apr 11-16
Individual
1 John Whitaker (GB) on Henderson Milton
2 Pierre Durand (Fra) on Jappeloup
3 Franke Sloothaak (FRG) on Optiebuers Wazlerkoenig
Whitaker was the first British winner

SILK CUT DERBY
Hickstead, Aug 23-27
1 Joe Turi (GB) on Vital
2 Nick Skelton (GB) on Alan Paul Apollo
3 Herve Godignon (Fra) on Moet & Chandon Quidam
  Michael Whitaker (GB) on Henderson Monsanta
  Herve Godignon (Fra) on Moet & Chandon Prince

KING GEORGE V CUP
NEC, Birmingham, Jun 17
1 John Whitaker (GB) on Henderson Milton
2 Ludo Philippaert (Bel) on Optiebeurs Fidelgo
3 David Broome (GB) on Countryman

QUEEN ELIZABETH II CUP
NEC, Birmingham, Jun 17
1 Emma-Jane Mac (GB) on Everest Oyster
2 Liz Edgar (GB) on Everest Asher
3 Rosemary Tillson (GB) on Farasi Kuni

THREE-DAY EVENTING

BADMINTON HORSE TRIALS
(Whitbread Trophy)
Badminton, May 3-6
1 Nicola McIrvine (GB) on Middle Road
2 Blyth Tait (NZ) on Messiah
3 Mary Thomson (GB) on King Boris

BURGHLEY HORSE TRIALS
Burghley House, Sep 6-9
1 Mark Todd (NZ) on Face the Music
2 Mary Thomson (GB) on King Cuthbert
3 Richard Walker (GB) on Jacam

——— CHAMPIONS ———

OLYMPIC GAMES
Show Jumping
Individual

	Rider	Horse
1900	Aime Haegeman (Bel)	Benton II
1912	Jean Cariou (Fra)	Mignon
1920	Tommaso Lequio (Ita)	Trebecco
1924	Alphonse Gemuseus (Swi)	Lucette
1928	Frantisek Ventura (Cze)	Eliot
1932	Takeichi Nishi (Jap)	Uranus
1936	Kurt Hasse (Ger)	Tora
1948	Humberto Cortes (Mex)	Arete
1952	Pierre d'Oriola (Fra)	Ali Baba
1956	Hans-Gunter Winkler (Ger)	Halla
1960	Raimondo d'Inzeo (Ita)	Posillipo
1964	Pierre d'Oriola (Fra)	Lutteur B
1968	William Steinkraus (US)	Snowbound
1972	Graziano Mancinelli (Ita)	Ambassador
1976	Alwin Schockemohle (FRG)	Warwick Rex
1980	Jan Kowalczyk (Pol)	Artemor
1984	Joe Fargis (US)	Touch of Class
1988	Pierre Durand (Fra)	Jappeloup

Team

1912	Sweden
1920	Sweden
1924	Sweden
1928	Spain
1932	No medals awarded
1936	Germany
1948	Mexico
1952	Britain
1956	West Germany
1960	West Germany
1964	West Germany
1968	Canada
1972	West Germany
1976	France
1980	USSR
1984	United States
1988	West Germany

Most gold medals
5 Hans-Gunter Winkler (Team 1956, 1960, 1964, 1972; Individual 1956)

Three-Day Event
Individual

	Rider	Horse
1912	Axel Nordlander (Swe)	Lady Artist
1920	Helmer Morner (Swe)	Germania
1924	Adolph van der Voort van Zijp (Hol)	Silver Piece
1928	Charles P de Mortanges (Hol)	Marcroix
1932	Charles P de Mortanges (Hol)	Marcroix
1936	Ludwig Stubbendorff (Ger)	Nurmi
1948	Bernard Chevallier (Fra)	Aiglonne
1952	Hans von Blixen-Finecke (Swe)	Jubal
1956	Petrus Kastenman (Swe)	Iluster
1960	Lawrence Morgan (US)	Salad Days
1964	Mauro Checcoli (Ita)	Surbean
1968	Jean-Jacques Guyon (Fra)	Pitou
1972	Richard Meade (GB)	Laurieston
1976	Edmund Coffin (US)	Bally-Cor
1980	Federico Roman (Ita)	Rossinan
1984	Mark Todd (NZ)	Charisma
1988	Mark Todd (NZ)	Charisma

Team

1912	Sweden
1920	Sweden
1924	Holland
1928	Holland
1932	United States
1936	Germany
1948	United States
1952	Sweden
1956	Britain
1960	Australia
1964	Italy
1968	Britain
1972	Britain

1976	United States
1980	USSR
1984	United States
1988	West Germany

Most gold medals
4 Charles Pahud de Mortanges (Team 1924, 1928;
Individual 1928, 1932)

Dressage
Individual

	Rider	Horse
1912	Carl Bonde (Swe)	Emperor
1920	Janne Lundblad (Swe)	Uno
1924	Ernst Linder (Swe)	Piccolomini
1928	Carl von Langen (Ger)	Draufganger
1932	Xavier Lesage (Fra)	Taine
1936	Heinz Pollay (Ger)	Kronos
1948	Hans Moser (Swi)	Hummer
1952	Henri St Cyr (Swe)	Master Rufus
1956	Henri St Cyr (Swe)	Juli
1960	Sergey Filatov (USSR)	Absent
1964	Henri Chammartin (Swi)	Woermann
1968	Ivan Kizimov (USSR)	Ichor
1972	Liselott Linsenhoff (FRG)	Piaff
1976	Christine Stuckelberger (Swi)	Granat
1980	Elisabeth Theurer (Aut)	Mon Chérie
1984	Reiner Klimke (FRG)	Ahlerich
1988	Nicole Uphoff (FRG)	Rembrandt

Team

1928	Germany
1932	France
1936	Germany
1948	France
1952	Sweden
1956	Sweden
1960	Not held
1964	West Germany
1968	West Germany
1972	USSR
1976	West Germany
1980	USSR
1984	West Germany
1988	West Germany

Most gold medals
4 Henri St Cyr (Team 1952, 1956; Individual 1952, 1956)

WORLD CHAMPIONSHIPS
Show Jumping
Individual

	Rider	Horse
1953	Francisco Goyoago (Spa)	Quorum
1954	Hans-Günter Winkler (FRG)	Halla
1955	Hans-Günter Winkler (FRG)	Halla
1956	Raimondo d'Inzeo (Ita)	Merano
1960	Raimondo d'Inzeo (Ita)	Gowran Girl
1966	Pierre d'Oriola (Fra)	Pomone
1970	David Broome (GB)	Beethoven
1974	Hartwig Steenken (FRG)	Simona
1978	Gerd Wiltfang (FRG)	Roman
1982	Norbert Koof (FRG)	Fire II
1986	Gail Greenhough (Can)	Mr T
1990	Eric Navet (Fra)	Malesan Quito de Baussy

Women

	Rider	Horse
1965	Marion Coakes (GB)	Stroller
1970	Janou Lefèbvre (Fra)	Rocket
1974	Janou Tissot (née Lefèbvre) (Fra)	Rocket

Team

1978	Britain
1982	France
1986	United States
1990	France

Three-Day Event
Individual

	Rider	Horse
1966	Carlos Moratorio (Arg)	Chalon
1970	Mary Gordon-Watson (GB)	Cornishman V
1974	Bruce Davidson (US)	Irish Cap
1978	Bruce Davidson (US)	Might Tango
1982	Lucinda Green (GB)	Regal Realm
1986	Virginia Leng (GB)	Priceless
1990	Blyth Tait (NZ)	Messiah

Team

Dressage
Individual

	Rider	Horse
1966	Josef Neckermann (FRG)	Mariano
1970	Yelena Petouchkova (USSR)	Pepel
1974	Reiner Klimke (FRG)	Mehmed
1978	Christine Stuckelberger (Swi)	Granat
1982	Reiner Klimke (FRG)	Ahlerich
1986	Anne Grethe Jensen (Den)	Marzog
1990	Nicole Uphoff (FRG)	Rembrandt

Team

1966	West Germany	1978	West Germany
1970	USSR	1982	West Germany
1974	West Germany	1986	West Germany
		1990	West Germany

Carriage Driving
Individual

		Team
1972	Auguste Dubey (Swi)	Great Britain
1974	Sandor Fulop (Hun)	Great Britain
1976	Imre Abonyi (Hun)	Hungary
1978	Gyorgy Bardos (Hun)	Hungary
1980	Gyorgy Bardos (Hun)	Great Britain
1982	Tjeerd Velstra (Hol)	Holland
1984	Laszlo Juhasz (Hun)	Hungary
1986	Tjeerd Velstra (Hol)	Holland
1988	Ijsbrand Chardon (Hol)	Holland
1990	Ad Aarts (Hol)	Holland

Endurance
Individual

	Rider	Horse
1986	Cassandra Schuler (US)	Skikos Omar
1988	Becky Hart (US)	RO Grand Sultan
1990	Becky Hart (US)	RO GrandSultan

Team

1986	Great Britain
1988	United States
1990	Great Britain

Vaulting
Men's Individual

1986	Dietmar Ott (FRG)
1988	Christopher Pensing (FRG)
1990	Michael Lehner (FRG)

Women's Individual

1986	Silke Bernhard (FRG)
1988	Silke Bernhard (FRG)
1990	Silke Bernhard (FRG)

Team

1986	West Germany
1988	West Germany
1990	Switzerland

EUROPEAN CHAMPIONSHIPS
Show Jumping
Individual

	Rider	Horse
1957	Hans-Günter Winkler (FRG)	Sonnenglanz
1958	Fritz Thiedemann (FRG)	Meteor
1959	Piero d'Inzeo (Ita)	Uruguay
1961	David Broome (GB)	Sunsalve
1962	David Barker (GB)	Mister Softee
1963	Graziano Mancinelli (Ita)	Rockette
1965	Hermann Schridde (FRG)	Dozent
1966	Nelson Pessoa (Bra)	Gran Geste
1967	David Broome (GB)	Mister Softee
1969	David Broome (GB)	Mister Softee
1971	Hartwig Steenken (FRG)	Simona
1973	Paddy McMahon (GB)	Penwood Forge Mill
1975	Alwin Schockemohle (FRG)	Warwick
1977	Johan Heins (Hol)	Seven Valleys
1979	Gerhard Wiltfang (FRG)	Roman
1981	Paul Schockemohle (FRG)	Deister
1983	Paul Schockemohle (FRG)	Deister
1985	Paul Schockemohle (FRG)	Deister
1987	Pierre Durand (Fra)	Jappeloup
1989	John Whitaker (GB)	Next Milton

Women

	Rider	Horse
1957	Pat Smythe (GB)	Flanagan
1958	Giulia Serventi (Ita)	Doly
1959	Ann Townsend (GB)	Bandit
1960	Susan Cohen (GB)	Clare Castle
1961	Pat Smythe (GB)	Flanagan
1962	Pat Smythe (GB)	Flanagan
1963	Pat Smythe (GB)	Flanagan
1966	Janou Lefèbvre (Fra)	Kenavo
1967	Kathy Kusner (US)	Untouchable
1968	Anneli Drummond-Hay (GB)	Merely-a-Monarch
1969	Iris Kellett (Ire)	Morning Light
1971	Ann Moore (GB)	Psalm
1973	Ann Moore (GB)	Psalm

Team

1975	West Germany	1983	Switzerland
1977	Holland	1985	Britain
1979	Britain	1987	Britain
1981	West Germany	1989	Britain

Three-Day Event
Individual

	Rider	Horse
1953	Lawrence Rook (GB)	Starlight
1954	Albert Hill (GB)	Crispin
1955	Frank Weldon (GB)	Kilbarry
1957	Sheila Willcox (GB)	High and Mighty
1959	Hans Schwarzenbach (Swi)	Burn Trout
1962	James Templar (GB)	M'Lord Connolly
1965	Marian Babirecki (Pol)	Volt
1967	Eddie Boylan (Ire)	Durlas Eile
1969	Mary Gordon-Watson (GB)	Cornishman V
1971	HRH Princess Anne (GB)	Doublet
1973	Aleksandr Yevdokimov (USSR)	Jeger
1975	Lucinda Prior-Palmer (GB)	Be Fair
1977	Lucinda Prior-Palmer (GB)	George
1979	Nils Haagensen (Den)	Monaco
1981	Hansueli Schmutz (Swi)	Oran
1983	Rachel Bayliss (GB)	Mystic Minstrel
1985	Virginia Holgate (GB)	Priceless
1987	Virginia Leng (née Holgate) (GB)	Night Cap

1989	Virginia Leng (GB)	Master Craftsman

Team

1953	Britain	1973	West Germany
1954	Britain	1975	USSR
1955	Britain	1977	Britain
1957	Britain	1979	Ireland
1959	West Germany	1981	Britain
1962	USSR	1983	Sweden
1965	USSR	1985	Britain
1967	Britain	1987	Britain
1969	Britain	1989	Britain
1971	Britain		

Dressage
Individual

	Rider	Horse
1963	Henri Chammartin (Swi)	Wolfdietrich
1965	Henri Chammartin (Swi)	Wolfdietrich
1967	Reiner Klimke (FRG)	Dux
1969	Liselott Linsenhoff (FRG)	Piaff
1971	Liselott Linsenhoff (FRG)	Piaff
1973	Reiner Klimke (FRG)	Mehmed
1975	Christine Stuckelberger (Swi)	Granat
1977	Christine Stuckelberger (Swi)	Granat
1979	Elisabeth Theurer (Aut)	Mon Chérie
1981	Uwe Schulten-Baumer (FRG)	Madras
1983	Anne Grethe Jensen (Den)	Marzog
1985	Reiner Klimke (FRG)	Ahlerich
1987	Margrit Otto-Crepin (Fra)	Corlandus
1989	Nicole Uphoff (FRG)	Rembrandt

Team

1963	Britain
1965-89	West Germany

OTHER MAJOR SHOW JUMPING COMPETITIONS
British Derby
Hickstead

1961	Seamus Hayes (Ire)	Goodbye III
1962	Pat Smythe (GB)	Flanagan
1963	Nelson Pessoa (Bra)	Gran Geste
1964	Seamus Hayes (Ire)	Goodbye III
1965	Nelson Pessoa (Bra)	Gran Geste
1966	David Broome (GB)	Mister Softee
1967	Marion Coakes (GB)	Stroller
1968	Alison Westwood (GB)	The Maverick VII
1969	Anneli Drummond-Hay (GB)	Xanthos
1970	Harvey Smith (GB)	Mattie Brown
1971	Harvey Smith (GB)	Mattie Brown
1972	Hendrick Snoek (FRG)	Shirokko
1973	Alison Dawes (née Westwood) (GB)	Mr Banbury
1974	Harvey Smith (GB)	Salvador
1975	Paul Darragh (Ire)	Pele
1976	Eddie Macken (Ire)	Boomerang
1977	Eddie Macken (Ire)	Boomerang
1978	Eddie Macken (Ire)	Boomerang
1979	Eddie Macken (Ire)	Boomerang
1980	Michael Whitaker (GB)	Owen Gregory
1981	Harvey Smith (GB)	Sanyo Video
1982	Paul Schockemohle (FRG)	Deister
1983	John Whitaker (GB)	Ryan's Son
1984	John Ledingham (Ire)	Gabhram
1985	Paul Schockemohle (FRG)	Lorenzo
1986	Paul Schockemohle (FRG)	Next Deister
1987	Nick Skelton (GB)	Raffles
1988	Nick Skelton (GB)	Apollo
1989	Nick Skelton (GB)	Burmah Apollo
1990	Joe Turi (GB)	Vital

King George V Gold Cup
First held 1911. Winners since 1981

1981	David Broome (GB)	Mr Ross
1982	Michael Whitaker (GB)	Disney Way
1983	Paul Schockemohle (FRG)	Deister
1984	Nick Skelton (GB)	St James
1985	Malcolm Pyrah (GB)	Towerlands Angelzark
1986	John Whitaker (GB)	Next Ryan's Son
1987	Malcolm Pyrah (GB)	Towerlands Angelzark
1988	Robert Smith (GB)	Brook Street Boysie
1989	Michael Whitaker (GB)	Next Didi
1990	Michael Whitaker (GB)	Henderson Milton

Most wins
5 David Broome 1960, 1966, 1972, 1977, 1981

Queen Elizabeth II Cup
First held 1949. Winners since 1981

1981	Liz Edgar (GB)	Everest Forever
1982	Liz Edgar (GB)	Everest Forever
1983	Jean Germany (GB)	Mandingo
1984	Veronique Whitaker (GB)	Next's Jingo
1985	Sue Pountain (GB)	Ned Kelly
1986	Liz Edgar (GB)	Everest Rapier
1987	Gillian Greenwood (GB)	Monsanta
1988	Janet Hunter (GB)	Everest Lisnamarrow
1989	Janet Hunter (GB)	Everest Lisnamarrow
1990	Emma-Jane Mac (GB)	Everest Oyster

Most wins
5 Liz Edgar 1977, 1979, 1981-82, 1986

Volvo World Cup
Inaugurated 1979

1979	Hugo Simon (Aut)	Gladstone
1980	Conrad Homfeld (US)	Balbuco
1981	Mike Matz (US)	Jet Run
1982	Melanie Smith (US)	Calypso
1983	Norman Dello Joio (US)	I Love You
1984	Mario Deslauriers (Can)	Aramis
1985	Conrad Homfeld (US)	Abdullah
1986	Leslie Burr-Lenehan (US)	McLain
1987	Katherine Burdsall (US)	The Natural
1988	Ian Miller (Can)	Big Ben
1989	Ian Miller (Can)	Big Ben
1990	John Whitaker (GB)	Henderson Milton

Nations Cup
(Gucci Cup)
Inaugurated 1947. Winners since 1981

1981	West Germany
1982	West Germany
1983	Britain
1984	West Germany
1985	Britain
1986	Britain
1987	France
1988	France
1989	Britain

THREE-DAY EVENT
Badminton Horse Trials
(1956 event at Windsor)

1949	John Shedden (GB)	Golden Willow
1950	Tony Collings (GB)	Remus
1951	Hans Schwarzenbach (Swi)	Vae Victus
1952	Mark Darley (Ire)	Emily Little
1953	Lawrence Rook (GB)	Starlight
1954	Margaret Hough (GB)	Bambi
1955	Frank Weldon (GB)	Kilbarry

1956	Frank Weldon (GB)	Kilbarry
1957	Sheila Willcox (GB)	High and Mighty
1958	Sheila Willcox (GB)	High and Mighty
1959	Sheila Waddington (née Willcox) (GB)	Airs and Graces
1960	Bill Roycroft (Aus)	Our Solo
1961	Lawrence Morgan (Aus)	Salad Days
1962	Anneli Drummond-Hay (GB)	Merely-a-Monarch
1963	Susan Fleet (GB)	Gladiator#
1964	James Templer (GB)	M'Lord Connolly
1965	Eddie Boylan (Ire)	Durlas Eile
1966	Not held	
1967	Celia Ross-Taylor (GB)	Jonathan
1968	Jane Bullen (GB)	Our Nobby
1969	Richard Walker (GB)	Pasha
1970	Richard Meade (GB)	The Poacher
1971	Mark Phillips (GB)	Great Ovation
1972	Mark Phillips (GB)	Great Ovation
1973	Lucinda Prior-Palmer (GB)	Be Fair
1974	Mark Phillips (GB)	Columbus
1975	Cancelled after dressage	
1976	Lucinda Prior-Palmer (GB)	Wideawake
1977	Lucinda Prior-Palmer (GB)	George
1978	Jane Holderness-Roddam (née Bullen) (GB)	Warrior
1979	Lucinda Prior-Palmer (GB)	Killaire
1980	Mark Todd (NZ)	Southern Comfort
1981	Mark Phillips (GB)	Lincoln
1982	Richard Meade (GB)	Speculator III
1983	Lucinda Green (née Prior-Palmer) (GB)	Regal Realm
1984	Lucinda Green (GB)	Beagle Bay
1985	Virginia Holgate (GB)	Priceless
1986	Ian Stark (GB)	Sir Wattie
1987	cancelled	
1988	Ian Stark (GB)	Sir Wattie
1989	Virginia Leng (GB)	Master Craftsman
1990	Nicola McIrvine (GB)	Middle Road

reduced to a One-Day Event because of the weather

Burghley Horse Trials

1961	Anneli Drummond-Hay (GB)	Merely-a-Monarch
1962	European Championship	
1963	Harry Freeman-Jackson (Ire)	St Finbar
1964	Richard Meade (GB)	Barberry
1965	Jeremy Beale (GB)	Victoria Bridge
1966	World Championship	
1967	Lorna Sutherland (GB)	Popadom
1968	Sheila Willcox (GB)	Fair and Square
1969	Gillian Watson (GB)	Shaitan
1970	Judy Bradwell (GB)	Don Camillo
1971	European Championship	
1972	Janet Hodgson (GB)	Larkspur
1973	Mark Phillips (GB)	Maid Marion
1974	World Championship	
1975	Aly Pattinson (GB)	Carawich
1976	Jane Holderness-Roddam (GB)	Warrior
1977	Lucinda Prior-Palmer (GB)	George
1978	Lorna Clarke (née Sutherland) (GB)	Greco
1979	Andrew Hoy (Aus)	Davy
1980	Richard Walker (GB)	John of Gaunt
1981	Lucinda Prior-Palmer (GB)	Beagle Bay
1982	Richard Walker (GB)	Ryan's Cross
1983	Virginia Holgate (GB)	Priceless
1984	Virginia Holgate (GB)	Night Cap
1985	European Championship	
1986	Virginia Leng (née Holgate) (GB)	Murphy Himself

1987	Mark Todd (NZ)	Wilton Fair
1988	Jane Thelwall (GB)	Kings Jester
1989	European Championship	
1990	Mark Todd (NZ)	Face the Music

━━━━━━━━**1991**━━━━━━━━

May 2-6: Badminton Horse Trials (Badminton); *May 30-Jun 2:* Nations Cup show jumping (Hickstead); *Jun 13-16:* Royal International Horse Show (NEC, Birmingham); *Jul 17-21;*European Show Jumping Championships (La Baule, Paris); *Jul 26-28;* European Vaulting Championships (Berne); *Aug 6-10;* Nations Cup show jumping (Dublin); *Sep 6-9;* European Horse Trials Championships (Punchestown, Ireland); *Sep 12-15:* Burghley Horse Trials; *Oct 7-12* Horse of the Year Show (Wembley); *Dec 18-22:* Olympia International (Olympia)

FENCING

━━━━━ 1990 ━━━━━

WORLD CHAMPIONSHIPS
Lyon, France, Jul 6-16

Men
FOIL

Individual	Team
1 Philippe Omnes (Fra)	1 Italy
2 Andrea Borella (Ita)	2 Poland
3 Dimitri Chevtchenko (USSR)	3 USSR

EPEE

Individual	Team
1 Thomas Gerull (FRG)	1 Italy
2 Angelo Mazzoni (Ita)	2 France
3 Arndt Schmitt (FRG)	3 USSR

SABRE

Individual	Team
1 Gyorgy Nebald (Hun)	1 USSR
2 Georgiy Pogossov (USSR)	2 Hungary
3 Tonni Terenzi (Ita)	3 West Germany

Women
FOIL

Individual	Team
1 Anja Fichtel (FRG)	1 Italy
2 Giovanna Trillini (Ita)	2 USSR
3 Olga Velitchko (USSR)	3 China

EPEE

Individual	Team
1 Taime Chappe (Cub)	1 West Germany
2 Diane Eori (Hun)	2 Hungary
3 Maria Mazina (USSR)	3 Italy

Cuba's first gold medal since 1904

NATIONAL CHAMPIONSHIPS

Men
FOIL
Sheffield, May 12-13
1 Bill Gosbee (Salle Boston)
2 Austin Royle (Ashton FC)
3 Tony Bartlett (Salle Paul)

EPEE
de Beaumont Centre, London, Feb 10
1 Ralph Johnson (Boston)
2 Neil Mallett (Boston)
3 Mark Kingston (Llantwit Major)
Johnson's sixth title, equalling the record

SABRE
de Beaumont Centre, London, Mar 10-11
1 Gary Fletcher (Ashton)
2 Ian Williams (London Thames)
3 Mark Hoenigman (Bellahouston)

Women
FOIL
Sheffield, May 12-13
1 Linda Strachan (Salle Paul)
2 Fiona McIntosh (Salle Paul)
3 Linda McMahon (Salle Paul)

EPEE
de Beaumont Centre, May 26-27
1 Nicole Twigg (Chelsea & Westminster)
2 Penny Tomkinson (London Thames)
3 Alda Milner-Barry (London Thames)

SABRE
de Beaumont Centre, Mar 10-11
1 Sally Claxton (London Polytechnic)
2 Tanis John (Sherwood)
3 Ondine Francis (Blackheath)

━━━━━ CHAMPIONS ━━━━━

OLYMPIC GAMES

Men
FOIL

	Individual	Team
1896	Emile Gravelotte (Fra)	-
1900	Emile Coste (Fra)	-
1904	Ramon Fonst (Cub)	Cuba
1908	Not Held	
1912	Nedo Nadi (Ita)	-
1920	Nedo Nadi (Ita)	Italy
1924	Roger Ducret (Fra)	France
1928	Lucien Gaudini (Ita)	Italy
1932	Gustavo Marzi	France
1936	Giulio Gaudini (Ita)	Italy
1948	Jean Buhan (Fra)	France
1952	Christian d'Oriola (Fra)	France
1956	Christian d'Oriola (Fra)	Italy
1960	Viktor Zhadanovich (USSR)	USSR
1964	Egon Franke (Pol)	USSR
1968	Ion Drimba (Rom)	France
1972	Witold Woyda (Pol)	Poland
1976	Fabio Dal Zotto (Ita)	Italy
1980	Vladimir Smirnov (USSR)	USSR
1984	Mauro Numa (Ita)	Italy
1988	Stefano Cerioni (Ita)	USSR

SABRE

	Individual	Team
1896	Jean Georgiadis (Gre)	-
1900	Georges de la Falaise (Fra)	-
1904	Manuel Diaz (Cub)	-
1908	Jeno Fuchs (Hun)	Hungary
1912	Jeno Fuchs (Hun)	Hungary
1920	Nedo Naidi (Ita)	Italy
1924	Sandor Posta (Hun)	Italy
1928	Odon Tersztyanszky (Hun)	Hungary
1932	Gyorgy Piller (Hun)	Hungary
1936	Endre Kabos (Hun)	Hungary
1948	Aldar Gerevich (Hun)	Hungary
1952	Pal Kovacs (Hun)	Hungary
1960	Rudolf Karpati (Hun)	Hungary
1964	Tibor Pezsa (Hun)	USSR
1968	Jerzy Pawlowski (Pol)	USSR
1972	Viktor Sidiak (USSR)	Italy
1976	Viktor Krovopuskov (USSR)	USSR
1980	Viktor Krovopuskov (USSR)	USSR
1984	Jean-François Lamour (Fra)	Italy
1988	Jean-François Lamour (Fra)	Hungary

EPEE
First held 1900

	Undividual	Team
1900	Ramon Fonst (Cub)	-
1904	Ramon Fonst (Cub)	-
1908	Gaston Alibert (Fra)	France
1912	Paul Anspach (Bel)	Belgium
1920	Armand Massard (Fra)	Italy
1924	Charles Delport (Bel)	France
1928	Lucien Gaudin (Fra)	Italy
1932	Giancarlo Cornaggia-Medici (Ita)	France
1936	Franco Riccardi (Ita)	Italy
1948	Luigi Cantone (Ita)	France

1952	Edoardo Mangiarotti (Ita)	Italy
1956	Carlo Pavesi (Ita)	Italy
1960	Giuseppe Delfino (Ita)	Italy
1964	Grigoriy Kriss (USSR)	Hungary
1968	Gyozo Kulcsar (Hun)	Hungary
1972	Csaba Fenyvesi (Hun)	Hungary
1976	Alexander Pusch (FRG)	Sweden
1980	Johan Harmenberg (Swe)	France
1984	Philippe Boisse (Fra)	W Germany
1988	Arnd Schmitt (FRG)	France

Women
FOIL (ONLY)

	Individual	Team
1924	Ellen Osiier (Den)	-
1928	Helene Mayer (Ger)	-
1932	Ellen Preis (Aut)	-
1936	Ilona Elek (Hun)	-
1948	Ilona Elek (Hun)	-
1952	Irene Camber (Ita)	-
1956	Gillian Sheen (GB)	-
1960	Heidi Schmid (W.Ger)	USSR
1964	Ildiko Ujlaki-Rejto (Hun)	Hungary
1968	Yelena Novikova (USSR)	USSR
1972	Antonella Ragno-Lonzi (Ita)	USSR
1976	Ildiko Schwarczenberger (Hun)	USSR
1980	Pascale Trinquet (Fra)	France
1984	Luan Jujie (Chn)	W Germany
1988	Anja Fichtel (FRG)	W Germany

WORLD CHAMPIONSHIPS
(since 1981)
Olympic champions are automatic world champions

Men
FOIL

	Individual	Team
1981	Vladimir Smirnov (USSR)	USSR
1982	Aleksandr Romankov (USSR)	USSR
1983	Aleksandr Romankov (USSR)	W Germany
1985	Mauro Numa (Ita)	Italy
1986	Andrea Borella (Ita)	USSR
1987	Mathias Gey (FRG)	USSR
1989	Alexander Koch (FRG)	USSR
1990	Philippe Omnes (Fra)	Italy

EPEE

1981	Zoltan Szekely (Hun)	USSR
1982	Jeno Pap (Hun)	France
1983	Ellmar Bormann (FRG)	France
1985	Phillippe Boisse (Fra)	W Germany
1986	Phillippe Riboud (Fra)	W Germany
1987	Volker Fisher (FRG)	W Germany
1989	Manuel Pereira (Spa)	Italy
1990	Thomas Gerull (FRG)	Italy

SABRE

1981	Mariusz Wodke (Pol)	Hungary
1982	Viktor Krovopuskov (USSR)	Hungary
1983	Vasiliy Etropolski (Pol)	USSR
1985	Gyorgy Nebald (Hun)	USSR
1986	Sergey Mindirgassov (USSR)	USSR
1987	Jean-François Lamour (Fra)	USSR
1989	Grigoriy Kirienko (USSR)	USSR
1990	Gyorgy Nebald (Hun)	USSR

Women
FOIL

1981	Cornelia Hanisch (FRG)	USSR
1982	Nalia Galiazova (USSR)	Italy
1983	Dorina Vaccoroni	Italy
1985	Cornelia Hanisch (FRG)	W Germany
1986	Anja Fichtel (FRG)	USSR
1987	Elisabeta Tufan (Rom)	Hungary
1989	Olga Velitchko (USSR)	W Germany
1990	Anja Fichtel (FRG)	Italy

EPEE

1989	Anja Straub (Swi)	Hungary
1990	Taime Chappe (Cub)	W Germany

——— 1990 ———

ALL-IRELAND HURLING FINAL
Croke Park, Dublin, Sep 2
CORK 5-15 (30)   Galway   2-21 (27)

ALL-IRELAND GAELIC FOOTBALL CHAMPIONSHIP
Croke Park, Dublin, Sep 16
CORK 0-11 (11)   Meath   0-9 (9)

——— CHAMPIONS ———

	Hurling	Football
1887	Tipperary	Limerick
1888	Not held	
1889	Dublin	Tipperary
1890	Cork	Cork
1891	Kerry	Dublin
1892	Cork	Dublin
1893	Cork	Wexford
1894	Cork	Dublin
1895	Tipperary	Tipperary
1896	Tipperary	Limerick
1897	Limerick	Dublin
1898	Tipperary	Dublin
1899	Tipperary	Dublin
1900	Tipperary	Tipperary
1901	London Irish	Dublin
1902	Cork	Dublin
1903	Cork	Kerry
1904	Kilkenny	Kerry
1905	Kilkenny	Kildare
1906	Tipperary	Dublin
1907	Kilkenny	Dublin
1908	Tipperary	Dublin
1909	Kilkenny	Kerry
1910	Wexford	Louth
1911	Kilkenny	Cork
1912	Kilkenny	Louth
1913	Kilkenny	Kerry
1914	Clare	Kerry
1915	Laois	Wexford
1916	Tipperary	Wexford
1917	Dublin	Wexford
1918	Limerick	Wexford
1919	Cork	Kildare
1920	Dublin	Tipperary
1921	Limerick	Dublin
1922	Kilkenny	Dublin
1923	Galway	Dublin
1924	Dublin	Kerry
1925	Tipperary	Galway
1926	Cork	Kerry
1927	Dublin	Kildare
1928	Cork	Kildare
1929	Cork	Kerry
1930	Tipperary	Kerry
1931	Cork	Kerry
1932	Kilkenny	Kerry
1933	Kilkenny	Cavan
1934	Limerick	Galway
1935	Kilkenny	Cavan
1936	Limerick	Mayo
1937	Tipperary	Kerry
1938	Dublin	Galway
1939	Kilkenny	Kerry
1940	Limerick	Kerry
1941	Cork	Kerry
1942	Cork	Dublin
1943	Cork	Roscommon
1944	Cork	Roscommon
1945	Tipperary	Cork
1946	Cork	Kerry
1947	Kilkenny	Cavan
1948	Waterford	Cavan
1949	Tipperary	Meath
1950	Tipperary	Mayo
1951	Tipperary	Mayo
1952	Cork	Cavan
1953	Cork	Kerry
1954	Cork	Meath
1955	Wexford	Kerry
1956	Wexford	Galway
1957	Kilkenny	Louth
1958	Tipperary	Dublin
1959	Waterford	Kerry
1960	Wexford	Down
1961	Tipperary	Down
1962	Tipperary	Kerry
1963	Kilkenny	Dublin
1964	Tipperary	Galway
1965	Tipperary	Galway
1966	Cork	Galway
1967	Kilkenny	Meath
1968	Wexford	Down
1969	Kilkenny	Kerry
1970	Cork	Kerry
1971	Tipperary	Offaly
1972	Kilkenny	Offaly
1973	Limerick	Cork
1974	Kilkenny	Dublin
1975	Kilkenny	Kerry
1976	Cork	Dublin
1977	Cork	Dublin
1978	Cork	Kerry
1979	Kilkenny	Kerry
1980	Galway	Kerry
1981	Offaly	Kerry
1982	Kilkenny	Offaly
1983	Kilkenny	Dublin
1984	Cork	Kerry
1985	Offaly	Kerry
1986	Cork	Kerry
1987	Galway	Meath
1988	Galway	Meath
1989	Tipperary	Cork
1990	Cork	Cork

Teams underlined completed Hurling/Football 'double'

Wins (Hurling):
27 Cork (Corcaigh); 23 Tipperary (Tiobrad Arann), Kilkenny (Cill Chainnigh); 7 Limerick (Luimneach); 6 Dublin (Ath Cliath); 5 Wexford (Loch Garman); 4 Galway (Gaillimh); 2 Waterford (Port Lairge), Offaly (Uibh Fhrili); 1 Kerry (Ciarraidhe), London Irish (Lonndain), Clare (An Clar), Laois (Laois).

Wins (Football):
30 Kerry (Ciarraidhe); 21 Dublin (Ath Cliath); 7 Galway (Gaillimh); 6 Cork (Corcaigh); 5 Wexford (Loch Garman), Cavan (Cabhan), Meath (An Mhidhe); 4 Tipperary (Tiobrad Arann), Kildare (Cill Dara); 3 Louth (Lughbhaidh), Mayo (Muigheo), Down (An Dun), Offaly (Uibh Fhrili); 2 Limerick (Luimneach), Roscommon (Ros Comain)

GOLF

THE FALDO PHENOMENON

With the sun improbably bright over the auld grey toun and people filling every imaginable vantage point, Nick Faldo walked up the 18th fairway at St Andrews to claim not merely the Open Championship but the unchallenged title as the world's best golfer. At Augusta three months earlier Faldo had become the second man (after Jack Nicklaus) to retain the Masters title; at the US Open only a putt lipping out on the 72nd hole prevented him joining a play-off; at St Andrews he made no mistake whatever.

Faldo started level with Greg Norman after the second round for what appeared to be a shoot-out in the style set by Watson and Nicklaus at Turnberry 13 years earlier. But Norman shot himself, with a 76. Faldo was five strokes ahead before the final round and four ahead coming to the last green which, he said, is how he had dreamed it. It took the official computer a further seven weeks to accept that history had moved on and Faldo had displaced Norman as no. 1. No humans had any doubts.

A combination of soft greens and warm, almost windless days made the Old Course almost ridiculously tame, and scoring records were smashed throughout the tournament. Faldo landed in only one bunker all week - at the fourth on the final day - and never once three-putted, despite the huge St Andrews greens.

Faldo was the first man to win two majors in a year since Tom Watson in 1982 and acquired a position in golf almost unthinkable for a Briton a few years earlier when it would also have been unthinkable for a golfer to kiss his caddie quite so fulsomely. Fanny Sunesson, a leading Swedish amateur herself, did not mind at all.

Open week had started with Faldo being drawn with Scott Hoch, the man he beat in the 1989 Masters play-off. Hoch said Faldo was not quite his favourite person and was punished first by the newspapers slightly overstating his remarks (FALDO IS A PLONKER - *Daily Mirror*; WE ALL HATE NASTY NICK -*The Sun*) and then by the Road Hole, which cost him his place in the third round. Faldo simply carried on serenely. Faldo's rival in the 1990 Masters was the much more substantial figure of Raymond Floyd, widely regarded as the least flappable golfer in the game. Floyd was four ahead with five to play but Faldo took him to a play-off and at the second extra hole, the 11th, where Hoch missed a tiddling putt in 1989, Floyd failed even to get on to the green, hitting a seven-iron into the water. In an atmosphere more of disbelief than elation, Faldo found himself the Master again.

In the US Open the old man did win the play-off. Hale Irwin, 45 years and 15 days, became the tournament's oldest winner when he holed an eight-foot birdie at the 91st hole. Mike Donald had led for the most of the fourth round until he was bunkered on the 16th. Irwin was down the field but was playing with Greg Norman which, he said, helped inspire him on his Normanesque inward nine of 31. On the 72nd Irwin holed a 60-footer to draw level with Donald. The USGA still try and avoid sudden-death play-offs but on their fifth round, Irwin and Donald both took unspectacular 74s, so there was no alternative. Irwin was able to enter only under a special exemption as a former winner, a system which he had vigorously opposed some years earlier.

Had Faldo come first instead of third in the US Open, the last major of the year, the PGA, would have been an extraordinarily hyped-up golfing occasion. In the end Faldo came only 19th equal after a third round of 80, his highest score since 1979, though he compensated by having the lowest round on the final day on a course where the vicious rough provided a vivid contrast to St Andrews. But the Americans could not win this one either. Wayne Grady of Australia became the third overseas winner of the tournament, after Gary Player and David Graham. Grady had previously won only four tournaments but come second 29 times. Even if Grady had wanted to lose, he could

MASTER, OPEN CHAMPION, NUMBER ONE

❝By the grace of the good Lord, his own perseverance and a lousy seven-iron-shot..."
Clem Furman, Radio WANS, Augusta
"Believe me, it's the most devastating thing that's happened to me in my career, at any time....This would've meant so much to me, you can't imagine. To be the oldest, to win another major. Nothing has ever affected me like this."
Ray Floyd
"I honestly believe the Open trophy is destined for one place, Nick Faldo's mantelpiece in Ascot. I have never known a more dedicated golfer in my life. He is a phenomenon. He has moved on to a different plane than the others. He is where Watson and Nicklaus were once and that is as high as you can go."
TonyJacklin, before The Open

"This is the moment...all those people ...enjoy this one."
Faldo to his caddie on the 18th fairway
"Daddy's won again."
Natalie Faldo, age three, afterwards
"I just want you to know it was a pleasure to watch you play in the Open. Great stuff."
Jack Nicklaus to Faldo
"I think if I'd had some coaching I could have played county cricket as a bowler. Luckily, I didn't have any coaching."
Faldo
"Normally, when I come over here it's 'Oh, it's Faldo, let's have another hot dog.' Now it's whooping and hollering and clambering all over the place."
Faldo at the USPGA
"I've got to keep working on my game, fine-tune it over the next ten years. Golf is a funny business, it can bite your head off.❞
Faldo

hardly have helped himself: his last rival, Fred Couples, missed three four-footers on the closing holes.

The tournament will be mainly remembered for the controversy caused when it was discovered that the host club, Shoal Creek near Birmingham, Alabama, did not admit black members. This could hardly have come as a surprise to anyone, least of all the USPGA, but it led to a major outbreak of self-righteousness. Four large companies, led by IBM, withdrew TV advertising. Then, a week before the event, the club asked a local black businessman, Louis Willie, to become an honorary member. Willie had not played golf in 20 years and did not want to join, but agreed. By an amazing coincidence, Hord Hardin, chairman of Augusta National, discovered a black TV executive who was suitable for membership a few weeks later, and all the all-white clubs scheduled to host the next four PGA Championships also agreed to find minority members. Various black golfers said protesters should not have been so easily satisfied. "You need a tub of water and you get a teardrop," said Charlie Owens, a member of the senior tour. Some courses, including Cypress Point in California, preferred to stop hosting professional tournaments.

Back on the circuit, Faldo's rivals had a terrible time trailing in his wake. Sandy Lyle again had a wretched year: at the US Masters he missed the cut but hit three spectators. He eventually asked Faldo's guru David Leadbetter for help. Severiano Ballesteros, thought by some to be distracted by fatherhood, started to remodel his swing, to no obvious effect: at Shoal Creek he took 77 and 83. Norman's disaster at St Andrews seemed to enter his soul. For them all, the sight of Faldo, apparently impervious to all distractions, was a sort of Nemesis.

THE SPANISH CONNECTION

The year's second brightest star was José-Maria Olazabal, who rose to third place in the rankings. He won his first professional tournament in Britain, the Benson and Hedges, followed by the Irish Open and the World Series of Golf in Ohio, which he took by 12 shots, the largest margin on the US tour for 15 years. Two putts lipped out in his first round of 61. Ian Woosnam won two tournaments running just before the Open and the World Match Play. The new kid on the block was Robert Gamez, 21, who won his first US tour event as a cardholder, the Tucson Open, and won again at Bay Hill two months later when he eagled the 18th, supposedly the hardest hole in the entire tour, with a 176-yard seven-iron. Norman - who else? - had been leading by one stroke. At the other extreme of proficiency, the indefatigable Maurice G Flitcroft, barred from the Open for the absurd crime of not being good enough, beat the officials looking out for him and entered the regional qualifying at Ormskirk under the name James Beau Jolley. He was caught after playing two holes incompetently and given his £60 entrance fee back. "I have always believed in my potential," said Flitcroft, "but I was not warmed up properly." A Flitcroft protégé, Simon John-Dawson, reached the third hole after arriving on the first tee in trainers asking "Do you think 90 will qualify?" "These people are an irritation and a nuisance," said Michael Bonallack, the Royal and Ancient Club secretary, pompously.

A more promising young hopeful, Jack Nicklaus, emulated Palmer, Player and George Archer by winning his first Seniors tournament, the tradition in Arizona. Nicklaus ascribed his success partly to losing weight through giving up junk food, partly to a new Japanese driver acquired from Jumbo Ozaki. Nicklaus became the eighth honorary member of the R and A (joining the Dukes of Edinburgh and Kent, Kel Nagle, Arnold Palmer, Gene Sarazen, Peter Thomson and Roberto de Vicenzo). President Bush became the ninth.

The European Tour's first six-man play-off, in the Atlantic Open in Portugal, was won at the first extra hole by Stephen McAllister who managed a par when the other five failed. At the Tenerife Open, officials emulated Moses (Numbers 20:11) by turning rocks into water. They simply daubed red paint on them and designated them water hazards to prevent damage to players' clubs. At the Irish Open, Michel Krantz of Sweden hit the ball and then fell over on the first tee: "I was very silly," he admitted. "I was invited to an Irish party and it just went on from there." He eventually took 83, a very decent score under the circumstances. Norman disqualified himself while leading the Palm Meadows Cup in Australia after taking an incorrect drop from a lateral water hazard. Norman was 12 under par after two rounds. A Golf World survey of British professionals showed 35 out of 40 would vote Conservative with three Greens, two wouldn't-bothers and none for Labour.

The Belfry was chosen to stage the Ryder Cup for the third time running in Europe in 1993 after a split between the PGA and the European tour; Spain was sort-of promised the event for 1997. The brief era of American failure in all the transatlantic team competitions ended when the US crushed Britain and Ireland 14-4 in the women's competition, the Curtis Cup. The American lady golfer Muffin Spencer-Devlin was disqualified from the Ford Classic at Woburn after storming out, swearing, from the sponsors' dinner. She returned four months later for the Women's Open and went round in 71. She said she was fond of Britain because in a previous incarnation she had been King Arthur.

Two little-known American golfers, Tammie Green and Deborah McHaffie, were chosen from photos to compete in the Hennessy Ladies Cup in Paris: "The aesthetic element is important in terms of coverage," said the promoter Lionel Provost, "and we have had complaints from the French magazines that the players have not been up to scratch in this department in the past." Angela Uzielli, 50, became the oldest winner of the English women's championship.

ACE OF CLUBS

We now come to *The Sportspages Almanac's* traditional round-up of the year's more unlikely but apparently true holes-in-one. We salute the following:

Margaret Waldron, 74, who made two on successive days at the 87-yard seventh hole at Amelia Island Florida. Mrs Waldron is legally blind and has to be told where the flag is by her husband.

John Smith, 54, of Brierley Hill, who did one on his first full round of golf after a major heart attack (Stourbridge, 178-yard 15th)

Wendy Russell, 51, of Broadstone, Dorset, a member of the LGU executive council, who did two (127-yard 4th, 118-yard 8th) during the British Women's Senior Championship at Wrexham. She finished with a 78.

Brothers Tom and Oliver Plunkett, within minutes of each other at Elm Park, Dublin.

THE UNFORGIVING GAME

❝You play a lot of rounds as a kid thinking you're at Augusta. And I never shot THAT good.❞
Mike Donald, first-round leader at the Masters with 64

"The slums of Chicago are full of first-round leaders."
Peter Jacobsen

"I'm not carrying that bloody thing any more. You're a naturally gifted golfer. Stop mucking about."
Dave Musgrove, Sandy Lyle's caddie, advising his master on the use of the long-shafted putter

"If you can imagine a hole halfway down the bonnet of a VW beetle, and then you have to putt to it from the roof."
Nick Faldo, describing the greens at Royal Melbourne

"I could putt it off a tabletop and leave it short, halfway down a leg."
JC Snead

"It's a great golf hole. It gives you a million options, not one of them worth a damn."
Tom Kite on the 13th at St Andrews

"Golf is not a game, it's a punishment. Clubs are enemies, courses are haunted houses or torture chambers, tournaments are where one guy is happy and 150 are sad."
Jim Murray, Los Angeles Times

"I'm playing well again."
Mark Calcavecchia, after shooting a 64 in practice for the Memorial Tournament

"I'm outta here.❞
Mark Calcavecchia, after shooting an 88 in the first round of the Memorial Tournament

David Harrison and Ron Whadcock, playing together (131-yard 10th, Cosby, Leicester) followed by George Wynder on the same hole a few hours later. A J Peter Pratt claimed an in-off after his opponent's drive knocked his ball in (Thorpe Hall, Essex).

Edna Upward, for the first time in her life, aged 78 (113-yard 13th, Whitchurch, Cardiff).

Dennis Bulmer, 62, on the same hole in successive rounds (162-yard 10th Selby, Yorks).

Five members of the Hawarden Golf Club, North Wales, inside eight days: "It's like buses," said club secretary Tim Hinks-Edwards, "you wait for months and then five come along."

Bill Hatherly and his wife Joan, within minutes of each other at Ampfield, Hants.

John Morse, two in less than 20 minutes at Yorktown, Illinois - at the 117-yard eighth and the 130-yard 10th.

Len Perrett, two in the same round at Shirland, Derbyshire.

John Critchley, his eighth on his local course at Leigh, Lancs. Oh, and Severiano Ballesteros at the Monte Carlo Open - his first-ever (156-yard 2nd at Mont Agel).

THE GOLF CRISIS

The first golf course opened in the Soviet Union, a nine-holer outside Moscow, along with a driving range from which 100,000 balls were said to have been stolen by souvenir-hunters. The R and A said that before 2000 Britain would need 700 more 18-hole courses, enough to cover the Isle of Wight. Environmental groups began to protest at the proliferation of new courses both in Britain and elsewhere. In Japan "The Group to Protect Greenery and Streams" was launched.

Campaigners said that adding to the 1,640 courses in Japan caused the loss of flora and fauna and increased the risk of landslides and flooding, and complained that the chemicals used on courses polluted the air and water. There were also protests against a huge complex planned for the Coto Donana in Spain, home to 10,000 flamingoes. In Montreal a two-month siege by Mohawk Indians was sparked by plans to build a course on ancestral land; one policeman was shot dead. Florida opened its 1,000th golf course. In Japan membership of the top club, the Konganei, was reported to be worth £1.36 million at the height of the stock exchange boom. In France the government threatened to double-tax the sport as a "signe exterieure de richesse". In Kent there were complaints about men at the Lullingstone Park municipal course playing golf in their underpants.

The first World Scientific Congress of Golf was held at St Andrews. Dr Alistair

Cochran of Aston University told delegates that if the perfect golf ball were ever invented, even the best hitters could not get more than an extra 20 yards out of it. A New York firm introduced a device called Thermal Distance to heat golf balls. Bill Cohen, the inventor, said balls heated at 108 degrees F for 24 hours travelled eight per cent farther than normal; he insisted that putting them by a heater would not work. Mark Minnie, 17, tried to heat a golf ball in his mother's microwave; after 40 seconds it exploded all over the kitchen.

Ted Jarvis was matched with his old friend Cliff Pole in a contest at Minchinhampton, Gloucestershire, 45 years after Jarvis had seen Pole's fighter shot down over Normandy and assumed he had been killed. At Peacehaven Golf Club, Sussex, ten people were taken to hospital after a club member put cannabis in the Christmas cake. Jery Cochern, playing the par-four 17th at the Pasatiempo Golf Club, Santa Cruz during the California earthquake, was denied relief by his opponents despite being forced to putt across an eight-inch crevice. Golf Digest said that under Rule 25-1 b (iii) this should have been designated ground under repair. Oliver Anthony, 60, was held up at gunpoint on the eighth tee at the Davy Crockett Golf Club in Memphis, Tennessee. He later discovered a tear in his trousers and a bullet embedded in the spare ball in his pocket. Four baby crocodiles found in a pond at Chapman Golf Club, Zimbabwe, were rumoured to have been put there by a member anxious to expose caddies who fished balls out.

1990

THE MAJORS

US MASTERS
Augusta, Georgia, Apr 5-8
All from US unless otherwise stated

1	NICK FALDO (GB) 71-72-66-69	278
2	Ray Floyd 70-68-68-72	278

Faldo won play-off at 2nd extra hole

3	Lanny Wadkins 72-73-70-68	283
	John Huston 66-74-68-75	283
5	Fred Couples 74-69-72-69	284
6	Jack Nicklaus 72-70-79-74	285
7	Severiano Ballesteros (Spa) 74-73-68-71	286
	Tom Watson 77-71-67-71	286
	Curtis Strange 70-73-71-72	286
	Bill Britton 68-74-72-73	286
	Scott Simpson 74-71-68-73	286
	Bernard Langer (FRG) 70-73-69-74	286
13	José-Maria Olazabal (Spa) 72-73-68-74	287
	Ben Crenshaw 72-74-73-69	287
	Larry Mize 70-76-71-71	287
	Ronan Rafferty (GB) 72-74-69-73	287
	Craig Stadler 72-70-74-72	287
	Scott Hoch 71-68-73-76	287
	Tom Kite 75-73-66-74	287
20	Mark Calcavecchia 74-73-73-69	289
	Fuzzy Zoeller 72-74-73-70	289
	Steve Jones 77-69-72-71	289
23	Jumbo Ozaki (Jap) 70-71-77-72	290
24	Donnie Hammond 71-74-75-71	291
	Lee Trevino 78-69-72-72	291
	Gary Player (SA) 73-74-68-76	291
27	Andy North 71-73-77-71	292
	Jeff Sluman 78-68-75-71	292
	Wayne Grady (Aus) 72-75-72-73	292
30	Peter Jacobsen 67-75-76-75	293
	Jodie Mudd 74-70-73-76	293
	Ian Woosnam (GB) 72-75-70-76	293
33	Andy Bean 76-72-74-72	294
	Joe Ozaki (Jap) 75-73-74-72	294
	Bill Glasson 70-75-76-73	294
36	Mark McCumber 74-74-76-71	295
	Payne Stewart 71-73-77-74	295
38	Bob Tway 72-76-73-74	296
	Chip Beck 72-74-75-75	296

	Mark Lye 75-73-73-75	296
	Chris Patton (*) 71-73-74-78	296
42	John Mahaffey 72-74-75-76	297
	Peter Senior (Aus) 72-75-73-77	297
	Don Pooley 73-73-72-79	297
45	Tom Purtzer 71-77-76-74	298
	Mike Hulbert 71-71-77-79	298
47	Mike Donald 64-82-77-76	299
48	Larry Nelson 74-73-79-74	300
49	George Archer 70-74-82-75	301

(*) *Denotes amateur*
Leaders
Round 1: 64 Mike Donald
Round 2: 138 Ray Floyd
Round 3: 206 Ray Floyd
Notables who failed to make the cut:
Greg Norman, Paul Azinger, Billy Casper, Sandy Lyle, Arnold Palmer

BACK-TO-BACK WINNERS OF POST-WAR MAJORS

Bobby Locke (SA)	1949-50	British Open
Ben Hogan (US)	1950-51	US Open
Peter Thomson (Aus)	1954-56	British Open
Arnold Palmer (US)	1961-62	British Open
Jack Nicklaus (US)	1965-66	US Masters
Lee Trevino (US)	1971-72	British Open
Tom Watson (US)	1982-83	British Open
Curtis Strange (US)	1988-89	US Open
NICK FALDO (GB)	1989-90	US Masters

US OPEN
Medinah Country Club, Chicago, Jun 14-18
All from US unless otherwise stated

1	HALE IRWIN 67-70-72-71	280
2	Mike Donald 69-70-74-67	280

Play-off; Irwin 74, Donald 74. Irwin won at first extra hole

3	Nick Faldo (GB) 72-72-68-69	281
	Billy Ray Brown 69-71-69-72	281
5	Mark Brooks 68-70-72-73	283
	Tim Simpson 66-69-75-73	283

	Greg Norman (Aus) 72-73-69-69	284
8	Craig Stadler 71-70-72-71	284
	Steve Jones 67-76-74-67	284
	Scott Hoch 70-73-69-72	284
	Tom Sieckmann 70-74-68-72	284
	José-Maria Olazabal (Spa) 73-69-69-73	284
	Fuzzy Zoeller 73-70-68-73	284
14	Larry Mize 72-70-69-74	285
	Jim Benepe 72-70-73-70	285
	John Huston 68-72-73-72	285
	John Inman 72-71-70-72	285
	Scott Simpson 66-73-73-73	285
	Jeff Sluman 66-70-74-75	285
	Larry Nelson 74-67-69-75	285
21	Curtis Strange 73-70-68-75	286
	Ian Woosnam (GB) 70-70-74-72	286
	Steve Elkington (Aus) 73-71-73-69	286
24	Corey Pavin 74-70-73-70	287
	Billy Tuten 74-70-72-71	287
	Jumbo Ozaki (Jap) 73-72-74-68	287
	Webb Heintzelman 70-75-74-68	287
	Paul Azinger 72-72-69-74	287
29	Chip Beck 71-71-73-73	288
	Mike Hulbert 76-66-71-75	288
	Phil Mickelson (*) 74-71-71-72	288
	Brian Claar 70-71-71-76	288
33	Jim Gallagher, Jnr 71-69-72-77	289
	Ted Schulz 73-70-69-77	289
	Bob Lohr 71-74-72-72	289
	Isao Aoki (Jap) 73-69-74-73	289
	David Frost (SA) 72-72-72-73	289
	Bob Tway 68-72-74-74	289
	Kirk Triplett 72-70-75-72	289
	Tom Byrum 70-75-74-70	289
	Steve Pate 75-68-72-74	289
	Bobby Wadkins 71-73-71-74	289
	Severiano Ballesteros (Spa) 73-69-71-76	289
	Jack Nicklaus 71-74-68-76	289
45	Craig Parry (Aus) 72-71-68-79	290
46	Dave Rummels 73-71-70-77	291
	Robert Thompson 73-73-72-75	291
	Dave Barr 74-71-75-71	291
	Mark McCumber 76-68-74-73	291
50	Andy North 74-71-71-76	292
	Bill Glasson 71-73-72-76	292
	Ray Stewart 70-74-73-75	292
	Greg Twiggs 72-70-73-77	292
	Lanny Wadkins 72-72-70-78	292
55	Bob Gilder 71-70-74-78	293
	Gil Morgan 70-72-73-78	293
	David Duval (*) 72-72-72-77	293
	Blaine McCallister 71-72-75-75	293
	Tom Kite 75-70-74-74	293
60	Scott Verplank 72-69-77-76	294
	Robert Gamez 72-73-73-76	294
62	Ronan Rafferty (GB) 75-70-73-78	296
63	David Graham (Aus) 72-73-74-79	298
64	Howard Twitty 73-72-77-77	299
65	Brad Faxon 70-74-76-81	301
66	Mike Smith 72-72-82-80	306
67	Randy Wylie 70-75-81-82	308

(*) *Denotes amateur*
Leaders after each round:
Round 1: 66 Tim Simpson, Scott Simpson, Jeff Sluman
Round 2: 135 Tim Simpson
Round 3: 209 Mike Donald, Billy Ray Brown
Notables who failed to make the cut:
Hubert Green, Mark Calcavecchia, Payne Stewart, Tom Watson, Ben Crenshaw, Hal Sutton, Mark O'Meara, Raymond Floyd, Bernhard Langer, Sandy Lyle

WINNERS OF US MASTERS AND BRITISH OPEN IN SAME YEAR

Ben Hogan (US)	1953
Arnold Palmer (US)	1962
Jack Nicklaus (US)	1966
Gary Player (SA)	1974
Tom Watson (US)	1977
NICK FALDO (GB)	1990

THE 119TH OPEN CHAMPIONSHIP

St Andrews, Jul 19-22
(All British unless otherwise stated)

1	NICK FALDO 67-65-67-71	270
2	Mark McNulty (Zim) 74-68-68-65	275
	Payne Stewart (US) 68-68-68-71	275
4	Jodie Mudd (US) 72-66-72-66	276
	Ian Woosnam 68-69-70-69	276
6	Ian Baker-Finch (Aus) 68-72-64-73	277
	Greg Norman (Aus) 66-66-76-69	277
8	David Graham (Aus) 72-71-70-66	279
	Donnie Hammond (US) 70-71-68-70	279
	Steve Pate (US) 70-68-72-69	279
	Corey Pavin (US) 71-69-68-71	279
12	Paul Broadhurst 74-69-63-74	280
	Robert Gamez (US) 70-72-67-71	280
	Tim Simpson(US) 70-69-69-72	280
	Vijay Singh (Fij) 70-69-72-69	280
16	Peter Jacobsen (US) 68-70-70-73	281
	Steve Jones (US) 72-67-72-70	281
	Sandy Lyle 72-70-67-72	281
	Frank Nobilo (NZ) 72-67-68-74	281
	José Maria Olazabal (Spa) 71-67-71-72	281
	Mark Roe 71-70-72-68	281
22	Eamonn Darcy (Ire) 71-71-72-68	282
	Craig Parry (Aus) 68-68-69-77	282
	Jamie Spence 72-65-73-72	282
25	Fred Couples (US) 71-70-70-72	283
	Christy O'Connor, Jnr (Ire) 68-72-71-72	283
	Nick Price (Zim) 70-67-71-75	283
	Jose Rivero (Spa) 70-70-70-73	283
	Jeff Sluman (US) 72-70-70-71	283
	Lee Trevino (US) 69-70-73-71	283
31	Ben Crenshaw (US) 74-69-68-73	284
	Vicente Fernandez (Arg) 72-67-69-76	284
	Mark James 73-69-70-72	284
	Mark McCumber (US) 69-74-69-72	284
	Larry Mize (US) 71-72-70-71	284
	Bryan Norton (US) 71-72-68-73	284
	Greg Powers (US) 74-69-69-72	284
	Ronan Rafferty 70-71-73-70	284
39	Derrick Cooper 72-71-69-73	285
	Ray Floyd (US) 72-71-71-71	285
	Mike Hulbert (US) 70-70-70-75	285
	Andy North (US) 71-71-72-71	285
	Naomichi Ozaki (Jap) 71-71-74-69	285
	Don Pooley (US) 70-73-71-71	285
	Mike Reid (US) 70-67-73-75	285
	Scott Simpson (US) 73-70-69-73	285
	Sam Torrance 68-70-75-72	285
48	Paul Azinger (US) 73-68-68-77	286
	Peter Fowler (Aus) 73-68-71-74	286
	Bernhard Langer (FRG) 74-69-75-68	286
	Colin Montgomerie 72-69-74-71	286
	Mark O'Meara (US) 70-69-73-74	286
53	Michael Allen (US) 66-75-73-73	287
	John Bland (SA) 71-72-72-72	287
	Hale Irwin (US) 72-68-75-72	287
	Eduardo Ronero (Arg) 69-71-74-73	287
57	Mike Clayton (Aus) 72-71-72-73	288
	Blaine McCallister (US) 71-68-75-74	288
	Danny Mijovic (Can) 69-74-71-74	288
	David Ray 71-69-73-75	288
	Jim Rutledge (US) 71-69-76-72	288

	Anders Sorensen (Den) 70-68-71-79	288
63	Peter Baker 73-68-75-73	289
	David Canipe (US) 72-70-69-78	289
	Roger Chapman 72-70-74-73	289
	Jack Nicklaus (US) 71-70-77-71	289
	Martin Poxon 68-72-74-75	289
68	Jorge Berendt (Arg) 75-66-72-77	290
	David Feherty 74-69-71-76	290
70	Armando Saavedra (Arg) 72-69-75-75	291
71	Malcolm Mackenzie 70-71-76-75	292
72	José-Maria Canizares (Spa) 72-70-78-76	296

Leaders

Round 1: 66 Greg Norman, Michael Allen
Round 2: 132 Greg Norman, Nick Faldo
Round 3: 199 Nick Faldo
Notables who failed to make the cut:
Arnold Palmer, Tom Kite (both 144); Gary Player, Lanny Wadkins, Severiano Ballesteros, Tom Watson, Curtis Strange (all 145); Mark Calcavecchia (146); Tom Weiskopf (147); Bob Charles, Isao Aoki (both 151); Craig Stadler (153).
(Calcavecchia was the first reigning champion to miss the cut since Tom Watson in 1976.)

THE OPEN RECORDS

Faldo's score of 18 under par was the best at any Open. His total of 270 was the third lowest, behind Watson (268) and Nicklaus (269) in 1977 at Turnberry, where the par is 70. He beat the record for a St Andrews Open (276 by Ballesteros in 1984) by six.
Faldo's 54 -hole total of 199 beat the previous for any Open by three (202 by Watson at Muirfield in 1980).
Faldo and Norman's 36-hole total of 132 equalled the record set by Henry Cotton at Sandwich in 1934.
Paul Broadhurst's third-round 63 equalled the Championship record shared by Mark Hayes (Turnberry, 1977), Isao Aoki (Muirfield, 1980) and Greg Norman (Turnberry, 1986). The lowest in a St Andrews Open was 65 by Neil Coles in 1970. Jamie Spence equalled it in the second round. The cut, at one under par, came at the lowest figure ever. The previous record was two over par at Troon in 1989.
The crowd of 206,123 beat the previous record of 193,126 set at St Andrews in 1984.

US PGA CHAMPIONSHIP

Shoal Creek, Birmingham, Alabama, Aug 9-12
All from US unless otherwise stated

1	WAYNE GRADY (Aus) 72-67-72-71	282
2	Fred Couples 69-71-73-72	285
3	Gil Morgan 77-72-65-72	286
4	Bill Britton 72-74-72-71	289
5	Billy Mayfair 70-71-75-74	290
	Loren Roberts 73-71-70-76	290
	Chip Beck 71-70-78-71	290
8	Don Pooley 75-74-71-72	292
	Tim Simpson 71-73-75-73	292
	Mark McNulty (Zim) 74-72-75-71	292
	Payne Stewart 71-72-70-79	292
12	Hale Irwin 77-72-70-74	293
	Larry Mize 72-68-76-77	293
14	José-Maria Olazabal (Spa) 73-77-72-72	294
	Morris Hatalsky 73-78-71-72	294
	Corey Pavin 73-75-72-74	294
	Billy Andrade 75-73-72-74	294
	Fuzzy Zoeller 72-71-76-75	294
19	Blaine McCallister 75-73-74-73	295
	Nick Faldo (GB) 71-75-80-69	295
	Mark O'Meara 69-76-79-71	295
	Mark Wiebe 74-73-75-73	295
	Greg Norman (Aus) 77-69-76-73	295
	Tom Watson 74-71-77-73	295
	Bob Boyd 74-74-71-76	295
26	Brian Tennyson 71-77-71-77	296
	Mark Brooks 78-69-76-73	296
	Ray Stewart (Can) 73-73-75-75	296
	Chris Perry 75-74-72-75	296
	Peter Jacobsen 74-75-71-76	296
31	Ian Woosnam (GB) 74-75-70-78	297
	David Frost (SA) 76-74-69-78	297
	Steve Pate 71-75-71-80	297
	Paul Azinger 76-70-74-77	297
	Scott Verplank 70-76-73-78	297
	Jeff Sluman 74-74-73-76	297
	Tom Purtzer 74-74-77-72	297
	Dave Rummels 73-73-77-74	297
	Ben Crenshaw 74-70-78-75	297
40	John Mahaffey 75-72-76-75	298
	Isao Aoki (Jap) 72-74-78-74	298
	Tom Kite 79-71-74-74	298
	Davis Love 111 72-72-77-77	298
	Craig Parry (Aus) 74-72-75-77	298
45	Andrew Magee 75-74-73-77	299
	Ed Fiori 75-76-77-77	305
	Cary Hungate 72-77-79-77	305
	Jumbo Ozaki (Jap) 75-74-79-77	305

FALDO AT ST ANDREWS

	SCORE				HOLE	1	2	3	4	5	6	7	8	9	10	11	12	13	14	15	16	17	18
TOTAL	IN	OUT	PAR		PAR	4	4	4	4	5	4	4	3	4	4	3	4	4	5	4	4	4	4
67	32	35	-5		ROUND 1	4	4	4	4	4	4	3	4	3	3	3	5	4	4	5	2
65	33	32	-7		ROUND 2	4	3	4	4	4	3	3	3	4	3	4	4	5	3	3	4	4
67	34	33	-5		ROUND 3	3	4	4	4	4	4	3	4	3	4	2	4	4	5	4	3	5	3
71	36	35	-1		ROUND 4	3	4	4	5	4	4	4	3	4	4	4	3	4	5	3	4	5	4
270			-18																				

ST ANDREWS STATISTICS 1990

Most consecutive birdies:	Paul Broadhurst 6	(holes	5-10, round 3)
Most consecutive pars:	John Bland 15	(holes	4-18, round 1)
Most consecutive 3's:	Michael Allen 7	(holes	7-13, round 1)
Most consecutive 4's:	Bob Tway 10	(holes	1-10, round 1)
	Miguel Martin 10	(holes	9-18, round 1)
	Tommy Armour III 10	(holes	1-10, round 2)

A total of 5343 holes were played in par; there were 23 eagles, 1490 birdies, 1220 bogeys and 132 double bogeys or more. There were 201 rounds below par, 70 at par and 185 above par. The average score was 71.95 to a par of 72.

Leaders
Round 1: 68 Bobby Wadkins
Round 2: 139 Wayne Grady
Round 3: 211 Wayne Grady
Notables who failed to make the cut:
Hubert Green, Lanny Wadkins, Bernhard Langer, Mark Calcavecchia, Larry Nelson, Lee Trevino, Seve Ballesteros, Jack Nicklaus, Curtis Strange, Arnold Palmer

THE MOST SUCCESSFUL BRITISH GOLFERS

7 Harry Vardon (6 British Open, 1 US Open)
5 John H. Taylor (all British Open)
5 James Braid (all British Open)
4 Tom Morris, snr (all British Open)
4 Tom Morris, jnr (all British Open)
4 Willie Park, snr (all British Open)
4 NICK FALDO (2 US Masters, 2 British Open)

US PGA TOUR
All winners from US unless otherwise stated

Mony Tournament of Champions
La Costa, California, Jan 4-7
272 PAUL AZINGER; 273 Ian Baker-Finch (Aus); 276 Mark O'Meara

Northern Telecom Tuscon Open
Randolph Park, Arizona, Jan 11-14
270 ROBERT GAMEZ; 274 Mark Calcavecchia, Jay Haas
Gamez was the first player to win his debut professional event since Ben Crenshaw in 1973

Bob Hope Chrysler Classic
Palm Springs, California, Jan 17-21
339 PETER JACOBSEN; 340 Scott Simpson; Brian Tennyson

Phoenix Open
Scottsdale, Arizona, Jan 25-28
267 TOMMY ARMOUR III, 272 Jim Thorpe; 274 Fred Couples, Billy Ray Brown

AT & T Pebble Beach National Pro-Am
Pebble Beach, California, Feb 1-4
281 MARK O'MEARA; 283 Kenny Perry; 284 Payne Stewart, Tom Kite

Hawaiian Open
Waialee, Honolulu, Feb 8-11
279 DAVID ISHII; 280 Paul Azinger; 281 Jodie Mudd, Craig Stadler, Clark Dennis

Shearson Lehman Hutton Open
La Jolla, California, Feb 15-18
275 DAN FORSMAN; 277 Tommy Armour III; 278 Tom Byrum

Nissan Los Angeles Open
Riviera CC, Los Angeles, Feb 22-25
266 FRED COUPLES; 269 Gil Morgan; 270 Peter Jacobsen, Rocco Mediate

Doral Ryder Open
Miami, Florida, Mar 1-4
273 GREG NORMAN (Aus), Mark Calcavecchia, Paul Azinger, Tim Simpson
Norman won play-off at first extra hole

Honda Classic
Coral Springs, Florida, Mar 8-11
282 JOHN HUSTON; 284 Mark Calcavecchia; 285 Ray Floyd, Mark Brooks, Billy Ray Brown, Bruce Lietzke

The Players Championship
Ponte Vedra, Florida, Mar 15-18
278 JODIE MUDD; 279 Mark Calcavecchia; 284 Steve Jones, Tom Purtzer

The Nestlé Invitational
Orlando, Florida, Mar 22-25
274 ROBERT GAMEZ; 275 Greg Norman (Aus); 276 Larry Mize

Independent Insurance Agent Open
The Woodlands, Texas, Mar 29-Apr 1
204 TONY SILLS, Gil Morgan; 205 Brad Bryant, Ian Woosnam (GB), Seve Ballesteros (Spa), Larry Mize, Bruce Lietzke, Scott Simpson
Sills won play-off at first extra hole
Rain reduced play to 54 holes

Deposit Guarantee Golf Classic
Hattiesburg, Mississippi, Apr 5-8
268 GENE SAUERS; 270 Jack Ferenz; 271 David Ogrin, Mike McCullogh

MCI Heritage Classic
Hilton Head Island, South Carolina, Apr 12-15
276 PAYNE STEWART, Larry Mize, Steve Jones
Stewart won play-off at 2nd extra hole
Stewart became the first man to win the title in consecutive years

K-Mart Greater Greensboro Open
Greensboro, North Carolina, Apr 19-22
282 STEVE ELKINGTON (Aus); 284 Jeff Sluman, Mike Reid

USF&G Classic
New Orleans, Louisiana, Apr 26-29
276 DAVID FROST (SA); 277 Greg Norman (Aus); 279 Russ Cochran

GTE Byron Nelson Golf Classic
Irving, Texas, May 3-6
202 PAYNE STEWART; 204 Lanny Wadkins; 207 Mark Calcavecchia, Bruce Lietzke
Rain reduced play to 54 holes

Memorial Tournament
Dublin, Ohio, May 10-13
216 GREG NORMAN (Aus); 217 Payne Stewart; 218 Dan Pooley, Fred Couples, Brad Faxon, Mark Brooks
Rain reduced play to 54 holes

Southwestern Bell Colonial
Fort Worth, Texas, May 17-20
272 BEN CRENSHAW; 275 John Mahaffey, Corey Pavin, Nick Price (Zim)

Bell South Atlanta Golf Classic
Marietta, Georgia, May 24-27
275 WAYNE LEVI; 276 Larry Mize, Keith Clearwater, Nick Price (Zim)

Kemper Open
Potomac, Maryland, May 31-Jun 3
274 GIL MORGAN; 275 Ian Baker-Finch (Aus); 276 Scott Hoch, Hale Irwin

Centel Western Open
Oak Brook, Illinois, Jun 7-10
275 WAYNE LEVI; 279 Payne Stewart; 280 Peter Jacobsen, Loren Roberts

Buick Classic
Westchester CC, Rye, New York, Jun 21-24
269 HALE IRWIN; 271 Paul Azinger; 272 Kirk Triplett

Canon Greater Hartford Open
Cromwell, Connecticut, Jun 28-Jul 1
267 WAYNE LEVI; 269 Mark Calcavecchia, Rocco Mediate, Brad Fabel, Chris Perry

Anheuser-Busch Classic
Williamsburg, Virginia, Jul 5-8
266 LANNY WADKINS; 271 Larry Mize; 272 Scott Verplank, Bob Wolcott

Bank of Boston Classic
Sutton, Massachusetts, Jul 12-15
275 MORRIS HATALSKY; 276 Scott Verplank; 277 D A Weibring, Rick Fehr, Mike Smith

Buick Open
Warwick Hills, Michigan, Jul 26-29
272 CHIP BECK; 273 Hale Irwin, Mike Donald, Fuzzy Zoeller

Federal Express St Jude Golf Classic
Germantown, Memphis, Aug 2-5
269 TOM KITE, John Cook; 272 David Canipe
Kite won play-off at 1st extra hole
Kite became the first man to win $6 million on the US Tour

The International
Castle Pines, Colorado, Aug 16-19
14pts DAVIS LOVE 111; 11pts Steve Pate, Peter Senior (Aus), Eduardo Romero (Arg)

NEC World Series of Golf
Akron, Ohio, Aug 23-26
262 JOSÉ-MARIA OLAZABAL (Spa); 274 Lanny Wadkins; 277 Hale Irwin

Chattanooga Classic
Hixson, Tennessee, Aug 23-26
260 PETER PERSONS; 262 Richard Zokol; 264 Kenny Knox, Fred Funk

Greater Milwaukee Open
Franklin, Wisconsin, Aug 30-Sep 2
271 JIM GALLAGHER; 273 Ed Dougherty, Billy Mayfair
Gallagher won play-off at first extra hole

Hardee's Golf Classic
Coal Valley, Illinois, Sep 6-9
268 JOEY SINDELAR, Willy Wood
Sindelar won play-off at first extra hole.

Canadian Open
Oakville, Ontario, Sep 13-16
278 WAYNE LEVI; 279 Ian Baker-Finch (Aus), Jim Woodward

EUROPEAN PGA TOUR

All winners from Great Britian & Northern Ireland unless otherwise stated

Vinho Verde Atlantic Open
Estela, Portugal, Feb 15-18
288 STEPHEN McALLISTER, Richard Boxall, Ronan Rafferty, David Williams, Stephen Hamill, Anders Sorensen (Den)
6-way tie which McAllister won at the 1st extra hole

Emirates Airline Desert Classic
Dubai, Feb 22-25
276 EAMONN DARCY (Ire); 280 David Feherty; 282 Des Smyth, Seve Ballesteros (Spa)

American Express Mediterranean Open
Las Brisas, Spain, Mar 1-4
210 IAN WOOSNAM; 212 Eduardo Romero (Arg), Miguel Martin (Spa)

Open Renault De Baleares
Son Vida, Mallorca, Mar 8-11
269 SEVERIANO BALLESTEROS (Spa), Magnus Persson (Swe); 271 Juan Quiros (Spa)
Ballesteros won play-off at 1st extra hole
This was Ballesteros' 60th professional win of his career

Tenerife Open
Golf del Sur, Mar 15-18
282 VICENTE FERNANDEZ (Arg), Mark Mouland; 284 Christy O'Connor Jnr (Ire), Tony Charnley, Emmanuel Dusaart (Fra)
Fernandez won play-off at 3rd extra hole

Volvo Open
Florence, Italy, Mar 22-25
265 EDUARDO ROMERO (Arg); 266 Russell Claydon, Colin Montgomerie; 269 Rodger Davis (Aus), Mats Hallberg (Swe)

AGF Open
Montpelier, France, Mar 29-Apr 1
278 BRETT OGLE (Aus); 281 Bill Longmuir, Paul Curry

El Bosque Open
Valencia, Apr 5-8
278 VIJAY SINGH (Fiji); 280 Richard Boxall, Chris Williams

Credit Lyonnais Cannes Open
Cannes Mouins, France, Apr 13-16
280 MARK McNULTY (Zim); 281 Ronan Rafferty; 282 Mark Roe

Cepsa Madrid Open
Puerta de Hierro, Spain, Apr 19-22
270 BERNHARD LANGER (FRG); 271 Rodger Davis (Aus); 272 Brett Ogle (Aus)

Peugeot Spanish Open
Club de Campo, Madrid, Apr 26-29
277 RODGER DAVIS (Aus); 278 Nick Faldo, Bernhard Langer (FRG), Peter Fowler (Aus)

Benson & Hedges International Open
St Mellion, Cornwall, May 4-7
279 JOSÉ-MARIA OLAZABAL (Spa); 280 Ian Woosnam; 282 Bernhard Langer (FRG)

Trends Belgian Open
Royal Waterloo, Brussels, Belgium, May 10-13
272 OVE SELLBERG (Swe); 276 Ian Woosnam; 278 Eduardo Romero (Arg)

Lancia-Martini Italian Open
Monza, Italy, May 17-20
267 RICHARD BOXALL; 272 José-Maria Olazabal (Spa); 275 Eduardo Romero (Arg)

Volvo PGA Championship
Wentworth, May 25-28
271 MIKE HARWOOD (Aus); 272 John Bland (SA), Nick Faldo

Dunhill British Masters
Woburn, May 31-Jun 3
270 MARK JAMES; 272 David Feherty; 274 Carl Mason

Scandinavian Enterprise Open
Drottningholm, Sweden, Jun 7-10
268 CRAIG STADLER (US); 272 Craig Parry (Aus); 273 Ronan Rafferty

Wang Four Stars National Pro-Celebrity
Moor Park, Jun 14-17
271 RODGER DAVIS (Aus), Mark McNulty (Zim), Mike Clayton (Aus), Bill Malley (US)
Davis won play-off at seventh extra hole

Carrolls Irish Open
Portmarnock, Jun 21-24
282 JOSÉ-MARIA OLAZABAL (Spa); 285 Mark Calcavecchia (US), Frank Nobilo (NZ)

Peugeot French Open
Chantilly, Jun 28-Jul 1
275 PHILIP WALTON, Bernhard Langer (FRG); 276 Eduardo Romero (Arg)
Walton won play-off at 2nd extra hole

Torras Monte Carlo Open
Mont Agel, Monaco, Jul 4-7
258 IAN WOOSNAM; 263 Constantino Rocca (Ita); 264 Mark McNulty (Zim), Mark Mouland
Woosnam's final round of 60 equalled the European PGA Tour record and was one off the world record

GOLF

203

Bell's Scottish Open
Gleneagles, Jul 11-14
269 IAN WOOSNAM; 273 Mark McNulty (SA); 275 Gordon Brand Jnr, Malcolm McKenzie

KLM Dutch Open
Zandvoort, Jul 26-29
274 STEPHEN McALLISTER; 278 Roger Chapman; 279 José-Maria Olazabal (Spa)

PLM Open
Bokskogens, Sweden, Aug 2-5
270 RONAN RAFFERTY; 275 Bernhard Langer (FRG);.276 Fred Couples (US), Ove Sellberg (Swe)

Murphy's Cup
Fulford, Aug 9-12
50pts TONY JOHNSTONE (Zim); 48 Malcolm Mackenzie; 44 Russell Claydon; 40 Sandy Lyle

NM English Open
The Belfry, Aug 16-19
284 MARK JAMES, Sam Torrance; 285 David Feherty; 287 Severiano Ballesteros (Spa)
James won play-off at first extra hole

Volvo German Open
Hubbelrath, Düsseldorf, Aug 23-26
270 MARK McNULTY (Zim); 273 Craig Parry (Aus); Eamonn Darcy (Ire), Anders Forsbrand (Swe)

Ebel European Masters-Swiss Open
Crans-sur-Sierre, Aug 30-Sep 2
267 RONAN RAFFERTY; 269 John Bland; 270 Jamie Spence

Panasonic European Open
Sunningdale, Sep 6-9
267 PETER SENIOR (Aus); 268 Ian Woosnam; 269 José-Maria Canizares

Lancome Trophy
St Nom-la-Breteche, France, Sep 13-16
269 JOSÉ-MARIA OLAZABAL (Spa); 270 Colin Montgomerie; 271 Tony Johnstone (Zim)

Suntory World Match Play
Wentworth, Sep 20-23
IAN WOOSNAM beat Mark McNulty (Zim) 4&2
Woosnam first Briton to win trophy twice

BMW European Open
Munich, Sep 20-23
277 PAUL AZINGER (US), David Feherty; 278 Peter O'Malley (Aus)
Azinger won play-off at first extra hole.

US Tour Milestones
First to win $1 million: Arnold Palmer, Jul 21, 1968
First to win $2 million: Jack Nicklaus, Dec 1, 1973
First to win $3 million: Jack Nicklaus, May 22, 1977
First to win $4 million: Jack Nicklaus, Feb 6, 1983
First to win $5 million: Jack Nicklaus, Aug 20, 1988
First to win $6 million: TOM KITE, Aug 5, 1990

"A champion is not a champion because he wins, but how he conducts himself."
Doug Sanders
"Ken may dress like a nerd, look like a nerd, but he isn't a nerd."
Mrs Ken Green
"I'd say I've played the front nine in 33. Now I have to come home in 30."
Greg Norman, on turning 35
"The only difference between an amateur and a pro is that we call a shot that goes left-to-right a fade and an amateur calls it a slice."
Peter Jacobsen
"Last Sunday BBC 2's Grandstand showed something called the Weetabix British Women's Open Golf. I've have never seen such ugly swings, and so many three-putts outside my local golf course and if I want to witness such incompetence I'll go there and watch it live."
Dominic Lawson, Mail on Sunday
"One plot in $1,000 section of Santa Barbara cemetry. Will sell for $500. Wanted: Reasonably priced women's golf clubs."
Ad in Santa Barbara News-Press

SONY WORLD RANKINGS
(as at Sep 9 1990)
Figures in brackets are positions in September 1989
1 (3) Nick Faldo (GB); 2 (1) Greg Norman (Aus); 3 (9) José-Maria Olazabal (Spa); 4 (6) Ian Woosnam (GB); 5 (7) Payne Stewart (US); 6 (5) Mark Calcavecchia (US); 7 (8) Tom Kite (US); 8 (2) Severiano Ballesteros (Spa); 9 (13) Paul Azinger (US); 10 (15) Fred Couples (US); 11 (4) Curtis Strange (US); 12 (27) Mark McNulty (Zim); 13 (11) Masashi Ozaki (Jap); 14 (32) Larry Mize (US); 15 (10) Chip Beck (US); 16 (90) Hale Irwin (US); 17 (26) Ronan Rafferty (GB); 18 (18) Bernhard Langer (FRG); 19 (53) Tim Simpson (US); 20 (28) Lanny Wadkins (US)
Positions of other players in the top 20 in September 1989:
21 (14) David Frost (SA); 23 (16) Ben Crenshaw (US); 29 (12) Sandy Lyle (GB); 35 (17) Mark McCumber (US); 36 (19) Tom Watson (US); 48 (20) Larry Nelson (US)

OTHER EVENTS
President's Putter
Rye, Jan 7
Final
GUY WOULLET beat John Hampel 6 & 5
Halford Hewitt Cup
Royal Cinque Ports, Apr 8
Final
TONBRIDGE 3 Malvern 2
US PGA Seniors' Championship
Palm Beach Gardens, Florida, Apr 12-15
281 GARY PLAYER (SA); 283 Chi Chi Rodriguez; 285 Jack Nicklaus, Lee Trevino
English Amateur Sroke Play
(Brabazon Trophy)
Burnham & Berrow, May 17-20
287 OLIVIER EDMOND (Fra) and GARY EVANS (Eng) shared title; 288 Bobby Eggo (Gue), Don Gammon (SA), John Metcalfe (Eng)

British Amateur Championship
Muirfield, Jun 4-9
ROLF MUNTZ (Hol) beat Michael Macara (Wal) 7 & 6

Trusthouse Forte PGA Seniors' Championship
Brough, Jun 14-17
269 BRIAN WAITES (Notts); 273 Neil Coles (Unatt); 277 Christy O'Connor (Royal Dublin), Hugh Boyle (Royal Wimbledon)

Volvo Seniors British Open
Turnberry, Jul 26-29
280 GARY PLAYER (SA); 281 Deane Beman (US), Brian Waites

English Amateur Championship
Woodhall Spa, Jul 30-Aug 4
IAN GARBUTT (Wheatley) beat Gary Evans (Worthing) 8 & 7

US Amateur Championship
Engelwood, Colorado, Aug 23-26
PHIL MICKELSON beat Manny Zerman 5 & 4

WOMEN'S GOLF: THE MAJORS

Nabisco Dinah Shore
Mission Hills, California, Mar 29-Apr 1
283 BETSY KING; 285 Shirley Furlong, Kathy Postlewait

Du Maurier Classic
Kitchener, Ontario, Jun 28-Jul 1
276 CATHY JOHNSTON; 278 Patty Sheehan; 281 Beth Daniel

US Women's Open
Duluth, Georgia, Jul 12-15
284 BETSY KING; 285 Patty Sheehan; 286 Dottie Mochrie, Danielle Ammacappane
Sheehan led King by 11 shots with 33 holes to play

Mazda LPGA Championship
Bethesda, Maryland, Jul 26-29
280 BETH DANIEL; 281 Rosie Jones; 284 Dawn Coe; 285 Sue Ertl

OTHER WOMEN'S EVENTS

BRITISH WOMEN'S AMATEUR CHAMPIONSHIP
Dunbar, Jun 12-16
JULIE HALL (Felixstowe Ferry) beat Helen Wadsworth (Salford University) 3 & 2

CURTIS CUP
Somerset Hills, New Jersey, Jul 28-29
First Round Foursomes
(US names first)
Vicki Goetze & Ann Sander beat Helen Dobson & Catriona Lambert 4 & 3; Karen Noble and Margaret Platt lost to Julie Hall & Kathryn Imrie 2 & 1; Robin Weiss & Carol Semple Thompson beat Elaine Farquharson & Helen Wadsworth 3 & 1

First Round Singles
Vicki Goetze lost to Julie Hall 2 & 1; Katie Peterson beat Kathryn Imrie 3 & 2; Robin Weiss beat Linzi Fletcher 4 & 3; Brandie Burton beat Elaine Farquharson 3 & 1; Karen Noble beat Catriona Lambert 1 hole; Carol Semple Thompson lost to Vicki Thomas 1 hole

Second Round Foursomes
Vicki Goetze & Ann Sander beat Julie Hall & Kathryn Imrie 3 & 1; Margaret Platt & Karen Noble lost to Catriona Lambert & Helen Dobson 1 hole; Brandie Burton & Katie Peterson beat Helen Wadsworth & Elaine Farquharson 5& 4

Second Round Singles
Vicki Goetze beat Helen Dobson 4 & 3; Brandie Burton beat Catriona Lambert 4 & 3; Katie Peterson beat Kathryn Imrie 1 hole; Karen Noble beat Julie Hall 2 holes; Robin Weiss beat Elaine Farquharson 2 & 1; Carol Semple Thompson beat Vicki Thomas 3 & 1

United States beat Great Britian & Ireland 14-4

Weetabix British Women's Open
Woburn, Aug 2-5
288 HELEN ALFREDSSON (Swe), Jan Hill (Zim); 291 Laura Davis, Kitrina Douglas, Dan Lofland (US)
Alfredsson won play-off at fourth extra hole

British Women's Strokeplay Championship
Strathaven, Aug 21-24
287 VICKI THOMAS (Pennard); 288 Claire Hourihane (Woodbrook)

─────────── **1989** ───────────

EUROPEAN PGA TOUR

Lancome Trophy
St Nom la Brêteche, France, Sep 14-17
266 EDUARDO ROMERO (Arg); 267 Bernhard Langer (FRG), José-Maria Olazabal (Spa)

The Equity & Law Challenge
Richmond, Surrey, Sep 25-26
25pts BRETT OGLE (Aus); 21pts Colin Montgomerie; 20pts David Feherty, Richard Boxall

Motorola Classic
Burnham and Berrow, Sep 28-Oct 1
272 DAVID LLEWELLYN; 276 David Williams; 277 Russell Weir

Dunhill Cup
St Andrews, Sep 28-Oct 1
Semi-finals
UNITED STATES beat Ireland 2-1; JAPAN beat England 2-1
Third Place Play-off
ENGLAND beat Ireland 2-1
Final
UNITED STATES beat Japan $3^1/_2$-$2^1/_2$

German Masters
Monsheim, West Germany, Oct 5-8
276 BERNHARD LANGER (FRG); 277 Payne Stewart (US), José-Maria Olazabal (Spa)

Suntory World Match Play Championship
Wentworth, England, Oct 12-15
First Round
RONAN RAFFERTY (NI) beat Mike Reid (US) 3 & 2; JOSÉ-MARIA OLAZABAL (Spa) beat Scott Hoch (US) 4 & 2; CHIP BECK (US) beat Aki Okamachi (Jap) 8 & 6; DAVID FROST (SA) beat Ian Baker-Finch (Aus) 4 &3
Quarter-finals
RAFFERTY beat Sandy Lyle (Sco) 1 hole; IAN WOOSNAM (Wal) beat Olazabal 3 & 2; SEVERIANO BALLESTEROS (Spa) beat Beck 9 & 8; NICK FALDO (Eng) beat Frost at 38th
Semi-finals
FALDO beat Ballesteros 6 & 5; WOOSNAM beat Rafferty 2 & 1
Third Place Play-off
BALLESTEROS beat Rafferty 5 & 3
Final
FALDO beat Woosnam 1 hole
The first £100,000 1st prize in Britain. Faldo gave it all to children's charity.

BMW International Open
Munich, Oct 12-15
269 DAVID FEHERTY; 274 Fred Couples (US); 275
Philip Walton; 276 Eamonn Darcy

Portuguese Open
Quinto do Lago, Oct 19-22
264 COLIN MONTGOMERIE; 275 Mike Smith (US),
Manuel Moreno (Spa)

Volvo Masters
Sotogrande, Spain, Oct 26-29
282 RONAN RAFFERTY; 283 Nick Faldo; 287 José-
Maria Olazabal (Spa)

THE SENIORS

ffThe older you get, the stronger the wind
gets-and it's always in your face on every
hole."
Jack Nicklaus, on turning 50

"Here comes that kid again."
*Associated Press on Nicklaus's first Seniors
win*

"My way of life does not include cookies
anymore. I have not had one all year."
Nicklaus, explaining his success

"I don't fear anybody. I don't fear death. But I
can look at the records and add and
subtract."
*Chi Chi Rodriguez on Nicklaus's arrival on the
tour*

"These are my boys. I can go into the locker
room and bum a cigarette. You go inside
on the other tour and all they are doing is
drinking orange juice and eating
bananas."
Lee Trevino

"When I reach 60, I'm gonna buy a blue
blazer and a can of dandruff and run the
USGA."
Trevino

"Baseball players quit playing and they take
up golf. Basketball players quit, take up
golf. What are we supposed to take up
when we quit?**ff**
George Archer

US PGA TOUR
Southern Open
Columbus, Georgia, Sep 21-24
266 TED SCHULZ; 267 Jay Haas, Tim Simpson

Centel Classic
Tallahassee, Florida, Sep 28-Oct 1
200 BILL BRITTON; 204 Ronnie Black; 205 Gary
Hallberg
Play reduced to 54 holes

Texas Open
San Antonio, Oct 5-8
258 DONNIE HAMMOND; 265 Paul Azinger; 267 Bob
Lohr, Duffy Waldorf, Mark Wiebe

Walt Disney World/ Oldsmobile Classic
Lake Buena Vista, Florida, Oct 18-21
272 TIM SIMPSON; 273 Donnie Hammond; 274 Paul
Azinger, Fred Couples, Kenny Knox

Nabisco Championships
Hilton Head Island, South Carolina, Oct 26-29
276 TOM KITE, Payne Stewart; 278 Paul Azinger,
Wayne Levi
Kite won play-off at second extra hole

Isuzu Kapalua International
Maui, Hawaii, Nov 8-11
270 PETER JACOBSEN, Steve Pate; 272 Nick Price
(Zim)
Jacobsen won play-off at third extra hole

OTHER 1989 EVENTS
Asaahi Glass Four Tours World Championship of Golf
Tokyo, Japan, Nov 2-5
Third Place Play-off
PGA OF JAPAN 9 Australia/New Zealand PGA Tour 3
Final
UNITED STATES PGA 6 PGA EUROPEAN TOUR 6
US won on tie-break rule with 404 strokes to 416
Leading Individual: 265 Chip Beck (US)

World Cup
Las Brisas, Marbella, Spain, Nov 16-19
(Reduced to 36 holes due to bad weather)
Team
278 AUSTRALIA (Peter Fowler 137, Wayne Grady 141);
281 Spain (José-Maria Canizares 138, José-Maria
Olazabal 143); 287 United States (Paul Azinger 141,
Mark McCumber 146); 287 Sweden (Mats Lanner 142,
Ove Sellberg 145); 288 Wales (Phillip Parkin 144, Mark
Mouland 144)
Individual
137 PETER FOWLER (Aus); 138 José-Maria Canizares
(Spa); 138 Anders Sorensen (Den); 140 Miguel
Fernandez (Arg); 141 Mark Roe (Eng); 141 Paul Azinger
(US); 141 Wayne Grady (Aus)

Skins Game
PGA West, Palm Springs, Nov 26
1 CURTIS STRANGE $265,000; 2 Jack Nicklaus
$90,000; 3 Ray Floyd $60,000; 4 Lee Trevino $35,000

Australian Open
Melbourne, Nov 30-Dec 3
271 PETER SENIOR (Aus); 278 Peter Fowler (Aus); 279
Brett Ogle (Aus)

Million Dollar Challenge
Sun City, South Africa, Dec 7-10
276 DAVID FROST (SA); 278 Scott Hoch (US); 280
Tim Simpson (US); 291 Dan Pooley (US)

CHAMPIONS

BRITISH OPEN

Year	Winner	Score	Venue	Runner(s)-up/Score
1860	Willie Park, Snr	174	*Prestwick*	Tom Morris Snr 176
1861	Tom Morris, Snr	163	*Prestwick*	Willie Park 167
1862	Tom Morris, Snr	163	*Prestwick*	Willie Park 176
1863	Willie Park, Snr	168	*Prestwick*	Tom Morris Snr 170
1864	Tom Morris, Snr	167	*Prestwick*	Andrew Strath 169
1865	Andrew Strath	162	*Prestwick*	Willie Park 164
1866	Willie Park, Snr	169	*Prestwick*	David Park 171
1867	Tom Morris, Snr	170	*Prestwick*	Willie Park 172
1868	Tom Morris, Jnr	157	*Prestwick*	Bob Andrew 159
1869	Tom Morris, Jnr	154	*Prestwick*	Tom Morris Snr 157
1870	Tom Morris, Jnr	149	*Prestwick*	Bob Kirk, David Strath 161

Year	Winner	Score	Venue	Runner(s)-up/Score
1872	Tom Morris, Jnr	166	Prestwick	David Strath 169
1873	Tom Kidd	179	St Andrews	Jamie Anderson 180
1874	Mungo Park	159	Musselburgh	Tom Morris Jnr 161
1875	Willie Park, Snr	166	Prestwick	Bob Martin 168
1876	Bob Martin	176	St Andrews	David Strath 176
(Martin awarded title as Strath refused play-off)				
1877	Jamie Anderson	160	Musselburgh	Bob Pingle 162
1878	Jamie Anderson	157	Prestwick	Bob Kirk 157
1879	Jamie Anderson	170*	St Andrews	Andrew Kirkaldy 170
1880	Robert Ferguson	162	Musselburgh	Peter Paxton 167
1881	Robert Ferguson	170	Prestwick	Jamie Anderson 173
1882	Robert Ferguson	171	St Andrews	Willie Fernie 174
1883	Willie Fernie	159*	Musselburgh	Bob Ferguson 159
1884	Jack Simpson	160	Prestwick	William Fernie, Doublas Rolland 164
1885	Bob Martin	171	St Andrews	Archie Simpson, David Ayton 172
1886	David Brown	157	Musselburgh	Willie Campbell 159
1887	Willie Park, Jnr	161	Prestwick	Bob Martin 162
1888	Jack Burns	171	St Andrews	David Anderson, Ben Sayers 172
1889	Willie Park, Jnr	155*	Musselburgh	Andrew Kirkaldy 155
1890	John Ball	164	Prestwick	Willie Fernie, Archie Simpson 167
1891	Hugh Kirkaldy	166	St Andrews	Willie Fern, Andrew Kirkaldy 168
1892	Harold H. Hilton	305	Muirfield	John Ball Jnr, James Kirkaldy, Sandy Herd 308
1893	Willie Auchterlonie	322	Prestwick	Johnny Laidlay 324
1894	John H. Taylor	326	Sandwich	Douglas Rolland 331
1895	John H.Taylor	322	St Andrews	Sandy Herd 326
1896	Harry Vardon	316*	Muirfield	John H Taylor 316
1897	Harold H.Hilton	314	Hoylake	James Braid 315
1898	Harry Vardon	307	Prestwick	Willie Park 308
1899	Harry Vardon	310	Sandwich	Jack White 315
1900	John H Taylor	309	St Andrews	Harry Vardon 317
1901	James Braid	309	Muirfield	Harry Vardon 312
1902	Sandy Herd	307	Hoylake	Harry Vardon, James Braid 308
1903	Harry Vardon	300	Prestwick	Tom Vardon 306
1904	Jack White	296	Sandwich	James Braid, John H Taylor 297
1905	James Braid	318	St Andrews	John H Taylor, R Jones 323
1906	James Braid	300	Muirfield	John H Taylor 304
1907	Arnaud Massy (Fra)	312	Hoylake	John H Taylor 314
1908	James Braid	291	Prestwick	Tom Ball 299
1909	John H Taylor	295	Deal	James Braid 299
1910	James Braid	299	St Andrews	Sandy Herd 303
1911	Harry Vardon	303*	Sandwich	Arnaud Massy 303
1912	Ted Ray	295	Muirfield	Harry Vardon 299
1913	John H Taylor	304	Hoylake	Ted Ray 312
1914	Harry Vardon	306	Prestwick	John H Taylor 309
1920	George Duncan	303	Deal	Sandy Herd 305
1921	Jock Hutchison (US)	296*	St Andrews	Roger H Wethered 296
1922	Walter Hagen (US)	300	Sandwich	George Duncan, Jim Barnes (US) 301
1923	Arthur Havers	295	Troon	Walter Hagen (US) 296
1924	Walter Hagen (US)	301	Hoylake	Ernest R Whitcombe 302
1925	Jim Barnes (US)	300	Prestwick	Archie Compston 301
1926	Bobby Jones (US)	291	Royal Lytham	Al Watrous (US) 293
1927	Bobby Jones (US)	285	St Andrews	Aubrey Boomer, Fred Robson 291
1928	Walter Hagen (US)	292	Sandwich	Gene Sarazen (US) 294
1929	Walter Hagen (US)	292	Muirfield	John Farrell (US) 298
1930	Bobby Jones (US)	291	Hoylake	Leo Deigel (US), Macdonald Smith (US) 293
1931	Tommy Armour (US)	296	Carnoustie	Jose Jurado (Arg) 297
1932	Gene Sarazen (US)	283	Prince's	Macdonald Smith (US) 288
1933	Densmore Shute (US)	292*	St Andrews	Craig Wood (US) 292
1934	Henry Cotton	283	Sandwich	Sid F Brews (SA) 288
1935	Alfred Perry	283	Muirfield	Alfred Padgham 287
1936	Alfred Padgham	287	Hoylake	Jimmy Adams 288
1937	Henry Cotton	290	Carnoustie	Reg Whitcombe 292
1938	Reg Whitcombe	295	Sandwich	Jimmy Adams 297
1939	Dick Burton	290	St Andrews	Johnny Bulla (US) 292
1946	Sam Snead (US)	290	St Andrews	Bobby Locke (SA), Johnny Bulla (US) 294
1947	Fred Daly	293	Hoylake	Reg Horne, Frank Stranahan (US) 294
1948	Henry Cotton	284	Muirfield	Fred Daly 289
1949	Bobby Locke (SA)	283*	Sandwich	Harry Bradshaw 283
1950	Bobby Locke (SA)	279	Troon	Roberto de Vicenzo (Arg) 281
1951	Max Faulkner	285	Portrush	Tony Cerda (Arg) 287
1952	Bobby Locke (SA)	287	Royal Lytham	Peter Thomson (Aus) 288
1953	Ben Hogan (US)	282	Carnoustie	Frank Stranahan (US) 286
1954	Peter Thomson (Aus)	283	Royal Birkdale	Sid Scott, Dai Rees, Bobby Locke (SA) 284

Year	Winner	Score	Venue	Runner(s)-up/Score
1955	Peter Thomson (Aus)	281	*St.Andrews*	Johnny Fallon 283
1956	Peter Thomson (Aus)	286	*Hoylake*	Flory van Donck (Bel) 289
1957	Bobby Locke (SA)	279	*St Andrews*	Peter Thomson (Aus) 282
1958	Peter Thomson (Aus)	278*	*Royal Lytham*	David Thomas 278
1959	Gary Player (SA)	284	*Muirfield*	Flory van Donck (Bel), Fred Bullock 286
1960	Kel Nagle (Aus)	278	*St Andrews*	Arnold Palmer (US) 279
1961	Arnold Palmer (US)	284	*Royal Birkdale*	Dai Rees 285
1962	Arnold Palmer (US)	276	*Troon*	Kel Nagle (Aus) 282
1963	Bob Charles (NZ)	277*	*Royal Lytham*	Phil Rodgers (US) 277
1964	Tony Lema (US)	279	*St Andrews*	Jack Nicklaus (US) 284
1965	Peter Thomson (Aus)	285	*Royal Birkdale*	Christy O'Connor, Brian Huggett 287
1966	Jack Nicklaus (US)	282	*Muirfield*	David Thomas, Doug Sanders (US) 283
1967	Roberto de Vicenzo (Arg)	278	*Hoylake*	Jack Nicklaus (US) 280
1968	Gary Player (SA)	289	*Carnoustie*	Jack Nicklaus (US), Bob Charles (NZ) 291
1969	Tony Jacklin	280	*Royal Lytham*	Bob Charles (NZ) 282
1970	Jack Nicklaus (US)	283*	*St Andrews*	Doug Sanders (US) 283
1971	Lee Trevino (US)	278	*Royal Birkdale*	Lu Liang Huan (Tai) 279
1972	Lee Trevino (US)	278	*Muirfield*	Jack Nicklaus (US) 279
1973	Tom Weiskopf (US)	276	*Troon*	Neil Coles 279
1974	Gary Player (SA)	282	*Royal Lytham*	Peter Oosterhuis 286
1975	Tom Watson (US)	279*	*Carnoustie*	Jack Newton (Aus) 279
1976	Johnny Miller (US)	279	*Royal Birkdale*	Jack Nicklaus (US), Seve Ballesteros (Spa) 285
1977	Tom Watson (US)	268	*Turnberry*	Jack Nicklaus (US) 269
1978	Jack Nicklaus (US)	281	*St.Andrews*	Simon Owen (NZ), Ben Crenshaw (US), Ray Floyd (US), Tom Kite (US) 283
1979	Seve Ballesteros (Spa)	283	*Royal Lytham*	Jack Nicklaus (US), Ben Crenshaw (US) 286
1980	Tom Watson (US)	271	*Muirfield*	Lee Trevino (US) 275
1981	Bill Rogers (US)	276	*Sandwich*	Bernhard Langer (FRG) 280
1982	Tom Watson (US)	284	*Royal Troon*	Peter Oosterhuis, Nick Price (SA) 285
1983	Tom Watson (US)	275	*Royal Birkdale*	Hale Irwin (US), Andy Bean (US) 276
1984	Seve Ballesteros (Spa)	276	*St Andrews*	Bernhard Langer (FRG), Tom Watson (US) 278
1985	Sandy Lyle	282	*Sandwich*	Payne Stewart (US) 283
1986	Greg Norman (Aus)	280	*Turnberry*	Gordon Brand Jnr 285
1987	Nick Faldo	279	*Muirfield*	Paul Azinger (US), Rodger Davis (Aus) 280
1988	Seve Ballesteros (Spa)	273	*Royal Lytham*	Nick Price (Zim) 275
1989	Mark Calcavecchia (US)	275*	*Royal Troon*	Greg Norman (Aus), Wayne Grady (Aus) 275
1990	Nick Faldo	270	*St Andrews*	Mark McNulty (Zim),Payne Stewart (US) 275

*denotes won after play-off

British Open Records
Most wins
6 Harry Vardon; 5 James Braid, John H.Taylor, Peter Thomson, Tom Watson; 4 Willie Park, Tom Morris, Snr, Tom Morris, Jnr, Walter Hagen, Bobby Locke

Lowest 72 hole total: 268 Tom Watson, Turnberry 1977
Lowest 18 hole total: 63 Mark Hayes, Turnberry 1977; Isao Aoki, Muirfield 1980; Greg Norman, Turnberry 1986; Paul Broadhurst, St Andrews, 1990
Oldest winner: 46y 99d Tom Morris, Snr, 1867
Youngest Winner: 17y 161d Tom Morris, Jnr, 1868

THE OTHER MAJORS

US MASTERS		US OPEN		US PGA	
1895	–	Horace Rawlins	173	–	
1896	–	James Foulis	152	–	
1897	–	Joe Lloyd	162	–	
1898	–	Fred Herd	328	–	
1899	–	Willie Smith	315	–	
1900	–	Harry Vardon (GB)	313	–	
1901	–	Willie Anderson	331*	–	
1902	–	Laurie Auchterlonie	307	–	
1903	-	Willie Anderson	307*	–	
1904	-	Willie Anderson	303	–	
1905	-	Willie Anderson	314	–	
1906	-	Alex Smith	295	–	
1907	-	Alex Ross	302	–	
1908	-	Fred McLeod	322*	–	
1909	-	George Sargent	290	–	
1910	-	Alex Smith	298*	–	
1911	-	John McDermott	307*	–	
1912	-	John McDermott	294	–	
1913	-	Francis Ouimet	304*	–	
1914	-	Walter Hagen	290	–	
1915	-	Jerome Travers	297	–	
1916	-	Charles Evans Jnr	286	Jim Barnes	1 up
1919	-	Walter Hagen	301*	Jim Barnes	6 & 5
1920	-	Ted Ray (GB)	295	Jock Hutchison	1 up
1921	-	Jim Barnes	289	Walter Hagen	3 & 2

US MASTERS

Year	Winner	Score
1922	-	
1923	-	
1924	-	
1925	-	
1926	-	
1927	-	
1928	-	
1929	-	
1930	-	
1931	-	
1932	-	
1933	Johnny Goodman	287
1934	Horton Smith	284
1935	Gene Sarazen	282*
1936	Horton Smith	285
1937	Byron Nelson	283
1938	Henry Picard	285
1939	Ralph Guldahl	279
1940	Jimmy Demaret	280
1941	Craig Wood	280
1942	Byron Nelson	280*
1944	–	
1945	–	
1946	Herman Keiser	282
1947	Jimmy Demaret	281
1948	Claude Harmon	279
1949	Sam Snead	282
1950	Jimmy Demaret	283
1951	Ben Hogan	280
1952	Sam Snead	286
1953	Ben Hogan	274
1954	Sam Snead	289*
1955	Cary Middlecoff	279
1956	Jack Burke Jnr	289
1957	Doug Ford	282
1958	Arnold Palmer	284
1959	Art Wall Jnr	284
1960	Arnold Palmer	282
1961	Gary Player (SA)	280
1962	Arnold Palmer	280*
1963	Jack Nicklaus	286
1964	Arnold Palmer	276
1965	Jack Nicklaus	271
1966	Jack Nicklaus	288*
1967	Gay Brewer	280
1968	Bob Goalby	277
1969	George Archer	281
1970	Billy Casper	279*
1971	Charles Coody	279
1972	Jack Nicklaus	286
1973	Tommy Aaron	283
1974	Gary Player (SA)	278
1975	Jack Nicklaus	276
1976	Ray Floyd	271
1977	Tom Watson	276
1978	Gary Player (SA)	277
1979	Fuzzy Zoeller	280*
1980	Seve Ballesteros (Spa)	275
1981	Tom Watson	280
1982	Craig Stadler	284*
1983	Seve Ballesteros (Spa)	280
1984	Ben Crenshaw	277
1985	Bernhard Langer (FRG)	282
1986	Jack Nicklaus	279
1987	Larry Mize	285*
1988	Sandy Lyle (GB)	281
1989	Nick Faldo (GB)	283*
1990	Nick Faldo (GB)	278*

US OPEN

Year	Winner	Score
1922	Gene Sarazen	288
1923	Bobby Jones	296*
1924	Cyril Walker	297
1925	Willie Macfarlane	291*
1926	Bobby Jones	293
1927	Tommy Armour	301*
1928	Johnny Farrell	294*
1929	Bobby Jones	294*
1930	Bobby Jones	287
1931	Billy Burke	292*
1932	Gene Sarazen	286
1933	Gene Sarazen	5 & 4
1934	Olin Dutra	293
1935	Sam Parks Jnr	299
1936	Tony Manero	282
1937	Ralph Guldahl	281
1938	Ralph Guldahl	284
1939	Byron Nelson	284*
1940	Lawson Little	287
1941	Craig Wood	284
1942	–	
1944	–	
1945	–	
1946	Lloyd Mangrum	284*
1947	Lew Worsham	282*
1948	Ben Hogan	276
1949	Cary Middlecoff	286
1950	Ben Hogan	287*
1951	Ben Hogan	287
1952	Julius Boros	281
1953	Ben Hogan	283
1954	Ed Furgol	284
1955	Jack Fleck	287
1956	Cary Middlecoff	281
1957	Dick Mayer	282
1958	Tommy Bolt	283
1959	Billy Casper	282
1960	Arnold Palmer	280
1961	Gene Littler	281
1962	Jack Nicklaus	283*
1963	Julius Boros	293*
1964	Ken Venturi	278
1965	Gary Player (SA)	282*
1966	Billy Casper	278*
1967	Jack Nicklaus	275
1968	Lee Trevino	275
1969	Orville Moody	281
1970	Tony Jacklin (GB)	281
1971	Lee Trevino	280*
1972	Jack Nicklaus	290
1973	Johnny Miller	279
1974	Hale Irwin	287
1975	Lou Graham	287*
1976	Jerry Pate	277
1977	Hubert Green	278
1978	Andy North	285
1979	Hale Irwin	284
1980	Jack Nicklaus	272
1981	David Graham (Aus)	273
1982	Tom Watson	282
1983	Larry Nelson	280
1984	Fuzzy Zoeller	276*
1985	Andy North	279
1986	Ray Floyd	279
1987	Scott Simpson	277
1988	Curtis Strange	278*
1989	Curtis Strange	278
1990	Hale Irwin	280*

US PGA

Year	Winner	Score
1922	Gene Sarazen	4 & 3
1923	Gene Sarazen	1 up
1924	Walter Hagen	2 up
1925	Walter Hagen	6 & 5
1926	Walter Hagen	5 & 3
1927	Walter Hagen	1 up
1928	Leo Diegel	6 & 5
1929	Leo Diegel	6 & 4
1930	Tommy Armour	1 up
1931	Tom Creavy	2 & 1
1932	Olin Dutra	4 & 3
1933	-	
1934	Paul Runyan	1 up
1935	Johnny Revolta	5&4
1936	Densmore Shute	3 & 2
1937	Densmore Shute	1 up
1938	Paul Runyan	8 & 7
1939	Henry Picard	1 up
1940	Byron Nelson	1 up
1941	Vic Ghezzi	1 up
1942	Sam Snead	2 & 1
1944	Bob Hamilton	1 up
1945	Byron Nelson	4 & 3
1946	Ben Hogan	6 & 4
1947	Jim Ferrier	2 & 1
1948	Ben Hogan	7 & 6
1949	Sam Snead	3 & 2
1950	Chandler Harper	4 & 3
1951	Sam Snead	7 & 6
1952	Jim Turnesa	1 up
1953	Walter Burkemo	2 & 1
1954	Chick Harbert	4 & 3
1955	Doug Ford	4 & 3
1956	Jack Burke	3 & 2
1957	Lionel Hebert	2 & 1
1958	Dow Finsterwald	276
1959	Bob Rosburg	277
1960	Jay Hebert	281
1961	Jerry Barber	277*
1962	Gary Player (SA)	278
1963	Jack Nicklaus	279
1964	Bobby Nichols	271
1965	Dave Marr	280
1966	Al Geiberger	280
1967	Don January	281*
1968	Julius Boros	281
1969	Ray Floyd	276
1970	Dave Stockton	279
1971	Jack Nicklaus	281
1972	Gary Player (SA)	281
1973	Jack Nicklaus	277
1974	Lee Trevino	276
1975	Jack Nicklaus	276
1976	Dave Stockton	281
1977	Lanny Wadkins	282*
1978	John Mahaffey	276*
1979	David Graham (Aus)	272*
1980	Jack Nicklaus	274
1981	Larry Nelson	273
1982	Ray Floyd	272
1983	Hal Sutton	274
1984	Lee Trevino	273
1985	Hubert Green	278
1986	Bob Tway	276
1987	Larry Nelson	287*
1988	Jeff Sluman	272
1989	Payne Stewart	276
1990	Wayne Grady (Aus)	282

* denotes won after a play-off
There were no Majors in 1943

Most Majors

18 Jack Nicklaus (6 Masters; 5 US PGA; 4 US Open; 3 British Open)
11 Walter Hagen (5 US PGA; 4 British Open; 2 US Open)
 9 Ben Hogan (4 US Open; 2 Masters; 2 US PGA, 1 British Open)
 9 Gary Player (3 British Open; 3 Masters; 2 US PGA; 1 US Open)
 8 Tom Watson (5 British Open; 2 Masters; 1 US Open)

MOST MAJORS 1981-90

4 Nick Faldo (GB); 4 Tom Watson (US); 3 Seve Ballesteros (Spa); 3 Larry Nelson (US); 2 Raymond Floyd (US); 2 Sandy Lyle (GB); 2 Curtis Strange (US)

Nations
27 United States, 6 Great Britain, 3 Spain, Australia, 1 West Germany

RYDER CUP

United States versus Great Britain 1927-71; Great Britain and Ireland 1973-77;
versus Europe 1979- . Since 1963 played over three days.

	Venue	Day 1	Day 2	Day 3	GB/Europe	United States
		Running Scores			**Captains**	
		GB US	GB US			
1927	Worcester, Massachusetts	1 – 3	2¹/₂ – 9¹/₂	–	Ted Ray	Walter Hagen
1929	Moortown, Yorks	1¹/₂ – 2¹/₂	7 - 5	–	George Duncan	Walter Hagen
1931	Scioto, Ohio	1 – 3	3 – 9	–	Charles Whitcombe	Walter Hagen
1933	Southport and Ainsdale	2¹/₂ – 1¹/₂	6¹/₂ – 5¹/₂	–	John H Taylor	Walter Hagen
1935	Ridgewood, New Jersey	1 – 3	3 – 9	–	Charles Whitcombe	Walter Hagen
1937	Southport and Ainsdale	1¹/₂ – 2¹/₂	4 – 8	–	Charles Whitcombe	Walter Hagen*
1947	Portland, Oregan	0 – 4	1 – 11	–	Henry Cotton	Ben Hogan
1949	Ganton, Yorks	3 – 1	5 – 7	–	Charles Whitcombe*	Ben Hogan*
1951	Pinehurst, North Carolina	1 – 3	2¹/₂ – 9¹/₂	–	Arthur Lacey*	Sam Snead
1953	Wentworth, Surrey	1 – 3	5¹/₂ – 6¹/₂	–	Henry Cotton*	Lloyd Mangrum
1955	Thunderbird, California	1 – 3	4 – 8	–	Dai Rees	Chick Harbert
1957	Lindrick Club, Yorks	1 – 3	7¹/₂ – 4¹/₂	–	Dai Rees	Jack Burke
1959	Eldorado, California	1¹/₂ – 2¹/₂	3¹/₂ – 8¹/₂	–	Dai Rees	Sam Snead
1961	Royal Lytham & St Annes	2 – 6	9¹/₂ – 14¹/₂	–	Dai Rees	Jerry Barber
1963	Atlanta, Georgia	2 – 6	4 – 23	9 – 23	Johnny Fallon*	Arnold Palmer
1965	Royal Birkdale, Southport	4 – 4	7 – 9	12¹/₂ – 19¹/₂	Harry Weetman*	Byron Nelson*
1967	Houston, Texas	2¹/₂ – 5¹/₂	3 – 13	8¹/₂ – 23¹/₂	Dai J Rees*	Ben Hogan*
1969	Royal Birkdale, Southport	4¹/₂ – 3¹/₂	8 – 7¹/₂	16 – 16	Eric Brown*	Sam Snead*
1971	St Louis, Missouri	4¹/₂ – 3¹/₂	6 – 12¹/₂	13¹/₂ – 18¹/₂	Eric Brown*	Jay Hebert*
1973	Muirfield, Scotland	5¹/₂ – 2¹/₂	8 – 8	13 – 19	Bernard Hunt*	Jack Burke*
1975	Laurel Valley, Pennsylvania	1¹/₂ – 6¹/₂	3¹/₂ – 12¹/₂	11 – 21	Bernard Hunt*	Arnold Palmer*
1977	Royal Lytham & St Annes	1¹/₂ – 3¹/₂	2¹/₂ – 7¹/₂	7¹/₂ – 12¹/₂	Brian Huggett*	Dow Finsterwald*
1979	Greenbrier, West Virginia	2¹/₂ – 5¹/₂	7¹/₂ – 8¹/₂	11 – 17	John Jacobs*	Billy Casper*
1981	Walton Heath, Surrey	4¹/₂ – 3¹/₂	5¹/₂ – 10¹/₂	9¹/₂ – 18¹/₂	John Jacobs*	Dave Marr*
1983	PGA National, Florida	4¹/₂ – 3¹/₂	8 – 8	13¹/₂ – 14¹/₂	Tony Jacklin*	Jack Nicklaus*
1985	The Belfry, Sutton Coldfield	3¹/₂ – 4¹/₂	9 – 7	16¹/₂ – 11¹/₂	Tony Jacklin*	Lee Trevino*
1987	Muirfield Village, Ohio	6 – 2	10¹/₂ – 5¹/₂	15 – 13	Tony Jacklin*	Jack Nicklaus*
1989	The Belfry, Sutton Coldfield	5 – 3	9 – 7	14 – 14	Tony Jacklin*	Raymond Floyd*
1991	Kiawah Island, South Carolina				Bernard Gallagher*	Dave Stockton*

*Denotes non-playing captain

NO. 1 GOLFERS

Leaders of Sony World Rankings since system began: Apr 13 1986 Bernhard Langer (FRG); Apr 27 1986 Severiano Ballesteros (Spa); Sep 14 1986 Greg Norman (Aus); Nov 22 1987 Ballesteros; Nov 29 1987 Norman; Oct 30 1988 Ballesteros; Nov 6 1988 Norman; Nov 13 1988 Ballesteros; Mar 26 1989 Norman; Apr 2 1989 Ballesteros; Aug 20 1989 Norman; Sep 2 1990 Nick Faldo (GB)
Faldo was ranked 23rd in April 1986 but had fallen to 65th by April 1987.

WORLD MATCH PLAY CHAMPIONSHIP

Sponsors: Piccadilly 1964-76, Colgate 1977-8, Suntory 1979-

1964	Arnold Palmer (US) beat Neil Coles (GB) 2 & 1
1965	Gary Player (SA) beat Peter Thomson (Aus) 3 & 2
1966	Gary Player (SA) beat Jack Nicklaus (US) 6 & 4
1967	Arnold Palmer (US) beat Peter Thomson (Aus) 1 up
1968	Gary Player (SA) beat Bob Charles (NZ) 1 up
1969	Bob Charles (NZ) beat Gene Littler (US) 37th
1970	Jack Nicklaus (US) beat Lee Trevino (US) 2 & 1
1971	Gary Player (SA) beat Jack Nicklaus (US) 5 & 4
1972	Tom Weiskopf (US) beat Lee Trevino (US) 4 & 3
1973	Gary Player (SA) beat Graham Marsh (Aus) 40th
1974	Hale Irwin (US) beat Gary Player (SA) 3 & 1
1975	Hale Irwin (US) beat Al Geiberger (US) 4 & 2
1976	David Graham (Aus) beat Hale Irwin (US) 38th
1977	Graham Marsh (Aus) beat Ray Floyd (US) 5 & 3
1978	Isoa Aoki (Jap) beat Simon Owen (NZ) 3 & 2
1979	Bill Rogers (US) beat Isao Aoki (Jap) 1 up
1980	Greg Norman (Aus) beat Sandy Lyle (GB) 1 up
1981	Seve Ballesteros (Spa) beat Ben Crenshaw (US) 1 up
1982	Seve Ballesteros (Spa) beat Sandy Lyle (GB) 37th
1983	Greg Norman (Aus) beat Nick Faldo (GB) 3 & 2
1984	Seve Ballesteros (Spa) beat Bernhard Langer (FRG) 2 & 1
1985	Seve Ballesteros (Spa) beat Bernhard Langer (FRG) 6 & 5
1986	Greg Norman (Aus) beat Sandy Lyle (GB) 2 & 1
1987	Ian Woosnam (GB) beat Sandy Lyle (GB) 1 up
1988	Sandy Lyle (GB) beat Nick Faldo (GB) 2 & 1
1989	Nick Faldo (GB) beat Ian Woosnam (GB) 1 up
1990	Ian Woosnam (GB) beat Mark McNulty 4 & 2

Most wins
5 Gary Player; 4 Severiano Ballesteros; 3 Greg Norman; 2 Arnold Palmer, Hale Irwin, Ian Woosnam

LEADING MONEY WINNERS SINCE 1981

	UNITED STATES	$	EUROPE	£
1981	Tom Kite	375,698	Bernhard Langer	95,991
1982	Craig Stadler	446,462	Sandy Lyle	86,141
1983	Hal Sutton	426,668	Nick Faldo	140,761
1984	Tom Watson	476,260	Bernhard Langer	160,883
1985	Curtis Strange	542,321	Sandy Lyle	199,020
1986	Greg Norman	653,296	Seve Ballesteros	259,275
1987	Curtis Strange	925,941	Ian Woosnam	439,075
1988	Curtis Strange	1,147,644	Seve Ballesteros	502,000
1989	Tom Kite	1,395,278	Ronan Rafferty	400,311

WORLD CUP
(Formerly the Canada Cup)

1953	Argentina	1967	United States
1954	Australia	1968	Canada
1955	United States	1969	United States
1956	United States	1970	Australia
1957	Japan	1971	United States
1958	Ireland	1972	Taiwan
1959	Australia	1973	United States
1960	United States	1974	South Africa
1961	United States	1975	United States
1962	United States	1976	Spain
1963	United States	1977	Spain
1964	United States	1978	United States
1965	South Africa	1979	United States
1966	United States	1980	Canada
		1981	Not held
		1982	Spain

1983	United States
1984	Spain
1985	Canada
1986	Not held
1987	Wales
1988	United States
1989	Australia

Most wins

Team: 17 United States; 4 Spain; Australia, 3 Canada; 2 South Africa

Played on winning teams: 6 Jack Nicklaus, Arnold Palmer; 4 Sam Snead

Individual title: 3 Jack Nicklaus (US) 1963-64, 1971; 2 Stan Leonard (Can) 1954, 1959; Roberto de Vicenzo (Arg) 1962, 1970; Johnny Miller (US) 1973, 1975, Gary Player (SA) 1965, 1977

WALKER CUP

Year	Venue	Winners	Score
1922	Long Island, New York	US	8 – 4
1923	St Andrews, Scotland	US	6 1/2 – 5 1/2
1924	Garden City, New York	US	9 – 3
1926	St Andrews, Scotland	US	6 1/2 – 5 1/2
1928	Chicago GC, Illinois	US	11 – 1
1930	Royal St George's, England	US	10 – 2
1932	Brookline, Massachusetts	US	9 1/2 – 2 1/2
1934	St Andrews, Scotland	US	9 1/2 – 2 1/2
1936	Pine Valley, New Jersey	US	10 1/2 – 1 1/2
1938	St Andrews, Scotland	GB	7 1/2 – 4 1/2
1947	St Andrews, Scotland	US	8 – 4
1949	Winged Foot, New York	US	10 – 2
1951	Royal Birkdale, England	US	7 1/2 – 4 1/2
1953	Kittansett, Massachusetts	US	9 – 3
1955	St Andrews, Scotland	US	10 – 2
1957	Minikhada, Minnesota	US	8 1/2 – 3 1/2
1959	Muirfield, Scotland	US	9 – 3
1961	Seattle, Washington	US	11 – 1
1963	Turnberry, Scotland	US	14 – 10
1965	Baltimore, Maryland	Drawn	12 – 12
1967	Royal St George's, England	US	15 – 9
1969	Milwaukee, Wisconsin	US	13 – 11

1971	St Andrews, Scotland	GB	13 – 11
1973	Brookline, Massachusetts	US	14 – 10
1975	St Andrews, Scotland	US	15 1/2 – 8 1/2
1977	Shinnecock Hills, New York	US	16 – 8
1979	Muirfield, Scotland	US	15 1/2 – 8 1/2
1981	Cypress Point, California	US	15 – 9
1983	Royal Liverpool, England	US	13 1/2 – 10 1/2
1985	Pine Valley, Philadelphia	US	13 – 11
1987	Sunningdale, England	US	16 1/2 – 7 1/2
1989	Peachtree, Georgia	GB	12 1/2 – 11 1/2

Wins

28 United States; 3 Great Britain; 1 Drawn

THE AMATEUR CHAMPIONSHIP

Winners since 1981. All British unless otherwise stated

1981	Philippe Ploujoux
1982	Martin Thompson
1983	Andrew Parkin
1984	José-Maria Olazabal (Spa)
1985	Garth McGimpsey
1986	David Curry
1987	Paul Mayo
1988	Christian Hardin (Swe)
1989	Stephen Dodd
1990	Rolf Muntz (Hol)

US AMATEUR CHAMPIONSHIP

Winners (all US) since 1981

1981	Nathaniel Crosby
1982	Jay Sigel
1983	Jay Sigel
1984	Scott Verplank
1985	Sam Randolph
1986	Buddy Alexander
1987	Billy Mayfair
1988	Eric Meeks
1989	Chris Patton
1990	Phil Mickelson

WOMEN'S MAJORS

Winners since 1981

US Open	US LPGA	du Maurier	Nabisco Dinah Shaw
1981 Pat Bradley	Donna Caponi	Jan Stephenson	–
1982 Janet Alex	Jan Stephenson	Sandra Haynie	–
1983 Jan Stephenson (Aus)	Patty Sheehan	Hollis Stacey	Amy Alcott
1984 Hollis Stacey	Patty Sheehan	Julie Inkster	Julie Inkster
1985 Kathy Baker	Nancy Lopez	Pat Bradley	Alice Miller
1986 Jane Geddes	Pat Bradley	Pat Bradley	Pat Bradley
1987 Laura Davies (GB)	Jane Geddes	Jody Rosenthal	Betsy King
1988 Liselotte Nuemann (Swe)	Sherri Turner	Sally Little	Amy Alcott
1989 Betsy King	Nancy Lopez	Tammie Green	Julie Inkster
1990 Betsy King	Beth Daniel	Cathy Johnston	Betsy King

BRITISH WOMEN'S OPEN CHAMPIONSHIP

Winners since 1981

1981	Debbie Massey (US)
1982	Marta Figueras-Dotti (Spa)
1983	Not Held
1984	Ayako Okamoto (Jap)
1985	Betsy King (US)
1986	Laura Davies (GB)
1987	Alison Nicholas (GB)
1988	Corinne Dibnah (Aus)
1989	Jane Geddes (US)
1990	Helen Alfredsson (Swe)

──── 1991 ────

Apr 4-7 US Masters (Augusta); Jun 3-8 British Amateur Championship (Ganton); Jun 13-16 US Open (Hazeltine National GC, Chaska, Minnesota); Jul 18-21 OPEN CHAMPIONSHIP (Royal Birkdale); Aug 7-9 British Senior Championship (Prestwick); Aug 8-11 US PGA Championship (Indianapolis); Sep 5-6 Walker Cup (Portmarnock); Sep 27-29 RYDER CUP (Kiawah Island, South Carolina)

GOODWILL GAMES

The second Goodwill Games - following the inaugural event in Moscow in 1986 - were held in Seattle entirely due to the dynamism and determination of the American broadcasting magnate Ted Turner. They attracted 2,500 participants from nearly 50 countries for 21 sports and 17 days' competition, more than the Olympics. There was a total attendance of 800,000.

Turner spent $90 million and faced an estimated loss of $26 million. "Yes, we did lose some money," said Turner, "but in my opinion it's a reasonable down payment on an event that will grow in stature." Turner expected to back Goodwill III in the Soviet Union in 1994.

The athletes' opinion varied: Matt Biondi, the US swimmer, called the Games his most important event of the year; Biondi won four Gold medals. Soviet skater Sergei Grinkov said it was merely "an exhibition". Some countries hardly attended at all. The British presence was nominal. East Germany promised 23 of its top athletes but, taking advantage of their newly-delivered freedom, 14 refused.

The TV star of the games was Fu Mingxia, a 4ft 6in, 5st 5lb, 11-year-old diver from China, who became the youngest gold medallist of the Games when she smiled through the braces of her teeth and won the women's ten-metre platform diving. She attributed her success to "hard practice and diligent study"

GOODWILL GAMES 1990

Seattle, 21 Jul-5 Aug
Gold Medallists

ATHLETICS
Men
100 Metres:	Leroy Burrell (US) 10.05s
200 Metres:	Michael Johnson (US) 20.54s
400 Metres:	Roberto Hernández (Cub) 44.79s
800 Metres:	George Kersch (US) 1m 45.10s
1500 Metres:	Joe Falcon (US) 3m 39.97s
5000 Metres:	Paul Williams (Can) 13m 33.52s
10,000 Metres:	Hammou Boutayeb (Mor) 27m 26.43s
110 Metres Hurdles:	Roger Kingdom (US) 13.47s
400 Metres Hurdles:	Winthrop Graham (Jam) 48.78s
3000 Metres Chase:	Brian Diemer (US) 8m 23.24s
20km Walk:	Ernesto Canto (Mex) 1h 23m 13.12s
4x100 Metres Relay:	United States 38.45s
4x400 Metres Relay:	United States 2m 59.54s
Marathon:	Dave Morra (US) 2h 14m 49s
High Jump:	Hollis Conway (US) 2.33m
Long Jump:	Carl Lewis (US) 8.38m
Triple Jump:	Kenny Harrison (US) 17.72m
Pole Vault:	Rodion Gatauline (USSR) 5.92m
Javelin:	Boris Zaitsev (USSR) 84.16m
Shot:	Randy Barnes (US) 21.44m
Discus:	Romas Ubartas (USSR) 67.14m
Hammer:	Igor Astapkovich (USSR) 84.12m
Decathlon:	Dave Johnson (US) 8,402 pts

Women
100 Metres:	Carlette Guidry (US) 11.04s
200 Metres:	Danette Young (US) 22.64s
400 Metres:	Ana Quirot (Cub) 50.34s
800 Metres:	Ana Quirot (Cub) 1m 57.42s
1500 Metres:	Natalya Artemova (USSR) 4m 09.48s
3000 Metres:	Pattie Sue Plumer (US) 8m 51.59s
5000 Metres:	Yelena Romanova (USSR) 15m 02.33s
10,000 Metres:	Wanda Panfil (Pol) 32m 01.17s
100 Metres Hurdles:	Natalya Grigoreyeva (USSR) 12.70s
400 Metres Hurdles:	Sandra Patrick (US) 55.16s
10km Walk:	Nadezhda Ryashkina (USSR) 41m 56.21s

4x100 Metres Relay:	United States 42.46s
4x400 Metres Relay:	Soviet Union 3m 23.70s
Marathon:	Zoya Ivanova (USSR) 2h 34m 37.5s
High Jump:	Yelena Yelesina (USSR) 2.02m
Long Jump:	Inessa Kravets (USSR) 6.93m
Javelin:	Natalya Shikolenko (USSR) 61.62m
Shot:	Natalya Lisovskaya (USSR) 20.60m
Discus:	Ilke Wyludda (GDR) 68.08m
Heptathlon:	Jackie Joyner Kersee (US) 6,783pts

BASEBALL
Cuba

BASKETBALL
Men: Yugoslavia
Women: United States

BOXING
Light-flyweight:	Eric Griffin (US)
Flyweight:	Tim Austin (US)
Bantamweight:	Sergio Reyes (US)
Featherweight:	Oscar de la Hoya (US)
Lightweight:	Artur Grigoryan (USSR)
Light-welterweight:	Konstantin Tszyu (USSR)
Welterweight:	Fransisc Vastag (Romania)
Light-middleweight:	Israel Akopkohian (USSR)
Middleweight:	Orestes Solano (Cuba)
Light-heavyweight:	Andrei Kurnyavka (USSR)
Heavyweight:	Félix Savon (Cuba)
Super-heavyweight:	Yevgenyi Belousov (USSR)

CYCLING
Men
1km Time Trial:	Alexandr Kirichenko (USSR) 1m 04.722s
4km Team Pursuit:	Soviet Union 4m 19.68s
4km Individual Pursuit:	Steve Hegg (US) 4m 40.22s

Women
3km Individual Pursuit:	Jane Eichhoff (US) 3m 54.69s
Sprint:	Connie Paraskevin-Young (US) 13.70s, 12.59s

GYMNASTICS
Men
Team:	Soviet Union 176.50 pts
Overall:	Vitaly Sherbo (USSR) 59.20 pts
Floor:	Valeriy Lyukin (USSR) 9.90 pts
Pommel horse:	Valentin Mogilny (USSR) 9.97 pts
Rings:	Valeriy Belenki (USSR) 9.92 pts
Vault:	Vitaly Sherbo (USSR) 9.92 pts
Parallel bars:	GuoLinyao (Chn) & Valeriy Belenki (USSR) 9.87 pts
Horizontal bar:	Viyaly Sherbo (USSR) & Lance Ringnald (US) 9.90 pts

Women
Team:	Soviet Union 118.759pts
Overall:	Natalya Kalinini (USSR) 39,836 pts
Asymmetric Bars:	Xia Zhang (Chn) 9.96 pts
Floor:	Svetlana Boginskaya (USSR) & Natalya Kalinini (USSR) 9.96 pts
Beam:	Natalya Kalinini (USSR) 9.96 pts
Vault:	Oksana Chusovitna (USSR) 9.962 pts

Rhythmic
Individual:	Oksana Skaldina (USSR) 39.55 pts
Rope:	Oksana Skaldina (USSR) 9.90 pts
Hoop:	Oksana Skaldina (USSR) /Alexandra Timoshenko (USSR) /Mila Martinova (Bul) 9.90 pts
Ball:	Oksana Skaldina (USSR) 9.95 pts
Ribbons:	Alexandra Timoshenko (USSR) 10.00 pts

ICE HOCKEY
Soviet Union

ICE SKATING
Men:	Kurt Browning (Can)
Women:	Kristi Yamaguchi (US)
Pairs:	Ekaterina Gordeyeva & Sergey Grinkov (USSR)
Dance:	Marina Klimova & Sergey Ponomarenko (USSR)

JUDO
Men
60kg:	Amiran Totikashvili (USSR)
65kg:	Hyo San-kim (SKo)
71kg:	Y Yoshitaka (Jap)
78kg:	Bachir Varayev (USSR)
86kg:	Hirotaka Okada (Jap)
95kg:	D Knorrek (FRG)
Over 95kg:	S Kosorotov (USSR)

Women
52kg:	Chung Sung-hong (SKo)
61kg:	Elana Petrova (USSR)

MODERN PENTATHLON
Men:	Anatoly Starostin (USSR) 5,690 pts
Women:	Lori Norwood (US) 5.288 pts

ROWING
Men
Single Sculls:	Vaclav Chalupa (Cze) 6m 56.33s
Double Sculls:	Girt Vilks/Valeri Dosenko (USSR) 6m 17.59s
Quadruple Sculls:	Soviet Union 6m 01.16
Coxed Fours:	Soviet Union 6m 06.79
Coxless Fours:	East Germany 5m 55.75s
Eights:	West Germany 5m 44.16s
Lightweight Single Sculls:	Frans Geobel (Hol) 7m 10.83s
Lightweight Pairs:	Sabino Bellomo/Alfredo Striani (Ita) 7m 04.57s

Women
Single Sculls:	Titie Jordache (FRG) 7m 48.08s
Pairs:	Stefanie Werremeier/Ingeburt Althoff (FRG) 7m 28.93s
Coxless Fours:	East Germany 6m 57.62s
Double Sculls:	Sariya Zakirova/S Mazi (USSR) 6m 58.81s
Eights:	East Germany 6m 02.13s
Lightweight Single Sculls:	Mette Block Jenson (Den) 7m 48.72s
Lightweight Pairs:	G Andersen/E Fraas (Denm) 7m 38.09s

SWIMMING
Men
50 Metres Freestyle:	Matt Biondi (US) 22.10s
100 Metres Freestyle:	Matt Biondi (US) 49.02s
200 Metres Freestyle:	Artur Wojdat (Pol) 1m 48.19s
400 Metres Freestyle:	Artur Wojdat (Pol) 3m 48.61s
800 Metres Freestyle:	Jorg Hoffmann (GDR) 7m 54.73s
1500 Metres Freestyle:	Jorg Hoffmann (GDR) 15m 11.14s
100 Metres Backstroke:	Martin Lopez Zubero (Spa) 55.68s
200 Metres Backstroke:	Martin Lopez Zubero (Spa) 1m59.50s
100 Metres Breaststroke:	Alexei Matveev (USSR) 1m 02.34s
200 Metres Breaststroke:	Mike Barrowman (US) 2m 11.53s (WR)
100 Metres Butterfly:	Anthony Nesty (Sur) 53.42s
200 Metres Butterfly:	Melvin Stewart (US) 1m 57.05s
200 Metres Medley:	David Wharton (US) 2m 02.37s
400 Metres Medley:	David Wharton (US) & Patrick Kühl (GDR) 4m 17.74s
4x200 Metres Freestyle Relay:	United States 7m 16.26s
4x100 Metres Freestyle Relay:	United States 3m 17.50s
4x100 Metres Medley Relay:	United States 3m 40.97s
1m Springboard:	Sergey Lomonovski (USSR) 597.00pts
3m Springboard:	Tan Liangde (Chn) 650.01 pts
10m Platform:	Jan Hempel (GDR) 618.81 pts

Women
50 Metres Freestyle:	Leigh Ann Fetter (US) 25.71s
100 Metres Freestyle:	Nicole Haislett (US) 55.97s
200 Metres Freestyle:	Manuela Stellmach (GDR) 2m 00.38s
400 Metres Freestyle:	Janet Evans (US) 4m 05.84s
800 Metres Freestyle:	Janet Evans (US) 8m 28.47s
1500 Metres Freestyle:	Janet Evans (US) 15m 54.23s
100 Metres Backstroke:	Betsy Mitchell (US) 1m 01.46s

200 Metres Backstroke:	Krisztina Egerszegi (Hun) 2m 09.70s			

200 Metres Backstroke: Krisztina Egerszegi (Hun)
  2m 09.70s
100 Metres Breaststroke: Yulia Landik (USSR)
  1m 10.34s
200 Metres Breaststroke: Elena Volkova (USSR)
  2m 28.64s
100 Metres Butterfly: Janel Jorgenson (US)
  1m 00.98s
200 Metres Butterfly: Summer Sanders (US)
  2m 09.46s
200 Metres Medley: Summer Sanders (US)
  2m 14.06s
400 Metres Medley: Summer Sanders (US)
  4m 39.22s
4x100 Metres Freestyle Relay: East Germany 3m 44.28s
4x200 Metres Freestyle Relay: East Germany 8m 05.21s
4x100 Metres Medley Relay: United States 4m 06.94s
1m Springboard: Gao Min (Chn) 508.80 pts
3m Springboard: Gao Min (Chn) 525.78 pts
10m Platform: Fu Mingxia (Chn) 443.04 pts
Synchronised - Solo: Kristen Babb (US) 98.80 pts
Synchronised - Pairs: Karen and Sarah Josephson
  (US) 98.88 pts

VOLLEYBALL
Men: Italy
Women: Soviet Union

WATER POLO
Yugoslavia

WEIGHTLIFTING
Mixed weight class based on percentage of world record lifted by each man in his own particular weight category. Medals awarded for the snatch, clean and jerk and overall.
Snatch: Nicu Vlad (Rom) 100 kg (96.0%)
Clean & Jerk: Ivan Ivanov (Bul) 145 kg (93.5%)
Overall: Ivan Ivanov (Bul) 257.5 kg (94.4%)

WRESTLING (FREESTYLE)
Team: United States
48kg: Corey Baze (US)
52kg: Valentin Jordanov (Bul)
57kg: Khaltmaagin Battuul (Mon)
62kg: John Smith (US)
68kg: Nate Carr (US)
74kg: Park Yung-Jim (SKo)
82kg: Elamadie Jabraylow (USSR)
90kg: Makharbek Khardtzev (USSR)
100kg: Petyo Makedonov (Bul)
130kg: David Gobedishvili (USSR)

YACHTING
Men's Sailboard: Grzegorz Myszkowski (Pol)
  36.4pts
Women's Sailboard: Mireia Casas (Spa) 30.4pts
Men's Finn: Brian Ledbetter (US) 28.7pts
Men's 470: Nigel Cochrane & Jeff Eckard
  (Can) 29.7pts
Women's 470: Jody Swanson & Cory Fischer-Sertl
  (US) 20.4pts

LEADING MEDALLISTS

	G	S	B	Total
Soviet Union	66	68	54	188
United States	60	53	48	161
East Germany	11	8	24	43
Bulgaria	8	7	9	24
China	6	7	3	16
West Germany	4	3	8	15
Japan	2	3	10	15
Cuba	6	4	3	13
Canada	4	1	6	11
Romania	2	4	2	8

British Medallists
Silver: Nicola Fairbrother (56kg Judo); Diane Bell (61kg Judo)
Bronze: Mens Coxless Fours (Rowing); Penny Way (Boardsailing)

GREYHOUND RACING

DAILY MIRROR GREYHOUND DERBY
Wimbledon, Jun 23
480 metres

1 Slippy Blue	8-1	(Trap 4)
2 Druid's Johno	4-7f	(Trap 6)
3 Fair Hill Boy	4-1	(Trap 1)
4 Fires of War	10-1	(Trap 5)
5 Galtymore Lad	20-1	(Trap 3)
6 Burnt Oak Champ	14-1	(Trap 2)

Time: 28.70s
Trainer: Ken Linzell, Walthamstow

GRAND NATIONAL
Hall Green, Mar 30
474 Metres

1 Gizmo Pasha	4-5f	(Trap 6)
2 Columbokill Jet	16-1	(Trap 1)
3 Temple Garden	10-1	(Trap 2)

Time: 29.62s

BBC TELEVISION TROPHY
Walthamstow, Apr 4
820 Metres

1 Shropshire Lass	11-4	(Trap 3)
2 Sail on Valerie	10-11f	(Trap 6)
3 Trans Mercedes	3-1	(Trap 2)

Time: 52.18s

CHAMPIONS

GREYHOUND DERBY
At White City 1927-84, except 1940 at Harringay; at Wimbledon 1985 - Raced over 500yd 1927, 525yd 1928-74, 500m 1975-85, 480m 1986

		Price	Trap	Time
1927	Entry Badge	1-4f	5	29.01s
1928	Doher Ash	5-1	1	30.48s
1929	Mick the Miller	4-7f	4	29.96s
1930	Mick the Miller	4-9f	1	30.24s
1931	Seldom Lad	7-2	4	30.04s
1932	Wild Woolley	5-2	6	29.72s
1933	Future Cutlet	6-1	3	29.80s
1934	Davesland	3-1	4	29.81s
1935	Greta Ranee	4-1	3	30.18s
1936	Fine Jubilee	10-11f	3	29.48s
1937	Wattle Bark	5-2	6	29.26s
1938	Lone Keel	9-4	3	29.62s
1939	Highland Rum	2-1jf	6	29.35s
1940	G.R. Archduke	100-7	1	29.66s
1945	Ballyhennessy Seal	Evens f	1	29.56s
1946	Mondays News	5-1	3	29.24s
1947	Trev's Perfection	4-1	2	28.95s
1948	Priceless Border	1-2f	1	28.78s
1949	Narrogar Ann	5-1	2	28.95s
1950	Ballymac Ball	7-2	4	28.72s
1951	Ballylanigan Tanist	11-4	1	28.62s
1952	Endless Gossip	Evens f	6	28.50s
1953	Daws Dancer	10-1	5	29.20s
1954	Paul's Fun	8-15f	3	28.84s
1955	Rushton Mack	5-1	2	28.97s
1956	Dunmore King	7-2	3	29.22s
1957	Ford Spartan	Evens f	1	28.84s
1958	Pigalle Wonder	4-5f	1	28.65s
1959	Mile Bush Pride	Evens f	4	28.76s
1960	Duleek Dandy	25-1	4	29.15s
1961	Palm's Printer	2-1	1	28.84s
1962	The Grand Canal	2-1f	5	29.09s
1963	Lucky Boy Boy	Evens f	1	29.00s
1964	Hack Up Chieftain	20-1	1	28.92s
1965	Chittering Clapton	5-2	6	28.82s
1966	Faithful Hope	8-1	3	28.52s
1967	Tric-Trac	9-2	1	29.00s
1968	Camira Flash	100-8	4	28.89s
1969	Sand Star	5-4f	4	28.76s
1970	John Silver	11-4	2	29.01s
1971	Dolores Rocket	11-4	2	28.74s
1972	Patricia's Hope	7-1	5	28.55s
1973	Patricia's Hope	7-2	5	28.68s
1974	Jimsun	20-1	2	28.76s
1975	Tartan Khan	25-1	2	29.57s
1976	Mutts Silver	6-1	4	29.38s
1977	Balliniska Band	Evens f	5	29.16s
1978	Lacca Champion	6-4f	3	29.42s
1979	Sarah's Bunny	3-1	6	29.53s
1980	Indian Joe	13-8jf	6	29.68s
1981	Parkdown Jet	4-5f	6	29.57s
1982	Laurie's Panther	6-4f	1	29.60s
1983	I'm Slippy	6-1	4	29.40s
1984	Whisper Wishes	7-4f	4	29.43s
1985	Pagan Swallow	9-1	5	29.04s
1986	Tico	6-4jf	5	28.69s
1987	Signal Spark	14-1	4	28.83s
1988	Hit the Lid	3-1	6	28.53s
1989	Lartigue Note	Evens f	2	28.79s
1990	Slippy Blue	8-1	4	28.70s

BBC TELEVISION TROPHY
First Run 1956. Raced at various tracks and distances
Winners since 1981:

	Venue	Winner
1981	Perry Barr	Decoy Boom
1982	Belle Vue	Alfa My Son
1983	Walthamstow	Sandy Lane
1984	Wimbledon	Weston Prelude
1985	Wolverhampton	Scurlogue Champ
1986	Brough Park	Scurlogue Champ
1987	Oxford	Glenowen Queen
1988	Hall Green	Minnie's Siren
1989	Catford	Proud To Run
1990	Walthamstow	Shropshire Lass

Most wins: 2 Scurlogue Champ

1991

Group 1 Races. All dates provisional

Mar/Apr TV Trophy (tba); Apr 5 Grand National (Hall Green) 474m hurdles; May 2 Essex Vase (Romford) 400m; May 11 Scottish Derby (Shawfield) 500m; May 16 Regency (Hove) 740m; Jun 22 GREYHOUND DERBY (Wimbledon) 480m; Sep 21 Gold Collar (Catford) 555m; Sep 28 Cesarewitch (Belle Vue) 855m; Oct 12 Grand Prix (Walthamstow) 640m; Nov 15 St Leger (Wembley) 655m.

GYMNASTICS

1990

EUROPEAN CHAMPIONSHIPS
Lausanne, May 26-27

Men
Overall
1 Valentin Mogilny (USSR) 58.45pts
2 Sergei Kharkov (USSR) 58.30pts
3 Yuri Chechi (Ita) 58.20pts
Apparatus Champions
Floor: Vitaliy Sherbo (USSR) 9.825pts
Pommel Horse: Valentin Mogilny (USSR) 9.937pts
Rings: Yuri Chechi (Ita) 9.837pts
Parallel Bars: Valentin Mogilny (USSR) & Daniel
Giubellini (Swi) 9.800pts
High Bar: Vitaliy Sherbo (USSR) 9.912pts
Vault: Vitaliy Sherbo (USSR) 9.943pts
*Neil Thomas won Britain's first medal at the
Championships for 50 years when he took bronze in the
Vault. His team-mate James May finished fourth.*

Women
Overall
1 Svetlana Boginskaya (USSR) 39.874pts
2 Natalya Kalinina (USSR) 39.637pts
3 Henrietta Onodi (Hun) 39.636pts
Apparatus Champions
Floor: Svetlana Boginskaya (USSR) 10.000pts
Vault: Svetlana Boginskaya (USSR) 9.943pts
Beam: Svetlana Boginskaya (USSR) 10.000pts
Asymmetrical
Bars: Svetlana Boginskaya (USSR) 9.950

BRITISH WOMEN'S CHAMPIONSHIPS
Crawley, Mar 9-11

Overall
1 Sarah Mercer (Leatherhead) 75.975pts
2 Louise Redding (Telford) 75.425pts
3 Lorna Mainwaring (Telford) 74.675pts
Apparatus Champions
Vault: Louise Redding 9.637pts
Asymmetrical Bars: Sarah Mercer 9.725pts
Beam: Lorna Mainwaring 9.562pts
Floor: Sarah Mercer 9.850pts

BRITISH MEN'S CHAMPIONSHIPS
Gateshead, Mar 17

Overall
1 Neil Thomas (Lilleshall) 113.00pts
2 James May (Bristol) 112.15pts
3 Terry Bartlett (Lilleshall) 111.15pts
Apparatus Champions
Floor: James May & Terry Bartlett 9.45pts
Pommel Horse: Neil Thomas 9.5pts
Rings: Michael Bone (Eston) 9.4pts
Vault: Neil Thomas 9.65pts
Parallel Bars: Dave Cox (Liverpool) 9.5pts
High Bar: Marvin Campbell (Manchester) 9.45pts

BRITISH WOMEN'S RHYTHMICS CHAMPIONSHIPS
Individual
Bletchley, Jan 13-14
1 Alitia Sands (Coventry) 36.35pts
2 Viva Siefert (Hillingdon) 36.30pts
3 Gabrielle Yorath (Leeds) 35.25pts
*Gabrielle Yorath is the daughter of the football manager
Terry Yorath*

Team
Hinckley, Leics, Mar 24
1 Coventry 32.70pts
2 Northampton 32.40pts
3 Cheadle Hulme 30.45pts

1989

WORLD CHAMPIONSHIPS
Stuttgart, Oct

Men
Team
1 USSR 587.25pts
2 East Germany 580.85pts
3 China 579.30pts
Overall Individual
1 Igor Korobchinski (USSR) 59.250pts
2 Valentin Mogilny (USSR) 59.150pts
3 Li Jing (Chn) 58.800pts
Floor Exercise
1 Igor Korobchinski (USSR) 9.937pts
2 Vladimir Artemov (USSR) 9.875pts
3 Li Chunyang (Chn) 9.850pts
Pommel Horse
1 Valentin Mogilny (USSR) 10.000pts
2 Andreas Wecker (GDR) 9.962pts
3 Li Jing (Chn) 9.937pts
Rings
1 Andreas Aguilar (FRG) 9.875pts
2 Andreas Wecker (GDR) 9.862pts
3 Vitaliy Marnich (USSR) & Juri Chechi (Ita) 9.812pts
Vault
1 Jorg Behrendt (GDR) 9.881pts
2 Sylvio Kroll (GDR) 9.874pts
3 Vladimir Artemov (USSR) 9.868pts
Parallel Bars
1 Li Jing (Chn) & Vlademir Artemov (USSR) 9.900pts
3 Andreas Wecker (GDR) 9.887pts
High Bar
1 Li Chunyang (Chn) 9.950pts
2 Vladimir Artemov (USSR) 9.900pts
3 Yukio Iketani (Jap) 9.875pts

Women
Team
1 USSR 397.093pts
2 Romania 394.931pts
3 China 392.116pts
Overall Individual
1 Svetlana Boginskaya (USSR) 39.900pts
2 Natalya Laschenova (USSR) 39.862pts
3 Olga Strageva (USSR) 39.774pts
Vault
1 Olessia Dudnik (USSR) 9.987pts
2 Christina Bontas (Rom) & Brandy Johnson (USA)
9.950pts
Asymmetrical Bars
1 Fan Di (Chn) & Daniela Silivas (Rom) 10.000pts
3 Olga Strageva (USSR) 9.975pts
Beam
1 Daniela Silivas (Rom) 9.950pts
2 Olessia Dudnik (USSR) 9.937pts
3 Gabriella Potorac (Rom) 9.887pts
Floor
1 Daniela Silivas (Rom) & Svetlana Boginskaya (USSR)
10.000pts
3 Christina Bontas (Rom) 9.962pts

CHAMPIONS

OLYMPIC GAMES
Men
Combined
1900	Gustave Sandras (Fra)
1904	Julius Lenhart (Aut)
1908	Alberto Braglia (Ita)
1912	Alberto Braglia (Ita)
1920	Giorgio Zampori (Ita)
1924	Leon Stukelj (Yug)
1928	Georges Miez (Sui)
1932	Romeo Neri (Ita)
1936	Alfred Schwarzmann (Ger)
1948	Veikko Huhtanen (Fin)
1952	Viktor Chukarin (USSR)
1956	Viktor Chukarin (USSR)
1960	Boris Shakhlin (USSR)
1964	Yukio Endo (Jap)
1968	Sawao Kato (Jap)
1972	Sawao Kato (Jap)
1976	Nikolay Andrianov (USSR)
1980	Aleksandr Ditiatin (USSR)
1984	Koji Gushiken (Jap)
1988	Vladimir Artemov (USSR)

Floor
1932	Istavan Pelle (Hun)
1936	Georges Miez (Swi)
1948	Ferenc Pataki (Hun)
1952	William Thoresson (Swe)
1956	Valentin Muratov (USSR)
1960	Nobuyuki Aihara (Jap)
1964	Franco Menichelli (Ita)
1968	Sawao Kato (Jap)
1972	Nikolay Andrianov (USSR)
1976	Nikolay Andrianov (USSR)
1980	Roland Brückner (GDR)
1984	Li Ning (Chn)
1988	Sergey Kharikov (USSR)

Parallel Bars
1896	Alfred Flatow (Ger)
1904	George Eyser (US)
1908	August Güttinger (Swi)
1928	Ladislav Vacha (Cze)
1932	Romeo Neri (Ita)
1936	Konrad Frey (Ger)
1948	Mickael Reusch (Swi)
1952	Hans Eugster (Swi)
1956	Viktor Chukarin (USSR)
1960	Boris Shakhlin (USSR)
1964	Yukio Endo (Jap)
1968	Akinori Nakayama (Jap)
1972	Sawao Kato (Jap)
1976	Sawao Kato (Jap)
1980	Aleksandr Tkachev (USSR)
1984	Bart Conner (US)
1988	Vladimir Artemov (USSR)

Pommel Horse
1896	Louis Zutter (Swi)
1904	Anton Heida (US)
1924	Josef Wilhelm (Swi)
1928	Hermann Hanggi (Swi)
1932	Istvan Pelle (Hun)
1936	Konrad Frey (Ger)
1948	Paavo Aaltonen (Fin)
	Veikko Huhtanen (Fin) &
	Heikki Savolainen (Fin)
1952	Viktor Chukarin (USSR)

1956	Boris Shakhlin (USSR)
1960	Eugen Ekman (Fin) &
	Boris Shakhlin (USSR)
1964	Miroslav Cerar (Yug)
1968	Miroslav Cerar (Yug)
1972	Viktor Klimenko (USSR)
1976	Zoltán Magyar (Hun)
1980	Zoltán Magyar (Hun)
1984	Li Ning (Chn) &
	Peter Vidmar (US)
1988	Lyubomir Gueraskov (Bul)
	Zsolt Borkai (Hun) &
	Dmitri Belozerchev (USSR)

Rings
1896	Ioannis Mitropoulos (Gre)
1904	Hermann Glass (US)
1924	Francesco Martino (Ita)
1928	Leon Skutelj (Yug)
1932	George Gulack (US)
1936	Alois Hudec (Cze)
1948	Karl Frei (Swi)
1952	Grant Shaginyan (USSR)
1956	Albert Azaryan (USSR)
1960	Albert Azaryan (USSR)
1964	Takuji Hayata (Jap)
1968	Akinori Nakayama (Jap)
1972	Akinori Nakayama (Jap)
1976	Nikolay Andrianov (USSR)
1980	Aleksandr Ditiatin (USSR)
1984	Koji Gushiken (Jap) & Li Ning (Chn)
1988	Holger Behrendt (GDR) & Dmitri Belozerchev (USSR)

Horizontal Bar
1896	Hermann Weingärtner (Ger)
1904	Anton Heida (US) & Edward Hennig (US)
1924	Leon Stukelj (Yug)
1928	Georges Miez (Swi)
1932	Dallas Bixler (US)
1936	Aleksanteri Saavala (Fin)
1948	Josef Stadler (Swi)
1952	Jack Günthard (Swi)
1956	Takashi Ono (Jap)
1960	Takashi Ono (Jap)
1964	Boris Shakhlin (USSR)
1968	Mikhail Voronin (USSR) &
	Akinori Nakayama (Jap)
1972	Mitsuo Tsukahara (Jap)
1976	Mitsuo Tsukahara (Jap)
1980	Stoyan Deltchev (Bul)
1984	Shinji Morisue (Jap)
1988	Vladimir Artemov (USSR) &
	Valeri Lyukine (USSR)

Vault
1896	Carl Schumann (Ger)
1904	Anton Heida (US) George Eyser (US)
1924	Frank Kriz (US)
1928	Eugen Mack (Swi)
1932	Savino Guglielmetti (Ita)
1936	Alfred Schwarzmann (Ger)
1948	Paavo Aaltonen (Fin)
1952	Viktor Chukarin (USSR)
1956	Helmuth Bantz (Ger) & Valentin Muratov (USSR)
1960	Takashi Ono (Jap) & Boris Shakhin (USSR)
1964	Haruhiro Yamashita (Jap)
1968	Mikhail Voronin (USSR)
1972	Klaus Köste (GDR)
1976	Nikolay Andrianov (USSR)
1980	Nikolay Andrianov (USSR)
1984	Lou Yun (Chn)
1988	Lou Yun (Chn)

Team
1904	United States
1908	Sweden
1912	Italy
1920	Italy
1924	Italy
1928	Switzerland
1932	Italy
1936	Germany
1948	Finland
1952	USSR
1956	USSR
1960	Japan
1964	Japan
1968	Japan
1972	Japan
1976	Japan
1980	USSR
1984	United States
1988	USSR

Women
Combined
1952	Maria Gorokhovskaya (USSR)
1956	Larissa Latynina (USSR)
1960	Larissa Latynina (USSR)
1964	Vera Cáslavská (Cze)
1968	Vera Cáslavská (Cze)
1972	Lyudmila Tourischeva (USSR)
1976	Nadia Comaneci (Rom)
1980	Yelena Davydova (USSR)
1984	Mary Lou Retton (US)
1988	Yelena Shoushounova (USSR)

Asymmetrical Bars
1952	Margit Korondi (Hun)
1956	Agnes Keleti (Hun)
1960	Polina Astakhova (USSR)
1964	Polina Astakhova (USSR)
1968	Vera Cáslavská (Cze)
1972	Karin Janz (GDR)
1976	Nadia Comaneci (Rom)
1980	Maxi Gnauck (GDR)
1984	Ma Yanhong (Chn) & Julianne McNamara (US)
1988	Daniela Silivas (Rom)

Beam
1952	Nina Bocharova (USSR)
1956	Agnes Keleti (Hun)
1960	Eva Bosakova (Cze)
1964	Vera Cáslavská (Cze)
1968	Natalya Kuchinskaya (USSR)
1972	Olga Korbut (USSR)
1976	Nadia Comaneci (Rom)
1980	Nadia Comaneci (Rom)
1984	Simona Pauca (Rom) & Ecaterina Szabo (Rom)
1988	Daniela Silivas (Rom)

Floor
1952	Agnes Keleti (Hun)
1956	Larissa Latynina (USSR) & Agnes Keleti (Hun)
1960	Larissa Latynina (USSR)
1964	Larissa Latynina (USSR)
1968	Larissa Petrik (USSR) & Vera Cáslavská (Cze)
1972	Olga Korbut (USSR)
1976	Nelli Kim (USSR)
1980	Nelli Kim (USSR) & Nadia Comaneci (Rom)
1984	Ecaterina Szabo (Rom)
1988	Daniela Silivas (Rom)

Vault
1952	Yekaterina Kalinchuk (USSR)
1956	Larissa Latynina (USSR)
1960	Margarita Nikolayeva (USSR)
1964	Vera Cáslavská (Cze)
1968	Vera Cáslavská (Cze)
1972	Karin Janz (GDR)
1976	Nelli Kim (USSR)
1980	Natalya Shaposhnikova (USSR)
1984	Ecaterina Szabo (Rom)
1988	Svetlana Boginskaya (USSR)

Team
1928	Netherlands
1932	Not held
1936	Germany
1948	Czechoslovakia
1952	USSR
1956	USSR
1960	USSR
1964	USSR
1968	USSR
1972	USSR
1976	USSR
1980	USSR
1984	Romania
1988	USSR

Rhythmic Gymnastics
1984	Fung Lori (Can)
1988	Marina Lobatch (USSR)

WORLD CHAMPIONSHIPS
(First held 1903)
Men
Combined (post-war winners)
1950	Walter Lehmann (Swi)
1954	Vikton Chukarin (USSR)
1958	Boris Shakhlin (USSR)
1962	Yuriy Titov (USSR)
1966	Mikhail Voronin (USSR)
1970	Eizo Kenmotsu (Jap)
1974	Shigeru Kasamatsu (Jap)
1978	Nikolay Andrianov (USSR)
1979	Aleksandr Ditiatin (USSR)
1981	Yuriy Korolev (USSR)
1983	Dmitri Belozerchev (USSR)
1985	Yuriy Korolev (USSR)
1987	Dmitri Belozerchev (USSR)
1989	Igor Korobchinski (USSR)

Individual Disciplines
Winners since 1981
Floor
1981	Yuriy Korolev (USSR) & Li Yuejiu (Chn)
1983	Tong Fei (Chn)
1985	Tong Fei (Chn)
1987	Lou Yun (Chn)
1989	Igor Korobchinski (USSR)

Vault
1981	Ralf-Peter Hemmann (GDR)
1983	Artur Akopian (USSR)
1985	Yuriy Korolev (USSR)
1987	Slvio Kroll (GDR) & Lou Yun (Chn)
1989	Jorg Behrendt (GDR)

Rings
1981	Aleksandr Ditiatin (USSR)
1983	Dmitriy Belozerchev (USSR) & Koji Gushiken (Jap)
1985	Li Ning (Chn) & Yuriy Korolev (USSR)
1987	Yuriy Korolev (USSR)
1989	Andreas Aguilar (FRG)

Pommel Horse
1981	Michael Mikolay (GDR) & Li Xiaoping (Chn)
1983	Dmitriy Belozerchev (USSR)
1985	Valentin Mogilnyi (USSR)
1987	Dmitri Belozerchev (USSR) & Zsolt Borkai (Hun)
1989	Valentin Mognilny (USSR)

Team
1981	USSR
1983	China
1985	USSR
1987	USSR
1989	USSR

High Bar
1981	Aleksandr Tkachev (USSR)
1983	Dmitri Belozerchev (USSR)
1985	Tong Fei (Chn)
1987	Dmitri Belozerchev (USSR)
1989	Li Chunyang (Chn)

Parallel Bars
1981	Aleksandr Ditiatin (USSR) & Koji Gushiken (Jap)
1983	Vladimir Artemov (USSR) & Lou Yun (Chn)
1985	Silvio Kroll (GDR) & Valentin Mogilnyi (USSR)
1987	Vladimir Artemov (USSR)
1989	Vladimir Artemov (USSR) & Li Jing (Chn)

Women

Combined (post-war winners)
1950	Helena Rakoczy (Pol)
1954	Galina Roudiko (USSR)
1958	Larissa Latynina (USSR)
1962	Larissa Latynina (USSR)
1966	Vera Cáslavská (Cze)
1970	Lyudmila Tourischeva (USSR)
1974	Lyudmila Tourischeva (USSR)
1978	Yelena Mukhina (USSR)
1979	Nelli Kim (USSR)
1981	Olga Bicherova (USSR)
1983	Natalya Yurchenko (USSR)
1985	Oksana Omelianchuk (USSR) & Yelena Shoushounova (USSR)
1987	Aurelia Dobre (Rom)
1989	Svetlana Boginskaya (USSR)

Individual Disciplines
Winners since 1981

Vault
1981	Maxi Gnauck (GDR)
1983	Boriana Stoyanova (Bul)
1985	Yelena Shoushounova (USSR)
1987	Yelena Shoushounova (USSR)
1989	Olessia Dudnik (USSR)

Beam
1981	Maxi Gnauck (GDR)
1983	Olga Mostepanova (USSR)
1985	Daniela Silivas (Rom)
1987	Aurelia Dobre (Rom)
1989	Daniela Silivas (Rom)

Floor
1981	Natalya Ilyenko (USSR)
1983	Ecaterina Szabo (Rom)
1985	Oksana Omeliantchuk (USSR)
1987	Yelena Shoushounova (USSR) & Daniela Silivas (Rom)
1989	Daniela Silivas (Rom) & Svetlana Boginskaya (USSR)

Asymmetrical Bars
1981	Maxi Gnauck (GDR)
1983	Maxi Gnauck (GDR)
1985	Gabriela Fahnrich (GDR)
1987	Daniela Silivas (Rom) & Doerte Thumler (GDR)
1989	Fan Di (Chn) & Daniela Silivas (Rom)

Team (post-war)
1950	Sweden
1954	USSR
1958	USSR
1962	USSR
1966	Czechoslovakia
1970	USSR
1974	USSR
1978	USSR
1979	Romania
1981	USSR
1983	USSR
1985	USSR
1987	Romania
1989	USSR

EUROPEAN CHAMPIONS
(Inaugurated 1955)
Combined winners only

Men
1955	Boris Shakhlin (USSR)
1957	Jaochim Blume (Spa)
1959	Yuriy Titov (USSR)
1961	Miroslav Cerar (Yug)
1963	Miroslav Cerar (Yug)
1965	Franco Menichelli(Ita)
1967	Mikhail Voronin (USSR)
1969	Mikhail Voronin (USSR)
1971	Viktor Klimenko (USSR)
1973	Viktor Klimenko (USSR)
1975	Nikolay Andrianov (USSR)
1977	Vladimir Markelov (USSR)
1979	Stoyan Deltchev (Bul)
1981	Aleksandr Tkachev (USSR)
1983	Dmitriy Belozerchev (USSR)
1985	Dmitriy Belozerchev (USSR)
1987	Valeriy Lyukin (USSR)
1989	Igor Korobchinsky (USSR)
1990	Valentin Mogilny (USSR)

Women
1955	not held
1957	Larissa Latynina (USSR)
1959	Natalie Kot (Pol)
1961	Larissa Latynina (USSR)
1963	Mirjana Bilic (Yug)
1965	Vera Cáslavská (Cze)
1967	Vera Cáslavská (Cze)
1969	Karin Janz (GDR)
1971	Lyudmila Tourischeva (USSR) & Tamara Lazakovich (USSR)
1973	Lyudmila Tourischeva (USSR)
1975	Nadia Comaneci (Rom)
1977	Nadia Comaneci (Rom)
1979	Nadia Comaneci (Rom)
1981	Maxi Gnauck (GDR)
1983	OLga Bicherova (USSR)
1985	Yelena Shoushounova (USSR)
1987	Daniela Silivas (Rom)
1989	Svetlana Boginskaya (USSR)
1990	Svetlana Boginskaya (USSR)

HOCKEY

MEN'S WORLD CUP
Lahore, Feb 12–23

Pool A

HOLLAND 2 France 1
India 1 Soviet Union 1
AUSTRALIA 4 Argentina 1
HOLLAND 5 Soviet Union 2
AUSTRALIA 3 France 1
ARGENTINA 5 India 3
FRANCE 2 India 1
Argentina 3 Holland 3
AUSTRALIA 3 Soviet Union 0
HOLLAND 5 India 3
France 0 Soviet Union 0
AUSTRALIA 3 India 2
FRANCE 1 Argentina 0
AUSTRALIA 1 Holland 0
SOVIET UNION 3 Argentina 1

FINAL TABLE

	P	W	D	L	F	A	Pts
1 Australia	5	5	0	0	14	4	10
2 Holland	5	3	1	1	15	10	7
3 France	5	2	1	2	5	6	5
4 Soviet Union	5	1	2	2	6	10	4
5 Argentina	5	1	1	3	10	14	3
6 India	5	0	1	4	10	16	1

Australia & Holland qualified for semi-finals

Pool B

ENGLAND 2 Ireland 0
PAKISTAN 6 Spain 3
WEST GERMANY 4 Canada 1
PAKISTAN 2 Ireland 1
ENGLAND 2 Canada 0
WEST GERMANY 2 Spain 0
SPAIN 4 England 1
WEST GERMANY 4 Ireland 0
PAKISTAN 1 Canada 0
England 1 Pakistan 1
SPAIN 2 Ireland 1
WEST GERMANY 2 England 1
SPAIN 1 Canada 0
Canada 1 Ireland 1
WEST GERMANY 1 Pakistan 0

FINAL TABLE

	P	W	D	L	F	A	Pts
1 West Germany	5	5	0	0	13	2	10
2 Pakistan	5	3	1	1	10	6	7
3 Spain	5	3	0	2	10	10	6
4 England	5	2	1	2	7	7	5
5 Canada	5	0	1	4	2	9	1
6 Ireland	5	0	1	4	3	11	1

West Germany & Pakistan qualified for semi-finals

SEMI-FINALS

PAKISTAN 2 Australia 1
HOLLAND 3 West Germany 2 (aet)

THIRD PLACE PLAY-OFF

AUSTRALIA 2 West Germany 1

FINAL

HOLLAND 3 Pakistan 1

FINAL STANDINGS :

1 Holland
2 Pakistan
3 Australia
4 West Germany
5 England
6 USSR
7 France
8 Spain
9 Argentina
10 India
11 Canada
12 Ireland

WOMEN'S WORLD CUP
Sydney, Australia, May 2–13

Pool A

AUSTRALIA 3 China 0
ENGLAND 1 Argentina 0
WEST GERMANY 2 Japan 0
ENGLAND 1 Japan 0
Argentina 1 Australia 1
WEST GERMANY 3 China 1
ENGLAND 2 China 0
AUSTRALIA 2 West Germany 1
Argentina 0 Japan 0
England 0 West Germany 0
CHINA 2 Argentina 0
AUSTRALIA 2 Japan 0
WEST GERMANY 3 Argentina 1
CHINA 1 Japan 1
Australia 0 England 0

FINAL TABLE

	P	W	D	L	F	A	Pts
1 Australia	5	5	0	0	14	4	10
2 England	5	3	1	1	15	10	7
3 West Germany	5	2	1	2	5	6	5
4 China	5	1	2	2	6	10	4
5 Argentina	5	1	1	3	10	14	3
6 Japan	5	0	1	4	10	16	1

Australia & England qualified for semi-finals

Pool B

CANADA 1 New Zealand 0
SOUTH KOREA 7 Spain 0
HOLLAND 3 United States 0
NEW ZEALAND 1 South Korea 0
Canada 1 United States 1
HOLLAND 3 Spain 0
HOLLAND 3 New Zealand 0
SOUTH KOREA 1 Canada 0
SPAIN 3 United States 1
NEW ZEALAND 6 United States 1
Holland 0 South Korea 0
SPAIN 3 Canada 0
SOUTH KOREA 9 United States 0
SPAIN 1 New Zealand 1
HOLLAND 2 Canada 0

FINAL TABLE

	P	W	D	L	F	A	Pts
1 Holland	5	4	1	0	11	0	9
2 South Korea	5	3	1	1	17	1	7
3 New Zealand	5	2	1	2	8	6	5
4 Spain	5	2	1	2	7	12	5
5 Canada	5	1	1	3	2	7	3
6 United States	5	0	1	4	3	22	1

Holland & South Korea qualified for semi-finals

SEMI-FINALS

HOLLAND 5 England 0
AUSTRALIA 2 South Korea 1

THIRD PLACE PLAY-OFF

SOUTH KOREA 3 England 2

FINAL

HOLLAND 3 Australia 1

FINAL STANDINGS
1 Holland
2 Australia
3 South Korea
4 England
5 Spain
6 China
7 New Zealand
8 West Germany
9 Argentina
10 Canada
11 Japan
12 United States

EUROPEAN CLUBS CUP
Frankfurt, W. Germany, Jun 1-4
Men
FINAL
Uhlenhorst MULHEIM (FRG) 2 Athletico Terrassa (Spa) 0

FINAL STANDINGS
1 Uhlenhorst Mulheim
2 Athletico Terrassa
3 Bloemendaal (Hol)
4 Frankfurt 1880 (FRG)
5 Royal Leopold (Bel)
6 Southgate (Eng)
7 Dinamo Alma Ata (USSR)
8 Lisnagarvey (Ire)
Women
FINAL
AMSTERDAM (HOL) 4 Guytech Western (Sco) 0

FINAL STANDINGS :
1 Amsterdam
2 Guytech Western
3 Kolos Borispol (USSR)
4 Campo de Madrid (Spa)
5 Pegasus (Ire)
6 Ealing (Eng)
7 Swansea (Wal)
8 Frankfurt 1880 (FRG)

EUROPEAN CUP WINNER'S CUP FINAL
(Inaugurated 1990)
Frankfurt W. Germany Jun 3
HOUNSLOW 3 Amsterdam 2
MEN'S EUROPEAN INDOOR CUP
(Inaugurated 1990)
Amiens, Mar 2–4
ROTWEISS COLOGNE 8 Amsterdam 4

WOMEN'S EUROPEAN CLUB INDOOR CHAMPIONSHIP
(Inaugurated 1990)
Groningen, Holland, Feb 23–25
BRANDENBURG BERLIN 4 Slough 3
POUNDSTRETCHER CUP FINALS
Luton, May 6
First Division
HAVANT 3 Hounslow 2
Second Division
NESTON 3 St. Albans 2
NATIONWIDE ANGLIA HA CUP FINAL
Luton, Apr 8
HAVANT 3 Stourport 0

WOMEN'S NATIONAL CLUBS INDOOR CHAMPIONSHIP
Crystal Palace, Feb 9
IPSWICH 4 Hightown 3
WOMEN'S NATIONAL CLUB CHAMPIONSHIP
Bournemouth, Apr 20–22
SUTTON COLDFIELD 1 Hightown 0
MEN'S COUNTY CHAMPIONSHIP FINAL
Sheffield, May 13
MIDDLESEX 2 Yorkshire 1
Middlesex's 3rd successive title

POUNDSTRETCHER NATIONAL LEAGUE
First Division

	P	W	D	L	F	A	Pts
1 (3) **Hounslow**	15	10	4	1	52	12	34
2 (8) E. Grinstead	15	11	1	3	26	8	34
3 (2) Havant	15	9	2	4	41	23	29
4 (9) Slough	15	7	7	1	37	19	28
5 (1) Southgate	15	8	3	4	21	18	27
6 (11) Stourport	15	6	5	4	23	19	23
7 (7) Teddington	15	7	2	6	24	23	23
8 (10) Welton	15	6	4	5	22	14	22
9 (12) ISCA	15	6	4	5	21	23	22
10 (6) Bromley	15	6	2	7	27	33	20
11 (5) Indian Gymkhana	15	5	4	6	27	25	19
12 (P) Cannock	15	6	0	9	20	37	18
13 (4) Old Loughtonians	15	4	2	9	18	36	14
14 (14) Wakefield	15	3	4	8	14	29	13
15 (13) *Harborne*	15	3	1	11	12	32	10
16 (P) *Reading*	15	0	1	14	10	44	1

Last year's positions in brackets

CHAMPIONS

OLYMPIC GAMES
First contested 1908
Men
1908 England
1920 Great Britain
1928 India
1932 India
1936 India
1948 India
1952 India
1956 India
1960 Pakistan
1964 India
1968 Pakistan
1972 West Germany
1976 New Zealand
1980 India
1984 Pakistan
1988 Great Britain
Most wins: 8 India
Women
First contested 1980
1980 Zimbabwe
1984 Holland
1988 Australia

WORLD CUP
Men
1971 Pakistan
1973 Holland
1975 India
1978 Pakistan
1982 Pakistan
1986 Australia
1990 Holland
Women
1974 Holland
1976 West Germany
1978 Holland
1981 West Germany
1983 Holland
1986 Holland
1990 Holland

WOMEN'S WORLD CHAMPIONSHIP
1975 England
1979 Holland

EUROPEAN CLUBS CUP
Men
1971 Frankfurt 1880 (FRG)
1972 Frankfurt 1880 (FRG)
1973 Frankfurt 1880 (FRG)
1974 Frankfurt 1880 (FRG)
1975 Frankfurt 1880 (FRG)
1976 Southgate (Eng)
1977 Southgate (Eng)
1978 Southgate (Eng)
1979 Klein Zwitserland (Hol)
1980 Slough (Eng)
1981 Klein Zwitserland (Hol)
1982 Dinamo Alma-Ata (USSR)
1983 Dinamo Alma-Ata (USSR)
1984 TG 1846 Frankental (FRG)
1985 Atletico Tarrasa (Spa)
1986 Kampong Utrecht (Hol)
1987 Bloemendaal (Hol)
1988 Uhlenhorst (FRG)
1989 Uhlenhorst (FRG)
1990 Uhlenhorst (FRG)
Women
1974 Harvetschuder Hamburg (FRG)
1975 Amsterdam (Hol)
1976 Amsterdam (Hol)
1977 Amsterdam (Hol)
1978 Amsterdam (Hol)
1979 Amsterdam (Hol)
1980 Amsterdam (Hol)
1981 Amsterdam (Hol)
1982 Amsterdam (Hol)
1983 HGC Wassenaar (Hol)
1984 HGC Wassenaar (Hol)
1985 HGC Wassenaar (Hol)
1986 HGC Wassenaar (Hol)
1987 HGC Wassenaar (Hol)
1988 Amsterdam (Hol)
1989 Amsterdam (Hol)
1990 Amsterdam (Hol)

ENGLISH LEAGUE CHAMPIONS
(Known as National League from 1989)
Men
1975 Bedfordshire Eagles
1976 Slough
1977 Southgate
1978 Southgate
1979 ISCA

1980 Slough
1981 Slough
1982 Slough
1983 Slough
1984 Neston
1985 East Grinstead
1986 East Grinstead
1987 Slough
1988 Southgate
1989 Southgate
1990 Hounslow

ENGLISH WOMEN'S CHAMPIONS
1979 Chelmsford
1980 Norton
1981 Sutton Coldfield
1982 Slough
1983 Slough
1984 Sheffield
1985 Ipswich
1986 Slough
1987 Ealing
1988 Ealing
1989 Ealing
1990 Sutton Coldfield

HOCKEY ASSOCIATION (HA) CUP
Men
1972 Hounslow
1973 Hounslow
1974 Southgate
1975 Southgate
1976 Nottingham
1977 Slough
1978 Guildford
1979 Slough
1980 Slough
1981 Slough
1982 Southgate
1983 Neston
1984 East Grinstead
1985 Southgate
1986 Southgate
1987 Southgate
1988 Southgate
1989 Hounslow
1990 Havant

1991

Men: Feb 8-10 Senior Indoor World Masters (Kelvin Hall, Glasgow); *Feb 22-24* European Cup (Birmingham); *Apr 26-28* Six Nations Tournament (Berlin, prov); *May 12* Poundstretcher League Cup final (Luton Town FC); *Jun 1-23* European Cup (Paris); *Jul 4-16* GB tour to Pakistan (prov)
Women: Mar 1-3 Home Counties Senior Tournament (Durham); *Mar 16* England v France (Wembley); *May 3* European Cup (Brussels)

HORSE RACING

A FLATTISH FLAT SEASON

The great drought of 1990 helped ensure that it was far from a great flat racing season. No obvious personality dominated the summer, certainly not a four-legged one. Despite the performances of the filly Salsabil and the sprinter Dayjur, it was a season aptly summed up when the St Leger was won by a horse named Snurge, providing the best argument yet for abolishing the race. None of these animals remotely managed to approach the steeplechaser Desert Orchid for popularity or panache.

Salsabil became the 46th horse to win both fillies' classics, for which her trainer John Dunlop credited the owner Sheikh Hamdan, who insisted she should run in The Oaks though Dunlop had doubts whether she would stay. The two then staged the one real piece of theatre of the season by supplementing the horse for the Irish Derby. There Salsabil established her credentials by beating the colts, something no filly had done since Gallinaria in 1900. Salsabil pulled out of the King George at Ascot because of the firm ground ("Hamlet without the princess," said *The Times*) but returned to win her fifth Group One race, the Prix Vermeille at Longchamp before failing in the Prix de L'Arc de Triomphe behind Saumarez, a colt sold out of Henry Cecil's yard to France in the spring.

Among those trailing in Salsabil's wake at The Curragh was the Epsom Derby winner Quest for Fame who was beaten into fifth place and found to be lame. The horse was retired for the season with its reputation far from secure. The 1990 Derby was a mess with only 126 entries, the lowest in peacetime since 1845, and a set of ridiculously inconclusive trials. Every few days saw a new market leader who would then disappear in injury or disgrace. Derby Day itself was cold, damp and windy with the crowd way below normal and a dreadful betting market (the largest bet was only £10,000). Quest For Fame's win was convincing enough but his inability to build on it did nothing to help the race recover its prestige. William Hill announced that Derby Day had been displaced by Cheltenham Gold Cup day as the second-biggest occasion of the year behind the Grand National.

Quest for Fame's win, however, represented an exceptional training achievement for Roger Charlton, Jeremy Tree's assistant for 12 years and now, following Tree's retirement, in his first year in charge at Beckhampton. Three days earlier Charlton had won the French Derby, the Prix du Jockey Club at Chantilly with his first classic runner and his first runner in France, Sanglamore. It was a £633,000 double for the owner Khalid Abdullah, Charlton and their jockey Pat Eddery, last achieved by Marcel Boussac, Charles Semblat and Rae Johnstone in 1950 with Galcador and Scratch II. The best tribute came from Tree: "I didn't think I had left him with any top-class horses," he said.

Charlton's successes suggested there was still a little glorious uncertainty left on the Flat, as did the triumphs of Tirol who became the third horse to win both the English and Irish 2,000 Guineas. Tirol cost only £14,000 and was owned not by an Arab prince but by the Horgan brothers, Irish cattle-dealers, at least eight of whom were spotted at Newmarket. "They engulfed the winner's enclosure," wrote Paul Hayward in *The Independent,* "as if heralding the end of war or taxation." When Tirol won again at The Curragh, the Cork anthem "The Banks of My Own Lovely Lee" emerged from the unsaddling enclosure as the Horgans gathered.

Another unsheikhly horse, the two-year-old Timeless Times, trained by Bill O'Gorman, equalled the total of 16 wins in a season shared by The Bard and another O'Gorman horse Provideo. He equalled Spindrifter's mark of 13 at Pontefract in a race called the Spindrifter Stakes.

ARAB EMINENCE

However, the usual suspects dominated the rest of the season. In Salsabil's absence, horses trained by Henry Cecil did a 1-2 in the King George, the first time this has happened. Belmez beat Old Vic by a neck. The result made no difference to Sheikh Mohammed who won either way, but Belmez's win was more than normally remarkable. After banging his tendon before the Derby, the horse was officially retired. Another Maktoum family horse, Sheikh Hamdan's Dayjur, was the outstanding sprinter, smashing the York five-furlong record by over a second in the Nunthorpe Stakes, a feat widely hailed as the greatest sprint performance ever. Jon Freeman in the *Sunday Times* compared it to Bob Beamon's leap in Mexico.

Though the Arab princes had other more serious preoccupations at home, their domination of British racing looked like continuing. The favourites for the 1991 2,000 Guineas included Mujtahid, Majlood, Mukaddamah and Habaayib. Graham Goode, the Channel Four racereader, was quoted as saying he thought the Arab owners might be starting to take the mickey. The only two-year-old with a non-Arabic name among the crop trained for Sheikh Hamdan by Tom Jones was a filly called Mrs Thatcher.

Henry Cecil and his wife Julie divorced: Julie announced plans to start training in Newmarket herself. Jack Berry became the first Northern trainer since Dobson Peacock in 1932 to train 100 winners in a season. Pat Eddery led the jockeys' table throughout the summer, through sheer energy as much as anything. He completed a century of winners on June 27, the fastest since Sir Gordon Richards on June 17 1949 and was on target to become the first flat jockey to ride 200 winners in a season since Sir Gordon in 1952. But he was run close - and in terms of prize money eclipsed - by Willie Carson, who had a remarkable year, especially in the big races.

At Salisbury on May 22 Carson became the fourth man to ride 3,000 winners in Britain and on August 24 he overhauled Doug Smith to move third on the all-time list behind Sir Gordon and Lester Piggott. In between, he had a phenomenal run which included becoming the third jockey (after Sir Gordon, of course, and Alec Russell) to ride six in a day at a meeting. It happened at Newcastle on June 30 at accumulated odds of 3,266 to.1. The previous day Carson had ridden five winners at Newmarket and Goodwood and the following day he took the Irish Derby. Lanfranco Dettori, 19, became the first teenager to ride 100 Flat winners since Lester Piggott in 1955. Dettori reached his century on August 27, Piggott on October 26.

THE RETURN OF LESTER

Other jockeys found life a little less rosy. Eleven were fined a total of £6,000 for refusing to obey instructions to start at Beverley on a dangerous track in 1989. "If this is justice I am not only a banana," wrote Monty Court in the *Sporting Life*, "but Portman Square enquiries might as well be conducted by melons."

Steve Cauthen was fined £1000 for withdrawing from a race at Leicester in May after weighing out; his fellow-jockeys had teased him that the horse, Nicholas Payne, was a rogue. Ian Johnson and Paul Cook were both forced to retire as a result of their injuries sustained in the Portland Handicap at Doncaster in 1989.

One lightweight, Allan Mackay, was acquitted of a £7m conspiracy to smuggle cocaine; another, Martin Fry, learned that he would never ride again because of a crippling spinal disease. Bob Curant, 41, a jockey for 25 years, decided to emigrate to Macau after riding 197 consecutive losers. Marco Paganini, leading jockey in Italy in 1989, died after being brought down at the notoriously dangerous Grossetto racecourse. Lester Piggott, 54, made an improbable return to race riding in three races at the Monterrico track, Lima, Peru. He received £12 prize money for one third place. He also rode in a couple of veteran's races in Ireland. On October 11, Piggott was granted a licence to ride regularly again. Newmarket publicans introduced a voluntary ID card scheme so stable lads and jockeys could be served without arguments. An unnamed jockey was reported to have conned a British Rail clerk at King's Cross into selling him

THE DESSIE SHOW

❝ To object too much to the hoopla surrounding Desert Orchid casts one in the role of the miserable preacher in the Dylan Thomas short story, who stands on a box on a beach and tells everyone that holidays are bad.**❞**
Jamie Reid, Independent on Sunday

"What a pity he was not owned by one of the old timers who kept horses for the duty for which they are bred, namely racing. Only in recent years has the idea sprung up of not racing a handicap certainty in the Grand National."
Richard Baerlein, The Guardian, *on Desert Orchid*

"HOW THE WINGED ANGEL WAS BROUGHT TO EARTH BY A DONKEY OFF THE BEACH"
Sun *headline*

"A triumph of hope over expectation, of genuine affection over the bleak ritual of scientific preparation."
Michael Calvin, Daily Telegraph, *on Norton, Coin's win*

"He was a terrible tempered horse until we gave him the bantams."
Sirrell Griffiths, trainer of Norton's Coin

Col. Piers Bengough, Her Majesty's Representative at Ascot: "I used to ride a few point-to-pointers for you, Mrs Griffiths.'
Mrs Griffiths: "Well, you may have. But what's your name?"
Exchange after the Gold Cup

"If Norton's Coin was 100-1 to win the Gold Cup on form, then he must have been a million to one on breeding...it's the sort of thing that gives hope to everyone - though some would also say it's the sort of thing that only goes to encourage people to keep useless damn mares and go to useless damn horses: well, you never know, do you? Look at Norton's Coin."
Sue Montgomery, Racing Post

"The jockeys are being penalised for skill and excellence. Graham gave that horse an inspired ride. You've never seen a happier horse come into the winners' enclosure."
Michael Caulfield, secretary of the Jockey's Association after Graham McCourt was banned for excessive whipping of Norton's Coin

"I'm completely with the stewards....The whip should be used with intelligence, not by mindless flogging."
Stan Mellor

"Sir: Your racing correspondent, Michael Seely, in writing 'Cavvie's Clown, who had lost 20 lengths at the start by his mulish behaviour' reveals that he has never served with mules. If he had, he would have learned that the mule is intelligent, sensitive, resilient and even stoical. Does he know that a mule, Lord Fauntleroy, won in 1976 the Bicentennial Transcontinental Horse Race of 3,100 miles in the time of 98 days? No mule would have tolerated the whips used at Cheltenham.**❞**
Letter to The Times *from Lt-Col C H T MacFetridge*

a half-fare ticket to Edinburgh; he then tried to pay for the ticket by Access.

No one during the Flat season matched the charisma of the extraordinary steeplechaser Desert Orchid. The amazing grey had spectacular victories in both the King George VI Chase and the Irish Grand National (his 32nd win and 30th on a right-handed track) and the author Dr Desmond Morris suggested that a white horse should be carved on to chalk hillside to commemorate him.

Even when he lost he managed to do so in a quite improbably theatrical manner. Dessie's attempt to retain the Cheltenham Gold Cup ended when he was beaten into third place behind a 100 to 1 shot Norton's Coin, the longest-priced Gold Cup winner ever. The successful trainer was a Carmarthenshire farmer, Sirrell Griffiths, who only went for the big race by accident. The horse was ineligible for his first-choice race at the festival, the Cathcart, and he missed the deadline for his second-choice, the Mildmay of Flete. After getting up at 3.45 am to milk the cows, Griffiths drove the horse box to the races himself. He planned to spend the prize money on more cows. Norton's Coin himself was considered a foul-tempered brute until Griffiths put some bantams in with him to stop him from lashing out. The victory was soured when the winning jockey,

Graham McCourt, was suspended for three days for over-use of the whip.

AN OUTSIDER'S GOLD CUP

Longest-priced winners			Longest-priced placed horses		
33-1	Gay Donald	1955	100-1	Garde Toi	1950
33-1	L'Escargot	1970	100-1	Stoney Crossing	1965
100-1	Norton's Coin	1990	100-1	Sunset Cristo	1982
			100-1	Norton's Coin	1990

Norton Coin's sire, Mount Cassino, was mainly used to cover ponies and cobs and the dam, Grove Chance never raced. They just happened to be on the farm together one spring and produced their champion in the casual manner common in human mating but not among racehorses. In contrast, the Champion Hurdle winner, Kribensis, was the product of more scientific breeding and the slightly more upmarket combination of Sheikh Mohammed and Michael Stoute. He was the only jumper in Stoute's 191-strong yard. Course records were broken on the firm ground in 11 of the 18 Cheltenham Festival races.

NATIONAL HEROES

The Grand National went to Mr Frisk, owned by an 83-year-old American, Lois Duffy, and ridden by Marcus Armytage, Newmarket correspondent of the *Racing Post*. Durham Edition came second for the second time. Only one horse went down at the remodelled Becher's ("Becher's Drain" snorted one racegoer); the RSPCA received "dozens of phone calls". Two other horses died less obviously during the race and three horses were killed on the first day of the Aintree meeting, all in hurdle races. Mr Frisk went on to become the first horse to complete the National-Whitbread Gold Cup double. The Jockey Club announced that 174 horses were killed in national hunt racing in 1989, a slight drop.

The more workaday races were again dominated by the same pair: Martin Pipe and Peter Scudamore. Helped by the mildest winter in memory, Pipe trained the once-unthinkable figure of 224 winners, beating the record he set a year earlier by 16. No one was surprised by this any more: a £1 level stake on all his runners would have shown a loss of £13.78 before tax. His other half, Scudamore, actually declined slightly, dropping from 221 winners to a trifling 170, still far more than anyone else has ever ridden; he missed most of the last six weeks of the season with a wrist injury. Scudamore's big moment came when he equalled (Regal Ambition at Worcester) and then passed (Arden at Ascot) John Francome's total of 1,139 jumping winners. Of these, 552 had come since July 1986. Pipe insisted that he would not be trying to continue the pace of winners and suggested he might settle for about 100 in 1990-91. No one believed him. Fulke Walwyn retired 50 years after training his first winner.

Of Scudamore's rivals, Michael Hammond, Reg Crank, Phil Tuck and (through injury) Niall Madden all retired. Steve Smith-Eccles kept going, however, became the eighth jump jockey to pass 700 winners and, on the concrete going at the start of the 90-91 season, rode nine consecutive winners, one short of the record. The new jump season started at Bangor on the hottest day of the century; it took $4^1/4$ million gallons of water from the Dee to make the track raceable. During the drought, there were complaints about this kind of activity from householders banned from putting hosepipes on their lawns. Nick Lees, clerk of the course at Newmarket, suggested that beer-drinking should be banned rather than racing: "Do you know it takes 11 gallons of water for every pint?"

THE RISE AND RISE OF MARTIN PIPE

	Winners		PIPE'S LANDMARKS.
1974-5	1		
1975-6	5		**1988-89**
1976-7	5	50	Afford, Ascot Oct 29
1977-8	2	100	Delkusha, Taunton, Dec 29
1978-9	6	150	Beau Ranger, Worcester, Mar 1
1979-80	12	200	Anti Matter, Stratford, May 19
1980-1	14		
1981-2	20		**1989-90**
1982-3	23	50	Walk of Life, Wincanton, Oct 26
1983-4	32	100	King's Rank, Haydock, Dec 14
1984-5	51	150	Minnohoma, Newbury Mar 3
1985-6	79	200	Don't be Late or Walk of Life,
1986-7	106		simultaneous at Devon and Fontwell,
1987-8	129		3.07, May 7
1988-9	208		
1989-90	224		

All-weather racing came to Britain on dirt tracks at Lingfield and Southwell providing low-quality races for desperate horses and desperate punters. Early meetings were cancelled due to fog (November 14) rain (February 8) and gales (February 27), which rather defeated the object. At one Southwell race day, the attendance was only 137 and the experiment was in danger of being laughed out. It came into its own unexpectedly; in July Southwell staged unscheduled all-weather racing because the turf track was unfinished and achieved larger fields than rival meetings with hard ground. Trainers then demanded regular all-weather racing in summer.

Four great horses died: Brigadier Gerard (21), Allez France (19), The Minstrel (16) and Comedy of Errors (24). De Pluvinel, aged 17, won the Royal Artillery Gold Cup at Sandown. Three great racecourses died: Phoenix Park in Dublin, Suffolk Downs in Massachusetts and Hialeah in Florida. Comanche Indians planned to set up their own racecourse at Lawton Downs, Oklahoma; state governments cannot tax Indian gambling revenues. The first all-German race meeting since the building of the Berlin Wall was held at Hoppegarten, East Berlin. Racing resumed in Vietnam for the first time since the Communist takeover. Andy Orkney became the first British jockey to ride a winner in the Soviet Union on Altan at Piatygorsk in the Caucasus. The Palio in Siena, the bareback gallop round the city's main square which dates back to the Middle Ages, came under threat from animal rights campaigners.

SEX AND DRUGS....

On the day Mr Frisk won the Grand National, an horse called Mister Frisky equalled Citation's US record of 16 consecutive wins. However, Mister Frisky came only eighth in the Kentucky Derby behind Unbridled, whose trainer Carl Nafzger commentated for the 92-year-old wheelchair-bound owner Frances Genter. Jockey Sylvester Carmouche was suspended for ten years after a race in thick fog at Delta Downs, Louisiana, in which he rode round only once, sneaking into the pack on the final turn and winning by 24 lengths. Uptown Swell, one of the leading US steeplechasers, drowned during swimming exercise, apparently after being stung by a bee. "I always thought there were 200 ways you could lose a racehorse," said his owner Virginia Kraft Payson. "This was 201." America's greatest jockey, Willie Shoemaker, finally retired in February aged 58 after 40,351 races, 8,833 winners and an eight-month retirement tour that some people found rather tacky. A less great jockey, P J Lydon (7 stone 5 lbs), came third in an eating contest at Rusty's restaurant in Manhattan, devouring 25 baby back ribs in three minutes. The FBI clandestinely bought its own horse to run at Finger Lakes, New York, in the hope that it would perform badly and get involved in a race-fixing scheme; the plan failed because the horse started winning.

Gary Moore, former champion jockey in both France and Hong Kong, received a $5\frac{1}{2}$ year worldwide ban after being found guilty of 66 betting-related charges by the Hong Kong Royal Jockey Club. Gambling revenues collected by the club, the only legal betting outlet in the colony, reached £3,185 million in 1989, £55 per head of the population. Illegal off-course betting revenue is thought to be far higher. Three policemen in Hong Kong were charged with procuring a 17-year-old girl for sex with a jockey in exchange for racing tips. In nearby Macao, two Australian-born racing writers, Chris Collins and Ian Manning, were killed when their car disappeared from a bridge.

An equine vet, Dr Alistair Fraser, claimed that Devon Loch's famous collapse, yards from victory in the 1956 Grand National, was the result of an iliac thrombosis which can cause a horse's legs to give way suddenly. Two horses at the St Leger meeting, Norwich and Bravefoot, were found to have been doped by a common equine tranquiliser. A London car dealer, James Laming, on trial for cocaine dealing, was said in court to have invented an ultra-sonic stun gun disguised as a pair of binoculars which caused Ile de Chypre to swerve and fall while leading in the King George V Handicap at Ascot in 1988. The story was never proved or disproved but Laming was sentenced to 14 years in jail anyway.

Tim Smith, rider of Rossa Prince at Mr Groschen's Hunt point-to-point at Tweseldown managed to lose a walkover when his mount bolted out of his horsebox and was only caught after the race. Smith was also fined £25 for declaring the wrong colours. On the same day, a two-horse ladies' race produced no winner because the jockeys kept falling off; one of the riders retired because she injured herself with her own whip. Mrs Thatcher began attending race meetings and was spotted at Towcester and Newbury. Ascot banned jeans from the Tatts enclosure; a reader of the fanzine *Racing Ghost* suggested that Silver Ring punters should form vigilante groups and eject anyone wearing a suit and tie.

1990

THE CLASSICS
General Accident 1000 Guineas
Newmarket, May 3, 1 mile

1 SALSABIL	Willie Carson	6-4f
2 Heart of Joy	Walter Swinburn	4-1
3 Negligent	Pat Eddery	11-2
4 Free at Last	Tony Clark	16-1
5 Palace Street	John Williams	100-1
6 Sally Rous	Gary Carter	14-1
7 Raa	George Duffield	50-1
8 In the Groove	Steve Cauthen	11-1
9 Lakeland Beauty	Billy Newnes	100-1
10 Hasbah	Richard Hills	8-1

Trainer: John Dunlop, Arundel
Owner: Hamdan Al-Maktoum
Time: 1m 38,06s
Distance: 3/4 length
Carson became the 22nd jockey to ride the winners of all the British Classics

General Accident 2000 Guineas
Newmarket, May 5, 1 mile

1 TIROL	Michael Kinane	9-1
2 Machiavellian	Freddy Head	6-4f
3 Anshan	Walter Swinburn	6-1
4 Rock City	Bruce Raymond	14-1
5 Septieme Ciel	Guy Guignard	18-1
6 Welney	Gary Carter	66-1
7 Elmaamul	Willie Carson	12-1
8 Sure Sharp	Steve Cauthen	9-1
9 Now Listen	Pat Eddery	17-2
10 Rami	Michael Roberts	33-1

11 Lord of the Field	George Duffield	50-1
12 Dashing Blade	John Matthias	25-1
13 Raj Waki	Ray Cochrane	20-1
14 Swordsmith	Willie Ryan	250-1

Trainer: Richard Hannon, East Everleigh
Owner: John Horgan
Time: 1m 35,84s
(Fastest time since introduction of electric timing at Newmarket in 1952, beating Nashwan's 1989 record)
Distance: 2 lengths

Ever Ready Derby
Epsom, Jun 6, 1 mile 4f

1 QUEST FOR FAME	Pat Eddery	7-1
2 Blue Stag	Cash Asmussen	8-1
3 Elmaamul	Willie Carson	10-1
4 Kaheel	Michael Roberts	33-1
5 Karinga Bay	Brian Rouse	14-1
6 Duke of Paducah	Ray Cochrane	14-1
7 Zoman	Richard Quinn	6-1
8 Treble Eight	Bruce Raymond	66-1
9 Linamix	Gerald Mosse	11-2
10 Missionary Ridge	Michael Hills	50-1
11 Digression	Walter Swinburn	14-1
12 Sober Mind	Alan Munro	100-1
13 Bookcase	John Williams	150-1
14 Razeen	Steve Cauthen	9-2f
15 Bastille Day	Stephen Craine	100-1
16 River God	Michael Kinane	28-1
17 Aromatic	Tony Clark	100-1
18 Mr Brooks	Pat Shanahan	66-1

Trainer:Roger Charlton, Beckhampton
Owner: Prince Khalid Abdulla
Time: 2m 37.6s
Distance: 3 lengths

Gold Seal Oaks
Epsom, Jun 9, 1.mile 4f

1	SALSABIL	Willie Carson	2-1f
2	Game Plan	Basil Marcus	50-1
3	Knight's Baroness	Richard Quinn	16-1
4	In the Groove	Cash Asmussen	85-40
5	Ahead	Ray Cochrane	16-1
6	Cameo Performance	Pat Eddery	25-1
7	Gharam	Michael Roberts	12-1
8	Kartajana	Walter Swinburn	7-2

Trainer:John Dunlop, Arundel
Owner: Hamdan Al-Maktoum
Time: 2m 38,70s
Distance: 5 lengths

St.Leger
Doncaster, Sep 15, 1.mile 6f 127yd

1	SNURGE	Richard Quinn	7-2
2	Hellenic	Walter Swinburn	2-1f
3	River God	Steve Cauthen	100-30
4	Rubicund	Willie Carson	16-1
5	Great Marquess	Pat Eddery	11-1
6	Karinga Bay	Brian Rouse	11-1
7	Hajade	Lanfranco Dettori	9-1
8	Pier Damiani	Michael Roberts	100-1

Trainer: Paul Cole, Wantage
Owner: Martin Arbib
Time: 3m 08,78s
Distance: ³/₄ length
Snurge was the first maiden to win the St Leger since Night Hawk in 1913

❝ We wish to petition you regarding the serious plight of your subjects employed in the racing industry, many of whom are living on the edge, if not actually in poverty. The racing industry is not a poor one...We are sure you would not wish the pleasure of so many to depend on the hardship of so few.❞
Petition to the Queen from Labour MPs Patrick Duffy and Alan Meale

❝If the members of the Jockey Club were ever to appear on Mastermind it would be in their best interests not to choose racing as their specified subject.❞
Alistair Down, Sporting Life Weekender

❝They dope test 80 per cent of my winners and learn nothing. I don't want to know what makes them win, I want to know what stops them.❞
Jenny Pitman, trainer

❝We are in real danger of throwing away everything that made the game great a generation ago. It is ludicrous that virtually all the best horses are owned by the same few people and trained in the same few stables. It is ludicrous that entries for the Derby should be as low as 120-odd. It is ludicrous that only the favoured few, of breeders, owners and trainers, should be allowed even the opportunity of achieving success.❞
Tony Morris, Racing Post

❝You would never have guessed from the commentary during or after the race that anything had darkened the day except, perhaps 'they come to the Canal Turn where there's a major obstruction after an incident on the first circuit'. Any traveller on the Underground would recognise that we are now out of English and into euphemism. An incident means that some benighted soul has thrown himself under a train. Roll-A-Joint broke his neck at the Canal Turn.❞
Nancy Banks-Smith, The Guardian

❝From a spectator's point of view, Newmarket is the worst course in the country. No, let's not mess about, from a spectator's point of view Newmarket is the worst course in the world. It may even be that there is no sporting event anywhere on earth, except possibly the Whitbread Round the World yacht race and that 2,000-mile husky and sledge marathon across the north of Canada, in which the spectator has as little opportunity to see what is actually going on as he does in a race down the Rowley Mile, never mind an absurdity like the Cesarewitch.❞
Paul Haigh, Racing Post

❝Doncaster people don't get anything out of it, not even a special deal to get in. The councillors pretend to be tinpot sheikhs...It is an outrage to every Labour party member in the country.❞
Ron Rose, former Labour councillor, on the municipal racecourse

MOST CLASSIC WINS (JOCKEYS) 1946-90

	Derby	Oaks	1000	2000	Leger
29 Lester Piggott	9	6	2	4	8
15 Willie Carson	3	4	1	4	3
10 Rae Johnstone	3	3	2	0	2
9 Steve Cauthen	2	2	1	1	3
8 Pat Eddery	3	2	0	2	1
8 Joe Mercer	0	1	2	1	4
7 Edgar Britt	0	2	2	1	2
7 Yves Saint-Martin	1	2	2	1	1
7 Charlie Smirke	2	0	1	2	2
6 Harry Carr	1	1	1	0	3
6 Eddie Hide	1	1	2	0	2
6 Walter Swinburn	2	2	1	1	0

Prix de L'Arc de Triomphe
Longchamp, Oct 7, 2400 metres

1	SAUMAREZ	Gérald Mossé
2	Epervier Bleu	Dominic Boeuf
3	Snurge	Richard Quinn

Trainer: Nicholas Clement

IRISH CLASSICS
Airlie Coolmore 2000 Guineas
The Curragh, May 19, 1 mile
1 TIROL	Pat Eddery	5-4f
2 Royal Academy	John Reid	4-1
3 Lotus Pool	Michael Kinane	14-1

Trainer: Richard Hannon, Marlborough

Goffs 1000 Guineas
The Curragh, May 26, 1 mile
1 IN THE GROOVE	Steve Cauthen	5-1
2 Heart of Joy	Walter Swinburn	4-6f
3 Performing Arts	Michael Hills	5-1

Trainer: David Elsworth, Fordingbridge

Derby
The Curragh, Jul 1, 1 mile 4 furlongs
1 SALSABIL	Willie Carson	11-4
2 Deploy	Walter Swinburn	16-1
3 Belmez	Steve Cauthen	4-1

Trainer: John Dunlop, Arundel

Oaks
The Curragh, Jul 14, 1 mile 4 furlongs
1 KNIGHTS BARONESS	Richard Quinn	13-8f
2 Atoll	Gary Moore	5-1
3 Assertion	Declan Gillespie	50-1

Trainer: Paul Cole, Wantage

St.Leger
The Curragh, Sep 22, 1 mile 6 furlongs
1 IBN BEY	Richard Quinn	5-1
2 Mr. Pintips	Declan Gillespie	25-1
3 Braashee	Michael Roberts	5-1

Trainer: Paul Cole, Wantage

FRENCH CLASSICS
Poule d'Essai des Poulains (2000 Guineas)
Longchamp, May 6, 1600 metres
1 LINAMIX	Freddy Head	
2 Zoman	Tommy Quinn	
3 Funambule	Guy Guignard	

Trainer: Francois Boutin, France

Poule d'Essai des Pouliches (1000 Guineas)
Longchamp, May 13, 1600 metres
1 HOUSEPROUD	Pat Eddery	
2 Pont Aven	Alain Lequeux	
3 Gharam	Michael Roberts	

Trainer: André Fabré, France

Prix du Jockey Club (Derby)
Chantilly, June 3, 2400 metres
1 SANGLAMORE	Pat Eddery	
2 Epervier Bleu	Dominic Boeuf	
3 Erdelistan	Tony Cruz	

Trainer: Roger Charlton, Beckhampton

Prix de Diane Hermes (Oaks)
Chantilly, June 10, 2400 metres
1 RAHFA	Willie Carson	
2 Moon Cactus	Steve Cauthen	
3 Air de Rein	Alain Badel	

Trainer: Henry Cecil, Newmarket

US TRIPLE CROWN
Kentucky Derby
Churchill Downs, May 5, 1 mile 2 furlongs
1 UNBRIDLED	Craig Peret	
2 Summer Squall	Pat Day	
3 Pleasant Tap	Kent Desormeaux	

Trainer: Carl Nafzger

Preakness Stakes
Pimlico, Maryland, May 19, 1 mile $1^1/2$ furlongs
1 SUMMER SQUALL	Pat Day	
2 Unbridled	Craig Peret	
3 Mister Frisky	Gary Stevens	

Trainer: Neil Howard

Belmont Stakes
Belmont Park, New York, Jun 9, 1 mile 4 furlongs
1 GO AND GO	Michael Kinane	
2 Thirty Six Red	Mike Smith	
3 Baron de Vaux	Jean Cruguet	

Trainer: Dermot Weld, Ireland

HIT FOR SIX

GORDON RICHARDS		ALEC RUSSELL		WILLIE CARSON	
Chepstow, Oct 4 1933		Bogside, Jul 19 1957		Newcastle, Jun 30 1990	
Manner	4-6f	Double Up	2-5f	Arousal	Evens f
Brush Past	Evens f	Cligarry	2-1f	Soweto	5-2f
Miss B	7-4f	Wage Claim	100-8	Al Maheb	9-2
Arcona	4-6f	Courtlier	8-1	Terminus	8-1
Red Horizon	7-4f	Newton	8-13f	Tadwin	5-1
Delicia	5-4f	Roselime	11-8f	Hot Desert	4-7f

RICHARDS and RUSSELL went through the card. There were seven races at Newcastle; CARSON came last of six in the third race on Parliament Piece

THE BIG HANDICAPS

Venue/Date/Distance	Winner	Trainer	Jockey	Price
Doncaster, Mar 24, 1m William Hill LINCOLN HANDICAP	EVICHSTAR	Jimmy Fitzgerald	Alan Munro	33-1
Kempton Park, May 7, 1m JUBILEE HANDICAP STAKES	LANGTRY LADY	Michael Ryan	Neil Gwilliams	14-1
Chester, May 9, 2 m 2f 97 yd Ladbroke CHESTER CUP	TRAVELLING LIGHT	Lynda Ramsden	Alan Munro	5-2f
Royal Ascot, Jun 20, 1m ROYAL HUNT CUP	PONTENUOVO	David Elsworth	Gary Bardwell	50-1
Royal Ascot, Jun 22, 6f WOKINGHAM STAKES	KNIGHT OF MERCY	Richard Hannon	Pat Eddery	16-1

Newcastle, Jun 30, 2m
Newcastle Brown Ale

Race	Winner	Trainer	Jockey	Price
NORTHUMBERLAND PLATE	AL MAHEN	Alec Stewart	Willie Carson	9-2
York, Jul 14, 1m 2f 110yd				
John Smith's MAGNET CUP	ERADICATE	Peter Calver	Billy Newnes	15-2
Goodwood, Jul 31, 6f				
William Hill STEWARDS' CUP	KNIGHT OF MERCY	Richard Hannon	Bruce Raymond	14-1
Goodwood, Aug 2,1m				
Schweppes GOLDEN MILE	MARCH BIRD	John Sutcliffe	Nicky Adams	15-1
Ripon, Aug 18, 6f				
The Tote GREAT ST WILFRID HANDICAP	FASCINATION WALTZ	John Mackie	Gary Carter	9-2
York, Aug 22, 1m 6f				
Tote EBOR HANDICAP	FURTHER FLIGHT	Barry Hills	Michael Hills	7-1jf
Ayr, Sep 21, 6f				
Ladbroke AYR GOLD CUP	FINAL SHOT	Peter Easterby	John Lowe	12-1
Ascot, Sep 29, 1 m 4 f				
Tote FESTIVAL HANDICAP STAKES	SECRET SOCIETY	Maurice Camacho	Nicky Connorton	20-1

ffHe's fourth, Mrs Genter...he's third, Mrs Genter...he's second, Mrs Genter...he's taking the lead, Mrs Genter...he's a winner, he's a winner, he's a winner, you've won the Kentucky Derby for the 92-year-old, wheelchair-bound owner.

Carl Nafzger, trainer of Unbridled, commentating on the Kentucky Derby for the 92-year-old, wheelchair-bound owner.

"The publicity I am given is totally out of proportion to my ability as a rider - I honestly believe that if I were a man I would be given little or none at all."

Gee Armytage, woman jockey

"It's amazing. It's hard enough to train 100 winners in a season, let alone before Christmas."

Gordon Richards, trainer, on his rival Martin Pipe

"The policy is to run them. They are racehorses, aren't they? They win damn all in their boxes. If they are fit and well, run the buggers. If they don't come off on the Flat, you can soon jump the so-and-so's. Let's go to the races and have some fun."

Mike Channon, new trainer

"You know something? Sometimes I wake and think: God's been good."

Clive Brittain, trainer

"It's was hard to begin with. We all lived in a caravan and on Sundays I would boil a kettle of water for a wash and take the family out for a meal at the Forton service station on the M6."

Jack Berry, trainer

"This silly boy will not go on waving. I know, because I'll smack his face if he does.**ff**

John McCririck, Channel Four Racing

TWO-YEAR-OLD RACES

Venue/Date/Distance Race	Winner	Trainer	Jockey	Price
Royal Ascot, Jun 19, 6f				
COVENTRY STAKES	MAC'S IMP	Bill O'Gorman	Alan Munro	2-1f
Royal Ascot, Jun 20, 5f (fillies)				
QUEEN MARY STAKES	ON TIPTOES	Jim Leigh	Dean McKeown	8-1
Royal Ascot, Jun 21, 5f				
NORFOLK STAKES	LINE ENGAGED	David Elsworth	Steve Cauthen	14-1
Salisbury, Jun 28, 6f				
Veuve Cliquot CHAMPAGNE STAKES	ANJIZ	Alex Scott	Pat Eddery	1-2f
Newmarket, Jul 11 6f (fillies)				
Hillsdown CHERRY HINTON STAKES	CHICARICA	John Gosden	Walter Swinburn	9-4f
Newmarket, Jul 11 6f				
Anglia Television JULY STAKES	MUJTAHID	Robert Armstrong	Willie Carson	2-1
Goodwood, Aug 1, 6f				
Scottish Equitable RICHMOND STAKES	MAC'S IMP	Bill O'Gorman	Alan Munro	2-1f
York, Aug 22, 6f				
Scottish Equitable GIMCRACK STAKES	MUJTAHID	Robert Armstrong	Willie Carson	1-2f
York, Aug 23, 6f				
Pacemaker Update LOWTHER STAKES	ONLY YOURS	Richard Hannon	Bruce Raymond	8-1
Newmarket, Aug 25, 7f				
*Tattersalls Tiffany HIGHFLYER STAKES	FLYING BRAVE	John Dunlop	Willie Carson	2-1f
Doncaster, Sep 12, 1m (fillies)				
MAY HILL EBF STAKES	MAJMU	John Gosden	Willie Carson	6-1
Doncaster, Sep 13, 6f 110yd				
*Tattersalls Tiffany YORKSHIRE FILLIES STAKES	NAZOO	Jim Bolger	Christy Roche	6-1

Doncaster, Sep 14, 7f
Laurent-Perrier CHAMPAGNE STAKES   BOG TROTTER   Willie Haggas   Nigel Day   8-1
Doncaster, Sep 15, 5f
FLYING CHILDERS STAKES   DISTINCTLY NORTH   Jack Berry   Pat Eddery   6-4f
Ascot, Sep 29, 1m
Royal Lodge William Hill STAKES   MUJAAZIF   Michael Stoute   Walter Swinburn 11-2
Ascot, Sep 29, 1m
Brent Walker FILLIES' MILE   SHAMSHIR   Luca Comani   Frankie Dettori   11-2
*These races, officially worth only about £20,000, carried bonuses of £500,000 paid directly by the sponsors to the winning owners. These do not count in any lists of prize money but makes the races the richest in Britain by far.

THREE-YEAR-OLD RACES

Venue/Date/Distance Race	Winner	Trainer	Jockey	Price
Newmarket, Apr 17, 7f NELL GWYN STAKES	HEART OF JOY	Michael Stoute	Walter Swinburn	5-6f
Newmarket, Apr 18, 7f Ladbroke EUROPEAN FREE HANDICAP	ANSHAN	John Gosden	Pat Eddery	9-2
Newmarket, Apr 19, 1m Charles Heidsieck CRAVEN STAKES	TIROL	Richard Hannon	Pat Eddery	9-2
Newbury, Apr 20, 7f 60yd Gainsborough Stud FRED DARLING STAKES	SALSABIL	John Dunlop	Willie Carson	11-4
Newbury, Apr 21, 7f S & F GREENHAM STAKES	ROCK CITY	Richard Hannon	Pat Eddery	4-1
Sandown Park, Apr 21 1 m 2 f Guardian CLASSIC TRIAL	DEFENSIVE PLAY	Guy Harwood	Pat Eddery	7-4f
Chester, May 8, 1m 4f 65yd Dalham CHESTER VASE	BELMEZ	Henry Cecil	Steve Cauthen	8-13f
Lingfield Park, May 12, 1m 3f 106yd Calor DERBY TRIAL	ROCK HOPPER	Michael Stoute	Walter Swinburn	9-4
Lingfield Park, May 12, 1m 3f 106yd (fillies) Marley Roof Tile OAKS TRIAL STAKES	RAHFA	Henry Cecil	Steve Cauthen	3-13f
York, May 15, 1m 2f 110yd (fillies) Tattersalls MUSIDORA STAKES	IN THE GROOVE	David Elsworth	Ray Cochrane	15-2
York, May 16, 1m 2f 110yd William Hill DANTE STAKES	SANGLAMORE	Roger Charlton	Pat Eddery	11-2
Goodwood, May 23, 1 m 2 f NM Financial PREDOMINATE STAKES	RAZEEN	Henry Cecil	Steve Cauthen	7-2
York, Jun 16, 6f William Hill TROPHY HANDICAP	KATZAKEENA	Peter Makin	Bruce Raymond	7-2f
Royal Ascot, Jun 19, 1m 4f KING EDWARD VII STAKES	PRIVATE TENDER	Henry Cecil	Steve Cauthen	11-4f
Royal Ascot, Jun 19, 1m ST JAMES'S PALACE STAKES	SHAVIAN	Henry Cecil	Steve Cauthen	11-1
Royal Ascot, Jun 20, 1m CORONATION STAKES	CHIMES OF FREEDOM	Henry Cecil	Steve Cauthen	11-2
Royal Ascot, Jun 20, 7f JERSEY STAKES	SALLY ROUS	Geoff Wragg	Gary Carter	20-1
Royal Ascot, Jun 20, 2m 45yd QUEEN'S VASE	RIVER GOD	Henry Cecil	Steve Cauthen	6-4f
Royal Ascot, Jun 21, 1m 4 f RIBBLESDALE STAKES	HELLENIC	Michael Stoute	Walter Swinburn	6-1
Haydock Park, Jul 7, 1m 4f (fillies) LANCASHIRE OAKS	PHARIAN	Clive Brittain	Frankie Dettori	14-1
Goodwood, Jul 31, 1 m 4 f GORDON STAKES	KARINGA BAY	Denys Smith	Brian Rouse	13-2
Goodwood, Aug 3, 1m 2f Leslie & Godwin SPITFIRE HANDICAP	KAWTUBAN	Roger Charlton	Willie Carson	7-1
York, Aug 21, 1m 4f GREAT VOLTIGEUR STAKES	BELMEZ	Henry Cecil	Steve Cauthen	1-2f
York, Aug 22 1m 6f 127yd (fillies) Aston Upthorpe YORKSHIRE OAKS	HELLENIC	Michael Stoute	Willie Carson	100-30
Doncaster, Sep 12, 1m 6f 127yd (fillies) AF Budge PARK HILL STAKES	MADAME DUBOIS	Henry Cecil	Steve Cauthen	2-1f

OTHER MAJOR BRITISH RACES

Venue/Date/Distance Race	Winner	Trainer	Jockey	Price
Newmarket, Apr 18, 1m 1f				
EARL OF SEFTON EBF STAKES	TERIMON	Clive Brittain	Ray Cochrane	20-1
Newbury, Apr 21, 1m 4f				
Lanes End JOHN PORTER EBF STAKES	BRUSH ASIDE	Henry Cecil	Steve Cauthen	9-2f
Epsom, Apr 25, 1m 1f				
Racal-Vodaphone BLUE RIBAND TRIAL STAKES	ETON LAD	Neville Callaghan	Pat Eddery	6-1
Sandown Park, Apr 27, 1m				
Trusthouse Forte MILE	MARKOF--DISTINCTION	Luca Cumani	Frankie Dettori	6-4f
Newmarket, May 4, 1m 4f				
General Accident JOCKEY CLUB STAKES	ROSEATE TURN	Luca Cumani	Frankie Dettori	17-2
Newmarket, May 5, 5f				
PALACE HOUSE STAKES	STATOBLEST	Luca Cumani	Frankie Dettori	5-6f
Chester, May 10, 1m 5ft 88yd				
ORMONDE STAKES	BRAASHEE	Alec Stewart	Michael Roberts	6-1
York, May 17, 1m 6f				
Kosset YORKSHIRE CUP	BRAASHEE	Alec Stewart	Michael Roberts	11-8f
Newbury, May 18, 1m				
Juddmonte LOCKINGE STAKES	SAFAWAN	Michael Stoute	Walter Swinburn	5-1
Sandown Park, May 28, 2m				
Mappin & Webb HENRY II EBF STAKES	TEAMSTER	Michael Stoute	Walter Swinburn	2-1f
Epsom, Jun 7, 1 1m 4f				
Hanson CORONATION CUP	IN THE WINGS	André Fabré	Cash Asmussen	15-8f
Royal Ascot, Jun 19, 1m				
PRINCE OF WALES'S STAKES	BATSHOOF	Ben Hanbury	Pat Eddery	2-1f
Royal Ascot, Jun 21, 2m 4f				
GOLD CUP	ASHAL	Harry Thomson Jones	Richard Hills	14-1
Royal Ascot, Jun 21, 6f				
CORK AND ORRERY STAKES	GREAT COMMOTION	Alex Scott	Pat Eddery	5-1
Royal Ascot, Jun 22, 5f				
KING'S STAND STAKES	DAYJUR	Dick Hearn	Willie Carson	11-2
Royal Ascot, Jun 22, 1m 4f				
HARDWICKE STAKES	ASSATIS	Guy Harwood	Ray Cochrane	50-1
Sandown Park , Jul 7, 1m 2f				
Coral ECLIPSE STAKES	ELMAAMUL	Dick Hern	Willie Carson	13-2
Newmarket, Jul 10, 1m 4f				
PRINCESS OF WALES'S STAKES	SAPIENCE	Jimmy Fitzgerald	Pat Eddery	11-2
Newmarket, Jul 11, 1m				
CHILD STAKES	CHIMES OF FREEDOM	Henry Cecil	Steve Cauthen	4-6f
Newmarket, Jul 12, 6f				
Carroll Foundation JULY STAKES	ROYAL ACADEMY	Vincent O'Brien	John Reid	7-1
Chepstow, Jul 12, 1m 4f				
Welsh Brewers PREMIER STAKES	PIRATE ARMY	Luca Cumani	Frankie Dettori	4-9f
Royal Ascot, Jul 28, 1m 4f				
KING GEORGE VI & QUEEN ELIZABETH DIAMOND STAKES	BELMEZ	Henry Cecil	Michael Kinane	15-2
Goodwood, Aug 1, 1m				
SUSSEX STAKES	DISTANT RELATIVE	Barry Hills	Willie Carson	4-1
Goodwood, Aug 2, 2m 4f				
GOODWOOD CUP	LUCKY MOON	John Dunlop	Willie Carson	11-8f
Goodwood, Aug 4, 1m 2f				
Vodafone NASSAU STAKES	KARTAJANA	Michael Stoute	Walter Swinburn	11-2
Newbury, Aug 17, 7f 60yd				
Gardner Merchant HUNGERFORD STAKES	NORWICH	Barry Hills	Michael Hills	11-2
Newbury, Aug 18, 7f 60yd				
Walmac International GEOFFREY FREER STAKES	CHARMER	Clive Brittain	Frankie Dettori	4-1
York, Aug 21, 1m 2f 110 y				
Juddmonte INTERNATIONAL STAKES	IN THE GROOVE	David Elsworth	Steve Cauthen	4-1f
York, Aug 23, 5f				
Keeneland NUNTHORPE STAKES	DAYJUR	Dick Hern	Willie Carson	8-11f

Kempton Park, Sep 8, 1m 3f 30yd
BonusPrint SEPTEMBER STAKES   LORD OF THE FIELD   Jim Toller   Billy Newnes   6-1
Doncaster, Sep 13, 2m 2f
DONCASTER CUP   AL MAHEB   Alec Stewart   Michael Roberts   7-2
Ascot, Sep 29, 1m
QUEEN ELIZABETH II STAKES   MARKOF-
-DISTINCTION   Luca Cumani   Frankie Dettori   6-1
Ascot, Sep 29, 4f
Krug DIADEM STAKES   RON'S VICTORY   A.Falourd   Freddy Head   13-2

OVERSEAS RACES

Venue/Date/Distance *Race*	*Winner*	*Trainer*	*Jockey*	*Price*
Maisons-Lafitte, Jul 22, 5f 110yd, 2-y-o				
PRIX ROBERT PAPIN	DANSEUSE DU SOIR	Elie Lellouche	Dominic Boeuf	Evens f
Phoenix Park, Aug 12, 6f, 2-y-o				
Heinz 57 PHOENIX STAKES	MAC'S IMP	Bill O'Gorman	Alan Munro	Evens f
Deauville, Aug 19, 6f, 2-y-o				
PRIX MORNAY	HECTOR PROTECTOR	François Boutin	Freddie Head	6-4
Phoenix Park, Sep 1, 1m 2f				
EBF PHOENIX CHAMPIONS STAKES	ELMAAMUL	Dick Hern	Willie Carson	2-1f
Longchamp, Sep 2, 1m				
PRIX DU MOULIN	DISTANT RELATIVE	Berry Hills	Pat Eddery	5-2
Arlington, Illinois, Sep 2, 1 m 2 f				
ARLINGTON MILLION	GOLDEN PHEASANT	Charlie Whittingham	Gary Stevens	-
One of Golden Pheasant's co-owners is the ice hockey player Wayne Gretzky				
Longchamp, Sep 9, 7f , 2-y-o				
PRIX DE LA SALAMANDRE	HECTOR PROTECTOR	François Boutin	Freddy Head	4-6f
Longchamp, Sep 16, 3-y-o (fillies)				
PRIX VERMEILLE	SALSABIL	John Dunlop	Willie Carson	2-5f

THE WORLD'S RICHEST RACES-1989

Position Race	Place	Winner's prize
1 Breeders' Cup Classic	Gulfstream Pk (US)	£750,000
2 Japan Cup	Tokyo (Jap)	£592,478
3 Melbourne Cup	Flemington (Aus)	£571,816
4 Golden Slipper	Rosehill (Aus)	£525,966
5 W S Cox Plate	Moonee Valley (Aus)	£524,292
6 Breeders' Cup Turf	Gulfstream Pk (US)	£500,000
7 Tokyo Yuushun (Derby)	Tokyo (Jap)	£481,723
8 Autumn Tenno Sho	Tokyo (Jap)	£454,466
9 Takara Zuka Kinen	Hanshin (Jap)	£454,330
10 Arima Kinen	Nakayama (Jap)	£454,300
11 Prix de l'Arc de Triomphe	Longchamp (Fra)	£450,450
12 Spring Tenno Sho	Kyoto (Jap)	£441,435

Britain's richest race was the Derby, with a prize of £296,000. It was ranked 29th.
Source: *The Independent*

1989-90

NATIONAL HUNT RACING
Waterford Crystal Champion Hurdle
Cheltenham, Mar 13, 2 miles

1	KRIBENSIS	Richard Dunwoody	95-40
2	Nomadic Way	Peter Scudamore	8-1
3	Past Glories	John Quinn	150-1
4	Beech Road	Richard Guest	2-1f
5	Morley Street	Jimmy Frost	10-1
6	Jinxy Jack	Neale Doughty	50-1
7	Island Set	Chris Grant	40-1
8	Vagador	Amanda Harwood	16-1
9	Deep Sensation	Richard Rowe	33-1
10	Elementary	Tommy Carmody	22-1
11	Don Valentino	Hywel Davies	50-1
12	Space Fair	Willie McFarland	150-1
13	Sudden Victory	Kevin Moody	150-1
14	Redundant Pal	Con O' Dwyer	33-1
15	Dis Train	Mark Pitman	100-1
16	See You Then	Steve Smith-Eccles	25-1
F	Bank View	Graham McCourt	50-1
F	Cruising Altitude	Jamie Osborne	9-1
F	Persian Style	Peter Hobbs	150-1

Owner: Sheikh Mohammed
Trainer: Michael Stoute, Newmarket
Winning distance: 31
Time: 3m 50,7s (record)

TOTE CHELTENHAM GOLD CUP
Cheltenham, Mar 15, 3 miles 2 furlongs

1	NORTON'S COIN	Graham McCourt	100-1
2	Toby Tobias	Mark Pitman	8-1
3	Desert Orchid	Richard Dunwoody	10-11f
4	Cavvies Clown	Graham Bradley	10-1
5	Pegwell Bay	Brendan Powell	20-1
6	Maid of Money	Anthony Powell	25-1
7	Yahoo	Tom Morgan	40-1
8	Bonanza Boy	Peter Scudamore	15-2
F	Kildimo	Jimmy Frost	50-1
F	Ten of Spades	Kevin Mooney	20-1
P	Nick the Brief	Martin Lynch	10-1
P	The Bakewell Boy	Steve Smith-Eccles	200-1

Owner: Sirell Griffiths
Trainer: Sirrell Griffiths, Carmarthen
Winning distance: 3/4 l
Time: 6m 35.3s (record)

SEAGRAM GRAND NATIONAL
Aintree, Apr 7, 4 miles 4 furlongs

1	MR FRISK	Marcus Armytage	16-1
2	Durham Edition	Chris Grant	9-1
3	Rinus	Neale Doughty	13-1
4	Brown Windsor	John White	7-1f
5	Lastofthebrownies	Charlie Swan	20-1
6	Bigsun	Richard Dunwoody	15-2
7	Call Collect	Raymund Martin	14-1
8	Bartres	Michael Bowlby	66-1
9	Sir Jest	Brian Storey	66-1
10	West Tip	Peter Hobbs	20-1
11	Team Challenge	Ben de Haan	50-1
12	Charter Hardware	Norman Williamson	66-1
13	Gallic Prince	José Simo	100-1
14	Ghofar	Brendan Powell	14-1
15	Course Hunter	Graham Bradley	66-1
16	Bonanza Boy	Peter Scudamore	16-1
17	Solares	Paul McMahon	150-1
18	Gee-A	Declan Murphy	66-1
19	Mick's Star	Seamus O'Neill	66-1
20	BobTisdall	Kevin Mooney	66-1

The following horses fell, refused or were brought down:

f	1st Gala's Image	JohnShortt	66-1
f	3rd Conclusive	Steve Smith-Eccles	28-1
f	3rdThinking Cap	Pat Malone	100-1
pu	6th Torside	Jimmy Frost	66-1
f	6th Lanavoe	Paul Leech	100-1
pu	7th Young Driver	Jimmy Duggan	150-1
f	8th Roll-A-Joint	Simon McNeill	28-1
pu	13th Star's Delight	JohnLower	50-1
f	14th Gainsay	Mark Pitman	66-1
co	14th Monamore	Tom Taaffe	100-1
f	15th Huntworth	Alan Walter	66-1
pu	19th Hungary Hur	Tommy Carmody	50-1
ur	19th Joint Sovereignty	Lorcan Wyer	50-1
pu	21st Against the Grain	Jamie Osborne	25-1
ur	22ndUncle Merlin	Hywel Davies	16-1
pu	25th Polyfemus	Richard Rowe	18-1
f	27th Pukka Major	Mark Richards	50-1
f	27th Nautical Joke	Kenny Johnson	66-1

Owner: Mrs Lois Duffy
Trainer: Kim Bailey, East Ilsley
Time: 8m 47,80s (Record)
Distance: 3/4 length   38 ran

HORSES KILLED IN THE GRAND NATIONAL

Since 1981

1983	Duncreggan	Canal Turn	8th
1984	Earthstopper	collapsed after the race	
1987	Dark Ivy	Becher's	6th
1989	Seeandem	Becher's	6th
1989	Brown Trix	Becher's	6th
1990	Roll-A-Joint	Canal Turn	8th
1990	Hungary Hur	fell on flat before 19th	

11 horses died in the race between 1960 and 1980 (full list in the *1990 Almanac*)

NATIONAL HUNT TABLES 1989-90

Jockeys	Mounts	Wins
1 Peter Scudamore	523	170
2 Richard Dunwoody	604	102
3 Graham McCourt	435	100
4 Chris Grant	425	94
5 Mark Dwyer	378	74
6 Hywel Davies	406	60

Trainers	Runners	Winners	Prizemoney
1 Martin Pipe	639	224	£792,544
2 Jenny Pitman	335	93	£520,231
3 Arthur Stephenson	519	116	£479,016
4 Gordon Richards	374	78	£437,520
5 Josh Gifford	365	50	£362,584
6 David Elsworth	177	24	£351,658

LEADING POST WAR NATIONAL HUNT JOCKEYS

(Up to the end of 1989-90 season)

Wins	Jockey	Years
1233	Peter Scudamore	1978-
1138	John Francome	1970-85
1035	Stan Mellor	1954-72
923	Fred Winter	1947-64
911	Bob Davies	1966-82
885	Jonjo O'Neill	1972-86
823	Ron Barry	1964-83
726	Tim Molony	1946-58
710	Jeff King	1960-81

OTHER BIG JUMP RACES

STEEPLECHASES

	Winner	Trainer	Jockey	Price
Cheltenham, Nov 11, 2m 4f				
MACKESON GOLD CUP	JOINT SOVEREIGNTY	Peter Hobbs	Graham McCourt	10-1
Newbury, Nov 25, 3m 2f 82yd				
HENNESSY COGNAC GOLD CUP	GHOFAR	David Elsworth	Hywel Davies	5-1
Kempton Park, Dec 26, 3m				
KING GEORGE V1 Rank CHASE	DESERT ORCHID	David Elsworth	Richard Dunwoody	4-6f
Sandown Park, Jan 6, 3m 5f 18yd				
ANTHONY MILDMAY HANDICAP CHASE	COOL GROUND	Norman Mitchell	Anthony Tory	6-1
Haydock Park, Jan 20, 3m				
PETER MARSH CHASE	NICK THE BRIEF	John Upson	Martin Lynch	15-8f
Doncaster, Jan 27, 3m 122yd				
William Hill GOLDEN SPURS HANDICAP	MAN O'MAGIC	Kim Bailey	Mark Perrett	7-2
Newcastle, Feb 17, 4m 1f				
Tote EIDER HANDICAP CHASE	JELUPE	Robin Sandys-Clarke	Robin Sandys-Clarke	13-2
Kempton Park, Feb 24, 3m				
Racing Post CHASE HANDICAP	DESERT ORCHID	David Elsworth	Richard Dunwoody	8-11f
Haydock Park, Mar 3, 3m				
Greenall Whitley GOLD CUP HANDICAP	RINUS	Gordon Richards	Richard Dunwoody	11-2
Cheltenham, Mar 13, 2m				
ARKLE CHALLENGE TROPHY CHASE	COMANDATE	Josh Gifford	Peter Hobbs	9-2
Cheltenham, Mar 14, 3m				
Sun Alliance CHASE	GARRISON SAVANNAH	Jenny Pitman	Ben de Haan	12-1
Cheltenham, Mar 14, 2m				
QUEEN MOTHER CHAMPION CHASE	BARNBROOK AGAIN	David Elsworth	Hywel Davies	11-10f
Aintree, Apr 5, 3m 1f				
MARTELL CUP	TOBY TOBIAS	Jenny Pitman	Mark Pitman	Evens f
Chepstow, Apr 17, 2m				
WELSH NOVICE CHAMPIONSHIP CHASE	AL HASHIMI	David Nicholson	Richard Dunwoody	5-2
Ayr, Apr 21, 4m 120yd				
William Hill SCOTTISH GRAND NATIONAL	FOUR TRIX	Gordon Richards	Derek Byrne	25-1
Sandown Park, Apr 28, 3m 5f 18yd				
34th Whitbread GOLD CUP	MR FRISK	Kim Bailey	Marcus Armytage	9-2f

HURDLES

	Winner	Trainer	Jockey	Price
Kempton Park, Jan 20, 2m				
Bic Razor LANZAROTE HANDICAP HURDLE	ATLAAL	John Jenkins	Richard Dunwoody	10-1
Newbury, Feb 10, 2m 100 yd				
Tote GOLD TROPHY HANDICAP HURDLE	DEEP SENSATION	Josh Gifford	Richard Rowe	7-1
Wincanton, Feb 22, 2m				
KINGWELL HURDLE	KRIBENSIS	Michael Stoute	Richard Dunwoody	4-6f
Sandown Park, Mar 10, 2m				
William Hill IMPERIAL CUP	MOODY MAN	Peter Hobbs	Peter Hobbs	20-1
Cheltenham, Mar 13, 3m 1f				
Waterford Crystal STAYERS HURDLE	TRAPPER JOHN	Mouse Morris	Charlie Swann	15-2
Cheltenham, Mar 13, 2m				
Waterford Crystal SUPREME NOVICES HURDLE	FORESAT SUN	Toby Balding	Jimmy Frost	7-4f
Cheltenham, Mar 14, 2m 4f				
Sun Alliance NOVICE HURDLE	REGAL AMBITION	Martin Pipe	Peter Scudamore	3-1f
Cheltenham, Mar 15, 2m				
Daily Express TRIUMPH HURDLE	RARE HOLIDAY	Dermot Weld	Brendan Sheridan	25-1
Aintree, Apr 7, 2m 4f				
Sandeman AINTREE HURDLE	MORLEY STREET	Tony Balding	Jimmy Frost	4-5f
Haydock Park, May 7, 2m				
Swinton Insurance TROPHY	SYBILLIN	Jimmy Fitzgerald	Derek Byrne	8-1

IRISH RACING

	Winner	Trainer	Jockey	Price
Fairyhouse, Apr 16, 3m				
Jameson IRISH GRAND NATIONAL	DESERT ORCHID	David Elsworth	Richard Dunwoody	Evens f

1989

CIGA PRIX DE L'ARC DE TRIOMPHE
Longchamp, Oct 8, 2400 metres
1 Carroll House   Michael Kinane
2 Behera   Alain Lequeux
3 Saint Andrews   Eric Legrix
Trainer: Michael Jarvis, Newmarket

BREEDERS' CUP
Gulfstream Park, Florida, Nov 4
Sprint, 6f
1 Dancing Spree   Angel Cordero
2 Safely Kept   Craig Perret
3 Dispersal   Chris McCarron
Juvenile Fillies, 1m 110y
1 Go for Wand   Randy Romero
2 Sweet Roberta   Pat Day
3 Stella Madrid   Angel Cordero
Distaff, 1m 1f
1 Bayakoa   Laffit Pincay
2 Gorgeous   Eddie Delahoussaye
3 Open Mind   Angel Cordero
Mile
1 Steinlen   Jose Santos
2 Sabona   Chris McCarron
3 Most Welcome   Gary Carter
10th Breeders' Cup win for trainer D Wayne Lukas
Juvenile, 1m 110y
1 Rhythm   Craig Perret
2 Grand Canyon   Chris McCarron
3 Slavic   Jose Santos
Turf, 1m 4f
1 Prized   Eddie Delahoussaye
2 Sierra Roberta   Pat Eddery
3 Star Lift   Gary Stevens
Classic, 1m 4f
1 Sunday Silence   Chris McCarron
2 Easy Goer   Pat Day
3 Blushing John   Angel Cordero

MELBOURNE CUP
Flemington Park, Nov 7, 3,200 metres
1 Tawrrific   Shane Dye   30-1
2 Super Impose   Darren Bauchey   25-1
3 Kudz   Michael Clarke   50-1
Trainer: Lee Freedman (also trained second)
Time: 3m 17.1s (Record)
23 Ran

FINAL FLAT RACING STATISTICS 1989
Leading Owners

	Winners	Prizemoney
Sheikh Mohammed	130	£1,295,148
Hamdan Al-Maktoum	98	£1,222,212
Khalid Abdullah	61	£ 683,589
Maktoum Al-Maktoum	32	£ 484,696
HH Aga Khan	48	£ 484,588
Mana Al-Maktoum	5	£ 397,607

Leading Trainers

	Winners	Prizemoney
Michael Stoute	117	£1,999,664
Guy Harwood	109	£1,719,786
Henry Cecil	116	£1,606,248
Dick Hern	44	£1,262,532
Luca Cumani	88	£1,142,277
Barry Hills	73	£ 814,119
Clive Brittain	36	£ 736,004

Leading Jockeys

	Winners	Mounts
Pat Eddery	171	838
Steve Cauthen	163	661
Willie Carson	137	867
Ray Cochrane	121	682
Michael Roberts	106	811
Walter Swinburn	94	652

WINNERS OF OTHER LEADING BRITISH RACES
Oct 1, 1989 to Dec 31, 1989

Race	Horse	Jockey	Price
Tattersalls CHEVELEY PARK STAKES	DEAD CERTAIN	Cash Asmussen	11-2
Tattersalls MIDDLE PARK STAKES	BALLACOVE	Steve Cauthen	20-1
Cheveley Park Stud SUN CHARIOT STAKES	BRAISWICK	Gary Carter	4-1
William Hill CAMBRIDGESHIRE HANDICAP	RAMBO'S HALL	Dean McKeown	15-1
JOCKEY CLUB CUP	WELD	Bruce Ryamond	Evens f
Three Chimneys DEWHURST STAKES	DASHING BLADE	John Matthias	8-1
Dubai CHAMPION STAKES	LEGAL CASE	Ray Cochrane	5-1
Tote CESAREWITCH HANDICAP	DOUBLE DUTCH	Billy Newnes	15-2
Vodafone HORRIS HILL STAKES	TIROL	Pat Eddery	6-1
ST SIMON STAKES	SESAME	Gary Hind	14-1
RACING POST TROPHY	BE MY CHIEF	Steve Cauthen	4-7f
RACECALL GOLD TROPHY	OSARIO	Brian Rouse	12-1
William Hill NOVEMBER HANDICAP	FIESTA	Bruce Raymond	9-2f

CHAMPIONS

THE ENGLISH CLASSICS

	1000 Guineas	2000 Guineas	Derby	Oaks	St Leger
1776	-	-	-	-	Allabaculia
1777	-	-	-	-	Bourbon
1778	-	-	-	-	Hollandaise
1779	-	-	-	Bridget	Tommy
1780	-	-	Diomed	Tetoum	Ruler
1781	-	-	Young Eclipse	Faith	Serina
1782	-	-	Assassin	Ceres	Imperatrix
1783	-	-	Saltram	Maid of the Oaks	Phenomenon
1784	-	-	Sergeant	Stella	Omphale
1785	-	-	Aimwell	Trifle	Cowslip
1786	-	-	Noble	Yellow Filly	Paragon
1787	-	-	Sir Peter Teazle	Annette	Spadille
1788	-	-	Sir Thomas	Nightshade	Young Flora
1789	-	-	Skyscraper	Tag	Pewett
1790	-	-	Rhadamanthus	Hippolyta	Ambidexter
1791	-	-	Eager	Portia	Young Traveller
1792	-	-	John Bull	Volante	Tartar
1793	-	-	Waxy	Caelia	Ninety-Three
1794	-	-	Daedalus	Hermione	Beningbrough
1795	-	-	Spread Eagle	Platina	Hambletonian
1796	-	-	Didelot	Pasiot	Ambrosio
1797	-	-	(unnamed colt)	Nike	Lounger
1798	-	-	Sir Harry	Bellissima	Symmetry
1799	-	-	Archduke	Bellina	Cockfighter
1800	-	-	Champion	Ephemera	Champion
1801	-	-	Eleanor	Eleanor	Quiz
1802	-	-	Tyrant	Scotia	Orville
1803	-	-	Ditto	Theophania	Remembrancer
1804	-	-	Hannibal	Pelisse	Sancho
1805	-	-	Cardinal Beaufort	Meteora	Staveley
1806	-	-	Paris	Bronze	Fyldener
1807	-	-	Election	Briseis	Paulina
1808	-	-	Pan	Morel	Petronius
1809	-	Wizard	Pope	Maid of Orleans	Ashton
1810	-	Hephestion	Whalebone	Oriana	Octavian
1811	-	Trophonius	Phantom	Sorcery	Soothsayer
1812	-	Cwrw	Octavius	Manuella	Otterington
1813	-	Smolensko	Smolensko	Music	Altisidora
1814	Charlotte	Olive	Blucher	Medora	William
1815	Unnamed filly	Tigris	Whisker	Minuet	Fihlo da Puta
1816	Rhoda	Nectar	Prince Leopold	Landscape	The Duchess
1817	Neva	Manfred	Azor	Neva	Ebor
1818	Corinne	Interpreter	Sam	Corinne	Reveller
1819	Catgut	Antar	Tiresias	Shoveler	Antonio
1820	Rowena	Pindarrie	Sailor	Caroline	St Patrick
1821	Zeal	Reginald	Gustavus	Augusta	Jack Spigot
1822	Whizgig	Pastille	Moses	Pastille	Theodore
1823	Zinc	Nicolo	Emilius	Zinc	Barefoot
1824	Cobweb	Schahriar	Cedric	Cobweb	Jerry
1825	Tontine	Enamel	Middleton	Wings	Memnon
1826	Problem	Devise	Lapdog	Lilias	Tarrare
1827	Arab	Turcoman	Mameluke	Gulnare	Matilda
1828	Zoe	Cadland	Cadland	Turquoise	The Colonel
1829	Young Mouse	Patron	Frederick	Green Mantle	Rowton
1830	Charlotte West	Augustus	Priam	Variation	Birmingham
1831	Galantine	Riddlesworth	Spaniel	Oxygen	Chorister
1832	Galata	Archibald	St.Giles	Galata	Margrave
1833	Tarantella	Clearwell	Dangerous	Vespa	Rockingham
1834	May-Day	Glencoe	Plenipotentiary	Pussy	Touchstone
1835	Preserve	Ibrahim	Mundig	Queen of Trumps	Queen of Trumps
1836	Destiny	Bay Middleton	Bay Middleton	Cyprian	Elis
1837	Chapeau D'Espange	Achmet	Phosphorus	Miss Letty	Mango
1838	Barcarolle	Grey Momus	Amato	Industry	Don John
1839	Cara	The Corsair	Bloomsbury	Deception	Charles the Twelth
1840	Crucifix	Crucifix	Little Wonder	Crucifix	Launcelot
1841	Potentia	Ralph	Coronation	Ghunznee	Satirist

	1000 Guineas	*2000 Guineas*	*Derby*	*Oaks*	*St Leger*
1842	Firebrand	Meteor	Attila	Our Nell	The Blue Bonnet
1843	Extempore	Cotherstone	Cotherstone	Poison	Nutwith
1844	Sorella	The Ugly Buck	Orlando	The Princess	Foig a Ballagh
1845	Picnic	Idas	The Merry Monarch	Refraction	The Baron
1846	Mendicant	Sir Tatton Sykes	Pyrrhus the First	Mendicant	Sir Tatton Sykes
1847	Clementina	Conyngham	Cossack	Miami	VanTromp
1848	Canezou	Flatcatcher	Surplice	Cymba	Surplice
1849	The Flea	Nunnykirk	The Flying Dutchman	Lady Evelyn	The Flying Dutchman
1850	Lady Orford	Pitsford	Voltigeur	Rhedycina	Voltigeur
1851	Aphrodite	Hernandez	Teddington	Iris	Newminster
1852	Kate	Stockwell	Daniel O'Rourke	Songstress	Stockwell
1853	Mentmore Lass	West Australian	West Australian	Catherine Hayes	West Australian
1854	Virage	The Hermit	Andover	Mincemeat	Knight of St George
1855	Habena	Lord of the Isles	Wild Dayrell	Marchioness	Saucebox
1856	Manganese	Fazzoletto	Ellington	Mincepie	Warlock
1857	Imperieuse	Vedette	Blink Bonny	Blink Bonny	Imperieuse
1858	Governess	Fitzroland	Beadsman	Governess	Sunbeam
1859	Mayonaise	Promised Land	Musjid	Summerside	Gamester
1860	Sagitta	The Wizard	Thormanby	Butterfly	St Albans
1861	Nemesis	Diophantus	Kettledrum	Brown Duchess	Caller Ou
1862	Hurricane	The Marquis	Caractacus	Fue de Joie	The Marquis
1863	Lady Augusta	Marconi	Marconi	Queen Bertha	Lord Clifden
1864	Tomato	General Peel	Blair Athol	Fille de L'Air	Blair Athol
1865	Siberia	Gladiateur	Gladiateur	Regalia	Gladiateur
1866	Repulse	Lord Lyon	Lord Lyon	Tormentor	Lord Lyon
1867	Achievement	Vauban	Hermit	Hippia	Achievement
1868	Formosa	Moslem } Formosa } (dead heat)	Blue Gown	Formosa	Formosa
1869	Scottish Queen	Pretender	Pretender	Brigantine	Pero Gomez
1870	Hester	Macgregor	Kingcraft	Gamos	Hawthornden
1871	Hannah	Bothwell	Favonius	Hannah	Hannah
1872	Reine	Prince Charlie	Cremorne	Reine	Wenlock
1873	Cecilia	Gang Forward	Doncaster	Marie Stuart	Marie Stuart
1874	Apology	Atlantic	Gearge Frederick	Apology	Apology
1875	Spinaway	Camballo	Galopin	Spinaway	Craig Millar
1876	Camelia	Petrarch	Kisber	Enguerrande } Camelia } dead heat	Petrarch
1877	Belpheobe	Chamant	Silvio	Placida	Silvio
1878	Pilgrimage	Pilgrimage	Sefton	Jannette	Jannette
1879	Wheel of Fortune	Charibert	Sir Bevys	Wheel of Fortune	Rayon d'Or
1880	Elizabeth	Petronel	Bend Or	Jenny Howlet	Robert the Devil
1881	Thebais	Peregrine	Iroquois	Thebais	Iroquois
1882	St Marguerite	Shotover	Shotover	Geheimniss	Dutch Oven
1883	Hauteur	Galliard	St Blaise	Bonny Jean	Ossian
1884	Busybody	Scot Free	St Gatien } Harvester } dead heat	Busybody	The Lambkin
1885	Farewell	Paradox	Melton	Lonely	Melton
1886	Miss Jummy	Ormonde	Ormonde	Miss Jummy	Ormonde
1887	Reve d'Or	Enterprise	Merry Hampton	Reve d'Or	Kilwarlin
1888	Briarroot	Ayrshire	Ayrshire	Seabreeze	Seabreeze
1889	Minthe	Enthusiast	Donovan	L'Abbesse de Jouarre	Donovan
1890	Semolina	Surefoot	Sainfoin	Memoir	Memoir
1891	Mimi	Common	Common	Mimi	Common
1892	La Fleche	Bona Vista	Sir Hugo	La Fleche	La Fleche
1893	Siffleuse	Isinglass	Isinglass	Mrs Butterwick	Isinglass
1894	Amiable	Ladas	Ladas	Amiable	Throstle
1895	Galeottia	Kirkconnel	Sir Visto	La Sagesse	Sir Visto
1896	Thias	St Frusquin	Persimmon	Canterbury Pilgrim	Persimmon
1897	Chelandry	Galtee More	Galtee More	Limasol	Galtee More
1898	Nun Nicer	Disraeli	Jeddah	Airs and Graces	Wildfowler
1899	Sibola	Flying Fox	Flying Fox	Musa	Flying Fox
1900	Winifreda	Diamond Jubilee	Diamond Jubilee	La Roche	Diamond Jubilee
1901	Aida	Handicapper	Volodyovski	Caps and Bells II	Doricles
1902	Sceptre	Sceptre	Ard Patrick	Sceptre	Sceptre
1903	Quintessence	Rock Sand	Rock Sand	Our Lassie	Rock Sand
1904	Pretty Polly	St Amant	St Amant	Pretty Polly	Pretty Polly
1905	Cherry Lass	Vedas	Cicero	Cherry Lass	Challacombe
1906	Flair	Gorgos	Spearmint	Keystone II	Troutbeck

	1000 Guineas	*2000 Guineas*	*Derby*	*Oaks*	*St Leger*
1907	Witch Elm	Slieve Gallion	Orby	Glass Doll	Wool Winder
1908	Rhodora	Norman III	Signorinetta	Signorinetta	Your Majesty
1909	Electra	Minoru	Minoru	Perola	Bayardo
1910	Winkipop	Neil Gow	Lemberg	Rosedrop	Swynford
1911	Atmah	Sunstar	Sunstar	Cherimoya	Prince Palatine
1912	Tagalie	Sweeper II	Tagalie	Mirska	Tracery
1913	Jest	Louvis	Aboyeur	Jest	Night Hawk
1914	Princess Dorrie	Kennymore	Durbar II	Princess Dorrie	Black Jester
1915	Vaucluse	Pommern	Pommern	Snow Marten	Pommern
1916	Canyon	Clarissimus	Fifinella	Fifinella	Hurry On
1917	Diadem	Gay Crusader	Gay Crusader	Sunny Jane	Gay Crusader
1918	Ferry	Gainsborough	Gainsborough	My Dear	Gainsborough
1919	Roseway	The Panther	Grand Parade	Bayuda	Keysoe
1920	Cinna	Tetratema	Spion Kop	Charlebelle	Caligula
1921	Bettina	Criag an Eran	Humorist	Love in Idleness	Polemarch
1922	Silver Urn	St Louis	Captain Cuttle	Pogrom	Royal Lancer
1923	Tranquil	Ellangowan	Papyrus	Brownhylda	Tranquil
1924	Plack	Diophon	Sansovino	Straitlace	Salmon-Trout
1925	Saucy Sue	Manna	Manna	Saucy Sue	Solario
1926	Pillion	Colorado	Coronach	Short Story	Coronach
1927	Cresta Run	Adam's Apple	Call Boy	Beam	Book Law
1928	Scuttle	Flamingo	Fellstead	Toboggan	Fairway
1929	Taj Mah	Mr Jinks	Trigo	Pennycomequick	Trigo
1930	Fair Isle	Diolite	Blenheim	Rose of England	Singapore
1931	Four Course	Cameronian	Cameronian	Brulette	Sandwich
1932	Kandy	Orwell	April the Fifth	Udaipur	Firdaussi
1933	Bety Brown	Rodosto	Hyperion	Chatelaine	Hyperion
1934	Campanula	Colombo	Windsor Lad	Light Brocade	Windsor Lad
1935	Mesa	Bahram	Bahram	Quashed	Bahram
1936	Tide-Way	Pay Up	Mahmoud	Lovely Rosa	Boswell
1937	Exhibitionist	Le Ksar	Mid-day Sun	Exhibitionist	Chulmleigh
1938	Rockfel	Pasch	Bois Roussel	Rockfel	Scottish Union
1939	Galatea II	Blue Peter	Blue Peter	Galatea II	
1940	Godiva	Djebel	Pont l'Eveque	Godiva	Turkham
1941	Dancing Time	Lambert Simnel	Owen Tudor	Commotion	Sun Castle
1942	Sun Chariot	Big Game	Watling Street	Sun Chariot	Sun Chariot
1943	Herringbone	Kingsway	Straight Deal	Why Hurry	Herringbone
1944	Picture Play	Garden Path	Ocean Swell	Hycilla	Tehran
1945	Sun Stream	Court Martial	Dante	Sun Stream	Chamossaire
1946	Hypericum	Happy Knight	Airborne	Steady Aim	Airborne
1947	Imprudence	Tudor Minstel	Pearl Diver	Imprudence	Sayajirao
1948	Queenpot	My Babu	My Love	Masaka	Black Tarquin
1949	Musidora	Nimbus	Nimbus	Musidora	Ridge Wood
1950	Camaree	Palestine	Galcador	Asmena	Scratch II
1951	Belle of All	Ki Ming	Arctic Prince	Neasham Belle	Talma II
1952	Zabara	Thunderhead II	Tulyar	Frieze	Tulyar
1953	Happy Laughter	Nearula	Pinza	Ambiguity	Premonition
1954	Festoon	Darius	Never Say Die	Sun Cap	Never Say Die
1955	Meld	Our Babu	Phil Drake	Meld	Meld
1956	Honeylight	Gilles de Retz	Lavandin	Sicarelle	Cambremer
1957	Rose Royale II	Crepello	Crepello	Carrozza	Ballymoss
1958	Bella Paola	Pall Mall	Hard Ridden	Bella Paola	Alcide
1959	Petite Etoile	Taboun	Parthia	Petite Etoile	Cantelo
1960	Never Too Late	Martial	St. Paddy	Never Too Late	St Paddy
1961	Sweet Solera	Rockavon	Psidium	Sweet Solera	Aurelius
1962	Abermaid	Privy Councillor	Larkspur	Monade	Hethersett
1963	Hula Dancer	Only for Life	Relko	Noblesse	Ragusa
1964	Pourparler	Baldric II	Santa Claus	Homeward Bound	Indiana
1965	Night Off	Niksar	Sea Bird II	Long Look	Provoke
1966	Glad Rags	Kashmir II	Charlottown	Valoris	Sodium
1967	Fleet	Royal Palace	Royal Palace	Pia	Ribocco
1968	Caergwrle	Sir Ivor	Sir Ivor	La Lagune	Ribero
1969	Full Dress II	Right Tack	Blakeney	Sleeping Partner	Intermezzo
1970	Humble Duty	Nijinsky	Nijinsky	Lupe	Nijinsky
1971	Altesse Royale	Brigadier Gerard	Mill Reef	Altesse Royale	Athens Wood
1972	Waterloo	High Top	Roberto	Ginevra	Boucher
1973	Mysterious	Mon Fils	Morston	Mysterious	Peleid
1974	Highclere	Nonoalco	Snow Knight	Polygamy	Bustino
1975	Nocturnal Spree	Bolkonski	Grundy	Juliette Marny	Bruni
1976	Flying Water	Wollow	Empery	Pawneese	Crow

1977	Mrs McArdy	Nebbiolo	The Minstrel	Dunfermline	Dunfermline
1978	Enstone Spark	Roland Gardens	Shirley Heights	Fari Salinia	Julio Mariner
1979	One in a Million	Tap On Wood	Troy	Scintillate	Son of Love
1980	Quick as Lightning	Known Fact	Henbit	Bireme	Light Cavalry
1981	Fairy Footsteps	To-Agori-Mou	Shergar	Blue Wind	Cut Above
1982	On the House	Zino	Golden Fleece	Time Charter	Touching Wood
1983	Ma Biche	Lomond	Teenoso	Sun Princess	Sun Princess
1984	Pebbles	El Gran Senor	Secreto	Circus Plume	Commanche Run
1985	Oh So Sharp	Shaheed	Slip Anchor	Oh So Sharp	Oh So Sharp
1986	Midway Lady	Dancing Brave	Shahrastani	Midway Lady	Moon Madness
1987	Miesque	Don't Forget Me	Reference Point	Unite	Reference Point
1988	Ravinella	Doyoun	Kahyasi	Diminuendo	Minster Son
1989	Musical Bliss	Nashwan	Nashwan	Aliysa	Michelozzo
1990	Salsabil	Tirol	Quest for Fame	Salsabil	Snurge

Horses underlined won more than one classic

FASTEST TIMES FOR THE ENGLISH CLASSICS
Derby: 2m 33.80s Mahmoud (1936) HT
2m 33.84s Kahyasi (1988) ET
Oaks: 2m 34.21s Time Charter (1982) ET
1000 Guineas: 1m 36.85s Oh So Sharp (1985) ET
1m 35.80s My Babu (1948) HT
2000 Guineas: 1m 35.84s Tirol (1990) ET
St Leger: 3m 01.60s Coronach (1926) HT
3m 01.60s Windsor Lad (1934) HT

HT=Hand Timed, ET=Electronically Timed

THE TRIPLE CROWN: 2,000 GUINEAS, DERBY AND ST LEGER

Horse	Year	Jockey(s)
West Australian	1853	Frank Butler
Gladiateur	1865	Harry Grimshaw
Lord Lyon	1866	Harry Custance 2, R. Thomas 1
Ormonde	1886	Fred Archer 2, George Barrett 1
Common	1891	George Barrett
Isinglass	1893	Tommy Loates
Galtee More	1897	Charlie Wood
Flying Fox	1899	Morny Cannon
Diamond Jubilee	1900	Herbert Jones
Rock Sand	1903	Danny Maher 2, J Martin 1
Pommern	1915	Steve Donoghue
Gay Crusader	1917	Steve Donoghue
Gainsborough	1918	Joe Childs
Bahram	1935	Freddie Fox 2, Charlie Smirke 1
Nijinsky	1970	Lester Piggott

GRAND NATIONAL WINNERS (1836-1919)

1836 The Duke	1857 Emigrant	1878 Shifnal	1899 Manifesto
1837 The Duke	1858 Little Charley	1879 The Liberator	1900 Ambush II
1838 Sir William	1859 Half Caste	1800 Empress	1901 Grudon
1839 Lottery	1860 Anatis	1881 Woodbrook	1902 Shannon Lass
1840 Jerry	1861 Jealousy	1882 Seaman	1903 Drumcree
1841 Charity	1862 Huntsman	1883 Zoedone	1904 Moifaa
1842 Gay Lad	1863 Emblem	1884 Voluptuary	1905 Kirkland
1843 Vanguard	1864 Emblematic	1885 Roquefort	1906 Ascetic's Silver
1844 Discount	1865 Alcibiade	1886 Old Joe	1907 Eremon
1845 Cureall	1866 Salamander	1887 Gamecock	1908 Rubio
1846 Pioneer	1867 Cortolvin	1888 Playfair	1909 Lutteur III
1847 Matthew	1868 The Lamb	1889 Frigate	1910 Jenkinstown
1848 Chandler	1869 The Colonel	1890 Ilex	1911 Glenside
1849 Peter Simple	1870 The Colonel	1891 Come Away	1912 Jerry M
1850 Abd-el-Kader	1871 The Lamb	1892 Father O'Flynn	1913 Covetcoat
1851 Abd-el-Kader	1872 Casse Tete	1893 Cloister	1914 Sunloch
1852 Miss Mowbray	1873 Disturbance	1894 Why Not	1915 Ally Sloper
1853 Peter Simple	1874 Reugny	1895 Wild Man from Borneo	1916 Vermouth
1854 Bourton	1875 Pathfinder	1896 Soarer	1917 Ballymacad
1855 Wanderer	1876 Regal	1897 Manifesto	1918 Poethlyn
1856 Freetrader	1877 Austerlitz	1898 Drogheda	1919 Poethlyn

TIMEFORM RATINGS OF STEEPLECHASERS

1. Arkle   212
2. Flyingbolt   210
3. Mill House   191
4. Desert Orchid   187
5. Dunkirk   186
6. Burrough Hill Lad   184
7. Captain Christy   182
8. Badsworth Boy   179
9. Pendil   178
10. Bregawn   }
    The Dikler   }   177

GRAND NATIONAL AND OTHER BIG RACE WINNERS SINCE 1920

Grand National	Cheltenham Gold Cup	Champion Hurdle	Arc de Triomphe	Irish Derby
1920 Troytown	-	-	Comrade	He Goes
1921 Shaun Spadah	-	-	Ksar	Ballyheron
1922 Music Hall	-	-	Ksar	Spike Island
1923 Sergeant Murphy	-	-	Parth	Waygood
1924 Master Robert	Red Splash	-	Massine	Zodiac/Haine
1925 Double Chance	Balinode	-	Priori	Zionist
1926 Jack Horner	Koko	-	Biribi	Embargo
1927 Sprig	Thrown In	Blaris	Mon Talisman	Knight of the Grail
1928 Tipperary Tim	Patron Saint	Brown Jack	Kantar	Baytown
1929 Gregalach	Easter Hero	Royal Falcon	Ortello	Kopi
1930 Shaun Goilin	Easter Hero	Brown Tony	Motrico	Rock Star
1931 Grakle	-	-	Pearl Cap	Sea Serpent
1932 Forbra	Golden Miller		Motrico	Dastur
1933 Kellsboro' Jack	Golden Miller	Insurance	Crapom	Harninero
1934 Golden Miller	Golden Miller	Chenango	Brantome	Primero/Patriot King
1935 Reynoldstown	Golden Miller	Lion Courage	Samos	Museum
1936 Reynoldstown	Golden Miller	Victor Norman	Corrida	Raeburn
1937 Royal Mail	-	Free Fare	Corrida	Phidias
1938 Battleship	Morse Code	Our Hope	Eclair au Chocolat	Rosewell
1939 Workman	Brendan's Cottage	Africa Sister	-	Mondragon
1940 Bogskar	Roman Hackle	Solford	-	Turkhan
1941 -	Poet Prince	Seneca	La Pacha	Sol Oriens
1942 -	Medoc II	Forestation	Djebel	Windsor Slipper
1943 -	-	-	Verso II	The Phoenix
1944 -	-	-	Ardan	Slide On
1945 -	Red Rower	Brains Trust	Nikellora	Piccadilly
1946 Lovely Cottage	Prince Regent	Distel	Caracella	Bright News
1947 Caughoo	Fortina	National Spirit	Le Paillon	Sayajirao
1948 Sheila's Cottage	Cottage Rake	National Spirit	Migoli	Nathoo
1949 Russian Hero	Cottage Rake	Hatton's Grace	Coronation	Hindostan
1950 Freebooter	Cottage Rake	Hatton's Grace	Tantieme	Dark Warrior
1951 Nickel Coin	Silver Fame	Hatton's Grace	Tantieme	Fraise du Bois II
1952 Teal	Mont Tremblant	Sir Ken	Nuccio	Thirteen of Diamonds
1953 Early Mist	Knock Hard	Sir Ken	La Sorellina	Chamier
1954 Royal Tan	Four Ten	Sir Ken	Sica Boy	Zarathustra
1955 Quare Times	Gay Donald	Clair Soleil	Ribot	Panaslipper
1956 E.S.B.	Limber Hill	Doorknocker	Ribot	Panaslipper
1957 Sundew	Linwell	Merry Deal	Oreso	Ballymoss
1958 Mr What	Kerstin	Bandalore	Ballymoss	Sindon
1959 Oxo	Roddy Owen	Fare Time	Saint Crespin	Fidalgo
1960 Merryman II	Pas Seul	Another Flash	Pussaint Chef	Chamour
1961 Nicolaus Silver	Saffron Tartan	Ebornezeer	Molvedo	Your Highness
1962 Kilmore	Mandarin	Anzio	Soltikoff	Tambourine II
1963 Ayala	Mill House	Winning Fair	Exbury	Ragusa
1964 Team Spirit	Arkle	Magic Court	Prince Royal II	Santa Claus
1965 Jay Trump	Arkle	Kirriemuir	Sea Bird II	Meadow Court
1966 Anglo	Arkle	Salmon Spray	Bon Mot	Sodium
1967 Foinavon	Woodland Venture	Saucy Kit	Topyo	Ribocco
1968 Reg Alligator	Fort Leney	Persian War	Vaguely Noble	Ribero
1969 Highland Wedding	What a Myth	Persian War	Levmoss	Prince Regent
1970 Gay Trip	L'Escargot	Persian War	Sassafras	Nijinsky
1971 Specify	L'Escargot	Bula	Mill Reef	Irish Ball

Grand National	Cheltenham Gold Cup	Champion Hurdle	Arc de Triomphe	Irish Derby
1972 Well To Do	Glencaraig Lady	Bula	San San	Steel Pulse
1973 Red Rum	The Dikler	Comedy of Errors	Rheingold	Weaver's Hall
1974 Red Rum	Captain Christy	Lanzarote	Allez France	English Prince
1975 L'Escargot	Ten Up	Comedy of Errors	Star Appeal	Grundy
1976 Rag Trade	Royal Frolic	Night Nurse	Ivanjica	Malacate
1977 Red Rum	Davy Lad	Night Nurse	Alleged	The Minstrel
1978 Lucius	Midnight Court	Monksfield	Alleged	Shirley Heights
1979 Rubstic	Alverton	Monksfield	Three Troikas	Troy
1980 Ben Nevis	Master Smudge	Sea Pigeon	Detroit	Tyrnavos
1981 Aldaniti	Little Owl	Sea Pigeon	Gold River	Shergar
1982 Grittar	Silver Buck	For Auction	Akiyda	Assert
1983 Corbiere	Bregawn	Gaye Brief	All Along	Shareef Dancer
1984 Hallo Dandy	Burrough Hill Lad	Dawn Run	Sagace	El Gran Senor
1985 Last Suspect	Forgive N'Forget	See You Then	Rainbow Quest	Law Society
1986 West Tip	Dawn Run	See You Then	Dancing Brave	Shahrastani
1987 Maori Venture	The Thinker	See You Then	Trempolino	Sir Harry Lewis
1988 Rhyme N'Reason	Charter Party	Celtic Shot	Tony Bin	Kahyasi
1989 Little Polveir	Desert Orchid	Beech Road	Carroll House	Old Vic
1990 Mr Frisk	Norton's Coin	Kribensis	Saumarez	Salsabil

DERBY WINNERS SINCE 1981

	Jockey	Price	Distance	Time	Trainer	Owner
1981 Shergar	Walter Swinburn	10-11	101	2m 22.21s	Michael Stoute	HH Aga Khan
1982 Golden Fleece	Pat Eddery	3-1	31	2m 34.27s	Vincent O'Brien	Robert Sangster
1983 Teenoso	Lester Piggott	9-2	31	2m 49.07s	Geoffrey Wragg	Eric Moller
1984 Secreto	Christy Roche	14-1	sh	2m 39.12s	David O'Brien	Luigi Miglietti
1985 Slip Anchor	Steve Cauthen	9-4	71	2m 36.23s	Henry Cecil	Lord H de Walden
1986 Shahrastani	Walter Swinburn	11-2	1/2 1	2m 37.13s	Michael Stoute	HH Aga Khan
1987 Reference Point	Steve Cauthen	6-4	1¹/21	2m 33.90s	Henry Cecil	Louise Freedman
1988 Kahyasi	Ray Cochrane	11-1	1¹/21	2m 33.84s	Luca Cumani	HH Aga Khan
1989 Nashwan	Willie Carson	5-4	51	2m 34.90s	Dick Hern	Hamdan al Maktoum
1990 Quest for Fame	Pat Eddery	7-1	31	2m 37.60s	Roger Charlton	Khalid Abdullah

GRAND NATIONAL WINNERS SINCE 1981

	Horse	Age/Weight	Jockey	Price	Trainer	Owner
1981	Aldaniti	11-10-13	Bob Champion	10-1	Josh Gifford	Nick Embiricos
1982	Grittar	9-11-5	Mr Dick Saunders	7-1	Frank Gilman	Frank Gilman
1983	Corbiere	8-11-4	Ben De Haan	13-1	Mrs Jenny Pitman	Brian Burroughs
1984	Hallo Dandy	10-10-2	Neale Doughty	13-1	Gordon Richards	Richard Shaw
1985	Last Suspect	11-10-5	Hywel Davies	50-1	Tim Forster	Duchess of Westminster
1986	West Tip	9-10-11	Richard Dunwoody	15-2	Michael Oliver	Peter Luff
1987	Maori Venture	11-10-13	Steve Knight	28-1	Andy Turnell	Jim Joel
1988	Rhyme n' Reason	9-10-11	Brendon Powell	10-1	David Elsworth	Juliet Reed
1989	Little Polveir	12-10-3	Jimmy Frost	28-1	Toby Balding	Edward Harvey
1990	Mr Frisk	11-10-6	Marcus Armytage	16-1	Kim Bailey	Lois Duffy

CHAMPION FLAT RACE JOCKEYS 1840-1945

1840	Elnathan Flatman	50	1875	Fred Archer	172	1912	Frank Wootton	118
1841	Elnathan Flatman	68	1876	Fred Archer	207	1913	Danny Maher	115
1842	Elnathan Flatman	42	1877	Fred Archer	218	1914	Steve Donoghue	129
1843	Elnathan Flatman	60	1878	Fred Archer	229	1915	Steve Donoghue	62
1844	Elnathan Flatman	64	1879	Fred Archer	197	1916	Steve Donoghue	43
1845	Elnathan Flatman	81	1880	Fred Archer	120	1917	Steve Donoghue	42
1846	Elnathan Flatman	81	1881	Fred Archer	220	1918	Steve Donoghue	66
1847	Elnathan Flatman	89	1882	Fred Archer	210	1919	Steve Donoghue	129
1848	Elnathan Flatman	104	1883	Fred Archer	232	1920	Steve Donoghue	143
1849	Elnathan Flatman	94	1884	Fred Archer	241	1921	Steve Donoghue	141
1850	Elnathan Flatman	88	1885	Fred Archer	246	1922	Steve Donoghue	102
1851	Elnathan Flatman	78	1886	Fred Archer	170	1923	Steve Donoghue &	
1852	Elnathan Flatman	92	1887	Charlie Wood	151		Charlie Elliott	89
1853	John Wells	86	1888	Fred Barrett	108	1924	Charlie Elliott	106
1854	John Wells	82	1889	Tommy Loates	167	1925	Gordon Richards	118
1855	George Fordham	70	1890	Tommy Loates	147	1926	Tommy Weston	95
1856	George Fordham	108	1891	Morny Cannon	137	1927	Gordon Richards	164
1857	George Fordham	84	1892	Morny Cannon	182	1928	Gordon Richards	148
1858	George Fordham	91	1893	Tommy Loates	222	1929	Gordon Richards	135
1859	George Fordham	118	1894	Morny Cannon	167	1930	Freddy Fox	129
1860	George Fordham	146	1895	Morny Cannon	184	1931	Gordon Richards	145
1861	George Fordham	106	1896	Morny Cannon	164	1932	Gordon Richards	190
1862	George Fordham	166	1897	Morny Cannon	145	1933	Gordon Richards	259

1863	George Fordham	103
1864	Harry Grimshaw	164
1865	George Fordham	142
1866	S Kenyon	123
1867	George Fordham	143
1868	George Fordham	110
1869	George Fordham	95
1870	W Gray & Charlie Maidment	76
1871	George Fordham & Charlie Maidment	86
1872	Tommy Cannon	87
1873	Harry Constable	110
1874	Fred Archer	147

1898	Otto Madden	161
1899	Sam Loates	160
1900	Lester Reiff	143
1901	Otto Madden	130
1902	Willie Lane	170
1903	Otto Madden	154
1904	Otto Madden	161
1905	Elijah Wheatley	124
1906	Billy Higgs	149
1907	Billy Higgs	146
1908	Danny Maher	139
1909	Frank Wootton	165
1910	Frank Wootton	137
1911	Frank Wootton	187

1934	Gordon Richards	212
1935	Gordon Richards	217
1936	Gordon Richards	174
1937	Gordon Richards	216
1938	Gordon Richards	200
1939	Gordon Richards	155
1940	Gordon Richards	68
1941	Harry Wragg	71
1942	Gordon Richards	67
1943	Gordon Richards	65
1944	Gordon Richards	88
1945	Gordon Richards	104

CHAMPION FLAT RACE JOCKEYS, TRAINERS AND OWNERS 1946-89

	Jockey		Apprentice		Trainer	£	Owner	£
1946	Gordon Richards	212	Joe Sime	40	Frank Butters	56,140	HH Aga Khan	24,118
1947	Gordon Richards	269	Dennis Buckle	20	Fred Darling	65,313	HH Aga Khan	44,020
1948	Gordon Richards	224	Dennis Buckle	25	Noel Murless	66,542	HH Aga Khan	46,393
1949	Gordon Richards	261	Willie Snaith	31	Frank Butters	71,721	HH Aga Khan	68,916
1950	Gordon Richards	201	Lester Piggott	52	Charles Semblat	57,044	Marcel Boussac	57,044
1951	Gordon Richards	227	Lester Piggott	51	Jack Jarvis	56,397	Marcel Boussac	39,339
1952	Gordon Richards	231	Joe Mercer	26	Marcus Marsh	92,093	HH Aga Khan	92,518
1953	Gordon Richards	191	Joe Mercer	61	Jack Jarvis	71,546	Victor Sassoon	58,579
1954	Doug Smith	129	Eddie Hide	53	Cecil Boyd-Rochfort	65,326	HM The Queen	40,993
1955	Doug Smith	168	Philip Robinson	46	Cecil Boyd-Rochfort	74,424	Lady Zia Wernher	46,345
1975	Pat Eddery	164	Alan Bond	66	Peter Walwyn	382,527	Carlo Vittadi	209,492
1976	Pat Eddery	162	David Dineley	54	Henry Cecil	261,301	Dan Wildenstein	244,500
1977	Pat Eddery	176	Jimmy Bleasdale	67	Vincent O'Brien	439,124	Robert Sangster	348,023
1978	Willie Carson	182	Kevin Darley	70	Henry Cecil	382,812	Robert Sangster	160,405
1979	Joe Mercer	164	Philip Robinson	51	Henry Cecil	683,971	Michael Sobell	339,751
1980	Willie Carson	165	Philip Robinson	59	Dick Hern	831,964	Simon Weinstock	236,332
1981	Lester Piggott	179	Bryn Crossley	45	Michael Stoute	723,786	HH Aga Khan	441,654
1982	Lester Piggott	188	Billy Newnes	57	Henry Cecil	872,614	Robert Sangster	397,749
1983	Willie Carson	159	Michael Hills	39	Dick Hern	549,598	Robert Sangster	461,488
1984	Steve Cauthen	130	Tommy Quinn	62	Henry Cecil	551,939	Robert Sangster	395,901
1985	Steve Cauthen	195	Gary Carter & Willie Ryan	37	Henry Cecil	1,148,206	Shk Mohammed	1,082,502
1986	Pat Eddery	177	Gary Carter	34	Michael Stoute	1,266,807	Shk Mohammed	830,121
1987	Steve Cauthen	197	Gary Bardwell	27	Henry Cecil	1,882,116	Shk Mohammed	1,232,240
1988	Pat Eddery	183	Gary Bardwell	39	Henry Cecil	1,186,122	Shk Mohammed	1,143,343
1989	Pat Eddery	171	Lanfranco Dettori	75	Michael Stoute	1,999,664	Shk Mohammed	1,295,148

LEADING JOCKEYS IN BRITAIN

4,870	Sir Gordon Richards	1921-54
4,349	Lester Piggott	1948-85
3,126+	Willie Carson	1962-
3,111	Doug Smith	1932-67
2,870+	Pat Eddery	1969-
2,810	Joe Mercer	1950-85
2,748	Fred Archer	1870-86
2,591	Edward Hide	1951-85
2,587	George Fordham	1851-83
2,313	Eph Smith	1930-65

Carson and Eddery figures correct to Sep 17, 1990; winners abroad excluded

CHAMPION NATIONAL HUNT JOCKEYS & TRAINERS SINCE 1946

	Jockey		Trainer	£
1946	Fred Rimell	54	Tom Rayson	9,933
1947	Jack Dowdeswell	58	Fulke Walwyn	11,115
1948	Bryan Marshall	66	Fulke Walwyn	16,790
1949	Tim Molony	60	Fulke Walwyn	15,563
1950	Tim Molony	95	Peter Cazalet	18,427
1951	Tim Molony	83	Fred Rimell	18,381
1952	Tim Molony	99	Neville Crump	19,377
1953	Fred Winter	121	Vincent O'Brien	15,515
1954	Dick Francis	76	Vincent O'Brien	14,274
1955	Tim Molony	67	Ryan Price	13,888
1956	Fred Winter	74	Charlie Hall	15,807
1957	Fred Winter	80	Neville Crump	18,495
1958	Fred Winter	82	Fulke Walwyn	23,013
1959	Tim Brookshaw	83	Ryan Price	26,550
1960	Stan Mellor	68	Peter Cazalet	22,270
1961	Stan Mellor	118	Fred Rimell	34,811
1962	Stan Mellor	80	Ryan Price	40,950
1963	Josh Gifford	70	Keith Piggott	23,091
1964	Josh Gifford	94	Fulke Walwyn	67,129
1965	Terry Biddlecombe	114	Peter Cazalet	36,153
1966	Terry Biddlecombe	102	Ryan Price	42,267
1967	Josh Gifford	122	Ryan Price	41,222
1968	Josh Gifford	82	Denys Smith	37,944

1974	Ron Barry	94	Fred Winter	101,782
1975	Tommy Stack	82	Fred Winter	74,205
1976	John Francome	96	Fred Rimell	111,740
1977	Tommy Stack	97	Fred Winter	85,202
1978	Jonjo O'Neill	149	Fred Winter	145,915
1979	John Francome	95	Peter Easterby	150,746
1980	Jonjo O'Neill	115	Peter Easterby	218,258
1981	John Francome	105	Peter Easterby	236,867
1982	John Francome &	120	Michael Dickinson	296,028
	Peter Scudamore	120		
1983	John Francome	106	Michael Dickinson	358,837
1984	John Francome	131	Michael Dickinson	266,146
1985	John Francome	101	Fred Winter	218,978
1986	Peter Scudamore	91	Nicky Henderson	162,234
1987	Peter Scudamore	123	Nicky Henderson	162,234
1988	Peter Scudamore	132	David Elsworth	344,210
1989	Peter Scudamore	221	Martin Pipe	589,460
1990	Peter Scudamore	170	Martin Pipe	792,544

BILL SHOEMAKER

First ride....March 19 1949-fifth on Waxahachie at Golden Gate Fields, California.
Last ride....February 3 1990-fourth on Patchy Groundfog at Santa Anita, California in "The Legend's Last Ride Handicap".
Total rides: 40,351
Winners: 8,833 (world record)
Seconds: 6,136
Thirds: 4,987
Prize money: $123,368,024

US RACING
Triple Crown

The following horses have all won the Triple Crown:

Horse	Year	Jockey
Sir Barton	1919	John Loftus
Gallant Fox	1930	Earl Sande
Omaha	1935	W Saunders
War Admiral	1937	C Kurtsinger
Whirlaway	1941	Eddie Arcaro
Count Fleet	1943	Johnny Longden
Assault	1946	W Mehrtens
Citation	1948	Eddie Arcaro
Secretariat	1973	Ron Turcotte
Seattle Slew	1977	Jean Cruguet
Affirmed	1978	Steve Cauthen

Breeder's Cup

	Sprint	Mile	Juvenile	Juvenile Fillies
1984	Ellio	Royal Heroine	Chief's Crown	Outstandingly
1985	Precisionist	Cozzene	Tasso	Twilight Ridge
1986	Smile	Last Tycoon	Capote	Brave Raj
1987	Very Subtle	Miesque	Success Express	Epitome
1988	Gulch	Miesque	Is It True?	Open Mind
1990	Dancing Spree	Steinlen	Rhythm	Go for Wand

	Distaff	Classic	Turf
1984	Princess Rooney	Wild Again	Lashkari
1985	Life's Magic	Proud Truth	Pebbles
1986	Lady's Secret	Skywalker	Manila
1987	Sacahuista	Ferdinand	Theatrical
1988	Personal Ensign	Alysheba	Great Communicator
1989	Bayakoa	Sunday Silence	Prized

AMONGSTHORSESRACINGINTHEUNITEDSTATES...

Agirlfrommars
Haveigotadealforyou
Doyouseewhatisee
Akissforjose
Hookenonthehighway
Moreofthebest
Rootentootenwooten

(Other US Stakes winners in the past decade have included Scorched Panties (by Fire Dancer), Willy Wank (18 wins), Dumdedumdedum (out of Dumtadumtadum) and Arewehavingfunyet.
Source: *Racing Post/Sporting Life*

AUSTRALIAN RACING
Melbourne Cup

(Winners since 1981)

1981	Just a Dash
1982	Gurner's Lane
1983	Kiwi
1984	Black Night
1985	What a Nuisance
1986	At Talaq
1987	Kensei
1988	Empire Rose
1989	Tawrrific

─── RECORDS ───

Highest race speed: 43.26 mph by Big Racket over 0.25 mile carrying 114 lb at Mexico City, Feb 5 1945.
Most wins *Horse*: 137 Galgo jr, Puerto Rico, 1930-36. *Jockey*: 8833 Bill Shoemaker 1949-1990: 4870. *Jockey in Britain*: Sir Gordon Richards 1920-1954: 4349 (5200+ worldwide) Lester Piggott 1948-1985.

─── 1991 ───

BIG RACES

Mar 12	Champion Hurdle (Cheltenham)
Mar 14	Cheltenham Gold Cup
Mar 21	Flat season starts (Doncaster)
Apr 6	Grand National (Aintree)
Apr 16-18	Newmarket Craven meeting
May 2	1000 Guineas (Newmarket)
May 4	2000 Guineas (Newmarket)
Jun 5	The Derby (Epsom)
Jun 8	The Oaks (Epsom)
Jun 18-21	Royal Ascot
Jul 9-11	Newmarket July meeting
July 27	King George V1 and Queen Elizabeth Diamond Stakes (Ascot)
Jul 30-Aug 3	Glorious Goodwood
Aug 20-22	Ebor meeting (York)
Sep 14	St Leger (Doncaster)
Sep 20	Ayr Gold Cup
Sep 28	Festival of British Racing (Ascot)
Oct 5	The Cambridgeshire (Newmarket)
Oct 19	The Cesarewitch (Newmarket)
Nov 11	Flat season ends (Folkestone)

FULL RACING FIXTURES 1991

TURF MEETINGS
JANUARY

1 Catterick Bridge, Cheltenham, Devon & Exeter, Leicester, Windsor
2 Ayr
3 Ayr, Nottingham, Sedgefield
4 Edinburgh, Newton Abbot
5 Haydock Park, Market Rasen, Worcester, Sandown Park
7 Lingfield Park, Wolverhampton
8 Leicester, Chepstow
9 Kelso, Plumpton
10 Wincanton
11 Edinburgh, Ascot, Wetherby
12 Newcastle, Market Rasen, Ascot, Warwick
14 Carlisle, Fontwell Park
15 Sedgefield, Folkestone
16 Ludlow, Windsor
17 Taunton
18 Catterick Bridge, Kempton Park, Towcester
19 Catterick Bridge, Warwick, Kempton Park, Haydock Park
21 Leicester, Lingfield Park
22 Nottingham, Chepstow
23 Sedgefield, Wolverhampton
24 Huntingdon, Newton Abbot
25 Doncaster, Wincanton
26 Ayr, Cheltenham, Doncaster
28 Ayr, Plumpton
29 Sedgefield, Leicester
30 Nottingham, Windsor
31 Edinburgh, Towcester

FEBRUARY

1 Kelso, Bangor-on-Dee, Lingfield Park
2 Wetherby, Stratford-on-Avon, Chepstow, Sandown Park
4 Wolverhampton, Fontwell Park
5 Carlisle, Warwick
6 Ludlow, Ascot
7 Huntington, Wincanton
8 Sedgefield, Newbury
9 Ayr, Uttoxeter, Catterick Bridge, Newbury
11 Hereford, Plumpton
12 Towcester, Newton Abbot
13 Ayr, Worcester, Folkestone
14 Leicester, Sandown Park, Taunton
15 Edinburgh, Fakenham, Sandown Park
16 Newcastle, Nottingham, Chepstow, Windsor
18 Wolverhampton, Fontwell Park
19 Sedgefield, Huntingdon
20 Catterick Bridge, Warwick
21 Folkestone, Wincanton
22 Kelso, Kempton Park
23 Doncaster, Stratford-on-Avon, Kempton Park, Edinburgh
25 Doncaster, Leicester, Lingfield Park
26 Nottingham
27 Wetherby, Plumpton, Worcester
28 Ludlow

MARCH

1 Haydock Park, Newbury
2 Haydock Park, Hereford, Market Rasen, Newbury
4 Leicester, Windsor
5 Sedgefield, Warwick
6 Catterick Bridge, Bangor-on-Dee, Folkestone
7 Stratford-on-Avon, Wincanton
8 Carlisle, Market Rasen, Grand Military Meeting (Sandown Park)
9 Ayr, Chepstow, Doncaster, Grand Military Meeting (Sandown Park)
11 Ayr, Plumpton

12 Sedgefield, N.H. Meeting (Cheltenham)
13 N.H. Meeting (Cheltenham), Newton Abbot
14 Hexham, N.H. Meeting (Cheltenham)
15 Fakenham, Lingfield Park, Wolverhampton
16 Newcastle, Chepstow, Uttoxeter, Lingfield Park
18 Newcastle, Wolverhampton
19 Nottingham, Fontwell Park
20 Kelso, Worcester
21 DONCASTER, Towcester, Devon & Exeter
22 DONCASTER, Ludlow, Newbury
23 DONCASTER, Bangor-on-Dee, Hexham, Newbury
25 Hexham, LEICESTER, FOLKESTONE
26 LEICESTER, Royal Artillery Meeting (Sandown Park)
27 CATTERICK PARK, Worcester
28 Southwell, BRIGHTON, Taunton
30 Carlisle, Southwell, KEMPTON PARK, HAYDOCK PARK, Towcester, Newton Abbot, NEWCASTLE, Plumpton

APRIL

1 Carlisle, Fakenham, Chepstow, NEWCASTLE, Hereford, KEMPTON PARK, Wetherby, Huntingdon, Newton Abbot, Market Rasen, Plumpton, NOTTINGHAM, Wincanton, Towcester, Uttoxeter, Warwick
2 Wetherby, Uttoxeter, Chepstow, WARWICK
3 Hamilton Park, Worcester
4 Aintree, BRIGHTON
5 Aintree, Devon & Exeter, KEMPTON PARK
6 Aintree, Hereford, LINGFIELD PARK
8 Kelso, WOLVERHAMPTON, NEWCASTLE
9 PONTEFRACT, WOLVERHAMPTON
10 RIPON, Ludlow, Ascot
11 RIPON, Taunton
12 BEVERLEY, Plumpton, Wincanton
13 BEVERLEY, Southwell, Ascot, WARWICK
15 EDINBURGH, Huntingdon, FOLKESTONE, NOTTINGHAM
16 Sedgefield, NEWMARKET CRAVEN, Fontwell Park
17 AYR, Cheltenham, PONTEFRACT, NEWMARKET CRAVEN
18 AYR (MIXED), Cheltenham, NEWMARKET CRAVEN
19 Ayr, NEWBURY, THIRSK
20 Ayr, Bangor-on-Dee, NEWBURY, THIRSK, Stratford-on-Avon
22 HAMILTON PARK, Brighton
23 Perth, KEMPTON PARK
24 CATTERICK BRIDGE, KEMPTON PARK, Perth
25 BEVERLEY, Ludlow, +Wincanton, Perth
26 CARLISLE, Southwell, SANDOWN PARK, +Taunton
27 Hexham, LEICESTER, SANDOWN PARK (MIXED), RIPON, Market Rasen, +Worcester
29 Hexham, WOLVERHAMPTON, +WINDSOR, PONTEFRACT
30 Sedgefield, NOTTINGHAM, +Ascot, BATH

MAY

1 Kelso, +Cheltenham, ASCOT
2 REDCAR, NEWMARKET SPRING, +Newton Abbot, SALISBURY
3 HAMILTON PARK, NEWMARKET SPRING, Newton Abbot
4 HAYDOCK PARK, Hereford, +Hexham, NEWMARKET SPRING, THIRSK, Uttoxeter
6 DONCASTER, Ludlow, Devon & Exeter, HAYDOCK PARK (MIXED), Southwell, Fontwell Park, Newcastle,Towcester, Kempton Park, WARWICK
7 +Sedgefield, CHESTER, Chepstow, SALISBURY
8 +Wetherby, CHESTER, SALISBURY, +Worcester, +Sandown Park
9 CARLISLE, CHESTER, BRIGHTON, +Huntingdon,

+Uttoxeter
10 BEVERLEY, +Stratford-on-Avon, LINGFIELD PARK,
CARLISLE, +Taunton
11 BEVERLEY, +Market Rasen, BATH, +Newcastle,
NEWMARKET, LINGFIELD PARK, +Warwick
13 EDINBURGH, WOLVERHAMPTON, WINDSOR
14 YORK, +NOTTINGHAM, +United Hunts Meeting
(Folkestone), +Towcester, Newton Abbot
15 +Perth, Hereford, +KEMPTON PARK, YORK,
+Newton Park
16 Perth, +Huntingdon, York
17 THIRSK, NEWMARKET, NEWBURY, +Stratford-on-
Avon
18 +HAMILTON PARK, Bangor-on-Dee, +LINGFIELD
PARK, THIRSK, +SOUTHWELL, NEWBURY,
+Warwick
20 HAMILTON PARK, WOLVERHAMPTON, BATH,
FOLKESTONE
21 BEVERLEY, GOODWOOD
22 Worcester, GOODWOOD
23 CATTERICK BRIDGE, GOODWOOD
24 HAYDOCK PARK, Towcester, +PONTEFRACT,
Sedgefield
25 Cartmel, +SOUTHWELL, KEMPTON PARK,
DONCASTER, +WARWICK, +LINGFIELD PARK,
HAYDOCK PARK, Hexham
27 Cartmel, Fakenham, CHEPSTOW, DONCASTER,
Hereford, Devon & Exeter, +Hexham, Huntingdon,
Fontwell Park, REDCAR, LEICESTER, SANDOWN
PARK, Wetherby, Uttoxeter
28 REDCAR, LEICESTER, +SANDOWN PARK,
+Uttoxeter
29 Cartmel, BRIGHTON, +Ripon
30 CARLISLE, BRIGHTON
31 HAMILTON PARK, NOTTINGHAM,
+GOODWOOD, NEWCASTLE, +Stratford-on-Avon

JUNE
1 EDINBURGH, +Market Rasen, LINGFIELD PARK,
Stratford-on-Avon
3 +EDINBURGH, LEICESTER, REDCAR
4 YARMOUTH, FOLKESTONE
5 +BEVERLEY, YARMOUTH, EPSOM
6 BEVERLEY, EPSOM
7 CATTERICK BRIDGE, SOUTHWELL, EPSOM,
+HAYDOCK PARK, +GOODWOOD
8 +CARLISLE, +LEICESTER, EPSOM, CATTERICK
BRIDGE, HAYDOCK PARK
10 PONTEFRACT, NOTTINGHAM, +BRIGHTON
11 PONTEFRACT, SALISBURY
12 BEVERLEY, +KEMPTON PARK, +HAMILTON
PARK, NEWBURY
13 HAMILTON PARK, +CHEPSTOW, NEWBURY
14 +DONCASTER, SOUTHWELL, +GOODWOOD,
YORK, SANDOWN PARK
15 YORK, +NOTTINGHAM, BATH, +LINGFIELD
PARK, SANDOWN PARK
17 EDINBURGH, WOLVERHAMPTON, BRIGHTON,
+WINDSOR
18 THIRSK, ROYAL ASCOT
19 RIPON, ROYAL ASCOT
20 RIPON, ROYAL ASCOT
21 AYR, SOUTHWELL, ROYAL ASCOT, REDCAR
22 AYR, WARWICK, ASCOT, REDCAR, +LINGFIELD
PARK
24 EDINBURGH, NOTTINGHAM, +WINDSOR
25 YARMOUTH, BRIGHTON, +NEWBURY
26 CARLISLE, +CHESTER, +KEMPTON PARK,
SALISBURY
27 CARLISLE, SALISBURY
28 DONCASTER, NEWMARKET, +BATH

+NEWCASTLE, +GOODWOOD, LINGFIELD PARK
29 DONCASTER, NEWMARKET, CHEPSTOW,
NEWCASTLE, +WARWICK, +LINGFIELD PARK

JULY
1 EDINBURGH, WOLVERHAMPTON, +WINDSOR,
PONTEFRACT
2 CHEPSTOW, FOLKESTONE
3 +CATTERICK BRIDGE, WARWICK, YARMOUTH
4 CATTERICK BRIDGE, YARMOUTH, +BRIGHTON,
+HAYDOCK PARK
5 BEVERLEY, SOUTHWELL, SANDOWN PARK,
HAYDOCK PARK
6 BEVERLEY, +NOTTINGHAM, BATH, HAYDOCK
PARK, SANDOWN PARK
8 EDINBURGH, LEICESTER, WINDSOR, +RIPON
9 PONTEFRACT, NEWMARKET JULY
10 +REDCAR, NEWMARKET JULY, BATH,
+KEMPTON PARK
11 +HAMILTON PARK, NEWMARKET JULY,
+CHEPSTOW, KEMPTON PARK
12 HAMILTON PARK, +CHESTER, LINGFIELD PARK,
YORK, WARWICK
13 AYR, CHESTER, LINGFIELD PARK, YORK,
+SOUTHWELL, SALISBURY
15 AYR, WOLVERHAMPTON, WINDSOR,
+BEVERLEY
16 AYR, +LEICESTER, +FOLKESTONE, BEVERLEY
17 CATTERICK BRIDGE, +YARMOUTH, SANDOWN,
HAMILTON PARK
18 CATTERICK BRIDGE, +CHEPSTOW, HAMILTON
PARK, SANDOWN PARK
19 AYR, +NEWMARKET, NEWBURY, THIRSK
20 AYR, NEWMARKET, +LINGFIELD PARK, RIPON,
+SOUTHWELL, NEWBURY
22 AYR, +NOTTINGHAM, BATH, +WINDSOR
23 REDCAR, FOLKESTONE
24 DONCASTER, YARMOUTH, +SANDOWN PARK,
+REDCAR
25 +DONCASTER, YARMOUTH, BRIGHTON
26 CARLISLE, YARMOUTH, ASCOT, +PONTEFRACT
27 HAMILTON PARK,+SOUTHWELL, ASCOT,
NEWCASTLE, +WARWICK
29 NEWCASTLE, WOLVERHAMPTON, LINGFIELD
PARK, +WINDSOR
30 BEVERLEY, +LEICESTER, GOODWOOD
31 CATTERICK BRIDGE, +SOUTHWELL,
GOODWOOD

AUGUST
1 YARMOUTH, GOODWOOD
2 EDINBURGH, Bangor-on-Dee, GOODWOOD,
THIRSK, +NEWMARKET
3 +THIRSK, Market Rasen, GOODWOOD,
NEWMARKET, Newton Abbot, WINDSOR
5 RIPON, +NOTTINGHAM, Newton Abbot
6 REDCAR, +NOTTINGHAM, BRIGHTON
7 PONTEFRACT, BRIGHTON, Devon & Exeter,
+KEMPTON PARK
8 PONTEFRACT, +Uttoxeter, BRIGHTON
9 +HAYDOCK PARK, Market Rasen, Plumpton,
REDCAR, NEWMARKET
10 HAYDOCK PARK, NEWMARKET, LINGFIELD
PARK, REDCAR, +SOUTHWELL, +Worcester
12 +THIRSK, +LEICESTER, WINDSOR, Worcester
13 +CATTERICK BRIDGE, YARMOUTH, BATH,
+Fontwell Park
14 BEVERLEY, SOUTHWELL, FOLKESTONE,
SALISBURY
15 BEVERLEY, SOUTHWELL, Newton Abbot,
SALISBURY
16 +HAYDOCK PARK, SOUTHWELL, NEWBURY,

Perth
17 Perth, Bangor-on-Dee, LINGFIELD PARK, RIPON, +Market Rasen, NEWBURY, +WOLVERHAMPTON
19 HAMILTON PARK, WINDSOR
20 YORK, FOLKESTONE
21 YORK, YARMOUTH, Fontwell Park
22 YORK, YARMOUTH, +Salisbury
23 NEWMARKET AUGUST, Devon & Exeter, GOODWOOD
24 Cartmel, Hereford, GOODWOOD, NEWCASTLE, Market Rasen, +WINDSOR, NEWMARKET AUGUST
26 Cartmel, Huntingdon, CHEPSTOW, NEWCASTLE, Southwell, Newton Abbot, RIPON, WARWICK, Plumpton, WOLVERHAMPTON, SANDOWN PARK
27 RIPON, Newton Abbot
28 REDCAR, BRIGHTON, Newton Abbot
29 Worcester, LINGFIELD PARK
30 THIRSK, CHESTER, SANDOWN PARK
31 RIPON, CHESTER, SANDOWN PARK, Hereford

SEPTEMBER
2 Hexham, NOTTINGHAM
3 PONTEFRACT, BRIGHTON
4 YORK, Fontwell Park
5 YORK, Newton Abbot, SALISBURY
6 HAYDOCK PARK, KEMPTON PARK, Sedgefield
7 HAYDOCK PARK, SOUTHWELL, KEMPTON PARK, THIRSK, Stratford-on-Avon
9 HAMILTON PARK, WOLVERHAMPTON
10 CARLISLE, LEICESTER, LINGFIELD PARK
11 DONCASTER, Devon & Exeter, Royal Caledonian Hunt & Perth
12 DONCASTER, FOLKESTONE
13 DONCASTER, Worcester, GOODWOOD
14 DONCASTER, Bangor-on-Dee, CHEPSTOW, Worcester, GOODWOOD
16 EDINBURGH, LEICESTER, BATH, Plumpton
17 Sedgefield, YARMOUTH, Sandown Park
18 WESTERN MEETING (AYR), YARMOUTH, Devon & Exeter, BEVERLEY, SANDOWN PARK
19 WESTERN MEETING (AYR), Uttoxeter, LINGFIELD PARK, BEVERLEY, YARMOUTH
20 WESTERN MEETING (AYR), Huntingdon, NEWBURY, SOUTHWELL
21 WESTERN MEETING (AYR), Market Rasen, NEWBURY, CATTERICK BRIDGE, Worcester
23 PONTEFRACT, NOTTINGHAM, Folkestone
24 Nottingham, Kempton Park
25 Perth, Ludlow, BRIGHTON, Southwell
26 Perth, ASCOT, Taunton
27 HAYDOCK PARK, Hereford, ASCOT, REDCAR
28 Carlisle, Stratford-on-Avon, ASCOT, HAYDOCK PARK, REDCAR
30 Carlisle, WOLVERHAMPTON, BATH, HAMILTON PARK, Fontwell Park

OCTOBER
1 NEWCASTLE, WOLVERHAMPTON, BRIGHTON, Devon & Exeter
2 Sedgefield, Cheltenham, SALISBURY, NEWMARKET OCTOBER
3 Cheltenham, LINGFIELD PARK, NEWMARKET OCTOBER
4 Hexham, NEWMARKET OCTOBER, GOODWOOD
5 Kelso, NEWMARKET OCTOBER, Chepstow, Uttoxeter, GOODWOOD
7 PONTEFRACT, Southwell, Warwick
8 REDCAR, WARWICK, FOLKESTONE, Newton Abbot
9 HAYDOCK PARK, Towcester, Plumpton, YORK
10 HAYDOCK PARK, Wincanton, YORK
11 Carlisle, Market Rasen, Ascot
12 Ayr, Bangor-on-Dee, ASCOT, YORK, Southwell,

Worcester
14 AYR, LEICESTER, Fontwell Park
15 AYR, LEICESTER, CHEPSTOW, Sedgefield, Devon & Exeter
16 REDCAR, Cheltenham, Wetherby, WOLVERHAMPTON
17 Hexham, NEWMARKET HOUGHTON, Taunton, Uttoxeter
18 CATTERICK BRIDGE, Ludlow, NEWMARKET HOUGHTON
19 CATTERICK BRIDGE, NEWMARKET HOUGHTON, Kempton Park, Kelso, Southwell, Stratford-on-Avon
21 Fakenham, FOLKESTONE, NOTTINGHAM
22 CHESTER, CHEPSTOW, NOTTINGHAM, Plumpton
23 EDINBURGH, CHESTER, ASCOT, Newcastle
24 PONTEFRACT, Southwell, NEWBURY, Wincanton
25 DONCASTER, Hereford, Devon & Exeter, Newbury
26 Catterick Bridge, Huntingdon, NEWBURY, DONCASTER, Worcester
28 LEICESTER, BATH, LINGFIELD PARK
29 REDCAR, LEICESTER, SALISBURY
30 Sedgefield, YARMOUTH, Fontwell Park
31 NEWMARKET, Kempton Park, Stratford-on-Avon

NOVEMBER
1 Wetherby, Bangor-on-Dee, NEWMARKET
2 Wetherby, NEWMARKET, Chepstow, Warwick, Sandown Park
4 NEWCASTLE, Wolverhampton, Plumpton
5 HAMILTON PARK, Hereford, Devon & Exeter, Nottingham
6 Kelso, Newbury
7 EDINBURGH, Uttoxeter, Wincanton
8 DONCASTER, Cheltenham, Hexham, Market Rasen
9 DONCASTER, Cheltenham, Windsor, Newcastle
11 Carlisle, Wolverhampton, FOLKESTONE
12 Sedgefield
13 Haydock Park, Worcester, Newbury
14 Ayr, Towcester, Taunton
15 Ayr, Huntingdon, Ascot
16 Ayr, Warwick, Ascot, Catterick Bridge
18 Bangor-on-Dee, Windsor, Leicester
19 Wetherby, Nottingham, Newton Abbot
20 Haydock Park, Kempton Park, Kelso
21 Haydock Park, Ludlow, Wincanton
22 Sedgefield, Leicester, Newbury
23 Newcastle, Market Rasen, Newbury, Towcester
25 Catterick Bridge, Wolverhampton, Folkestone
26 Huntingdon, Stratford-on-Avon, Devon & Exeter
27 Hexham, Hereford, Plumpton
28 Carlisle, Warwick, Taunton
29 Bangor-on-Dee, Sandown Park
30 Wetherby, Nottingham, Chepstow, Sandown Park

DECEMBER
2 Kelso, Worcester
3 Newcastle, Leicester, Fontwell Park
4 Catterick Bridge, Huntingdon, Ludlow
5 Uttoxeter, Taunton, Windsor
6 Doncaster, Cheltenham, Devon & Exeter
7 Doncaster, Cheltenham, Lingfield, Towcester
9 Edinburgh, Warwick
10 Sedgefield, Plumpton
11 Haydock Park, Worcester
12 Haydock Park
13 Catterick Bridge, Fakenham, Hereford
14 Edinburgh, Nottingham, Ascot
16 Ludlow, Newton Abbot
17 Folkestone
18 Bangor-on-Dee
19 Kelso, Towcester

20 Hexham, Hereford, Uttoxeter
21 Edinburgh, Uttoxeter, Chepstow, Lingfield Park
26 Sedgefield, Huntingdon, Kempton Park, Wetherby, Market Rasen, Newton Abbot, Wolverhampton, Wincanton
27 Wetherby, Wolverhampton, Kempton Park, Taunton
28 Newcastle, Folkestone, Stratford-on-Avon, Newbury
30 Carlisle, Warwick, Fontwell Park, Newbury
31 Catterick Bridge, Cheltenham, Plumpton, Leicester
Flat meetings in capitals
+ = Evening meetings
(c) The Jockey Club 1990

ALL-WEATHER MEETINGS
LINGFIELD PARK-FLAT
Jan 1, 5, 12, 19, 22, 25
Feb 2, 5, 9, 16, 19, 23
Mar 2, 5, 9, 12, 23
Nov 7, 14, 28
Dec 5, 14, 18, 27

SOUTHWELL-FLAT
Jan 2, 4, 11, 16, 18, 25, 30
Feb 1, 8, 13, 15, 22, 27
Mar 1, 6, 16, 20
Nov 12, 19, 29
Dec 4, 12, 17, 28

LINGFIELD PARK-NH
Jan 3, 8, 10, 15, 17, 24, 29, 31
Feb 7, 12, 14, 21, 26, 28
Dec 7, 21

SOUTHWELL-NH
Jan 7, 9, 14, 21, 23, 28
Feb 4, 6, 11, 18, 20, 25

ICE HOCKEY

OIL AND ICE

The Edmonton Oilers, once regarded as Wayne Gretzky and a few others, won the 1990 Stanley Cup without Gretzky with an unexpected but decisive 4-1 victory over the Boston Bruins. It was the Oilers' fifth title in seven years but, more significantly, it was the first since the club traded the Great One to the Los Angeles Kings in 1988.

The Oilers did not even win their division and were up against the team with the best regular-season record. But they began by winning the longest game in Stanley Cup history (third period of overtime, 1.23 am) and, helped by magnificent work from the goaltender Bill Ranford, went on from there to give John Muckler a triumph in his first year as coach. This glory can be short-lived; the loudmouthed Terry Crisp, who led the Calgary Flames to the Cup in 1989, was fired in 1990.

Gretzky was also happy. he became the NHL's highest-ever scorer when he passed Gordie Howe's record of 1,850 points in the game against the Oilers (having taken 11 seasons to get there against Howe's 26) and he signed a $29.7m contract that could keep him with the Kings until 1998. He lost the chance of another $100,000 by refusing to do an advert saying "I'm going to Disneyland" immediately after the goal. The Kings, losing $5m a year until Gretzky joined, expected to make $5m in 1990. Gretzky paid tribute to Howe - "Gordie still is the greatest". Howe, 61, mused about making a comeback so he could play in six decades.

Nine Soviet players played in the National Hockey League, but mostly struggled, partly because of their reluctance to join in the local custom of fighting rather than playing. Vyacheslav Fetisov of the New Jersey Devils declined to retaliate when hit by Wendel Clark of the Toronto Maple Leafs. "Wendel didn't want to hurt him, just punch him a couple of times," said a shocked Canadian TV commentator.

The Kings and the Oilers had 86 penalties in one game, beating the record 84 set between Minnesota and Boston in 1981. Seven players were ejected and one punch-up included both goaltenders. The fans actually booed and threw rubbish on to the ice. "Sometimes fighting can bring the team closer together," said the Los Angeles assistant coach Cap Reader. "I thought the fights made it a real spiritual game," said his wing Marty McSorley. The Minnesota North Stars and the Chicago Blackhawks got into a brawl at the end of the warm-up session. "I think our guys are edgy just now," said the Minnesota coach Pierre Page.

Brett Hull of the St Louis Blues emulated his father Bobby by passing 50 goals in a season, and became only the sixth player to pass 70. It was reported from Minnesota that nitrogen oxide given off by faulty ice-scraping machines was suspected of causing respiratory problems which affected two-thirds of the players and cheerleaders at two high school games.

In Britain the Cardiff Devils, in their first Premier Division season, won the League under their 29-year-old Canadian founder, John Lawless, who started the club only in 1986. The Devils also beat the Murrayfield Racers to win the Heineken Championship on a penalty shoot-out. The Whitley Bay - Ayr game had to be abandoned after home fans apparently attacked a visiting player. The local MP, Neville Trotter, said the Government might have to intervene. Keith Gretzky, the younger brother, signed for Ayr after playing in Finland. His contract was worth less than $29.7m.

1989-90

WORLD CHAMPIONSHIPS (A GROUP)
Berne/Freiburg, Switzerland, Apr 16-May 2

ROUND ROBIN RESULTS
SOVIET UNION 9 Norway 1; CANADA 5 West Germany 1; SWEDEN 4 Norway 3; CZECHOSLOVAKIA 4 Finland 2; FINLAND 4 West Germany 2; CANADA 6 United States 3; CZECHOSLOVAKIA 9 Norway 1; CANADA 6 Finland 5; SOVIET UNION 5 West Germany 2; SWEDEN 6 West Germany 0; CANADA 8 Norway 0; SWEDEN 6 United States 1; SOVIET UNION 10 United States 1; CZECHOSLOVAKIA 3 West Germany 0; SOVIET UNION 6 Finland 1; CANADA 3 Sweden 1; UNITED STATES 6 West Germany 3; SOVIET UNION 4 Czechoslovakia 1; SWEDEN 4 Finland 2; CANADA 5 Czechoslovakia 3; NORWAY 7 West Germany 3; Finland 3 Norway 3; CZECHOSLOVAKIA 7 United States 1, SWEDEN 3 Soviet Union *1 Soviet Union's first defeat in 5 years in the World Championship;* UNITED STATES 2 Finland 1; Canada 3 Soviet Union 3; SWEDEN 5 Czechoslovakia 1

STANDINGS
	P	W	D	L	F	A	Pts
1 Canada	7	6	1	0	36	16	13
2 Sweden	7	6	0	1	29	11	12
3 Soviet Union	7	5	1	1	38	12	11
4 Czechoslovakia	7	4	0	3	28	18	8
5 United States	7	3	0	4	23	37	6
6 Finland	7	1	1	5	18	27	3
7 Norway	7	1	1	5	19	45	3
8 West Germany	7	0	0	7	11	36	0

Canada, Sweden, Soviet Union and Czechoslovakia qualified for Medal round.

MEDAL ROUND
CZECHOSLOVAKIA 3 Canada 2; SOVIET UNION 3 Sweden 0; Czechoslovakia 5 Sweden 5; SOVIET UNION 7 Canada 1; SOVIET UNION 5 Czechoslovakia 0; SWEDEN 6 Canada 4

FINAL POSITIONS (MEDAL GROUPS)
	P	W	D	L	F	A	Pts
1 Soviet Union	3	3	0	0	15	1	6
2 Sweden	3	1	1	1	11	12	3
3 Czechoslovakia	3	1	1	1	8	12	3
4 Canada	3	0	0	3	7	16	0

Norway finished bottom of the Relegation Group and are now relegated to Group B in 1991.

NATIONAL HOCKEY LEAGUE
Final Standings (last year's positions in brackets)
Wales Conference
Patrick Division

	P	W	L	T	Pts
1 (3) NY Rangers	80	36	31	13	85
2 (5) New Jersey	80	37	34	9	83
3 (1) Washington	80	36	38	6	78
4 (3) NY Islanders	80	31	38	11	73
5 (2) Pittsburgh	80	32	40	8	72
6 (4) Philadelphia	80	30	39	11	71

Play offs
NEW YORK RANGERS 4 New York Islanders 1; WASHINGTON CAPITALS 4 New Jersey Devils 2;
Divisional Final
WASHINGTON CAPITALS 4 New York Rangers 1

Wales Conference
Adams Division

	P	W	L	T	Pts
1 (2) Boston	80	46	25	9	101
2 (3) Buffalo	80	45	27	8	98
3 (1) Montreal	80	41	28	11	93
4 (4) Hartford	80	38	33	9	85
5 (5) Quebec	80	12	61	7	31

Play-offs
MONTREAL CANADIENS 4 Buffalo Sabres 2; BOSTON BRUINS 4 Hartford Whalers 3
Divisional Final
BOSTON BRUINS 4 Montreal Canadiens 0

WALES CONFERENCE FINAL
Boston Bruins 4 Montreal Canadiens 1

Campbell Conference
Norris Division

	P	W	L	T	Pts
1 (4) Chicago	80	41	33	6	88
2 (2) St Louis	80	37	34	9	83
3 (5) Toronto	80	38	38	4	80
4 (3) Minnesota	80	36	40	4	76
5 (1) Detroit	80	28	38	14	70

Play-offs
CHICAGO BLACKHAWKS 4 Minnesota North Stars 3; ST LOUIS BLUES 4 Toronto Maple Leafs 1
Divisional Final
CHICAGO BLACKHAWKS 4 St Louis Blues 3

Smythe Division

	P	W	L	T	Pts
1 (1) Calgary	80	42	23	15	99
2 (3) Edmonton	80	38	28	14	90
3 (5) Winnipeg	80	37	32	11	85
4 (2) Los Angeles	80	34	39	7	75
5 (4) Vancouver	80	25	41	14	64

Play-offs
EDMONTON OILERS 4 Winnipeg Jets 3; LOS ANGELES KINGS 4 Calgary Flames 1;
Divisional Final
EDMONTON OILERS 4 Chicago Blackhawks 2

CONFERENCE FINAL
EDMONTON OILERS 4 Chicago Blackhawks 2

THE GENTLE SPORT

❝Some sportscasters believe that unless they show a hockey fight on television every night, people won't be able to fall asleep. They must believe they're performing some charitable or medical act - such as serving warm milk before beddy-bye".
Ira Berkow, New York Times

"I do know this about fighting in the NHL: If the NHL wants to do anything about it, fine. And if they don't want to do anything about it, fine".
Wayne Gretzky

"If I was a mineworker and he was the pit boss, I'd put my pick through his forehead.❞
Unnamed Calgary player on Flames coach Terry Crisp

STANLEY CUP
Game 1: Boston Bruins 2 EDMONTON OILERS 3
* *Longest Stanley Cup game in history at 5hr 32m*
Game 2: Boston Bruins 2 EDMONTON OILERS 7
Game 3: Edmonton Oilers 1 BOSTON BRUINS 2
Game 4: EDMONTON OILERS 5 Boston Bruins 1
Game 5: Boston Bruins 1 EDMONTON OILERS 4
Edmonton won best-of-seven games series 4-1
Conn Smythe Trophy for MVP in play-offs: Bill Ranford (Edmonton)
Hart Trophy for NHL MVP: Mark Messier (Edmonton)

LEADING SCORERS
1989-90 REGULAR SEASON
Most Goals: 72 Brett Hull (St Louis)
(Record: 92 Wayne Gretzky (Edmonton) 1981-82)
Most Assists: 102 Wayne Gretzky (Los Angeles)
(Record: 163 Wayne Gretzky (Edmonton) 1985-86)
Most Points: 142 Wayne Gretzky (Los Angeles)
(Record: 215 Wayne Gretzky (Edmonton) 1985-86)

HEINEKEN LEAGUE

	P	W	D	L	F	A	Pts
1 Cardiff Devils	32	28	3	1	304	146	57
2 Murrayfield Racers	32	23	6	3	273	169	49
3 Durham Wasps	32	20	10	2	261	209	42
4 Solihull Barons	32	16	15	1	218	209	33
5 Fife Flyers	32	14	15	3	226	264	31
6 Nottingham Panthers	32	12	18	2	183	185	26
7 Ayr Raiders	32	9	19	4	181	229	22
8 Peterborough Pirates	32	7	25	0	174	281	14
9 Whitley Bay Warriors	32	6	24	2	202	330	14

HEINEKEN BRITISH CHAMPIONSHIP
Wembley April 20-22
SEMI-FINAL
CARDIFF DEVILS 5 Fife Flyers 1; MURRAYFIELD RACERS 5 Nottingham Panthers 4
FINAL
CARDIFF DEVILS 6 Murrayfield Racers 6 (OT)
Cardiff won 6-5 on penalty shots
Att: 9,000

CHAMPIONS

WORLD CHAMPIONSHIPS

1920 Canada	1950 Canada	1966 USSR
1924 Canada	1951 Canada	1967 USSR
1928 Canada	1952 Canada	1968 USSR
1930 Canada	1953 Sweden	1970 USSR
1931 Canada	1954 USSR	1971 USSR
1932 Canada	1955 Canada	1972 Czechoslovakia
1933 United States	1956 USSR	1973 USSR
1934 Canada	1957 Sweden	1974 USSR
1935 Canada	1958 Canada	1975 USSR
1936 Great Britain	1959 Canada	1976 Czechoslovakia
1937 Canada	1960 United States	1977 Czechoslovakia
1938 Canada	1961 Canada	1978 USSR
1939 Canada	1962 Sweden	1979 USSR
1947 Czechoslovakia	1963 USSR	1980 United States
1948 Canada	1964 USSR	1981 USSR
1949 Czechoslovakia	1965 USSR	1982 USSR

1983 USSR
1984 USSR
1985 Czechoslovakia
1986 USSR
1987 Sweden
1988 USSR
1989 USSR
1990 USSR
Most wins:
24 USSR; **19** Canada

STANLEY CUP
(First contested 1985)
Post-war winners

1945-46	Montreal Canadiens
1946-47	Toronto Maple Leafs
1947-48	Toronto Maple Leafs
1948-49	Toronto Maple Leafs
1949-50	Detroit Red Wings
1950-51	Toronto Maple Leafs
1951-52	Detroit Red Wings
1952-53	Montreal Canadiens
1953-54	Detroit Red Wings
1954-55	Detroit Red Wings
1955-56	Montreal Canadiens
1956-57	Montreal Canadiens
1957-58	Montreal Canadiens
1958-59	Montreal Canadiens
1959-60	Montreal Canadiens
1960-61	Chicago Blackhawks
1961-62	Toronto Maple Leafs
1962-63	Toronto Maple Leafs
1963-64	Toronto Maple Leafs
1964-65	Montreal Canadiens
1965-66	Montreal Canadiens
1966-67	Toronto Maple Leafs
1967-68	Montreal Canadiens
1968-69	Montreal Canadiens
1969-70	Boston Bruins
1970-71	Montreal Canadiens
1971-72	Boston Bruins
1972-73	Montreal Canadiens
1973-74	Philadelphia Flyers
1974-75	Philadelphia Flyers
1975-76	Montreal Canadiens
1976-77	Montreal Canadiens
1977-78	Montreal Canadiens
1978-79	Montreal Canadiens
1979-80	New York Islanders
1980-81	New York Islanders
1981-82	New York Islanders
1982-83	New York Islanders
1983-84	Edmonton Oilers
1984-85	Edmonton Oilers
1985-86	Montreal Canadiens
1986-87	Edmonton Oilers
1987-88	Edmonton Oilers
1988-89	Calgary Flames
1989-90	Edmonton Oilers

Most Wins:
23 Montreal Canadiens; 11 Toronto Maple Leafs; 7 Detroit
Red Wings; 6 Ottawa Senators; 5 Montreal Victorias;
Boston Bruins; Edmonton Oilers

HEINEKEN BRITISH CHAMPIONSHIP
1982	Dundee Rockets
1983	Dundee Rockets
1984	Dundee Rockets
1985	Fife Flyers
1986	Murrayfield Racers
1987	Durham Wasps
1988	Durham Wasps
1989	Nottingham Panthers
1990	Cardiff Devils

JUDO

1990

EUROPEAN CHAMPIONSHIPS
Frankfurt, May 10-13
Winners
Men

Open Class:	Laszlo Tolnai (Hun)
Heavyweight/over 95kg:	Sergei Kosorotov (USSR)
Light-heavyweight/under 95kg:	Stephane Traineau (Fra)
Middleweight/under 86kg:	Waldemar Legien (Pol)
Light-middleweight/under 78kg:	Bachir Varayev (USSR)
Lightweight/under 71kg:	Guido Schumacher (FRG)
Featherweight/under 65kg:	Bruno Carabetta (Fra)
Bantamweight/under 60kg:	Philippe Pradayrol (Fra)

Women

Open Class:	Sharon Lee (GB)
Heavyweight/over 72kg:	Christine Cicot (Fra)
Light-heavyweight/under 72kg:	Karin Krueger (FRG)
Middleweight/under 66kg:	Alexandra Schreiber (FRG)
Light-middleweight/under 61kg:	Begona Gomez (Spa)
Lightweight/under 56kg:	Catherine Arnaud (Fra)
Featherweight/under 52kg:	Sharon Rendle (GB)
Bantamweight/under 48kg:	Cecile Nowak (Fra)

BRITISH OPEN CHAMPIONSHIPS
Crystal Palace, Apr 7-8
Winners
Men

Bantamweight/under 60kg:	T Dibert (Fra)
Featherweight/under 65kg:	Mark Preston (GB)
Lightweight/under 71kg:	C M'Bani (Fra)
Light-middleweight/under 78kg:	Ryan Birch (GB)
Middleweight/under 86kg:	M Liebnitz (Fra)
Light-heavyweight/under 95kg:	Ray Stevens (GB)
Heavyweight/over 95kg:	D Douillet (Fra)

Women

Bantamweight/under 48kg:	Karen Briggs (GB)
Featherweight/under 52kg:	Sharon Rendle (GB)
Lightweight/under 56kg:	Nicola Fairbrother (GB)
Light-middleweight/under 61kg:	Diane Bell (GB)
Middleweight/under 66kg:	Kate Howey (GB)
Light-heavyweight/under 72kg:	E Essombe (Fra)
Heavyweight/over 72kg:	Sharon Lee (GB)

1989

WORLD CHAMPIONSHIPS
Belgrade, Oct 10-16

FINALS
Men
Open
Naoyo Ogawa (Jap) beat Akaky Kibordiladze (USSR)
Over 95kg
Naoyo Ogawa (Jap) beat Francesco Moreno (Cub)
Under 95kg
Koba Kurtanidze (USSR) beat Odvog Baljuynnyan (Mon)
Under 86kg
Fabian Canu (Fra) beat Ben Spijkers (Hol)
Under 78kg
Byung-ju Kim (SKo) beat Tatsuto Mochida (Jap)
Under 71kg
Toshihiko Koga (Jap) beat Mike Swain (US)
Under 65kg
Drago Becanovic (Yug) beat Udo Quellmalz (GDR)
Under 60kg
Amiran Totikashvilli (USSR) beat Todanori Koshino (Jap)

Women
Open
Estela Rodriguez (Cub) beat Sharon Lee (GB)
Over 72kg
Fenglian Gao (Chn) beat Regine Sigmund (FRG)
Under 72kg
Ingrid Berghmans (Bel) beat Yoko Tanabe (Jap)
Under 66kg
Emanuela Pierantozzi (Ita) beat Hakiri Sasaki (Jap)
Under 61kg
Catherine Fleury (Fra) beat Elena Petrova (USSR)
Under 56kg
Catherine Arnaud (Fra) beat Ann Hughes (GB)
Under 52kg
Sharon Rendle (GB) beat Alessandra Giungi (Ita)
Under 48kg
Karen Briggs (GB) beat Fumiko Esaki (Jap)

EUROPEAN TEAM CHAMPIONSHIP
Vienna, Oct 28
Men
1 USSR
2 France
3 East Germany & Great Britain
Women
1 France
2 Great Britain
3 Austria & Italy

CHAMPIONS

OLYMPIC GAMES
Open

1964	Anton Geesink (Hol)
1972	Willem Ruska (Hol)
1976	Haruki Uemura (Jap)
1980	Dietmar Lorenz (GDR)
1984	Yasuhiro Yamashita (Jap)

Heavyweight/Over 95kg

1964	Isao Inokuma (Jap)
1972	Willem Ruska (Hol)
1976	Sergey Novikov (USSR)
1980	Angelo Parisi (Fra)
1984	Hitoshi Saito (Jap)
1988	Hitoshi Saito (Jap)

Half-heavyweight/Under 95kg

1972	Shota Chochoshvili (USSR)
1976	Kazuhiro Ninomiya (Jap)
1980	Robert Van de Walle (Bel)
1984	Hyeung-Zoo Ha (SKo)
1988	Aurelio Miguel (Bra)

Middleweight/Under 86kg

1964	Isao Okano (Jap)
1972	Shinobu Sekine (Jap)
1976	Isamu Sonoda (Jap)
1980	Jurg Rothlisberger (Swi)
1984	Peter Seisenbacher (Aut)
1988	Peter Seisenbacher (Aut)

Half-middleweight/Under 78kg

1980	Shota Khabareli (USSR)
1984	Frank Weineke (FRG)
1988	Waldemar Legien (Pol)

Lightweight/Under 71kg

1964	Takehide Nakatani (Jap)
1972	Toyokazu Nomura (Jap)
1976	Vladimir Nevzorov (USSR)
1980	Ezio Gamba (Ita)
1984	Byeong-Kuen Ahn (SKo)
1988	Marc Alexandre (Fra)

Half-lightweight/Under 65kg
1972   Takao Kawaguchi (Jap)
1976   Hector Rodriguez (Cub)
1980   Nikoli Soludukhin (USSR)
1984   Yoshiyuki Matsuoda (Jap)
1988   Lee Kuung-Keun (SKo)

Extra-lightweight/Under 60kg
1980   Thierry Rey (Fra)
1984   Shinji Hosokawa (Jap)
1988   Kim Jae-Yup (SKo)

WORLD CHAMPIONSHIPS
Winners since 1981

Men
Open
1981   Yasuhiro Yamashita (Jap)
1983   Hitoshi Saito (Jap)
1985   Yoshimi Masaki (Jap)
1987   Naoya Ogawa (Jap)
1989   Naoya Ogawa (Jap)

Heavyweight/Over 95kg
1981   Yasuhiro Yamashita (Jap)
1983   Yasuhiro Yamashita (Jap)
1985   Yong-Chul Cho (SKo)
1987   Grigori Vertichev (USSR)
1989   Naoya Ogawa (Jap)

Half-heavyweight/Under 95kg
1981   Tengiz Khubuluri (USSR)
1983   Valerily Divisenko (USSR)
1985   Hitoshi Sugai (Jap)
1987   Hitoshi Sugai (Jap)
1989   Koba Kurtanidze (USSR)

Middleweight/Under 86kg
1981   Bernard Tchoullouyan (Fra)
1983   Detlef Ultsch (GDR)
1985   Peter Seisenbacher (Aut)
1987   Fabian Canu (Fra)
1989   Fabian Canu (Fra)

Half-middleweight/Under 78kg
1981   Neil Adams (GB)
1983   Nobutoshi Hikage (Jap)
1985   Nobutoshi Hikage (Jap)
1987   Hirotaka Okada (Jap)
1989   Byung-ju Kim (SKo)

Lightweight/Under 71kg
1981   Chong-Hak Park (SKo)
1983   Hidetoshi Nakanishi (Jap)
1985   Byeong-Kuen Ahn (SKo)
1987   Mike Swain (US)
1989   Toshihiko Koga (Jap)

Half-lightweight/Under 65kg
1981   Katsuhiko Kashiwazaki (Jap)
1983   Nikolai Soludukhin (USSR)
1985   Yuriy Sokolov (USSR)
1987   Yosuke Yamamoto (Jap)
1989   Drago Becanovic (Yug)

Extra-lightweight/Under 60kg
1981   Yasuhiko Moriwaki (Jap)
1983   Khazret Tletseri (USSR)
1985   Shinji Hosokawa (Jap)
1987   Kim Jae-Yup (SKo)
1989   Amiran Totikashvilli (USSR)

Women
Open
1982   Ingrid Berghmans (Bel)
1984   Ingrid Berghmans (Bel)
1987   Fenglian Gao (Chn)
1988   Ingrid Berghmans (Bel)

1989   Estela Rodriguez (Cub)

Heavyweight/Over 72kg
1982   Natalina Lupino (Fra)
1984   Maria-Teresa Motta (Ita)
1986   Fenglian Gao (Chn)
1987   Fenglian Gao (Chn)
1989   Fenglian Gao (Chn)

Half-heavyweight/Under 72kg
1982   Barbara Classen (FRG)
1984   Ingrid Berghmans (Bel)
1986   Irene de Kok (Hol)
1987   Irene de Kok (Hol)
1989   Ingrid Berghmans (Bel)

Middleweight/under 66kg
1982   Brigitte Deydier (Fra)
1984   Brigitte Deydier (Fra)
1986   Brigitte Deydier (Fra)
1987   Alexandra Schreiber (FRG)
1989   Emanuela Pierantozzi (Ita)

Half-middleweight/Under 61kg
1982   Martine Rothier (Fra)
1984   Natasha Hernandez (Ven)
1986   Diane Bell (GB)
1987   Diane Bell (GB)
1989   Catherine Fleury (Fra)

Lightweight/Under 56kg
1982   Beatrice Rodriguez (Fra)
1984   Ann-Maria Burns (US)
1986   Ann Hughs (GB)
1987   Catherine Arnaud (Fra)
1989   Catherine Arnaud (Fra)

Half-lightweight/Under 52kg
1982   Loretta Doyle (GB)
1984   Kaori Yamaguchi (Jap)
1986   Dominique Brun (Fra)
1987   Sharon Rendle (GB)
1989   Sharon Rendle (GB)

Extra-lightweight/Under 48kg
1982   Karen Briggs (GB)
1984   Karen Briggs (GB)
1986   Karen Briggs (GB)
1987   Zhang Li (Chn)
1989   Karen Briggs (GB)

─────────── 1991 ───────────

May 16-19 European championships, men and women
(Prague, Czechoslovakia); *Jul 25-28* World
Championships (Barcelona); *Nov 14-17* Junior European
championships, men and women (Finland)

LACROSSE

The Iroquois national team, banned from international competition almost a century ago for using professionals, competed in the World Championships and became firm favourites with the crowds despite losing all their games. The Iroquois used wooden sticks instead of modern aluminium or fibre glass. They will host the Championships in 2002. One of the Iroquois squad, Tyler Sunday, once beat Mike Tyson in an amateur boxing bout.

1990

Men's Lacrosse

WORLD CHAMPIONSHIP
Perth, Australia Jul 8-15
Third Place Play-off
AUSTRALIA 16 England 6
Final
UNITED STATES 19 Canada 15
Final Standings:
1 United States; 2 Canada; 3 Australia; 4 England; 5 Iroquois Nationals

AVON INSURANCE NORTHERN SENIOR FLAGS
Didsbury, Apr 8
CHEADLE 7 Mellor 6

SOUTHERN SENIOR FLAGS
Leyton, Apr 7
HAMPSTEAD 19 London University 16

BRINE NORTHERN LEAGUE
Champions: HEATON MERSEY

ENGLISH CLUB CHAMPIONSHIP
(Iroquois Cup)
Battersea Park, May 13
CHEADLE 23 Hampstead 6

Women's Lacrosse

HOME INTERNATIONAL SERIES
1 ENGLAND; 2 Scotland; 3 Wales

HATTERSLEY SALVER
Berkhamsted, Mar 31-Apr 1
Final Placings
1 EAST; 2 West; 3 South; 4 Combined Universities; 5 North; 6 Midlands

SAC CLUBS & COLLEGES TROPHY
Cobham, Surrey, Apr 28
WEST LONDON 2 Centaurs 1 (aet)

NATIONAL SCHOOLS CHAMPIONSHIP
Luton, Mar 17
QUEEN ANNE'S (Caversham) 2 Berkhamstead 1 (sudden death)

WOMEN'S WORLD CUP
1982	United States
1986	Australia
1989	United States

IROQUOIS CUP
(English Men's Club Championship, first contested 1890)
Winners since 1981:
1981	Cheadle
1982	Sheffield University
1983	Sheffield University
1984	Cheadle
1985	Cheadle
1986	Heaton Mersey
1987	Stockport
1988	Mellor
1989	Stockport
1990	Cheadle

Most wins:
17 Stockport; 11 South Manchester; 10 Old Hulmeians, Mellor; 7 Old Waconians; 6 Heaton Mersey, Cheadle

1991

Mar 9-10 Hattersley Salver (Hughton, Merseyside); Apr 6-7 Hattersley Salver (Reading University); Apr 27-28 Clubs and Colleges Trophy (Cobham, Surrey); Mar 16 National Schools Final (Luton).

CHAMPIONS

MEN'S WORLD CHAMPIONSHIP
(First held 1967)
1967	United States
1974	United States
1978	Canada
1982	United States
1986	United States
1990	United States

MODERN PENTATHLON

1990

Men

WORLD CHAMPIONSHIP
Finland, Jul 25-29

Individual
1 Gianluca Tiberti (Ita) 5,441pts
2 Anatoly Starostin (USSR) 5,403pts
3 Milan Kadlec (Cze) 5,402pts

Team
1 USSR 16,041pts
2 Italy 16,035pts
3 Poland 15,971pts

BRITISH CHAMPIONSHIP
Barnet, Jun 8-10

Individual
1 Richard Phelps (Spartan) 5,524pts
2 Graham Brookhouse (Spartan) 5,435pts
3 Dominic Mahoney (Army) 5,410pts

Team
1 Army MPA 15,408pts
2 Spartan MPC 15,367pts
Only two teams classified

Women

WORLD CHAMPIONSHIP
Sweden, Aug 23-26

Individual
1 Eva Fjellerup (Den) 5,478pts
2 Lori Norwood (US) 5,333pts
3 Dorota Idzi (Pol) 5,264pts

Team
1 Poland 15,527pts
2 USSR 15,134pts
3 West Germany 15,095pts

BRITISH CHAMPIONSHIP
Wantage, May 25-27

Individual
1 Sarah Cox 5,448pts
2 Kath Young 5,261pts
3 Alison Hollington 5,046pts

Team
1 Pegasus MPC Junior 13,153pts
2 Newton Hall 11,689pts
3 Wessex Wyvern MPC 10,884pts

CHAMPIONS

WORLD CHAMPIONSHIPS
(Not held in Olympic years)

Men - Individual
1981	Janusz Pyciak-Peciak (Pol)
1982	Daniele Masala (Ita)
1983	Anatoliy Starostin (USSR)
1985	Attila Mizser (Hun)
1986	Carlo Massullo (Ita)
1987	Joel Bouzou (Fra)
1989	Laszlo Fabian (Hun)
1990	Gianluca Tiberti (Ita)

Men - Team
1981	Poland
1982	USSR
1983	USSR
1985	USSR

1986	Italy
1987	Hungary
1989	Hungary
1990	USSR

Women - Individual
1981	Anne Ahlgren (Swe)
1982	Wendy Norman (GB)
1983	Lynn Chernobrywy (Can)
1984	Svetlana Jakovleva (USSR)
1985	Barbara Kotowska (Pol)
1986	Irina Kisselyeva (USSR)
1987	Irina Kisselyeva (USSR)
1988	Dorota Idzi (Pol)
1989	Lori Norwood (US)
1990	Eva Fjellerup (Den)

Women - Team
1981	Britain
1982	Britain
1983	Britain
1984	USSR
1985	Poland
1986	France
1987	USSR
1988	Poland
1989	Poland
1990	Poland

OLYMPIC GAMES
Men Only

Individual
1912	Gosta Lilliehook (Swe)
1920	Gustaf Dryssen (Swe)
1924	Bo Lindman (Swe)
1928	Sven Thofelt (Swe)
1932	Johan Oxenstierna (Swe)
1936	Gotthardt Handrick (Ger)
1948	Willie Grut (Swe)
1952	Lars Hall (Swe)
1956	Lars Hall (Swe)
1960	Ferenc Nemeth (Hun)
1964	Ferenc Torok (Hun)
1968	Bjorn Ferm (Swe)
1972	Andras Balczo (Hun)
1976	Janusz Pyciak-Peciak (Pol)
1980	Anatoly Starostin (USSR)
1984	Daniele Masala (Ita)
1988	Janos Martinek (Hun)

Team
1952	Hungary
1956	USSR
1960	Hungary
1964	USSR
1968	Hungary
1972	USSR
1976	Britain
1980	USSR
1984	Italy
1988	Hungary

1991

Jul 12-14	British Championship - men (Corby)
Aug 21-23	World Championship - men (US)
Sep 20-22	British Championship - women (Knutsford)
Nov 1-5	World Championship - women (Australia)

MOTOR CYCLING

The 29-year-old Californian Wayne Rainey became the new world 500cc champion after only three laps of the Czechoslovak Grand Prix, the third last, when his only possible challenger Kevin Schwantz slid off the track and out of contention. Rainey won the race in style anyway. It was his seventh win of the year and his worst position until then had been third.

The 1989 champion Eddie Lawson, who had switched from Honda to become Rainey's Yamaha team-mate, lost his chance at the start of the season. He was brought down in the Japanese Grand Prix and chipped a bone in his ankle; then he broke a heel in practice for the US race. Schwantz won five races on his Suzuki but was again inconsistent. The Australian Wayne Gardner lost his chance in practice for the German Grand Prix. "Bad luck is following me around at the moment," he had just moaned to reporters. Then he broke his right foot in nine places. He said he felt like a bag of crisps.

Enos Manfredini, 21, of Italy was killed in a 13-machine pile-up at the first bend of a European Championship 250cc race in Yugoslavia. The International Motor Cycling Federation decided to abolish its jury system, comprising delegates from national federations, and replace it with a six-man committee. "I've been waiting ten years to see this happen," said Kenny Roberts. "At last we may see the professionalism that we need now that the holidaymakers are out of the way."

1990

WORLD CHAMPIONSHIP GRANDS PRIX
500cc

Japanese GP
Suzuka, Mar 25
1 Wayne Rainey (US) Yamaha 98.27mph/158.15kph
2 Wayne Gardner (Aus) Honda
3 Kevin Schwantz (US) Suzuki

United States GP
Laguna Seca, California, Apr 8
1 Wayne Rainey (US) Yamaha 90.56mph/145.74kph
2 Michael Doohan (Aus) Honda
3 Pier Fancisco Chili (Ita) Honda

Spanish GP
Jerez, May 6
1 Wayne Gardner (Aus) Honda 86.10mph/138.56kph
2 Wayne Rainey (US) Yamaha
3 Kevin Schwantz (US) Suzuki

Italian GP
Misano, May 19-20
1 Wayne Rainey (US) Yamaha 101.00mph/162.54kph
2 Kevin Schwantz (US) Suzuki
3 Michael Doohan (Aus) Honda

West German GP
Nurburgring, May 27
1 Kevin Schwantz (US) Suzuki 100.98mph/162.51kph
2 Wayne Rainey (US) Yamaha
3 Niall Mackenzie (GB) Suzuki

Austrian GP
Salzburg, Jun 10
1 Kevin Schwantz (US) Suzuki 119.53mph/192.36kph
2 Wayne Rainey (US) Yamaha
3 Michael Doohan (Aus) Honda

Yugoslav GP
Rijeka, Jun 10
1 Wayne Rainey (US) Yamaha 103.15mph/166.00kph
2 Kevin Schwantz (US) Suzuki
3 Niall Mackenzie (GB) Suzuki

Dutch GP
Assen, Jun 30
1 Kevin Schwantz (US) Suzuki 108.62mph/174.81kph
2 Wayne Rainey (US) Yamaha
3 Eddie Lawson (US) Yamaha

Belgian GP
Spa - Francorchamps, Jul 8
1 Wayne Rainey (US) Yamaha 92.90mph/149.51kph
2 Jean-Phillippe Ruggia (Fra) Yamaha
3 Eddie Lawson (US) Yamaha

French GP
Le Mans, Jul 22
1 Kevin Schwantz (US) Suzuki 96.11mph/138.66kph
2 Wayne Gardner (Aus) Honda
3 Wayne Rainey (US) Yamaha

British GP
Donington Park, Aug 5
1 Kevin Schwantz (US) Suzuki 93.82mph/153.22kph
2 Wayne Rainey (US) Yamaha
3 Eddie Lawson (US) Yamaha

Swedish GP
Anderstorp, Aug 12
1 Wayne Rainey (US) Yamaha 97.80mph/157.40kph
2 Eddie Lawson (US) Yamaha
3 Wayne Gardner (Aus) Honda

Czechoslovak GP
Brno, Aug 26
1 Wayne Rainey (US) Yamaha 96.61mph/155.48kph
2 Wayne Gardner (Aus) Honda
3 Eddie Lawson (US) Yamaha

Hungarian GP
Budapest, Sep 2
1 Michael Doohan (Aus) Honda 84.17mph/135.46kph
2 Eddie Lawson (US) Yamaha
3 Kevin Schwantz (US) Suzuki

Australian GP
Philip Island, Sep 16
1 Wayne Gardner (Aus) Honda 104.12mph/167.56kph
2 Michael Doohan (Aus) Honda
3 Wayne Rainey (US) Yamaha

FINAL CHAMPIONSHIP STANDINGS
1 Wayne Rainey (US) Yamaha   255pts
2 Kevin Schwantz (US) Suzuki   188pts
3 Michael Doohan (Aus) Honda   179pts
4 Niall Mackenzie (GB) Yamaha   140pts
5 Wayne Gardner (Aus) Honda   138pts
6 Juan Garriga (Spa) Yamaha   121pts

THE OTHER WORLD CHAMPIONS
250cc
1 John Kocinski (US) Yamaha   223pts
2 Carlos Cardus (Spa) Honda   208pts
3 Luca Cadalora (Ita) Yamaha   184pts

125cc
1 Loris Capirossi (Ita) Honda   182pts
2 Hans Spaan (Hol) Honda   173pts
3 Stefan Prein (FRG) Honda   169pts
Capirossi, 17, became youngest ever world champion

Sidecars
1 Alain Michel (Fra)/Simon Birchall (GB) Krauser 178pts
2 Egbert Streuer/Geral de Haas (Hol) and Scott Whiteside (GB) Krauser 167pts
3 Steve Webster (GB)/Gavin Simmons (GB) Krauser 166pts

TT Formula One World Championship
1 Carl Fogarty (GB) Honda   71pts
2 Joey Dunlop (GB) Honda   54pts
3 Robert Dunlop (GB) Honda   49pts

ISLE OF MAN TT RACES
May 28-Jun 8
Supersport 600
1 Brain Reid (Yamaha) 111.98mph/180.21kph
2 Johnny Rea (Honda)
3 Steve Cull (Yamaha)
Ulstermen filled the first four places

Supersport 400
1 Dave Leach (Yamaha) 107.73mph/173.37kph
2 Nick Jefferies (Loctite Yamaha)
3 Robert Dunlop (Norton)

Sidecar TT (I)
1 Dave Saville/Nick Roche (Yamaha). 100.72mph/162.09kph
2 Mick Boddice/Dave Wells (Honda)
3 Neil Smith/Steven Mace (Yamaha)

Sidecar TT (II)
1 Dave Saville/Nick Roche (Yamaha) 100.17mph/161.21kph
2 Geoff Bell/Jim Cochrane (Yamaha)
3 Peter Krukowski/Chris McGahan (Yamaha)

125cc
1 Robert Dunlop (Honda) 103.41mph/166.42kph
2 Ian Newton (Honda)
3 Michael Topping (Honda)

Junior TT
1 Ian Lougher (Yamaha) 115.16mph/185.33kph
2 Steve Hislop (Honda)
3 Eddie Laycock (Yamaha)

Senior TT
1 Carl Fogarty (Honda) 110.95mph/178.56kph
2 Trevor Nation (Norton)
3 Dave Leach (Yamaha)

MOTO CROSS
500cc
1 Eric Geboers (Bel) Honda   393pts
2 Kurt Nicoll (GB) KTM   294pts
3 Kirk Geukens (Bel) Honda   247pts

250cc
1 Alessandro Puzar (Ita) Suzuki   362pts
2 Pekka Vehkonen (Fin) Yamaha   256pts
3 John van den Berk (Hol) Suzuki 246pts
Puzar is the first Italian to win a moto cross world title

125cc
1 Donny Schmit (US) Suzuki   285pts
2 Bobby Moore (FRG) KTM   214pts
3 Stefan Everts (Bel) Suzuki   161pts

World Team Championship
1 United States   9pts
2 Belgium   10pts
3 Sweden   12pts

——— CHAMPIONS ———

WORLD CHAMPIONS

1949

125cc	Nello Pagani (Ita)	Mondial
250cc	Bruno Ruffo (Ita)	Guzzi
350cc	Freddie Frith (GB)	Velocette
500cc	Leslie Graham (GB)	AJS
Sidecar	Eric Oliver (GB)	Norton

1950

125cc	Bruno Ruffo (Ita)	Mondial
250cc	Dario Ambrosini (Ita)	Benelli
350cc	Bob Foster (GB)	Velocette
500cc	Umberto Masetti (Ita)	Gilera
Sidecar	Eric Oliver (GB)	Norton

1951

125cc	Carlo Ubbiali (Ita)	Mondial
250cc	Bruno Ruffo (Ita)	Guzzi
350cc	Geoff Duke (GB)	Norton
500cc	Geoff Duke (GB)	Norton
Sidecar	Eric Oliver (GB)	Norton

1952

125cc	Cecil Sandford (GB)	MV
250cc	Enrico Lorensetti (Ita)	Guzzi
350cc	Geoff Duke (UK)	Norton
500cc	Umberto Masetti (Ita)	Gilera
Sidecar	Cyril Smith (GB)	Norton

1953

125cc	Werner Haas (FRG)	NSU
250cc	Werner Haas (FRG)	NSU
350cc	Fergus Anderson (GB)	Guzzi

500cc	Geoff Duke (GB)	Gilera
Sidecar	Eric Oliver (GB)	Norton

1954

125cc	Rupert Hollaus (Aut)	NSU
250cc	Werner Haas (FRG)	NSU
350cc	Fergus Anderson (GB)	Guzzi
500cc	Geoff Duke (GB)	Gilera
Sidecar	Wilhelm Noll (FRG)	BMW

1955

125cc	Carlo Ubbiali (Ita)	MV
250cc	Herman Muller (FRG)	NSU
350cc	Bill Lomas (GB)	Guzzi
500cc	Geoff Duke (GB)	Gilera
Sidecar	Wilhelm Faust (FRG)	BMW

1956

125cc	Carlo Ubbiali (Ita)	MV
250cc	Carlo Ubbiali (Ita)	MV
350cc	Bill Lomas (GB)	Guzzi
500cc	John Surtees (GB)	MV
Sidecar	Wilhelm Noll (FRG)	BMW

1957

125cc	Tarquinio Provini (Ita)	Mondial
250cc	Cecil Sandford (GB)	Mondial
350cc	Keith Campbell (Aus)	Guzzi
500cc	Libero Liberati (Ita)	Gilera
Sidecar	Fritz Hillebrand (FRG)	BMW

1958

125cc	Carlo Ubbiali (Ita)	MV
250cc	Tarquinio Provini (Ita)	MV
350cc	John Surtees (GB)	MV
500cc	John Surtees (GB)	MV
Sidecar	Walter Schneider (FRG)	BMW

1959

125cc	Carlo Ubbiali (Ita)	MV
250cc	Carlo Ubbiali (Ita)	MV
350cc	John Surtees (GB)	MV
500cc	John Surtees (GB)	MV
Sidecar	Walter Schneider (FRG)	BMW

1960

125cc	Carlo Ubbiali (Ita)	MV
250cc	Carlo Ubbiali (Ita)	MV
350cc	John Surtees (GB)	MV
500cc	John Surtees (GB)	MV
Sidecar	Helmut Fath (FRG)	BMW

1961

125cc	Tom Phillis (Aus)	Honda
250cc	Mike Hailwood (GB)	Honda
350cc	Gary Hocking (Rho)	MV
500cc	Gary Hocking (Rho)	MV
Sidecar	Max Deubel (FRG)	BMW

1962

50cc	Ernst Degner (FRG)	Suzuki
125cc	Luigi Taveri (Swi)	Honda
250cc	Jim Redman (Rho)	Honda
350cc	Jim Redman (Rho)	Honda
500cc	Mike Hailwood (GB)	MV
Sidecar	Max Deubel (FRG)	BMW

1963

50cc	Hugh Anderson (NZ)	Suzuki
100cc	Hugh Anderson (NZ)	Suzuki
125cc	Hugh Anderson (NZ)	Suzuki

250cc	Jim Redman (Rho)	Honda
350cc	Jim Redman (Rho)	Honda
500cc	Mike Hailwood (GB)	MV
Sidecar	Max Deubel (FRG)	BMW

1964

50cc	Hugh Anderson (NZ)	Suzuki
125cc	Luigi Taveri (Swi)	Honda
250cc	Phil Read (GB)	Yamaha
350cc	Jim Redman (Rho)	Honda
500cc	Mike Hailwood (GB)	MV
Sidecar	Max Deubel (FRG)	BMW

1965

50cc	Ralph Bryans (Ire)	Honda
125cc	Hugh Anderson (NZ)	Suzuki
250cc	Phil Read (GB)	Yamaha
350cc	Jim Redman (Rho)	Honda
500cc	Mike Hailwood (GB)	MV
Sidecar	Fritz Scheidegger (Swi)	BMW

1966

50cc	Hans-Georg Anscheidt (FRG)	Suzuki
125cc	Luigi Taveri (Swi)	Honda
250cc	Mike Hailwood (GB)	Honda
350cc	Mike Hailwood (GB)	Honda
500cc	Giacomo Agostini (Ita)	MV
Sidecar	Fritz Scheidegger (Swi)	BMW

1967

50cc	Hans-Georg Anscheidt(FRG)	Suzuki
125cc	Bill Ivy (GB)	Yamaha
250cc	Mike Hailwood (GB)	Honda
350cc	Mike Hailwood (GB)	Honda
500cc	Giacomo Agostini (Ita)	MV
Sidecar	Klaus Enders (FRG)	BMW

1968

50cc	Hans-Georg Anscheidt (FRG)	Suzuki
125cc	Phil Read (GB)	Yamaha
250cc	Phil Read (GB)	Yamaha
350cc	Giacomo Agostini (Ita)	MV
500cc	Giacomo Agostini (Ita)	MV
Sidecar	Helmut Fath (FRG)	URS

1969

50cc	Angel Nieto (Spa)	Derbi
125cc	Dave Simmonds (GB)	Kawasaki
250cc	Kel Carruthers (Aus)	Benelli
350cc	Giacomo Agostini (Ita)	MV
500cc	Giacomo Agostini (Ita)	MV
Sidecar	Klaus Enders (FRG)	BMW

1970

50cc	Angel Nieto (Spa)	Derbi
125cc	Dieter Braun (FRG)	Suzuki
250cc	Rod Gould (GB)	Yamaha
350cc	Giacomo Agostini (Ita)	MV
500cc	Giacomo Agostini (Ita)	MV
Sidecar	Klaus Enders (FRG)	BMW

1971

50cc	Jan de Vries (Hol)	Kreidler
125cc	Angel Nieto (Spa)	Derbi
250cc	Phil Read (GB)	Yamaha
350cc	Giacomo Agostini (Ita)	MV
500cc	Giacomo Agostini (Ita)	MV
Sidecar	Horst Owesle (FRG)	Munch

1972

50cc	Angel Nieto (Spa)	Derbi

125cc	Angel Nieto (Spa)	Derbi
250cc	Jarno Saarinen (Fin)	Yamaha
350cc	Giacomo Agostini (Ita)	MV
500cc	Giacomo Agostini (Ita)	MV
Sidecar	Klaus Enders (FRG)	BMW

1973

50cc	Jan de Vries (Hol)	Kreidler
125cc	Kent Andersson (Swe)	Yamaha
250cc	Dieter Braun (FRG)	Yamaha
350cc	Giacomo Agostini (Ita)	MV
500cc	Phil Read (GB)	MV
Sidecar	Klaus Enders (FRG)	BMW

1974

50cc	Henk van Kessell (Hol)	Kreidler
125cc	Kent Andersson (Swe)	Yamaha
250cc	Walter Villa (Ita)	H-Davidson
350cc	Giacomo Agostini (Ita)	Yamaha
500cc	Phil Read (GB)	MV
Sidecar	Klaus Enders (FRG)	Busch BMW

1975

50cc	Angel Nieto (Spa)	Kreidler
125cc	Paolo Pileri (Ita)	Morbidelli
250cc	Walter Villa (Ita)	H-Davidson
350cc	Johnny Cecotto (Ven)	Yamaha
500cc	Giacomo Agostini (Ita)	Yamaha
Sidecar	Rolf Steinhausen (FRG)	Konig

1976

50cc	Angel Nieto (Spa)	Bultaco
125cc	Pier-Paolo Bianchi (Ita)	Morbidelli
250cc	Walter Villa (Ita)	H-Davidson
350cc	Walter Villa (Ita)	H-Davidson
500cc	Barry Sheene (GB)	Suzuki
Sidecar	Rolf Steinhausen (FRG)	Busch Konig

1977

50cc	Angel Nieto (Spa)	Bultaco
125cc	Pier-Paolo Bianchi (Ita)	Morbidelli
250cc	Mario Lega (Ita)	Morbidelli
350cc	Takazumi Katayama (Jap)	Yamaha
500cc	Barry Sheene (GB)	Suzuki
750cc	Steve Baker (US)	Yamaha
F1	Phil Read (GB)	Honda
Sidecar	George O'Dell (GB)	Yamaha

1978

50cc	Ricardo Tormo (Spa)	Bultaco
125cc	Eugenio Lazzarini (Ita)	MBA
250cc	Kork Ballington (SA)	Kawasaki
350cc	Kork Ballington (SA)	Kawasaki
500cc	Kenny Roberts (US)	Yamaha
750cc	Johnny Cecotto (Ven)	Yamaha
F1	Mike Hailwood (GB)	Ducati
Sidecar	Rolf Biland (Swi)	Yamaha

1979

50cc	Eugenio Lazzarini (Ita)	Kreidler
125cc	Angel Nieto (Spa)	Morbidelli
250cc	Kork Ballington (SA)	Kawasaki
350cc	Kork Ballington (SA)	Kawasaki
500cc	Kenny Roberts (US)	Yamaha
750cc	Patrick Pons (Fra)	Yamaha
F1	Ron Haslam (GB)	Honda
Sidecar	Rolf Biland (Swi)	Yamaha

1980

50cc	Eugenio Lazzarini (Ita)	Kreidler
125cc	Pier-Paolo Bianchi (Ita)	MBA

250cc	Anton Mang (FRG)	Kawasaki
350cc	John Ekerold (SA)	Yamaha
500cc	Kenny Roberts (US)	Yamaha
F1	Graeme Crosby (NZ)	Suzuki
Sidecar	Jock Taylor (GB)	Yamaha

1981

50cc	Ricardo Tormo (Spa)	Bultaco
125cc	Angel Nieto (Spa)	Minarelli
250cc	Anton Mang (FRG)	Kawasaki
350cc	Anton Mang (FRG)	Kawasaki
500cc	Marco Lucchinelli (Ita)	Suzuki
F1	Graeme Crosby (NZ)	Suzuki
Sidecar	Rolf Biland (Swi)	Yamaha

1982

50cc	Stefan Dorflinger (Swi)	MBA
125cc	Angel Nieto (Spa)	Garelli
250cc	Jean-Louis Tournadre (Fra)	Yamaha
350cc	Anton Mang (FRG)	Kawasaki
500cc	Franco Uncini (Ita)	Suzuki
F1	Joey Dunlop (Ire)	Honda
Sidecar	Werner Schwarzel (FRG)	Yamaha

1983

50cc	Stefan Dorflinger (Swi)	Kreidler
125cc	Angel Nieto (Spa)	Garelli
250cc	Carlos Lavado (Ven)	Yamaha
500cc	Freddie Spencer (US)	Honda
F1	Joey Dunlop (Ire)	Honda
Sidecar	Rolf Biland (Swi)	Yamaha

1984

80cc	Stefan Dorflinger (Swi)	Zundapp
125cc	Angel Nieto (Spa)	Garelli
250cc	Christain Sarron (Fra)	Yamaha
500cc	Eddie Lawson (US)	Yamaha
F1	Joey Dunlop (Ire)	Honda
Sidecar	Egbert Streuer (Hol)	Yamaha

1985

80cc	Stefan Dorflinger (Swi)	Krauser
125cc	Fausto Gresini (Ita)	Garelli
250cc	Freddie Spencer (US)	Honda
500cc	Freddie Spencer (US)	Honda
F1	Joey Dunlop (Ire)	Honda
Sidecar	Egbert Streuer (Hol)	Yamaha

1986

80cc	Jorge Martinez (Spa)	Derbi
125cc	Luca Cadalora (Ita)	Garelli
250cc	Carlos Lavado (Ven)	Yamaha
500cc	Eddie Lawson (US)	Yamaha
F1	Joey Dunlop (Ire)	Honda
Sidecar	Egbert Streuer (Hol)	Yamaha

1987

80cc	Jorge Martinez (Spa)	Derbi
125cc	Fausto Gresini (Ita)	Garelli
250cc	Anton Mang (FRG)	Honda
500cc	Wayne Gardner (Aus)	Honda
F1	Virginio Ferrari (Ita)	Yamaha
Sidecar	Steve Webster (GB)	LCR Krauser

1988

80cc	Jorge Martinez (Spa)	Derbi
125cc	Jorge Martinez (Spa)	Derbi
250cc	Sito Pons (Spa)	Honda
500cc	Eddie Lawson (US)	Yamaha
F1	Carl Fogarty (GB)	Honda
Sidecar	Steve Webster (GB)	LCR Krauser

1989

80cc	Champi Herreros (Spa)	Derbi
125cc	Alex Crivelle (Spa)	Cobas
250cc	Sito Pons (Spa)	Honda
500cc	Eddie Lawson (US)	Honda
Sidecar	Steve Webster (GB)	Krauser

1990

125cc	Loris Capirossi (Ita)	Honda
250cc	John Kocinski (US)	Yamaha
500cc	Wayne Rainey (US)	Yamaha
Sidecar	Alain Michel (Fra)	Krauser

ISLE OF MAN - SENIOR TT WINNERS

All winners British Isles unless stated

1911	Oliver Godfrey, Indian 47.63mph
1912	Frank Applebee, Scott 48.69mph
1913	Tim Wood, Scott 48.27mph
1914	Cyril Pullin, Rudge 49.49mph
1915-19	Not held
1920	Tommy De La Hay, Sunbeam 51.48mph
1921	Howard Davies, AJS 54.50mph
1922	Alec Bennett, Sunbeam 58.31mph
1923	Tom Sheard, Douglas 55.55mph
1924	Alec Bennett, Norton 61.64mph
1925	Howard Davies, HRD 66.13mph
1926	Stanley Woods, Norton 67.54mph
1927	Alec Bennett, Norton 68.41mph
1928	Charlie Dodson, Sunbeam 62.98mph
1929	Charlie Dodson, Sunbeam 72.05mph
1930	Wal Handley, Rudge Whitworth 74.24mph
1931	Tim Hunt, Norton 77.90mph
1932	Stanley Woods, Norton 79.38mph
1933	Stanley Woods, Norton 77.16mph
1934	Jimmy Guthrie, Norton 78.01mph
1935	Stanley Woods, Moto Guzzi 84.68mph
1936	Jimmy Guthrie, Norton 85.80mph
1937	Freddie Frith, Norton 88.21mph
1938	Harold Daniell, Norton 89.11mph
1939	Georg Meir (Ger), BMW 89.38mph
1940-46	Not held
1947	Harold Daniell, Norton 82.81mph
1948	Artie Bell, Norton 84.97mph
1949	Harold Daniell, Norton 86.93mph
1950	Geoff Duke, Norton 92.27mph
1951	Geoff Duke, Norton 93.83mph
1952	Reg Armstrong, Norton 92.97mph
1953	Ray Amm (SRho), Norton 93.85mph
1954	Ray Amm (SRho), Norton 88.12mph
1955	Geoff Duke, Gilara 97.93mph
1956	John Surtees, Gilera 96.57mph
1957	Bob McIntyre, Gilera 98.99mph
1958	John Surtees, MV Agusta 98.63mph
1959	John Surtees, MV Agusta 87.94mph
1960	John Surtees, MV Agusta 102.44mph
1961	Mike Hailwood, Norton 100.60mph
1962	Gary Hockling (SRho), MV Agusta 103.51mph
1963	Mike Hailwood, MV Agusta 104.64mph
1964	Mike Hailwood, MV Agusta 100.95mph
1965	Mike Hailwood, MV Agusta 91.69mph
1966	Mike Hailwood, Honda 103.11mph

1967	Mike Hailwood, Honda 105.62mph
1968	Giacomo Agostini (Ita), MV Agusta 101.63mph
1969	Giacomo Agostini (Ita), MV Agusta 104.75mph
1970	Giacomo Agostini (Ita), MV Agusta 101.52mph
1971	Giacomo Agostini (Ita), MV Agusta 102.59mph
1972	Giacomo Agostini (Ita), MV Agusta 104.02mph
1973	Jack Findlay (Aus), Suzuki 101.55mph
1974	Phil Carpenter, Yamaha 96.99mph
1975	Mick Grant, Kawasaki 100.27mph
1976	Tom Herron, Yamaha 105.16mph
1977	Phil Read, Suzuki 106.98mph
1978	Tom Herron, Suzuki 111.74mph
1979	Mike Hailwood, Suzuki 111.75mph
1980	Graeme Crosby (NZ), Suzuki 109.65mph
1981	Mike Grant, Suzuki 106.14mph
1982	Norman Brown, Suzuki 110.98mph
1983	Not held
1984	Rob McElnea, Suzuki 115.66mph
1985	Joey Dunlop, Honda 113.69mph
1986	Roger Burnett, Honda 113.98mph
1987	Joey Dunlop, Honda 99.85mph
1988	Joey Dunlop, Honda 117.38mph
1989	Steve Hislop, Honda 118.23mph
1990	Carl Fogarty, Honda 110.95mph

Most wins:
7 Mike Hailwood; 5 Giacomo Agostini (Ita); 4 Stanley Woods, John Surtees; 3 Alec Bennett, Harold Daniell, Geoff Duke, Joey Dunlop

Outright lap record: 122.63mph/197.35kph Steve Hislop, Honda, 1990

———— 1991 ————

(all dates provisional)

Mar 24	Japanese Grand Prix (Suzuka);
Apr 7	Australian Grand Prix (Eastern Creek);
Apr 23	US Grand Prix (Laguna Seca);
May 12	Spanish Grand Prix (Cataluna);
May 19	Italian Grand Prix (Santa Monica);
May 31-Jun 7	Isle of Man TT;
May 26	German Grand Prix (Hockenheim);
Jun 9	Austrian Grand Prix (Salzburgring);
Jun 15	Yugoslav Grand Prix (Rijeka);
Jun 29	Dutch TT (Assen);
Jul 7	Belgian Grand Prix (Spa-Francorchamps);
Jul 21	French Grand Prix (Le Castellet);
Aug 4	BRITISH GRAND PRIX (Donington Park);
Aug 25	Czech Grand Prix (Brno);
Sep 1	Hungarian Grand Prix (Budapest);
Sep 15	Brazilian Grand Prix (Interlagos);
Sep 29	FIM Coupe d'Endurance Championship, Six hours (Donington Park).

MOTOR RACING & RALLYING

SENNA TAKES COMMAND

Ayrton Senna spent most of the 1990 season apparently accelerating smoothly to regain the World Championship he lost in 1989. Senna won six grands prix to establish a commanding lead over the reigning champion Alain Prost before Prost hit back to win the Spanish Grand Prix and keep the Championship open.

But events on the track were constantly overshadowed by the sport's machinations, feuds and politics. And perhaps the most dramatic moment of the year came when the two great protagonists, Senna and Prost, shook hands publicly after the Italian Grand Prix for the first time in more than twelve months.

Senna's win at Monza had made it very probable that he would be champion. He had started the season in tremendous style at Phoenix, made a lightning getaway at Monaco, missed a pile-up and beat Jean Alesi by a second, and then won the Canadian Grand Prix quite masterfully. However, Prost followed with a hat-trick of victories - in Mexico, France and Britain - to take the lead briefly and give Ferrari their 99th, 100th and 101st successes. Next race, at Hockenheim, however, Senna was back on top.

The duel between Prost and Senna was often accompanied by an extraordinary, sometimes sad, sometimes comic, subplot from inside the Ferrari camp. Prost's team-mate Nigel Mansell frequently felt that most of the world's humans and all its machines were against him. He discovered almost every imaginable way to lose a race. He had problems with the Ferrari's engine, gearbox, steering...Some felt the problems were in his head and, indeed, just before Imola, he cut that open and needed stitches.

After a storming drive at Silverstone where he was forced to withdraw through gearbox trouble when only three seconds behind Prost, he announced his retirement, saying he wanted to quit while at the top. This brought about a new frenzy of speculation both about Mansell's real intentions and about the movement that would result if he really did retire. In October, the sport's more cynical observers were proved right and Mansell returned to the fold by signing for Williams. And he had some consolation for his frustrations when he won the Portuguese Grand Prix.

Ferrari first announced that Alessandro Nannini would be Prost's team-mate in 1991. This came after Alesi, the much-hyped young Frenchman, had contrived to sign contracts with both Ferrari and Williams while still being committed to Tyrrell for 1991; he could have been in the interesting position of being forced by lawyers to drive three cars simultaneously. But Ferrari eventually bought him out from the other two companies.

At Monza, Derek Warwick had the most dramatic smash since Gerhard Berger at Imola in 1988 but he was able to rejoin the race. The latest safety improvements to the petrol tanks, added to those changes which had kept Formula One fatality-free for eight years, were given the credit for his escape. Others were less lucky. The Belfast driver Martin Donnelly received multiple fractures after hitting a safety barrier head-on at 170mph in practice for the Spanish Grand Prix. A spectator was killed at Donington Park during an International Formula 3000 race when the Scottish driver Allan McNish crashed over a retaining wall. Guy Renard, the Belgian driver, was killed when his car exploded at the Spa-Francorchamps 24-hour touring car endurance race; the fuel tank in endurance cars is inside the driver's cockpit and Renard had no chance of escape. Rich Vogler, 39, was killed during a US Auto Club sprint car race; Vogler's father Don was killed racing at Indianapolis in 1981.

Arie Luyendyk of the Netherlands won the Indy 500. It was the first Indy to last less that three hours: Luyendyk needed just over two hours 41 minutes. Jaguar won Le Mans for the seventh time just as the firm's new owners were trying to decide whether to invest in a new sports car. Stirling Moss needed three metal pins in a broken thigh after being hit by a car in London while doing 20mph on his 80cc motor bike, thus giving rise to endless "Who do you think you are?" jokes.

1990

FORMULA ONE WORLD CHAMPIONSHIP
United States GP
Phoenix, Mar 11
1 Ayrton Senna (Bra) McLaren
90.50 mph/145.65 kph
2 Jean Alesi (Fra) Tyrrell
3 Thierry Boutsen (Bel) Williams
4 Nelson Piquet (Bra) Benetton
5 Stefan Modena (Ita) Brabham
6 Satoru Nakajima (Jap) Tyrrell
Tyrrell's best finish for seven years
Pole Position: Gerhard Berger (Aut) McLaren
Championship leaders:
1 Senna 9pts; 2 Alesi 6pts; 3 Boutsen 4pts

Brazilian GP
Sao Paulo, Mar 25
1 Alain Prost (Fra) Ferrari
117.56 mph/189.19 kph
2 Gerhard Berger (Aut) McLaren
3 Ayrton Senna (Bra) McLaren
4 Nigel Mansell (GB) Ferrari
5 Thierry Boutsen (Bel) Williams
6 Nelson Piquet (Bra) Benetton
Prost's 40th Grand Prix win
Pole Position: Senna
Championship leaders:
1 Senna 13pts; 2 Prost 9pts; 3 Alesi, Berger & Boutsen 6pts

San Marino GP
Imola, May 13
1 Riccardo Patrese (Ita) Williams
126.06 mph/ 202.88 kph
2 Gerhard Berger (Aut) McLaren
3 Alessandro Nannini (Ita) Benetton
4 Alain Prost (Fra) Ferrari
5 Nelson Piquet (Bra) Benetton
6 Jean Alesi (Ita) Tyrrell
Pole Position: Senna
Championship leaders:
1 Senna 13pts; 2 Prost & Berger 12pts

Monaco GP
Monte Carlo, May 27
1 Ayrton Senna (Bra) McLaren
85.83 mph/138.10 kph
2 Jean Alesi (Fra) Tyrrell
3 Gerhard Berger (Aut) McLaren
4 Thierry Boutsen (Bel) Williams
5 Alex Caffi (Ita) Arrows
6 Eric Bernard (Fra) Larrousse
Pole Position: Senna
Senna on pole for the 45th time in his career
Championship leaders:
1 Senna 22pts; 2 Berger 16pts; 3 Alesi 13pts

Canadian GP
Montreal, Jun 10
1 Ayrton Senna (Bra) McLaren
111.95 mph/180.16 kph
2 Nelson Piquet (Bra) Benetton
3 Nigel Mansell (GB) Ferrari
4 Gerhard Berger (Aut) McLaren
5 Alain Prost (Fra) Ferrari
6 Derek Warwick (GB) Lotus
Pole Position: Senna
Championship leaders:
1 Senna 31pts; 2 Berger 19pts; 3 Prost 14pts

Gerhard Berger finished first but was penalised one minute for jumping the start and placed fourth

Mexican GP
Mexico City, Jun 24
1 Alain Prost (Fra) Ferrari
123.54 mph/197.66kph
2 Nigel Mansell (GB) Ferrari
3 Gerhard Berger (Aut) McLaren
4 Alessandro Nannini (Ita) Benetton
5 Thierry Boutsen (Bel) Williams
6 Nelson Piquet (Bra) Benetton
Pole Position: Berger
Championship leaders:
1 Senna 31pts; 2 Berger, Prost 23pts

French GP
Paul Ricard, Le Castellet, Jul 8
1 Alain Prost (Fra) Ferrari
121.67 mph/196.76 kph
2 Ivan Capelli (Ita) Leyton House
3 Ayrton Senna (Bra) McLaren
4 Nelson Piquet (Bra) Benetton
5 Gerhard Berger (Aut) McLaren
6 Riccardo Patrese (Ita) Williams
Pole Position: Nigel Mansell (GB) Ferrari
Championship leaders:
1 Senna 35pts; 2 Prost 32pts; 3 Berger 25pts
Ferrari's 100th Formula One win

THE TON UP

José Froilan Gonzalez drove the first Ferrari to win a Grand Prix at Silverstone in 1951. Alain Prost drove the 100th at Le Castellet in 1990. Leading drivers of the first 100:
15 Niki Lauda (Aut) 1974-77; 13 Alberto Ascari (Ita) 1951-53; 6 Jacky Ickx (Bel) 1968-72, Gilles Villeneuve (Can) 1978-81; 5 Carlos Reutemann (Arg) 1977-78; 4 John Surtees (GB) 1963-66, Clay Regazzoni (Swi) 1970-76, Gerhard Berger (Aut) 1987-89.

British GP
Silverstone, Jul 15
1 Alain Prost (Fra) Ferrari
145.25 mph/233.76 kph
2 Thierry Boutsen (Bel) Williams
3 Ayrton Senna (Bra) McLaren
4 Eric Bernard (Fra) Larrousse
5 Nelson Piquet (Bra) Benetton
6 Aguri Suzuki (Jap) Larrousse
Pole Position: Nigel Mansell (GB) Ferrari
Championship leaders:
1 Prost 41pts; 2 Senna 39pts; 3 Berger 25pts

West German GP
Hockenheim, Jul 29
1 Ayrton Senna (Bra) McLaren
141.26 mph/227.33 kph
2 Alessandro Nannini (Ita) Benetton
3 Gerhard Berger (Aut) McLaren
4 Alain Prost (Fra) Ferrari
5 Riccardo Patrese (Ita) Williams
6 Thierry Boutsen (Bel) Williams
Pole Position: Senna
Championship leaders:
1 Senna 48pts; 2 Prost 44pts; 3 Berger 29pts

Hungarian GP
Budapest, Aug 12
1 Thierry Boutsen (Bel)   Williams
 104.02 mph/167.40 kph
2 Ayrton Senna (Bra)   McLaren
3 Nelson Piquet (Bra)   Benetton
4 Riccardo Patrese (Ita)   Williams
5 Derek Warwick (GB)   Lotus
6 Eric Bernard (Fra)   Larrousse
Pole Position: Boutsen
Championship leaders:
1 Senna 54pts; 2 Prost 44pts; 3 Berger 29pts

Belgian GP
Spa-Francorchamps, Aug 26
1 Ayrton Senna (Bra)   McLaren
 131.57 mph/211.73 kph
2 Alain Prost (Fra)   Ferrari
3 Gerhard Berger (Aut)   McLaren
4 Alessandro Nannini (Ita)   Benetton
5 Nelson Piquet (Bra)   Benetton
6 Maurizio Gugelmin (Bra)Leyton House
Pole Position: Senna
Championship leaders:
1 Senna 63pts; 2 Prost 50pts; 3 Berger 33pts

Italian GP
Monza, Sep 9
1 Ayrton Senna (Bra)   McLaren
 147.00 mph/236.57 kph
2 Alain Prost (Fra)   Ferrari
3 Gerhard Berger (Aut)   McLaren
4 Nigel Mansell (GB)   Ferrari
5 Riccardo Patrese (Ita)   Williams
6 Satoru Nakajima (Jap)   Tyrrell
Pole Position: Senna
Championship leaders:
1 Senna 72pts; 2 Prost 56pts; 3 Berger 37pts

Portuguese GP
Estoril, Sep 23
1 Nigel Mansell (GB)   Ferrari
 121.07 mph/199.84 kph
2 Ayrton Senna (Bra)   McLaren
3 Alain Prost (Fra)   Ferrari
4 Gerhard Berger (Aut)   McLaren
5 Nelson Piquet (Bra)   Benetton
6 Alessandro Nannini (Ita)   Benetton
Pole Position: Mansell
Championship leaders:
1 Senna 78pts; 2 Prost 60pts; 3 Berger 40pts

Spanish GP
Jerez, Sep 30
1 Alain Prost (Fra)   Ferrari
 106.27 mph/171.02 kph
2 Nigel Mansell (GB)   Ferrari
3 Alessandro Nannini (Ita)   Benetton
4 Thierry Boutsen (Bel)   Williams
5 Riccardo Patrese (Ita)   Williams
6 Agori Suzuki (Jap)   Larrousse
Pole Position: Ayrton Senna (Bra) McLaren
Senna's 50th pole
Championship leaders:
1 Senna 78pts; 2 Prost 69pts; Berger 40pts

OH, NIGEL
Nigel Mansell's record in 1990 Grand Prix
UNITED STATES: Did not finish, engine problems. "It'll be different when we get back on the proper circuits."
BRAZIL: Fourth, despite a 22-second stop to repair a damaged roll bar in front suspension.
SAN MARINO: Badly baulked by de Cesaris (lap 27) and Berger (lap 36). Out of race (lap 39) when engine blew.
MONACO: Early pit stop. Rose from 16th to fourth then pulled out - electrical problems in the gearbox.
CANADA: No problems. Third.
MEXICO: No problems. Second.
FRENCH: Retired eight laps from home. "It's the worst engine I've had all season," he said.
BRITISH: Gearbox trouble. Retired eight laps from finish. Announced retirement.
GERMAN: Track debris caused damage to car's undertray and front wing. Pulled out after 30 of the 45 laps.
HUNGARIAN: Pushed off the track by Berger when third with five laps to go.
BELGIAN: Driven into the first corner by Piquet and had to take up spare Ferrari. Pulled out after 19 laps complaining of "massive oversteer".
ITALIAN: Throttle problems. Finished fourth.
PORTUGUESE: A win, at last!
SPANISH:... And second.

WORLD SPORTSCAR CHAMPIONSHIP
Round One: *Suzuka, Japan, Apr 8*
Jean-Louis Schlesser (Fra)/Mauro Baldi (Ita) Sauber-Mercedes
Round Two: *Monza, Apr 29*
Jean-Louis Schlesser (Fra)/Mauro Baldi (Ita) Sauber-Mercedes
Round Three: *Silverstone, May 20*
Martin Brundle (GB)/Alain Ferte (Fra) Silk Cut Jaguar
Round Four: *Spa-Francorchamps, Jun 3*
Jochen Maas (FRG)/Karl Wendlinger (Aut) Sauber-Mercedes
Round Five: *Dijon, Jul 22*
Jean-Louis Schlesser (Fra)/Mauro Baldi (Ita) Sauber-Mercedes
Round Six: *Nurburgring, Aug 19*
Jean-Louis Schlesser (Fra)/Mauro Baldi (Ita) Sauber-Mercedes
Round Seven: *Donington Park, Sep 2*
Jean-Louis Schlesser (Fra)/Mauro Baldi (Ita) Sauber-Mercedes
Round Eight: *Montreal, Sep 23*
Jean-Louis Schlesser (Fra)/Mauro Baldi (Ita) Sauber-Mercedes
Round Nine: *Mexico City, Oct 7*
Jochen Maas (Ger)/M Schumacher (Ger) Sauber-Mercedes
Champion: Schlesser

FIA FORMULA 3000 CHAMPIONSHIP

(Winners only)
Round One: *Donington Park, Apr 22*
Erik Comas (Fra) Lola
Round Two: *Silverstone, May 20*
Allan McNish (GB) Lola
Round Three: *Pau, France, Jun 4*
Eric van de Poel (Bel) Reynard
Round Four: *Jerez, Spain, Jun 17*
Erik Comas (Fra) Lola
Round Five: *Monza, Italy, Jun 24*
Erik Comas (Fra) Lola
Round Six: *Enna, Italy, Jul 22*
Gianni Morbidelli (Ita) Lola
Round Seven: *Hockenheim, West Germany, Jul 29*
Eddie Irvine (GB) Reynard
Round Eight: *Brands Hatch, Aug 19*
Allan McNish (GB) Lola
Round Nine: *Birmingham, Aug 27*
Eric van de Poel (Bel) Reynard
Round Ten: *Nogaro, France, Oct 7*
Eric van der Poel (Bel)
Champion: Comas

OTHER MAJOR RESULTS
Daytona 24 Hours
Daytona International Speedway, Florida, Feb 4
1 Jan Lammers (Hol)/Davy Jones (US)/Andy Wallace (GB) Jaguar 112.86mph/181.63kph
2 Price Cobb (US)/Martin Brundle (GB)/John Nielsen (Den) Jaguar
3 Dominic Dobson (US)/Sarel van der Merwe (SA)/Bob Wollek (Fra) Porsche

Daytona 500
Daytona International Speedway, Florida, Feb 18
1 Derrike Cope (Chevrolet Lumina) 165.76mph/266.76kph
2 Terry Labonte (Oldsmobile Cutlass)
3 Bill Elliot (Ford Thunderbird)

Indianapolis 500
Indianapolis Raceway, May 27
1 Arie Luyendyk (Hol) Lola-Chevrolet 185.90mph/299.17kph (record)
2 Bobby Rahal (US) Lola-Chevrolet
3 Emerson Fittipaldi (Bra) Penske-Chevrolet
For the first time four members of one family qualified: Mario Andretti, his sons Michael & Jeff, and nephew John.

Le Mans 24 Hour Race
Le Mans, Jun 16-17
1 John Nielsen (Den)/Price Cobb (US)/Martin Brundle (GB) Jaguar; 359 laps, 3,034 miles, 126.80mph/204.06kph
2 Jan Lammers (Hol)/Andy Wallace (GB)/Franz Konrad (FRG) Jaguar
3 Tiff Needall/David Sears/Anthony Reid (all GB) Porsche

❝This remarkable old gentleman controls his sport absolutely... power makes you odd; absolute power makes you completely barking.❞
Simon Barnes, The Times, on Jean-Marie Balestre

"One car is working perfectly and...I have to be very careful what I say here...but I don't understand why I've had these problems."
Nigel Mansell after the British Grand Prix

"I may have fought with him but I respect him because he is a great driver, one of the greatest in Formula One."
Ayrton Senna on Mansell

"He's one of the top three drivers in the world because of his amazing ability. Nigel's a winner and no one can take that away from him."
Derek Warwick on Mansell

"He has got the intelligence of a mosquito."
Nelson Piquet on Mansell

"There's no amount of money in the world which pays to kill yourself...and that car was dangerous."
Mansell, retiring from the Belgian Grand Prix

"If the old regulations had still been in force - the ones which were used before Berger's crash last year - the tank would have burst and there would have been a fire. Under the new regulations the skins of the fuel tanks are four times as tough and that's what saved him. He's a very lucky guy."
Charlie Whiting, scrutineer, on Derek Warwick's crash at Monza

"There has not been a fatality in a grand prix since 1982, a statistic which is a tribute to the safety reforms. The danger is, however, that the resulting complacency can lead to the belief that grand prix racing is a relatively safe business. Warwick's accident, and others like it, at least serve to show that tragedy is only a millimetre away."
Maurice Hamilton, The Independent

"Ayrton Senna is as peculiar in his emotional make-up as Lester Piggott, as driven as John McEnroe, more complete in his self-centredness than Brian Clough."
Neil Lyndon, Sunday Correspondent

"At my first marriage I had six ushers who were all racing drivers. I think nowadays if I were racing, I'd find it hard to find anyone who would come along, never mind being an usher.❞
Stirling Moss

—— RALLYING 1990 ——

Paris-Dakar Rally
Dec 25-Jan 14
1 Ari Vatanen (Fin) Peugeot 39h 08m 59s
2 Bjorn Waldegaard (Swe) Peugeot 40h 18m 30s
3 Alain Ambrosino (Fra) Peugeot 43h 05m 45s

Monte Carlo Rally
Jan 19-26
1 Didier Auriol (Fra) Lancia 5h 56m 52s
2 Carlos Sainz (Spa) Toyota 5h 57m 44s
3 Miki Biasion (Ita) Lancia 6h 00m 31s

Portuguese Rally
Mar 6-11
1 Miki Biasion (Ita) Lancia
2 Didier Auriol (Fra) Lancia
3 Juha Kankkunen (Fin) Lancia

Safari Rally
Kenya, Apr 12-16
1 Bjorn Waldegaard (Swe) Toyota 8h 39m 11s
2 Juha Kankkunen (Fin) Lancia 9h 17m 23s
3 Mikael Ericsson (Swe) Toyota 11h 26m 58s
Waldegaard's 4th victory in the race

Tour of Corsica
May 6-10
1 Didier Auriol (Fra) Lancia 6h 45m 16s
2 Carlos Sainz (Spa) Toyota 6h 45m 52s
3 Francois Chatriot (Fra) BMW 6h 49m 05s

Acropolis Rally
Greece, Jun 2-7
1 Carlos Sainz (Spa) Toyota 7h 34m 44s
2 Juha Kankkunen (Fin) Lancia 7h 35m 30s
3 Miki Biasion (Ita) Lancia 7h 37m 42s

New Zealand Rally
Jun 29-Jul 14
1 Carlos Sainz (Spa) Toyota 6h 48m 26s
2 Inquar Carlsson (Swe) Mazda 6h 49m 57s
3 Erwin Weber (FRG) Volkswagen 6h 56m 24s

Argentine Rally
Jul 23-29
1 Miki Biasion (Ita) Lancia 6h 51m 27s
2 Carlos Sainz (Spa) Toyota 6h 59m 29s
3 Didier Auriol (Fra) Lancia 7h 26m 22s

Rally of 1000 Lakes
Finland, Aug 22-27
1 Carlos Sainz (Spa) Toyota 4h 40m 55s
2 Ari Vatanen (Fin) Mitsubishi 4h 41m 14s
3 Kenneth Eriksson (Swe) Mitsubishi 4h 45m 53s

Australian Rally
Sep 13-17
1 Juha Kankkunen (Fin) Lancia 5h 43m 48s
2 Carlos Sainz (Spa) Toyota 5h 45m 28s
3 Alex Fiorio (Ita) Lancia 5h 49m 28s

—— 1989 ——

FORMULA ONE GRAND PRIX
Spanish GP
Jerez, Oct 1
1 Ayrton Senna (Bra)   McLaren
107.11mph/172.37kph
2 Gerhard Berger (Aut)   Ferrari
3 Alain Prost (Fra)   McLaren

Japanese GP
Suzuka, Oct 22
1 Alessandro Nannini (Ita) Benetton
122.50mph/197.14kph
2 Riccardo Patrese (Ita)   Williams
3 Thierry Boutsen (Bel)   Williams
*Ayrton Senna first home but disqualified after taking
illegal track following shunt with Alain Prost*

Australian GP
Adelaide, Nov 5
1 Thierry Boutsen (Fra)   Williams
2 Alessandro Nannini (Ita) Benetton
3 Riccardo Patrese (Ita)   Williams
81.96mph/131.90kph

FINAL STANDINGS
Leading Positions

Drivers
1 Alain Prost 76 pts
2 Ayrton Senna 60 pts
3 Riccardo Patrese 40 pts
4 Nigel Mansell 38 pts
5 Thierry Boutsen 37 pts
6 Alessandro Nannini 32 pts

Constructors
1 McLaren 141 pts
2 Williams 77 pts
3 Ferrari 59 pts
4 Benetton 39 pts
5 Tyrrell 16 pts
6 Lotus 15 pts

Lombard RAC Rally
Finished Nottingham, Nov 23
1 Pentti Arikkala (Fin)/Ronan McNamee (Ire) Mitsubishi
6h 19m 22s
2 Carlos Sainz/Luis Moya (Spa) Toyota, 6h 20m 50s
3 Juha Kankkunen/Juha Piironen (Fin) Toyota 6h 23m 11s

—— CHAMPIONS ——

FORMULA ONE WORLD CHAMPIONSHIP
World Champion Drivers

Year	Winner	Car	Runner-up	Third
1950	Giuseppe Farina (Ita)	Alfa Romeo	Juan Manuel Fangio (Arg)	Luigi Fagioli (Ita)
1951	Juan Manuel Fangio (Arg)	Alfa Romeo	Alberto Ascari (Ita)	Jose Gonzalez (Arg)
1952	Alberto Ascari (Ita)	Ferrari	Giuseppe Farina (Ita)	Piero Taruffi (Ita)
1953	Alberto Ascari (Ita)	Ferrari	Juan Manuel Fangio (Arg)	Giuseppe Farina (Ita)
1954	Juan Manuel Fangio (Arg)	Maserati/Mercedes	Jose Gonzalez (Arg)	Mike Hawthorn (GB)
1955	Juan Manuel Fangio (Arg)	Mercedes-Benz	Stirling Moss (GB)	Eugenio Castellotti (Ita)
1956	Juan Manuel Fangio (Arg)	Lancia-Ferrari	Stirling Moss (GB)	Peter Collins (GB)
1957	Juan Manuel Fangio (Arg)	Maserati	Stirling Moss (GB)	Luigi Musso (Ita)
1958	Mike Hawthorn (GB)	Ferrari	Stirling Moss (GB)	Tony Brooks (GB)
1959	Jack Brabham (Aus)	Cooper-Climax	Tony Brooks (GB)	Stirling Moss (GB)
1960	Jack Brabham (Aus)	Cooper-Climax	Bruce McLaren (NZ)	Stirling Moss (GB)

1961	Phil Hill (US)	Ferrari	Wolfgang von Trips (FRG)	Stirling Moss (GB)
1962	Graham Hill (GB)	BRM	Jim Clark (GB)	Bruce McLaren (NZ)
1963	Jim Clark (GB)	Lotus-Climax	Graham Hill (GB)	Richie Ginther (US)
1964	John Surtees (GB)	Ferrari	Graham Hill (GB)	Jim Clark (GB)
1965	Jim Clark (GB)	Lotus-Climax	Graham Hill (GB)	Jackie Stewart (GB)
1966	Jack Brabham (Aus)	Brabham-Repco	John Surtees (GB)	Jochen Rindt (Aut)
1967	Denny Hulme (NZ)	Brabham-Repco	Jack Brabham (Aus)	Jim Clark (GB)
1968	Graham Hill (GB)	Lotus-Ford	Jackie Stewart (GB)	Denny Hulme (NZ)
1969	Jackie Stewart (GB)	Matra-Ford	Jacky Ickx (Bel)	Bruce McLaren (NZ)
1970	Jochen Rindt (Aut)	Lotus-Ford	Jacky Ickx (Bel)	Clay Regazzoni (Swi)
1971	Jackie Stewart (GB)	Tyrrell-Ford	Ronnie Peterson (Swe)	Francois Cevert (Fra)
1972	Emerson Fittipaldi (Bra)	Lotus-Ford	Jackie Stewart (GB)	Denny Hulme (NZ)
1973	Jackie Stewart (GB)	Tyrrell-Ford	Emerson Fittipaldi (Bra)	Ronnie Peterson (Swe)
1974	Emerson Fittipaldi (Bra)	McLaren-Ford	Clay Regazzoni (Swi)	Jody Scheckter (SA)
1975	Niki Lauda (Aut)	Ferrari	Emerson Fittipaldi (Bra)	Carlos Reutemann (Arg)
1976	James Hunt (GB)	McLaren-Ford	Niki Lauda (Aut)	Jody Scheckter (SA)
1977	Niki Lauda (Aut)	Ferrari	Jody Scheckter (SA)	Mario Andretti (US)
1978	Mario Andretti (US)	Lotus-Ford	Ronnie Peterson (Swe)	Carlos Reutemann (Arg)
1979	Jody Scheckter (SA)	Ferrari	Gilles Villeneuve (Can)	Alan Jones (Aus)
1980	Alan Jones (Aus)	Williams-Ford	Nelson Piquet (Bra)	Carlos Reutemann (Arg)
1981	Nelson Piquet (Bra)	Brabham-Ford	Carlos Reutemann (Arg)	Alan Jones (Aus)
1982	Keke Rosberg (Fin)	Williams-Ford	Didier Pironi (Fra) and John Watson (GB)	
1983	Nelson Piquet (Bra)	Brabham-BMW	Alain Prost (Fra)	Rene Arnoux (Fra)
1984	Niki Lauda (Aut)	McLaren-TAG	Alain Prost (Fra)	Elio de Angelis (Ita)
1985	Alain Prost (Fra)	McLaren-TAG	Michele Alboreto (Ita)	Keke Rosberg (Fin)
1986	Alain Prost (Fra)	McLaren-TAG	Nigel Mansell (GB)	Nelson Piquet (Bra)
1987	Nelson Piquet (Bra)	Williams-Honda	Nigel Mansell (GB)	Ayrton Senna (Bra)
1988	Ayrton Senna (Bra)	McLaren-Honda	Alain Prost (Fra)	Gerhard Berger (Aut)
1989	Alain Prost (Fra)	McLaren-Honda	Ayrton Senna (Bra)	Riccardo Patrese (Ita)

Most titles: 5 Fangio; **3** Brabham, Stewart, Lauda, Piquet, Prost; **2** Clark, Ascari, Graham Hill, Fittipaldi

Constructors' Cup

1958 Vanwall	1959 Cooper-Climax	1960 Cooper-Climax	1961 Ferrari	1962 BRM
1963 Lotus-Climax	1964 Ferrari	1965 Lotus-Climax	1966 Brabham-Repco	1967 Brabham-Repco
1968 Lotus-Ford	1969 Matra-Ford	1970 Lotus-Ford	1971 Tyrrell-Ford	1972 Lotus-Ford
1973 Lotus-Ford	1974 McLaren-Ford	1975 Ferrari	1976 Ferrari	1977 Ferrari
1978 Lotus-Ford	1979 Ferrari	1980 Williams-Ford	1981 Williams-Ford	1982 Ferrari
1983 Ferrari	1984 McLaren-Porsche	1985 McLaren-TAG	1986 Williams-Honda	1987 Williams-Honda
1988 McLaren-Honda	1989 McLaren-Honda			

Most titles: 8 Ferrari; **7** Lotus (**5** Lotus-Ford; **2** Lotus-Climax); **5** McLaren (**1** McLaren-TAG; **1** McLaren-Ford; **2** McLaren-Honda; **1** McLaren-Porsche); **4** Williams (**2** Williams-Ford; **2** Williams-Honda)

HIGHEST PLACED BRITONS IN THE FORMULA ONE WORLD CHAMPIONSHIP

1976	**James Hunt**	**1st**
1977	**James Hunt**	**5th**
1978	**John Watson**	**6th**
1979	**John Watson**	**9th**
1980	**John Watson**	**jt.10th**
1981	**John Watson**	**6th**
1982	**John Watson**	**jt. 2nd**
1983	**John Watson**	**jt. 6th**
1984	**Derek Warwick**	**7th**
1985	**Nigel Mansell**	**6th**
1986	**Nigel Mansell**	**2nd**
1987	**Nigel Mansell**	**2nd**
1988	**Derek Warwick**	**jt. 7th**
1989	**Nigel Mansell**	**4th**

THE RACE WINNERS
(up to and including Sep 1990)

ALBORETO, Michele (5)
1982 Las Vegas; 1983 Detroit (both Tyrrell); 1984 Belgian; 1985 Canadian, German (all Ferrari)

ANDRETTI, Mario (12)
1971 South African (Ferrari); 1976 Japanese; 1977 United States (West), Spanish, French, Italian; 1978 Argentine, Belgian, Spanish, French, German, Dutch (all Lotus)

ARNOUX, Rene (7)
1980 Brazilian, South African; 1982 French, Italian (all Renault); 1983 Canadian, German, Dutch (all Ferrari)

ASCARI, Alberto (13)
1951 German, Italian; 1952 Belgian, French, British, German, Dutch, Italian; 1953 Argentine, Dutch, Belgian, British, Swiss (all Ferrari)

BAGHETTI, Giancarlo (1)
1961 French (Ferrari)

BANDINI, Lorenzo (1)
1964 Austrian (Ferrari)

BELTOISE, Jean-Pierre (1)
1972 Monaco (BRM)

BERGER, Gerhard (5)
1986 Mexican (Benetton); 1987 Japanese, Australian; 1988 Italian; 1989 Portuguese (all Ferrari)

BONNIER, Jo (1)
1959 Dutch (BRM)

BOUTSEN, Thierry (2)
1989 Canadian, Australian (both Williams)

BRABHAM, Jack (14)
1959 Monaco, British; 1960 Dutch, Belgian, French, British, Portuguese (all Cooper); 1966 French, British, Dutch, German; 1967 French, Canadian; 1970 South African (all Brabham)

BRAMBILLA, Vittorio (1)
1975 Austrian (March)

BROOKS, Tony (6)
1957 British*; 1958 Belgian, German, Italian (all Vanwall); 1959 French, German (both Ferrari)

CEVERT, Francois (1)
1971 United States (Tyrrell)

CLARK, Jim (25)
1962 Belgian, British, United States; 1963 Belgian, Dutch, French, British, Italian, Mexican, South African; 1964 Dutch, Belgian, British; 1965 South African, Belgian, French, British, Dutch, German; 1966 United States; 1967 Dutch, British, United States, Mexican; 1968 South African (all Lotus)

COLLINS, Peter (3)
1956 Belgian, French (both Lancia-Ferrari); 1968 British (Ferrari)

DE ANGELIS, Elio (2)
1982 Austrian; 1985 San Marino (both Lotus)

DEPAILLER, Patrick (2)
1978 Monaco (Tyrrell); 1979 Spanish (Ligier)

FAGIOLI, Luigi (1)
1951 French* (Alfa Romeo)

FANGIO, Juan Manuel (24)
1950 Monaco, Belgian, French; 1951 Swiss, French, Spanish (all Alfa Romeo); 1953 Italian (Maserati); 1954 Argentine, Belgian (both Maserati), French, German, Swiss, Italian; 1955 Argentine, Belgian, Dutch, Italian (all Mercedes-Benz); 1956 Argentine*, British, German (all Lancia-Ferrari); 1957 Argentine, Monaco, French, German (all Maserati)

FARINA, Giuseppe (5)
1950 British, Swiss, Italian; 1951 Belgian (all Alfa Romeo); 1953 German (Ferrari)

FITTIPALDI, Emerson (14)
1970 United States; 1972 Spanish, Belgian, British, Austrian, Italian; 1973 Argentine, Brazilian, Spanish (all Lotus); 1974 Brazilian, Belgian, Canadian; 1975 Argentine, British (all McLaren)

GETHIN, Peter (1)
1971 Italian (BRM)

GINTHER, Richie (1)
1965 Mexican (Honda)

GONZALEZ, Jose Froilan (2)
1951 British; 1954 British (both Ferrari)

GURNEY, Dan (4)
1962 French (Porsche); 1964 French, Mexican (both Brabham); 1967 Belgian (Eagle)

HAWTHORN, Mike (3)
1953 French; 1954 Spanish; 1958 French (all Ferrari)

HILL, Graham (14)
1962 Dutch, German, Italian, South African; 1963 Monaco, United States; 1964 Monaco, United States; 1965 Monaco, United States (all BRM); 1968 Spanish, Monaco, Mexican; 1969 Monaco (all Lotus)

HILL, Phil (3)
1960 Italian; 1961 Belgian, Italian (all Ferrari)

HULME, Denny (8)
1967 Monaco, German (both Brabham); 1968 Italian, Canadian; 1969 Mexico; 1972 South African; 1973 Swedish; 1974 Argentine (all McLaren)

HUNT, James (10)
1975 Dutch (Hesketh); 1976 Spanish, French, German, Dutch, Canadian, United States; 1977 British, United States; Japanese (all McLaren)

ICKX, Jacky (8)
1968 French (Ferrari); 1969 German, Canadian (both Brabham); 1970 Austrian, Canadian, Mexican; 1971 Dutch; 1972 German (all Ferrari)

IRELAND, Innes (1)
1961 United States (Lotus)

JABOUILLE, Jean-Pierre (2)
1979 French; 1980 Austrian (both Renault)

JONES, Alan (12)
1977 Austrian (Shadow); 1979 German, Austrian, Dutch, Canadian; 1980 Argentine, French, British, Canadian,

United States; 1981 United States (West), Las Vegas (all Williams)

LAFFITE, Jacques (6)
1977 Swedish; 1979 Argentine, Brazilian; 1980 German (all Ligier); 1981 Austrian, Canadian (both Talbot-Ligier)

LAUDA, Niki (25)
1974 Spanish, Dutch; 1975 Monaco, Belgian, Swedish, French, United States; 1976 Brazilian, South African, Belgian, Monaco, British; 1977 South African, German, Dutch (all Ferrari); 1978 Swedish, Italian (both Brabham); 1982 United States (West), British; 1984 South African, French, British, Austrian, Italian; 1985 Dutch (all McLaren)

McLAREN, Bruce (4)
1959 United States; 1960 Argentine; 1962 Monaco (all Cooper); 1968 Belgian (McLaren)

MANSELL, Nigel (16)
1985 European, South African; 1986 Belgian, Canadian, French, British, Portuguese; 1987 San Marino, French, British, Austrian, Spanish, Mexican (all Williams); 1989 Brazilian, Hungarian; 1990 Portuguese (all Ferrari)

MASS, Jochen (1)
1975 Spanish (McLaren)

MOSS, Stirling (16)
1955 British (Mercedes-Benz); 1956 Monaco, Italian (both Maserati); 1957 British*, Pescara, Italian (all Vanwall); 1958 Argentine (Cooper), Dutch, Portuguese, Moroccan (all Vanwall); 1959 Portuguese, Italian (Cooper); 1960 Monaco, United States; 1961 Monaco, German (all Lotus)

MUSSO, Luigi (1)
1956 Argentine* (Lancia-Ferrari)

NANNINI, Alessandro (1)
1989 Japanese (Benetton)

NILSON, Gunnar (1)
1977 Belgian (Lotus)

PACE, Carlos (1)
1975 Brazilian (Brabham)

PATRESE, Riccardo (3)
1982 Monaco; 1983 South African (both Brabham) 1990 San Marino (Williams)

PETERSON, Ronnie (10)
1973 French, Austrian, Italian, United States; 1974 Monaco, French, Italian (all Lotus); 1976 Italian (March); 1978 South African, Austrian (both Lotus)

PIRONI, Didier (3)
1980 Belgian (Ligier); 1982 San Marino, Dutch (both Ferrari)

PIQUET, Nelson (20)
1980 United States (West), Dutch, Italian; 1981 Argentine, San Marino, German; 1982 Canadian; 1983 Brazilian, Italian, European, Detroit; 1985 French (all Brabham); 1986 Brazilian, German, Hungarian, Italian; 1987 German, Hungarian, Italian (all Williams)

PROST, Alain (44)
1981 French, Dutch, Italian; 1982 South African, Brazilian; 1983 French, Belgian, British, Austrian (all Renault); 1984 Brazilian, San Marino, Monaco, German, Dutch, European, Portuguese; 1985 Brazilian, Monaco, British, Austrian, Italian; 1986 San Marino, Monaco, Austrian, Australian; 1987 Brazilian, Belgian, Portuguese;1988 Brazilian, Monaco, Mexican, French, Portuguese, Spanish, Australian; 1989 United States, French, British, Italian (all McLaren); 1990 Brazilian, Mexican, French, British, Spanish (all Ferrari)

REGAZZONI, Clay (5)
1970 British; 1974 German; 1975 Italian; 1976 United States (West) (all Ferrari); 1979 British (Williams)

REUTEMANN, Carlos (12)
1974 South African, Austrian, United States; 1975 German (all Brabham); 1977 Brazilian; 1978 Brazilian, United States (West), British, United States (all Ferrari); 1980

Monaco; 1981 Brazilian, Belgian (all Williams)
REVSON, Peter (2)
1973 British, Canadian (both McLaren)
RINDT, Jochen (6)
1969 United States; 1970 Monaco, Dutch, French, British, German (all Lotus)
RODRIGUEZ, Pedro (2)
1967 South African (Cooper); 1970 Belgian (BRM)
ROSBERG, Keke (5)
1982 Swiss; 1983 Monaco; 1984 Dallas; 1985 Detroit, Australian (all Williams)
SCARFIOTTI, Ludovico (1)
1966 Italian (Ferrari)
SCHECKTER, Jody (10)
1974 Swedish, British; 1975 South African; 1976 Swedish (all Tyrrell); 1977 Argentine, Monaco, Canadian (all Wolf); 1979 Belgian, Monaco, Italian (all Ferrari)
SENNA, Ayrton (25)
1985 Portuguese, Belgian; 1986 Spanish, Detroit; 1987 Monaco, United States (all Lotus); 1988 San Marino, Canadian, United States, British, German, Hungarian, Belgian, Japanese; 1989 San Marino, Monaco, Mexican, German, Belgian; 1990 United States, Monaco, Canadian, German, Belgian, Italian (all McLaren)
SIFFERT, Jo (2)
1968 British (Lotus); 1971 Austrian (BRM)
STEWART, Jackie (27)
1965 Italian; 1966 Monaco (both BRM); 1968 Dutch, German, United States; 1969 South African, Spanish, Dutch, French, British, Italian (all Matra); 1970 Spanish (March); 1971 Spanish, Monaco, French, British, German, Canadian; 1972 Argentine, French, Canadian, United States; 1973 South African, Belgian, Monaco, Dutch, German (all Tyrrell)
SURTEES, John (6)
1963 German; 1964 German, Italian; 1966 Belgian (all Ferrari), Mexican (Cooper); 1967 Italian (Honda)
TAMBAY, Patrick (2)
1982 German; 1983 San Marino (both Ferrari)
TARUFFI, Piero (1)
1952 Swiss (Ferrari)
TRINTIGNANT, Maurice (2)
1955 Monaco (Ferrari); 1958 Monaco (Cooper)
VILLENEUVE, Gilles (6)
1978 Canadian; 1979 South African, United States (West), United States; 1981 Monaco, Spanish (all Ferrari)
VON TRIPS, Wolfgang (2)
1961 Dutch, British (both Ferrari)
WATSON, John (5)
1976 Austrian (Penske); 1981 British; 1982 Belgian, Detroit; 1983 United States West (all McLaren)

* denotes shared drive
  only half points awarded
Figures in brackets () indicate total wins
Most wins in a season
8 Ayrton Senna (Bra) 1988; 7 Jim Clark (GB) 1963, Alain Prost (Fra) 1984, 1988; 6 Alberto Ascari (Ita) 1952, Juan Manuel Fangio (Arg) 1954, Jim Clark (GB) 1965, Jackie Stewart (GB) 1969, 1971, James Hunt (GB) 1976, Mario Andretti (US) 1978, Nigel Mansell (GB) 1987, Ayrton Senna (Bra) 1990 (up to and incl - Spanish GP)
Most successive wins
9 Alberto Ascari (Ita) 1952-3; 5 Jack Brabham (Aus) 1960, Jim Clark (GB) ;965
Most pole positions
50 Ayrton Senna (Bra); 33 Jim Clark (GB); 29 Juan Manuel Fangio (Arg); 24 Niki Lauda (Aut), Nelson Piquet (Bra)

CARS
Race Wins
103 Ferrari 1951-90; 86 McLaren 1968-90; 79 Lotus 1960-87; 44 Williams 1979-90; 35 Brabham 1964-85; 23 Tyrrell 1971-83; 17 BRM 1959-72; 16 Cooper 1958-67; 15 Renault 1979-83; 10 Alfa Romeo 1950-51; 9 Mercedes-Benz 1954-55; Maserati 1953-57; Vanwell 1957-58; Matra 1968-69; 8 Ligier 1977-81; 3 Wolf 1970-76; 3 March 1970-76; 2 Honda 1965-67; 2 Benetton 1986-89; 1 Porsche 1962; Eagle 1967; Hesketh 1975; Penske 1976; Shadow 1977
Most wins in a season
15 McLaren-Honda 1988; 12 McLaren-Porsche 1984; 10 McLaren-Honda 1989; 9 Williams-Honda 1986, 1987; 8 Lotus-Ford 1978; 7 Ferrari 1952,1953; Lotus-Climax 1963; Tyrrell-Ford 1971; Lotus-Ford 1973
Most successive wins
14 Ferrari 1952-3; 11 McLaren-Honda 1988; 9 Alfa Romeo 1950-51; 8 McLaren-TAG 1984-85

ENGINES
Wins
155 Ford; 103 Ferrari; 58 Honda; 40 Climax; 26 Porsche/TAG; 24 Renault; 18 BRM; 12 Alfa Romeo; 11 Maserati, Offenhauser; 9 BMW, Mercedes-Benz, Vanwall; 8 Repco; 3 Matra; 1 Westlake

BRITISH GRAND PRIX WINNERS
1950-54, 1956, 1958, 1960, 1963, 1965, 1967, 1969, 1971, 1973, 1975, 1977, 1979, 1981, 1983, 1985, 1987, 1988, 1989 at Silverstone; 1955, 1957, 1959, 1961-62 at Aintree; 1964, 1966, 1968, 1970, 1972, 1974, 1976, 1978, 1980, 1982, 1984, 1986 at Brands Hatch

1950	Giuseppe Farina (Ita)	Alfa Romeo
1951	Jose Froilan Gonzalez (Arg)	Ferrari
1952	Alberto Ascari (Ita)	Ferrari
1953	Alberto Ascari (Ita)	Ferrari
1954	Jose Froilan Gonzalez (Arg)	Ferrari
1955	Stirling Moss (GB)	Mercedes-Benz
1956	Juan Manuel Fangio (Arg)	Lancia-Ferrari
1957	Stirling Moss (GB) &	
	Tony Brooks (GB)	Vanwall
1958	Peter Collins (GB)	Ferrari
1959	Jack Brabham (Aus)	Cooper-Climax
1960	Jack Brabham (Aus)	Cooper-Climax
1961	Wolfgang Von Trips (FRG)	Ferrari
1962	Jim Clark (GB)	Lotus-Climax
1963	Jim Clark (GB)	Lotus-Climax
1964	Jim Clark (GB)	Lotus-Climax
1965	Jim Clark (GB)	Lotus-Climax
1966	Jack Brabham (Aus)	Brabham-Repco
1967	Jim Clark (GB)	Lotus-Ford
1968	Jo Siffert (Swi)	Lotus-Ford
1969	Jackie Stewart (GB)	Matra-Ford
1970	Jochen Rindt (Aut)	Lotus-Ford
1971	Jackie Stewart (GB)	Tyrrell-Ford
1972	Emerson Fittipaldi (Bra)	Lotus-Ford
1973	Peter Revson (US)	McLaren-Ford
1974	Jody Scheckter (SA)	Tyrrell-Ford
1975	Emerson Fittipaldi (Bra)	McLaren-Ford
1976	Niki Lauda (Aut)	Ferrari
1977	James Hunt (GB)	McLaren-Ford
1978	Carlos Reutemann (Arg)	Ferrari
1979	Clay Regazzoni (Swi)	Williams-Ford
1980	Alan Jones (Aus)	Williams-Ford
1981	John Watson (GB)	McLaren-Ford
1982	Niki Lauda (Aut)	McLaren-Ford
1983	Alain Prost (Fra)	Renault
1984	Niki Lauda (Aut)	McLaren-TAG
1985	Alain Prost (Fra)	McLaren-TAG

1986	Nigel Mansell (GB)	Williams-Honda
1987	Nigel Mansell (GB)	Williams-Honda
1988	Ayrton Senna (Bra)	McLaren-Honda
1989	Alain Prost (Fra)	McLaren-Honda
1990	Alain Prost (Fra)	Ferrari

WORLD SPORTSCAR CHAMPIONS

Inaugurated for types in 1953. A drivers' championship was introduced in 1981

Drivers

1981	Bob Garretson (US) Porsche
1982	Jacky Ickx (Bel) Porsche
1983	Jacky Ickx (Bel) Porsche
1984	Stefan Bellof (FRG) Porsche
1985	Derek Bell (GB) & Hans Stuck (FRG) Porsche
1986	Derek Bell (GB) & Hans Stuck (FRG) Porsche
1987	Raul Boesel (Bra) Jaguar
1988	Martin Brundle (GB) Jaguar
1989	Jean-Louis Schlesser (Fra) Mercedes

Cars

1953	Ferrari	1974	Matra-Simca
1954	Ferrari	1975	Alfa Romeo
1955	Mercedes-Benz	1976	Porsche
1956	Ferrari	1977	Porsche
1957	Ferrari	1978	Porsche
1958	Ferrari	1979	Porsche
1959	Aston Martin	1980	Lancia
1960	Ferrari	1981	Porsche
1961	Ferrari	1982	Porsche
1962-67	Not held	1983	Porsche
1968	Gord	1984	Porsche
1969	Porsche	1985	Rothmans-Porsche
1970	Porsche	1986	Brun Motorsport
1971	Porsche	1987	Silk Cut Jaguar
1972	Ferrari	1988	Silk Cut Jaguar
1973	Matra-Simca	1989	Sauber-Mercedes

FIA FORMULA 3000 INTERNATIONAL CHAMPIONSHIP

Inaugurated 1985

1985	Christian Danner (FRG) March-Smith
1986	Ivan Capelli (Ita) March-Mader
1987	Stefano Modena (Ita) March-Cosworth
1988	Roberto Moreno (Bra) Reynard-Nicholson
1989	Jean Alesi (Fra) Reynard-Mugen

LE MANS 24 HOUR RACE

First held 1923
Winners since 1981

1981	Derek Bell (GB)/Jacky Ickx (Bel) Porsche
1982	Derek Bell (GB)/Jacky Ickx (Bel) Porsche
1983	Hurley Haywood/Al Holbert (both US)/Vern Schuppan (Aut) Porsche
1984	Klaus Ludwig (FRG)/Henri Pescarolo (Fra) Porsche
1985	Paulo Barillo (Ita)/Klaus Ludwig/John Winter (both FRG) Porsche
1986	Derek Bell (GB)/Al Holbert (US)/Hans Stuck (FRG) Porsche
1987	Derek Bell (GB)/Al Holbert (US)/ Hans Stuck (FRG) Porsche
1988	Jan Lammers (Hol)/Johnny Dumfries/Andy Wallace (both GB) Jaguar
1989	Stanley Dickens (Swe)/Jochen Mass/Manuel Reuter (both FRG) Mercedes
1990	John Nielsen (Den)/Price Cobb (US)/Martin Brundle (GB) Jaguar

Most wins
6 Jacky Ickx 1969, 1975-77, 1981-82; 5 Derek Bell 1975, 1981-82, 1986-87; 4 Olivier Gendebien (Bel) 1958, 1960-62, Henri Pescarolo 1972-74, 1984

INDIANAPOLIS 500

First held 1911
Winners since 1981. US unless otherwise stated

1981	Bobby Unser	Penske
1982	Gordon Johncock	Wildcat
1983	Tom Sneva	March
1984	Rick Mears	March
1985	Danny Sullivan	March
1986	Bobby Rahal	March
1987	Al Unser	March
1988	Rick Mears	Penske
1989	Emerson Fittipaldi (Bra)	Penske
1990	Arie Luyendyk (Hol)	Chevrolet

Most wins
4 A J Foyt 1961, 1964, 1967, 1977; Al Unser 1970-71, 1978, 1987; 3 Louis Meyer 1928, 1933, 1936; Mauri Rose 1941, 1947-48; Bobby Unser 1968, 1975, 1981; Johnny Rutherford 1974, 1976, 1980; Rick Mears 1979, 1984, 1988

RALLYING

MONTE CARLO RALLY

Inaugurated 1911
Winners since 1981

1981	Jean Ragnotti (Fra)	Renault
1982	Walter Rohrl (FRG)	Opel
1983	Walter Rohrl (FRG)	Opel
1984	Walter Rohrl (FRG)	Audi
1985	Ari Vatanen (Fin)	Peugeot
1986	Henri Toivonen (Fin)	Lancia
1987	Miki Biasion (Ita)	Lancia
1988	Bruno Saby (Fra)	Lancia
1989	Miki Biasion (Ita)	Lancia
1990	Didier Auriol (Ita)	Lancia

Most wins
4 Sandro Munari (Ita) 1972, 1975-77; Walter Rohr (FRG); 3 Jean Trevoux (Fra) 1939, 1949, 1951

LOMBARD RAC RALLY

Inaugurated 1951
Winners since 1981

1981	Hannu Mikkola (Fin)	Audi
1982	Hannu Mikkola (Fin)	Audi
1983	Stig Blomqvist (Swe)	Audi
1984	Ari Vatanen (Fin)	Peugeot
1985	Henri Toivonen (Fin)	Lancia
1986	Timo Salonen (Fin)	Peugeot
1987	Juha Kankkunen (Fin)	Lancia
1988	Markku Alen (Fin)	Lancia
1989	Pentti Arikkala (Fin)	Mitsubishi

Most wins
4 Hannu Mikola (Fin) 1978-79, 1981-82; 3 Erik Carlsson (Swe) 1960-62, Timo Makinen (Fin) 1973-75

SAFARI RALLY

Inaugurated 1953
Winners since 1981

1981	Shekhar Mahta (Ken)	Datsun
1982	Shekhar Mahta (Ken)	Datsun
1983	Ari Vatanen (Fin)	Opel
1984	Bjorn Waldegaard (Swe)	Toyota
1985	Juha Kankkunen (Fin)	Toyota
1986	Bjorn Waldegard (Swe)	Toyota
1987	Hannu Mikkola (Fin)	Audi
1988	Miki Biasion (Ita)	Lancia
1989	Miki Biasion (Ita)	Lancia
1990	Bjorn Waldegaard (Swe)	Toyota

Most wins
5 Shekhar Mehta; 4 Bjorn Waldegard 1977, 1984, 1986, 1990; 3 Joginder Singh 1965, 1974, 1974, 1976

WORLD RALLY CHAMPIONS
Drivers
1977   Sandro Munari (Ita)
1978   Markku Alen (Fin)
1979   Bjorn Waldegaard (Swe)
1980   Walter Rohrl (FRG)
1981   Ari Vatanen (Fin)
1982   Walter Rohrl (FRG)
1983   Hannu Mikkola (Fin)
1984   Stig Blomqvist (Swe)
1985   Timo Salonen (Fin)
1986   Juha Kankkunen (Fin)
1987   Juha Kankunnen (Fin)
1988   Miki Biasion (Ita)
1989   Miki Baision (Ita)

——— 1991 ———

FORMULA ONE GRANDS PRIX

(all dates provisional)
Mar 17: US Grand Prix (Phoenix)
Mar 31: Brazilian Grand Prix (Interlagos)
Apr 21: San Marino Grand Prix (Imola)
May 12: Monaco Grand Prix (Monaco)
Jun 2: Canadian Grand Prix (Montreal)
Jun 16: Mexican Grand Prix (Mexico City)
Jul 7: French Grand Prix (Paul Ricard or Magny-Cours)
Jul 14: British Grand Prix (Silverstone)
Jul 28: German Grand Prix (Hockenheim)
Aug 11: Hungarian Grand Prix (Budapest)
Aug 25: Belgian Grand Prix (Spa)
Sep 8: Italian Grand Prix (Monza)
Sep 22: Portuguese Grand Prix (Estoril)
Sep 29: Spanish Grand Prix (Jerez or Montmelo)
Oct 27: Japanese Grand Prix (Suzuka)
Nov 10: Australian Grand Prix (Adelaide)

NETBALL

OLYMPIC GAMES

1996

On September 18, the International Olympic Committee chose Atlanta, Georgia to host the 1996 Olympics, defeating Athens, the Modern Games' inventors, who desperately wanted to stage the modern Games' centenary. The decision was widely criticised as a sell-out to financial interests.

VOTING
Ballots

	1	2	3	4	5
Atlanta	19	20	26	34	51
Athens	23	23	26	30	35
Toronto	14	17	18	22	
Melbourne	12	21	16		
Manchester	11	5			
Belgrade	7				

> **We would have accepted victory for Melbourne. It would have been good for sport. But not Atlanta. We'll never accept it because it's victory for industry and money."**
> *Spyros Metaxas, head of the Athens bid*

> **"This is not about money."**
> *Maynard Jackson, mayor of Atlanta*

> **"We had to decide whether to look back to the last century or to look forward to the next. It was a vote for the next century."**
> *Dick Pound, vice-president of the IOC*

> **"I remained undismayed...Without covering itself in glory, Manchester had made a fight of it.**
> *Bob Scott, head of the Manchester bid*

RECORDS

OLYMPIC VENUES
I Athens 1896; II Paris 1900; III St Louis 1904; (extra Games Athens 1906); IV London 1908; V Stockholm 1912; VI Berlin 1916 (cancelled); VII Antwerp 1920; VIII Paris 1924; IX Amsterdam 1928; X Los Angeles 1932; XI Berlin 1936; XII Tokyo then Helsinki 1940 (cancelled); XIII London 1944 (cancelled); XIV London 1948; XV Helsinki 1952; XVI Melbourne 1956; XVII Rome 1960; XVIII Tokyo 1964; XIX Mexico City 1968; XX Munich 1972; XXI Montreal 1976; XXII Moscow 1980; XXIII Los Angeles 1984; XXIV Seoul 1988; XXV Barcelona 1992 (Jul 25-Aug 9); XXVI Atlanta 1996 (July 20 - Aug 4.)

WINTER GAMES
(From 1994 to be held in between summer celebrations) Chamonix 1924; St Moritz 1928; Lake Placid 1932; Garmisch-Partenkirchen 1936; St Moritz 1948; Oslo 1952; Cortina d'Ampezzo 1956; Squaw Valley 1960; Innsbruck 1964; Grenoble 1968; Sapporo 1972; Innsbruck 1976; Lake Placid 1980; Sarajevo 1984; Calgary 1988; Albertville 1992; Lillehammer 1994.

1990

ENGLISH COUNTIES LEAGUE
First Division

	P	W	D	L	F	A	Pts
1 (5) Bedfordshire	7	5	1	1	300	238	29
2 (2) Essex Met	7	5	1	1	267	249	29
3 (3) Surrey	7	5	0	2	360	290	27
4 (1) Birmingham	7	5	0	2	324	307	27
5 (P) Middlesex	7	4	0	3	314	257	23
6 (P) Cheshire	7	2	0	5	250	289	15
7 (6) Hants North	7	1	0	6	237	305	11
8 (4) Herts	7	0	0	7	263	380	7

Second Division

	P	W	D	L	F	A	Pts
1 (4) South Yorks	7	5	0	2	320	255	27
2 (R) Kent	7	5	0	2	313	261	27
3 (6) Warwicks	7	5	0	2	266	243	27
4 (R) East Essex	7	4	0	3	307	268	23
5 (3) Gloucs	7	3	0	4	280	287	19
6 (P) Northants	7	3	0	4	260	270	19
7 (7) Derbys	7	3	0	4	283	300	19
8 (5) South Staffs	7	0	0	7	182	327	7

Last season's positions in brackets
Northern Division champs: Humberside
Southern Division champs: Mid Hants
Eastern Division champs: Notts
Western Division Champs: West Yorks
After play-offs West Yorkshire and Humberside were promoted to Division Two instead of South Staffs and Derbys

NATIONAL CLUBS' KNOCKOUT CUP FINAL
Manchester, May 12
NEW CAMPBELL GRASSHOPPERS (Essex Met) 49
Linden (Birmingham) 43

EVIAN INTER COUNTIES TOURNAMENT
Anerley, London, Apr 21-22
Seniors
1 MIDDLESEX; 2 Bedfordshire; 3 Essex Met; 4 Birmingham
Under-21
1 EAST SUSSEX; 2 Kent; 3 Derbyshire; 4 Surrey

CHAMPIONS

WORLD CHAMPIONSHIPS
First held 1963

1963	Australia
1967	New Zealand
1971	Australia
1975	Australia
1979	Australia, New Zealand and Trinidad & Tobago

(all shared the title)

1983	Australia
1987	New Zealand

ENGLISH COUNTIES LEAGUE
(Formerly National League)

1985	Birmingham
1986	Birmingham
1987	Birmingham
1988	Surrey
1989	Birmingham
1990	Bedfordshire

1991

April 1-19 England tour to New Zealand; Jun 29- Jul 13 World Championships (Sydney).

ORIENTEERING	POLO

ORIENTEERING

1990

TSB BRITISH CHAMPIONSHIPS
Sheffield, Mar 24
Men
1 Steve Hale (Perth)
2 Andy Kitchen (INT)
3 Richard Jones (GUOC)
Hale's third successive title
Women
1 Yvette Hague (EUOC)
2 Jill Hayle (CLOK)
3 Clare Bolland (EUOC)

TSB JAN KJELLSTROM INTERNATIONAL FESTIVAL
Perth, Apr 13-16
Men
1 Steve Hale (GB)
2 Jürgen Mortensen (Swe)
3 Häkan Ericsson (Swe)
Women
1 Yvette Hague (GB)
2 Maine Westlund (Nor)
3 Claire Bolland (GB)

CHAMPIONS

WORLD CHAMPIONS
Inaugurated 1966

Men - Individual		Team
1966	Age Hadler (Nor)	Sweden
1968	Karl Johansson (Swe)	Sweden
1970	Stig Berge (Nor)	Norway
1972	Age Hadler (Nor)	Sweden
1974	Bernt Frilen (Swe)	Sweden
1976	Egil Johansen (Nor)	Sweden
1978	Egil Johansen (Nor)	Norway
1979	Oyvin Thon (Nor)	Sweden
1981	Oyvin Thon (Nor)	Norway
1983	Morten Berglia (Nor)	Norway
1985	Kari Sallinen (Fin)	Norway
1987	Kent Olsson (Swe)	Norway
1989	Peter Thoresen (Nor)	Norway

Women - Individual		Team
1966	Ulla Lindqvist (Swe)	Sweden
1968	Ulla Lindqvist (Swe)	Norway
1970	Ingrid Hadler (Nor)	Sweden
1972	Sarolta Monspart (Hun)	Finland
1974	Mona Norgaard (Den)	Sweden
1976	Lia Veijalainen (Fin)	Sweden
1978	Anne Berit Eid (Nor)	Finland
1979	Outi Bergonstrom (Fin)	Finland
1981	Annichen Kringstad (Nor)	Sweden
		Sweden
1983	Annichen Kringstad-Svensson (Swe)	Sweden
1985	Annichen Kringstad-Svensson (Swe)	Sweden
1987	Arja Hannus (Swe)	Norway
1989	Marita Skogum (Swe)	Sweden

1991

Mar 29 - Apr 1 Jan Kjellstrom Festival (Chesterfield);
May 4 - 5 British Championships (Alnwick, Northumberland).

POLO

1990

BRITISH OPEN
(Davidoff Cup)
Cowdray Park, Jun 30-Jul 22
Semi-finals
COWDRAY PARK 8 Diamond D 7; HILDON 9 Pendell 8
Final
HILDON 10 Cowdray Park 9 (aet)

COWDRAY PARK CHALLENGE CUP
Cowdray Park, Aug 5
ROSAMUNDO 5 1/2 Sante Fe 4

OTHER TOURNAMENTS
Finals
Queen's Cup: SANTE FE 12 Rosamundo 7
Prince of Wales Trophy: TRAMONTANA 10
Champagne Pommery 8
Warwickshire Cup: ELLERSTON WHITE 9 Hildon 7

TOP HANDICAP PLAYERS IN BRITAIN IN 1990

10 goals: Carlos Gracida (Mex/Cowdray Park), G Gracida (Mex/Cowdray Park), Ernesto Heguy (Arg/Royal Berkshire), Marcos Heguy (Arg/Royal Berkshire), A Pieres (Arg/Cowdray Park), Gonzalo Pieres (Arg/Cowdray Park), Ernesto Trotz (Arg/Cirencester); **9 goals:** Alejandro Alberdi (Arg/Guards), Hector Crotto (Arg/Guards), J Crotto (Arg/Royal Berkshire), Gabriele Donoso (Chi/Royal Berkshire), Howard Hipwood (Eng/Royal Berkshire), Owen Rinehart (US/Cowdray Park), R Walton (Guards)

CHAMPIONS

WORLD CUP
Inaugurated 1987
1987 Argentina
1989 United States

BRITISH OPEN
Winners since 1981
1981 Falcons
1982 Southfield
1983 Falcons
1984 Southfield
1985 Maple Leafs
1986 Tramontana
1987 Tramontana
1988 Tramontana
1989 Tramontana
1990 Hildon

OLYMPIC GAMES
Dropped after 1936
1900 Great Britain
1908 Great Britain
1920 Great Britain
1924 Argentina
1936 Argentina

RACKETS

━━━━━ 1990 ━━━━━
WORLD DOUBLES CHAMPIONSHIP
Queen's Club, Feb 15-18
JAMES MALE & JOHN PRENN (UK) beat Neil Smith & Shannon Hazell (UK) 8-15 7-15 14-17 15-8 15-10 15-12 15-3

RANK XEROX PROFESSIONAL SINGLES
Marlborough, Feb 11-12
SHANNON HAZELL (Clifton) beat Neil Smith (Queen's) 1-15 15-1 15-12 11-15 15-6

LACOSTE OPEN SINGLES
Queen's Club, Mar 9-25
NEIL SMITH beat Willie Boone 15-5 15-7 15-9 15-11
Boone's 10th final. Smith won after three successive years as runner-up.

OPEN DOUBLES
Queen's Club, Apr 21-29
JOHN PRENN & JAMES MALE beat Neil Smith & Shannon Hazell 15-9 15-9 5-15 15-10 15-9

AMATEUR DOUBLES CHAMPSIONSHIP
Queen's Club, Jan 31-Feb 11
JOHN PRENN & JAMES MALE beat Charles Hue Williams & Mark Hue Williams 7-15 15-1 15-6 15-0 15-9

━━━━━ CHAMPIONS ━━━━━

WORLD CHAMPIONS
Organised on a challenge basis. All winners British unless otherwise stated.
Winners

1820	Robert Mackay
1825	Thomas Pittman
1834	John Pittman
1838	John Lamb
1846	L C Mitchell
1860	Francis Erwood
1862	William Hart Dyke
1863	Henry Gray
1866	William Gray
1876	H B Fairs
1878	Joseph Gray
1887	Peter Latham
1903	J Jamsetjhi (Ind)
1911	Charles Williams
1913	Jock Soutar (US)
1929	Charles Williams
1937	David Milford
1947	James Dear
1954	Geoffrey Atkins
1972	William Surtees (US)
1973	Howard Angus
1974	William Surtees (US)
1981	John Prenn
1984	Willie Boone
1986	John Prenn
1988	James Male

REAL TENNIS

━━━━━ 1990 ━━━━━
WOMEN'S DOUBLES CHAMPIONSHIP
Canford, Jan 5-7
ALEX WARREN-PIPER & MELISSA BRIGGS beat Magda Groszek & Jo Page 6-1 6-4

HENRY LEAF CUP
Queen's Club, Jan 23
RADLEY beat Winchester 6-3 6-2

UNIVERSITY MATCH
Leamington, Mar 2-3
OXFORD UNIVERSITY beat Cambridge University 3-2

GEORGE WIMPEY AMATEUR SINGLES
Queen's Club, Mar 31-Apr 8
FINAL
JAMES MALE beat John Snow 6-4 6-4 6-4

BATHURST CUP
Queen's Club, Apr 15
ENGLAND beat Australia 3-0

BRITISH PROFESSIONAL SINGLES
Holyport, Apr 30-May 6
LACHLAN DEUCHAR beat David Johnson 6-1 6-0 6-3

TAYLOR CUP
Holyport, May 6
MARK DEVINE beat Nick Wood 6-4 5-6 6-2

━━━━━ CHAMPIONS ━━━━━

WORLD CHAMPIONS
Organised on a challenge basis
Men

1740	Clerge (Fra)
1765	Raymond Masson (Fra)
1785	Joseph Barcellon (Fra)
1816	Marchesio (Ita)
1819	Phillip Cox (GB)
1829	Edmond Barre (Fra)
1862	Edmund Tomkins (GB)
1871	George Lambert (GB)
1885	Tom Pettitt (US)
1890	Charles Saunders (GB)
1895	Peter Latham (GB)
1905	Cecil Fairs (GB)
1907	Peter Latham (GB)
1908	Cecil Fairs (GB)
1912	Fred Covey (GB)
1914	Jay Gould (US)
1916	Fred Covey (GB)
1928	Pierre Etchebaster (Fra)
1955	James Dear (GB)
1957	Albert Johnson (GB)
1959	Northrup Knox (US)
1969	Pete Bostwick (US)
1972	Jimmy Bostwick (US)
1976	Howard Angus (GB)
1981	Chris Ronaldson (GB)
1987	Wayne Davies (Aus)

Women
First held 1985, contested biennially

1985	Judy Clarke (Aus)
1987	Judy Clarke (Aus)
1989	Penny Fellows (GB)

PROFESSIONAL DOUBLES CHAMPIONSHIP
Canford, Jan 5-7
PETE BRAKE & CLIFF BRAY beat Nick Wood & Peter

ROWING

1990

NATIONAL CHAMPIONSHIPS
Nottingham, Jul 21-22

Men

Single Sculls	Simon Larkin Notts County 'A' 7m 02.38s
Double Sculls	Molesey 6m 32.03s
Quadruple Sculls	Upper Thames 'A' 6m 07.47s
Coxless Pairs	Lea/Tyrian 6m 48.57s
Coxed Pairs	Thames Tradesmen 7m 26.88s
Coxless Fours	Notts County 6m 03.86s
Coxed Fours	Lea 'A' 6m 17.62s
Eights	Notts County 5m 38.05s
Lightweight Single Sculls	Philip Ashmore St Ives 7m 10.45s
Lightweight Double Sculls	Notts County 6m 37.38s
Lightweight Quadruple Sculls	Auriol Kensington 6m 19.11s
Lightweight Coxless Fours	Notts County 6m 06.55s
Lightweight Eights	Notts County 5m 47.37s

Women

Single Sculls	Patricia Reid GB National Squad 'A' 7m 48.86s
Double Sculls	GB National Squad 7m 03.75s
Quadruple Sculls	Tideway Scullers 'A' 6m 49.37s
Coxless Pairs	GB National Squad 'B' 7m 31.38s
Coxless Fours	GB National Squad 6m 48.01s
Coxed Fours	University of London 7m 11.82s
Eights	Cambridge University 'A' 6m 30.99s
Lightweight Single Sculls	Claire Parker Notts County 7m 54.63s
Lightweight Double Sculls	Marlow/Thames 7m 15.36s
Lightweight Coxless Pairs	Birmingham 7m 45.80s
Lightweight Coxless Fours	Thames Tradesmen 7m 05.41s

BOAT RACE

Putney to Mortlake, Mar 31

OXFORD UNIVERSITY beat Cambridge University by 2 $\frac{1}{4}$ lengths (7 secs), Time 17m 15s

Crews

Oxford

Cox:	M W Watts (Westminster & Oriel) 7st 9lb
Stroke:	M Gaffney (US Naval Academy & Hertford) 15st 4lb
No.7:	J W C Searle (Hampton & Christ Church) 13st 10lb
No.6:	C J Heathcote (Allhallows, Coventry & Jesus) 17st 5lb
No.5:	R A Hull (Robinson College, Cambridge & Oriel) 15st 7lb
No.4:	M C Pinsent (Eton & St Catherine's) 15st 7lb
No.3:	D G Miller III (State University, New York & University) 14st 13lb
No.2:	R J Obholzer (Hampton & St Catherine's) 13st 12lb
Bow:	T G Slocock (Shrewsbury & St. Johns) 14st 6lb

Average Weight: 14st 12lb

The Oxford crew was the heaviest ever and Christopher Heathcote (Oxford No.6) was the heaviest person ever to compete in the race at 17st 5lb. He was two stone heavier than the boat.

Cambridge

Cox:	L Ross-Magenty (Godolphin and Latimer & New Hall) 7st 10lb
Stroke:	A J Wright (King Edward VI, Norwich & Corpus Christi) 13st 2lb
No.7:	S L Fowler (Eton & Robinson) 12st 12lb
No.6:	G R Pooley (Berkhamsted, Imperial College, London & LMBC) 12st 11lb
No.5:	P M Mant (Cheltenham & Selwyn) 11st 10lb
No.4:	E C Clark (Shrewsbury & Trinity) 11st 10lb
No.3:	D E Hole (Foster's GS, Sherborne & Selwyn), 13st 3lb
No.2:	R J Staite (Prince Henry's, Evesham & St. Catharine's) 11st 3lb
Bow:	R C Young (Bedford & Downing) 12st 13lb

Average weight: 12st 10 $\frac{1}{2}$lb

Reserve Race
GOLDIE (Cambridge) won after Isis (Oxford) disqualified for cutting across.

TALES FROM THE TIDEWAY

"You've got to manipulate eight enormous thugs and make them move like ballerinas."
Lisa Ross-Magenty, Cambridge cox

"It's like Barnet taking on Nottingham Forest at soccer - that's the sort of chance we've got...there is a lot of arrogance and apathy in the Cambridge camp."
Mark Lees, Cambridge coach

"They were fabulous. They rowed above themselves. That crew shouldn't have even been there."
Mark Lees on his crew's narrow defeat

"It's not a big thing for me. It's much more important to win the Olympics."
Jonny Searle, Oxford president

"At least I am fat and happy while he looks ill and likely to drop dead."
Ross-Magenty (7st 10lb) on Martin Watts, the Oxford cox (7st 9lb)

WOMEN'S BOAT RACE
Henley, Mar 25
CAMBRIDGE UNIVERSITY beat Oxford University by
3$^1/_4$ lengths (7m 17s)
Reserve Race
BLONDIE (Cambridge) beat Osiris (Oxford)
1$^1/_4$ lengths (7m 34s)
151st HENLEY ROYAL REGATTA
Jul 4-8
FINALS
Ladies Plate
HARVARD UNIVERSITY (US) beat University of
London by 3$^2/_3$l, 6m 35s
Visitors' Cup
UNIVERSITY OF LONDON 'A' beat Goldie, not rowed
out, 7m 17s
Thames Cup
NOTTINGHAM COUNTY beat Harvard University 'A'
(US) by 2l, 6m 50s
Henley Prize
Inaugurated 1990
IMPERIAL COLLEGE, LONDON beat Trinity College,
Dublin by 1$^3/_4$l, 7m 00s
Prince Philip Cup
HANSA DORTMUND (FRG) beat Levski Spartak (Bul)
by 4l, 7m 27s
Wyfold Cup
LONDON ROWING CLUB 'A' beat Notts County by
1$^1/_3$l, 7m 26s
Britannia Cup
UNIVERSITY COLLEGE, GALWAY (Ire) beat
Cappoquin (Ire) by 2l, 7m 47s
Stewards' Cup
STAR CLUB & LEANDER 'A' beat Star Club & Leander
'B' by 4$^3/_4$l, 7m 16s
Grand Challenge Cup
HANSA DORTMUND (FRG) beat Leander & University
of London by 2l, 6m 36s
Princess Elizabeth Cup
ETON COLLEGE beat Westminster School by $^2/_3$l, 6m
58s
Queen Mother Cup
DANMARK ROCENTER ROKLUB (Den) beat ASR
Nereus & Skadi (Hol) by $^1/_2$l, 7m 01s
Silver Goblets & Nickalls'
KARL SINZINGER & HERMANN BAUER
(Heeresportverein Kapsch Linz, Austria) beat Martin Cross
& Tim Foster (Thames Tradesmen & Star) by 1ft, 7m 39s
Diamond Sculls
ERIC VERDONK (Moru, New Zealand) beat Wim van
Belleghem (Bruges Trimmen, Belgium) by 3/4l, 8m 21s
Double Sculls Cup
ANDREW RUDKING & PHILLIP KITTERMASTER
(Tideway Scullers' School & Barclay's Bank) beat Mark
Alloway & Chris Williams (Tideway Scullers' School) by
1$^3/_4$l, 8m 28s

——— CHAMPIONS ———

OLYMPIC GAMES
Men
Single Sculls
1900 Henri Barrelet (Fra)
1904 Frank Greer (US)
1908 Harry Blackstaffe (GB)
1912 William Kinnear (GB)
1920 John Kelly Snr (US)
1924 Jack Beresford Jr (GB)
1928 Henry Pearce (Aus)
1932 Henry Pearce (Aus)
1936 Gustav Schäfer (Ger)
1948 Mervyn Wood (Aus)
1952 Yuriy Tyukalov (USSR)
1956 Vyacheslav Ivanov (USSR)
1960 Vyacheslav Ivanov (USSR)
1964 Vyacheslav Ivanov (USSR)
1968 Henri Jan Wienese (Hol)
1972 Yuriy Malishev (USSR)
1976 Pertti Karppinen (Fin)
1980 Pertti Karppinen (Fin)
1984 Pertti Karppinen (Fin)
1988 Thomas Lange (GDR)
Double Sculls
1904 John Mulcahy/William Varley (US)
1920 Paul Costello/John Kelly (US)
1924 Paul Costello/John Kelly (US)
1928 Paul Costello/Charles McIlvaine (US)
1932 William Garrett Gilmore/Kenneth Myers (US)
1936 Jack Beresford/Leslie Southwood (GB)
1948 Richard Burnell/Herbert Bushnell (GB)
1952 Tranquilo Capozzo/Eduardo Guerrero (Arg)
1956 Aleksandr Berkutov/Yuriy Tyukalov (USSR)
1960 Vaclav Kozak/Pavel Schmidt (Cze)
1964 Boris Dubrovsky/Oleg Tyurin (USSR)
1968 Anatoliy Sass/Aleksandr Timoshinin (USSR)
1972 Gennadiy Korshikov/Aleksandr Timoshinin (USSR)
1976 Alf Hansen/Frank Hansen (Nor)
1980 Joachim Dreifke/Klaus Kroppelien (GDR)
1984 Bradley Lewis/Paul Enquist (US)
1988 Ronald Florjin/Nicolaas Rienks (Hol)
Coxless Pairs
1904 Robert Farnam/Joseph Ryan (US)
1908 John Fenning/Gordon Thomson (GB)
1924 Antonie Beijnen/Wilhelm Rosingh (Hol)
1928 Kurt Moeschter/Bruno Muller (Ger)
1932 Lewis Clive/Arthur Edwards (GB)
1936 Willie Eichorn/Hugo Strauss (Ger)
1948 George Laurie/John Wilson (GB)
1952 Charles Logg/Thomas Price (US)
1956 James Fifer/Duvall Hecht (US)
1960 Valentin Boreyko/Oleg Golovanov (USSR)
1964 George Hungerford/Roger Jackson
1968 Heinz-Jürgen Bothe/Jorg Lucke (GDR)
1972 Siegfried Brietzke/Wolfgang Mager (GDR)
1976 Bernd Landvoigt/Jorg Landvoigt (GDR)
1980 Petru Iosub/Valer Toma (Rom)
1988 Andrew Holmes/Steven Redgrave (GB)
Coxed Pairs
1900 Holland
1906 Italy
1920 Italy
1924 Switzerland
1928 Switzerland
1932 United States
1936 Germany
1948 Denmark

1952 France
1956 United States
1960 Germany
1964 United States
1968 Italy
1972 East Germany
1976 East Germany
1980 East Germany
1984 Italy
1988 Italy

Quadruple Sculls
1976 East Germany
1980 East Germany
1984 West Germany
1988 Italy

Coxless Fours
1904 United States
1908 Great Britain
1924 Great Britain
1928 Great Britain
1932 Great Britain
1936 Germany
1948 Italy
1952 Yugoslavia
1956 Canada
1960 United States
1964 Denmark
1968 East Germany
1972 East Germany
1976 East Germany
1980 East Germany
1984 New Zealand
1988 East Germany

Coxed Fours
1900 Germany
1900† France
1912 Germany
1920 Switzerland
1924 Switzerland
1928 Italy
1932 Germany
1936 Germany
1948 United States
1952 Czechoslovakia
1956 Italy
1960 Germany
1964 Germany
1968 New Zealand
1972 West Germany
1976 USSR
1980 East Germany
1984 Great Britain
1988 East Germany
† There were two finals in 1900

Eights
1900 United States
1904 United States
1908 Great Britain
1912 Great Britain
1920 United States
1924 United States
1928 United States
1932 United States
1936 United States
1948 United States
1952 United States
1956 United States
1960 Germany
1964 United States

1968 West Germany
1972 New Zealand
1976 East Germany
1980 East Germany
1984 Canada
1988 West Germany

Women
Single Sculls
1976 Christine Scheiblich (GDR)
1980 Sanda Toma (Rom)
1984 Valeria Racila (Rom)
1988 Jutta Behrendt (GDR)

Double Sculls
1976 Svetla Otzetova/Zdravka Yordanova (Bul)
1980 Yelena Khlopsteva/Larisa Popova (USSR)
1984 Marioara Popescu/Elisabeta Oleniuc (Rom)
1988 Birgit Peter/Martina Schroeter (GDR)

Coxless Pairs
1976 Stoyanka Grouitcheva/Siika Kelbetcheva (Bul)
1980 Cornelia Klier/Ute Steindorf (GDR)
1984 Rodica Arba/Elena Horvat (Rom)
1988 Rodica Arba/Olga Homeghi (Rom)

Quadruple Sculls
1976 East Germany
1980 East Germany
1984 Romania
1988 East Germany

Coxed Fours
1976 East Germany
1980 East Germany
1984 Romania
1988 East Germany

Eights
1976 East Germany
1980 East Germany
1984 United States
1988 East Germany

WORLD CHAMPIONSHIPS
First held for men 1962, and for women 1974. Not held in Olympic years. Winners in heavyweight classes since 1981:

Men
Single Sculls
1981	Peter-Michael Kolbe (FRG)
1982	Rudiger Reiche (GDR)
1983	Peter-Michael Kolbe (FRG)
1985	Pertti Karppinen (Fin)
1986	Peter-Michael Kolbe (FRG)
1987	Thomas Lange (GDR)
1989	Thomas Lange (GDR)

Double Sculls
1981	Klaus Kroppelien/Joachim Dreifke (GDR)
1982	Alf Hansen/Rolf Thorsen (Nor)
1983	Thomas Lange/Uwe Heppner (GDR)
1985	Thomas Lange/Uwe Heppner (GDR)
1986	Alberto Belgori/Igor Pescialli (Ita)
1987	Danayl Yordanov/Vassil Radev (Bul)
1989	Lars Bjoeness/Rol Bent Thorsen (Nor)

Coxless Pairs
1981	Yuriy Pimenov/Nikolay Pimenov (USSR)
1982	Magnus Grepperud/Sverre Loken (Nor)
1983	Carl Ertel/Ulf Sauerbrev (GDR)
1985	Nikolay Pimenov/Yuriy Pimenov (USSR)
1986	Nikolay Pimenov/Yuriy Pimenov (USSR)
1987	Andrew Holmes/Steven Redgrave (GB)
1989	Thomas Jung/Uwe Kellner (GDR)

Coxed Pairs
1981	Italy
1982	Italy
1983	East Germany
1985	Italy
1986	Great Britain
1987	Italy
1989	Italy

Coxless Pairs
1981	USSR
1982	Switzerland
1983	West Germany
1985	West Germany
1986	United States
1987	East Germany
1989	East Germany

Coxed Fours
1981	East Germany
1982	East Germany
1983	New Zealand
1985	USSR
1986	East Germany
1987	East Germany
1989	Romania

Quadruple Sculls
1981	East Germany
1982	East Germany
1983	West Germany
1985	Canada
1986	USSR
1987	USSR
1989	Holland

Eights
1981	USSR
1982	New Zealand
1983	New Zealand
1985	USSR
1986	Australia
1987	United States
1989	West Germany

Women
Single Sculls
1981	Sanda Toma (Rom)
1982	Irina Fetissova (USSR)
1983	Jutta Hampe (GDR)
1985	Cornelia Linse (GDR)
1986	Jutta Hampe (GDR)
1987	Magdalena Georgieva (Bul)
1989	Elisabeta Lipa (Rom)

Double Sculls
1981	Margarita Kikarevitha/Antonina Makhina (USSR)
1982	Yelena Braticko/Antonina Makhina (USSR)
1983	Jutta Scheck/Martina Schroter (GDR)
1985	Sylvia Schurabe/Martina Schroter (GDR)
1986	Sylvia Schurabe/Beate Schramm (GDR)
1987	Steska Madina/Violeta Ninova (Bul)
1989	Jana Sorgers/Beate Schramm (GDR)

Coxless Pairs
1981	Sigrid Anders/Iris Rudoph (GDR)
1982	Silvia Frohlich/Marita Sandig (GDR)
1983	Silvia Frohlich/Marita Sandig (GDR)
1985	Rodica Arba/Elena Florea (Rom)
1986	Rodica Arba/Olga Homeghi (Rom)
1987	Rodica Arba/Olga Homeghi (Rom)
1989	Kathrin Haaker/Judith Zeidler (GDR)

Quadruple Sculls
1981	USSR
1982	USSR
1983	USSR
1985	East Germany
1986	East Germany
1987	East Germany
1989	East Germany

Coxed Fours
1981	USSR
1982	USSR
1983	East Germany
1985	East Germany
1986	Romania
1987	Romania
1989	-

Coxless Fours
1986	United States
1987	-
1989	East Germany

Eights
1981	USSR
1983	USSR
1985	USSR
1986	USSR
1987	Romania
1989	Romania

UNIVERSITY BOAT RACE
Cambridge wins (69):
1836,1839-41,1845-46,1849,1856,1858,1860,
1870-74,1876,1879,1884,1886-89,1899-1900,
1902-04,1906-08,1914,1920-22,1924-36,1939,
1947-51,1953,1955-58,1961-62,1964,1968-73,1975,1986
Oxford wins (66):
1829,1842,1849,1852,1854,1857,1859,1861-69,
1875,1878,1880-83,1885,1890-98,1901,1905,1909-13,
1923,1937-38,1946,1952,1954,1959-60,1963,1965-67,
1974,1976-85,1987-90
There was a dead-heat in 1877
Fastest Time: 16 min 45 sec, Oxford (1984)
Biggest winning margin: 20 lengths, Cambridge (1900)
Most winning boats: 6 Boris Rankov (Oxford) 1978-83

Grand Challenge Cup
First held 1839. Winners since 1981
1981	Oxford University/Thames Tradesmen (GB)
1982	Leander/London RC (GB)
1983	London RC/University of London (GB)
1984	Leander/London RC (GB)
1985	Harvard University (US)
1986	Nautilus (GB)
1987	Soviety Army (USSR)
1988	Leander/University of London (GB)
1989	RC Hansa Dortmund (FRG)
1990	RC Hansa Dortmund (FRG)

Most wins
31 Leander Club 1840, 1875, 1880, 1891-94, 1896, 1898-1901, 1903-05, 1913, 1922, 1924-26, 1929, 1932, 1934, 1946, 1949, 1952-53, 1975†, 1982†, 1984†, 1988†
(† Boat shared with either Thames Tradesmen, London RC or University of London)

1991

Mar 30: University Boat Race (Putney to Mortlake, 1.20pm); Jul 3-7: Henley Royal Regatta; Aug 1-4: World Junior Championships (Banyolas, Spain); Aug 20-25: World Championships (Vienna).

RUGBY LEAGUE

THE WONDER OF WIGAN

This was Wigan's year. They won the Championship, the Challenge Cup and the competition now known as the Regal Trophy, an unprecedented treble and one which re-established beyond question their pre-eminence in the English game. Widnes, who had outflanked Wigan the previous season, had a successful start and finish, becoming world club champions and winning their third successive Premiership but neither they nor Leeds – who finished runners-up – ever matched Wigan's consistency.

Wigan's two Cup finals were both marked by marvellous performances from Ellery Hanley. But Hanley's pelvic injury kept him out of the first half of the season and forced him to withdraw from Great Britain's summer tour, leading to a constant undercurrent of doubt about his future. That ran alongside speculation that Wigan would stage a clean sweep of the major trophies, which lasted until Bradford Northern kept them out of the Premiership final. When the season ended, Leeds launched a frontal assault on Wigan's status by signing John Gallagher, the London-born All-Black full-back, in a world record £350,000 deal; Wigan countered by getting another All-Black, Frano Botica.

Jonathan Davies, Rugby League's most publicised convert, had an uncomfortable year with Widnes due to hamstring injuries and uncertainty about his best position – he fluctuated between full-back, centre, wing and stand-off. He was, however, included in the summer touring party. His Test debut turned into a disaster for Great Britain when they were beaten 20-18 by Papua New Guinea in a match marked by violence from the crowd, who threw stones, the police who responded with teargas, and – more dangerously – the opposition who were accused by the British of using illegal "spear-tackles" in which players were lifted and thrown head-first to the ground. Mike Gregory, the captain, complained that one PNG player tried to pull his eye out.

Gregory's team had revenge in the second game – the only one counting for World Cup points – and left, gladly, for New Zealand where Great Britain won the first two Tests but lost the one that counted for the World Cup, 21-18. They would have won but for a schoolboy mistake by Martin Offiah; under no pressure, he dropped the ball when on the brink of completing a try – "like robbing the bank and dropping the cash," as Alex Murphy put it on a similar occasion. Murphy himself was in the news as ever. After four years, he left his job as coach of St Helens, saying he had been "shown the door" and complaining about directors' interference. He returned to Leigh for the fourth time.

Referees in England tried to clamp down on violent play. Gary Charlton, the Whitehaven forward, was banned *sine die* for breaking Gary Steadman of Castleford's nose and jaw while Steve Hampson, the Wigan full-back, was sent off twice in two days after 12 clean years, and then went again seven weeks later. "I am no psycho," he insisted. Barrow and Runcorn Highfield tried to match each other for incompetence. Barrow were relegated from the First Division with one win out of 26. Second Division Runcorn, without a win since October 1988, lost all their 28 games; against Rochdale Hornets they went down 92-0.

The original Rugby League World Cup, last seen in 1970 when it was stolen from a Bradford hotel, was discovered – in mint condition except for the missing base – by a motorist, Trevor Uttley, 44, who had stopped to urinate. Mr Uttley did not know what the cup was and officials only knew of the find when he was pictured with it in a local paper.

Perry and Mason played together for Wakefield Trinity. It was revealed that St Helens players drank sherry before each game to improve their throats. Bob Cooper, formerly second row forward for Western Suburbs in Sydney, won a court decision when he claimed his beer and food bills against tax because he had been ordered to put on weight to retain his first-team place. A drugs raid on the South Sydney Club by the Australian Sports Drug Agency revealed one test positive for cocaine (Scott Wilson, the full-back, was sacked) and nine for marijuana.

A group of nuns, the Society of Sisters Faithful Campanions of Jesus, played a team of vicars in Milton Keynes to raise money for an ecumenical church. Yorkshire TV issued a correction to their TV schedules: Delete Beauty and the Beast, insert Wigan v Leeds. Sheffield Eagles' ground at Owlerton Stadium was temporarily closed under safety regulations; the programme notes said spectators would "have to put up with a certain amount of incontinence". Wally Lewis, the Australian captain, admitted substituting flat lager for a urine sample at a random dope test in Brisbane in 1986; no one had noticed.

1989-90

STONES BITTER CHAMPIONSHIP
Division One

			P	W	D	L	F	A	Pts	Av. Home Attendance	Players Sent Off
1	(2)	**WIGAN**	26	20	0	6	699	349	40	13,973	3
2	(3)	Leeds	26	18	0	8	704	383	36	12,251	8
3	(1)	Widnes	26	16	2	8	659	423	34	7,858	6
4	(8)	Bradford Northern	26	17	0	9	614	416	34	5,584	5
5	(7)	St Helens	26	17	0	9	714	544	34	8,555	6
6	(4)	Hull	26	16	1	9	577	400	33	6,218	3
7	(5)	Castleford	26	16	0	10	703	448	32	6,428	6
8	(11)	Warrington	26	13	1	12	424	451	27	5,412	4
9	(9)	Wakefield Trinity	26	12	1	13	502	528	25	5,428	6
10	(6)	Featherstone Rovers	26	10	0	16	479	652	20	4,269	4
11	(P)	Sheffield Eagles	26	9	1	16	517	588	19	4,038	3
12	(P)	*Leigh*	26	9	1	16	442	642	19	4,568	7
13	(10)	*Salford*	26	4	1	21	421	699	9	3,720	4
14	(P)	*Barrow*	26	1	0	25	201	1133	2	1,997	5

Last season's positions in brackets

LEADING SCORERS 1989-90

Tries		Goals		Points	
45	Martin Offiah (Widnes)	145	Paul Loughlin (St Helens)	358	Paul Loughlin (St Helens)
33	Mark Preston (Wigan)	114	Colin Maskell (Leeds)	290	Paul Eastwood (Hull)
32	Gerald Cordle (Bradford N)	107	Mark Conway (Wakefield T)	260	Jonathan Davies (Widnes)

Results: Division One

	Barrow	Bradford N	Castleford	Featherstone	Hull	Leeds	Leigh	St Helens	Salford	Sheff E	Wakefield T	Warrington	Widnes	Wigan
Barrow	x	6-60	14-42	0-46	6-38	10-32	6-44	6-46	2-36	10-22	10-26	0-9	4-34	0-66
Bradford N	36-24	x	24-16	32-10	30-12	14-13	30-10	28-18	18-12	28-12	19-18	38-10	16-6	15-16
Castleford	58-6	32-13	x	20-22	18-10	38-18	44-18	34-24	65-0	24-22	16-18	40-6	22-30	34-10
Featherstone	22-29	24-16	12-6	x	10-24	20-22	16-30	23-24	20-33	12-37	15-8	20-13	30-22	20-26
Hull	48-0	24-0	16-6	36-10	x	8-7	28-24	24-34	44-8	15-6	34-17	44-16	11-26	30-20
Leeds	90-0	13-8	25-18	25-14	18-2	x	38-16	50-14	34-28	44-2	14-22	30-6	26-12	14-21
Leigh	42-16	22-16	6-40	35-26	14-24	14-26	x	30-18	10-18	28-16	6-24	10-25	20-20	7-44
St Helens	62-18	32-10	24-26	50-11	19-12	32-26	12-6	x	40-16	42-26	44-21	14-23	8-18	35-10
Salford	36-4	12-36	18-24	14-15	5-21	18-38	19-6	10-25	x	20-20	18-28	5-16	16-28	12-56
Sheffield E	40-2	14-34	14-18	20-30	4-32	16-27	46-0	20-36	17-12	x	24-10	8-12	31-6	10-22
Wakefield T	30-16	12-36	22-14	22-14	30-14	17-36	32-0	21-24	28-4	16-28	x	32-8	10-10	14-23
Warrington	58-6	18-17	32-10	9-15	12-12	9-6	16-8	3-15	18-15	22-36	33-2	x	10-22	2-8
Widnes	48-0	14-40	24-16	59-8	30-12	8-20	16-18	34-16	46-18	53-20	30-12	32-20	x	10-11
Wigan	62-6	12-0	20-22	40-14	30-2	16-12	34-16	38-6	32-26	30-2	38-10	6-18	8-22	x

Division Two

			P	W	D	L	F	A	Pts	Av. Home Attendance	Players Sent Off
1	(R)	**HULL KINGSTON ROVERS**	28	25	0	3	1102	190	50	4,851	3
2	(9)	Rochdale Hornets	28	24	0	4	977	422	48	2,510	3
3	(R)	Oldham	28	24	0	4	879	325	48	4,401	6
4	(4)	Ryedale-York	28	20	1	7	653	338	41	2,495	7
5	(R)	Halifax	28	20	0	8	741	360	40	5,921	8
6	(5)	Swinton	28	20	0	8	673	405	40	1,678	5
7	(13)	Dewsbury	28	19	1	8	503	411	39	1,227	3
8	(15)	Fulham	28	16	2	10	496	488	34	841	4

9	(6)	Doncaster	28	15	2	11	533	399	32	1,965	2
10	(16)	Trafford Borough	28	15	0	13	551	551	30	780	9
11	(18)	Huddersfield	28	14	0	14	469	441	28	1,634	7
12	(12)	Batley	28	13	0	15	466	476	26	1,506	1
13	(10)	Bramley	28	11	0	17	413	623	22	982	4
14	(14)	Hunslet	28	10	0	18	431	585	20	1,046	6
15	(-)	Chorley	28	10	0	18	399	618	20	806	3
16	(7)	Whitehaven	28	10	0	18	396	710	20	961	6
17	(11)	Carlisle	28	9	0	19	511	625	18	574	0
18	(17)	Workington Town	28	6	0	22	311	708	12	691	8
19	(8)	Keighley	28	6	0	22	436	837	12	936	10
20	(19)	Nottingham City	28	4	0	24	323	1032	8	577	5
21	(20)	Runcorn Highfield	28	0	0	28	216	935	0	453	3

Last season's positions in brackets

Note:

Ryedale York known as York 1988-89; Trafford Borough known as Chorley Borough 1988-89; Nottingham City known as Mansfield Marksmen 1988-89. Chorley newly elected into League 1989-90.

LEADING SCORERS 1989-90

Tries		Goals		Points	
38	Greg Austin (Hull KR)	199	Mike Fletcher (Hull KR)	450	Mike Fletcher (Hull KR)
35	Anthony Sullivan (Hull KR)	126	Duncan Platt (Oldham)	283	Duncan Platt (Oldham)
29	Paul Lord (Oldham)	98	Steve Turner (Rochdale H)		

"IF ONLY EVERYTHING IN LIFE WAS AS RELIABLE AS RUNCORN HIGHFIELD."

(Headline in Runcorn World*)*

1989

3 Sep	Div 2	Carlisle (a)	Lost	14-54
6 Sep	Div 2	Batley (h)	Lost	0-9
10 Sep	Div 2	Trafford B (a)	Lost	10-46
17 Sep	LC	St Helens (a)	Lost	10-78
24 Sep	Div 2	Doncaster (h)	Lost	6-46
1 Oct	Div 2	Huddersfield (h)	Lost	0-42
8 Oct	Div 2	Oldham (h)	Lost	6-34
15 Oct	Div 2	Dewsbury (a)	Lost	10-34
22 Oct	Div 2	Nottingham (h)	Lost	14-17
5 Nov	Div 2	Rochdale H (a)	Lost	0-92
12 Nov	Div 2	Batley (a)	Lost	14-46
19 Nov	Div 2	Bramley (h)	Lost	11-12
26 Nov	Div 2	Nottingham (a)	Lost	6-13
3 Dec	RT	Whitehaven (h)	Lost	10-20
17 Dec	Div 2	Whitehaven (h)	Lost	10-28
26 Dec	Div 2	Carlisle (h)	Lost	9-18

1990

1 Jan	Div 2	Chorley (a)	Lost	12-46
7 Jan	Div 2	Huddersfield (a)	Lost	10-22
14 Jan	Div 2	Dewsbury (h)	Lost	6-28
21 Jan	Div 2	Ryedale - York (h)	Lost	24-27
28 Jan	CC	Bradford N (h)	Lost	12-22
4 Feb	Div 2	Whitehaven (a)	Lost	8-20
18 Feb	Div 2	Hull KR (a)	Lost	6-36
25 Feb	Div 2	Trafford B (h)	Lost	7-18
4 Mar	Div 2	Rochdale H (h)	Lost	0-28
11 Mar	Div 2	Bramley (a)	Lost	6-29
18 Mar	Div 2	Oldham (a)	Lost	2-60
25 Mar	Div 2	Doncaster (h)	Lost	2-29
1 Apr	Div 2	Ryedale - York (a)	Lost	11-52
8 Apr	Div 2	Hull KR (h)	Lost	12-38
16 Apr	Div 2	Chorley (h)	Lost	2-11

Total Matches:

Played 31; Won 0; Drew; Lost 31; For 250; Against 1055
LC: Lancashire Cup; RT: Regal Trophy; CC: Challenge Cup.

SILK CUT CHALLENGE CUP

PRELIMINARY ROUND

Millom 0 BISONS 4; FULHAM 23 Doncaster 16; Leeds 8 BRADFORD NORTHERN 24; OLDHAM 30 Huddersfield 8; ST HELENS 39 Castleford 12

FIRST ROUND

Barrow 12 SHEFFIELD EAGLES 22; Bramley 14 ST HELENS 22; Chorley 6 KEIGHLEY 12; FULHAM 14, 16 Ryedale York 14, 12; HULL 46 Halifax 0; Hull Kingston Rovers 4 WIGAN 6; Nottingham City 2 DEWSBURY 32; OLDHAM 30 Workington Town 8; ROCHDALE HORNETS 38 Carlisle 6; Runcorn Highfield 12 BRADFORD NORTHERN 22; SALFORD 56 Bisons 6; Swinton 10, 4 WAKEFIELD TRINITY 10, 32; TRAFFORD BOROUGH 14 Hunslet 7; WARRINGTON 20 Featherstone Rovers 12; WHITEHAVEN 23 Leigh 22; WIDNES 26 Batley 10

SECOND ROUND

Fulham 2 BRADFORD NORTHERN 20; Hull 12 ST HELENS 24; Salford 7 OLDHAM 18; WAKEFIELD TRINITY 27 Sheffield Eagles 12; WARRINGTON 20 Trafford Borough 11; WHITEHAVEN 46 Keighley 10; WIDNES 22 Rochdale 16; WIGAN 30 Dewsbury 6

QUARTER-FINALS

Bradford Northern 10 WARRINGTON 12; ST HELENS 44 Whitehaven 10; Wakefield Trinity 14 WIGAN 26; Widnes 4 OLDHAM 16

SEMI-FINALS

St Helens 14 WIGAN 20 (Att:26,489); Oldham 6 WARRINGTON 10 (Att: 15,631)

FINAL

Wembley, Apr 28

WIGAN 36 Warrington 14

Wigan: Hampson; Lydon, Iro, Bell, Preston (Gildart); Edwards (Goulding), Gregory; Shelford, Dermott (Goulding, Dermott), Platt, Betts, Goodway, Hanley

Scorers: Tries: Preston (2), Iro (2), Betts, Hanley Goals: Lydon (6)

Warrington: Lyon; Drummond, Mercer, Darbyshire, Forster; Crompton, Bishop (McGinty); Burke (Jackson, Burke), Mann, Harmon, Jackson (Thomas), Sanderson, Gregory

Scorers: *Tries:* Gregory, Lyon *Goals:* Bishop (2), Darbyshire

Referee: John Holdsworth (Kippax)
Attendance: 77,749
Lance Todd Trophy: Andy Gregory (Wigan)
Team underlined beat a team from a higher division

WIGAN'S CUP FINAL RECORDS
* Andy Gregory is only the second dual Lance Todd winner after Gerry Helme (Warrington 1950, 1954) and the first to win the award twice at Wembley. He also collected his record fifth winners' medal in his sixth appearance at Wembley.
* Wigan were the first club to win Challenge Cup three years in succession.
* Wigan first club to win Championship and Challenge Cup in same season since the split into two divisions in 1973 and the only club to win Championship, Challenge Cup and Regal (formerly John Player) Trophy in same season.
* Wigan coach John Monie became the first man to be in charge of Sydney Grade Final winners (Parramatta, 1986) and Challenge Cup winners.
* Kevin Iro extended his number of Cup Final tries to six, three more than the next best total.

STONES BITTER PREMIERSHIP
First Division
FIRST ROUND
BRADFORD NORTHERN 25 St Helens 8; LEEDS 24 Castleford 16; WIDNES 18 Hull 8; WIGAN 28 Warrington 26

SEMI-FINALS
Leeds 7 WIDNES 27; Wigan 0 BRADFORD NORTHERN 9

FINAL
Old Trafford, May 13
WIDNES 28 Bradford Northern 6
Attendance: 40,796
Harry Sunderland Trophy: Alan Tait (Widnes)
Second Division
FIRST ROUND
HULL KR 40 Fulham 6; OLDHAM 32 Swinton 10; Rochdale Hornets 18 DEWSBURY 20; RYEDALE-YORK 24 Halifax 7

SEMI-FINALS
HULL KR 36 Dewsbury 8; OLDHAM 32 Ryedale-York 8

FINAL
Old Trafford, May 13
OLDHAM 30 HULL KR 29
Attendance: 40,796

REGAL TROPHY
SEMI-FINALS
St Helens 9 HALIFAX 10; Castleford 10 WIGAN 24

FINAL
Headingley, Jan 13
WIGAN 24 Halifax 12
Attendance: 17,810

GRUNHALLE LANCASHIRE CUP
SEMI-FINALS
OLDHAM 19 Wigan 18; WARRINGTON 28 Widnes 6

FINAL
Knowsley Road, St Helens, Oct 14
WARRINGTON 24 Oldham 16
Attendance: 9,895

JOHN SMITH'S YORKSHIRE CUP
SEMI-FINALS
Halifax 16, 4 BRADFORD NORTHERN 16, 26;

FEATHERSTONE ROVERS 18, 28 Castleford 18, 26

FINAL
Headingley, Leeds, Nov 5
BRADFORD NORTHERN 20 Featherstone Rovers 14
Attendance: 12,055

RODSTOCK WAR OF THE ROSES
Central Park, Wigan, Sep 20
Lancashire 12 YORKSHIRE 56
Attendance: 10,182

NEW ZEALAND TOUR TO GREAT BRITAIN 1989

Date	Opponents	Results	Score	Attendance
Oct 3	St Helens	lost	26-27	7,040
Oct 3	Castleford	won	22-20	5,993
Oct 8	Wigan	lost	14-24	15,013
Oct 11	Bradford N	won	26-8	3,498
Oct 15	Leeds	won	34-4	9,632
Oct 17	Cumbria	won	28-2	3,983
Oct 21	GREAT BRITAIN	won	24-16	18,273
Oct 28	GREAT BRITAIN	lost	6-26	13,073
Nov 1	Hull	won	44-8	5,894
Nov 5	Widnes	won	26-18	9,905
Nov 7	Featherstone	won	44-20	2,773
Nov 11	GREAT BRITAIN	lost	6-10	20,346

GREAT BRITAIN V NEW ZEALAND

FIRST TEST
Old Trafford, Manchester, Oct 21
Great Britain 16 NEW ZEALAND 24
Great Britain: Tait, Ford (Newlove), Currier (Edwards), Loughlin, Offiah; D Hulme, A Gregory; Skerrett, K Beardmore, Hobbs, Goodway, Platt, M Gregory
T: Tait, Ford, Offiah; G: Loughlin 2
New Zealand: Williams (Kemp); Iro, Bell, Sherlock, Mercer; K Shelford, Freeman, Goulding, Mann, Todd, Stewart, Sorensen, McGahan
T: Iro, Shelford, Freeman, Goulding, McGahan
G. Sherlock

SECOND TEST
Elland Road, Leeds, Oct 28
GREAT BRITAIN 26 New Zealand 6
Great Britain: Hampson; Ford, Newlove, Loughlin, Offiah; Edwards, D Hulme; Skerrett (Hobbs), R.Hulme (Fox), Platt, Goodway, Powell, M Gregory
T: Goodway 2, Offiah, Edwards; G: Loughlin 5
New Zealand: Williams; Iro, Bell, Sherlock (Kemp); Mercer; K Shelford, Freeman; A Shelford (Faimalo), Mann, Todd, Sorensen, Stewart, McGahan
T: McGahan; G: Sherlock

THIRD TEST
Central Park, Wigan, Nov 11
GREAT BRITAIN 10 New Zealand 6
Great Britain: Tait; Ford, Newlove (Lydon), Loughlin, Offiah; Edwards, D Hulme; Skerrett (England), P Hulme, Platt, Goodway, Powell, M Gregory
T: Tait, Offiah; G: Loughlin
New Zealand: Kemp; Iro, Bell, Williams, Mercer; K Shelford (Clark), Freeman; Todd, Mann, Faimalo (Leota), Sorensen, Stewart, McGahan
T: Shelford; G: Shelford

GREAT BRITAIN V FRANCE

FIRST TEST
Gilbert Brutus Stadium, Perpignan, Mar 18
France 4 GREAT BRITAIN 8
France: Pougeau; Ratier, Delauney, Fraisse, Pons; Dumas, Entat; Buttignol, Valéro, Rabot (Aillères), Divet,

Cabestany, Molinier
T: Pons
Great Britain: Tait; Lydon, Schofield, Loughlin, Offiah;
Edwards, A Gregory; Skerrett, B Beardmore, Platt, M
Gregory, Goodway, Hanley
T: Offiah; G: Schofield 2
SECOND TEST
Headingley, Apr 7
Great Britain   18   FRANCE   25
Great Britain: Tait; Cordle (Irwin), Schofield, C Gibson,
Offiah; Steadman, Edwards; Skerrett (Bishop), B
Beardmore, Platt, M Gregory, Goodway, Hanley
T: Tait, Cordle, Offiah; G: Steadman 3
France: Fraisse; Ratier, Delauney, Bienes, Pons; Dumas,
Entat; Buttignol, Valéro, Rabot, Divet, Cabestany (Frison),
Molinier
T: Pons, Rabot, Divet; G: Fraisse 5, Dumas; DG: Dumas
*France's first win on British soil since Mar 4, 1967 when
they won 23-13 at Wigan*

GREAT BRITAIN TOUR
Port Moresby, May 20
Southern Zone   18   GREAT BRITAIN   40
T: Igo, Las, Ganiga   T: Schofield 3, Gibson
G: Lae 3   Eastwood 2, Davies
                                            G: Davies 6

Lae, May 23
Combined Northen &
Highland Zones   10   GREAT BRITAIN   24
T: Elara   T: Bibb, Dixon, Simpson
G: Sambu 3   Davies
                                     G: Eastwood 4
FIRST TEST, Goroka, May 27
PAPUA NEW GUINEA 20   Great Britain   18
Papua New Guinea: Wanega; Krewanty, Boge (Kool),
Numapo, Morea; Haru, Ongogo; Ako, M Matmillo, Evei
(Arigae), Gispe, Taumaku (capt)
T: Evei, Haru; G: Numapo 5; DG: Numapo, Haru
Great Britain: Tait; Eastwood, D Powell (Irwin), Davies,
Gibson; Schofield, Goulding, R Powell, Jackson, Dixon,
Betts, Fairbank (England), M Gregory (capt)
T: Eastwood, Davies, Goulding; G: Davies 3
Referee: D Hale (New Zealand)

Rabaul, New Britain, May 30
Islands Zone   4   GREAT BRITAIN   50
G: Eremas 2   T: Devereux 2, Betts 2
                              Price, Fox, Irwin
                              Eastwood, Simpson,
                              Gibson
                              G: Eastwood 5

SECOND TEST
Port Moresby, Jun 2
Papua New Guinea   8   GREAT BRITAIN   40
Papua New Guinea: Wanega; Krewanty, Boge, Numapo,
Morea; Haru, Ongogo; Lomutopa (Tiri), Matmillo,
Evei, Gispe, Taumaku (capt), Angra
T: Ongogo; G: Numapo 2
Great Britain: Tait; Eastwood, D Powell, Davies, Gibson;
Schofield, Goulding; R Powell, Jackson (Fox), England,
Betts, Dixon, M Gregory (capt) (Clarke)
T: Gibson 2, Eastwood, Goulding, Dixon, D Powell,
Schofield; G: Davies 6
Referee: D Hale (New Zealand)
*World Cup points at stake

Napier, Jun 10
NZ President's XIII   22   GREAT BRITAIN   23
T: Nixon 2, Panapi   T: Davies, Gibson,
Tuimavave   Dermott
G: Edwards 3   G: Davies 5
                                       DG: Dermott

Christchurch, Jun 13
CANTERBURY   18   Great Britain   10
T: Dorreen, Whittaker   T: Bishop, Tait
Leck
G: Culley 3   G: Eastwood

Auckland, Jun 17
AUCKLAND   24   Great Britain   13
T: Panapa, Patten,   T: Skerrett, Goulding
Nikau   G: Davies 2
G: Brown 4   DG: Davies

Hamilton, Jun 20
Kiwi Colts   10   GREAT BRITAIN   22
T: Ropati, Fisher   T: Eastwood 3, Clarke
G: Shelford   G: Davies 3

FIRST TEST
Palmerston North, Jun 24
New Zealand   10   GREAT BRITAIN   11
New Zealand: Williams; A Iro (Edwards), K Iro, Kemp,
Panapa; Clark, Freeman; Brown, D Mann, Todd (G Mann),
Horo, Nicku, McGahan
T: Panapa, K Iro; G: Brown;
Great Britain: Bibb; Davies, Lydon (D Powell), Gibson,
Offiah; Schofield, Goulding; Skerrett (R Powell), Dermott,
England, Betts, Dixon, Gregory
T: Davies, Gibson; G: Davies; DG: Schofield

Wellington, Jun 27
WELLINGTON   30   Great Britain   22
T: Edwards, Tangira,   T: Fairbank, Smales
Aramoana, Molemau   Davies, Lyon
G: Gilbert 7   G: Davies 3

Rotorua, Jul 1
New Zealand Maoris   12   GREAT BRITAIN   20
T: Tangira, Aramoana   T: Eastwood, Offiah,
G: Edwards 2   Schofield
                                      G: Eastwood 4

New Plymouth, Jul 4
Taranaki Invitation   0   GREAT BRITAIN   24
                                   T: Simpson, Lyon,
                                   Fairbank, Irwin
                                   G: Eastwood 4

SECOND TEST
Auckland, Jul 8
New Zealand   14   GREAT BRITAIN   16
New Zealand: Ridge; Panapa, K Iro, Williams, A Iro;
Clark (Lonergan), Freeman; Brown, D Mann, Todd
(Kemp), Nicku, Horo, McGahan
T: Horo; G: Ridge 5;
Great Britain: Lydon; Davies, Gibson (Irwin), D Powell,
Offiah; Schofield, Goulding; Skerrett, Jackson, England,
Betts, Dixon (R Powell), Gregory
T: Schofield, Betts, Offiah; G: Davies 2

THIRD TEST
Christchurch, Jul 15
NEW ZEALAND   21   Great Britain   18
New Zealand: Ridge; A Iro, K Iro (Edwards), Williams,
Panapa; Kemp, Freeman; Brown, D Mann, Todd

(Lonergan), Nicku, Horo, McGahan
T: Kemp, Nicku; G: Ridge 6; DG: McGahan
Great Britain: Lydon; Davies, Gibson, D Powell, Offiah; Schofield, Goulding; Skerrett (Dixon), Dermott, England, Betts, R Powell, Gregory
T: Schofield, R Powell, Offiah; G: Davies 3
* World Cup points at stake

WORLD CUP STANDINGS

		P	Pts
1	Australia	2	4
2	Great Britain	3	4
3	New Zealand	4	4
4	France	2	0
5	Papua New Guinea	1	0

BARLA LEAGUE CUP FINAL
Barrow, Apr 15
WIGAN ST PATRICK'S 11 Askam 6

AWARDS
Man of Steel: Shaun Edwards (Wigan)
Coach of the Year: John Monie (Wigan)
First Division Player of the Year: Andy Goodway (Wigan)
Second Division Player of the Year: John Woods (Rochdale H)
Young Player of the Year: Bobby Goulding (Wigan)
Referee of the Year: Robin Whitfield (Widnes)

━━━ CHAMPIONS ━━━

CHALLENGE CUP
11 Wigan 1924, 1929, 1948, 1951, 1958-59, 1965, 1985, 1988-90; **10** Leeds 1910, 1923, 1932, 1936, 1941-42, 1957, 1968, 1977-78; **7** Widnes 1930, 1937, 1964, 1975, 1979, 1981, 1984; **6** Huddersfield 1913, 1915, 1920, 1933, 1945, 1953; **5** Halifax 1903-4, 1931, 1939, 1987; St Helens 1956, 1961, 1966, 1972, 1976; Wakefield Trinity 1909, 1946, 1960, 1962-63; Warrington 1905, 1907, 1950, 1954, 1974; **4** Bradford Northern 1906, 1944, 1947, 1949; Castleford 1935, 1969-70, 1986; **3** Batley 1897-98, 1901; Featherstone Rovers 1967, 1973, 1983; Oldham 1899, 1925, 1927; Swinton 1900, 1926, 1928; **2** Broughton Rangers 1902, 1911; Dewsbury 1912, 1943; Hull 1914, 1982; Hunslet 1908, 1934; Leigh 1921, 1971; **1** Barrow 1955; Hull KR 1980; Rochdale Hornets 1922; Salford 1938; Workington T 1952

PREMIERSHIP TROPHY
6 Widnes 1980, 1982-83, 1988-90; **3** St Helens 1976-77, 1985; **2** Hull KR 1981, 1984; Leeds 1975, 1979; **1** Bradford Northern 1978; Warrington 1986; Wigan 1987

DIVISION TWO PREMIERSHIP
2 Oldham 1988, 1990; **1** Swinton 1987, Sheffield E 1989

CHAMPIONSHIP
(1906-73)
9 Wigan 1909, 1922, 1926, 1934, 1946-47, 1950, 1952, 1960 **7** Huddersfield 1912-13, 1915, 1929-30, 1949, 1962 **6** St Helens 1932, 1953, 1959, 1966, 1970-71 **5** Hull 1920-21, 1936, 1956, 1958 **4** Salford 1914, 1933, 1937, 1939; Swinton 1927-28, 1931, 1935 **3** Leeds 1961, 1969, 1972; Oldham 1910-11, 1957; Warrington 1948, 1954-55 **2** Halifax 1907, 1965; Hull KR 1923, 1925; Hunslet 1908, 1938; Wakefield Trinity 1967-68 **1** Batley 1924, Dewsbury 1973; Leigh 1906; Workington Town 1951
Not Held 1963-64

DIVISION ONE
1974-90
3 Hull KR 1979, 1984-85; Widnes 1978, 1988-89 **2** Bradford Northern 1980-81; Salford 1974, 1976; Wigan 1987, 1990 **1** Featherstone Rovers 1977; Halifax 1986; Hull 1983; Leigh 1982; St Helens 1975

DIVISION TWO
1974-90
3 Leigh 1978, 1986, 1989 **2** Barrow 1976, 1984; Hull 1977, 1979; Oldham 1982, 1988 **1** Bradord Northern 1974; Huddersfield 1975; Featherstone Rovers 1980; York 1981; Fulham 1983; Swinton 1985; Hunslet 1987; Hull KR 1990

REGAL TROPHY
(Formerly John Player Special Trophy)
5 Wigan 1983, 1986-87, 1989-90 **3** Warrington 1974, 1978, 1981; **2** Bradford Northern 1975, 1980; Leeds 1973, 1984; Widnes 1976, 1979 **1** Castleford 1977; Halifax 1972; Hull 1982; Hull KR 1985; St Helens 1988

LANCASHIRE COUNTY CUP
Wins:
20 Wigan 1906, 1909-10, 1913, 1923, 1929, 1939, 1947-52, 1967, 1972, 1974, 1986-89; **10** St Helens 1927, 1954, 1961-65, 1968-69, 1985; **9** Oldham 1908, 1911, 1914, 1920, 1925, 1934, 1957-59; **9** Warrington 1922, 1930, 1933, 1938, 1960, 1966, 1981, 1983, 1990; **6** Widnes 1946, 1975-77, 1979-80; **5** Salford 1932, 1935-37, 1973; **4** Leigh 1953, 1956, 1971, 1982; Swinton 1926, 1928, 1940, 1970; **3** Rochdale Hornets 1912, 1915, 1919; **2** Barrow 1955, 1984; **1** Workington Town 1978

YORKSHIRE COUNTY CUP
Wins:
17 Leeds 1922, 1929, 1931, 1933, 1935-36, 1938, 1959, 1969, 1971, 1973-74, 1976-77, 1980-81, 1989; **12** Huddersfield 1910, 1912, 1914-15, 1919-20, 1927, 1932, 1939, 1951, 1953, 1958; **12** Bradford Northern 1907, 1941-42, 1944, 1946, 1949-50, 1954, 1966, 1979, 1988, 1990; **9** Wakefield Trinity 1911, 1925, 1947-48, 1952, 1957, 1961-62, 1965; **7** Hull KR 1921, 1930, 1967-68, 1972, 1975, 1986; **5** Halifax 1909, 1945, 1955-56, 1964; Hull 1924, 1970, 1983-85; **3** Castleford 1978, 1982, 1987; Dewsbury 1926, 1928, 1943; Hunslet 1906, 1908, 1963; York 1923, 1934, 1937; **2** Featherstone Rovers 1940, 1960; **1** Batley 1913
(Years indicate second half of season.)

CHARITY SHIELD
Winners:
1985 Wigan; 1986 Halifax; 1987 Wigan; 1988 Widnes; 1989 Widnes; 1990 Widnes

WORLD CUP
Wins:
6 Australia 1957, 1968, 1970, 1975*, 1977, 1988:
3 Great Britain 1954, 1960, 1972
* Known as The International Championship

SYDNEY PREMIERSHIP
Wins:
20 South Sydney 1908-09, 1914, 1918, 1925-29, 1931-32, 1950-51, 1953-55, 1967-68, 1970-71; **15** St George 1941, 1949, 1956-66, 1977, 1979; **11** Balmain 1915-17, 1919-20, 1924, 1939, 1944, 1946-47, 1969; Eastern Suburbs 1911-13, 1923, 1935-37, 1940, 1945, 1974-75

CLUBS WHO HAVE JOINED AND LEFT THE RUGBY LEAGUE SINCE THE WAR
1945   **In** Workington Town
        Out St Helens Recs, Leigh

1946	**In** Leigh
1948	**In** Whitehaven
1951	**In** Cardiff, Doncaster
1952	**Out** Cardiff
1954	**In** Blackpool Borough
1955	**Out** Belle Vue Rangers
1963	**Out** Bradford Northern
1964	**In** Bradford Northern (*)
1980	**In** Fulham
1981	**In** Cardiff City, Carlisle
1983	**In** Kent Invicta
1984	**In** Mansfield Marksmen, Sheffield Eagles
1985	**Out** Southend (formerly Kent Invicta), Bridgend (formerly Cardiff City)
1989	**In** Chorley

(*) Bradford Northern disbanded after 13 matches of the 1963-64 season but were re-formed for the start of the 1964-65 season.

LANCE TODD/HARRY SUNDERLAND WINNERS
(Since 1976)

	Lance Todd*	Harry Sunderland+
1976	Geoff Pimblett *St Helens*	George Nicholls *St Helens*
1977	Steve Pitchford *Leeds*	Geoff Pimblett *St Helens*
1978	George Nicholls *St Helens*	Bob Haigh *Bradford Northern*
1979	Dave Topliss *Wakefield Trinity*	Kevin Dick *Leeds*
1980	Brain Lockwood *Hull Kingston Rovers*	Mal Aspey *Widnes*
1981	Mick Burke *Widnes*	Len Casey *Hull Kingston Rovers*
1982	Eddie Cunningham *Widnes*	Mick Burke *Widnes*
1983	David Hobbs *Featherstone Rovers*	Tony Myler *Widnes*
1984	Joe Lydon *Widnes*	John Dorahy *Hull Kingston Rovers*
1985	Brett Kenny *Wigan*	Harry Pinner *St Helens*
1986	Bob Beardmore *Castleford*	Les Boyd *Warrington*
1987	Graham Eadie *Halifax*	Joe Lydon *Wigan*
1988	Andy Gregory *Wigan*	David Hulme *Widnes*
1989	Ellery Hanley *Wigan*	Alan Tait *Widnes*
1990	Andy Gregory *Wigan*	Alan Tait *Widnes*

* Man of match in Challenge Cup Final
+ Man of match in Premiership Final

MAN OF STEEL

1978	George Nicholls (St Helens)
1979	Doug Laughton (Widnes)
1980	George Fairbairn (Wigan)
1981	Ken Kelly (Warrington)
1982	Mick Morgan (Oldham)
1983	Allan Agar (Featherstone R)
1984	Joe Lydon (Widnes)
1985	Ellery Hanley (Bradford N)
1986	Gavin Miller (Hull KR)
1987	Ellery Hanley (Wigan)
1988	Martin Offiah (Widnes)
1989	Ellery Hanley (Wigan)
1990	Shaun Edwards (Wigan)

RECORDS

ALL FIRST-CLASS MATCHES
Single Game Records
Biggest win: 119-2 Huddersfield v Swindon Park Rangers (Challenge Cup) 1914; **Most tries in a match:** 11 George Henry West, Hull Kingston Rovers v Brookland Rovers (Challenge Cup) 1905; **Most goals in a match:** 22 Jim Sullivan, Wigan v Flimby & Fothergill (Challenge Cup, 1925: **Most points in a match:** 53 George Henry West (as above)

Season Records
Most tries: 80 Albert Rosenfeld (Huddersfield) 1913-14; **Most goals:** 221 David Watkins (Salford) 1972-3; **Most points:** 496 (194 goals, 36 tries) Lewis Jones (Leeds) 1956-7

Career Records
Most tries: 796 Brian Bevan (Warrington & Blackpool Borough) 1946-64; **Most goals:** 2,859 Jim Sullivan (Wigan) 1921-46; **Most points:** 6,220 Neil Fox (Wakefield Trinity, Bradford Northern, Hull Kingston Rovers, York, Bramley, Huddersfield) 1956-79; **Most appearances:** 921 Jim Sullivan (Wigan) 1921-46; **Most consecutive club appearances:** 239 Keith Elwell (Widnes) May 1977-Sep 1982; **Most consecutive games scoring points:** 92 David Watkins (Salford) Aug 1972-Apr 1974

INTERNATIONAL MATCHES
Most appearances: 60 Jim Sullivan, Wales, Great Britain & Other Nationalities, 1921-39; **Most tries:** 45 Mick Sullivan, Great Britain & England 1954-63; **Most goals:** 160 Jim Sullivan; **Most points:** 329 Jim Sullivan; **Biggest win:** 70-8 Australia v Papua New Guinea, 1988

ALL-TIME WORST RUGBY LEAGUE RECORDS
(Min. qualification 20 matches)

		P	W	D	L	F	A	Pts
1906-07	Liverpool C	30	0	0	30	76	1398	0
1989-90	**RUNCORN H**	**28**	**0**	**0**	**28**	**216**	**935**	**0**
1912-13	Coventry	27	0	1	26	157	896	1
1914-15	Runcorn	27	0	1	26	84	590	1
1989-90	**BARROW**	**26**	**1**	**0**	**25**	**201**	**1133**	**2**
1984-85	Bridgend	28	1	0	27	258	966	2
1976-77	Doncaster	26	1	0	25	243	704	2
1943-44	St Helens	20	1	0	19	123	446	2
1979-80	Doncaster	26	1	1	24	196	733	3
1974-75	Doncaster	26	1	1	24	147	745	3

1991

Jan 12 Regal Trophy Final; Jan 26 France v Great Britain, under - 21 (Limoux); Jan 27 France v Great Britain, Test match (Perpignan); Feb 9 Challenge Cup First Round; Feb 15 Great Britain v France, under - 21 (Huddersfield); Feb 16 Great Britain v France, Test match (Headingley); Feb 23 Challenge Cup second round; Mar 9 Challenge Cup third round; Mar 23 and 30 Challenge Cup semi – finals; Apr 14 First and Second Division season ends; Apr 21 Premiership First Round; Apr 27 CHALLENGE CUP FINAL (Wembley); May 5 Premiership semi – final; May 12 Premiership Final (Old Trafford).

RUGBY UNION

OH, CALCUTTA

The most exciting climax ever to a Five Nations season came on an extraordinary spring afternoon at Murrayfield. For the first time two teams came together at the end of the tournament unbeaten and contending for everything. This, like 1989, was supposed to be England's year; having trampled all over Ireland, France and Wales they were expected to wipe out the Scots who had scored the same three wins far less convincingly.

It did not work out that way. Scotland applied unexpected and effective psychology before the game: walking not running on to the field and singing two verses of Flower of Scotland (with enormous gusto) instead of one. Then they raced into the lead and despite enormous English pressure never lost it. The English were confident enough to run penalties near the Scottish line instead of kicking them, but Scotland scored a crucial try seconds after half-time and took the Calcutta Cup, their third Grand Slam, tenth Triple Crown and 21st Championship. Yet they had bumbled through much of the season, hitting the front against Ireland only ten minutes from time, and secured a mere four-point margin against Wales. Spirit carried them through. "No one would accuse Scotland of being a delight to the naked eye or even a team of rich entertainment," summed up Stephen Jones in the *Sunday Times*. "It was their storming approach that was wonderfully compelling."

Before Murrayfield England were the only team anyone talked about. Their 90 points was the biggest total ever (or since 1914, with adjustments for the different scoring system) and their play against France and Wales gave rise to an optimism not seen in English rugby circles for years. "If you had put black shirts on them they could have passed for the All-Blacks," said Jacques Fouroux, the French coach, after the win in Paris. At Twickenham against Wales, England were even more stunning and won 34-6, the heaviest-ever Welsh defeat in the Championship. An Englishman trying to get in illegally to watch the last half-hour was just being led away by security men when he was met by two Welsh spectators who handed over a ticket: "We've had enough," they said.

That was England's high point. In the summer a half-strength team sent to Argentina lost three of their five provincial matches and split the Test series 1-1 against a country that had only lately lost to Canada. "I couldn't believe what I was seeing," said the manager Geoff Cooke after England were beaten by a Buenos Aires XV. The reputation of England's young captain Will Carling remained sky-high but neither the ageing figures round him at home nor their possible successors sent to Argentina encouraged any continuation of February's high hopes.

But there were always Wales's troubles to cheer everyone up. Two days after the England game John Ryan resigned as Welsh coach, to be replaced by Ron Waldron of Neath, who filled the team with his own club players and managed to restrict the last two games to defeats rather than humiliations. Nonetheless, Wales lost all four games for the first time ever and in the summer were quite lucky not to get beaten by Namibia as well. The "Big Five" selection committee was abolished.

Fouroux resigned as French coach in September, to be replaced by Daniel Dubroca. The pressure had been on Fouroux as France continued to struggle, often quite literally. Three French players were sent off in internationals. Alain Carminati, who stamped on John Jeffrey at Murrayfield, was banned until September (as was Kevin Moseley of Wales, despatched a month earlier by the same referee, Fred Howard). However, the flanker Benazzi, also sent off, also for stamping, but this time in Sydney, was suspended for only nine days.

A year before the World Cup there was still only one team in world rugby. New Zealand's unbeaten sequence in internationals was halted at 23 when they lost unexpectedly to Australia in Wellington. But before then they had swept through their

European tour in the autumn and followed with two wins against Scotland (who ran them dangerously close at Auckland) and two against Australia before the Wallabies surprised them. But even the All-Blacks had their problems. In May, four key players took the traditional exit route to rugby league including both John Gallagher, who joined Leeds for a record fee, and his deputy at full-back, Matthew Ridge, who went to Australia.

Referees were assaulted after two successive All-Black matches in Wales, at Neath and Llanelli, and the referee in the Cardiff international that followed almost blew the final whistle from the dressing room. "It seems," wrote Robert Armstrong in *The Guardian*, "that Welsh rugby has begun to acquire some of the character defects associated with English soccer." This point was emphasised by the treatment of Welsh senior club coaches: 12 were sacked.

The Romanian captain Florica Murariu was among six gifted rugby players killed during the revolution against the Ceausescu regime. Murariu was shot by mistake by a frightened recruit at a roadblock. Five months later the Romanians beat France for the first time, winning 12-6 in Auch.

IF YOU CAN COPE WITH TRIUMPH AND DISASTER...

❝People will remember 1990 for Scotland's grand slam, not for the team who came second."
David Sole, Scotland captain

"The most outstanding performance any of us have witnessed from any England side in any era."
Roger Uttley, England coach, on the win over Wales

"No side I have seen from the British Isles have played with such a sustained, invigorating, bonny presumption and panache since the Welsh team's grandeur nearly two decades ago. It was a golden afternoon for a crowd so long fed on dross."
Frank Keating, The Guardian

"I've learned the true meaning of the word gutted."
Uttley after the Calcutta Cup

"There's been no trouble. The English are very timid. A lot of them have brought roses but that's for their wreath tonight."
Edinburgh policeman the same day

David Sole, Scotland captain;
"We dedicated this not only to the whole of Scotland but to every Scot in outposts around the world, from New Zealand, Canada, South America, all over the globe."

Bob Munro, chairman of selectors:
"Even Wales."

"We were beaten by an outstanding side, genuine world champions. All I hope is that the players have learned something on the day and take it home with them. The commitment was there. We have just got to look at their game and learn."
John Ryan, Welsh coach, after losing to New Zealand

"On the sliding scale of mediocrity by which England have come to be gauged, this final effort failed even to register. England's defeat... was their most tactically illiterate performance yet."
Chris Rea, Independent on Sunday, on the defeat against Argentina

"I was delighted that the Scottish response afterwards was one of extreme disappointment that we did not beat them. Many a side would have come here and been quite happy to lose by only three points.❞
Finlay Calder after Scotland's narrow defeat in Auckland, his last international.

Bath remained the leading team in English club rugby but were deposed as league champions by Wasps. The kingmakers were Nottingham, inconsistent themselves, who achieved vital springtime wins over first Bath and then Gloucester. Wasps' chances had been described, two games before the end, as "very remote" by the club's own press officer. The celebrations were muted: only two weeks earlier the club's talented young wing Raphael Tsagane had been killed in a car crash. Bath made their point at Twickenham in the Cup final against Gloucester, not merely winning (for the sixth time in seven years) but doing so 48-6. The captain Stuart Barnes said this was Bath's best team yet. They might have stamped all over the opposition but Gloucester's John Gadd got caught doing that first: he was sent off. At Leicester Les Cusworth, the former England fly-half, followed his team-mate Dusty Hare into retirement.

Neath dominated Welsh rugby, failing to equal their previous season's record of 345 tries by one and winning 37 successive games culminating in a Cup final win over Bridgend. Neath's Andrew Kembery became the first man sent off in a Welsh Cup final. The Welsh RU abandoned its experiment with a sin-bin.

An Australian rugby supporter wrote to "Mr M Gorbachev, The Kremlin, Moscow" to express his disgust about the Soviet team's behaviour on their tour of Australia, especially over the incident which left Nick Farr-Jones, the Australian captain, with a broken jaw. He received a letter back from a Soviet official saying "We can only agree with you that rugby is a game for gentlemen", and announcing that the coach Victor Masyura had been sacked and two players dropped. Farr-Jones was horrified: "Masyura was the future of Soviet rugby and one of the nicest guys I have met. It's crazy."

The referee Clive Norling was wired for sound as an experiment at a Bath-Toulon game so he could announce who was being penalised for what; he was enthusiastic about extending the idea. Andy Haden admitted that he cheated in the 1978 New Zealand-Wales game to get a winning penalty in the closing minutes. England and Ireland made an apparently doomed attempt to resist new International Board guidelines allowing quasi-professionalism including compensation for loss of earnings.

The South African Rugby Board at last agreed to halt all tours as a prelude to unification with the mainly black group, SARU. The Board also proposed new rules for schoolboy rugby, punishing all deliberate fouls with a kick in front of the posts. In Britain headmasters started either abolishing old boys' fixtures or banning older, fatter men from the games to prevent injuries to their players.

Paul Setter, playing for Ivybridge 2nd XV in Devon, successfully proposed to his girlfriend Lisa when she brought on the half-time oranges. Don Manning, playing for Old Colstonians in Bristol, had to leave the game at half-time to get married. He went down the aisle with a cut head. Maggie Waugh was married and immediately went off to play as hooker in the Sale women's team.

The three Liverpool University teams were disbanded for the year after the annual all-day pub crawl ended with students vandalising pubs, gatecrashing a vice-chancellor's reception and dropping their trousers. Members of the Lesbian and Gay Society meeting nearby, were said to be terrified.

INTERNATIONAL CHAMPIONSHIP

National Stadium, Cardiff, Jan 20
Wales 19 FRANCE 29
Wales: P Thorburn; M Titley, M Ring, M Hall, A Emyr; D Evans, R Jones (capt); M Griffiths (H Williams-Jones), K Phillips, D Young, A Allen, K Moseley, P Davies, M Jones, G Jones
T: Titley; P: Thorburn 4; DG: Evans
France: J-B Lafond; M Andrieu, P Sella, D.Charvet, P Lagisquet; D Camberabero, P Berbizier (capt); P Ondarts, L Armary, J-P Garuet, T Devergie, D Erbani, E Champ, O Roumat, L Rodriquez
T: Lafond, Sella, Camberabero, Lagisquet, Rodriguez; C: Camberabero 3; P: Camberabero
Kevin Moseley, the Welsh lock, sent off after 32 minutes. He was banned until September 1.

Twickenham, Jan 20
ENGLAND 23 Ireland 0
England: S Hodgkinson; R Underwood, W Carling (capt), J Guscott, M Bailey; R Andrew, R Hill; P Rendall, B Moore, J Probyn, W Dooley, P Ackford, M Skinner, D Egerton, P Winterbottom
T: Probyn, Egerton, Underwood, Guscott; C.Hodgkinson 2; P: Hodgkinson

Ireland: K Murphy; M Kiernan, B Mullin, D Irwin K Crossan; P Russell, F Aherne; D Fitzgerald, S Smith (J McDonald), G Halpin, N Francis, W Anderson (capt), P Matthews, N Mannion, P O'Hara
England scored three tries in the last ten minutes.

Parc des Princes, Feb 3
France 7 ENGLAND 26
France: S Blanco; M Andrieu, P Sella, D Charvet, P Lagisquet; F Mesnel, P Berbizier (capt); P Ondarts, L Armary (P Marocco), J-P Garuet, T Devergie, D Erbani, E Champ, L Rodriguez, O Roumat
T: Lagisquet; P: Charvet
England: S Hodgkinson; R Underwood, W Carling (capt), J Guscott, M Bailey; R Andrew, R Hill; P Rendall, B Moore, J Probyn, W Dooley, P Ackford M Skinner, P Winterbottom, M Teague
T: Underwood, Guscott, Carling; C: Hodgkinson; P: Hodgkinson 4
France's heaviest defeat at Parc des Princes

Lansdowne Road, Feb 3
Ireland 10 SCOTLAND 13
Ireland: K Murphy; M Kiernan, B Mullin, D Irwin K Crossan; B Smith, F Aherne; J Fitzgerald, J McDonald, D Fitzgerald, D Lenihan, W Anderson (capt), P Matthews, P

O'Hara (P Collins), N Mannion
T: J Fitzgerald; P: Kiernan 2
Scotland: G Hastings; A Stanger, S Hastings, S Lineen, I Tukalo; C Chalmers, G Armstrong; D Sole (capt), K Milne, A Burnell, C Gray, D Cronin, J Jeffrey, F Calder, D White
T: White 2: C: Chalmers; P: Chalmers
Kiernan hooked a straightforward penalty wide near the end and Ireland missed the chance to draw.

Twickenham, Feb 17
ENGLAND 34 Wales 6
England: S Hodgkinson; S Halliday, W Carling (capt), J Guscott, R Underwood; R Andrew, R Hill; P Rendall, B Moore, P Probyn, W Dooley, P Ackford, M Skinner, P Winterbottom, M Teague
T: Underwood 2, Carling, Hill; P: Hodgkinson 4; C: Hodgkinson 3
Wales: P Thorburn; M Titley, M Ring, M Hall, A Emyr; D Evans, R Jones (capt); M Griffiths, K Phillips, L Delaney, A Allen, G Llewellyn, P Davies, R Collins, M Jones
T: Davies; C: Thorburn
Wales's heaviest championship defeat

Murrayfield, Feb 17
SCOTLAND 21 France 0
Scotland: G Hastings; A Stanger, S Hastings, S Lineen, I Tukalo; C Chalmers, G Armstrong; D Sole (capt), K Milne, A Burnell, C Gray, D Cronin, J Jeffrey, F Calder, D White, D Turnbull
T: Calder, Tukalo; C: Chalmers 2; P: Chalmers 2, G Hastings
France: S Blanco; P Hontax, P Sella, F Mesnel, P Lagisquet, D Camberabero, H Sanz; M Pujolle, L Armary, P Ondarts, T Devergie, O Roumat, J-M Lhermet, A Carminati, L Rodriguez
Alain Carminati sent off for stamping, 48 minutes, when Scotland only 3-0 up.

National Stadium, Cardiff, Mar 3
Wales 9 SCOTLAND 13
Wales: P Thorburn; M Hall, M Ring, A Bateman, A Emyr; D Evans (A Clement), R Jones (capt); B Williams, K Phillips, J Pugh, P Davies, G Llewellyn, M Perego, R Collins, M Jones
T: Emyr; C: Thorburn; P: Thorburn
Scotland: G Hastings; A Stanger, S Hastings, S Lineen, I Tukalo; C Chalmers, G Armstrong; D Sole (capt), K Milne, A Burnell, C Gray, D Cronin, J Jeffrey, F Calder, D White
T: Cronin; P: Chalmers 3

Parc des Princes, Mar 3
FRANCE 31 Ireland 12
France: S Blanco (M Andrieu); P Hontax, P Sella, F Mesnel, P Lagisquet; D Camberabero, H Sanz; M Pujolle, L Armary, P Ondarts, T Devergie, J-M Lhermet (E Melville), O Roumat, L Rodrigues (capt)
T: Mesnel 2, Lagisquet; C: Camberabero 2; P: Camberabero 5
Ireland: K Murphy; K Hooks, M Kiernan, P Danaher, K Crossan; B Smith, F Aherne; J Fitzgerald, T Kingston, D Fitzgerald, N Francis,D Lenihan (capt), D McBride, P O'Hara, N Mannion
P: Kiernan 4
Ireland's heaviest defeat in this fixture

Murrayfield, Mar 17
SCOTLAND 13 England 7
Scotland: G Hastings; A Stanger, S Hastings, S Lineen, I Tukalo; C Chalmers, G Armstrong; D Sole (capt), K Milne, A Burnell, C Gray, D Cronin, J Jeffrey, F Calder, D White (DTurnbull)
T: Stanger; P: Chalmers 3

England: S Hodgkinson; S Halliday, W Carling (capt), J Guscott (M Bailey), R Underwood; R Andrew, R Hill, P Rendall, B Moore, J Probyn, W Dooley, P Ackford, M Skinner, P Winterbottom, M Teague
T: Guscott; P: Hodgkinson
The first time two sides have met for the Championship, Triple Crown and Grand Slam.

Lansdowne Road, Mar 25
IRELAND 14 Wales 8
Ireland: K Murphy; K Hooks, M Kiernan, B Mullin, K Crossan; B Smith, M Bradley (F Aherne); J Fitzgerald, T Kingston, D Fitzgerald, D Lenihan (capt), N Francis, D McBride, P O'Hara, N Mannion
T: Smith, McBride, Kingston; C: Kiernan
Wales: P Thorburn (A Clement); S Ford, M Ring, A Bateman, A Emyr; D Evans (A Edmunds), R Jones (capt); B Williams, K Phillips, H Williams-Jones, A Allen, G Llewellyn, M Morris, R Collins, M Jones
T: Ford, Llewellyn

This defeat completed Wales's first-ever four-game championship whitewash

FINAL TABLE

			P	W	D	L	F	A	Pts
1	(2=)	Scotland	4	4	0	0	60	26	8
2	(2=)	England	4	3	0	1	90	26	6
3	(1)	France	4	2	0	2	67	78	4
4	(4=)	Ireland	4	1	0	3	36	75	2
5	(4=)	Wales	4	0	0	4	42	90	0

Last season's positions in brackets

ALL BLACKS TOUR OF BRITAIN

Date	Opponents	Result
Oct 14	Cardiff	won 25-15
Oct 13	Pontypool	won 47-6
Oct 21	Swansea	won 37-22
Oct 25	Neath	won 26-25
Oct 28	Llanelli	won 11-0
Oct 31	Newport	won 54-9
Nov 4	WALES (Cardiff)	won 34-9
Nov 8	Leinster (Dublin)	won 36-9
Nov 11	Munster (Cork)	won 31-9
Nov 14	Connacht (Galway)	won 40-6
Nov 18	IRELAND (Dublin)	won 23-6
Nov 21	Ulster (Belfast)	won 21-3
Nov 25	Barbarians (Twickenham)	won 21-10

Test Match details

Wales 9 NEW ZEALAND 34
Wales: P H Thorburn; M R Hall, M G Ring, D W Evans, A Emyr; A Clement, R N Jones (capt); M Griffiths, K H Phillips, D Young, P T Davies, G O Llewellyn, P Pugh, G Jones, M A Jones
P: Thorburn 3
New Zealand: J A Gallagher; C R Innes, J T Stanley, N J Schuster, T J Wright; G J Fox, G T M Bachop; S C McDowell, S B T Fitzpatrick, R W Loe, M J Pierce, G W Whetton, A T Earl, M R Brewer, W T Shelford (Capt)
T: Innes 2, Bachop; Wright C: Fox 3; P: Fox 4

Ireland 6 NEW ZEALAND 23
Ireland: P I Rainey; K J Hooks (P P A Danaher), B J Mullin, D G Irwin, K C Crossan; B A Smith, L F P Aherne; N J Popplewell (D C Fitzgerald), S J Smith, J J McCoy, D G Lenihan, W A Anderson (capt), P M Matthews, P T J O'Hara, N P Mannion
P: Smith 2
New Zealand: J A Gallagher; C R Innes, J T Stanley, N J Schuster, T J Wright; G J Fox, G T M Bachop; S C McDowell, S B T Fitzpatrick, R W Loe, M J Pierce, G W

Whetton, A T Earl, M R Brewer, W T Shelford (Capt)
T: Gallagher, Wright, Shelford; C: Fox: P: Fox 3

FIJI IN ENGLAND
Twickenham, Nov 4
ENGLAND 58 Fiji 23
S Hodgkinson; R Underwood, J C Guscott, W D C Carling (capt), M D Bailey (S Halliday); C R Andrew, R J Hill; M S Linnett, B C Moore, A R Mullins, W A Dooley, P J Ackford, M G Skinner, P J Winterbottom (G Rees), D W Egerton
T: Underwood 5, Skinner, Bailey, Linnett, Ackford, Guscott; C: Hodgkinson 5, Andrew; P:Hodgkinson 2
Fiji: M Natuilagilagi; T Lovo, L Erenavula, N Nadruka, T Venolagi; S Koroduadua, L Vasuwulagi; M Taga, S Naivilawasa, S Naituku, I Savai, M Rasari, N Matirawa, A Dere, E Teleni (capt)
T: Erenavula, Teleni, Rasari, Savai; C: Koroduadua 2; P: Koroduadua

AUSTRALIA IN FRANCE
First Test
Strasbourg, Nov 4
France 15 AUSTRALIA 32
France: S Blanco; S Weller, P Sella, F Mesnel, P Lagisquet; D Camberabero (T Lacroix), P Berbizier (capt); L Rodriguez, M Cecillon, J Condom, G Bourguignon, E Champ, L Seigne, L Armary, M Pujolle
P: Camberabero 4; DG: Camberabero
Australia: G Martin; I Williams (D Junee), J Little, T Horan, D Campese; M Lynagh, N Farr-Jones (capt); T Gavin, B Nasser, P FitzSimons, R McCall, D Carter, M Hartill, P Kearns, T Daly
T: Horan 2, Williams, Campese; C: Lynagh 2; P: Lynagh 4

Second Test
Lille, Nov 11
FRANCE 25 Australia 19
France: P Sella; S Weller, F Mesnel, M Andrieu, P Lagisquet; T Lacroix, H Sanz (capt); D Boet, L Armary, P Ondarts, A Lorieux, D Erbani, E Champ, A Carminati, T Devergie
T: Lagisquet; Andrieu; C: Lacroix; P: Lacroix 5
Australia: G Martin; I Williams (D Junee), J Little, T Horan, D Campese; M Lynagh, N Farr-Jones (capt); T Daly, P Kearns, M Hartill, R McCall, P FitzSimons, D Carter, B Nasser, T Gavin
T: Kearns, Farr-Jones; C: Lynagh; P: Lynagh 3

FRANCE IN AUSTRALIA
First Test
Sydney, Jun 9
AUSTRALIA 21 France 9
Australia: G Martin; I Williams, J Little, T Horan (A Herbert), P Carozza, M Lynagh, N Farr-Jones (capt); A Daly, P Kearns, E McKenzie, R McCall, P FitzSimons,J Miller, B Nasser, T Gavin
T: T Martin; C: Lynagh; P: Lynagh 5
France: S Blanco (capt.); S Weller, P Sellal, J Langlade, P Lagisquet; D Camberabero, H Sanz ; M Pujolle, L Armary, P Gellart, T Devergie, O Roumat, E Melville, A Benazzi, C Deslandes
P: Camberabero 3
Benazzi sent off for stamping

Second Test
Brisbane, Jun 24
AUSTRALIA 48 France 31
Australia: D Campese; I Williams, J Little, P Cornish, P Carozza; M Lynagh, N Farr-Jones (capt); A Daly, P Kearns, E McKenzie, R McCall, P FitzSimons, S Scott-Young, B Nasser, T Gavin
T: Carozza, Cornish, Gavin, Little, Campese, Pen try; C:

Lynagh 6; P: Lynagh 4
France: S Blanco (capt); P Lacombe, P Sella, F Mesnel, P Lagisquet; D Camberabero, H Sanz ; M Pujolle, L Armary, F Heyer (P Gallart), T Devergie, J Condom, E Melville, A Benazzi, O Roumat
T: Blanco 2, Armary, Lacombe; C: Camberabero 3; P: Camberabero 3

Third Test
Sydney, Jun 30
Australia 19 FRANCE 28
Australia: D Campese; I Williams, J Little, P Cornish, P Carozza (G Martin); M Lynagh, N Farr-Jones (capt); A Daly, P Kearns, E McKenzie, R McCall, P FitzSimons, J Miller, B Nasser, T Gavin (S Scott-Young)
T: Campese, Daly; C: Lynagh; P: Lynagh 2; DG: Lynagh
France: S Blanco (capt) (J Lafond); P Saint-Andre, P Sella, F Mesnel, P Lagisquet; D Camberabero, A Hueber ; D Bouet, L Armary, P Gallart, T Devergie (J Condom), O Roumat, X Blond, A Benazzi, E Melville
T: Camberabero, Mesnel; C: Camberabero; P: Canberabero 2, Blanco; DG: Camberabero 3
Gallart sent off for punching by referee Clive Norling

GAUL AND WORMWOOD

❝If it was in my hands, I'd change all 15 players for the second Test.❞
Albert Ferrasse, head of the French rugby federation, after defeat by Australia in Strasbourg

"Changes are only of any use in a winning side."
Jacques Fouroux, French coach

"Who will take his place? There are no lack of takers for his job but there are not so many who would be prepared to work for months and months for no financial gain. All those squealing simpletons who are so good at giving advice are not so clever when it comes to the crunch."
Ferrasse defending Fouroux

"Fouroux sorted out the real talents from the fluffy nothings. He stopped French tempers blowing French excellence.....he was an infinitely better bet than the skulking failed artists who formed the basis of the opposition faction."
Stephen Jones, Sunday Times

"By being made to play like donkeys, they have become donkeys. They no longer have the potential to dream. And when you take that away from a French rugby man, you take away his soul."
Daniel Herrero, Toulon coach

"The joy of the visitors [Romania] and the pitiful sight of France being soundly beaten reminded you of the conventional wisdom in rugby that the only two areas still to move for freedom in Europe are Albania and the French Rugby Federation.❞
Stephen Jones, Sunday Times

SCOTLAND IN NEW ZEALAND

Gisborne, May 30
Poverty Bay/East Coast 0   SCOTLAND   45
                             T: Marshall 2. Oliver, Dods,
                             Chalmers, Lineen, K Milne,
                             Turnbull
                             C: Dods 5
                             P: Dods

Wellington, Jun 2
Wellington   16   Scotland   16
T: Tregaskis, Tacaloa,   T: Allan
Bradbrook   P: G Hastings 4
C: Pokere 2

Nelson, Jun 6
Nelson Bays/Marlboro 6   SCOTLAND   23
P: Stark 2   T: Moore 2, Marshall
                             Buchanan-Smith
                             C: Dods 2
                             P: Dods

Christchurch, Jun 9
Canterbury   12   SCOTLAND   21
P: Deans 4   T: Calder, Pen try
                             C: G Hastings 2
                             P: G Hastings 3

Invercargill, Jun 12
Southland   12   SCOTLAND   45
T: Laidlaw   T: S Hastings 2, Moore
C: McKenzie   Dods, Shiel
P: McKenzie   P: Dods 5
DG: Laidlaw   P: Dods 3
                             DG: Wylie 2

First Test
Dunedin, Jun 16
NEW ZEALAND   31   Scotland   16
New Zealand: K Crowley, J Kirwan, J Stanley, W Little,
T Wright, G Fox, G Bachop, S McDowell, S Fitzpatrick, R
Loe, G Whetton, I Jones, A Whetton, M Brewer, W
Shelford (capt)
T: Kirwan 2, Crowley, Fox, Jones; C: Fox 4; P: Fox
Scotland: G Hastings, A Stanger, S Hastings, S Lineen, I
Tukalo, C Chalmers, G Armstrong, D Sole (capt), J Allan,
I Milne, C Gray, D Cronin, J Jeffrey, F Calder, D White
T: Lineen, Gray, Sole; C: G Hastings 2

Palmerston North, Jun 19
Manawatu   4   SCOTLAND   19
T: Konia   T: K Milne, Richardson
                             C: Dods
                             P: Dods 3

Second Test
Auckland, Jun 23
NEW ZEALAND   21   Scotland   18
New Zealand: K Crowley, J Kirwan, J Stanley, W Little,
T Wright; G Fox, G Bachop, S McDowell, S Fitzpatrick, R
Loe, I Jones, G Whetton, A Whetton, M Brewer, W
Shelford (capt)
T: Loe; C: Fox; P: Fox 5
Scotland: G Hastings, A Stanger, S Hastings, S Lineen; A
Moore; C Chalmers, G Armstrong (G Oliver); D Sole
(capt); K Milne, I Milne, C Gray, D Cronin, J Jeffrey, F
Calder, D White
T: Stanger, Moore, C: G Hastings 2; P: G Hastings 2

WALES TOUR OF NAMIBIA

Swakopmund, May 23
Welwitschia   0   WALES   73
                             T: Feeley 3, O Williams 2,
                             Ford 2, Llewellyn,
                             Ring, A Williams,
                             Bowling, R Phillips,
                             Buckett
                             C: Rayer 7, A Williams 2
                             P: Rayer

Windhoek, May 26
Namibia 'B'   18   WALES   35
T: Swartz   T: Parfitt 2, Emyr 2,
C: McCulley   Bateman
P: McCulley 3   C: Thorburn 3
DG: McCulley   P: Thorburn 3

Windhoek, May 30
Central Region   6   WALES   43
P: J Coetzee   T: Parfitt, Morris, Emyr,
DG: J Coetzee   Ring, Fealey, Reynolds
                             C: Rayer 5
                             P: Rayer 3

Windhoek, Jun 2
Namibia   9   WALES   18
T: Mans   T: Thorburn, Bridges
C: McCulley   C: Thorburn 2
P: McCulley   P: Thorburn 2

Tsumeb, Jun 5
Northern Region   9   WALES   67
T: Jeffery   T: Rayer 2, A Williams 2,
C: Olivier   Morris 2, Gregory,
P: Olivier   Pugh, S Williams,
                             Parfitt, O Williams
                             C: Rayer 7
                             P: Rayer 2
                             DG: A Willaims

Windhoek, Jun 9
Namibia   30   WALES   34
T: Swartz 2, Mans   T: Emyr 2, O Williams,
C: J Coetzee 2,   Pen try
   McCulley   C: Thorburn 3
P: McCulley 2,   P: Thorburn 3
   J Coetzee   DG: Clement
DG: J Coetzee

A TROUBLED GAME

“ They have devised a simple system of meeting each year and changing one law and making a cock-up of it so that they have to meet the next year to put it right.”
Clive Norling, referee, on the International Board

“The old idea of a ticket tout being someone in a dirty raincoat making a few bob on the side has long since been overtaken. We are talking about organised crime.”
Dudley Wood, RFU secretary

“If any All Black went to Rugby League then John Gallagher would be the last man I would say would make the change.”
Murray Deaker, Radio New Zealand

“July and August...is the worst time for European players to tour and what is even more reprehensible was that by the time next year's World Cup season has ended, England's leading players will have been committed to maintaining peak match fitness for three years without a break. This is far more than is asked of a professional soccer team like Liverpool. For it to be asked of players who are supposed to be amateurs cuts the bridge from under the feet of the RU who have been posturing in defence of the amateur ethic.”
John Reason, Daily Telegraph

“It often seems to escape the game's administrators that Union has spawned all the disadvantages of professionalism with precious few of the benefits.”
Robert Armstrong, The Guardian

“I like being modelled on King Canute, he is one of my favourite characters.”
Dudley Wood

“Amateurism is dead and they know it. But they're ready to let us leave a game we love so they can keep up the pretence. It's bloody shameful.”
Anonymous international, quoted by Patrick Collins, Mail on Sunday

“Even dirtier than the British Lions.”
Steve Cutler, Australian lock, on the Soviet team

“The day cannot dawn too soon when a player, besides being sent off the field in disgrace, is arrested and charged with grievous bodily harm.”
John Mason, Daily Telegraph

“There were only two of us in that pack of eight (Penzance, after the war) who had not knowingly killed at least one of the enemy. Yet that scrum was the safest place I've ever been in my life. Violence at rugby was unheard of by those men. Now I look at the game and see it being played often by mean-spirited young men who've learnt mean-spirited tricks **”**
John Kendall-Carpenter, shortly before his death

ENGLAND TOUR OF ARGENTINA

Buenos Aires, Jul 15

BANCO NACION	29	England	21
T: Gentile, Gomez		T: Robinson, Lilley,	
P: Porta 5		Buckton, Kimmins	
DG: Porta 2		C: Pears	
		P: Pears	

Tucuman, Jul 19

Tucuman	14	ENGLAND	19
T: M Teran, G Teran		T: Olver	
P: Martinez 2		P: Hodgkinson 3, Pears 2	

Buenos Aires, Jul 22

BUENOS AIRES SELECT	26	England	23
T: Cubelli, S Ezcurra		T: Ryan, Carling,	
Laborde		Egerton, Heslop	
C: Angaut		C: Pears 2	
P: Angaut 4		P: Pears	

Mendoza, Jul 24

DUYO	22	England	21
T: Alejandro, Bertranou		P: Hodgkinson 7	
C: G Filizzola			
P: G Filizzola 3			
DG: G Filizzola			

First Test
Buenos Aires, Jul 28

Argentina	12	ENGLAND	25

Argentina: A Scolni; H Vidou, M Loffreda (capt), D Cuesta Silva, S Salvat; R Madero; F Gomez; A Rocca, J-J Angelillo, L Molina, E Branca, A Lachetti, P Garreton, M Bertranou, M Baeck
P: Vidou 4
England: S D Hodgkinson; N J Heslop, W D C Carling (capt), J R Buckton, C Oti; D Pears, R J Hill; J Leonard, B C Moore, J A Probyn, N C Redman, W A Dooley, M G Skinner, P J Winterbottom, D Ryan
T: Ryan, Oti; C: Hodgkinson; P: Hodgkinson 5

Cordoba, Jul 31

Cordoba	12	ENGLAND	15
P: Cosa 4		T: Kimmins	
		C: Liley	
		P: Liley 3	

Second Test
Buenos Aires, Aug 4

ARGENTINA	15	England	13

Argentina: A Scolni, S Salvat, M Loffreda (capt), D Cuesta Silva, H Vidou, R Madero, F Gomez, M Aguirre, J-J Angelillo, D Cash, E Branca, A Lachetti, P Garreton, M Bertranou, M Baeck
P: Vidou 5
England: S D Hodgkinson; N J Heslop, W D C Carling (capt), J R Buckton, C Oti; D Pears, R J Hill; J Leonard, B C Moore, J A Probyn, N C Redman, W A Dooley, M G Skinner, P J Winterbottom, D Ryan
T: Hodgkinson, Heslop; C: Hodgkinson; P: Hodgkinson

NEW ZEALAND V AUSTRALIA

First Test
Christchurch, Jul 21

NEW ZEALAND	21	Australia	6

New Zealand: K Crowley; J Kirwan, C Innes, W Little T Wright; G Fox, G Bachop; S McDowell, F Fitzpatrick, R Loe, I Jones, G Whetton (capt), A Whetton, M Brewer, Z Brooke
T: Fitzpatrick, Innes, Crowley, Kirwan; C: Fox ; P: Fox
Australia: G Martin; I Williams, T Horan, P Cornish,

D Campese; M Lynagh, N Farr-Jones (capt); T Daly, P Kearns, E McKenzie, R McCall, P FitzSimons, W Ofahengaue, S Tuynman, T Gavin
P: Lynagh 2

Second Test
Auckland, Aug 4
NEW ZEALAND 27 *Australia* 17
New Zealand: K Crowley; J Kirwan,C Innes, W Little T Wright; G Fox, G Bachop; S McDowell, F Fitzpatrick, R Loe, G Whetton (capt), I Jones, A Whetton, M Brewer, Z Brooke (K Schuler)
T: Fitzpatrick, Brooke, Bachop C; Fox 3; P: Fox 2; DG: Fox

Australia: D Campese; J Flett, A Herbert, T Horan, P Carozza; M Lynagh, N Farr-Jones (capt); T Daly, P Kearns, E McKenzie, W Campbell, R McCall, W Ofahengaue, P Nasser, T Gavin
T: Horan, Ofahengaue; P: Lynagh 2; DG: Lynagh

Third Test
Wellington, Aug 18
New Zealand 9 AUSTRALIA 21
New Zealand: K Crowley; J Kirwan, C Innes, W Little; T Wright; G Fox, G Bachop; S McDowell, F Fitzpatrick, R Loe, G Whetton (capt), I Jones, A Whetton, M Brewer, Z Brooke
P: Fox 2; DG: Fox

Australia: D Campese; J Flett, A Herbert, T Horan, P Carozza; M Lynagh, N Farr-Jones (capt); E McKenzie, P Kearns, T Daly, V Ofahengaue, R McCall, S Scott-Young, T Gavin, B Campbell
T: Kearns, C; Lynagh, P: Lynagh 5

❝Six Borderers in Scottish XV to play Fifi."
Headline in Borders Gazette

"When he's holding the ball in the middle of the field and there's nothing on and he must be tackled suddenly, he floats off into a different space. I could never call it anything as crude as a change of pace."
Simon Halliday on Jeremy Guscott

"It has been a disaster, particularly to those averse to running. No rain fell before December, consequently games were at relatively high speed on bone-jarring ground. After Christmas no games were cancelled due to weather. This is unacceptable. In addition, many games were played in gale-force winds, making grounds even firmer. As I cannot wait for either global warming to be rectified or pitches to be watered, I am retiring....in protest against the greenhouse effect."
John Gronow, Harlequins veteran

"You report that it is customary for New Zealand club sides to respond in kind to a haka. I wonder if the home sides could learn from this.....The sight of the Barbarians performing a Morris Dance, for example, would certainly give the All Blacks pause for thought when they next meet.❞
Letter to The Independent *from Carol Jarvis of Bristol*

NEW ZEALAND'S RECORD BREAKING RUN

May 22	1987	Italy	won 70-6 (†)
May 27	1987	Fiji	won 74-13 (†)
Jun 1	1987	Argentina	won 46-15 (†)
Jun 6	1987	Scotland	won 30-3 (†)
Jun 14	1987	Wales	won 49-6 (†)
Jun 20	1987	France	won 29-9 (†)
Jul 25	1987	Australia	won 30-16
May 2	1988	Wales	won 52-3
Jun 11	1988	Wales	won 54-9
Jul 3	1988	Australia	won 32-7
Jul 16	1988	Australia	drew 19-19
Jul 30	1988	Australia	won 30-9
Jun 17	1989	France	won 25-17
Jul 1	1989	France	won 34-20
Jul 15	1989	Argentina	won 60-9
Jul 29	1989	Argentina	won 49-12
Aug 5	1989	Australia	won 24-12
Nov 4	1989	Wales	won 34-9
Nov 11	1989	Ireland	won 23-6
Jun 16	1990	Scotland	won 31-16
Jun 23	1990	Scotland	won 21-18
July 21	1990	Australia	won 21-6
Aug 4	1990	Australia	won 27-17
Aug 18	1990	Australia	lost 9-21

Played 23 won 2 drew 1 lost 1
(†) indicates World Cup Match

PILKINGTON CUP
Third Round
BATH 9 Harlequins 0; Bedford 7 RICHMOND 12; BRISTOL 29 Liverpool St Helens 0; Fylde 15 GOSFORTH 17; Harrogate 3 WEST HARTLEPOOL 12; HEADINGLEY 12 North Walsham 0; London Welsh 3 LEICESTER 43; Metropolitan Police 4 NORTHAMPTON 16; MOSELEY 28 Berry Hill 11; Nuneaton 7 SARACENS 16; Plymouth Albion 0 ORRELL 7; Rosslyn Park 3 NOTTINGHAM 30; SALE 26 Blackheath 16; Vale of Lune 13 EXETER 18; WAKEFIELD 16 Rugby 9; Wasps 19 GLOUCESTER 23

Fourth Round
BATH 25 Headingley 3; BRISTOL 26 Exeter 3; Gosforth 15 GLOUCESTER 26; LEICESTER 43 West Hartlepool 15; MOSELEY 10 Saracens 6; NORTHAMPTON 22 Wakefield 10; NOTTINGHAM 12 Orrell 6; RICHMOND 14 Sale 12

Fifth Round
MOSELEY 15 Bristol 13; NORTHAMPTON 23 Leicester 7; Nottingham 16 GLOUCESTER 26; Richmond 3 BATH 35

Semi-finals
Moseley 7 BATH 21; Northampton 12 GLOUCESTER 17
Final
Twickenham, May 5

BATH	48	Gloucester	6
T: Withey, Guscott		T: Dunn	
Callard, Swift (2)		C: T Smith	
Dawe, Redman, Ubogu			
C: Barnes (4), Halliday			
PG: Barnes (2)			

BATH'S CUP RECORDS

* **Highest score in the final**
* **Biggest winning margin in the final**
* **Most tries (8) in the final**
* **The final was Bath's 50th JPS/Pilkington Cup tie. Won 38, scored 984 points, conceded 448**
* **In the last seven seasons they have won 32 cup ties out of 33.**

SCHWEPPES WELSH CUP
Fifth Round
BRIDGEND 30 Llandovery 4; CARDIFF 15 Llanelli 4;
Ebbw Vale 3 PONTYPOOL 12; Maesteg Celtic 6 NEATH
19; SWANSEA 15 Glamorgan Wanderers 9; TUMBLE 19
Llanharan 6; ABERAVON 15 Newbridge 9; NEWPORT
12 Pontypridd 3
Sixth Round
ABERAVON 18 Pontypool 12; BRIDGEND 31 Tumble 4;
NEATH 22 Cardiff 6; SWANSEA 28 Newport 14
Semi-finals
Aberavon 6 BRIDGEND 12; NEATH 24 Swansea 16
Final
National Stadium, Cardiff, May 5

NEATH	16	Bridgend	10
T: Morris, Bridges		T: Ellis	
P: Thorburn		DG: A Williams (2)	
C: Thorburn			
DG: Ball			

TOSHIBA COUNTY CHAMPIONSHIP
Semi-finals
LANCASHIRE 26 Warwickshire 14; Cornwall 15
MIDDLESEX 15 (Middlesex won on better try ratio)
Final
Twickenham, Apr 8
LANCASHIRE 32 Middlesex 9
Under-21 Final
EASTERN COUNTIES 28 Yorkshire 12

CATHAY PACIFIC HONG KONG SEVENS
Hong Kong, Apr 1
Quarter Finals
NEW ZEALAND 20 Scottish Borderers 12;
BARBARIANS 18 Western Samoa 10; FIJI 28 Tonga 12;
WALES 16 Australia 10
Semi-Finals
NEW ZEALAND 24 Barbarians 6; FIJI 34 Wales 6
Final
FIJI 22 New Zealand 10

SAVE & PROSPER MIDDLESEX SEVENS
Twickenham, May 12
HARLEQUINS 26 Rosslyn Park 10
Harlequins' fifth successive win and 13th in total

FRENCH CHAMPIONSHIP
Paris, May 26
RACING CLUB DE FRANCE 22 Agen 12 (aet)

COMMERCIAL UNION UAU FINAL
Twickenham, Mar 14
LOUGHBOROUGH UNIVERSITY 25 Swansea
University 16

WOMEN'S CUP FINAL
Rosslyn Park, Apr 3
WASPS 10 Richmond 3

VARSITY MATCH
Twickenham, Dec 12
CAMBRIDGE 22 Oxford 13

COURAGE CLUBS CHAMPIONSHIP
Division One

			P	W	D	L	F	A	Pts	P	W	D	L	F	A
1	(3)	WASPS	11	9	0	2	250	106	18	38	27	0	11	887	521
2	(2)	Gloucester	11	8	1	2	214	139	17	46	34	2	10	1090	665
3	(1)	Bath	11	8	0	3	258	104	16	42	35	1	6	1116	363
4	(P)	Saracens	11	7	1	3	168	167	15	32	19	2	11	654	486
5	(6)	Leicester	11	6	0	5	248	184	12	36	27	0	9	1031	480
6	(4)	Nottingham	11	6	0	5	187	148	12	37	25	0	12	848	606
7	(8)	Harlequins	11	6	0	5	218	180	12	35	22	0	13	693	610
8	(5)	Orrell	11	5	0	6	221	132	10	38	24	0	14	903	465
9	(7)	Bristol	11	4	0	7	136	144	8	44	27	1	16	1012	550
10	(9)	Rosslyn Park	11	4	0	7	164	243	8	37	19	1	17	717	676
11	(10)	*Moseley*	11	2	0	9	138	258	4	42	12	2	28	561	921
12	(P)	*Bedford*	11	0	0	11	70	467	0	38	6	1	31	388	1083

FULL PLAYING RECORD

DIVISION ONE RESULTS

Home team	*Away team* Bath	Bedford	Bristol	Gloucs	Quins	Leics	Moseley	Nott'm	Orrell	Rosslyn P	Saracens	Wasps
BATH	-	76-0	-	-	32-12	26-15	27-9	-	-	34-6	-	-
BEDFORD	-	-	6-16	-	8-71	-	0-24	-	7-25	-	3-22	9-44
BRISTOL	13-14	-	-	6-13	-	11-13	-	13-9	-	6-15	-	21-22
GLOUCESTER	13-6	37-6	-	-	24-9	-	-	-	16-10	41-12	21-21	-
HARLEQUINS	-	-	13-7	-	-	15-12	-	22-27	15-9	19-16	-	12-9
LEICESTER	-	60-3	-	16-26	-	-	38-20	15-6	-	-	34-6	-
MOSELEY	-	-	10-16	12-16	22-21	-	-	6-22	-	-	-	0-42
NOTTINGHAM	12-9	47-16	-	12-3	-	-	-	-	9-25	6-11	25-12	-
ORRELL	6-9	-	12-15	-	33-10	25-13	-	-	64-14	-	-	-
ROSSLYN PARK	-	45-12	-	-	9-23	18-9	-	-	-	13-15	6-14	
SARACENS	9-7	-	17-12	-	15-9	-	33-13	-	12-6	-	-	-
WASPS	9-18	-	-	29-4	-	29-12	-	16-12	12-6	-	24-6	-

Division Two

			P	W	D	L	F	A	Pts	P	W	D	L	F	A
1	(3)	NORTHAMPTON	11	9	1	1	192	135	19	38	23	1	14	753	386
2	(R)	L'POOL ST. HELENS	11	8	2	1	154	106	18	40	30	2	8	765	451
3	(9)	Richmond	11	7	1	3	282	135	15	35	21	3	11	741	508
4	(5)	Coventry	11	6	1	4	206	185	13	41	20	1	20	738	693
5	(6)	London Irish	11	6	0	5	228	247	12	34	15	1	18	565	806
6	(P)	Rugby	11	5	0	6	238	172	10	35	21	1	13	644	567
7	(P)	Plymouth Albion	11	5	0	6	206	164	10	31	18	0	13	776	447
8	(7)	Headingley	11	5	0	6	161	226	10	42	17	1	24	627	747
9	(4)	Sale	11	4	0	7	153	182	8	37	20	0	17	762	661
10	(8)	Blackheath	11	3	2	6	141	205	8	33	16	4	13	713	540
11	(R)	Waterloo	11	3	0	8	147	193	6	40	17	1	22	634	670
12	(10)	Gosforth	11	1	1	9	108	266	3	40	17	1	22	526	724

FULL PLAYING RECORD

Divison Three

			P	W	D	L	F	A	Pts	P	W	D	L	F	A
1	(R)	LONDON SCOTTISH	11	11	0	0	258	92	22	28	17	0	11	528	447
2	(3)	WAKEFIELD	11	7	1	3	210	126	15	41	29	1	11	853	505
3	(4)	West Hartlepool	11	5	2	4	175	110	12	37	21	2	14	691	516
4	(6)	Sheffield	11	6	0	5	176	174	12	37	26	2	9	706	446
5	(8)	Askeans	11	6	0	5	170	235	12	36	22	0	14	703	595
6	(9)	Exeter	11	5	1	5	149	153	11	31	17	1	13	509	517
7	(P)	Roundhay	11	5	0	6	156	166	10	41	18	1	22	558	625
8	(10)	Fylde	11	5	0	6	169	222	10	37	24	2	11	658	565
9	(7)	Vale of Lune	11	4	0	7	154	219	8	38	13	0	25	555	853
10	(5)	Nuneaton	11	4	0	7	127	196	8	35	12	1	22	566	689
11	(P)	Lydney	11	3	0	8	153	166	6	42	23	1	18	759	577
12	(R)	London Welsh	11	3	0	8	141	179	6	35	12	1	22	604	772

FULL PLAYING RECORD

Last season's positions in brackets
P = Promoted 1988 - 89
R = Relegated 1988 - 89

ALL THE OTHER CHAMPIONS

Area North	BROUGHTON PARK
Area South	METROPOLITAN POLICE
North 1	OTLEY
North 2	ROTHERHAM
North East 1	STOCKTON
North East 2	BRAMLEY*
North West 1	SANDBACH
North West 2	MANCHESTER
Midlands 1	HEREFORD
Midlands 2 East	TOWCESTRIANS*
Midlands 2 West	CAMP HILL
E Midlands/Leics	BIGGLESWADE*
Staffs/Warwicks	LEAMINGTON
Notts/Lincs/Derbys	CHESTERFIELD*
N Midlands	WORCESTER
South West 1	MAIDENHEAD
South West 2	GORDON LEAGUE*
Western Counties	PENRYN
Southern Counties	MARLOW
Cornwall/Devon	PENZANCE
Gloucs/Somerset	COMBE DOWN
Berks/Dorset/Wilts	SHERBORNE*
Bucks/Oxon	GROVE
London Division 1	NORTH WALSHAM
London 2 North	THURROCK
London 2 South	OLD MID-WHITGIFTIANS*
London 3 North West	TABARD*
London 3 North East	CHINGFORD*
London 3 South West	DORKING
London 3 South East	WESTCOMBE PARK

* Won division with 100% record - 10 wins out of 10

CHAMPIONS

RUGBY UNION

Year	Winners	Grand Slam	Triple Crown
1883	England	-	England
1884	England	-	England
1885	-	-	-
1886	England	-	-
	Scotland	-	
1887	Scotland	-	-
1888	-	-	-
1889	-	-	-
1890	England	-	-
	Scotland		
1891	Scotland	-	Scotland
1892	England	-	England
1893	Wales	-	Wales
1894	Ireland	-	Ireland
1895	Scotland	-	Scotland
1896	Ireland	-	-
1897	-	-	-
1898	-	-	-
1899	Ireland	-	Ireland
1900	Wales	-	Wales
1901	Scotland	-	Scotland
1902	Wales	-	Wales
1903	Scotland	-	Scotland
1904	Scotland	-	-
1905	Wales	-	Wales
1906	Ireland	-	-
	Wales	-	
1907	Scotland	-	Scotland
1908	Wales	Wales	Wales
1909	Wales	Wales	Wales
1910	England	-	-
1911	Wales	Wales	Wales
1912	England	-	-
	Ireland		
1913	England	England	England

Year	Winners	Grand Slam	Triple Crown
1914	England	England	England
1920	England	-	-
	Scotland		
	Wales		
1921	England	England	England
1922	Wales	-	-
1923	England	England	England
1924	England	England	England
1925	Scotland	Scotland	Scotland
1926	Scotland	-	-
	Ireland		
1927	Scotland	-	-
	Ireland		
1828	England	England	England
1929	Scotland	-	-
1930	England	-	-
1931	Wales	-	-
1932	England	-	-
	Wales		
	Ireland		
1933	Scotland	-	Scotland
1934	England	-	England
1935	Ireland	-	-
1936	Wales	-	-
1937	England	-	England
1938	Scotland	-	Scotland
1939	England	-	-
	Wales		
	Ireland		
1947	Wales	-	-
	England		
1948	Ireland	Ireland	Ireland
1949	Ireland	-	Ireland
1950	Wales	Wales	Wales
1951	Ireland	-	-
1952	Wales	Wales	Wales
1953	England	-	-
1954	England	-	England
	Wales		
	France		
1955	Wales	-	-
	France		
1956	Wales	-	-
1958	England	-	-
1959	France	-	-
1960	France	-	England

Year	Winners	Grand Slam	Triple Crown
	England		
1961	France	-	-
1962	France	-	-
1963	England	-	-
1964	Scotland	-	-
	Wales		
1965	Wales	-	Wales
1966	Wales	-	-
1967	France	-	-
1968	France	France	-
1969	Wales	-	Wales
1970	Wales	-	-
	France		
1971	Wales	Wales	Wales
1972	-	-	-
1973	Quintuple tie	-	-
1974	Ireland	-	-
1975	Wales	-	-
1976	Wales	Wales	Wales
1977	France	France	Wales
1978	Wales	Wales	Wales
1979	Wales	-	Wales
1980	England	England	England
1981	France	France	-
1982	Ireland	-	Ireland
1983	France	-	-
	Ireland		
1984	Scotland	Scotland	Scotland
1985	Ireland	-	Ireland
1986	France	-	-
	Scotland		
1987	France	France	-
1988	Wales	-	Wales
	France		
1989	France	-	-
1990	Scotland	Scotland	Scotland

WINS

32 Wales	8 Wales	17 Wales
27 England	8 England	15 England
21 Scotland	4 France	10 Scotland
18 Ireland	3 Scotland	6 Ireland
17 France	1 Ireland	

France first played all four home nations in 1910. They withdrew from the Championship because of a dispute over professionalism from 1932 until after the war.

THE INTERNATIONAL CHAMPIONSHIP - THE LAST TEN YEARS:

	ENG V IRE	SCO V ENG	ENG V WAL	IRE V SCO	IRE V WAL
1982	15-16	9-9	17-7	21-12	20-12
1984	12-9	18-6	15-24	9-32	9-18
1986	25-20	33-6	21-18	9-10	12-19
1988	35-3	6-9	3-11	22-18	9-12
1990	23-0	13-7	34-6	10-13	14-8
	IRE V ENG	ENG V SCO	WAL V ENG	SCO V IRE	WAL V IRE
1981	6-10	23-17	21-19	10-9	9-8
1983	23-15	12-22	13-13	15-18	9-21
1985	13-10	10-7	24-15	15-18	11-15
1987	17-0	21-12	19-12	16-12	11-15
1989	3-16	12-12	12-9	37-21	13-19
	WAL V SCO	FRA V ENG	FRA V IRE	SCO V FRA	WAL V FRA
1982	18-34	15-27	22-9	16-7	22-12
1984	9-15	32-18	25-12	21-12	16-21
1986	22-15	29-10	29-9	18-17	15-23
1988	25-20	10-9	25-6	23-12	9-10
1990	9-13	7-26	31-12	21-0	19-29
	SCO V WAL	ENG V FRA	IRE V FRA	FRA V SCO	FRA V WAL
1981	15-6	12-16	13-19	16-9	19-15
1983	15-19	15-19	22-16	19-15	16-9
1985	21-25	9-9	15-15	11-3	14-3
1987	21-14	15-19	13-19	28-22	16-9
1989	23-7	11-0	21-26	19-3	31-12

WORLD CUP
Inaugurated 1987
1987   New Zealand 29 France 9

COUNTY CHAMPIONSHIP
1889	Yorkshire
1890	Yorkshire
1891	Lancashire
1892	Yorkshire
1893	Yorkshire
1894	Yorkshire
1895	Yorkshire
1896	Yorkshire
1897	Kent
1898	Northumberland
1899	Devon
1900	Durham
1901	Devon
1902	Durham
1903	Durham
1904	Kent
1905	Durham
1906	Devon
1907	Devon & Durham (shared)
1908	Cornwall
1909	Durham
1910	Gloucestershire
1911	Devon
1912	Devon
1913	Gloucestershire
1914	Midlands
1915-19	Not held
1920	Gloucestershire
1921	Gloucestershire
1922	Gloucestershire
1923	Somerset
1924	Cumberland
1925	Leicestershire
1926	Yorkshire
1927	Kent
1928	Yorkshire
1929	Middlesex
1930	Gloucestershire
1931	Gloucestershire
1932	Gloucestershire
1933	Hampshire
1934	East Midlands
1935	Lancashire
1936	Hampshire
1937	Gloucestershire
1938	Lancashire
1939	Warwickshire
1940-46	Not held
1947	Lancashire
1948	Lancashire
1949	Lancashire
1950	Cheshire
1951	East Midlands
1952	Middlesex
1953	Yorkshire
1954	Middlesex
1955	Lancashire
1956	Middlesex
1957	Devon
1958	Warwickshire
1959	Warwickshire
1960	Warwickshire
1961	Cheshire
1962	Warwickshire
1963	Warwickshire
1964	Warwickshire
1965	Warwickshire
1966	Middlesex
1967	Surrey & Durham
1968	Middlesex
1969	Lancashire
1970	Staffordshire
1971	Surrey
1972	Gloucestershire
1973	Lancashire
1974	Gloucestershire
1975	Gloucestershire
1976	Gloucestershire
1977	Lancashire
1978	North Midlands
1979	Middlesex
1980	Lancashire

Finals since 1981
1981	Northumberland	15	Gloucestershire	6
1982	Lancashire	7	Gloucestershire	6
1983	Gloucestershire	19	Yorkshire	7
1984	Gloucestershire	36	Somerset	18
1985	Middlesex	12	Notts, Lincs, Derbys	9
1986	Warwickshire	16	Kent	6
1987	Yorkshire	22	Middlesex	7
1988	Lancashire	23	Warwickshire	18
1989	Durham	13	Cornwall	9
1990	Lancashire	32	Middlesex	9

Most wins: 15 Gloucestershire; **14** Lancashire; **11** Yorkshire; **9** Warwickshire; **8** Durham (including two shared), Middlesex; **7** Devon (including one shared)

PILKINGTON CUP
Formerly John Player Cup
1972	Gloucester	17	Moseley	16
1973	Coventry	27	Bristol	15
1974	Coventry	26	London Scottish	6
1975	Bedford	28	Rosslyn Park	12
1976	Gosforth	27	Rosslyn Park	14
1977	Gosforth	27	Waterloo	11
1978	Gloucester	6	Leicester	3
1979	Leicester	15	Moseley	12
1980	Leicester	21	London Irish	9
1981	Leicester	22	Gosforth	15
1982	Gloucester	12	Moseley	12(shared)
1983	Bristol	28	Leicester	22
1984	Bath	10	Bristol	9
1985	Bath	24	London Welsh	15
1986	Bath	25	Wasps	17
1987	Bath	19	Wasps	12
1988	Harlequins	28	Bristol	22
1989	Bath	10	Leicester	6
1990	Bath	48	Gloucester	6

Most wins: 6 Bath; **3** Leicester, Gloucester (including one shared)

SCHWEPPES WELSH CUP
1972	Neath	15	Llanelli	9
1973	Llanelli	30	Cardiff	7
1974	Llanelli	12	Aberavon	10
1975	Llanelli	15	Aberavon	6
1976	Llanelli	15	Swansea	4
1977	Newport	16	Cardiff	15
1978	Swansea	13	Newport	9
1979	Bridgend	18	Pontypridd	12
1980	Bridgend	15	Swansea	9
1981	Cardiff	14	Bridgend	6
1982	Cardiff*	12	Bridgend	12
1983	Pontypool	18	Swansea	6
1984	Cardiff	24	Neath	19
1985	Llanelli	15	Cardiff	14
1986	Cardiff	28	Newport	21
1987	Cardiff	16	Swansea	15aet
1988	Llanelli	28	Neath	13
1989	Neath	14	Llanelli	13
1990	Neath	16	Bridgend	10

* Winners on more tries rule
Most wins: 6 Llanelli; **5** Cardiff

COURAGE CLUBS CHAMPIONSHIPS

Formerly National Merit Tables

	League 1	League 2	League 3
1985-6	Gloucester	Orrell	
1986-7	Bath	Waterloo	Vale of Lane
1987-8	Leicester	Rosslyn Park	Wakefield
1988-9	Bath	Saracens	Plymouth Alb
1989-90	Wasps	Northampton	London Scottish

UNIVERSITY MATCH

Results since 1981

1981	Cambridge	9	Oxford	9
1982	Cambridge	20	Oxford	13
1983	Cambridge	20	Oxford	9
1984	Cambridge	32	Oxford	6
1985	Oxford	7	Cambridge	6
1986	Oxford	15	Cambrdige	10
1987	Cambridge	15	Oxford	10
1988	Oxford	27	Cambridge	7
1989	Cambridge	22	Oxford	13

Wins: 49 Cambridge; **45** Oxford; **13** Drawn

————1991————

Jan 19	WALES v ENGLAND (Cardiff); FRANCE v SCOTLAND (Paris)
Jan 26	RFU Cup fourth round; Welsh Cup fifth round
Feb 2	IRELAND v FRANCE (Dublin); SCOTLAND v WALES (Murrayfield)
Feb 16	ENGLAND v SCOTLAND (Twickenham); WALES v IRELAND (Cardiff)
Feb 23	RFU and Welsh Cups, quarter-finals
Mar 2	FRANCE v WALES (Paris); IRELAND v ENGLAND (Dublin)
Mar 16	ENGLAND v FRANCE (Twickeham); SCOTLAND v IRELAND (Murrayfield)
Mar 23-24	Hong Kong Sevens
Apr 6	RFU and Welsh Cup semi-finals
Apr 20	County Championship final (Twickenham)
May 4	RFU Cup final (Twickenham); WRU Cup final (Cardiff)
May 11	Middlesex Sevens final (Twickenham)
Jun 22	Romania v France

COURAGE LEAGUE FIRST DIVISION

Jan 12	Bath v Moseley; Liverpool St Helens v Gloucester; Northampton v Leicester; Orrell v Harlequins; Rosslyn Park v Nottingham; Saracens v Wasps.
Feb 9	Gloucester v Bath; Harlequins v Bristol; Leicester v Orrell; Moseley v Northampton; Nottingham v Saracens; Wasps v Liverpool St Helens.
Mar 9	Bath v Wasps; Bristol v Leicester; Liverpool St Helens v Nottingham; Northampton v Gloucester; Orrell v Moseley; Saracens v Rosslyn Park.
Mar 23	Gloucester v Orrell; Leicester v Harlequins; Moseley v Bristol; Nottingham v Bath; Rosslyn Park v Liverpool St Helens; Wasps v Northampton.
Apr 13	Bath v Rosslyn Park; Bristol v Gloucester; Harlequins v Moseley; Liverpool St Helens v Saracens; Northampton v Nottingham; Orrell v Wasps.
Apr 27	Gloucester v Harlequins; Moseley v Leicester; Nottingham v Orrell; Rosslyn Park v Northampton; Saracens v Bath; Wasps v Bristol.

HEINEKEN LEAGUE PREMIER DIVISION

Jan 12	Abertillery v Glamorgan Wanderers; Bridgend v Cardiff; Neath v Llanelli; Newbridge v Swansea; Pontypridd v Pontypool.
Feb 9	Cardiff v Pontypridd; Glamorgan Wanderers v Llanelli; Newbridge v Neath; Pontypool v Abertillery; Swansea v Bridgend.
Mar 9	Abertillery v Cardiff; Bridgend v Newbridge; Llanelli v Pontypool; Neath v Glamorgan Wanderers; Swansea v Abertillery.
Mar 23	Bridgend v Neath; Cardiff v Llanelli; Newbridge v Pontypridd; Pontypool v Glamorgan Wanderers; Swansea v Abertillery.
Apr 13	Abertillery v Newbridge; Glamorgan Wanderers v Cardiff; Llanelli v Swansea; Neath v Pontypool; Pontypridd v Bridgend.
Apr 20	Bridgend v Abertillery; Cardiff v Pontypool; Newbridge v Llanelli; Pontypridd v Neath; Swansea v Glamorgan Wanderers.
Apr 27	Abertillery v Pontypridd; Glamorgan Wanderers v Newbridge; Llanelli v Bridgend; Neath v Cardiff; Pontypool v Swansea.

WORLD CUP

Pool 1	Pool 2	Pool 3	Pool 4
England	Scotland	Wales	France
New Zealand	Ireland	Australia	Fiji
Italy	Zimbabwe	Argentina	Canada
US	Japan	Western Samoa	Romania

All kick-off times are local and subject to change

Sun Sep 29	Opening Ceremony (Twickenham)
Thu Oct 3	England v New Zealand (Twickenham, 3pm)
Fri Oct 4	Australia v Argentina (Llanelli, 2pm); France v Romania (Beziers, 8pm)
Sat Oct 5	Italy v US (Otley, 1pm); Scotland v Japan (Murrayfield, 3pm); Fiji v Canada (Bayonne, 8pm)
Sun Oct 6	Wales v Western Samoa (Cardiff, 1pm); Ireland v Zimbabwe (Dublin, 3pm).
Tue Oct 8	New Zealand v US (Gloucester, 1pm); England v Italy (Twickenham, 3pm); France v Fiji (Grenoble, 8pm).
Wed Oct 9	Wales v Argentina (Cardiff, 1pm); Scotland v Zimbabwe (Murrayfield, 3pm); Ireland v Japan (Dublin, 6pm); Australia v Western Samoa (Pontypool, 8pm); Canada v Romania (Toulouse, 8pm).
Fri Oct 11	England v US (Twickenham, 3pm)
Sat Oct 12	Scotland v Ireland (Murrayfield, 1pm); Wales v Australia (Cardiff, 3pm); France v Canada (Agen, 8pm).
Sun Oct 13	New Zealand v Italy (Leicester, 1pm); Fiji v Romania (Brive, 8pm).
Mon Oct 14	Zimbabwe v Japan (Belfast, 5pm); Argentina v Western Samoa (Pontypridd, 7pm).
Sat Oct 19	Winner Pool 2 v Runner-up Pool 3 (Murrayfield, 1pm); Winner Pool 4 v Runner-up Pool 1 (Paris, 2.45pm).
Sun Oct 20	Winner Pool 3 v Runner-up Pool 2 (Dublin, 1pm); Winner Pool 1 v Runner-up Pool 4 (Lille, 2.45pm).
Sat Oct 26	Dublin winner v Murrayfield winner (Murrayfield, 2.30pm); Lille winner v Paris winner (Dublin, 2.30pm).
Wed Oct 30	Third-place play-off (Cardiff, 2.30pm). Sat Nov 2 WORLD CUP FINAL (Twickenham, 2.30pm).

SHOOTING

WORLD CHAMPIONSHIPS
Moscow, Aug 6-20

Men

	Individual	Team
300m Free Rifle (3 x 40 shots):	Malcolm Cooper (GB) 1168	USSR 3467
300m Free Rifle (40 shots standing):	Glen Dubis (US) 385	France 1129
300m Free Rifle (40 shots kneeling):	Malcolm Cooper (GB) 392Sweden 1162	
300m Free Rifle (60 shots prone):	Harald Srevaag (Nor) 600	Norway 1786
Great Britain finished 3rd in the team event		
300m Standard Rifle (3 x 30 shots):	Glen Dubis (US) 582	United States 1719
Malcolm Cooper (GB) finished 3rd in the individual event		
50m Free Rifle (3 x 40 shots):	Eun-chul Lee (SKo) 1267.8	USSR 3490
50m Free Rifle (40 shots standing):	Eun-chul Lee (SKo) 387	USSR 1138
50m Free Rifle (40 shots kneeling):	Hubert Bichler (FRG) 393	West Germany 1170
50m Free Rifle (60 shots prone):	Viacheslav Bochkarev (USSR) 701.8 USSR 1784	
10m Air Rifle (60 shots):	Hannes Riederer (FRG) 697.4	West Germany 1766
Free Pistol (60 shots):	Spas Koprinkov 671	Hungary 1695
25m Rapid Fire Pistol (60 shots):	Ralf Schumann (GDR) 885	USSR 1766
10m Air Pistol (60 shots):	Bernardo Tobar (Col) 682.6	USSR 1732
25m Centre Fire Pistol (30 + 30 shots):	Sergey Pyzhianov (USSR) 590USSR 1762	
25m Standard Pistol (3 x 20 shots):	Miroslav Ignatyuk (USSR) 577USSR 1723	
10m Running Target (30 + 30 shots):	Manfred Kurzer (GDR) 664	China 1694
50m Running Target (30 + 30 shots):	Alexsey Poslov (USSR) 594Hungary 1767	
50m Running Target (40 shots mixed):	Ronghui Zang (Chn) 396	USSR 1174
Olympic Trap (200 targets):	Jorg Damme (GDR) 200	Italy 441
Skeet (200 targets):	Andrea Benelli (Ita) 198	Czechoslovakia 439
Double Trap (200 targets):	Bret Erickson (US) 175	France 364
Kevin Gill (GB) was 2nd in the individual event		

Women

	Individual	Team
50m Standard Rifle (3 x 20 shots):	Vesella Letcheva (USSR) 678.2	Bulgaria 1738
50m Standard Rifle (60 shots prone):	Irina Shilova (USSR) 596	USSR 1786
10m Air Rifle (40 shots):	Eva Joo (Hun) 496.4	United States 1171
25m Sport Rifle (30 + 30 shots):	Marina Logvimenko (USSR) 685	USSR 1751
10m Air Pistol (40 shots):	Jasna Sekaric (Yug) 483.8	USSR 1157
Olympic Trap 200 targets:	Pia Baldisserri (Ita) 189	Italy 414
Skeet 200 targets:	Svetlana Demina (USSR) 195	Hungary 429
Double Trap 160 targets:	Satu Pusila (Fin) 132	USSR 246

Leading Medal Positions

Total		G	S	B
46	USSR	20	15	11
17	United States	5	5	7
14	China	2	6	6

Britain were 11th equal in the table with two golds, one silver and two bronzes.

121ST NATIONAL RIFLE ASSOCIATION MEETING
Bisley, Jul 14-28
Queen's Prize: John Bloomfield (North London RC)
Hopton Challenge Cup: Stuart Collings (Windsor)
Elcho Challenge Shield: England
Ashburton Shield: Epsom College

King George V Challenge Cup: Surrey
Daily Telegraph Challenge Cup: Paul Kent (Old Epsomians)
Centenary Overseas Match: Britain
Inter Services Long Range Challenge Cup: UK Cadets
Mackinnon Challenge Cup: Canada
St George's Vase: Anthony Ringer (Uppingham Veterans)

MALCOLM COOPER'S TITLES

Commonwealth Games
1982 Small Bore Rifle (Prone) Pairs (with Mike Sullivan)
1982 Small Bore Rifle (3 Position) Pairs (with Barry Dagger)
1986 Small Bore Rifle (3 Position)
1986 Small Bore Rifle (3 Position) Pairs (with Sarah Cooper)

Olympic Games
1984 Small Bore Rifle (3 Position)
1988 Small Bore Rifle (3 Position)

World Championships
1978 Free Rifle
1982 Free Rifle
1986 Free Rifle (3 x 40)
1986 Free Rifle (3 x 20)
1986 English Match Standard Rifle
1990 Free Rifle (3 x 40)

CHAMPIONS

OLYMPIC GAMES
Men
Free Pistol
1896	Sumner Paine (US)
1900	Conrad Roderer (Swi)
1908	Paul von Asbroeck (Bel)
1912	Alfred Lane (US)
1920	Karl Frederick (US)
1936	Torsten Ullmann (Swe)
1948	Edwin Vazquez Cam (Per)
1952	Huelet Benner (US)
1956	Pentti Linnosvuo (Fin)
1960	Aleksey Gushchin (USSR)
1964	Vaino Markkanen (Fin)
1968	Grigory Kossykh (USSR)
1972	Ragner Skanakar (Swe)
1976	Uwe Potteck (GDR)
1980	Aleksandr Melentyev (USSR)
1984	Xu Haifeng (Chn)
1988	Sorin Babii (Rom)

Rapid Fire Pistol
1896	Jean Phrangoudis (Gre)
1900	Maurice Larrouy (Fra)
1912	Alfred Lane (US)
1920	Guilherme Paraense (Bra)
1924	Henry Bailey (US)
1932	Renzo Morigi (Ita)
1936	Cornelius van Oyen (Ger)
1948	Karoly Takacs (Hun)
1952	Karoly Takacs (Hun)
1956	Stefan Petrescu (Rom)
1960	William McMilliam (US)
1964	Pentti Linnosvuo (Fin)
1968	Jozef Zapedzki (Pol)
1972	Jozef Zapedzki (Pol)
1976	Norbert Klaar (GDR)
1980	Corneliu Ion (Rom)
1984	Takeo Kamachi (Jap)
1988	Afanasi Kouzmine (USSR)

Trap
1900	Roger de Barbarian (Fra)
1908	Walter Ewing (Can)
1912	James Graham (US)
1920	Mark Arie (US)
1924	Gyula Halasy (Hun)
1952	George Genereux (Can)
1956	Galliano Rossini (Ita)
1960	Ion Dumitrescu (Rom)
1964	Ennio Mattarelli (Ita)
1968	Bob Braithwaite (GB)
1972	Angelo Scalzone (Ita)
1976	Don Haldeman (US)
1980	Luciano Giovanetti (Ita)
1984	Luciano Giovanetti (Ita)
1988	Dmitri Monakov (USSR)

Running Game Target
1900	Louis Debray (Fra)
1972	Yokov Zheleznial (USSR)
1976	Aleksandr Gazov (USSR)
1980	Igor Sokolov (USSR)
1984	Li Yuwei (Chn)
1988	Tor Heiestad (Nor)

Small Bore Rifle (Prone)
1908	A. A. Carnell (GB)
1912	Frederick Hird (US)
1920	Lawrence Nuesslein (US)

1924	Pierre Coquelin de Lisle (Fra)
1932	Bertil Ronnmark (Swe)
1936	Willy Rogeberg (Nor)
1948	Arther Cook (US)
1952	Iosif Sarbu (Rom)
1956	Gerald Ouellette (Can)
1960	Peter Kohnke (FRG)
1964	Kaszlo Hammerl (Hun)
1968	Jan Kurka (Cze)
1972	Jo-Jun Li (NKo)
1976	Karl_Heinz Smieszek (FRG)
1980	Karoly Varga (Hun)
1984	Edward Etzel (US)
1988	Miroslav Varga (Cze)

Small Bore Rifle (Three Position)
1952	Erling Kongshaug (Nor)
1956	Anatoliy Bogdanov (USSR)
1960	Viktor Shamburkin (USSR)
1964	Lones Wigger (US)
1968	Bernd Klingner (FRG)
1972	John Writer (US)
1976	Lanny Bassham (US)
1980	Viktor Vlasov (USSR)
1984	Malcolm Cooper (GB)
1988	Malcolm Cooper (GB)

Skeet
1968	Yevgeniy Petrov (USSR)
1972	Konrad Wirnhier (FRG)
1976	Josef Panacek (Cze)
1980	Jans Kjeld Rasmussen (Den)
1984	Matthew Dryke (US)
1988	Axel Wegner (GDR)

Air Rifle
1984	Philippe Heberle (Fra)
1988	Goran Maksimovic (Yug)

Air Pistol
1988	Taniou Kiriakov (Bul)

Women
Sport Pistol
1984	Linda Thom (Can)
1988	Non Saluokvadze (USSR)

Small Bore Rifle (Three Position)
1984	Wu Xiaoxuan (Chn)
1988	Silvia Sperber (FRG)

Air Rifle
1984	Pat Spurgin (US)
1988	Irina Chilova (USSR)

Air Pistol
1988	Jasna Sekaric (Yug)

Most Olympic Medals
11 Carl Osburn (US)
8 Konrad Staheli (Swi)
8 Otto Olsen (Nor)

QUEEN'S PRIZE
*Principal event at the NRA meeting at Bisley every July.
Winners since 1981. (All British unless otherwise stated):*
1981	Geoffrey Ayling (Aus)
1982	Lindsay Peden
1983	Alain Marion (Can)
1984	David Richards
1985	John Bloomfield
1986	Geoffrey Cox
1987	Andrew Tucker
1988	John Pugsley
1989	Jeremy Thompson
1990	John Bloomfield

SNOOKER

GOODBYE STEVE, HELLO STEPHEN

Just when the British public appeared to be wearying of the script a little, snooker's soap opera took a fascinating turn by providing a new, young, and brilliant champion. Stephen Hendry, aged only 21, beat Jimmy White in the final of the World Championship at Sheffield to become the youngest winner and the first man in a decade who appeared not to be just a temporary usurper of Steve Davis's crown but a genuine successor.

Hendry beat White 18-12 ("his 18-12 overture", as someone put it) to set up the possibility of earning about £1½ million in the next year, but his manager Ian Doyle insisted Hendry would not be diverted by financial greed from his aim of winning more titles. White had put up the performance of the tournament in the semi-finals to withstand a storming comeback by Davis and win 16-14. But interest for the future centred on whether Davis would still be hungry enough to be able to retain his title. Hendry's triumph came only 6½ years after Doyle spotted him playing at Spencer's Club in Stirling, introduced himself and transformed both their lives. He is the first Scottish champion since Walter Donaldson in 1950; when the game languished in the years that followed, Donaldson converted his snooker room into a cowshed. Hendry should be luckier.

Davis passed one major landmark: the Rothmans Grand Prix was his 50th professional title and he won it by beating Dean Reynolds 10-0, his 31st whitewash. But he also had a number of surprising defeats including one to Hendry in the UK Open which many people, including the winner, saw as significant. "I had to prove I could beat Steve over a long distance," said Hendry. The technically-minded ascribed Davis's decline to a tendency to over-cut when potting to the left; others to the distraction of his impending marriage.

Another former champion had things far, far worse. Alex Higgins was banned for the whole of the 1990-91 season by the World Professional Billiards and snooker Association's one man disciplinary body, Gavin Lightman QC, after admitting threats of violence (to Dennis Taylor); actual violence (to the WPBSA's Press Officer), abusing the WPBSA's new chairman John Spencer and bringing the Association and snooker into disrepute. Higgins was docked 25 ranking points and ordered to pay £5,000 costs. There had been other incidents (the previous October he had grabbed a journalist round the neck and threatened another with a heavy ashtray; he was also fined £50 by Stockport magistrates after he admitted throwing a skateboard through his ex-wife's window) and there had been suggestions of a lifetime ban. The major trouble came in the World Cup at Bournemouth when Higgins apparently threatened to have Taylor shot after a dispute about money. He remained allowed to play exhibitions and minor events.

John Virgo, the chairman, and David Taylor were voted off the WPBSA board, which was abused by more level-headed people than Higgins. It was revealed that the Association had lost £553,408 and had been paying directors' car expenses at £1 a mile. Fred Davis, 76, had to end his 60-year professional career - probably a record in any sport - when he lost in the pro-ticket play-offs. However, two months later the professional closed shop was abolished and replaced with open snooker with regional qualifiers for each ranking tournament. This created space for both Davis and Allison Fisher, the women's world champion.

Soviet Colonel Vladimir Liakhov, Hero of the USSR, who spent a total of a year in space as a cosmonaut, was chosen to head the All-Union Billiards and Snooker Federation. Although pocket billiards is popular in the USSR, there were said to be only four full-sized snooker tables in Moscow and none anywhere else. Sister Simeon of The Adorers of the Sacred Heart became the first convent snooker champion when she beat Sister Mary John at the Tyburn Convent in West London. The Kenilworth Conservative Club withdrew its team from the local league in Warwickshire because, it was reported, visiting opponents were too scruffy.

1989-90

EMBASSY WORLD PROFESSIONAL CHAMPIONSHIP
Crucible Theatre, Sheffield, Apr 13-29

FIRST ROUND
STEVE DAVIS (Eng) beat Eddie Charlton (Aus) 10-1;
JOHN PARROTT (Eng) beat Mark Bennett (Wal) 10-9;
STEVE JAMES (Eng) beat Alex Higgins (NI) 10-5;
DEAN REYNOLDS (Eng) beat Peter Francisco (SA) 10-7;
WILLIE THORNE (Eng) beat Tony Drago (Mal) 10-4;
DOUG MOUNTJOY (Wal) beat Brady Gollan (Can) 10-8;
NEAL FOULDS (Eng) beat Dennis Taylor (NI) 10-8;
CLIFF THORBURN (Can) beat Cliff Wilson (Wal) 10-6;
MIKE HALLETT (Eng) beat Steve Newbury (Wal) 10-9;
TERRY GRIFFITHS (Wal) beat Nigel Gilbert (Eng) 10-4;
DARREN MORGAN (Wal) beat Joe Johnson (Eng) 10-8;
TONY KNOWLES beat Tony Chappel (Wal) 10-4; JOHN
VIRGO (Eng) beat Gary Wilkinson 10-6; STEPHEN
HENDRY (Sco) beat Alain Robidoux (Can) 10-7; TONY
MEO (Eng) beat Wayne Jones (Wal) 10-8; JIMMY
WHITE (Eng) beat Danny Fowler (Eng) 10-4.
*Steve James (v Higgins) had the first 16-red clearance in
recognised tournament play. This is only available after a
foul snooker, enabling the opponent to count a colour as
red.*

SECOND ROUND
DAVIS beat James 13-7; PARROTT beat Reynolds 13-11;
FOULDS beat Thorne 13-11; THORBURN beat Mountjoy
13-12; GRIFFITHS beat Knowles 13-6; MORGAN beat
Hallett 13-8; WHITE beat Virgo 13-6; HENDRY beat Meo
13-7.

QUARTER-FINALS
DAVIS beat Foulds 13-8; HENDRY beat Morgan 13-6;
WHITE beat Griffiths 13-5; PARROTT beat Thorburn 13-6.

SEMI-FINALS
WHITE beat Davis 16-14; HENDRY beat Parrott 16-11.

FINAL
HENDRY beat White 18-12
*Players underlined beat a player with a higher ranking
First Prize £120,000*

HIGHEST BREAKS
140 John Parrott; 135 Steve James; 131 Terry Griffiths
(Nigel Gilbert compiled a 135 break in the pre-television
rounds)

THE HURRICANE BLOWS OUT

**"I'm the most talented snooker player who
has ever been born. If I'd had Barry Hearn
as my Manager, I'd probably be the
richest too".**
Alex Higgins

**"I come from the Shankhill, you come from
Coalisland. The next time you are back in
Northern Ireland I will have you shot".**
*Higgins's alleged remark to Dennis Taylor after
a dispute during the World Cup final*

**"In my estimation Dennis Taylor is not a
snooker person. He is a money
person...He put money before country. He
belongs back in Coalisland. He's not fit to
wear this badge, the red hand of Ulster."**
*Higgins's public statement after World Cup
final*

"The crazy thing is that most people still side
with Higgins because they don't know
what sort of person he is. If they really
knew him he would not get the support
he does."
Taylor on Higgins

**"That's the last you'll see of the Hurricane.
Let's see how you do without me...it's the
most corrupt game in the world. The
Department of Trade and Industry should
look into the whole thing".**
Higgins, threatening to retire

**"Absolute tossers doing jobs for exorbitant
money."**
Higgins on the WPBSA executive

**"He will be reduced to exhibitions and
hustling in low-life billiard halls for a few
quid, a pitiable conclusion to a career
which for some time has been clearly
heading for self- destruction".**
Clive Everton, The Guardian

NEW HIGGINS SENSATION
**"The world of snooker was rocked to its
foundations last night when the crowded
auditorium of the Sheffield Crucible
witnessed amazing scenes involving
snooker's 'bad boy' Mr Alex 'Hurricane'
Higgins. Halfway through the first frame,
spectators and TV viewers gasped as the
veteran Northern Ireland ace and former
World Champion bent down over the table
and deliberately hit a ball. Said one close
observer: "I couldn't believe my eyes.
Alex had been behaving quite normally up
until then...."**
Private Eye

OTHER RANKING TOURNAMENTS
(All players from UK unless otherwise stated)

Hong Kong Open
Hong Kong, Aug 13
SEMI-FINALS
MIKE HALLETT beat Jimmy White 5-2; DENE O'KANE
(NZ) beat Gary Wilkinson 5-3
FINAL
HALLETT beat O'Kane 9-8
Highest Break: 135 Mike Hallett

555 Asian Open
Bangkok, Aug 27
SEMI-FINALS
STEPHEN HENDRY beat Gary Wilkinson 5-4; JAMES
WATTANA (Tha) beat Terry Griffiths 5-0
FINAL
HENDRY beat Wattana 9-6
Highest Break: 140 Stephen Hendry

BCE International
Trentham Gardens, Stoke-on-Trent, Sept 30
SEMI-FINALS
STEVE DAVIS beat Alain Robidoux (Can) 6-3;
STEPHEN HENDRY beat Nigel Bond 6-5
FINAL
DAVIS beat Hendry
Highest Break: 139 John Parrott

Rothmans Grand Prix
Hexagon Theatre, Reading, Oct 22
SEMI-FINALS
STEVE DAVIS beat Danny Fowler 9-2; DEAN
REYNOLDS beat James Wattana (Tha) 9-8
FINAL
DAVIS beat Reynolds 10-0
Highest Break: 141 Willie Thorne

Dubai Duty Free Classic
Al Nasr Stadium, Dubai, Nov 3
SEMI-FINALS
DOUG MOUNTJOY beat John Parrott 5-4; STEPHEN
HENDRY beat Danny Fowler 5-4
FINAL
HENDRY beat Mountjoy 9-2
Highest Break: 135 Tony Chappel

Stormseal UK Open
Guildhall, Preston, Dec 3
SEMI-FINALS
STEPHEN HENDRY beat Terry Griffiths 9-7; STEVE
DAVIS beat Gary Wilkinson 9-8
FINAL
HENDRY beat Davis 16-12
Highest Break: 141 Stephen Hendry

Mercantile Credit Classic
Blackpool, Jan 14
SEMI-FINALS
STEVE JAMES beat Steve Davis 6-4; WARREN KING
(Aus) beat Silvino Francisco (SA) 6-5
FINAL
JAMES beat King 10-6
Highest Break: 141 Steve James

Pearl Assurance British Open
Assembly Rooms, Derby, Mar 4
SEMI-FINALS
ALEX HIGGINS beat Steve James 9-3; BOB
CHAPERON (Can) beat Robert Marshall 9-5
FINAL
CHAPERON beat Higgins 10-8
Highest Break: 139 Steve Davis

European Open
Lyon, France, Mar 18
SEMI-FINALS
STEPHEN HENDRY beat Steve Davis 6-3; JOHN
PARROTT beat Steve James 6-3
FINAL
PARROTT beat Hendry 10-6
Highest break: 134 Nick Terry

ALEX HIGGINS - THE HIGHS AND LOWS

Highs

1968	Northern Ireland amateur champion
1972	Youngest ever World champion
1978	Benson & Hedges Masters champion
1980	British Gold Cup winner
1981	Benson & Hedges Masters champion
1982	World champion
1983	Irish Professional and UK champion
1984	World Doubles champion, with Jimmy White
1985,6,7	Member of winning Irish World Cup team
1989	Irish Professional and Irish Masters champion

Lows

1973	Fined £100 for misconduct during the World Championship
1980	Fined £200 for abusive language and bringing the game into disrepute. Fined £200 following complaints about him during the Tolly Cobbold Classic and Gus Demmy Pro-am
1981	Fined £200 and had two ranking points deducted for ungentlemanly conduct at an exhibition match at the Herringthorpe Leisure Centre.
1982	Fined £1000 following incidents at Irish Masters and World Championships
1984	Suspended from competing in New Zealand and Australian events
1985	Fined £1500 for swearing during the Benson & Hedges Masters
1986	Fined £2000 for bringing the game into disrepute following incidents at the Mercantile Credit Classic
1987	Fined £12,000 and suspended from five tournaments for various offenses, including head-butting Paul Hatherell, a WPBSA official, at the UK Open
1988	Severely reprimanded and given a £1500 suspended fine for refusing to take a drug test during a non-ranking event at Glasgow
1989	Fined £500 for being abusive to Kevin Norton, tournament director of the Irish Masters. Fined £3000 and reprimanded for his failure to attend press conferences, foul and abusive language to journalists, assaulting a journalist, and foul and abusive language to two WPBSA officials
1990	Banned for ten months, had 25 ranking points deducted and ordered to pay £5000 costs after admitting (a) punching the WPBSA Press Officer Colin Randle; (b) bringing the WPBSA and snooker into disrepute with his comments after that; (c) abusing the WPBSA Chairman John Spencer and (d) threatening Dennis Taylor with violence at Bournemouth

OTHER TOURNAMENTS

Regal Masters
STEPHEN HENDRY beat Terry Griffiths 10-1

Norwich Union Grand Prix
JOE JOHNSON beat Stephen Hendry 5-3

World Amateur Championship
KEN DOHERTY (Ire) beat Jonathan Birch (Eng) 11-2

Everest World March-Play Championship
JIMMY WHITE beat John Parrott 18-9

Benson & Hedges Masters
STEPHEN HENDRY beat John Parrott 9-4
Hendry's £70,000 winner's cheque took his career earnings past £1 million

Senator Windows Welsh Professional Championship
DARREN MORGAN beat Doug Mountjoy 9-7

Benson & Hedges Irish Masters
STEVE DAVIS beat Dennis Taylor 9-4

Continental Airlines London Masters
STEPHEN HENDRY beat John Parrott 4-2

Stormseal Matchroom League
1st: STEVE DAVIS 2nd: Stephen Hendry
Relegated: John Parrott and Cliff Thorburn (Can)

BCE English Amateur Championship
JOE SWAIL (Ire) beat Alan McManus (Sco) 13-11
Swail was the first Irish winner for 38 years

WOMEN'S SNOOKER

British Open
ALLISON FISHER beat Georgina Alpin 3-1

Pontin's World Championship
ALLISON FISHER beat Anne-Marie Farren 6-5

WPBSA British Championship
ALLISON FISHER beat Stacey Hillyard 4-1

UK Championship
ALLISON FISHER beat Stacey Hillyard 5-0
Fisher's fifth title

WORLD RANKINGS 1990-91

(Last seasons figures in brackets)

1 **Stephen Hendry (3)**
2 **Steve Davis (1)**
3 **John Parrott (2)**
4 **Jimmy White (4)**
5 **Doug Mountjoy (10)**
6 **Terry Griffiths (5)**
7 **Mike Hallett (6)**
8 **Dean Reynolds (15)**
9 **Steve James (16)**
10 **Dennis Taylor (8)**
11 **Willie Thorne (9)**
12 **Martin Clarke (17)**
13 **Neal Foulds (20)**
14 **John Virgo (13)**
15 **Tony Meo (14)**
16 **Alain Robidoux (35)**

Alex Higgins originally 14th (24) but subsequently had 25 ranking points deducted.

YOUNGEST WORLD CHAMPIONS

21yr 3m Stephen Hendry (1990)
23yr 1m Alex Higgins (1972)
23yr 8m Steve Davis (1981) *
26yr 1m Joe Davis (1927)
31yr 6m Terry Griffiths (1979)

Davis also won when he was 25, 26, 29 and 30

──── CHAMPIONS ────

WORLD PROFESSIONAL CHAMPIONSHIP

(Embassy World Professional Championship since 1976)
All winners British unless otehwise stated

1927	Joe Davis	20-11	Tom Dennis
1928	Joe Davis	16-13	Fred Lawrence
1929	Joe Davis	19-14	Tom Dennis
1930	Joe Davis	25-12	Tom Dennis
1931	Joe Davis	25-21	Tom Dennis
1932	Joe Davis	30-19	Clark McConachy (NZ)
1933	Joe Davis	25-18	Willie Smith
1934	Joe Davis	25-23	Tom Newman
1935	Joe Davis	25-20	Willie Smith
1936	Joe Davis	34-27	Horace Lindrum (Aus)
1937	Joe Davis	32-29	Horace Lindrum (Aus)
1938	Joe Davis	37-24	Sidney Smith
1939	Joe Daivis	43-30	Sidney Smith
1940	Joe Davis	37-36	Fred Davis
1946	Joe Davis	78-67	Horace Lindrum (Aus)
1947	Walter Donaldson	82-63	Fred Davis
1948	Fred Davis	84-61	Walter Donaldson
1949	Fred Davis	80-65	Walter Donaldson
1950	Walter Donaldson	51-46	Fred Davis
1951	Fred Davis	58-39	Walter Donaldson
1952	Horace Lindrum	94-49	Clark McConachy (NZ)

Professional Match-Play Championship

1952	Fred Davis	38-35	Walter Donaldson
1953	Fred Davis	37-34	Walter Donaldson
1954	Fred Davis	39-21	Walter Donaldson
1955	Fred Davis	37-34	John Pulman
1956	Fred Davis	38-35	John Pulman
1957	John Pulman	39-34	Jackie Rea

Challenge Matches

1964	John Pulman	19-16	Fred Davis
1964	John Pulman	40-33	Rex Williams
1965	John Pulman	37-36	Fred Davis
1965	John Pulman	25-22	Rex Williams
1965	John Pulman	39-12	Freddie van Rensburg (SA)
1966	John Pulman	5-2	Fred Davis
1968	John Pulman	39-34	Eddie Charlton (Aus)
1969	John Spencer	37-34	Gary Owen
1970	Ray Reardon	37-33	John Pulman
1971	*John Spencer	37-29	Warren Simpson (Aus)
1972	Alex Higgins	37-32	John Spencer
1973	Ray Reardon	38-32	Eddie Charlton (Aus)
1974	Ray Reardon	22-12	Graham Miles
1975	Ray Reardon	31-30	Eddie Charlton (Aus)
1976	Ray Reardon	27-16	Alex Higgins
1977	John Spencer	25-21	Cliff Thorburn (Can)
1978	Ray Reardon	25-18	Perrie Mans (SA)
1979	Terry Griffiths	24-16	Dennis Taylor
1980	Cliff Thorburn (Can)	18-16	Alex Higgins
1981	Steve Davis	18-12	Doug Mountjoy
1982	Alex Higgins	18-15	Ray Reardon
1983	Steve Davis	18-6	Cliff Thorburn (Can)
1984	Steve Davis	18-16	Jimmy White
1985	Dennis Taylor	18-17	Steve Davis
1986	Joe Johnson	18-12	Steve Davis
1987	Steve Davis	18-14	Joe Johnson
1988	Steve Davis	18-11	Terry Griffiths
1989	Steve Davis	18-3	John Parrott
1990	Stephen Hendry	18-12	Jimmy White

* *Played November 1970*

RANKING TOURNAMENT WINNERS

BCE International

1981-84 Jameson International; 1985 Goya International; 1986 BCE International; 1987-88 Fidelity Unit Trust International

1982 Tony Knowles
1983 Steve Davis
1984 Steve Davis
1985 Cliff Thorburn (Can)
1986 Neal Foulds
1987 Steve Davis
1988 Steve Davis
1989 Steve Davis

> **"** We shall not be following a totally commercial trial. With Stephen it's all about winning matches, winning titles and being No. 1"
> *Ian Doyle, Stephen Hendry's Manager*

"I said someone would have to play their head off to beat me and someone just did".
Steve Davis after losing to Jimmy White at Sheffield

"This is war. But we are not going to take it lying down and intend to get the title back".
Barry Hearn, Davis's Manager

"Sir, may a wine merchant question your snooker correspondent, Steve Acteson. He reported that Hendry missed 'potable reds'. Should this not have been 'pottable'?...If Mr Hendry was really missing 'potable' reds - a condition with which I heartily sympathise - I should recommend Cahors, Fitou or Côtes du Ventoux".
Letters to The Times *from Peter F Portwood of Truro*

"That's it. I don't play for fun."
Fred Davis, on losing his professional status after 60 years

"Yeh, I go to the toilet, I know what you must be thinking, but that's the price I pay. **"**
Kirk Stevens, former cocaine user.

Rothmans Grand Prix
1982-83 Professional Player's Tournament; 1984-Rothmans Grand Prix

1982	Ray Reardon
1983	Tony Knowles
1984	Dennis Taylor
1985	Steve Davis
1986	Jimmy White
1987	Stephen Hendry
1988	Steve Davis
1989	Steve Davis

Mercantile Credit Classic
1984 Lada Classic; 1985-Mercantile Credit Classic

1984	Steve Davis
1985	Willie Thorne
1986	Jimmy White
1987	Steve Davis
1988	Steve Davis
1989	Doug Mountjoy
1990	Steve James

Stormseal United Kingdom Open
1984-85 Coral UK Open; 1986-88 Tennents UK Open

1984	Steve Davis
1985	Steve Davis
1986	Steve Davis
1987	Steve Davis
1988	Doug Mountjoy
1989	Stephen Hendry

Pearl Assurance British Open
1985-87 Dulux British Open; 1988 MIM Britannia British Open; 1989 Anglian British Open

1985	Silviano Francisco (SA)

1986	Steve Davis
1987	Jimmy White
1988	Stephen Hendry
1989	Tony Meo
1990	Bob Chaperon (Can)

BCE Canadian Masters
1988	Jimmy White

European Open
1989	John Parrott
1990	John Parrott

RANKING TOURNAMENT WINS

22	**Steve Davis**
6	**Stephen Hendry**
5	**Ray Reardon**
4	**Jimmy White**
2	**Tony Knowles**
2	**Doug Mountjoy**
2	**Dennis Taylor**
2	**Cliff Thorburn (Can)**
2	**John Parrott**
1	**Neal Foulds**
1	**Silviano Francisco (SA)**
1	**Tony Meo**
1	**Willie Thorne**
1	**John Spencer**
1	**Alex Higgins**
1	**Terry Griffiths**
1	**Joe Jackson**
1	**Mike Hallett**
1	**Steve James**
1	**Bob Chaperon (Can)**

OTHER MAJOR TOURNAMENTS
Pot Black

1969	Ray Reardon
1970	John Spencer
1971	John Spencer
1972	Eddie Charlton (Aus)
1973	Eddie Charlton (Aus)
1974	Graham Miles
1975	Graham Miles
1976	John Spencer
1977	Perrie Mans (SA)
1978	Doug Mountjoy
1979	Ray Reardon
1980	Eddie Charlton (Aus)
1981	Cliff Thorburn (Can)
1982	Steve Davis
1983	Steve Davis
1984	Terry Griffiths
1985	Doug Mountjoy
1986	Jimmy White

(discontinued)

Benson & Hedges Masters

1975	John Spencer
1976	Ray Reardon
1977	Doug Mountjoy
1978	Alex Higgins
1979	Perrie Mans (SA)
1980	Terry Griffiths
1981	Alex Higgins
1982	Steve Davis
1983	Cliff Thorburn (Can)

1984	Jimmy White
1985	Cliff Thorburn (Can)
1986	Cliff Thorburn (Can)
1987	Dennis Taylor
1988	Steve Davis
1989	Stephen Hendry
1990	Stephen Hendry

Coral UK Championship
Sponsored by Coral since 1978

1977	Patsy Fagan
1978	Doug Mountjoy
1979	John Virgo
1980	Steve Davis
1981	Steve Davis
1982	Terry Griffiths
1983	Alex Higgins

Became a ranking event in 1984

Benson & Hedges Irish Masters

1978	John Spencer
1979	Doug Mountjoy
1980	Terry Griffiths
1981	Terry Griffiths
1982	Terry Griffiths
1983	Steve Davis
1984	Steve Davis
1985	Jimmy White
1986	Jimmy White
1987	Steve Davis
1988	Steve Davis
1989	Alex Higgins
1990	Steve Davis

British Car Rental World Cup
Previously sponsored by five different firms

1979	Wales (Griffiths, Reardon, Mountjoy)
1980	Wales (Griffiths, Reardon, Mountjoy)
1981	England (S.Davis, Taylor, Spencer)
1982	Canada (Thorburn, Stevens, Werbeniuk)
1983	England (Knowles, Meo, S.Davis)
1984	Not held
1985	All-Ireland (Higgins, Taylor, Hughes)
1986	Ireland 'A' (Higgins, Taylor, Hughes)
1987	Ireland 'A' (Higgins, Taylor, Hughes)
1988	England (S.Davis, Foulds, White)
1989	England (S.Davis, Foulds, White)
1990	Canada (Thorburn, Robidoux, Chaperon)

Lada Classic

1980	John Spencer
1981	*Steve Davis
1982	Terry Griffiths
1983	Steve Davis

*Played in December 1980
Became ranking event in 1984

Everest World Match-Play Championship

1988	Steve Davis
1989	Jimmy White

WORLD AMATEUR CHAMPIONS

1963	Gary Owen
1966	Gary Owen
1968	David Taylor
1970	Jonathan Barron
1972	Ray Edmonds
1974	Ray Edmonds
1976	Doug Mountjoy
1978	Cliff Wilson
1980	Jimmy White
1982	Terry Parsons
1984	O B (Omprakash) Agrawal (Ind)
1985	Paul Mifsud (Malta)
1986	Paul Mifsud (Malta)
1987	James Wattana (Tha)
1989	Ken Doherty (Ire)

OFFICIAL MAXIMUM BREAKS

22 Jan	1955	Joe Davis (Exhibition)
22 Dec	1965	Rex Williams (Exhibition)
11 Jan	1982	Steve Davis (Lada Classic)
23 Apr	1983	Cliff Thorburn (Embassy W/Champs)
28 Jan	1984	Kirk Stevens (B&H Masters)
17 Nov	1987	Willie Thorne (Tennents UK Champs)
20 Feb	1988	Tony Meo (Matchroom League)
24 Sep	1988	Alain Robidoux (European Open)
18 Feb	1989	John Rea (Scottish Pro Champs)
8 Mar	1989	Cliff Thorburn (Matchroom League)

——— 1991 ———

Jan 1-12 Mercantile Credit Classic (Blackpool); *Jan 13-26* World Masters (NEC Birmingham); *Feb 3-10* Benson and Hedges International Masters (Wembley); *Feb 17 - Mar 2* Pearl Assurance British Open (Derby); *Apr 2-7* Benson and Hedges Irish Masters (Kill, Co. Kildare); *Apr 20 - May 6* EMBASSY WORLD PROFESSIONAL CHAMPIONSHIP (Crucible Theatre, Sheffield)

SPEEDWAY

WORLD CHAMPIONSHIPS
Individual
Odsal, Bradford, Sep 1
1 Per Jonsson (Reading/Sweden) 13pts
2 Shawn Moran (Belle Vue/US) 13pts
(Jonsson won run-off)
3 Todd Wiltshire (Reading/Aus) 12pts
4 Hans Nielsen (Oxford/Den) 11pts
5 Jimmy Nilsen (Swindon/Swe) 10pts
6 Henrik Gustafsson (Swe) 9pts
  Kelvin Tatum (Coventry/Eng) 9pts

Pairs
Landshut, West Germany, Jul 21
1 Hans Nielsen & Jan Pedersen (Denmark) 43pts
2 Todd Wiltshire & Leigh Adams (Australia) 41pts
3 Zoltan Andorjan & Sandor Tihany (Hungary) 34pts

Long Track
Herxheim, West Germany, Aug 19
1 Simon Wigg (Eng) 37pts
2 Karl Maier (FRG) 30pts
3 Hans-Otto Pingel (FRG) 30pts

Team
Pardubice, Czechoslovakia, Sep 15
1 United States 37pts
(Kevin Moran, Sam Ermolenko, Shawn Moran, Billy Hamill, Rick Miller)
2 England 34pts
3 Denmark 30pts

NATIONAL LEAGUE RIDERS' CHAMPIONSHIP
Coventry, Sep 15
1 Andy Grahame (Wimbledon) 14pts
2 Chris Louis (Ipswich) 13pts
3 Craig Boyce (Poole) 11pts

SUNBRITE TEST MATCHES
First Test
Oxford, Apr 18
ENGLAND 63 Denmark 45
Second Test
Bradford, Apr 22
ENGLAND 62 Denmark 46
Third Test
Wolverhampton, Apr 30
ENGLAND 61 Denmark 47
England won the series 3-0

SUNBRITE BRITISH LEAGUE

	P	W	D	L	Pts
1 Oxford	32	22	1	9	58
2 Wolverhampton	32	19	2	11	52
3 Cradley Heath	32	19	3	10	51
4 Belle Vue	32	19	2	11	50
5 Coventry	32	15	3	14	41
6 Swindon	32	12	1	19	33
7 Reading	32	13	1	18	32
8 Bradford	32	9	2	21	23
9 King's Lynn	32	8	1	23	20

Points total includes bonus points

NATIONAL LEAGUE

	P	W	D	L	Pts
1 Poole	33	26	1	7	53
2 Wimbledon	34	23	2	9	48
3 Berwick	34	23	0	11	46
4 Ipswich	34	23	0	11	46
5 Exeter	34	19	1	14	39
6 Hackney	34	19	1	14	39
7 Eastbourne	34	19	0	15	38
8 Edinburgh	34	19	0	15	38
9 Glasgow	34	17	0	17	34
10 Stoke	34	16	1	17	33
11 Peterborough	33	16	0	18	32
12 Arena Essex	34	15	2	17	32
13 Middlesbrough	34	14	0	20	28
14 Rye House	34	13	0	21	26
15 Newcastle	34	11	2	21	24
16 Mildenhall	34	10	1	23	21
17 Long Eaton	34	9	1	24	19
18 Milton Keynes	34	7	2	25	16

CHAMPIONS

BRITISH SPEEDWAY LEAGUE
Champions since formation of two divisions in 1968. Known as British League and National League since 1968.

	British League	National League
1968	Coventry	Belle Vue Colts
1969	Poole	Belle Vue Colts
1970	Belle Vue	Canterbury
1971	Belle Vue	Eastbourne
1972	Belle Vue	Crewe
1973	Reading	Boston
1974	Exeter	Birmingham
1975	Ipswich	Birmingham
1976	Ipswich	Newcastle
1977	White City	Eastbourne
1978	Coventry	Canterbury
1979	Coventry	Mildenhall
1980	Reading	Rye House
1981	Cradley Heath	Middlesbrough
1982	Belle Vue	Newcastle
1983	Cradley Heath	Newcastle
1984	Ipswich	Long Eaton
1985	Oxford	Ellesmere Port
1986	Oxford	Eastbourne
1987	Coventry	Eastbourne
1988	Coventry	Hackney
1989	Oxford	Poole

Most Titles
Division One/British League
10 Belle Vue; **8** Wembley; **7** Wimbledon; Coventry

BRITISH LEAGUE RIDERS' CHAMPIONSHIP

1965	Barry Briggs (Swindon)	1978	Ole Olsen (Coventry)
1966	Barry Briggs (Swindon)	1979	John Louis (Ipswich)
1967	Barry Briggs (Swindon)	1980	Les Collins (Leicester)
1968	Barry Briggs (Swindon)	1981	Kenny Carter (Halifax)
1969	Barry Briggs (Swindon)	1982	Kenny Carter (Halifax)
1970	Barry Briggs (Swindon)	1983	Erik Gundersen (Cradley Heath)
1971	Ivan Mauger (Belle Vue)	1984	Chris Morton (Belle Vue)
1972	Ole Olsen (Wolverhampton)	1985	Erik Gundersen (Cradley Heath)
1973	Ivan Mauger (Exeter)	1986	Hans Nielsen (Oxford)
1974	Peter Collins (Belle Vue)	1987	Hans Nielsen (Oxford)
1975	Peter Collins (Belle Vue)	1988	Jan Pedersen (Cradley Heath)
1976	Ole Olsen (Coventry)	1989	Shawn Moran (Belle Vue)
1977	Ole Olsen (Coventry)		

WORLD CHAMPIONS

	Individual	*Pairs*	*Team*	*Long Track*
1936	Lionel Van Praag (Aus)	-	-	-
1937	Jack Milne (US)	-	-	-
1938	Bluey Wilkinson (Aus)	-	-	-
1949	Tommy Price (Eng)	-	-	-
1950	Freddie Williams (Wal)	-	-	-
1951	Jack Young (Aus)	-	-	-
1952	Jack Young (Aus)	-	-	-
1953	Freddie Williams (Wal)	-	-	-
1954	Ronnie Moore (NZ)	-	-	-
1955	Peter Craven (Eng)	-	-	-
1956	Ove Fundin (Swe)	-	-	-
1957	Barry Briggs (NZ)	-	-	-
1958	Barry Briggs (NZ)	-	-	-
1959	Ronnie Moore (NZ)	-	-	-
1960	Ove Fundin (Swe)	-	Sweden	-
1961	Ove Fundin (Swe)	-	Poland	-
1962	Peter Craven (Eng)	-	Sweden	-
1963	Ove Fundin (Swe)	-	Sweden	-
1964	Barry Briggs (NZ)	-	Sweden	-
1965	Bjorn Knutsson (Swe)	-	Poland	-
1966	Barry Briggs (NZ)	-	Poland	-
1967	Ove Fundin (Swe)	-	Sweden	-
1968	Ivan Mauger (NZ)	-	Great Britain	-
1969	Ivan Mauger (NZ)	-	Poland	-
1970	Ivan Mauger (NZ)	New Zealand (Moore/Mauger)	Sweden	-
1971	Ole Olsen (Den)	Poland (Szczakiel/Wyglenda)	Great Britain	Ivan Mauger (NZ)
1972	Ivan Mauger (NZ)	England (Wilson/Betts)	Great Britain	Ivan Mauger (NZ)
1973	Jerzy Szczakiel (Pol)	Sweden (Michanek/Jansson)	Great Britain	Ole Olsen (Den)
1974	Anders Michanek (Swe)	Sweden (Michanek/Sjosten)	England	Egon Muller (FRG)
1975	Ole Olsen (Den)	Sweden (Michanek/Jansson)	England	Egon Muller (FRG)
1976	Peter Collins (Eng)	England (Simmons/Louis)	Australia	Egon Muller (FRG)
1977	Ivan Mauger (NZ)	England (Simmons/Collins)	England	Anders Michanek (Swe)
1978	Ole Olsen (Den)	England (Simmons/Kennett)	Denmark	Egon Muller (FRG)
1979	Ivan Mauger (NZ)	Denmark (Olsen/Nielsen)	New Zealand	Alois Weisbock (FRG)
1980	Michael Lee (Eng)	England (Jessup/Collins)	England	Karl Maier (FRG)
1981	Bruce Penhall (US)	United States (Penhall/Schwartz)	Denmark	Michael Lee (Eng)
1982	Bruce Penhall (US)	United States (Sigalos/Schwartz)	United States	Karl Maier (FRG)
1983	Egon Muller (FRG)	England (Carter/Collins)	Denmark	Shawn Moran (US)
1984	Erik Gundersen (Den)	England (Collins/Morton)	Denmark	Erik Gundersen (Den)
1985	Erik Gundersen (Den)	Denmark (Gundersen/Knudsen)	Denmark	Simon Wigg (Eng)
1986	Hans Nielsen (Den)	Denmark (Gundersen/Nielsen)	Denmark	Erik Gundersen (Den)
1987	Hans Nielsen (Den)	Denmark (Gundersen/Nielsen)	Denmark	Karl Maier (FRG)
1988	Erik Gundersen (Den)	Denmark (Gundersen/Nielsen)	Denmark	Karl Maier (FRG)
1989	Hans Nielsen (Den)	Denmark (Gundersen/Nielsen)	England	Simon Wigg (Eng)
1990	Per Jonsson (Swe)	Denmark (Nielsen/Pedersen)	United States	Simon Wigg (Eng)

Most Wins

Individual	6 Ivan Mauger; 5 Ove Fundin; 4 Barry Briggs; 3 Ole Olsen, Hans Nielsen, Erik Gundersen
Pairs	- Team: 7 England, Denmark; 3 Sweden
	- Ind: 5 Erik Gundersen (Den), Hans Nielsen (Den); 4 Peter Collins (Eng)
Team	- Team: 8 Denmark; 6 Sweden; 5 England; 4 Britain
	- Ind: 8 Hans Nielsen (Den); 7 Erik Gundersen (Den); 6 Ove Fundin (Swe)
Long Track:	4 Egon Muller (FRG), Karl Maier (FRG); 3 Simon Wigg (Eng)

SQUASH

Jahangir Khan achieved his greatest ambition when he won a record ninth British Open title aged only 26. Afterwards he was embraced by his father Roshan Khan (the 1956 champion) who was visiting England for the first time in 25 years. Jahangir dismissed thoughts of retirement for "another three or four years".

"This is the best day of my life," he said. "I don't feel I want to stop yet." However, only a week later he was beaten by Chris Dittmar in the European Open semi-finals. Susan Devoy won her seventh successive All-England title when she beat the 12th seed Suzanne Horner, who was hoping to become the first British winner in 29 years. Martine Le Moignan, the 1989 world champion, posed in camisole and French knickers for the cover of *Squash Player International*.

1990

HI-TEC BRITISH OPEN
Wembley Conference Centre, Apr 14-23
Men

QUARTER-FINALS
CHRIS DITTMAR (Aus) beat Tristan Nancarrow (Aus) 9-0 9-1 9-1; JAHANGIR KHAN (Pak) beat Jason Nicolle (Eng) 9-0 9-1 9-3; RODNEY MARTIN (Aus) beat Chris Robertson (Aus) 9-2 9-5 6-9 9-4; JANSHER KHAN (Pak) beat Chris Walker (Eng) 9-1 9-1 9-1

SEMI-FINALS
JAHANGIR beat Dittmar 9-6 9-6 9-5; MARTIN beat Jansher 1-9 10-8 9-0 10-9

FINAL
JAHANGIR beat Martin 9-6 10-8 9-1
Jahangir won title for a record 9th time

Women

QUARTER-FINALS
SUSAN DEVOY (NZ) beat Alison Cumings (Eng) 9-5 9-2 9-5; MICHELLE MARTIN (Aus) beat Lisa Opie (Eng) 9-6 6-9 9-4 2-9 9-2; SUZANNE HORNER (Eng) beat Robyn Lambourne (Aus) 9-1 8-10 4-9 9-2 9-4; LUCY SOUTTER (Eng) beat Danielle Drady (Aus) 4-9 2-9 9-6 9-3 9-5

SEMI-FINALS
DEVOY beat Martin 5-9 10-8 9-4 9-5; HORNER beat Soutter 9-2 9-5 9-1

FINAL
DEVOY beat Horner 9-2 1-9 9-3 9-3
Devoy's seventh consecutive title

HI-TEC EUROPEAN OPEN
Karlsruhe, West Germany, Apr 30

SEMI-FINALS
CHRIS DITTMAR (Aus) beat Jahangir Khan (Pak) 15-9 15-10 4-15 13-15 15-9; CHRIS ROBERTSON (Aus) beat Brett Martin (Aus) 15-9 9-15 15-9 15-9

FINAL
ROBERTSON beat Dittmar 15-10 10-15 15-6 15-6

EUROPEAN TEAM CHAMPIONSHIPS
Zurich, May 2-6
Men

THIRD PLACE PLAY-OFF
FINLAND   5   Sweden   0

FINAL
ENGLAND   **5**   West Germany   0
This was the first time since 1977 that the final has not been between England and Sweden.

Women

THIRD PLACE PLAY-OFF
FINLAND   3   Ireland   0

FINAL
ENGLAND   3   Holland   0
This was the first time since competition started in 1978 that the final has not been between England and Ireland. England have won every championship.

PIMMS PREMIER LEAGUE

Final Table		P	W	L	F	A	Pts
1	Wizards	14	12	2	51	19	75
2	Cannons	14	12	2	49	21	73
3	Village	14	11	3	49	21	71
4	Lambs	14	8	6	43	27	59
5	Abbeydale	14	6	8	28	42	40
6	Edgbaston	14	3	11	24	46	30
7	Northern	14	3	11	21	49	27
8	Surbiton	14	1	13	15	55	17

WORLD RANKINGS
(Summer 1990)
Men
1 Jahangir Khan (Pak)
2 Jansher Khan (Pak)
3 Chris Robertson (Aus)
4 Chris Dittmar (Aus)
5 Rodney Martin (Aus)
Women
1 Susan Devoy (NZ)
2 Lisa Opie (GB)
3 Danielle Drady (Aus)
4 Martine Le Moignan (GB)
5 Robyn Lambourne (Aus)

1989

MEN'S WORLD CHAMPIONSHIP
Kuala Lumpur, Oct 3-8

QUARTER-FINALS
CHRIS DITTMAR (Aus) beat Rodney Eyles (Aus) 15-3 15-8 10-15 15-12; JAHANGIR KHAN (Pak) beat Mark Maclean (Sco) 15-11 15-11 15-12; JANSHER KHAN (Pak) beat Bryan Beeson (Eng) 15-7 15-2 15-3; CHRIS ROBERTSON (Aus) beat Brett Martin (Aus) 15-12 17-15 8-15 15-13

SEMI-FINALS
DITTMAR beat Jahangir 9-15 15-12 9-15 15-9 15-12; JANSHER KHAN beat Robertson 15-3 15-12 15-6

FINAL
JANSHER beat Dittmar 10-15 6-15 15-4 15-11 15-10

WORLD TEAM CHAMPIONSHIP
Singapore, Oct 9-17

SEMI-FINALS
PAKISTAN beat England 3-0; AUSTRALIA beat New Zealand 3-0

THIRD PLACE PLAY-OFF
ENGLAND beat New Zealand 2-1

FINAL
AUSTRALIA beat Pakistan 3-0

——— CHAMPIONS ———

WORLD OPEN CHAMPIONSHIP
(Not held 1978)
Men
1976	Geoff Hunt (Aus)
1977	Geoff Hunt (Aus)
1979	Geoff Hunt (Aus)
1980	Geoff Hunt (Aus)
1981	Jahangir Khan (Pak)
1982	Jahangir Khan (Pak)
1983	Jahangir Khan (Pak)
1984	Jahangir Khan (Pak)
1985	Jahangir Khan (Pak)
1986	Ross Norman (NZ)
1987	Jansher Khan (Pak)
1988	Jahangir Khan (Pak)
1989	Jansher Khan (Pak)

Women
1976	Heather McKay (Aus)
1979	Heather McKay (Aus)
1981	Rhonda Thorne (Aus)
1983	Vicki Cardwell (Aus)
1985	Susan Devoy (NZ)
1987	Susan Devoy (NZ)
1989	Martine Le Moignan (GB)

WOMEN'S WORLD TEAM CHAMPIONSHIP
1979	Great Britain
1981	Australia
1983	Australia
1985	England
1987	England
1989	England

WORLD AMATEUR/ISRF CHAMPIONSHIPS
From 1987 a Team competition only
Individual
1967	Geoff Hunt (Aus)
1969	Geoff Hunt (Aus)
1971	Geoff Hunt (Aus)
1973	Cam Nancarrow (Aus)
1975	Kevin Shawcross (Aus)
1977	Maqsood Ahmed (Pak)
1979	Jahangir Khan (Pak)
1981	Steve Bowditch (Aus)
1983	Jahangir Khan (Pak)
1985	Jahangir Khan (Pak)

Team
1967	Australia
1969	Australia
1971	Australia
1973	Australia

1975	Great Britain
1977	Pakistan
1979	Great Britain
1981	Pakistan
1983	Pakistan
1985	Pakistan
1987	Pakistan
1989	Australia

BRITISH OPEN CHAMPIONSHIPS
First held in 1922 for women; 1930 for men
Winners since 1971
Men
1971	Jonah Barrington (GB)
1972	Jonah Barrington (GB)
1973	Jonah Barrington (GB)
1974	Geoff Hunt (Aus)
1975	Qamar Zaman (Pak)
1976	Geoff Hunt (Aus)
1977	Geoff Hunt (Aus)
1978	Geoff Hunt (Aus)
1979	Geoff Hunt (Aus)
1980	Geoff Hunt (Aus)
1981	Geoff Hunt (Aus)
1982	Jahangir Khan (Pak)
1983	Jahangir Khan (Pak)
1984	Jahangir Khan (Pak)
1985	Jahangir Khan (Pak)
1986	Jahangir Khan (Pak)
1987	Jahangir Khan (Pak)
1988	Jahangir Khan (Pak)
1989	Jahangir Khan (Pak)
1990	Jahangir Khan (Pak)

Most wins
9 Jahangir Khan; **8** Geoff Hunt; **7** Hashim Khan; **6** Abdel Fattah Amr Bey, Jonah Barrington

Women
1971	Heather McKay (Aus)
1972	Heather McKay (Aus)
1973	Heather McKay (Aus)
1974	Heather McKay (Aus)
1975	Heather McKay (Aus)
1976	Heather McKay (Aus)
1977	Heather McKay (Aus)
1978	Susan Newman (Aus)
1979	Barbara Well (Aus)
1980	Vicki Hoffman (Aus)
1981	Vicki Hoffman (Aus)
1982	Vicki Cardwell (née Hoffman) (Aus)
1983	Vicki Cardwell (Aus)
1984	Susan Devoy (NZ)
1985	Susan Devoy (NZ)
1986	Susan Devoy (NZ)
1987	Susan Devoy (NZ)
1988	Susan Devoy (NZ)
1989	Susan Devoy (NZ)
1990	Susan Devoy (NZ)

Most wins
16 Heather McKay; **9** Janet Morgan; **7** Susan Devoy; **6** Margot Lumb.

——— 1991 ———

Jan 28-Feb 4 World Cup (Dubai); Apr 13-22 British Open (Wembley Conference Centre); May 11-16 National League play-offs; Nov 16-20 World Open (Finland).

STUDENT GAMES

The XVI Universiade, the World Student Games, is to be held in Sheffield starting on July 14. This is the second largest participation event in world sport (next to the Olympics) and has never before been held in Britain. The estimated 4,500 competitors and 1,500 officials are to be housed in the city's huge refurbished housing complex at Hyde Park. Preparation for the Games has been dogged by financial problems and the organisation was taken over by the City Council in 1990 after the original company, Universiade GB, went into voluntary liquidation.

1991

All timings provisional

OPENING CEREMONY: Sheffield International Stadium, Don Valley, Jul 14, 2pm.
ASSOCIATION FOOTBALL: Hillsborough; Bramall Lane; Elland Road, Leeds; Valley Parade, Bradford; Leeds Road, Huddersfield; Meadow Lane, Nottingham; Glanford Park, Scunthorpe; Belle Vue RL ground, Wakefield. Jul 13-24. Final, Hillsborough, Jul 24, 6.30pm.
ATHLETICS: Don Valley, Jul 19, 20, 21, 23, 24, 25. Marathon (start and finish Don Valley) Jul 21, 9am, incorporating Sheffield City Marathon.
BASKETBALL: Concord Sports Centre, Sheffield; The Dome, Doncaster; Barnsley Metrodome; Herringbone Centre, Rotherham; North Bridge Centre, Halifax; Leeds University; Sheffield Indoor Arena, Jul 15-24. Finals Sheffield Indoor Arena Jul 24: Men's - 8.30pm; Women's 3pm.
DIVING: Ponds Forge Centre, Jul 18-24.
FENCING: Preliminaries - Norton Tennis Centre; Finals Pine Grove, Jul 15-24.
GYMNASTICS: Sheffield Indoor Arena, Jul 15-19.
HOCKEY: Concord Sports Centre and Abbeydale Park, Jul 15-24. Finals at Concord. Men's Final - Jul 24, 7pm; Women's final - Jul 24, 4.30pm.
SWIMMING: Ponds Forge, Jul 15-21.
TENNIS: Norton Tennis Centre, Jul 15-21. Singles finals Jul 21, 2pm.
VOLLEYBALL: Ponds Forge; Hillsborough Leisure Centre; Waltheof Sports Centre; Huddersfield Sports Centre; Dewsbury Sports Centre; Harvey Hadden Stadium, Nottingham; Sheffield Indoor Arena. Jul 15-23. Finals at Sheffield Indoor Arena, Jul 23. Women's - 6.30pm, men's - 8.30pm.
WATER POLO: Hillsborough Leisure Centre and Ponds Forge, Jul 15-23. Final, Ponds Forge, Jul 23, 5pm.
CLOSING CEREMONY: Don Valley, Jul 25, 6.30pm.

RECORDS

Universiades

I Turin 1959; II Sofia 1961; III Porto Alegre, Brazil 1963; IV Budapest 1965; V Tokyo 1967; VI Turin 1970; VII Moscow 1973; VIII Rome, 1975; IX Sofia 1977; X Mexico City 1979; XI Bucharest, 1981; XII Edmonton, Alberta 1983; XIII Kobe, Japan 1985; XIV Zagreb, Yugoslavia 1987; XV Duisburg, West Germany 1989; XVI Sheffield 1991.

SURFING

1990

WORLD AMATEUR CHAMPIONSHIPS
Japan, Apr 6-7

Men
1	Heifara Tahutini (Tah)
2	Craig McMillan (Aus)
3	P Paiva (Bra)

Ladies
1	Kathy Newman (Aus)
2	Horeau Anne Galle (Fij)
3	Haylie Tasker (Aus)

Kneeboarders
1	Simon Farrer (Aus)
2	M Gardeazabal (Bra)
3	Timmy Tanaka (Hai)

Team
1	Australia
2	United States
3	Brazil

CHAMPIONS

WORLD PROFESSIONAL CHAMPIONS

Men
1970	Robert Young (Aus)
1971	Paul Neilsen (Aus)
1972	Jonathan Paarman (SA)
1973	Ian Cairns (Aus)
1974	Reno Abelira (Haw)
1975	Mark Richards (Aus)
1976	Peter Townend (Aus)
1977	Shaun Thomson (SA)
1978	Wayne Bartholomew (Aus)
1979	Mark Richards (Aus)
1980	Mark Richards (Aus)
1981	Mark Richards (Aus)
1983	Mark Richards (Aus)
1984	Tom Carroll (Aus)
1985	Tom Carroll (Aus)
1986	Tommy Curren (US)
1987	Damien Hardman (Aus)
1988	Barton Lynch (Aus)
1989	Martin Potter (GB)

Women
1979	Margo Oberg (Haw)
1980	Lyne Boyer (Haw)
1981	Margo Oberg (Haw)
1983	Margo Oberg (Haw)
1984	Kim Mearig (US)
1985	Frieda Zamba (US)
1986	Frieda Zamba (US)
1987	Wendy Botha (SA)
1988	Frieda Zamba (US)
1989	Wendy Botha (SA)

No winner in 1982 because event became a season-long competition

SWIMMING

1990

EUROPEAN OPEN CUP
Rome, Aug 9-12
Note: Goodwill and Commonwealth Games results can be found in their respective sections.

Men
50 Metres Freestyle:	Dano Halsall (Swi) 22.71s
100 Metres Freestyle:	Anders Holmertz (Swe) 49.95s
200 Metres Freestyle:	Anders Holmertz (Swe) 1m 47.28s
400 Metres Freestyle:	Anders Holmertz (Swe) 3m 35. 15s
1500 Metres Freestyle:	Ian Wilson (GB) 15m 16.05s
100 Metres Butterfly:	Mark Henderson (US) 54.04s
200 Metres Butterfly:	Ray Carey (US) 1m 59.65s
100 Metres Breaststroke:	Adrian Moorhouse (GB) 1m 02.22s
200 Metres Breaststroke:	Nick Gillingham (GB) 2m 14.95s
100 Metres Backstroke:	Jeff Rousse (US) 55.42s
200 Metres Backstroke:	Stefano Battistelli (Ita) 1m 59.48s
200 Metres Ind. Medley:	Eric Namesnik (US) 2m 02.67s
400 Metres Ind. Medley:	Eric Namesnik (US) 4m 16.81s
4x100 Metres Freestyle Relay:	Sweden 3m 21.40s
4x200 Metres Freestyle Relay:	Italy 7m 20.90s
4x100 Metres Medley Relay:	United States 3m 40.06s

Women
50 Metres Freestyle:	Jenny Thompson (US) 25.97s
100 Metres Freestyle:	Jenny Thompson (US) 56.03s
200 Metres Freestyle:	Whitney Hedgepeth (US) 2m 01.12s
400 Metres Freestyle:	Irene Dalby (Nor) 4m 12.86s
800 Metres Freestyle:	Irene Dalby (Nor) 8m 33.36s
100 Metres Butterfly:	Chrissy Ahmann-Leighton (US) 1m 00.92s
200 Metres Butterfly:	Trina Radke (US) 2m 11.24s
100 Metres Breaststroke:	Manuela Dalla Valle (Ita) 1m 09.88s
200 Metres Breaststroke:	Svetlana Kouzmina (USSR) 2m 29.37s
100 Metres Backstroke:	Beth Barr (US) 1m 03.02s
200 Metres Backstroke:	Beth Barr (US) 2m 13.00s
200 Metres Ind. Medley:	Nancy Sweetman (Can) 2m 16.54s
400 Metres Ind. Medley:	Anamariza Petriceva (Yug) 4m 47.13s
4x100 Metres Freestyle Relay:	United States 3m 45.20s
4x200 Metres Freestyle Relay:	United States 8m 08.28s
4x100 Metres Medley Relay:	United States 4m 11.46s

Team:

Men	*Women*	*Overall*
1 United States 404 pts	1 United States 411 pts	1 United States 815 pts
2 Canada 245 pts	2 Great Britain 232 pts	2 Canada 476 pts
3 Italy 225 pts	3 Canada 231 pts	3 Great Britain 421 pts

TSB NATIONAL CHAMPIONSHIPS
Crystal Palace. Jul 26-29

50 Metres Freestyle:	Nicholas Sanders (New Zealand) 23.51s
100 Metres Freestyle:	John Steel (New Zealand) 51.45s
200 Metres Freestyle:	Paul Howe (City of Birmingham) 1m 51.07s
400 Metres Freestyle:	Paul Howe (City of Birmingham) 3m 55.10s
1500 Metres Freestyle:	Ian Wilson (Borough of Sunderland) 15m 25.92s
100 Metres Butterfly:	Nicholas Sanders (New Zealand) 54.97s
200 Metres Butterfly:	Paul Howe (City of Birmingham) 2m 04.23s
100 Metres Breaststroke:	Adrian Moorhouse (City of Leeds) 1m 01.49s
	Moorhouse equalled world record
200 Metres Breaststroke:	Nick Gillingham (City of Birmingham) 2m 16.48s
100 Metres Backstroke:	Martin Harris (Barnet Copthall) 57.87s
200 Metres Backstroke:	Tamas Deutsch (Hungary) 2m 04.92s
200 Metres Individual Medley:	Grant Robins (Portsmouth Northsea) 2m 05.99s
400 Metres Individual Medley:	John Munro (New Zealand) 4m 26.84s
Club Freestyle Relay:	Barnet Copthall 3m 30.50s
Club Medley Relay:	City of Leeds 3m 51.08s

Women
50 Metres Freestyle:	Caroline Woodcock (Barnet Copthall) 26.54s
100 Metres Freestyle:	Karen Pickering (Ipswich) 57.60s
200 Metres Freestyle:	Karen Pickering (Ipswich) 2m 03.02s
400 Metres Freestyle:	Karen Mellor (City of Sheffield) 4m 17.96s
800 Metres Freestyle:	Karen Mellor (City of Sheffield) 8m 44.98s

100 Metres Butterfly:	Madelaine Scarborough (Portsmouth Northsea) 1m 02.00s
200 Metres Butterfly:	Madelaine Scarborough (Portsmouth Northsea) 2m 15.71s
100 Metres Breaststroke:	Lara Hooiveld (City of Leeds) 1m 11.03s
200 Metres Breaststroke:	Suki Brownsdon (Wigan Wasps) 1m 04.34s
100 Metres Backstroke:	Sharon Page (Wigan Wasps) 1m 04.34s
200 Metres Backstroke:	Anna Simcic (New Zealand) 2m 15.53s
200 Metres Individual Medley:	Zara Long (Beckenham) 2m 19.74s
400 Metres Individual Medley:	Zara Long (Beckenham) 4m 54.34s
Club Freestyle Relay:	Portsmouth Northsea 4m 00.93s
Club Medley Relay:	City of Southampton 4m 21.40s

Bill Juba Memorial Trophy (Outstanding Competitor at the Championships: Adrian Moorhouse)

CHAMPIONS

OLYMPIC CHAMPIONS
Men
50 Metres Freestyle
1988	Matt Biondi (US) 22.39s

100 Metres Freestyle
1896	Alfred Hajos (Hun) 1m 22.2s
1904	Zoltan von Halmay (Hun) 1m 22.08s
1908	Charles Daniels (US) 1m 05.6s
1912	Duke Kahanamoku (US) 1m 03.4s
1920	Duke Kahanamoku (US) 1m 01.4s
1924	Johnny Weissmuller (US) 59.0s
1928	Johnny Weissmuller (US) 58.6s
1932	Yasuji Miyazaki (Jap) 58.2s
1936	Ferenc Csik (Hun) 57.6s
1948	Walter Ris (US) 57.3s
1952	Clarke Scholes (US) 57.4s
1956	Jon Henricks (Aus) 55.4s
1960	John Devitt (Aus) 55.2s
1964	Don Schollander (US) 53.4s
1968	Mike Wenden (Aus) 52.2s
1972	Mark Spitz (US) 51.22s
1976	Jim Montgomery (US) 49.99s
1980	Jörg Woithe (GDR) 50.4s
1984	Rowdy Gaines (US) 49.80s
1988	Matt Biondi (US) 48.63s

200 Metres Freestyle
1900	Frederick Lane (Aus) 2m 25.2s
1904	Charles Daniels (US) 2m 44.2s
1968	Mike Wenden (Aus) 1m 55.2s
1972	Mark Spitz (US) 1m 52.78s
1976	Bruce Furniss (US) 1m 50.29s
1980	Sergey Koplyakov (USSR) 1m 49.81s
1984	Michael Gross (FRG) 1m 47.44s
1988	Duncan Armstrong (Aus) 1m 47.25s

400 Metres Freestyle
1896	Paul Neumann (Aut) 8m 12.6s(500m)
1904	Charles Daniels (US) 6m 16.2s
1908	Henry Taylor (GB) 5m 36.8s
1912	George Hodgson (Can) 5m 24.4s
1920	Norman Ross (US) 5m 24.4s
1924	Johnny Weissmuller (US) 5m 04.2s
1928	Alberto Zorilla (Arg) 5m 01.6s
1932	Buster Crabble (US) 4m 48.4s
1936	Jack Medica (US) 4m 44.5s
1948	William Smith (US) 4m 41.0s
1952	Jean Boiteux (Fra) 4m 30.7s
1956	Murray Rose (Aus) 4m 27.3s
1960	Murray Rose (Aus) 4m 18.3s
1964	Don Schollander (US) 4m 12.2s
1968	Mike Burton (US) 4m 09.0s
1972	Brad Cooper (Aus) 4m 00.27s
1976	Brian Goodell (US) 3m 51.93s
1980	Vladimir Salnikov (USSR) 3m 51.31s
1984	George Dicarlo (US) 3m 51.23s
1988	Uwe Dassler (GDR) 3m 46.95s

1500 Metres Freestyle
1896	Alfred Hajos (Hun) 18m 22.2s (1200m)
1900	John Jarvis (GB) 13m 40.2s (1000m)
1904	Emil Rausch (Ger) 27m 18.2s (1 Mile)
1908	Henry Taylor (GB) 22m 48.4s
1912	George Hodgson (Can) 22m 00.0s
1920	Norman Ross (US) 22m 23.2s
1924	Andrew Charlton (Aus) 20m 06.6s
1928	Arne Borge (Swe) 19m 51.8s
1932	Kusuo Kitamura (Jap) 19m 12.4s
1936	Noboru Terada (Jap) 19m 13.7s
1948	James McLane (US) 19m 18.5s
1952	Ford Konno (US) 18m 30.0s
1956	Murray Rose (Aus) 17m 58.9s
1960	John Konrads (Aus) 17m 19.6s
1964	Bob Windle (Aus) 17m 01.7s
1968	Mike Burton (US) 16m 38.9s
1972	Mike Burton (US) 15m 52.58s
1976	Brian Goodell (US) 15m 02.40s
1980	Vladimir Salnikov (USSR) 14m 58.27s
1984	Michael O'Brien (US) 15m 05.20s
1988	Vladimir Salnikov (USSR) 15m 00.40s

100 Metres Backstroke
1904	Walter Brack (Ger) 1m 16.8s
1908	Arno Bieberstein (Ger) 1m 24.6s
1912	Harry Hebner (US) 1m 21.2s
1920	Warren Kealoha (US) 1m 15.2s
1924	Warren Kealoha (US) 1m 13.2s
1928	George Kojac (US) 1m 08.2s
1932	Masaji Kiyokawa (Jap) 1m 08.6s
1936	Adolf Kiefer (US) 1m 05.9s
1948	Allen Stack (US) 1m 06.4s
1952	Yoshinobu Oyakawa (US) 1m 05.4s
1956	David Thiele (Aus) 1m 02.2s
1960	David Thiele (Aus) 1m 01.9s
1968	Roland Matthes (GDR) 58.7s
1972	Roland Matthes (GDR) 56.58s
1976	John Naber (US) 55.49s
1980	Bengt Baron (Swe) 56.33s
1984	Rick Carey (US) 55.79s
1988	Daichi Suzuki (Jap) 55.05s

200 Metres Backstroke
1900	Ernst Hoppenberg (Ger) 2m 47.0s
1964	Jed Graef (US) 2m 10.3s
1968	Roland Matthes(GDR) 2m 09.6s
1972	Roland Matthes (GDR) 2m 02.82s
1976	John Naber (US) 1m 59.19s
1980	Sandor Wladar (Hun) 2m 01.93s
1984	Rick Carey (US) 2m 00.23s
1988	Igor Polianski (USSR) 1m 59.37s

100 Metres Breaststroke
1968	Don McKenzie (US) 1m 07.7s
1972	Nobutaka Taguchi (Jap) 1m 04.94s
1976	John Hencken (US) 1m 03.11s
1980	Duncan Goodhew (GB) 1m 03.34s
1984	Steve Lundquist (US) 1m 01.65s
1988	Adrian Moorhouse (GB) 1m 02..04s

200 Metres Breaststroke

1908	Frederick Holman (GB) 3m 01.8s
1912	Walter Bathe (Ger) 3m 01.8s
1920	Haken Malmroth (Swe) 3m 04.4s
1924	Robert Skelton (US) 2m 56.5s
1928	Yoshiyuki Tsuruta (Jap) 2m 48.8s
1932	Yoshiyuki Tsuruta (Jap) 2m 45.4s
1936	Tetsuo Hamuro (Jap) 2m 41.5s
1948	Joseph Verdeur (US) 2m 39.3s
1952	John Davies (Aus) 2m 34.4s
1956	Masaru Furukawa (Jap) 2m 34.7s
1960	William Mulliken (US) 2m 37.4s
1964	Ian O'Brien (Aus) 2m 27.8s
1968	Felipe Munoz (Mex) 2m 28.7s
1972	John Hencken (US) 2m 21.55s
1976	David Wilkie (GB) 2m 15.11s
1980	Robertas Zhulpa (USSR) 2m 15.85s
1984	Victor Davis (Can) 2m 13.34s
1988	Jozef Szabo (Hun) 2m 13.52s

100 Metres Butterfly

1968	Doug Russell (US) 55.9s
1972	Mark Spitz (US) 54.27s
1976	Matt Vogel (US) 54.35s
1980	Pär Arvidsson (Swe) 54.92s
1984	Michael Gross (FRG) 53.08s
1988	Anthony Nesty (Sur) 53.0s

200 Metres Butterfly

1956	William Yorzyk (US) 2m 19.3s
1960	Mike Troy (US) 2m 12.8s
1964	Kevin Berry (Aus) 2m 06.6s
1968	Carl Robie (US) 2m 08.7s
1972	Mark Spitz (US) 2m 00.70s
1976	Mike Bruner (US) 1m 59.76s
1980	Sergey Fesenko (USSR) 1m 59.76s
1984	Jon Sieben (Aus) 1m 57.04s
1988	Michael Gross (FRG) 1m 56.94s

200 Metres Individual Medley

1968	Charles Hickcox (US) 2m 12.0s
1972	Gunnar Larsson (Swe) 2m 07.17s
1984	Alex Baumann (Can) 2m 01.42s
1988	Tamas Darnyi (Hun) 4m 14.75s

400 Meters Individual Medley

1964	Richard Roth (US) 4m 45.4s
1968	Charles Hickcox (US) 4m 48.4s
1972	Gunnar Larsson (Swe) 4m 31.98s
1976	Rod Strachen (US) 4m 23.68s
1980	Aleksandr Sidorenko (USSR) 4m 22.89s
1984	Alex Baumann (Can) 4m 17.41s
1988	Tamas Darnyi (Hun) 4m 14.75s

4 x 100 Metres Freestyle Relay

1964	United States 3m 33.2s
1968	United States 3m 31.7s
1972	United States 3m 26.42s
1984	United States 3m 19.03s
1988	United States 3m 16.53s

4 x 200 Metres Freestyle Relay

1908	Great Britain 10m 55.6s
1912	Australasia 10m 11.6s
1920	United States 10m 04.4s
1924	United States 9m 53.4s
1928	United States 9m 36.2s
1932	Japan 8m 58.4s
1936	Japan 8m 51.5s
1948	United States 8m 46.0s
1952	United States 8m 31.1s
1956	Australia 8m 23.6s
1960	United States 8m 10.2s
1964	United States 7m 52.1s
1968	United States 7m 52.3s

1972	United States 7m 35.78s
1976	United States 7m 23.22s
1980	USSR 7m 23.50s
1984	United States 7m 15.69s
1988	United States 7m 12.51s

4 x 100 Metres Medley Relay

1960	United States 4m 05.4s
1964	United States 3m 58.4s
1968	United States 3m 54.9s
1972	United States 3m 48.16s
1976	United States 3m 42.22s
1980	Australia 3m 45.70s
1984	United States 3m 39.30s
1988	United States 3m 36.93s

Springboard Diving

1908	Albert Zurner (Ger)
1912	Paul Günther (Ger)
1920	Louis Kuehn (US)
1924	Albert White (US)
1928	Peter Desjardin (US)
1932	Michael Galitzen (US)
1936	Richard Degener (US)
1948	Bruce Harlan (US)
1952	David Browning (US)
1956	Robert Clotworthy (US)
1960	Gary Tobian (US)
1964	Kenneth Sitzberger (US)
1968	Bernard Wrightson (US)
1972	Vladimir Vasin (USSR)
1976	Phil Boggs (US)
1980	Aleksandr Portnov (USSR)
1984	Greg Louganis (US)
1988	Greg Louganis (US)

Platform Diving

1904	George Sheldon (US)
1908	Hjalmar Johansson (Swe)
1912	Erik Adlerz (Swe)
1920	Clarence Pinkston (US)
1924	Albert White (US)
1928	Peter Desjardins (US)
1932	Harold Smith (US)
1936	Marshall Wayne (US)
1948	Samuel Lee (US)
1952	Samuel Lee (US)
1956	Joaquin Capilla Perez (Mex)
1960	Robert Webster (US)
1964	Robert Webster (US)
1968	Klaus Dibiasi (Ita)
1972	Klaus Dibiasi (Ita)
1976	Klaus Dibiasi (Ita)
1980	Falk Hoffmann (GDR)
1984	Greg Louganis (US)
1988	Greg Louganis (US)

Women

50 Metres Freestyle

1988	Kristin Otto (GDR) 25.49s

100 Metres Freestyle

1912	Fanny Durack (Aus) 1m 22.2s
1920	Etheleda Bleibtrey (US0 1m 13.6s
1924	Ethel Lackie (US) 1m 12.4s
1928	Albina Osipowich (US) 1m 11.0s
1932	Helene Madison (US) 1m 06.8s
1936	Hendrika Mastenbroek (Hol) 1m 05.9s
1948	Greta Andersen (Den) 1m 06.3s
1952	Katalin Szöke (Hun) 1m 06.8s
1956	Dawn Fraser (Aus) 1m 02.0s
1960	Dawn Fraser (Aus) 1m 01.2s
1964	Dawn Fraser (Aus) 59.5s
1968	Jan Henne (US) 1m 00.0s

1972	Sandra Neilson (US) 58.59s
1976	Kornelia Ender (GDR) 55.65s
1980	Barbara Krause (GDR) 54.79s
1984	Nancy Hogshead (US) & Carrie Steinseifer (US) 55.92s
1988	Kristin Otto (GDR) 54.93s

200 Metres Freestyle

1968	Debbie Meyer (US) 2m 10.5s
1972	Shane Gould (Aus) 2m 03.56s
1976	Kornelia Ender (GDR) 1m 59.26s
1980	Barbara Krause (GDR) 1m 58.33s
1984	Mary Wayte (US) 1m 59.23s
1988	Heike Freidrich (GDR) 1m 57.65s

400 Metres Freestyle

1920	Ethelda Bleibtrey (US) 4m 34..0s (300m)
1924	Martha Norelius (US) 6m 02..2s
1928	Martha Norelius (US) 5m 42.8s
1932	Helene Madison (US) 5m 28.5s
1936	Hendrika Mastenbroek (Hol) 5m 26.4s
1948	Ann Curtis (US) 5m 17.8s
1952	Valeria Gyenge (Hun) 5m 12.1s
1956	Lorraine Crapp (Aus) 4m 54.6s
1960	Chris von Saltza (US) 4m 50.6s
1964	Virginia Duenkel (US) 4m 43.3s
1968	Debbie Meyer (US) 4m 31.8s
1972	Shane Gould (Aus) 4m 19.04s
1976	Petra Thümer (GDR) 4m 09.89s
1980	Ines Diers (GDR) 4m 08.76s
1984	Tiffany Cohen (US) 4m 07.10s
1988	Janet Evans (US) 4m 03.85s

800 Metres Freestyle

1968	Debbie Mayer (US) 9m 24.0s
1972	Keena Rothhammer (US) 8m 53.68s
1976	Petra Thümer (GDR) 8m 37.14s
1980	Michelle Ford (Aus) 8m 28.90s
1984	Tiffany Cohen (US) 8m 24.95s
1988	Janet Evans (US) 8m 20.20s

100 Metres Backstroke

1924	Sybil Bauer (US) 1m 23.2s
1928	Maria Braun (Hol) 1m 22.0s
1932	Eleanor Holm (US) 1m 19.4s
1936	Nida Senff (Hol) 1m 18.9s
1948	Karen Harup (Den) 1m 14.4s
1952	Joan Harrison (SA) 1m 14.3s
1956	Judy Grinham (GB) 1m 12.9s
1960	Lynn Burke (US) 1m 09.3s
1964	Cathy Ferguson (US) 1m 07.7s
1968	Kaye Hall (US) 1m 06.2s
1972	Melissa Belote (US) 1m 05.78s
1976	Ulrike Richter (GDR) 1m 01.83s
1980	Rica Reinisch (GDR) 1m 00.86s
1984	Theresa Andrews (US) 1m 02.55s
1988	Kristin Otto (GDR) 1m 00.89s

200 Metres Backstroke

1968	Pokey Watson (US) 2m 24.8s
1972	Melissa Belote (US) 2m 19.19s
1976	Ulrike Richter (GDR) 2m 13.43s
1980	Rica Reinisch (GDR) 2m 11.77s
1984	Jolanda de Rover (Hol) 2m 12.38s
1988	Tania Dangalakova (Bul) 1m 07.95

200 Metres Breaststroke

1924	Lucy Morton (GB) 3m 33.2s
1928	Hilde Schrader (Ger) 3m 12.6s
1932	Claire Dennis (Aus) 3m 06.3s
1936	Hideko Maehata (Jap) 3m 03.6s
1948	Petronella van Vliet (Hol) 2m 57.2s
1952	Eva Szekely (Hun) 2m 51.7s
1956	Ursula Happe (FRG) 2m 53.1s
1960	Anita Lonsbrough (GB) 2m 49.5s

1964	Galima Prozumenschikova (USSR) 2m 46.4s
1968	Sharon Wichman (US) 2m 44.4s
1972	Beverley Whitfield (Aus) 2m 41.71s
1976	Marina Koshevayua (USSR) 2m 33.35s
1980	Lina Kachushite (USSR) 2m 29.54s
1984	Anne Ottenbrite (Can) 2m 30.38s
1988	Silke Hoerner (GDR) 2m 26.71s

100 Metres Butterfly

1956	Shelley Mann (US) 1m 11.0s
1960	Carolyn Schuler (US) 1m 09.5s
1964	Sharon Stouder (US) 1. 04.7s
1968	Lynette McClements (Aus) 1m 05.0s
1972	Mayumi Aoki (Jap) 1m 03.34s
1976	Kornelia Ender (GDR) 1m 00.13s
1980	Caren Metschuck (GDR) 1m 00.42s
1984	Mary T. Meagher (US) 59.26s
1988	Kristin Otto (GDR) 59.00s

200 Metres Butterfly

1968	Ada Kok (Hol) 2m 24.7s
1972	Karen Moe (US) 2m 15.57s
1976	Andrea Pollack (GDR) 2m 11.41s
1980	Ines Geissler (GDR) 2m 10.44s
1984	Mary T. Meagher (US) 2m 06.90s
1988	Kathleen Nord (GDR) 2m 16.23s

200 Metres Individual Medley

1968	Claudia Kolb (US) 2m 24.7s
1972	Sharon Gould (Aus) 2m 23.07s
1984	Tracy Caulkins (US) 2m 12.64s
1988	Daniela Hunger (GDR) 2m 16.23s

400 Metres Individual Medley

1964	Donna De Varona (US) 5m 18.7s
1968	Claudia Kolb (US) 5m 08.5s
1972	Gail Neall (Aus) 5m 02.97s
1976	Ulrike Tauber (GDR) 4m 42.77s
1980	Petra Schneider (GDR) 4m 36.29s
1984	Tracy Caulkins (US) 4m 39.24s
1988	Janet Evans (US) 4m 37.36s

4 x 100 Metres Freestyle Medley

1912	Great Britain 5m 52.8s
1920	United States 5m 11.6s
1924	United States 4m 58.8s
1928	United States 4m 47.6s
1932	United States 4m 38.0s
1936	Netherlands 4m 36.0s
1948	United States 4m 29.2s
1952	Hungary 4m 24.4s
1956	Australia 4m 17.1s
1960	United States 4m 08.9s
1964	United States 4m 03.8s
1968	United States 4m 02.5s
1972	United States 3m 55.19s
1976	United States 3m 44.82s
1980	East Germany 3m 42. 71s
1984	United States 3m 43. 43s
1988	East Germany 3m 40.63s

4 x 100 Metres Medley Relay

1960	United States 4m 41.1s
1964	United States 4m 33.9s
1968	United States 4m 28.3s
1972	United States 4m 20.75s
1976	East Germany 4m 07.95s
1980	East Germany 4m 06.67s
1984	United States 4m 08.34s
1988	East Germany 4m 03.74s

Springboard Diving

1920	Aileen Riggin (US)
1924	Elizabeth Becker (US)
1928	Helen Meany (US)
1932	Georgia Coleman (US)

1936	Marjorie Gestring (US)
1948	Victoria Draves (US)
1952	Pat McCormick (US)
1956	Pat McCormick (US)
1960	Ingrid Krämer (GDR)
1964	Ingrid Engel (née Krämer) (GDR)
1968	Sue Gossick (US)
1972	Micki King (US)
1976	Jennifer Chandler (US)
1990	Irina Kalinina (USSR)
1984	Sylvie Bernier (Can)
1988	Goa Min (Chn)

Platform Diving

1912	Greta Johansson (Swe)
1920	Stefani Fryland-Clausen (Den)
1924	Caroline Smith (US)
1928	Elizabeth Pinkston (US)
1932	Dorothy Poynton (US)
1936	Dorothy Hill (née Poynton) (US)
1948	Victoria Draves (US)
1952	Pat McCormick (US)
1956	Pat McCormick (US)
1960	Ingrid Krämer (GDR)
1964	Lesley Bush (US)
1968	Milena Duchkova (Cze)
1972	Ulrike Knape (Swe)
1976	Elena Vaytsekhovskaya (USSR)
1980	Martina Jäschke (GDR)
1984	Zhou Jihong (Chn)
1988	Xu Yanmei (Chn)

Synchronised - Solo

| 1984 | Tracie Ruiz (US) |
| 1988 | Carolyn Waldo (Can) |

Synchronised - Duet

| 1984 | Candy Costie & Tracie Ruiz (US) |
| 1988 | Michelle Cameron & Carolyn Waldo (Can) |

WORLD CHAMPIONS

Note: 1990 Championships now being held January 1991

Men

50 Metres Freestyle
| 1986 | Tom Jager (US) 22.49s |

100 Metres Freestyle
1973	Jim Montgomery (US) 51.70s
1975	Andrew Coan (US) 51.25s
1978	David McCagg (US) 50.24s
1982	Jorg Woithe (GDR) 50.18s
1986	Matt Biondi (US) 48.94s

200 Metres Freestyle
1973	Jim Montgomery (US) 1m 53.02s
1975	Tim Shaw (US) 1m 51.04s
1978	William Forrester (US) 1m 51.04s
1982	Michael Gross (FRG) 1m 49.84s
1986	Michael Gross (FRG) 1m 47.92s

400 Metres Freestyle
1973	Rick DeMont (US) 3m 58.18s
1975	Tim Shaw (US) 3m 54.88s
1978	Vladimir Salnikov (USSR) 3m 51.94s
1982	Vladimir Salnikov (USSR) 3m 51.30s
1986	Rainer Henkel (FRG) 3m 50.05s

1500 Metres Freestyle
1973	Steve Holland (Aus) 15m 31.85s
1975	Tim Shaw (US) 15m 28.92s
1978	Vladimir Salnikov (USSR) 15m 03.99s
1982	Vladimir Salnikov (USSR) 15m 01.77s
1986	Rainer Henkel (FRG) 15m 05.31s

100 Metres Backstroke
1973	Roland Matthes (GDR) 57.47s
1975	Roland Matthes (GDR) 58.15s
1978	Robert Jackson (US) 56.36s
1982	Dirk Richter (GDR) 55.95s
1986	Igor Polianski (USSR) 55.58s

200 Metres Backstroke
1973	Roland Matthes (GDR) 2m 01.87s
1975	Zoltan Verraszto (Hun) 2m 05.05s
1978	Jesse Vassallo (US) 2m 02.16s
1982	Rick Carey (US) 2m 00.82s
1986	Igor Polianski (USSR) 1m 58.78s

100 Metres Breaststroke
1973	John Hencken (US) 1m 04.02s
1975	David Wilkie (GB) 1m 04.26s
1978	Walter Kusch (GDR) 1m 03.56s
1982	Steve Lundquist (US) 1m 02.75s
1986	Victor Davis (Can) 1m 02.71s

200 Metres Breaststroke
1973	David Wilkie (GB) 2m 19.28s
1975	David Wilkie (GB) 2m 18.23s
1978	Nick Nevid (US) 2m 18.37s
1982	Victor Davis (Can) 2m 14.77s
1986	Jozsef Szabo (Hun) 2m 14.27s

100 Metres Butterfly
1973	Bruce Robertson (Can) 55.69s
1975	Greg Jagenburg (US) 55.63s
1978	Joe Bottom (US) 54.30s
1982	Matt Gribble (US) 53.88s
1986	Pablo Morales (US) 53.54s

200 Metres Butterfly
1973	Robin Backhaus (US) 2m 03.32s
1975	William Forrester (US) 2m 01.95s
1978	Michael Bruner (US) 1m 59.38s
1982	Michael Gross (FRG) 1m 58.85s
1986	Michael Gross (FRG) 1m 56.53s

200 Metres Individual Medley
1973	Gunnar Larsson (Swe) 2m 08.36s
1975	Andras Hargitay (Hun) 2m 07.72s
1978	Graham Smith (Can) 2m 03.65s
1982	Aleksey Sidorenko (USSR) 2m 03.30s
1986	Tamas Darnyi (Hun) 2m 01.57s

400 Metres Individual Medley
1973	Andras Hargitay (Hun) 4m 31.11s
1975	Andras Hargitay (Hun) 4m 32.57s
1978	Jesse Vassallo (US) 4m 20.05s
1982	Ricardo Prado (Bra) 4m 19.78s
1986	Tamas Darnyi (Hun) 4m 18.98s

4 x 100 Metres Freestyle Relay
1973	United States 3m 27.18s
1975	United States 3m 24.85s
1978	United States 3m 19.74s
1982	United States 3m 19.26s
1986	United States 3m 19.89s

4 x 200 Metres Freestyle Relay
1973	United States 7m 33.22s
1975	West Germany 7m 39.44s
1978	United States 7m 20.82s
1982	United States 7m 21.09s
1986	East Germany 7m 15.91s

4 x 100 Metres Medley Relay
1973	United States 3m 49.49s
1975	United States 3m 49.0s
1978	United States 3m 44.63s
1982	United States 3m 40.84s
1986	United States 3m 41.25s

Springboard Diving
1973	Phil Boggs (US)
1975	Phil Boggs (US)
1978	Phil Boggs (US)
1982	Greg Louganis (US)
1986	Greg Louganis (US)

Platform Diving
1973 Klaus Dibiasi (Ita)
1975 Klaus Dibiasi (Ita)
1978 Greg Louganis (US)
1982 Greg Louganis (US)
1986 Greg Louganis (US)
Women
50 Metres Freestyle
1986 Tamara Costache (Rom) 25.28s
100 Metres Freestyle
1973 Kornelia Ender (GDR) 57.54s
1975 Kornelia Ender (GDR) 56.50s
1978 Barbara Krause (GDR) 55.68s
1982 Birgit Meineke (GDR) 55.79s
1986 Kristin Otto (GDR) 55.05s
200 Metres Freestyle
1973 Keena Rothhammer (US) 2m 04.99s
1975 Shirley Babashoff (US) 2m 02.50s
1978 Cynthia Woodhead (US) 1m 58.53s
1982 Annemarie Verstappen (Hol) 1m 59.53s
1986 Heike Friedrich (GDR) 1m 58.26s
400 Metres Freestyle
1973 Heather Greenwood (US) 4m 20.28s
1975 Shirley Babashoff (US) 4m 16.87s
1978 Tracey Wickham (Aus) 4m 06.28s
1983 Carmela Schmidt (GDR) 4m 08.98s
1986 Heike Friedrich (GDR) 4m 07.45s
800 Metres Freestyle
1973 Novella Calligaris (Ita) 8m 52.97s
1975 Jenny Turrall (Aus) 8m 44.75s
1978 Tracey Wickham (Aus) 8m 24.94s
1982 Kim Linehan (US) 8m 27.48s
1986 Astrid Strauss (GDR) 8m 28.24s
100 Metres Backstroke
1973 Ulrike Richter (GDR) 1m 05.42s
1975 Ulrike Richter (GDR) 1m 03.30s
1978 Linda Jezek (US) 1m 02.55s
1982 Kristin Otto (GDR) 1m 01.30s
1986 Betsy Mitchell (US) 1m 01.74s
200 Metres Backstroke
1973 Melissa Belote (US) 2m 20.52s
1975 Birgit Treiber (GDR) 2m 15.46s
1978 Linda Jezek (US) 2m 11.93s
1982 Cornelia Sirch (GDR) 2m 09.91s
1986 Cornelia Sirch (GDR) 2m 11.37s
100 Metres Breaststroke
1973 Renate Vogel (GDR) 1m 13.74s
1975 Hannalore Anke (GDR) 1m12.72s
1978 Julia Bogdanova (USSR) 1m 10.31s
1982 Ute Geweniger (GDR) 1m 09.14s
1986 Sylvia Gerasch (GDR) 1m 08.11s
200 Metres Breaststroke
1973 Renate Vogel (GDR) 2m 40.01s
1975 Hannalore Anke (GDR) 2m 37.25s
1978 Lina Kachushite (USSR) 2m 31.42s
1982 Svetlana Varganova (USSR) 2m 28.82s
1986 Silke Hoerner (GDR) 2m 27.40s
100 Metres Butterfly
1973 Kornelia Ender (GDR) 1m 02.53s
1975 Kornelia Ender (GDR) 1m 01.24s
1978 Mary-Joan Pennington (US) 1m 00.20s
1982 Mary T. Meagher (US) 59.41s
1986 Kornelia Gressler (GDR) 59.51s
200 Metres Butterfly
1973 Rosemarie Kother (GDR) 2m 13.76s
1975 Rosemarie Kother (GDR) 2m 13.82s
1978 Tracy Caulkins (US) 2m 09.87s
1982 Ines Geissler (GDR) 2m 08.66s
1986 Mary T. Meagher (US) 2m 08.41s

200 Metres Individual Medley
1973 Angela Hubner (GDR) 2m 20.51s
1975 Kathy Heddy (US) 2m 19.80s
1978 Tracy Caulkins (US) 2m 14.07s
1982 Petra Schneider (GDR) 2m 11.79s
1986 Kristin Otto (GDR) 2m 15.56s
400 Metres Individual Medley
1973 Gudrun Wegner (GDR) 4m 57.31s
1975 Ulrike Tauber (GDR) 4m 52.76s
1978 Tracy Caulkins (US) 4m 40.83s
1982 Petra Schneider (GDR) 4m 36.10s
1986 Kathleen Nord (GDR) 4m 43.75s
4 x 100 Metres Freestyle Relay
1973 East Germany 3m 52.45s
1975 East Germany 3m 49.37s
1978 United States 3m 43.43s
1982 East Germany 3m 43.97s
1986 East Germany 3m 40.57s
4 x 200 Metres Freestyle Relay
1986 East Germany 7m 59.33s
4 x 100 Metres Medley Relay
1973 East Germany 4m 16.84s
1975 East Germany 4m 14.74s
1978 United States 4m 08.21s
1982 East Germany 4m 05.88s
1986 East Germany 4m 04.82s
Springboard Diving
1973 Christine Kohler (GDR)
1975 Irina Kalinina (USSR)
1978 Irina Kalinina (USSR0
1982 Megan Meyer (US)
1986 Gao Min (Chn)
Platform Diving
1973 Ulrike Knape (Swe)
1975 Janet Ely (US)
1978 Irina Kalinina (USSR)
1982 Wendy Wyland (US)
1986 Lin Chen (Chn)
Synchronised - Solo
1973 Teresa Andersen (US)
1975 Gail Buzonas (US)
1978 Helen Vanderburg (Can)
1982 Tracie Ruiz (US)
1986 Carolyn Waldo (Can)
Synchronised - Duet
1973 United States
1975 United States
1978 Canada
1982 Canada
1986 Canada
Synchronised - Team
1973 United States
1975 United States
1978 United States
1982 Canada
1986 Canada

WORLD RECORDS
(September 1990)
Men
50 Metres Freestyle:
21.81s Tom Jager (US). Nashville Tennessee. Mar 24.1990
100 Metres Freestyle:
48.24s Matt Biondi (US). Austin. Texas. Aug 10. 1988
200 Metres Freestyle:
1m 46.69s Giorgio Lamberti (Ita). Bonn. Aug 15.1989
400 Metres Freestyle:
3m 46.95s Uwe Dassler (GDR). Moscow. Feb 22 1983

800 Metres Freestyle:
7m 50.64s Vladimir Salnikov (USSR). Moscow. Jul 24 1986
1500 Metres Freestyle:
14m 54.76s Vladimir Salnikov (USSR). Moscow. Feb 22. 1983
100 Metres Backstroke:
54.51s David Berkoff (US). Seoul. Sep 24. 1988
200 Metres Backstroke:
1m 58.14s Igor Polianski (USSR). Erfurt. GDR. Mar 3. 1985
100 Metres Breaststroke:
1m 01.49s Adrian Moorhouse (GB). Bonn. Aug 15. 1989
200 Metres Breaststroke:
2m 11.53s Mike Barrowman (US). Seattle. Jul 21. 1990
100 Metres Butterfly:
52.84s Pablo Morales (US). Orlando. Florida. Jun 23. 1986
200 Metres Butterfly:
1m 56.24s Michael Gross (FRG). Hanover. Jun 27. 1986
200 Metres Medley:
2m 00.11s Dave Wharton (US). Tokyo. Aug 20. 1989
400 Metres Medley:
4m 14.75s Tamas Darnyi (Hun). Seoul. Sep 21. 1988
4 x 100 Metres Free
3m 16.53s United States. Seoul. Sep 23. 1988
4 x 200 Metres Free:
7m 12.51s United States. Seoul. Sep 21. 1988
4 x 100 Metres Medley:
3m 16.93s United States. Seoul. Sep 25. 1988

Women
50 Metres Freestyle:
24.98s Yang Wenyi (Chn). Guangzhou. China. Apr 11. 1988
100 Metres Freestyle:
54.73s Kristin Otto (GDR). Madrid. Aug 19. 1986
200 Metres Freestyle:
1m 57.55s Heike Friedrich (GDR). East Berlin. Jun 18. 1986
400 Metres Freestyle:
4m 03.85s Janet Evans (US). Seoul. Sep 22. 1988
800 Metres Freestyle:
8m 16.22s Janet Evans (US). Tokyo. Aug 20. 1989
1500 Metres Freestyle:
15m 52.10s Janet Evans (US). Orlando. Florida. Mar 26 1988
100 Metres Backstroke:
1m 00.59s Ina Kleber (GDR). Moscow. Aug 24. 1984
200 Metres Backstroke:
2m 08.60s Betsy Mitchell (US). Orlando. Florida. Jun 27. 1986
100 Metres Breaststroke:
1m 07.91s Silke Hoerner (GDR). Strasbourg. Aug 21. 1987

200 Metres Breaststroke:
2m 26.71s Silke Hoerner (GDR). Seoul. Sep 21. 1988
100 Metres Butterfly:
57.93s Mary Meagher (US). Milwaukee. Wisconsin. Aug 16. 1981
200 Metres Butterfly:
2m 05.96s Mary Meagher (US). Milwaukee. Wisconsin. Aug 13. 1981
200 Metres Medley:
2m 11.73s Ute Geweniger (GDR). East Berlin. Jul 4. 1981
400 Metres Medley:
4m 36.10s Petra Schneider (GDR). Guayaquil. Ecuador. Aug 1. 1982
4 x 100 Metres Free:
3m 40.57s East Germany. Madrid. Aug 19. 1986
4 x 200 Metres Free:
7m 55.47s East Germany. Strasbourg. Aug 18. 1987
4 x 100 Metres Medley:
4m 03.69s East Germany. Moscow. Aug 24. 1984

Glen Housman of Australia unofficially beat the 1.500 metre freestyle world record in Adelaide but his time could not be ratified because the timing mechanism broke. The 22-second barrier in the 50 metres freestyle was cracked three times in 24 hours in Nashville. Tom Jager became the first man to beat 22 seconds. beating his own record with 21.98; he then did 21.81 in the final. Matt Biondi,. who beat Jager in Seoul., did 21.85.

Adrian Moorhouse equalled his 100 metres breaststroke record of 1: 01.49 for the second time at the National Championship at Crystal Palace on July 26.

1991

Jan 3-13	World Championships (Perth, Australia)
Jul 1-4	ASA National Championships (Leeds)
Aug 5-10	National Age Group Championships (Coventry)
Sept 4-8	European Masters (Coventry)
Oct 18-20	ASA National Masters (Sheffield, prov)
Nov 14-17	ASA National Winter Championships (Barnet).

TABLE TENNIS

1990

WORLD TEAM CUP
Osaka, Japan, May 23
Men
Semi-finals
CHINA 3 North Korea 0; SWEDEN 3 England 0
Final
SWEDEN 3 China 2
Women
Semi-finals
CHINA 3 Japan 0; NORTH KOREA 3 South Korea 0
Final
CHINA 3 North Korea 0

EUROPEAN CHAMPIONSHIPS
Gothenburg, Sweden, Apr 8-16
Men's Singles
MIKAEL APPELGREN (Swe) beat Andrzej Grubba (Pol)
21-15 15-21 21-14 21-19
Appelgren won title for third time
Men's Doubles
ILIJA LUPELESCU & ZORAN PRIMORAC (Yug) beat
Joerg Rosskopf & Steffen Fetzner (FRG) 22-20 22-20
Women's Singles
DANIELA GUERGUELCHEVA (Bul) beat Yong Tu
(Swi) 17-21 21-15 21-18 21-16
Women's Doubles
GABRIELLA WIRTH & CSILLA BATORFI (Hun) beat
Elena Timina & Irena Palina (USSR) 15-21 21-18 21-16

LEEDS ENGLISH NATIONAL CHAMPIONSHIPS
Oldham, May 5-6
Men's Singles
DESMOND DOUGLAS (Warwicks) beat Carl Prean (Isle
of Wight) 8-21 21-17 21-17 17-21 21-12
Douglas won title for a record 11th time
Men's Doubles
ALAN COOKE (Derbys) & DESMOND DOUGLAS
(Warwicks) beat Nicky Mason (Surrey) & Skylet Andrew
(Essex) 21-15 21-18
Women's Singles
FIONA ELLIOTT (Staffs) beat Andrea Holt (Lancs) 12-21
23-21 21-11 21-14
Women's Doubles
LISA LOMAS (Beds) & FIONA ELLIOTT (Staffs) beat
Alison Gordon (Berks) & Andrea Holt (Lancs) 19-21 21-
19 21-19

CHAMPIONS

SWAYTHLING CUP
Men's World Team Championship

1927	Hungary
1928	Hungary
1929	Hungary
1930	Hungary
1931	Hungary
1932	Czechoslovakia
1933	Hungary
1934	Hungary
1935	Hungary
1936	Austria
1937	United States
1938	Hungary
1939	Czechoslovakia
1940-46	Not held
1947	Czechoslovakia
1948	Czechoslovakia
1949	Hungary
1950	Czechoslovakia
1951	Czechoslovakia
1952	Hungary
1953	England
1954	Japan
1955	Japan
1956	Japan
1957	Japan
1959	Japan
1961	China
1963	China
1965	China
1967	Japan
1969	Japan
1971	China
1973	Sweden
1975	China
1977	China
1979	Hungary
1981	China
1983	China
1985	China
1987	China
1989	Sweden
Most wins	
12 Hungary	

CORBILLON CUP
Women's World Team Championship

1934	Germany
1935	Czechoslovakia
1936	Czechoslovakia
1937	United States
1938	Czechoslovakia
1939	Germany
1940-46	Not held
1947	England
1948	England
1949	United States
1950	Romania
1951	Romania
1952	Japan
1953	Romania
1954	Japan
1955	Romania
1956	Romania
1957	Japan
1959	Japan
1961	Japan
1963	Japan
1965	China
1967	Japan
1969	USSR
1971	Japan
1973	South Korea
1975	China
1977	China
1979	China
1981	China
1983	China
1985	China
1987	China
1989	China
Most wins	
9 China	

WORLD CHAMPIONSHIPS

Men's Singles

1927	Roland Jacobi (Hun)
1928	Zoltan Mechlovits (Hun)
1929	Fred Perry (Eng)
1930	Victor Barna (Hun)
1931	Miklos Szabados (Hun)
1932	Victor Barna (Hun)
1933	Victor Barna (Hun)
1934	Victor Barna (Hun)
1935	Victor Barna (Hun)
1936	Standa Kolar (Cze)
1937	Richard Bergmann (Aut)
1938	Bohumil Vana (Cze)
1939	Richard Bergmann (Aut)
1940-46	Not held
1947	Bohumil Vana (Cze)
1948	Richard Bergmann (Eng)
1949	Johnny Leach (Eng)
1950	Richard Bergmann (Eng)
1951	Johnny Leach (Eng)
1952	Hiroji Satoh (Jap)
1953	Ferenc Sido (Hun)
1954	Ichiro Ogimura (Jap)
1955	Toshiaki Tanaka (Jap)
1956	Ichiro Ogimura (Jap)
1957	Toshiaki Tanaka (Jap)
1959	Jung-Kuo-tuan (Chn)
1961	Chuang Tse-tung (Chn)
1963	Chuang Tse-tung (Chn)
1965	Chuang Tse-tung (Chn)
1967	Nobuhiko Hasegawa (Jap)
1969	Shigeo Ito (Jap)
1971	Stellan Bengtsson (Swe)
1973	Hsi En-Ting (Chn)
1975	Istvan Jonyer (Hun)
1977	Mitsuru Kohno (Jap)
1979	Seiji Ono (Jap)
1981	Guo Yue-Hua (Chn)
1983	Guo Yue-Hua (Chn)
1985	Jiang Jialiang (Chn)
1987	Jiang Jialiang (Chn)
1989	Jan-Ove Waldner (Swe)

Most wins
5 Victor Barna

Women's Singles

1927	Maria Mednyanszky (Hun)
1928	Maria Mednyanszky (Hun)
1929	Maria Mednyanszky (Hun)
1930	Maria Mednyanszky (Hun)
1931	Maria Mednyanszky (Hun)
1932	Anna Sipos (Hun)
1933	Anna Sipos (Hun)
1934	Marie Kettnerova (Cze)
1935	Marie Kettnerova (Cze)
1936	Ruth Aarons (US)
1937	-
1938	Trudi Pritzi (Aut)
1939	Vlasha Depetrisova (Cze)
1940-46	Not held
1947	Gizi Farkas (Hun)
1948	Gizi Farkas (Hun)
1949	Gizi Farkas (Hun)
1950	Angelica Rozeanu (Rom)
1951	Angelica Rozeanu (Rom)
1952	Angelica Rozeanu (Rom)
1953	Angelica Rozeanu (Rom)
1954	Angelica Rozeanu (Rom)
1955	Angelica Rozeanu (Rom)
1956	Timo Okawa (Jap)
1957	Fujie Eguchi (Jap)
1959	Kimiyo Matsuzaki (Jap)
1961	Chiu Chang-Hui (Chn)
1963	Kimiyo Matsuzaki (Jap)
1965	Naoko Fukazu (Jap)
1967	Sachiko Morisawa (Jap)
1969	Toshiko Kowada (Jap)
1971	Lin Hui-Ching (Chn)
1973	Hu Yu-Lan (Chn)
1975	Pak Yung-Sun (NKo)
1977	Pak Yung-Sun (NKo)
1979	Ge Hsin-Ai (Chn)
1981	Tong Ling (Chn)
1983	Cao Yan-Hua (Chn)
1985	Cao Yan-Hua (Chn)
1987	He Zhili (Chn)
1989	Qiao Hong (Chn)

Most wins
6 Angela Rozeanu

Men's Doubles

Winners since 1981

1981	Cai Zhen-Hua/Li Zhen-Shi (Chn)
1983	Dragutin Surbek/Zoran Kalinic (Yug)
1985	Mikael Appelgren/Ulf Carlsson (Swe)
1987	Chen Longcan/Wei Quingguang (Chn)
1989	Joerg Rosskopf/Steffan Fetzner (FRG)

Most wins
8 Barna (Hun) 1929-35, 1939

Women's Doubles

Winners since 1981

1981	Zhang Deijing/Cao Yanhua (Chn)
1983	Shen Jianping/Dai Lili (Chn)
1985	Dai Lili/Geng Lijuan (Chn)
1987	Yang Young-Ja/Hyun Jung-Hua (SKo)
1989	Qiao Hong/Deng Yaping (Chn)

Most wins
7 Maria Mednyanszky (Hun) 1928, 1930-35

Mixed Doubles

Winners since 1981

1981	Huang Junquin/Xie Saike (Chn)
1983	Ni Xialin/Guo Yue-Hua (Chn)
1985	Cao Yan-Hua/Cai Zhenhua (Chn)
1987	Hui Jun/Geng Lijuan (Chn)
1989	Hyun Jung-Hua/Yoo Nam-Kyu (SKo)

Most wins
6 Maria Mednyansky (Hun) 1927-28, 1930-31, 1933-34

OLYMPIC GAMES

First included 1988

Men's Singles

1988	Yoo Nam-Kyu (SKo)

Women's Singles

1988	Chen Jing (Chn)

Men's Doubles

1988	Chen Longcan/Wei Qingguang (Chn)

Women's Doubles

1988	Hyung Jung-Hwa (SKo)/Yang Young-Ja (SKo)

——— 1991 ———

Feb 1-3 European Top 12 (s-Hertenbosch, Netherlands); Mar 9-10 National Championships (Crystal Leisure Centre, Stourbridge); Apr 10-17 Commonwealth Championships (Nairobi); Apr 24-May 6 World Championships (Chiba City, Japan).

THE YEAR OF CONFUSION

A year that began with Boris Becker and Steffi Graf apparently poised to dominate tennis in the early '90s ended with both players in partial eclipse and a new and exciting uncertainty surrounding the highest reaches of the sport.

For the first time since 1966 eight different players won the eight different Grand Slam singles titles and it was impossible to discern any pattern linking the winners. In Paris 16-year-old Monica Seles became the youngest-ever winner of the women's event, but Andres Gomez won the men's at 30, older than any winner since 1972. Gomez had originally planned to commentate for Ecuadorian TV and only decided to play when Ivan Lendl withdrew. Pete Sampras, 19 years 28 days, became the youngest winner of the US Open but the two teenage Paris champions of 1989, Michael Chang and Arantxa Sanchez-Vicario, both faded into the background.

The fact that Graf won only one Grand Slam event, the Australian, was probably a bigger surprise than Becker's inability to win any at all. Everyone expects men's tennis to be competitive but there was a new spice about the women's game as well. It was good news for tennis and everyone in it. Except Graf.

The rise of the new prodigies, led by Seles and the extraordinary 14-year-old reincarnation of Chris Evert, Jennifer Capriati, was the dominant feature. But Wimbledon belonged to the old lady: Martina Navratilova knew she could win again and proved it to the world. She found someone else to do the dirty work for her: the unlikely figure of Zina Garrison, one of life's quarter-finalists, who beat first Seles (who had previously won 36 times in a row and got to match point) and finally, on a cold, blustery Thursday, the great Graf herself. The final was less of a triumph for Garrison. There was some embarrassment beforehand because both finalists were wearing the same clothing design; and there was some embarrassment later because Navratilova completely outclassed her opponent. It was her ninth Championship, which surpassed Helen Wills Moody's record.

There had been signs beforehand that all was not well with Graf. The pressures had been getting to her: in the winter she had broken her hand skiing, evidently trying to avoid photographers. Even so, she came back strongly enough; before the final of the Berlin Open she had taken her unbeaten run to 66 games (eight short of Navratilova's record). But her sinuses were bothering her and so was a curious - and vehemently denied - paternity suit against her father. She flew home during the middle weekend of Wimbledon to see a specialist (the following week she had an operation) but apparently to avoid pressmen as well. In New York everything was fine until she was ambushed in the final by Gabriela Sabatini, whose new coach, the Brazilian Carlos Kirmayr, had suddenly turned her into a player who attacked the net.

Graf retained as much innocence and dignity as could reasonably be expected, and no one suggested she was not still the world's best female tennis player. It was only her own high standards that were slipping. In August she won her 50th professional singles title and in September she recorded her 160th consecutive week at No. 1, a record for either sex. She also posed in *Vogue* at her father's instigation ("She is more woman than tennis machine," he said) showing more bosom than nose, but her father did reject an offer of $750,000 from *Playboy* for her to pose naked. When she lost the first set of the French Open final her dog Roland, sitting by the TV set in the players' lounge, stood up and yapped.

The male side of Wimbledon was dominated by Ivan Lendl's magnificent obsession - a phrase he rejected but too apt to resist - about winning the tournament. He began as a hot favourite after demolishing Becker in the final at Queen's Club but he failed yet again, losing in the semi-final to Stefan Edberg. But Lendl succeeded in a manner no one expected, becoming an improbably humorous and affectionately-regarded loser as though he were Christine Truman in drag. Edberg then won a thrilling final, surviving a

Becker comeback from two sets down, at which point the silence was pierced by a shout of "Where's Boom-Boom?" and occasional cries of anguish from Becker.

The final, however, took place on the same day as the World Cup final and most of the planet's sports-watchers were otherwise preoccupied. It was the lowest-key Wimbledon for many years. Total attendance fell by more than 52,000 to 349,979, the lowest since 1972. The All-England Club was trying to discourage spectators because of new safety regulations. The decision to make six courts all-reserved and the abolition of standing room on Centre Court removed some of the character from the fortnight. But the fall was greater than expected, and the TV audience fell sharply too. The absence of characters among the men - ten out of the top 24 in the rankings were missing - was as much a factor as the competition from the football. The customary Wimbledon lunacies were not entirely absent: the Centre Court's resident pied wagtails upset both the Cyclops service monitor and losers anxious for an excuse. A fashion for eating bananas started among the players: David Wheaton ate nine during one five-setter. Fred Perry received a request for a signed photo "because you are currently appearing in pantomime"; Kevin Curren was fined $500 for kicking a photocopier in the referee's office.

HEROES AND VILLAINS

Among the missing characters, after the first round, was John McEnroe, who lost to Derrick Rostagno. It was not his most spectacular exit of the year. Playing Mikael Penfors in the fourth round of the Australian Open, he was thrown out of the tournament for swearing at officials, the first time anyone has been defaulted in a Grand Slam tournament. But the man would not lie down. At the US Open, where he was unseeded, McEnroe stormed through to reach the semi-finals before losing to Sampras. Yes, good old Mac was back: in the second round he was fined another $400 for smashing his racket against a glass panel in front of the president's box.

“Everybody, and rightly so, says Boris Becker is no.1. I am the first to say that. I am no.1 on the computer but that's wrong.”
Ivan Lendl at the Australian Open

“I have only one ambition left in life and that is coming in July.”
Lendl, before Wimbledon

“So long as I'm playing, I'll give it my best shot.”
Lendl, after Wimbledon

“Lendl's Wimbledon experiences tend to resemble the by-election history of Screaming Lord Sutch: A plus for effort and attendance, B minus for achievement.”
Patrick Collins, Mail on Sunday

“The first thing I'll do is kick his arse. Then we'll see how he copes with it between his ears.”
Tony Pickard, Stefan Edberg's coach, after first-round defeat at the French Open.

“This feels really, really good.”
Edberg, after Wimbledon

“The way he played today, he should come back to Vegas with me. We'll go to the casino.”
Andre Agassi on Pete Sampras after losing the US Open final

“Finally, an American winner of the US Open to love. Or at least to respect and enjoy without serious reservation. Thank you, Pete Sampras.”
Thomas Boswell, Washington Post

However, the traditionalists had a new, brash young man to hate. Andre Agassi arrived for his first-round game at Flushing Meadow wearing a lime-green outfit and his subsequent appearances were described in a mixture of outrage and the fashion comments normally reserved for the Queen at Ascot. He helped the process by spitting at an official. In Paris, playing Todd Woodbridge, he had worn black denim shorts over pink cycling pants with a pink, white and black shirt, matching headband, designer stubble and a punk hairdo. Agassi hinted that he would end his boycott of Wimbledon in 1991 in the unlikely event of Nike being able to design an outfit that would reconcile his sartorial tastes and those of the All-England club. There was widespread relief among the establishment when he lost the US final to Sampras, a teenager even more clean cut and wholesome than Michael Chang but with a service of sheer venom. Sampras, seeded 12th, had previously won only two tournaments and the victory almost doubled his career prize money. He has power to add. The other two heroes of the US Open were the Mayor of New York, David Dinkins, who persuaded the aviation authorities to redirect planes away from the courts, and James Nelson, 54, who became the world's oldest ball boy. He rang up and asked the age limit and was told the minimum age was 14 with no maximum.

THE WONDERGIRL

To some tournament players Sampras seemed like an ancient. The phenomenon of the year was Jennifer Capriati who made her professional debut 23 days short of her 14th birthday - by special concession because the tournament was in her home state of Florida - and five days later reached her first final. In July she won her first tournament and she swept up the rankings without appearing to lose her little-girl wonder at the world except when she was hitting a tennis ball.

But all round her there were reminders about what happens to yesterday's young heroes. Bjorn Borg, 34, won libel damages from his ex-girlfriend who accused him of having a cocaine habit, but he still found himself in deep financial trouble and was said to be considering a comeback to pay his debts. At Wimbledon an American TV commentator stopped by to wish Capriati good luck. Jennifer looked blank. "I'm Andrea Jaeger," said the stranger. Even Becker began to lose some of his teenage zip and mused about early retirement. It was a difficult year for all the leading men. Edberg displaced Lendl as no.1 in the ranking but contrived to be eliminated in the first round in both Paris and New York.

Any British player would have enjoyed the problems of superstardom. No Briton of either sex made the third round at Wimbledon for the first time ever. The last survivor was actually one Neil Broad, who qualified as a South African, but announced, in a thick accent, that "he had always wanted to play for England". He promptly lost. The LTA "temporarily suspended" the Wightman Cup after Britain's 11th consecutive defeat by the Americans. It is to be reinstated in 1991 as a US v Europe match along the lines of the Ryder Cup. Ladbrokes offered 1,000 to 1 against a British man winning Wimbledon in 1990, and 2,000 to 1 against a British woman. Their odds against aliens landing before the year 2000 are 100 to 1.

A spectator at the Australian Open returned £700 worth of Centre Court tickets because he found himself next to a heavy smoker; "Give the refund to charity," he told the tournament director, Colin Stubbs. Yannick Noah said he visited a witchdoctor in the Cameroon jungle to cure his chronic tendonitis: "He got a panther's tail and beat the shit out of my knees. Then he rubbed some oil into them and I've never had any problems since then."

------------ **1990** ------------

THE ALL ENGLAND CHAMPIONSHIPS

Wimbledon, Jun 25-Jul 8

Men's Singles

Third Round
BRAD GILBERT (US) [7] beat Paul Haarhuis (Hol) 6-1 3-6 6-1 6-2; BORIS BECKER (FRG) [2] beat Dan Goldie (US) 6-3 6-4 4-6 7-5; PAT CASH (Aus) beat Juan Aguilera (Spa) 6-1 6-1 6-4; DAVID WHEATON (US) beat Jonas Svensson (Swe) [10]; MARK WOODFORDE (Aus) beat Jim Courier (US) [9] 7-5 5-7 7-5 6-4; STEFAN EDBERG (Swe) [3] beat Amos Mansdorf (Isr) 6-4 5-7 3-6 6-2 9-7; CHRISTIAN BERGSTROM (Swe) beat Jim Grabb (US) 7-6 6-4 6-2; IVAN LENDL (Cze) [1] beat Bryan Sheldon

(US) 7-6 6-7 6-4 6-4; BRAD PEARCE (US) beat Milan Srejber (Cze) 6-3 6-3 6-1; MICHAEL CHANG (US) [13] beat Mark Kratzmann (Aus) 3-6 4-6 6-4 6-2 6-2; KEVIN CURREN (US) beat Karel Novacek (Cze) 6-2 4-6 1-6 7-5 6-3; GORAN IVANISEVIC (Yug) beat Derrick Rostagno (US) 6-2 6-2 6-4; ALEXANDR VOLKOV (USSR) beat Marc Rosset (Swi) 6-3 6-4 7-5; GUY FORGET (Fra) [11] beat Michael Stich (FRG) 3-6 7-5 6-2 4-6 6-3; ALEX ANTONITSCH (Aut) beat David Pate (US) 6-4 6-4 7-6; MARK KOEVERMANS (Hol) beat Niclas Kroon (Swe) 6-7 6-4 6-7 6-4 6-3

How the other seeds fell:
Yannick Noah (Fra) [16] lost to Wayne Ferreira (SA), Andres Gomez (Ecu) [5] lost to Jim Grabb (US), Tim Mayotte (US) [6] lost to Gary Muller (SA), Petr Korda (Cze) [14] lost to Gilad Bloom (Isr), Pete Sampras (US)

(12) lost to Christo Van Rensburg (SA), John McEnroe (US) [4] lost to Derrick Rostagno (US) *(all 1st Round)*; Henri Leconte (Fra) [15] lost to Alex Antonitsch (Aut) *(2nd Round)*; Aaron Krickstein (US) [8] withdrew following elbow injury

Fourth Round

IVANISEVIC beat Koevermans 4-6 6-3 6-4 7-6; BECKER beat Cash 7-6 6-1 6-4; BERGSTROM beat Forget 6-4 3-6 6-3 7-5; CURREN beat Volkov 6-4 7-6 7-6; EDBERG beat Chang 6-3 6-2 6-1; GILBERT beat Wheaton 6-7 3-6 6-1 6-4 13-11; PEARCE beat Woodforde 6-4 6-4 6-4; LENDL beat Antonitsch 3-6 6-4 6-3 6-4
Only 6 seeds reached their allocated places in the last 16

Quarter - finals

EDBERG beat Bergstrom 6-3 6-2 6-4; BECKER beat Gilbert 6-4 6-4 6-1; LENDL beat Pearce 6-4 6-4 5-7 6-4; IVANISEVIC beat Curren 4-6 6-4 6-4 6-7 6-3
Ivanisevic became the first unseeded player in the semi-finals since Zivojinovic in 1986. He aced Curren 26 times

Semi-finals

EDBERG beat Lendl 6-1 7-6 6-3; BECKER beat Ivanisevic 4-6 7-6 6-0 7-6

Final

EDBERG beat Becker 6-2 6-2 3-6 3-6 6-4
The final lasted two hours 58 minutes

Women's Singles

Third Round

In the first round Jennifer Capriati became the youngest player to win a match at Wimbledon. She beat Helen Kelesi 6-3 6-1, aged 14 years 89 days, two days younger than Kathy Rinaldi in 1981.
JANA NOVOTNA (Cze) [13] beat Jo-Anne Faull (Aus) 6-2 6-1; HELENA SUKOVA (Cze) [10] beat Alexia Dechaume (Fra) 6-4 6-3; JENNIFER CAPRIATI (US) [12] beat Robin White (US) 7-5 6-7 6-3; MONICA SELES (Yug) [3] beat Anne Minter (US) 6-3 6-3; STEFFI GRAF (FRG) [1] beat Claudia Kohde-Kilsch (FRG) 6-0 6-4; GABRIELA SABATINI (Arg) [4] beat Catherine Tanvier (Fra) 6-4 6-2; MARTINA NAVRATILOVA (US) [2] beat Karin Kschwendt (Lux) 6-1 6-1; NATHALIE HERREMAN (Fra) beat Lori McNeil (US) 6-4 6-3; BRENDA SCHULTZ (Hol) beat Betsy Nagelsen (US) 6-1 6-4; NATALYA ZVEREVA (USSR) [11] beat Gretchen Magers (US) 2-6 6-2 6-4; KATERINA MALEEVA (Bul) [7] beat Ann de Vries (Bel) 6-2 6-0; JUDITH WIESNER (Aut) [14] beat Laura Gildemeister (Per) 6-2 7-6; NATHALIE TAUZIAT (Fra) beat Amy Frazier (US) 3-6 6-2 7-5; ZINA GARRISON (US) [5] beat Andrea Leand (US) 6-0 6-3; PATTY FENDICK (US) beat Angelica Gavaldon (US) 6-1 6-1; ANN HENRICKSSON (US) beat Elna Reinach (SA) 3-6 6-3 6-3
How the other seeds fell;
Barbara Paulus (Aut) [16] lost to Sarah Loosemore (GB), Manuela Maleeva (Swi) [8] lost to Sara Gomer (GB), Arantxa Sanchez-Vicario (Spa) [6] lost to Betsy Nagelsen (US), Mary-Joe Fernandez (US) lost to Nathalie Herreman (Fra) *(all 1st Round)*; Ros Fairbank (US) [15] lost to Amy Frazier (US) *(2nd Round)*

Fourth Round

SELES beat Henricksson 6-1 6-0; MALEEVA beat N Herreman 6-3 6-0; ZVEREVA beat Schultz 6-2 6-2; GARRISON beat Sukova 6-3 6-3; NOVOTNA beat Fendick 6-2 6-4; NAVRATILOVA beat Wiesner 6-3 6-3; GRAF beat Capriati 6-2 6-4; SABATINI beat Tauziat 6-2 7-6

Quarter-finals

GRAF beat Novotna 7-5 6-2; GARRISON beat Seles 3-6 6-3 9-7; NAVRATILOVA beat Maleeva 6-1 6-1;

SABATINI beat Zvereva 6-2 2-6 8-6

Semi-finals

GARRISON beat Graf 6-3 3-6 6-4; NAVRATILOVA beat Sabatini 6-3 6-4

Final

NAVRATILOVA beat Garrison 6-4 6-1
Navratilova's ninth title. The final lasted 75 minutes. It was Navratilova's 28th win out of 29 against Garrison.

Steffi Graf lost only 11 matches between the start of 1987 and the US Open in September 1990. Her conquerors were:

Gabriela Sabatini	4
Martina Navratilova	2
Monica Seles	2
Zina Garrison	1
Pam Shriver	1
Arantxa Sanchez-Vicario	1

Men's Doubles

Final

RICK LEACH & JIM PUGH (US) [1] beat Pieter Aldrich & Danie Visser (SA) [2] 7-6 7-6 7-6

Women's Doubles

Final

JANA NOVOTNA & HELENA SUKOVA (Cze) [1] beat Kathy Jordan (US) and Elizabeth Smylie (Aus) 6-3 6-4 [6]

Mixed Doubles

Final

RICK LEACH & ZINA GARRISON (US) [3] beat John Fitzgerald & Elizabeth Smylie (Aus) [4] 7-5 6-2

The Other Finals

Men's Over 35s Singles
TOM GULLIKSON (US) beat Tim Gullikson 4-6 6-2 7-6

Men's Over 35s Doubles
PETER McNAMARA & PAUL McNAMEE (Aus) beat Tim & Tom Gullikson (US) 6-7 7-6 13-11

Ladies Over 35s Doubles
WENDY TURNBULL (Aus) & VIRGINIA WADE (GB) beat Rosie Casals & Sharon Walsh-Pete (US) 6-2 6-4

Junior Boys' Singles
LEANDER PAES (Ind) beat Marcos Ondruska (SA) 7-5 2-6 6-4

Junior Boys' Doubles
SEBASTIEN LAREAU & SEBASTIEN LEBLANC (Can) beat Clinton Marsh & Marcos Ondruska (SA) 7-6 4-6 6-3

Junior Girls' Singles
ANDREA STRNADOVA (Cze) beat Kirrily Sharpe (Aus) 6-2 6-4

Junior Girls' Doubles
KATRINA HABSUDOVA & ANDREA STRNADOVA (Cze) beat Nicole Pratt & Kirrily Sharpe (Aus) 6-3 6-2

AUSTRALIAN OPEN
Melbourne, Jan 15-28

Men's Singles

Fourth Round

IVAN LENDL (Cze) [1] beat Simon Youl (Aus) 6-1 6-3 6-1; ANDREI CHERKASOV (USSR) beat Andres Gomez (Ecu) [9] 2-6 6-3 7-6 7-6; YANNICK NOAH (Fra) [12] beat Pete Sampras (US) 6-3 6-4 3-6 6-2; MIKAEL

PERNFORS (Swe) beat John McEnroe (US) [4] 1-6 6-4 5-7 4-2 disq; STEFAN EDBERG (Swe) [3] beat Jonas B Svensson (Swe) 6-2 6-2 6-4; DAVID WHEATON (US) beat Aaron Krickstein (US) [5] 7-6 6-4 6-3; MATS WILANDER (Swe) [8] beat Veli Paloheimo (Fin) 7-5 6-4 6-0; BORIS BECKER (FRG) [2] beat Miloslav Mecir (Cze) [16] 4-6 6-7 6-4 6-1 6-1

Quarter-finals
LENDL beat Cherkasov 6-3 6-2 6-3; NOAH beat Pernfors 6-3 7-5 6-2; EDBERG beat Wheaton 7-5 7-6 3-6 6-2; WILANDER beat Becker 6-4 6-4 6-2;

Semi-finals
LENDL beat Noah 6-1 6-1 6-2; EDBERG beat Wilander 6-4 6-1 6-2

Final
LENDL beat Edberg 4-6 7-6 5-2 (retired)
Edberg had a pulled stomach muscle. He was the second player to retire from the final of a Grand Slam tournament. The other was H Roper Barrett who quit the 1911 Wimbledon final through exhaustion.

Women's Singles
Fourth Round
STEFFI GRAF (FRG) [1] beat Raffaella Reggi (Ita) [13] 6-2, 6-3; PATTY FENDICK (US) beat Barbara Paulus (Aut) [16] 7-5 6-2; HELENA SUKOVA (Cze) [4] beat Kimiko Date (Jap) 6-4 6-3; KATERINA MALEEVA (Bul) [9] beat Rachel McQuillan (Aus) 3-6 6-4 6-1; MARY-JOE FERNANDEZ (US) [6] beat Donna Faber (US) 6-4 6-2; ZINA GARRISON (US) [3] beat Catherine Tanvier (Fra) 6-2 2-0 rtd; ANGELICA GAVALDON (US) beat Gigi Fernandez (PR) [15] 6-3 1-6 6-2; CLAUDIA PORWICK (FRG) beat Dinky van Rensburg (SA) 7-6 3-6 6-4

Quarter-finals
GRAF beat Fendick 6-3 7-5; SUKOVA beat Maleeva 6-4 6-3; FERNANDEZ beat Garrison 6-2 2-0 (retired); PORWICK beat Gavaldon 6-4 6-3

Semi-finals
GRAF beat Sukova 6-4 3-6 6-4; FERNANDEZ beat Gavaldon 6-2 6-1

Final
GRAF beat Fernandez 6-3 6-4

Men's Doubles
Final
PIETER ALDRICH & DANIE VISSER (SA) [2] beat Grant Connell & Glenn Michibata (Can) [13] 6-4 4-6 6-1 6-4

Women's Doubles
Final
JANA NOVOTNA & HELENA SUKOVA (Cze) [1] beat Patty Fendick and Mary-Joe Fernandez (US) [5] 7-6 7-6

Mixed Doubles
Final
JIM PUGH (US) & NATALYA ZVEREVA (USSR) [1] beat Rick Leach & Zina Garrison (US) [2] 4-6 6-2 6-3

JOHNNY...

"Can we breathe, John?"
Spectator at the McEnroe-Pernfors match in Melbourne

"Code violation, verbal abuse, default Mr McEnroe. Game, set, match."
Umpire Gerry Armstrong, a few moments later

"I used a little four-letter word. He could have let me off, he could have figured it was in the heat of the moment."
John McEnroe

"When I walk out there on court I become a maniac. It is obvious I have a problem and need help...Something just comes over me, it's weird...I've been trying to clean up my act for 12 years now, but I just can't control myself."
McEnroe to his biographer

"In him you can see yourself. He is human and yet his personality is stronger and bigger than anyone's. That is why Johnny is Johnny."
Sergio Palmieri, McEnroe's agent

"There's a lot of act to get together."
McEnroe on being beaten at Wimbledon

"The risk is that his legend burns out long before his candle ever does."
Tony Kornheiser, Washington Post

"The magic, it has come back into his hand."
Antonio Palafox, McEnroe's coach, at the US Open

"There's no doubt in my mind what I've achieved. I don't have to sit here and tell everyone about it. It's my record and my personality combined with my ability. That's about it."
McEnroe

...AND ANDRE

"He looked horrible - absolutely terrible. He has taken outrageous clothes so far it has almost become an insult."
Philippe Chatrier, ITF president, on Andre Agassi

"Because I haven't been there, it speaks for itself what I think of the people who run Wimbledon...If they changed the dress code, I would have to consider whether I'd want to play...It seems those bozos will look for anything to talk about."
Agassi

"He is a very nice young man, 20 years old. I ask you to think back to Jimmy Connors or John McEnroe. Agassi is a prince of a person compared to either one of them."
Mark McCormack

"I still laugh at his reasons for not playing. This is Wimbledon. It's like a football player who skips the Super Bowl because he has to get ready for spring training."
Martina Navratilova on Agassi

FRENCH OPEN
Roland Garros, Paris, May 28-Jun 10
Men's Singles
Boris Becker and Stefan Edberg were the first No. 1 and 2 seeds both to be eliminated in the first round of a Grand Slam event. Becker lost to Goran Ivanisevic (Yug) and Edberg to Sergi Bruguera (Spa), both teenagers.

Fourth Round
ANDRE AGASSI (US) [3] beat Jim Courier (US) [13] 6-7 6-1 6-4 6-0; MICHAEL CHANG (US) [11] beat Javier Sanchez (Spa) 6-4 6-4 6-2; ANDRES GOMEZ (Ecu) [4] beat Magnus Gustafsson (Swe) beat Guillermo Perez-Roldan (Arg) 2-6 6-4 6-2 6-2; HENRI LECONTE (Fra) beat Andrei Chesnokov (USSR) [7] 6-4 6-3 4-6 2-6 6-3; THIERRY CHAMPION (Fra) beat Karel Novacek (Cze) 6-3 4-6 3-6 7-6 6-3; THOMAS MUSTER (US) [8] beat Martin Jaite (Arg) [10] 7-6 6-3 6-3; GORAN IVANISEVIC (Yug) beat Niclas Kroon (Swe) 6-2 6-4 7-5

Quarter-finals
AGASSI beat Chang 6-2 6-1 4-6 6-2; SVENSSON beat Leconte 3-6 7-5 6-3 6-4; MUSTER beat Ivanisevic 6-2 4-6 6-4 6-3; GOMEZ beat Champion 6-3 6-3 6-4

Semi-finals
GOMEZ beat Muster 7-5 6-1 7-5; AGASSI beat Svensson 6-1 6-4 3-6 6-3

Final
GOMEZ beat Agassi 6-3 2-6 6-4 6-4

Women's Singles
Fourth Round
STEFFI GRAF (FRG) [1] beat Nathalie Tauziat (Fra) [15] 6-4 6-2; CONCHITA MARTINEZ (Spa) [9] beat Wiltrud Probst (FRG) 6-3 6-3; KATERINA MALEEVA (Bul) [8] beat Nicole Provis (Aus) 3-6 6-3 6-3; MARY-JOE FERNANDEZ (US) [7] beat Ann Grossmann (US) 6-3 6-2; JENNIFER CAPRIATI (US) beat Mercedes Paz (Arg) 6-0 6-3; MANUELA MALEEVA (Swi) [6] beat Natalya Zvereva (USSR) [10] 6-4 6-2; JANA NOVOTNA (Cze) [11] beat Gabriela Sabatini (Arg) [4] 6-4 7-5; MONICA SELES (Yug) [2] beat Laura Gildemeister (Per) [16] 6-4 6-0

Quarter-finals
GRAF beat Martinez 6-1 6-3; SELES beat M Maleeva 3-6 6-1 7-5; NOVOTNA beat K Maleeva 4-6 6-2 6-4; CAPRIATI beat Fernandez 6-2 6-4
Capriati became youngest ever Grand Slam quarter-finalist at 14, then she became youngest ever semi-finalist. The Maleevas became the first sisters to reach a Grand Slam quarter-final since the Budings in the 1956 French Open.

Semi-finals
GRAF beat Novotna 6-1 6-2; SELES beat Capriati 6-2 6-2
Combined ages of Seles and Capriati: 30

Final
SELES beat Graf 7-6 6-4
Seles, at 16yr 6mth, became the youngest winner of a Grand Slam event since Lottie Dod in 1887.

Men's Doubles
Final
SERGIO CASAL & EMILIO SANCHEZ (Spa) [7] beat Goran Ivanisevic (Yug) & Petr Korda (Cze) [16] 7-5 6-3

Women's Doubles
Final
JANA NOVOTNA & HELENA SUKOVA (Cze) [1] beat Larissa Savchenko & Natalya Zvereva (USSR) [2] 6-4 7-5

Mixed Doubles
Final
JORGE LOZANO (Mex) & ARANTXA SANCHEZ VICARIO (Spa) [4] beat Danie Visser (SA) & Nicole Provis (Aus) 7-6 7-6 [2]

UNITED STATES OPEN
Flushing Meadow, New York, Aug 27-Sep 9
Men's Singles
Fourth Round
The top seed Stefan Edberg lost in the first round to Alexandr Volkov.
BORIS BECKER (FRG) [2] beat Darren Cahill (Aus) 2-6 6-2 6-3 3-6 6-4; ANDREI CHERKASOV (USSR) beat Christo van Rensburg (SA) 6-4 6-4 7-5; ANDRE AGASSI (US) [4] beat Jay Berger (US) [13] 7-5 6-0 6-2; AARON KRICKSTEIN (US) [9] beat Amos Mansdorf (Isr) 6-3 6-4 6-4; JOHN McENROE (US) beat Emilio Sanchez (Spa) [7] 7-6 3-6 4-6 6-4 6-3; DAVID WHEATON (US) [12] beat Kevin Curren (US) 7-5 7-6 4-6 6-4; PETE SAMPRAS (US) [12] beat Thomas Muster (Aut) [6] 6-7 7-6 6-4 6-3; IVAN LENDL (Cze) [3] beat Gilad Bloom (Isr) 6-0 6-3 6-4

Quarter-finals
McENROE beat Wheaton 6-1 6-4 6-4; SAMPRAS beat Lendl 6-4 7-6 3-6 4-6 6-2; AGASSI beat Cherkasov 6-2 6-2 6-3; BECKER beat Krickstein 3-6 6-3 6-2 6-3
Lendl, seeded only three (his lowest since 1983), failed to reach the final for the first time since 1981

Semi-finals
AGASSI beat Becker 6-7 6-3 6-2 6-3; SAMPRAS beat McEnroe 6-2 6-4 3-6 6-3

Final
SAMPRAS beat Agassi 6-4 6-3 6-2
Sampras was the tournament's youngest winner, at 19yrs 28 days, beating the record set by Oliver Campbell (19yrs 6mths) exactly 100 years earlier.

1990 GRAND SLAM RECORDS

	Aust	French	Wim	US
Ivan Lendl	W	-	SF	QF
Andres Gomez	4	W	1	1
Stefan Edberg	F	1	W	1
Pete Sampras	4	-	1	W
and				
Boris Becker	QF	1	F	SF
Steffi Graf	W	F	SF	F
Monica Seles	-	W	QF	3
Martina Navratilova	-	-	W	4
Gabriela Sabatini	3	4	SF	W

Women's Singles
Fourth Round
JANA NOVOTNA (Cze) [12] beat Katerina Maleeva (Bul) [7] 6-4 6-2; STEFFI GRAF (FRG) [1] beat Jennifer Capriati (US) [13] 6-1 6-2; ZINA GARRISON (US) [4] beat Nathalie Tauziat (Fra) 6-1 7-5; ARANTXA SANCHEZ VICARIO (Spa) [6] beat Barbara Paulus (Aut) [16] 6-4 6-3; MARY-JOE FERNANDEZ (US) [8] beat Judith Wiesner (Aut) [15] 6-3 6-2; MANUELA MALEEVA-FRAGNIERE (Swi) [9] beat Martina Navratilova (US) [2] 7-5 3-6 6-3; GABRIELA SABATINI (Arg) [5] beat Helena Sukova (Cze) [11] 6-2 6-1; LEILA MESHKI (USSR) beat Linda Ferrando (Ita) 7-6 6-1

Quarter-finals
FERNANDEZ beat Maleeva-Fragniere 6-2 2-6 6-1; GRAF

LADIES ONLY

❝If it wasn't for her I wouldn't be playing. She's my curse as well as my blessing.❞
Martina Navratilova on Steffi Graf

"I was destroyed by an adversary who wasn't even on the court. I didn't do any harm to these press people."
Graf on her defeats in Paris and Berlin

"I feel like I've been run over by a truck."
Navratilova, after losing to Monica Seles at the Italian Open

"If Monica had Steffi's serve, we'd all be gone."
Navratilova

"Monica is going to be no. 1 and I hope that it will happen soon so that it won't be boring for you."
Graf, after losing to Seles in Berlin

"I still can't believe it's true. I don't have to be depressed about Czechoslovakia any more."
Navratilova, after going home

"I'm like an orange without juice."
Hana Mandlikova, announcing her retirement

"To be just 21 and have to play so much younger girls. Its strange because I don't feel old. It's just weird."
Graf

"I can't comprehend even one title. It's just amazing that someone can win it nine times."
Zina Garrison, after losing the Wimbledon final to Navratilova

"I'm going for double digits. Why not?"
Navratilova, after winning

"She is a great player, but I'd like to see somebody at the top to whom the younger players look up ...If I had a daughter on the circuit I'd want to be there. There are now some players who don't even go to the tournament changing rooms because of the problem."
Margaret Court on Navratilova's lesbianism

"I pity the neighbours on her wedding night.❞
Peter Ustinov on Seles' grunting

---

beat Novotna 6-3 6-1; SABATINI beat Meshki 7-6 6-4; SANCHEZ VICARIO beat Garrison def.

Semi-finals
GRAF beat Sanchez Vicario 6-1 6-2; SABATINI beat Fernandez 7-5 5-7 6-3

Final
SABATINI beat Graf 6-2 7-6

Men's Doubles

Final
PIETER ALDRICH & Danie Visser (SA) [2] beat Paul Annacone & David Wheaton (US) 6-2 7-6 6-2

Women's Doubles

Final
GIGI FERNANDEZ (PR) & MARTINA NAVRATILOVA (US) [2] beat Jana Novotna & Helena Sukova (Cze) [1] 6-2 6-4

Mixed Doubles

Final
TODD WOODBRIDGE & ELIZABETH SMYLIE (Aus) [8] beat Jim Pugh (US) & Natalya Zverova (USSR) [1] 6-4 6-2

OTHER MAJOR EVENTS 1989-90
Men

Geneva Open *Geneva, Sep 17*
Mark Rosset (Swi) beat Guillermo Perez-Roldan (Arg) 6-4 7-5

Volvo Tournament *Los Angeles, Sep 24*
Aaron Krickstein (US) beat Michael Chang (US) 2-6 6-4 6-2

Volvo Tournament *San Francisco, Oct 1*
Brad Gilbert (US) beat Anders Jarryd (Swe) 7-5 6-2

Prudential-Bache Securities Classic *Orlando, Oct 8*
Andre Agassi (US) beat Brad Gilbert (US) 6-2 6-1

Nabisco Grand Prix *Vienna, Oct 22*
Paul Annacone (US) beat Kelly Evernden (NZ) 6-7 6-4 6-1 2-6 6-3

European Community Championship *Antwerp, Oct 29*
Ivan Lendl (Cze) beat Miloslav Mecir (Cze) 6-2 6-2 1-6

6-4

Paris Open *Paris, Nov 5*
Boris Becker (FRG) beat Stefan Edberg (Swe) 6-4 6-3 6-3

Silk Cut Championship *Wembley, Nov 12*
Michael Chang (US) beat Guy Forget (Fra) 6-2 6-1 6-1

Stockholm Open *Stockholm, Nov 12*
Ivan Lendl (Cze) beat Magnus Gustafsson (Swe) 7-5 7-0 6-3

South African Open *Johannesburg, Nov 19*
Christo van Rensburg (SA) beat Paul Chamberlin (US) 6-4 7-6 6-3

BP Nationals *Wellington, Jan 1*
Emilio Sanchez (Spa) beat Richey Reneberg (US) 6-7 6-4 4-6 6-4 6-1

New South Wales Open *Sydney, Jan 14*
Yannick Noah (Fra) beat Carl-Uwe Steeb (FRG) 5-7 6-3 6-4

Italian Indoor Championship *Milan, Feb 11*
Ivan Lendl (Cze) beat Tim Mayotte (US) 6-3 6-2

Skydrome World Tournament *Toronto, Feb 18*
Ivan Lendl (Cze) beat Tim Mayotte (US) 6-3 6-0

Belgian Indoor Championship *Brussels, Feb 18*
Boris Becker (FRG) beat Carl-Uwe Steeb (FRG) 7-5 6-2 6-2

Stuttgart Classic *Stuttgart Feb 25*
Boris Becker (FRG) beat Ivan Lendl (Cze) 6-2 6-2

Ebel US Professional Indoor Championship *Philadelphia, Feb 25*
Pete Sampras (US) beat Andres Gomez (Ecu) 7-6 7-5 6-2

Volvo Indoor Tournament *Memphis, Mar 4*
Michael Stitch (FRG) beat Wally Masur (Aus) 6-7 6-4 7-6

Newsweek Champions Cup *Indian Wells, California, Mar 11*
Stefan Edberg (Swe) beat Andre Agassi (US) 6-4 5-7 7-6 7-6

Players' Championship *Key Biscayne, Florida, Mar 25*
Andre Agassi (US) beat Stefan Edberg (Swe) 6-1 6-4 0-6 6-2

Volvo Tournament *Chicago, Apr 1*
Michael Chang (US) beat Jim Grabb (US) 7-6 1-6 6-4

Prudential - Bache Securities Classic *Orlando, Apr 8*
Brad Gilbert (US) beat Christo van Rensburg (SA) 6-2 6-1

Estoril Open *Estoril, Portugal, Apr 8*

Emilio Sanchez (Spa) beat Franco Davin (Arg) 6-3 6-1
Japan Open *Tokyo, Apr 15*
Stefan Edberg (Swe) beat Aaron Krickstein (US) 6-4 7-5
Philips Open *Nice, Apr 22*
Juan Aguilera (Spa) beat Guy Forget (Fra) 2-6 6-3 6-4
Monte Carlo Open *Monaco, Apr 29*
Andrei Chesnokov (USSR) beat Thomas Muster (Aut) 7-5
6-3 6-3
*Chesnokov became the first Soviet winner of a major
recognised men's tournament.*
BMW German Open *Hamburg, May 13*
Juan Aguilera (Spa) beat Boris Becker (FRG) 6-1 6-0 7-6
US Claycourt Championships *Kiawah Island, South
Carolina, May 13*
David Wheaton (US) beat Mark Kaplan (US) 6-4 6-4
Italian Open *Rome, May 20*
Thomas Muster (Aut) beat Andrei Chesnokov (USSR) 6-1
6-3 6-1
Beckenham Tournament *Beckenham, England, Jun 10*
Ivan Lendl (Cze) beat Darren Cahill (Aus) 6-3 6-5
Stella Artois Grasscourt Championship *Queen's Club,
London, Jun 17*
Ivan Lendl (Cze) beat Boris Becker (FRG) 6-3 6-2
Wentworth Classic *Wentworth, Jun 23*
Guy Forget (Fra) beat Henri Leconte (Fra) 7-5 3-6 6-3
Swedish Open *Bastad, Jul 15*
Richard Fromberg (Aus) beat Magnus Larsson (Swe) 6-2
7-6
Sovran Bank Classic *Washington DC, Jul 22*
Andre Agassi (US) beat Jim Grabb (US) 6-7 6-1 6-4 7-6
Players' International *Toronto, Jul 29*
Michael Chang (US) beat Jay Berger (US) 4-6 6-3 7-6
Volvo Tournament *Los Angeles, Aug 5*
Stefan Edberg (Swe) beat Michael Chang (US) 7-6 2-6 7-6
ATP Championship *Masen, Ohio, Aug 12*
Stefan Edberg (Swe) beat Brad Gilbert (US) 6-1 6-1
US Hardcourt Championship *Indianapolis, Aug 19*
Boris Becker (FRG) beat Peter Lundgren (Swe) 6-3 6-4
Tournament of Champions *New York, Aug 26*
Ivan Lendl (Cze) beat Aaron Krickstein (US) 6-4 6-7 6-3

Women

Virginia Slims of Arizona *Chandler, Arizona, Sep 17*
Conquita Martinez (Spa) beat Elise Burgin (US) 3-6 6-4
6-2
Virginia Slims of Dallas *Dallas, Sep 24*
Martina Navratilova (US) beat Monica Seles (Yug) 7-6 6-3
BMW European Indoor Championship *Zurich, Oct 22*
Steffi Graf (FRG) beat Jana Novotna (Cze) 6-1 7-6
Midland Bank Championship *Brighton, England, Oct 29*
Steffi Graf (FRG) beat Monica Seles (Yug) 7-5 6-4
New England Tournament *Worcester, Massachusetts,
Nov 5*
Martina Navratilova (US) beat Zina Garrison (US) 6-2 6-3
Virginia Slims of Chicago *Chicago, Nov 12*
Zina Garrison (US) beat Larissa Savchenko (USSR) 6-3
2-6 6-4
Nokia Masters *Essen, Nov 26*
Monica Seles (Yug) beat Manuela Maleeva (Bul) 6-1 7-5
Queensland Open *Brisbane, Jan 1*
Natalya Zvereva (USSR) beat Rachel McQuillan (Aus) 6-4
6-0
New South Wales Open *Sydney, Jan 14*
Natalya Zvereva (USSR) beat Barbara Paulus (Aut) 4-6
6-1 6-3
Toray Pan-Pacific Open *Tokyo, Feb 4*
Steffi Graf (FRG) beat Arantxa Sanchez Vicario (Spa) 6-1
6-2
Virginia Slims of Chicago *Chicago, Feb 18*
Martina Navratilova (US) beat Manuela Maleeva (Bul) 6-3
6-2

Virginia Slims of Washington *Washington, Feb 25*
Martina Navratilova (US) beat Zina Garrison (US) 6-1 6-0
Virginia Slims of Indian Wells *Indian Wells, California,
Mar 4*
Martina Navratilova (US) beat Helena Sukova (Cze) 6-2
5-7 6-1
Virginia Slims of Florida *Boca Raton, Florida, Mar 11*
Gabriela Sabatini (Arg) beat Jennifer Capriati (US) 4-6 7-5
*Capriati, 13 years 347 days, was the youngest-ever
professional finalist, beating the record of her opponent –
14 years 11 months.*
Players' Championship *Key Biscayne, Florida, Mar 25*
Monica Seles (Yug) beat Judith Wiesner (Aut) 6-1 6-2
Virginia Slims of Houston *Houston, Apr 1*
Katerina Maleeva (Bul) beat Arantxa Sanchez Vicario
(Spa) 6-1 1-6 6-4
Family Circle Cup *Hilton Head, South Carolina, Apr 8*
Martina Navratilova (US) beat Jennifer Capriati (US) 6-2
6-4
Navratilova's 150th professional title.
Japan Open *Tokyo, Apr 15*
Katarina Lundqvist (Swe) beat Elizabeth Smylie (Aus) 6-3
6-2
Bausch & Lomb Championship *Amelia Island, Florida,
Apr 15*
Steffi Graf (FRG) beat Arantxa Sanchez Vicario (Spa) 6-1
6-0
Eckerd Open *Largo, Florida, Apr 22*
Monico Seles (Yug) beat Katerina Maleeva (Bul) 6-1 6-0
Citizen Cup *Hamburg, May 6*
Steffi Graf (Fra) beat Arantxa Sanchez Vicario (Spa) 5-7 6-
0 6-1
Italian Open *Rome, May 13*
Monica Seles (Yug) beat Martina Navratilova (US) 6-1 6-1
BMW German Open *West Berlin, May 20*
Monica Seles (Yug) beat Steffi Graf (FRG) 6-4 6-3
Seles ended Steffi Graf's record of 66 consecutive victories
Beckenham Tournament *Beckenham, England, Jun 10*
Ros Fairbank (US) beat Gigi Fernandez (PR) 7-5 6-4
Dow Classic *Edgbaston, England, Jun 17*
Zina Garrison (US) beat Helena Sukova (Cze) 6-4 6-1
Eastbourne Classic *Eastbourne, England, Jun 23*
Martina Navratilova (US) beat Gretchen Magers (US) 6-0
6-2
Swedish Open *Bastad, Jul 15*
Sandra Cecchini (Ita) beat Csilla Bartos (Swi) 6-1 6-4
Virginia Slims Newport *Newport, Rhode Island, Jul 22*
Arantxa Sanchez Vicario (Spa) beat Jo Durie (GB) 7-6 4-6
7-5
Player's Challenge *Montreal, Aug 5*
Steffi Graf (FRG) beat Katerina Maleeva (Bul) 6-1 6-7 6-3
Virginia Slims of Albuquerque *Albuquerque, Aug 12*
Jana Novotna (Cze) beat Laura Gildermeister (Per) 6-4 6-4
Great American Bank Classic *San Diego, Aug 12*
Steffi Graf (FRG) beat Manuela Maleeva-Fragniere (Swi)
6-3 6-2
Graf's 50th professional title
Virginia Slims of Los Angeles *Manhattan Beach,
California, Aug 19*
Monica Seles (Yug) beat Martina Navratilova (US) 6-4 3-6
7-6
Pathmark Classic *Manwah, New Jersey, Aug 26*
Steffi Graf (FRG) beat Jennifer Capriati (US) 6-3 5-7 6-4

THE BABY BOOM

" Jennifer Capriati is the best American prospect since Tracy Austin."
Tracy Austin

"She's happy, that's her secret weapon."
Mary Carillo, US commentator on Capriati

"Its obscene, but wonderful."
Mary Francis, chief women's umpire on Capriati

"She is a good deal more mature than our mourned, maligned and gone-back-to-Manhattan anti-hero. McEnroe had mislaid his genius; Capriati was only missing her puppy."
Sue Mott, Sunday Times, on Capriati at Wimbledon

"Thank God England doesn't have a Capriati. The whole nation would grind to a halt."
Martina Navratilova

Jack Kramer, being interviewed about the new US tennis prodigy Venus Williams: "She has all the basic physical requirements to play that special kind of tennis. She's very quick, she has a good sense of tactics and she has a natural service motion. For being 14, she's pretty good."
Interviewer: "She's 10."
Kramer: "Oh my gosh. "

MEN'S RANKINGS
After US Open

1 Stefan Edberg; 2 Boris Becker; 3 Ivan Lendl; 4 Andre Agassi; 5 Andres Gomez; 6 Pete Sampras; 7 Thomas Muster; 8 Emilio Sanchez; 9 Brad Gilbert; 10 Aaron Krickstein; 11 John McEnroe; 12 Michael Chang; 13 Andrei Chesnokov; 14 Goran Ivanisevic; 15 Guillermo Perez-Roldan.

Edberg became the eighth player to be ranked no. 1 on the ATP computer on August 13. The others with, the dates they first became no. 1, were:

Ilie Nastase	August 1973
John Newcombe	June 1974
Jimmy Connors	July 1974
Bjorn Borg	August 1977
John McEnroe	March 1980
Ivan Lendl	February 1983
Mats Willander	September 1988

DAVIS CUP

WORLD GROUP
First Round *Feb 2-4*

New Zealand	3	Yugoslavia	2
Australia	3	France	2
Austria	3	Spain	2
West Germany	3	Holland	2
Argentina	3	Israel	0
(unfinished)			

Czechoslovakia	5	Switzerland	0
United States	4	Mexico	0
(unfinished)			
Italy	3	Sweden	

2Quarter-finals Mar 30-Apr 1

Australia	3	New Zealand	2
United States	4	Czechoslovakia	1
Austria	5	Italy	0
Argentina	3	West Germany	2

Semi-finals Sep 21-23

Australia	5	Argentina	0
United States	3	Austria	2

Final
Nov 30-Dec 2, 1990

BRITAIN IN THE DAVIS CUP

EUROPEAN/AFRICAN ZONE SEMI-FINAL
Bucharest, May 2-4

Romania	2	Great Britain	3

Results: (*British names first*)
Danny Sapsford beat Georg Gosac 4-6 6-1 6-2 6-3; Jeremy Bates lost to Florin Segarceanu 5-7 1-6 1-6; Bates & Andrew Castle beat Segarceanu & Gosac 6-3 6-3 6-2; Bates beat Gosac 6-1 6-2 6-2; Sapsford lost to Segarceanu 3-6 6-4 3-6

World Group Qualifying Round
Queen's Club, Sep 21-23

Great Britain	0	France	5

Results: (*British names first*)
Nick Brown lost to Henri Leconte 3-6 6-7 2-6; Jeremy Bates lost to Guy Forget 6-2 6-7 4-6 1-6; Andrew Castle & Bates lost to Forget & Leconte 1-6 4-6 4-6; Bates lost to Leconte 6-7 0-6; Brown lost to Forget 3-6 2-6

FEDERATION CUP
Atlanta, Georgia, July 22-29

First Round
UNITES STATES 3 Poland 0; BELGIUM 2 Sweden 1; AUSTRALIA 2 Indonesia 0; CZECHOSLOVAKIA 3 South Korea 0; AUSTRIA 3 Bulgaria 0; JAPAN 3 China 0; GREAT BRITAIN 3 Dominican Republic 0; ITALY 3 Finland 0; WEST GERMANY 2 Argentina 1; HOLLAND 2 Switzerland 1; HONG KONG 3 Hungary 0; SOVIET UNION 3 Brazil 0; FRANCE 3 Formosa 0; NEW ZEALAND 3 Greece 0; ISRAEL 2 Denmark 1; SPAIN 2 Canada 1

Second Round
UNITED STATES 3 Belgium 0; CZECHOSLOVAKIA 2 Australia 1; AUSTRIA 2 Japan 1; GREAT BRITAIN 2 Italy 1; HOLLAND 2 West Germany 1; SOVIET UNION 3 Hong Kong 0; FRANCE 3 New Zealand 0; SPAIN 3 Israel 0

Quarter-finals
UNITED STATES 2 Czechoslovakia 1; AUSTRIA 2 Great Britain 1; SOVIET UNION 2 Holland 1; SPAIN 3 France 0

Semi-finals
UNITED STATES 2 Austria 0; SOVIET UNION 2 Spain 1

Final
UNITED STATES 2 Soviet Union 1
Jennifer Capriati beat Leila Meshki 7-6 6-2; Zina Garrison lost to Natalya Zvereva 4-6 6-3 6-3; Garrison and Gigi Fernandez beat Zvereva and Savchenko 6-4 6-3

RULE BRITANNIA

" I just want to have good, interesting conversations with normal people."
Valda Lake, Britain's no. 11, announcing her retirement aged 21

"My God, if I'm Britain's no.1, it's pretty bad really."

Jo Durie

"If only we knew why, we'd do something about it."

Ann Jones, British women's captain

"These people are debating issues of life and death and we're talking about serve and volley. You have to come to a place like this to find out what's really important. God, I feel so pathetic."

Andrew Castle, after playing Davis Cup in Romania

"No wonder we don't lead the world tennis league when players like Andrew Castle blame their defeats on the balls, the court and tiredness. How pathetic can you get! Oh, for a player with the guts and backbone of a Jimmy Connors instead of whingers like Castle."

Letter in The Sun from A.M. Bye of Romford

"I reckon that we won about five per cent of the important points in the matches I watched, and in professional tennis that simply won't get you anywhere."

Warren Jacques, team coach, on the British men at Wimbledon

"This, to put it bluntly, is why British tennis isn't anywhere. The dominant ethos is not participation but exclusion. Little or no attempt is made to appeal to the average 11-year-old...Wimbledon is not the solution to the problems of British tennis, it is part of the problem."

Martin Jacques, Sunday Times

"Nobody in Britain can serve – you don't need to be Einstein to see that."

Ian Barclay, Australian coach

"He's got all the talent, but somehow it doesn't come through in the matches. "

David Lloyd on Jeremy Bates

1989

VIRGINIA SLIMS FINAL
New York, Nov 19
STEFFI GRAF (FRG) beat Martina Navratilova (US) 6-4 7-5 2-6 6-2

NABISCO MASTERS
New York, Dec 3
Semi - finals
BORIS BECKER (FRG) beat John McEnroe (US) 6-4 6-4;
STEFAN EDBERG (Swe) beat Ivan Lendl (Cze) 7-6 7-5
Final
EDBERG beat Becker 4-6 7-6 6-3 6-1

NABISCO MASTERS DOUBLES
London, Dec 10
PATRICK McENROE & JIM GRABB (US) beat Anders Jarryd (Swe) & John Fitzgerald (Aus) 7-5 7-6 5-7 6-3

DAVIS CUP FINAL
Stuttgart, Dec 15-17
WEST GERMANY beat Sweden 3-2
Results: (West German names first)
Carl-Uwe Steeb lost to Mats Wilander 7-5 6-7 7-6 2-6 3-6; Boris Becker beat Stefan Edberg 6-2 6-2 6-4; Becker and Eric Jelen beat Jan Gunnarsson and Jarryd 7-6 6-4 3-6 6-7 6-4; Becker beat Wilander 6-2 6-0 6-2; Steeb lost to Edberg 2-6 4-6

CHAMPIONS

THE ALL ENGLAND CHAMPIONSHIPS, WIMBLEDON
Men's Singles
(Until 1922 defending champions played only one challenge match against the winners of the open competition)

1877	Spencer Gore (GB) beat W C Marshall (GB) 6-1 6-2 6-4	
1878	Frank Hadow (GB) beat Spencer Gore (GB) 7-5 6-1 9-7	
1879	Rev John Hartley (GB) beat St L Goold (GB) 6-2 6-4 6-2	
1880	Rev John Hartley (GB) beat Herbert Lawford (GB) 6-3 6-2 2-6 6-3	
1881	William Renshaw (GB) beat Rev John Hartley (GB) 6-0 6-1 6-1	
1882	William Renshaw (GB) beat Ernest Renshaw (GB) 6-1 2-6 4-6 6-2 6-2	
1883	William Renshaw (GB) beat Ernest Renshaw (GB) 2-6 6-3 6-3 4-6 6-3	
1884	William Renshaw (GB) Herbert Lawford (GB) 6-0 6-4 9-7	
1885	William Renshaw (GB) beat Herbert Lawford (GB) 7-5 6-2 4-6 7-5	
1886	William Renshaw (GB) beat Herbert Lawford (GB) 6-0 5-7 6-3 6-4	
1887	Herbert Lawford (GB) beat Ernest Renshaw (GB) 1-6 6-3 3-6 6-4 6-4	
1888	Ernest Renshaw (GB) beat Herbert Lawford (GB) 6-3 7-5 6-0	
1889	William Renshaw (GB) beat Ernest Renshaw (GB) 6-4 6-1 3-6 6-0	
1890	Willoughby Hamilton (GB) beat William Renshaw (GB) 6-8 2-6 3-6 6-1 6-1	
1891	Wilfred Baddeley (GB) beat Joshua Pim (GB) 6-4 1-6 7-5 6-0	
1892	Wilfred Baddeley (GB) beat Joshua Pim (GB) 4-6 6-3 6-3 6-2	
1893	Joshua Pim (GB) beat Wilfred Baddeley (GB) 3-6 6-1 6-3 6-2	
1894	Joshua Pim (GB) beat Wilfred Baddeley (GB) 10-8 6-2 8-6	
1895	Wilfred Baddeley (GB) beat W V Eaves (GB) 4-6 2-6 8-6 6-2 6-3	
1896	Harold Mahoney (GB) beat Wilfred Baddeley (GB) 6-2 6-8 5-7 8-6 6-3	

1897	Reginald Doherty (GB) beat Harold Mahoney (GB) 6-4 6-4 6-3
1898	Reginald Doherty (GB) beat Lawrence Doherty (GB) 6-3 6-3 2-6 7-5 6-1
1899	Reginald Doherty (GB) beat Arthur Gore (GB)1-6 4-6 6-2 6-3 6-3
1900	Reginald Doherty (GB) beat Sidney Smith (GB) 6-8 6-3 6-1 6-2
1901	Arthur Gore (GB) beat Reginald Doherty (GB) 4-6 7-5 6-4 6-4
1902	Lawrence Doherty (GB) beat Arthur Gore (GB) 6-4 6-3 3-6 6-0
1903	Lawrence Doherty (GB) beat Frank Risely (GB) 7-5 6-3 6-0
1904	Lawrence Doherty (GB) beat Frank Risely (GB) 6-1 7-5 8-6
1905	Lawrence Doherty (GB) beat Norman Brookes (Aus) 8-6 6-2 6-4
1906	Lawrence Doherty (GB) beat Frank Riseley (GB) 6-4 6-2 6-3
1907	Norman Brookes (Aus) beat Arthur Gore (GB) 6-4 6-2 6-2
1908	Arthur Gore (GB) beat H Roper Barrett (GB) 6-3 6-2 4-6 3-6 6-4
1909	Arthur Gore (GB) beat Josiah Ritchie (GB) 6-8 1-6 6-2 6-2 6-2
1910	Tony Wilding (NZ) beat Arthur Gore (GB) 6-4 7-5 4-6 6-2
1911	Tony Wilding (NZ) beat H Roper Barrett (GB) 6-4 4-6 2-6 6-2 retired
1912	Tony Wilding (NZ) beat Arthur Gore (GB) 6-4 6-4 4-6 6-4
1913	Tony Wilding (NZ) beat M McLoughlin (US) 8-6 6-3 10-8
1914	Norman Brookes (Aus) beat Tony Wilding (NZ) 6-4 6-4 7-5
1919	Gerald Patterson (Aus) beat Norman Brookes (Aus) 6-3 7-5 7-2
1920	Bill Tilden (US) beat Gerald Patterson (Aus) 2-6 6-3 6-2 6-4
1921	Bill Tilden (US) beat Brian Norton (SA) 4-6 2-6 6-1 6-0 7-5
1922	Gerald Patterson (Aus) beat Randolph Lycett (GB) 6-3 6-4 6-2
1923	William Johnston (US) beat Frank Hunter (US) 6-0 6-3 6-1
1924	Jean Borotra (Fra) beat René Lacoste (Fra) 6-1 3-6 6-1 3-6 6-4
1925	René Lacoste (Fra) beat Jean Brotra (Fra) 6-3 6-3 4-6 8-6
1926	Jean Borotra (Fra) beat Howard Kinsey (US) 8-6 6-1 6-3
1927	Henri Cochet (Fra) beat Jean Borotra (Fra) 4-6 4-6 6-3 6-4 7-5
1928	René Lacoste (Fra) beat Henri Cochet (Fra) 6-1 4-6 6-4 6-2
1929	Henri Cochet (Fra) beat Jean Borotra (Fra) 6-4 6-3 6-4 ·
1930	Bill Tilden (US) beat William Allison (US) 6-3 9-7 6-4
1931	Sidney Wood (US) beat Frank Shields (US) w.o.
1932	Ellsworth Vines (US) beat Bunny Austin (GB) 6-4 6-2 6-0
1933	Jack Crawford (Aus) beat Ellsworth Vines (US) 4-6 11-9 6-2 2-6 6-4
1934	Fred Perry (GB) beat Jack Crawford (Aus) 6-3 6-0 7-5
1935	Fred Perry (GB) beat Gottfried von Cramm (Ger) 6-2 6-4 6-4
1936	Fred Perry (GB) beat Gottfried von Cramm (Ger) 6-1 6-1 6-0
1937	Donald Budge (US) beat Gottfried von Cramm (Ger) 6-3 6-4 6-2
1938	Donald Budge (US) beat Bunny Austin (GB) 6-1 6-0 6-3
1939	Bobby Riggs (US) beat Ellwood Cooke (US) 2-6 8-6 3-6 6-3 6-2
1946	Yvon Petra (Fra) beat Geoffrey Brown (Aus) 6-2 6-4 7-9 5-7 6-4
1947	Jack Kramer (US) beat Tom Brown (US) 6-1 6-3 6-2
1948	Bob Falkenburg (US) beat John Bromwich (Aus) 7-5 0-6 6-2 3-6 7-5
1949	Ted Schroeder (US) beat Jaroslav Drobny (Cze) 3-6 6-0 6-3 4-6 6-4
1950	Budge Patty (US) beat Frank Sedgman (Aus) 6-1 8-10 6-2 6-3
1951	Dick Savitt (US) beat Ken McGregor (Aus) 6-4 6-4 6-4
1952	Frank Sedgman (Aus) beat Jaroslav Drobny (Egy) 4-6 6-2 6-3 6-2
1953	Vic Seixas (US) beat Kurt Nielson (Den) 9-7 6-3 6-4
1954	Jaroslav Drobny (Egy) beat Ken Rosewall (Aus) 13-11 4-6 6-2 9-7
1955	Tony Trabert (US) beat Kurt Nielsen (Den) 6-3 7-5 6-1
1956	Lew Hoad (Aus) beat Ken Rosewall (Aus) 6-2 4-6 7-5 6-4
1957	Lew Hoad (Aus) beat Ashley Cooper (Aus) 6-2 6-1 6-2
1958	Ashley Cooper (Aus) beat Neale Fraser (Aus) 3-6 6-3 6-4 13-11
1959	Alex Olmedo (US) beat Rod Laver (Aus) 6-4 6-3 6-4
1960	Neale Fraser (Aus) beat Rod Laver (Aus) 6-4 3-6 9-7 7-5
1961	Rod Laver (Aus) beat Chuck McKinley (US) 6-3 6-1 6-4
1962	Rod Laver (Aus) beat Martin Mulligan (Aus) 6-2 6-2 6-1
1963	Chuck McKinley (US) beat Fred Stolle (Aus) 9-7 6-1 6-4
1964	Roy Emerson (Aus) beat Fred Stolle (Aus) 6-4 12-10 4-6 6-3
1965	Roy Emerson (Aus) beat Fred Stolle (Aus) 6-2 6-4 6-4
1966	Manuel Santana (Spa) beat Dennis Ralston (US) 6-4 11-9 6-4
1967	John Newcombe (Aus) beat Wilhelm Bungert (FRG) 6-3 6-1 6-1
1968	Rod Laver (Aus) beat Tony Roche (Aus) 6-3 6-4 6-2
1969	Rod Laver (Aus) beat John Newcombe (Aus) 6-4 5-7 6-4 6-4
1970	John Newcombe (Aus) beat Ken Rosewall (Aus) 5-7 6-3 6-2 3-6 6-1
1971	John Newcombe (Aus) beat Stan Smith (US) 6-3 5-7 2-6 6-4 6-4
1972	Stan Smith (US) beat Ilie Nastase (Rom) 4-6 6-3 6-3 4-6 7-5
1973	Jan Kodes (Cze) beat Alex Metreveli (USSR) 6-1 9-8 6-3
1974	Jimmy Connors (US) beat Ken Rosewall (Aus) 6-1 6-1 6-4
1975	Arthur Ashe (US) beat Jimmy Connors (US) 6-1 6-1 5-7 6-4
1976	Bjorn Borg (Swe) beat Ilie Nastase (Rom) 6-4 6-2 9-7
1977	Bjorn Borg (Swe) beat Jimmy Connors (US) 3-6 6-2 6-1 5-7 6-4
1978	Bjorn Borg (Swe) beat Jimmy Connors (US) 6-2 6-2 6-3